JOSEPHINE

JOSEPHINE

The Hungry Heart

JEAN-CLAUDE BAKER
and CHRIS CHASE

RANDOM HOUSE NEW YORK

Photos without attributions are from the private
collection of Jean-Claude Baker.

Grateful acknowledgment is made to the following for permission to reprint
previously published material: JACQUES ABTEY: Excerpts from *La Guerre Secrete
de Josephine Baker* by Jacques Abtey (Paris and Havana: Editions Siboney, 1948)
and from unpublished notes and the original manuscript. Any further reproduction of this material is strictly prohibited. Reprinted by permission. CENTRE
NATIONAL JEAN MOULIN, BORDEAUX, FRANCE: Letter from M. Brandin contained
in the archives of Jean Moulin housed at the Centre National Jean Moulin,
Bordeaux, France. Reprinted by permission. INSTITUT CHARLES DE GAULLE:
Excerpt from personal letters from General Charles de Gaulle to Josephine
Baker. Any further reproduction of this material is prohibited. Reprinted by
permission. SOPHIE REAGAN-HERR: Excerpts from an unpublished work entitled
La Revue Nègre by Caroline Dudley. Reprinted by permission of Sophie
Reagan-Herr. EMI SAWADA-KAMIYA: Personal correspondence and photos from
her mother, Miki Sawada. Reprinted by permission. YALE UNIVERSITY: Excerpts
from material regarding Josephine Baker from the files of Henry Hurford James
housed at the Yale Collection of American Literature, Beinecke Rare Book and
Manuscript Library, Yale University. Reprinted by permission.

Library of Congress Cataloging-in-Publication Data
Baker, Jean-Claude.
Josephine : the hungry heart / by Jean-Claude Baker and Chris Chase.
p.   cm.
Includes index.
ISBN 0-679-40915-7
1. Baker, Josephine, 1906–1975. 2. Dancers—France—Biography.
3. Afro-American entertainers—France—Biography. I. Chase, Chris. II. Title.
GV1785.B3B35   1993   792.8′028′092—dc20   92-56797
[B]

Manufactured in the United States of America on acid-free paper
Book design by J. K. Lambert
2 4 6 8 9 7 5 3

First Edition

To both my mothers, with all my love

I am become a name;

For always roaming with a hungry heart.

ALFRED, LORD TENNYSON

ACKNOWLEDGMENTS

In the course of researching this book over the last twenty years, I was privileged to meet and spend time with a number of Josephine Baker's contemporaries in America. These remarkable African-Americans inspired me, especially in view of the racial injustices they were called upon to bear. Their response was not one of submissiveness but of deep and abiding faith: "Jean-Claude," they repeatedly told me, "the Lord in His own time will reward us." I sincerely pray He will. I wish to thank them for their kindness and generosity. I would also like to acknowledge everyone all over the world who helped on this endeavor. My apologies to anyone I may have inadvertently left out. Please, you know you are all in my heart.

I would've been lost without the invaluable help of librarians. Their tireless and often thankless efforts fuel the writing of history and no one is more representative of their lifelong dedication than Jean Blackwell Hutson, the former chief of Schomburg Center for Research in Black Culture in New York City, and her colleagues Deborah Willis-Thomas, Alice Adamczyk, and Jim Murray. I was greatly assisted by the following institutions: St. Louis Public Schools (Thomas J. O'Keefe and Ornelle L. Meishon); Harris-Stowe State College (Martin Knorr); St. Louis Historical Museum (Ernestine Hardge); Missouri Historical Society (Robert R. Archibald and Suzanne Stolar); St. Louis Public Library; Arkansas History Commission State Archives; Arkansas Baptist College Library; Little Rock Public Library; Memphis Shelby County Public

Library (Patricia M. Lapointe); New Orleans Hogan Jazz Archive (Curtis D. Jerde); Detroit Public Library (Jean Currie Church); University of Chicago, Department of Music (John Steiner); Chicago Historical Society; *The Lakeville Journal* Library (Robert H. Estabrook, editor); Fisk University (Ann Allen Shockley, Janice Ayer Jackson); Rutgers University Institute of Jazz Studies (Edward Berger); Yale University Beinecke Rare Book and Manuscript Library (Patricia Willis); Theatre Historical Society of America (Irvin R. Glazer); Free Library of Philadelphia (Geraldine Duclow and Lee Stanley); Philadelphia Department of Records (Ward J. Childs); the Estate of Dr. Martin Luther King, Jr. (Michele Clark Jenkins); Schubert Archive (Maryann Chach, Reagan Fletcher); Museum of the City of New York; Library for the Performing Arts, Lincoln Center; University of Western Ontario; National Library of Canada (Franceen Goudet); Metropolitan Toronto Library Board (Anne Goluska); Arthur Prevost Archive, Quebec; Robert Brady Museum, Cuernavaca (Sally Sloan); Bibliothèque de l'Arsenal, Paris; Fondation Nationale des Arts Graphiques et Plastiques (Françoise Bertrand-Py); Institut Charles de Gaulle (L'Amiral de Gaulle, Le Général de Boissieu, Catherine Trouiller, and Mademoiselle de Bea); Centre National Jean Moulin (Geneviève Thieuleux); Archives Départementales de la Dordogne; Cinémathèque de la Danse (Patrick Bensard); Bibliothèque Royale Albert I (Jean M. Horemans and N. Tassoul); Cunard Archives Liverpool; Landesarchiv Berlin (Sabine Preuss); Dansmuseet Stockholm, Ralf de Mare collection (Lilavati Hager); the many who helped me in the passport offices and with F.B.I. files; and a special thanks to DHL, who allowed me to travel for free as a courier when I was short on cash.

To the following individuals, my heartfelt thanks: the Reverend Charles F. Rehkopf, Vergie Johnson-Kiger, Helen Englander, Albernice A. Fagan, Beredester Harvey, Louise King (the Sherlock Holmes of geneology), Joyce McDuffy Parker, Frank Driggs, Eddie Barefield, Tony Benford, Art Russell (one of the Three Dukes), Ruth Ellington, Claude Hopkins, Jr., Jean-Pierre and Eliane Laffont, Arthur Mitchell, Bobby Mitchell, Liane Mitchell, Barbara Mitchell Raskin, Hank O'Neal, Tommy Benford, Banjo Ikey Robinson, Eddie Durham, Robert S. Rappaport, Alice Staar and Ingeborg von Zitzenwitz (my favorite translators), Robert Kimball, Louis Martien, Albert Murray, Maranantha Marion Douglas-Cook, Thelma Meers-Meachum, Mabel Mercer, Jose

Orraca, Renee Epstein, Richard Mardus, Ed Wynn, Tommy Wonder, Don Dellair, Harry Watkins, Marlene Brody, Bernadette Mertl, Barry Gray, Colette Martin, George Jones, Harriette Jones-Marin, Maurice Russell, Charlotte Cohen, Bruce Kellner, Anne Leroux, Joseph Moran, Jim Neagle, George Reich, Noble Sissle, Jr., Cynthia Sissle, Dolores H. James-Johnson, Roger and Diane Green, Delilah Jackson, Harold and Fayard Nicholas, Antoine Blech, Luciano Stemberger and Capotorto G. Benedetto (who served me sympathy along with my pasta), Maurice Bataille, Christiane Fort, Alain Carrier, Rainer E. Lotz, Dominique Deschamps, Dr. Gudrun Boysen, Dr. Ole Thage, Dr. François Jarricot, Jun Hattory, Lucien R. le Lievre, Nicole Devilaine, John and Fabienne Ho, Serge Lifar, Yvette Mallet, Jean-Louis Menier, Abdelhafid El Aloui, Jaffa and Kamal Menebhi, Ali Bel Maalmem Attourti, Mohamed ben Abdelkador Alaoui, Jonathan Raskin, Georges and Marguerite Dejean, Henri Chapin, Elie Raynal, Madame Leon Burg, Josette Affergan, Father Charpagne, Consul Jean-Claude Lenoir, Jean Rumeau, Jean-Michel Rouziere, Eugene Browne, Jean-Louis Rico, Consul Celio Sandate, Consul Patricia R. Clark, Jeanne Aubert, Monsieur Coudert, Jeannine Walch, Marie Louise Hugues, Herve and Marie Charlotte Bolot, Suzanne Dubois, Jacqueline Stone, Ishii Yoshiko, André Pousse, Donald Goodwin, Nicol Rayney, Julio Sendin, Isaac Martinez, Peter Nowotny, Hisao Sawada, Catherine Favalelli, William and Elaine Cannan, Michael and Françoise Schmidt, and Georges Vikar. A salute to my devoted team and the guests at Chez Josephine who never tired of listening to my stories.

I owe a special debt of gratitude to Jacqueline Deslauriers, Fiametta Ponti, Anne Lacombe, Hilda Eftikides, Serge and Danielle Bellanger, Sophie Reagan-Herr and family, the Rodriguez Guignery family, Bernard Houdeline, Dr. and Mrs. David C. Baker, Dr. Francis Mas, Gene Lerner, Hank Kaufman, the Lamghari-Menebhi family, the Malaury family, the Garrigou-Battut family, Roger Prigent, Al Hirschfeld, Marie and Gerard Spiers, Danielle Charbonnel, John Hawkins, Randi and Tor Hultin, Peter Jackson, Bryan and Mireille Miller, Gwin Joh Chin, Patrick Pacheco, Steven Gaines, Helen Braun, Maude Russell, Donald and Marian Wyatt, Esther James and family, John J. O'Connor, Seymour Barofsky, Clive Panton, Ronald Woodberry, Rosario and Antonella Acquista, Jacques and Jacqueline Abtey and family, Helen Morris, Emi Sawada-Kamiya, William Melvin Kelley, Barry Tarshis, William Wright,

Ernest Brawley, Richard M. Sudhalter, Helen Gary Bishop, Hank Wittemore, Howard Kissel, Howard Sanders (who along with the departed Jack Jordan were my first American bosses), Betty Lee Hunt, Maryse Bouillon, Arthur and Janie Martin and daughter Vertel, Richard Martin, Jr., Clifford Martin, Margaret Martin-Wallace and her daughter, Rama, and the Richard Martin, Sr., family in France—Patrick, Guylaine, Alain, Laurence, Catherine and my darling godchild, Nais. I would also like to bow before Mademoiselle Bauche and Madame Lion, who first opened the magic world of books for a young boy in St. Symphorien. I hope somewhere they are proud of their student. Family, too, has always been important to me and to this book. My heart belongs to my two mothers and my two families: the Tronville-Rouzauds and the Bouillon-Bakers.

This book would not have been published were it not for the trust and confidence placed in me by a number of people. First, by the editors of *The New York Times Book Review,* who gave me the chance to explore its possibilities in their pages (February 4, 1990)—Rebecca Sinkler, Richard Flaste, and Michael Anderson, *merci.* Owen Laster gave me the benefit of his expertise and I am honored to be associated with the legendary Robert Loomis, my editor, who understood with both his mind and heart what this book was all about (and, to his assistant Barbé Hammer, a big kiss). Needless to say, I am grateful to my co-writer, Chris Chase.

CONTENTS

INTRODUCTION:
AN OVERVIEW

"She is like Salome, she has seven veils"

Who am I to think I have to write a book on Josephine Baker when I'm not even her legal son? She had thousands of lovers; I've never been her lover, I've never even been her fan. I was a fan of Edith Piaf, not of Josephine Baker. And I'm certainly not the first person to try to capture her on paper. There have been more than a dozen books written about her. She herself turned out five autobiographies, a novel, and a collection of fairy tales that expressed her vision of universal brotherhood. Since she died in 1975, seven volumes by other people have appeared.

Because I loved her, hated her, and wanted desperately to understand her, I read them all. And they made me crazy. It's hard to read a life of anyone you have known and be entirely satisfied with the account; you recognize too many half-truths, you find too little illumination. Gradually it became clear to me that if I wanted to come to terms with my memories of Josephine, I was going to have to become a biographer myself, and I set out to track down stories, fill in the gaps in what had already been reported.

I was ridiculed ("He wasn't really her son"), I went broke, but I persisted; even when a writer with a contract for a Baker book offered me fifty thousand dollars to share what I had found, I refused.

I once said on a television documentary that Josephine was like the sun. We need the sun for the flowers to grow, for the birds to sing, but if you come too close, you can get burned, you can die. Everyone who came too close to Josephine got burned.

We first met in 1958. I was fourteen years old and she was fifty-two. I was working at the Hôtel Scribe in Paris, running errands, and I was called to her room. When I got there, I saw a woman in a bathrobe, and someone at her feet giving her a pedicure. The woman sent me to the drugstore to buy something, and when I came back, she was alone. She said, "Do you love your mother, little one?" I was shocked, because nobody gave a damn about me, and I was missing my mother back in my village every day. Five minutes later, I was sitting on the bed next to her, telling her my story.

I was born Jean-Claude Julien Leon Tronville, a bastard. It was a tragedy for my thirty-five-year-old mother, who was very pure and Catholic, and would have become a nun if Hitler had not come along. Once the war started, the convent sent her back to her family in Paris, and at the train station she met a gentleman who looked like Rudolph Valentino. Nine months later, I came into the world in Dijon. Because of the war, my parents moved to a little village in Burgundy. Everyone else had been there two hundred years; I never felt I belonged.

When I was seven, my father married my mother and the school-teacher told me my name was Rouzaud. I didn't like that name. I planned three things for when I grew up: I would not do my military service. I would have a statue of myself like Napoléon III on a horse. And I would not bear the name of my father.

Soon after my parents' marriage, my father left us to go back to Paris to work in a restaurant. At first, he came home toward the end of each month, loaded like Santa Claus with toys for me and my sisters, but I would resent that because it was not Christmastime. He was never there at Christmas. After a while, he was never there at all. When I was fourteen, I made a big decision. I did not want to work in the fields or the factory, so I wrote my father and told him we needed to have a man-to-man talk.

He mailed me a third-class ticket to Paris, and my mother brought me to Dijon to the train station, but when my train pulled in, she started to cry in front of everyone. She said, "Ladies and gentlemen, I'm not a bad mother, it's just I have three little girls at home, so I can't go to Paris with my Jean-Claude; please keep an eye out for him."

I was so ashamed, and she ran along beside the train until it left the station, and then I cried too, and that's the way I arrived in Paris. And what happened was, I found my father living in a hotel for prostitutes, where they rented rooms by the hour; he had gambled away all his money. Three days later, he disappeared, and didn't come back.

Josephine listened to all this, and then she said, "Don't be worried, my little one, you have no father, but from today on, you will have two mothers."

But the fact is that I didn't find her again—we didn't become close—until the last seven years of her life. The Josephine I knew was an old lady who had adopted children from all over the world and called them her Rainbow Tribe. But sometimes, she would open a door to the past, talk about private things. So I gathered bits of the puzzle, told by her in the nights when she couldn't sleep. She was always afraid to be alone, afraid of the darkness.

She was like a piece of Ming china. You know nothing about it, you think it's beautiful, six hundred years old, a treasure, but if you look through a jeweler's loupe, you see it's been cracked. That was Josephine. When she died, something was taken from me, I suffered a loss and I wanted to know who she was, that woman I had witnessed in so many ways, sometimes a criminal, sometimes a saint. My real detective work began then, when she was gone and questions could not hurt her anymore, or threaten to expose the secrets she had hidden so fiercely.

After her funeral, I came back to New York. One day I walked into an antique shop, and on a hunch, I said, "Do you have anything about Josephine Baker?" The proprietor brought out a small volume in French—the earliest of three autobiographies Josephine had written in collaboration with Marcel Sauvage. It told how she came from St. Louis, joined a show called *Shuffle Along,* spent her first three nights in New York in a park where she ran from shadows and slept cold, hungry, "exhausted in the grass. . . ." Published in 1927 and filled with such fancies, that book also said Josephine had to go to Paris to become famous, though the truth was, she left New York with a star's contract in her pocket.

Later, I discovered the other books, filled with more myths Josephine had planted herself, the misinformation repeated by writer after writer. I was more and more intrigued, picking my way through the discrepancies.

By then, I had settled permanently in New York, and I read that the old blues singer Alberta Hunter was appearing at the Cookery on

University Place, and I went and asked her if she remembered Josephine Baker.

"Of course," she said. "We used to be roommates."

It seemed too good to be true, but that was how my American odyssey began. Through Alberta and the people she steered me toward, a dead world came alive. In Harlem, she would point out the windows of an apartment over a funeral parlor. "We used to live here. And Lena Horne's mother lived there, and Langston Hughes lived in that building, and this is the beauty parlor where I have had my hair done since 1923."

Witness after witness, many frail with age, shared their memories with me. Josephine's story is not hers alone, it's the story of all those people. I had to capture them before they disappeared. One day, I called the director of jazz studies at Rutgers University and asked him if he knew anyone still alive who had been with *La Revue Nègre*, the show that had taken Josephine to France. "Why don't you talk to Claude Hopkins?" he said. "He was musical director." I was irritated. "Monsieur," I said, "everybody knows Claude Hopkins is dead." His voice remained kind. "Mr. Baker, Claude Hopkins is in Parkview Nursing Home in the Bronx."

The next day, trembling, I walked into the Parkview Nursing Home. In a nursing home, you smell overcooked food, cheap perfume, medicine, and you see old people talking to themselves; the life there is a kind of going away, a ship leaving the harbor and it's too late to get off. I was directed to Claude's room. He was half asleep, and a nurse came in, shook him, and said, "Wake up, Claude, you have a visitor."

He opened his eyes, I said, "*Bonjour,* I'm Jean-Claude Baker," and we talked, but he was incoherent, rambling. I found a nurse. "Is he always like that?"

She shook her head. "He needs dialysis every day, and we don't have a machine here, so they come and take him once a week. The day before he goes, his blood is full of poisons, but if you come to see him after his treatment, he thinks as clearly as anyone. In fact," she said, starting to laugh, "he runs down the halls naked, chasing nurses."

I was there the next afternoon when they brought Claude back from dialysis, and his head worked better than mine. He answered all my questions, he even gave me addresses of two of the show's chorus girls who were still alive. And he admitted that, on the boat to Paris, he had become Josephine's lover, despite the misery this had caused his wife, Mabel. "I was bad to Mabel," he said, "but we were so young then, we were all so young."

Before I left, I asked if he remembered where they had rehearsed in New York. "232 West 138th Street," he said. "At William Spiller's. He had a jazz group."

Next day, I went uptown and rang the bell at 232 West 138th Street. A dignified old lady came to the door. "Is this William Spiller's house?" I asked. She said yes, William Spiller had been her brother-in-law. He was dead. "My name is Bessie Taliaferro," she said, and invited me in.

She was ninety-seven years old, living in the basement that had been *La Revue Nègre*'s rehearsal studio. She told me most of the cast had not believed in Josephine, they did not think the French would love her. "They were wrong, eh?" she said.

In that basement was a Chickering piano made in 1885, the piano Claude Hopkins had played for rehearsals. "He was so good-looking," Bessie said, "and Sidney Bechet stood right over there with his clarinet." I was transported, I could see them, I could hear them. Three years later, on her hundredth birthday, Bessie sold me the piano for a dollar. She thought I was the right one to have it.

I was getting used to miracles. In Philadelphia, I found an old woman (she looked like Popeye, sitting in her rocking chair, smoking a pipe) who had been a waitress at one of Josephine's weddings. Her name was Ethel Lockman, her nickname was the Duchess. "I used to work at the Green Dragon," she said. "It was a speakeasy, but I quit because every morning when we closed, I would have to step over a dead body, and I was too tired to wipe up the blood on the floor. That's why I went to work in the Bakers' restaurant on South Street. It was Mr. Baker who told his good-for-nothing son Billy he had to marry Josephine. He said, 'You have to marry her, or get out of my house.'

"Josephine was a nice girl," said the Duchess. "She didn't smoke."

In Atlantic City, I found Maude Russell, known in her prime as the Slim Princess. She had been a soubrette at the Standard Theater in Philadelphia when Josephine arrived there, fresh off the road from her first professional tour. Maude remembered Josephine's opening night, April 25, 1921. "She was dressed like a ragamuffin, but she killed them all the way up to the peanut gallery. Next day, her picture was out in front of the theater."

My research led me to St. Louis, and then back to Paris, where, out of the blue, a respected art dealer phoned to offer me a cache of letters—hundreds of pages—from Josephine to her lawyer, written between 1954 and 1961, most of them while she was on tour. In those letters, she was alive again, manipulating, cajoling, literally counting sheep. She had one ram, one ewe, twelve lambs—why were there only eleven mentioned in his last letter? Every night, she wrote that lawyer ten-page documents. She said she had fallen. "Do you know how hard it is to dance on your two feet when your ankles are swollen like sausages?" she demanded. "But I can't call a doctor, we need all the money. How are the children? I miss them so much."

At the end of seven years, Josephine terminated the lawyer's services with one last letter. Thank you, don't need you anymore, goodbye. And she never paid him. That was Josephine.

I said earlier that she had hurt me too. Like the lawyer, I was dumped. This was a pattern I only came to understand—and forgive—much later.

One trail led me to Commandant Jacques Abtey, who had been Josephine's boss in the French underground during World War II. He told me that when he first interviewed her for the job, she said, "France is the country that adopted me without reservation, I am willing to give my life for her."

Through Jacques, I met soldiers, spies, nurses—the world of the Resistance—who had gone on fighting against Hitler even after France was defeated, and they spoke of Josephine's courage, the way she had risked her life and lifted the morale of all around her. For five years, Jacques said, Josephine had been his lover; they shared not only affection but grief that they could not have a child.

Listening, I thought of a night in 1973 when Josephine and I came back from a party to the villa where the family was living on the Riviera. We kissed good-night, and after a minute, I heard a knock at my bedroom door. Josephine stood there, tears streaking her face. "Come, darling," she said, and led me to her room. Her bed had two big pillows. On one, Stellina (at nine, the youngest member of the Rainbow Tribe) was sleeping, curly brown hair framing her angelic face. On the other was a piece of paper with a message in pink crayon. "Little Mother," it said, "by the time you get home, the Sandman will have taken me away. But I wanted you to know I love you very much. Your daughter, Stellina."

Josephine looked at me and whispered, "You see, my Jean-Claude, no lover can give me that, no jewels." And after a pause, almost with regret, "Not even my public." We stood there holding each other, tears running together. Today, eighteen years after my search for Josephine began, I think I have discovered something. I think we were crying not for Stellina, but for the child in each of us who was forever gone with the Sandman.

I met the choreographer George Balanchine, who had known Josephine in the thirties, and although he refused to be interviewed on tape—he was ashamed of his accent—he told me how she had invited him, on a Sunday, to Le Vésinet, the suburb of Paris where she had a house called Le Beau Chêne. Balanchine, who was poor then, put on his best suit, took the train, and arrived at the mansion with two big iron gates. Josephine's name was spelled out in flowers on either side of the entrance, and everywhere there were life-size naked statues. Mostly of Josephine.

Balanchine went up the stairs, knocked on the door, and nobody answered, so he started yelling, "Josephine, Josephine—" Suddenly, in one of the tall ground-floor windows, Josephine appeared, naked except for three flowers glued on in strategic places. "Yes, yes, yes, *chéri*, I'm coming." She said she had given the servants the day off, and she had been baking bread.

A half century later, recounting the story, Balanchine turned a little pink. "Yes, *maître*," I said. "And then what happened?" He smiled. "Well," he said, "I think we had lunch."

I told him how I was discovering Josephine, and he said yes, "she is like Salome. She has seven veils. If you lift one, there is a second, and what you discover is even more mysterious, and you go to the third, and you still don't know where you are. Only at the end, if you keep looking faithfully, will you find the true Josephine."

JOSEPHINE

Chapter 1

—

PARIS, OCTOBER 1925: ALL HELL BREAKS LOOSE

"She had no shame in front of those crackers"

uel cul elle a!" What an ass! Excuse the expression, but that is the cry that greeted Josephine as she exploded onstage in "La Danse de Sauvage." (Sixty years later, her friend and sometime lover, Maurice Bataille, would say to me, "Ah! *ce cul* . . . it gave all of Paris a hard-on.")

It is October 2, 1925, at the Théâtre des Champs-Élysées, opening night of *La Revue Nègre*. Everyone is here, painters, writers, music hall stars—Léger, Gertrude Stein, Chevalier—diplomats, princes, expatriate Americans (of whom there are forty-three thousand in Paris). At home, there is Prohibition; in France, drink and sex seem free. For one American dollar, you get twenty-five francs.

The theater is sold out, all two thousand mauve-colored velvet seats. Earlier, a voice has roared a message—"Full! Only folding chairs left"—into the avenue Montaigne. So many flowers arrive that they are put on the street, there is no more place for them inside. Ticket holders walk to the entrance across a red carpet flanked by white rose trees, the men in full dress, the women with bobbed hair, lips and nails lacquered scarlet, arms flashing those narrow diamond bracelets the cynical of the age call "service stripes."

Backstage, producer Caroline Dudley Reagan paces. She has given herself the role of narrator. "Side by side with my artists." Years later, she will say of *La Revue Nègre*'s success, "It wasn't me, but the phoenix inside Josephine, that bird of paradise. It wasn't me, but Bechet's saxophone, and his soul. It wasn't me, but Louis Douglas, my choreographer. . . . He had already danced in Russia, even for the czarina. . . . Decidedly, God was with me."

In the first row are students from L'École des Beaux-Arts. They have rented twenty seats for the entire two weeks *La Revue Nègre* is expected to run. One tall blond boy—Maurice Blech—will come back every night until Josephine invites him to her dressing room, and then to her bed.

The show begins. "On one side of the stage," reports the man from *Le Figaro,* "before a curtain on which thick-lipped faces with immense black eyes stand out among the geometric designs in dazzling colors applied by some local Picasso in Tallahassee or Honolulu, eight musicians in red tailcoats take their seats."

The "local Picasso" is, in fact, the Mexican painter Covarrubias, the eight musicians are Claude Hopkins and his orchestra, and once they begin to play, *Le Figaro*'s critic loses all objectivity. "The music seems to have captured the echoes of the jungle and to mingle the moan of the breeze, the patter of rain, the crackling of leaves . . ."

The curtain rises to reveal a backdrop of two Mississippi riverboats. Down front is a wharf where people rest in the sun. A man comes on pushing a wheelbarrow full of flowers. It's Sidney Bechet. He picks his horn off the cart, bends his head to the mouthpiece, a short fat Pan inciting his listeners to revelry, filling the theater with genius.

The chorus girls are young, supple, they laugh as they dance the Charleston (Paris is crazy about the Charleston), but some in the audience are disappointed that the performers are so fair. Because of the word *nègre* in the title, the French are expecting black Africans, not American mulattoes. These dancers are creamy-skinned, beige-skinned, and for the ten days since they got off the boat they have moved from astonishment to astonishment, going to the Galeries Lafayette where they can try on clothes and no one forbids it, going to the cafés, where they are served politely, walking in the streets, where they are openly admired.

Josephine, the star, is darker than the other girls, a clown with rubber legs and rubber face. She works hard in a sketch about an abandoned bride, singing "Yes Sir, That's My Baby" (badly, because she is not yet a singer), offering a "darky impression" in blackface. She crosses her eyes, pushes her knees together, does splits, her pants rolled high. She's part Jerry Lewis, part Chaplin, competing with Louis Douglas (they say he has "talking feet") for the laughter of spectators already dazzled by music, speed, colors.

The critic Pierre de Regnier describes Josephine as a strange figure "who walks with bended knees . . . and looks like a boxing kangaroo. . . . Is this a man? Is this a woman? Her lips are painted black, her skin is the color of a banana, her hair, already short, is stuck to her head as if made of caviar, her voice is high-pitched, she shakes continually, and her body slithers like a snake. . . . The sounds of the orchestra seem to come from her. . . .

"Is she horrible? Is she ravishing? Is she black? Is she white? . . . Nobody knows for sure. There is no time to know. She returns as she left, quick as a one-step dance, she is not a woman, she is not a dancer, she is something extravagant and passing, just like the music. . . ."

"Electric greens," writes another critic, "burning pinks . . . what rapture. No rest for the eyes or for the ears."

But the real sensation of the night—the finale, a "Charleston Cabaret"—is still to come. Suddenly, Josephine, that funny girl, is being carried onstage by Joe Alex, a strong black dancer from Africa. She is naked except for a few feathers tied to her waist and ankles, and she is wrapped around Joe's body like a vine around a tree in the forest. He is half naked, too, bent over almost double, a hunter with his prey on his back.

First, you feel sorry that the lovely animal is dead, the shape of the body is so perfect, the color, the stillness. Then she starts to come alive, the muscular body begins to move, the music begins to pound. ("The jazz gets stronger and stronger, the blood pressure goes up six points," a doctor in the audience said later.)

She slides down Joe's body. Shameless, she seems to be making love to him in front of everyone. Joe has been chasing Josephine since rehearsals began, but he is not real to her. The one she wants to make jealous, Claude, is upstage of them, playing the piano, as their frenzy builds.

For Pierre de Regnier, the "Danse de Sauvage" is "barbaric . . .

naughty . . . a return to the customs of the dark ages," and he tells his readers how Josephine achieves a "silent declaration of love by a simple forward movement of her belly, with her arms raised above her head, and the quiver of her entire rear."

This is the way Josephine herself will recall the occasion: "The first time I had to appear in front of the Paris audience . . . I had to execute a dance rather . . . savage. I came onstage and . . . a frenzy took possession of me . . . seeing nothing, not even hearing the orchestra, I danced!"

Some people in the audience scream for more, others rise, wrapping themselves in indignation and little furs, and stalk from the theater, muttering that jazz and blacks are going to destroy white civilization. Josephine doesn't care. First, she doesn't understand a word of French, so she can't tell what they're saying, and second, she and Joe take the noise as a kind of participation in their ritual, it gives an extra energy to their wild mating dance.

In the wings, André Daven, the director of the theater, knows he has seen theatrical history being made. "It was like the revelation of a new world," Daven says. "Eroticism finding a style. Josephine was laughing, she was crying, and the audience stood and gave her such an ovation that she trembled, and could not leave the stage. We had to bring the curtain down."

Backstage, the chorus girls are amazed. Most feel sorry for Claude Hopkins's wife, Mabel, because Claude has been cheating on her with this crazy Josephine. Besides being amazed, the girls are embarrassed. Lydia Jones remembers the feeling. "We were horrified at how disgusting Josie was behaving in front of this French audience, doing her nigger routine. She had no self-respect, no shame in front of these crackers, and would you believe it, they loved her."

They did love her. Berenice Abbott, the American photographer, called the night electric. "Josephine came out with these feathers on her tail and this beautiful little body, and people went wild. The French were kind of tired and a little bit decadent, it's hard to get them excited, but everybody just wanted to leap over the balcony; a great spontaneous combustion took place."

In *Le Crapouillot,* Louis Cheronnet wrote that he had never seen anything more sensual than the dance where Josephine "mimics love, the gift of herself, while a black man wraps her in his passionate movements, his frantic desire. . . ."

In *L'Art Vivant*, André Levinson spoke of Josephine's having "the splendor of an ancient animal, until the movements of her behind and her grin of a benevolent cannibal make admiring spectators laugh."

Reviewing for *The New Yorker*, Janet Flanner found the music "tuneless" and the finale "dull," but later reversed herself. In 1972, forty-seven years after the fact, she described the moment when Joe Alex set Josephine down on the stage. "She was an unforgettable female ebony statue. A scream of salutation spread through the theater."

It's all in the perspective. One man's scream of salutation is another man's "What an ass!"

The belated Flanner homage continued: "Within a half hour of the final curtain on opening night, the news and meaning of her arrival had spread by the grapevine up to the cafés on the Champs-Élysées, where the witnesses of her triumph sat over their drinks excitedly repeating their report of what they had just seen. . . ."

News tearing through the streets, my God, it's like Napoléon, when he was fighting. And yet, Josephine's triumph was real. And she had made it look easy, effortless, so spontaneous that some observers were fooled into thinking the performance they had just seen was an expression of her nature, not a product of her art. They were mistaken. Josephine was not a natural child, she was a complicated, driven nineteen-year-old. She herself had created that "magnificent dark body," out of will and her need to be noticed. And the day leading up to her conquest of Paris had been one of the worst she had ever lived.

Chapter 2

—

TERROR BEFORE
THE OPENING

"Josephine, don't you jump out that window!"

here is a truth behind every legend that is different from what
you might imagine. The legend, for instance, of the night a dancer with
a body "possessed by the devil" seduced a jaded public.

In the twenty-four hours before the opening of *La Revue Nègre,* it
was Josephine who was feeling seduced and abandoned.

But let us step back a moment. Most of the cast had been drinking
since they got off the SS *Berengaria* in Cherbourg. It had been ten days
of nonstop party, though it began quietly. In a manuscript she never
published, Caroline Dudley Reagan wrote of "our modest arrival in Paris
at the Gare St. Lazare. . . . There was no fanfare, nor anybody to notice
. . . the performers were a little bewildered, lost. . . . It was Mr. Daven
who told me he had reserved rooms, two here, three there . . . and we
were on our way to the hotels—in Montmartre, in the section of artists
of all colors and all races, no prejudice, no racism—at the right time,
without a fuss."

Even during the rehearsal period, there were celebrations every night, one at a cabaret where Maurice Chevalier bought caviar for the cast. "I liked it on those little pieces of toast," says Evelyn Anderson. "I was eighteen years old, and it was great to be onstage and in France."

Josephine wasn't so sure. Claude Hopkins had been her lover all the way across the ocean (even with his wife, Mabel, right there, only a step behind them), but almost as soon as the *Berengaria* docked, he discovered the brothel of Madame Blanche. Now, every evening after rehearsal, he would lie to Mabel (and to Josephine) about where he was going, and show up at Madame Blanche's door.

The first time he went, there were five or six other patrons. After a few days, he decided he didn't want to be part of a crowd, asked, "How much for the house?" and a deal was made. A sultan with a harem, Claude spent blissful hours sitting naked at a gold piano, one girl perched on top of the gaudy upright, her legs around his neck, another girl on his knee.

If Mabel guessed what was going on, she kept her own counsel. Josephine was different. For a week, she had been raging to Lydia Jones about Claude's disappearances. She was also beginning to worry about the reception she might receive at the hands of the opening-night crowd. The company had already given a preview for an invited audience, and the responses had not been uniformly enthusiastic. (One journalist wrote of "dancers, singers and musicians who perform their sketches terribly"; another complained about the "infernal racket" made by the band.)

The day before the opening, dress rehearsal seemed to go well enough, but the theater was swarming with photographers and, as soon as the final curtain fell, Josephine made her escape. Claude was nowhere to be seen, but maybe he would show up at her place later.

Josephine, being the star, was booked into a different hotel than the chorus; she had a living room, a bedroom with a mirrored ceiling, and a bathroom with a bidet. In the bidet, she had installed a few goldfish; she always had some kind of livestock around.

Even though she had invited Lydia Jones to be her roommate (as always, she disliked spending nights alone), the two were not particularly compatible, and one of the things they disagreed about was the mirrored ceiling. Lydia was somewhat moralistic—"Claude used to come sleep in the bed with Josephine, and I would be in the next bed, that made me sick, you know"—and did not like to see endless reflections of herself. Josephine, on the other hand, admired her body day and night, loving it from every angle.

Waiting for Claude, who did not arrive, she put a hair straightener, Mary's Congolene, on her hair, and fell asleep. When she woke—was it noon? 2 P.M.?—she was not thinking of the opening of *La Revue Nègre*, only hours away; she was thinking of running. Anyplace.

For one thing, the Congolene had left her almost bald, her scalp badly burned. It was meant to be combed through and rinsed out, not slept in. And Lydia, her small pretty face so set in disapproval, was not the person to comfort a wild woman, so Josephine fled, making for Evelyn Anderson's hotel, on rue Pigalle.

Evelyn lived with Joe Hayman, Claude's saxophone player, and they were in bed on the fifth floor when the banging on the door woke them up. *Bam! bam! bam!* like a machine gun. Half asleep, Evelyn opened the door, and there like a fury came Josephine, eyes puffy, screaming a torrent of words.

"She was talkin' about Claude, she was so upset because she couldn't have him, and she'd had some champagne, I guess, and she went to the window, and I said, 'What are you gonna do, Josephine?' I said, 'Don't you act like no fool and jump out that window, you come on back here.' She was on the verge. Ain't no doubt about it, she really was."

Roused from sleep, Joe Hayman's reaction was fury. When Josephine opened the shutters and leaned over the balcony railing, he leaped naked from the bed, grabbed her, and nearly went off the balcony with her. He managed to yank the bellowing Josephine back inside—Evelyn remembers his yelling, "Stupid cow, you almost got me killed!"—and he hurled her onto the bed, where she continued to sob.

"She's having a nervous breakdown," said Evelyn.

"Get the cognac," said Joe.

Evelyn brought the bottle, then telephoned Caroline Reagan, who came rushing over and put in a call to her friend Antoine, the most famous hairdresser in Paris. She said she was bringing Miss Baker to see him. But after one look at Josephine, Antoine shook his head. Alas, Madame must forgive him, he could do nothing for that poor burned skin. He was desolate, he regretted—and then, all at once, an inspiration.

He fetched some paper, took up his scissors. He cut out a cap, complete with the spit curls that would become famous, lacquered it black, and gently glued it to Josephine's temples. A little black helmet so cleverly fashioned that from far away it would look like hair.

Crisis averted. Josephine had one more cognac, courtesy of Antoine, and went home. Caroline wanted her to get some rest before she came to the theater. Came, as it turned out, to be greeted by flowers and crowds and bravos and controversy and adulation.

She did not yet know that her life would never again be simple. Half an hour after the last curtain came down, she was slipping through the crowds, laughing, flirting, no more the naked savage, but a queen in a gold lamé dress by Poiret.

André Daven and Rolf de Maré, the theater's owner, had turned the place into a giant club (supper on the balcony, dancing on the stage) for three hundred invited guests. Mistinguett, queen of the music halls, who had just opened at the Moulin Rouge, came straight from her own show just in time to discover that she had, at last, a rival.

Josephine, however, was enjoying herself, even though, at 3 A.M., she went home alone. Tonight, of course, Claude had been with Mabel at the party, but Josephine had other things to think about.

The disastrous day had ended well. Until she went into her bathroom at the hotel. Hearing her scream, "Call a doctor!" Lydia Jones ran to help. "Look!" cried Josephine, pointing. The goldfish were lying dead in the bidet, which was empty of water. One more failure of communication. How could a simple child of St. Louis be expected to understand the mysteries of French plumbing?

As the worst and the best twenty-four hours of her life came to an end, Josephine reviled the universe for having murdered her goldfish. That she herself had put the fish in the bidet was not a subject Lydia brought up. It was better, she decided, to go to bed and think about finding a less volatile roommate.

Years before, in St. Louis, Josephine's mother had had the same thought.

Chapter 3

—

ELVIRA, CARRIE, THE BEGINNINGS

"Grandma often talked about slave days"

here is only one picture of Josephine Baker as a baby, and nobody is sure if that one is authentic.

She was born Freda J. McDonald on June 3, 1906, in the Female Hospital, which had opened as the St. Louis Social Evil Hospital, a treatment center for prostitutes suffering from venereal disease.

She died on April 12, 1975, in the Salpêtrière hospital, which had been built to care for the prostitutes, beggars, and criminal women of Paris.

But what a dance in between! Though even through the years of wine and roses, she could not forget the slums she had run so fast and so far to escape. Despite herself, she thought about them. Despite herself because, a friend said, "Miss Baker does not like to remember. She lives . . . in the present."

So much did Josephine "not like to remember" that when she left America, she erased all evidence of her early life. Pictures, papers, cut up, torn up, burnt. Goodbye.

And still, this impulse to cover her tracks was at war with her impulse to get the world's attention. She would alter her story again and again, reshaping history as she went. Marcel Sauvage told me how they worked on the first memoirs, a collection of "notes, impressions, images," when she was twenty. "Around 5 P.M., I would go to her hotel. That was when she got up. The maid would bring breakfast, and Josephine, half naked, her pink nightgown all open, laughing, playing with a parrot, would start to remember."

And what did she remember, in the shadows of those late afternoons?

She said her father and mother were married (they were not), and she said she sent a check home every month (at the time, she did). "Now, dear, you understand . . . I am the great man of the family."

She said that kings walked with pointed shoes in her dreams. "And the queens were blond . . . sometimes I cried because I too would have liked to be a queen."

She said she became a dancer "because I was born in a cold city. . . ."

She said her childhood was filled with "stories of cemeteries. A black childhood is always a little sad."

Even when the sadness was once removed. Her grandmother, Elvira, "often talked about slave days. I adored Grandma. The songs she sang as she rocked me to sleep . . . told of the freedom that would someday come."

As a child on a tobacco plantation, Elvira had seen a pregnant woman put in a hole, belly down, and beaten. Her great-grandson, Richard Martin, Jr., told me she repeated that story over and over. "She used to say, 'Poor Miz So-and-So, why is Master beating her on the back that way?' And she would cry, and I would just be amazed, it was as though she was living through the whole thing.

"I had no idea of slaves, but the way she was telling it made me feel very sad, not for the woman being beaten on the back, but for my great-grandmother. Each time, after she told that story, my grandmother Carrie would give her a peppermint to make her feel better." (No matter how terrible the past, Elvira at least had family; many former slaves had lost all trace of relatives. The government cared for some of these old people in homes like the one called Blue Plains, near Washington, D.C.)

Elvira had been born on a tobacco plantation in Holly Springs, Arkansas (when she died in 1936, the death certificate listed her as being "about ninety"), and Josephine would always be in conflict about her, partly proud, partly ashamed that her grandmother had been a slave. She sometimes claimed that Elvira was an Indian—hadn't the red man been in America when the first white man came ashore? In fact, the tiny five-foot-tall woman may have been part Indian; she had long, straight, black hair.

During the period that Josephine was mistress of the château Les Milandes, one of the men who worked for her told me she grew tobacco by the front door. She never revealed that the tobacco was a tribute to Elvira.

Elvira grew up to marry a Virginian, an older man named Richard McDonald. They could not have children, and in 1886, in Little Rock, Arkansas, they adopted a baby, naming her for Richard's sister, Caroline. (Caroline and her husband, Charles Crook—also a much older man— had had two children, but both died in infancy.) In time, the two couples and baby Carrie moved together from Little Rock to St. Louis.

At the end of the nineteenth century (we know the family was there as early as 1896, because of Carrie's school records), St. Louis was a rapidly growing city. In 1849, it had survived a cholera epidemic that killed four thousand people, and a waterfront fire that spread from burning steamboats to destroy hundreds of buildings in the narrow streets along the Mississippi. By 1874, the Eads Bridge had been built across the river, which meant the city could be reached by train from Cincinnati, rather than by ferry. The population of St. Louis was polyglot; the French settlers had been followed by Spaniards, Germans, Irish, and British. There was also, in the mid-1800s, an influx of blacks like the McDonalds and the Crooks from the rural South. By 1900, there were 575,238 people in the city, 35,516 of them black.

Charles Crook had a government pension of fourteen dollars a month. He had been one of 186,017 black soldiers to join the Union army during the Civil War; he had fought with Company D of the Sixty-first United States Colored Infantry, and suffered a gunshot wound in his left hand. In St. Louis, he found a job as a porter in a store; his two incomes established him as head of the household. He, his wife, and the McDonalds shared a third-floor railroad flat in a row house at 1534 Gratiot Street. Richard McDonald worked as a laborer, Elvira worked as a laundress, and little Carrie was left at home in the care of Caroline Crook.

When Carrie McDonald was seventeen years old, a conductor working for the St. Louis Transit Company—electric cars were replacing the old horse cars—was paid twenty-one cents an hour, and the city was playing host to a World's Fair. The fair—technically the Louisiana Purchase Exposition of 1904—brought visitors from all over the globe, but did not treat them all equally. One restaurant on the exposition grounds posted a sign, NO COLORED PEOPLE SERVED, and the company with the fresh-water concession refused to set out water for blacks "even when they offered to drop a cent in the slot, as do white folks."

Slavery was long gone, but many people of color felt that true freedom came only to those with light skins. A member of the black press who called himself Dr. Midnight wrote in *The Indianapolis Recorder* that he had visited a lady friend in St. Louis and been appalled to find her ironing her hair. "These men here don't go with kinks," she told him, "so if you want to shine in St. Louis, you must do away with kinks and get straight. I also have a preparation for making my face white by degrees."

"Some of our women look like circus riders," Dr. Midnight railed in another newspaper. "Rosy cheeks, ashy faces and wigs seem to be the go . . . Negroes clamouring for recognition in this world, but they will not get it as long as they are getting away from themselves. It is disgusting to hear colored women say, 'He's too black.' "

Other black editors reflected on white people's fear of "Negro domination." The *Gazetteer and Guide* printed the words of a white man named Tom Watson—he had run for vice president under the banner of the Populist party in 1896—who agreed that such fears were baseless. "What words," asked Watson, "can paint the cowardice of the Anglo-Saxon who would deny 'equal and exact justice' to the ignorant, helpless, poverty-cursed Negro, in whose ears the clank of chains have scarcely ceased domination. . . ."

By then, Carrie McDonald, who was without racial prejudice—she liked pretty boys, no matter what color they were—would have been able to follow Dr. Midnight's musings if she had stumbled across them; she was the first person in the Crook-McDonald household to learn to read and write. Coal black, pretty, tall, slender, full of life, the only child cared for by four adults, she was a bit spoiled.

She and Elvira adored each other. Aunt Caroline was the disciplinarian, demanding that Carrie study hard. To catch up with the white world, one had to fight.

But Carrie was young, and the streets of St. Louis were filled with music, especially if you went down to the red-light district (Market Street, Chestnut Street) where there were gambling joints, gin mills, and the sounds of ragtime pianos pounding through the nights. During the summers, ladies of the evening would stand outside the houses where they worked and sing blues songs. To Carrie, all this was a lot more fascinating than staying home listening to Aunt Caroline's sermons.

Or going to school. Carrie loved to dance, and one of her boyfriends, Eddie Carson (thought by many to be Josephine's father), was a good dancer. Years later, Josephine's half-sister Margaret would remember, "Mama was the most popular girl at the dance hall on Sundays. No one could dance like she could, with a glass of water balanced on her head, not spilling a drop."

But Carrie worked, too. By the time she was nineteen, she was employed as a laundress. An improvident laundress, because she got pregnant, and Aunt Caroline turned her out. Elvira had nothing to say about it; Caroline ruled the roost, and was fierce in judgment. Hadn't she warned Carrie a hundred times? Wasn't Carrie too wild? Hadn't the family given her everything, and hadn't she returned bad for good?

In St. Louis, I was lucky. I found Helen Morris (née Williams), whose mother had been Carrie's friend. "Mama's name was Emma Williams," says Helen, "and she and Carrie worked together at the laundry owned by my aunt Josephine Cooper. When Carrie's folks put her out, she ended up at Aunt Jo's house, she didn't have anywhere else to go. She stayed there until the baby was born, and that's when Aunt Jo said, 'Carrie, if it's a girl, name it after me,' and Carrie said, 'I will.' "

The records of the city of St. Louis tell an almost unbelievable story. They show that Carrie McDonald ("colored"), twenty years old, was admitted to the Female Hospital (at that time, almost exclusively white) on May 3, 1906, diagnosed as pregnant. She was discharged on June 17, her baby, Freda J. McDonald, having been born two weeks earlier. The baby's father was identified simply as "Edw." Why six weeks in the hospital? Especially for a black woman who would customarily have had her baby at home with the help of a midwife? Obviously, there had been problems with the pregnancy, but Carrie's chart reveals no details.

I think Josephine's father was white—so did Josephine, so did her family—and I think he cared about Carrie. He's the one who must have got her into that hospital and paid to keep her there all those weeks.

Also, her baby's birth was registered by O. H. Elbrecht, head of the hospital, at a time when most black births were not. Besides, Freda sounds German to me, and people in St. Louis say Carrie had worked for a German family. (Although it certainly didn't matter; Josephine was never called Freda.)

I have unraveled many mysteries associated with Josephine Baker, but the most painful mystery of her life, the mystery of her father's identity, I could not solve.

The secret died with Carrie, who refused till the end to talk about it. She let people think Eddie Carson was the father, and Carson played along.

Josephine knew better, though her version was also folklore. "My father was Eddie Moreno, a good-looking boy with olive skin," she would say. Or: "My father was a Spanish dancer." Helen Morris says, "You could look at Tumpy and tell she was not entirely black."

(Tumpy was the nickname given Josephine as a baby; she always said it was because "I was fat as Humpty Dumpty." But if she was fat, she was also lucky. At that time, according to the records of the health department in St. Louis, three out of five children died before the age of three. A Dr. Temms, writing in *The St. Louis Argus,* described the city's more poverty-stricken sections as "a great breeding ground," saying, "Next to the Russian Jews in point of being prolific came the Negroes and then the Italians.")

When Carrie was discharged from the hospital, she brought her baby back to the apartment on Gratiot Street, and left her in the reluctant care of Aunt Caroline Crook.

The McDonalds were heartbroken. They had been living for thirteen years at the same address, providing a stable home for their adopted child; they had hoped she would get an education so she wouldn't have to do the kind of manual labor in which they were trapped. This was a new age, opportunities were opening for women of color; at the very least Carrie might have been an elevator operator wearing white gloves and mixing with the elite of St. Louis in a department store.

On October 12, 1907, to the further dismay of her relatives, Carrie had a second baby, a boy named Richard Alexander, whose birth was not recorded. Neither was the place where he was born. His father was a black man named James Alexander Perkins, but he and Carrie did not marry, and Carrie did not change her errant ways

Baby Richard, called Brothercat, might not have had such a good start in life if it had not been for Helen Morris's beneficent mother. "Mama claimed we were all family," Helen says. "You know we colored people had been separated and moved around so much, and then life brought us together like a family. And Mama nursed Brothercat. See, she was nursing my brother Buddy at the same time, so after Aunt Carrie's milk dried up—she was flittin' and flyin'—Mama nursed Carrie's baby. Mama always said that's why he loved her."

Josephine, who was light brown, the color of café au lait, the color of honey, envied her new brother. "He had black skin . . . he was the welcome one."

Her mother didn't entirely forget about Josephine, but visits were hard on both of them. After a day's work at the laundry, Carrie would sometimes stop by, only to be greeted by a furious Aunt Caroline. "Who gave you permission to come in here, lazy demon?" When Elvira tried to defend her daughter, Caroline would scream at her too. "Be quiet! Your daughter, with a white man! . . . She has dishonored us as much as she possibly could."

"I was used to these accusations against my mother," Josephine remembered, "but I did not understand yet what was humiliating or dishonorable about my birth."

Some eight months after Richard was born, Carrie finally became a bride. She and Arthur Martin, a burly, 220-pound, twenty-three-year-old, were married by a duly ordained minister of the gospel, W. H. Piner, and on December 23, they got an early Christmas present: Carrie was delivered of baby Marguerite, who was always called Margaret. She was as black as her parents.

The new family settled into an apartment at 1526 Gratiot, just a few houses down from the Crook-McDonald ménage. Arthur hauled gravel with his horse and wagon, Carrie continued to do laundry, got pregnant again, had a miscarriage. It was 1910, the year she would try to turn her family into a tidy legal entity. When the census taker came to 1526 Gratiot, she assured him that she and Arthur Martin had been married for five years, and had three Martin children. On July 18, 1910, she gave birth to Willie Mae, a pretty baby and, like Richard and Margaret, black.

At this point, Carrie reclaimed Josephine to help out with the little ones. "Mama took me back with her," Josephine said. "Then she said since I was the oldest, I had to do the dishes."

If the five-year-old Josephine felt she didn't belong anywhere, it wasn't surprising. Now she was home again, but did Carrie love her or did she just need a servant? Always, the child was being sent mixed messages: Aunt Caroline moralizing, Elvira comforting, Carrie alternately fond and furious, with a temper so terrible that she almost beat Richard to death when she discovered he had stolen a bicycle. She was guilty about all her "flittin' and flyin'," and forever trying to regain the respect and control of her children. As for Arthur, he wasn't strong enough to manage his wife, whose moods came and went like summer storms.

Helen Morris says Arthur, nicknamed Weatherbird, had some domestic talent, which was lucky because "Aunt Carrie, she didn't let any grass grow under her feet, she had a good time. Sometimes she would go away with a man and stay for a month, and Mama and Weatherbird would take care of the kids. He was left-handed, and he could clean like a woman, everything was spotless."

Although they were not his own children, both Josephine and Richard called Arthur "Papa." And right from the beginning, the young family struggled to live. "We were very, very poor," Richard remembered.

All four children slept on a single bedbug-ridden mattress on the floor, in the same room with their parents. Richard laughed about it. "I used to put my big toe in Tumpy's face, I would try to wiggle it up her nose, and she would scream till Papa or Mama got up and beat both of us.

"At five o'clock in the morning, Josephine and I would go down to the Soulard market three blocks away and pick up vegetables that had fallen on the ground. She was a good sister. She worked, and didn't make much money, maybe fifty cents a week, and when she got it, she would buy things for us."

The enterprising Josephine went out ringing doorbells at the mansions of the rich white people on Westmoreland Avenue—"Can I sweep your steps? Can I shovel the snow?"—and often, she and Richard and their gang, all boys except for her, would cross the railroad tracks to steal coal from freight cars. Josephine was the daring one, climbing to the top of a train: "I start throwing big chunks to the ground, the others fill the bags."

Down below, the boys, frightened that the train is already in motion, yell to her, "Tumpy, jump!"—and still she stays, hurling the coal down faster as the train picks up speed, testing herself as she would always do, straining against limits. Finally: "I throw myself. The train was just accelerating . . . I fall on the ground."

Sometimes, she did odd jobs in a house where there were other servants. In one place, a black housekeeper scolded her for kissing a white baby. This was hard for a young child to comprehend. "They're so soft," Josephine said, "they're warm, the little white children, and so fragile." (She was puzzled also by the sign over the door to Aunt Jo Cooper's laundry that read WE WASH FOR WHITE PEOPLE ONLY. But white people would not have sent their laundry to be washed in the same tubs with the clothes of black people. And the black housekeeper might have lost her job if the white mother had caught Josephine kissing her baby.)

Still, the Martins' neighborhood wasn't segregated, and the census reflected its makeup. Listed under race or color were three categories: *B* for black, *W* for white, *MU* for mulatto. "We grew up," says Helen Morris, "in a kind of United Nations. Russian families, German families, blacks. There were poor people, not so poor people. There was Izzy the Jew, and Lukie Skeel, he was an Irishman, and Mexican Robert; I remember Mexican Robert would put me on his knee and sing 'The Wang Wang Blues' to me, and I was a little bitty thing."

Josephine loved the life of those streets. She played hooky from school, ranging through the neighborhoods of St. Louis with "some other little starvelings. Saturday was a party all over, everywhere accordions, banjos, harmonicas."

There were rent parties, where grown-ups paid to dance and drink, thus providing the host with cash for his landlord. Josephine remembered one night when her gang—Brothercat, Carl, Freckles, Sonny, Skinny, Fatty—stared, fascinated, through an open door at a piano player wearing yellow shoes, and a lady singing, "Do that one little thing Papa a long time."

Freckles, who had red hair, was Josephine's first crush, but when she told him, "I like you," he said, "You're a nigger!" and ran away. She didn't brood. The crap games in the back of the grocery store were even more interesting than love, and so was the church where Holy Rollers hollered. "At the height of their emotion, they raise their legs and kick in the air," Josephine recalled. "Really, they are terribly funny. One of their friends rushes forward to hold their skirts in place, it's more proper.

" 'How can you laugh?' the pastor erupts. 'Leave here and don't ever darken this doorway again as long as you live!' "

In the cellar on Gratiot Street, Josephine did some fancy kicking of her own. "Tumpy made a theater in the basement," her sister Margaret said. "She made costumes out of Grandma's cast-off dresses, and she'd sweep regally across the stage. 'Every show is alike, Tumpy,' Richard and I would complain. 'We're sick of it, we're not coming tonight.' . . . She would shove us down the steps. 'Get in there and take a seat. If you move, I'll slap your faces.' "

"Tumpy made benches out of boards on boxes," Richard told me, "and about three or four kids would come; sometimes one would bring a penny, or a pin, anything so she would let them come in. And she would sing and dance and look cross-eyed. That's a true fact."

Other times, she performed in the open air, in the backyard of Aunt Emma's house. "Mama would give her old pieces of clothes and run-down shoes," Helen says. "Tumpy would go to the neighbors, ask for a potato, a carrot, or an onion, and she would cook them. Then while she performed, my three brothers and Brothercat would eat what she had cooked, and afterward, Tumpy would have a fit and cry. Mama would laugh and say, 'Come on, Tumpy, I'll cook you some more food.' We didn't have much in those days, but we shared what we had."

Listening to this, I got goose pimples. Here are the beginnings of Josephine, the entertainer. Didn't Molière say, "What is theater but two boards and a passion?"

Josephine had three passions—theater, animals, and little children. "Animals interest me," she said, "because they are as simple and as uncomplicated as babies."

She, however, was not simple or uncomplicated. Often, she was difficult and uncontrollable, and at a wake for a local man known as Uncle Joe, she made a memorable scene.

A kind neighbor, wanting to give Carrie a peaceful Sunday at home, had offered to take the hyperactive Josephine to the vigil. They found Uncle Joe ensconced in his coffin, supported by four chairs, in the living room. Mrs. Joe was serving booze, coffee, and cake to the mourners, and all the children were sent out to play. In the yard, a snake wriggled by, and Josephine, picking it up, rushed into the house. She had a present for Uncle Joe.

Seeing the snake, women screamed, and one in her fright kicked a chair out from under the coffin, which fell. Uncle Joe rolled onto the floor, whereupon Josephine dropped the snake, and a man stomped on it. Josephine ran to the man and beat at him. "You killed my friend!" she howled.

Eventually, Uncle Joe was put back in place, but the damage had been done. When the tired neighbor lady restored Josephine to her mother, she said, "Carrie, I feel sorry for you! She's such a monster, you can't take her nowhere."

Soon, Carrie banished the monster again. "I know someone who's looking for a child to work for them, and they'll provide room and board," she told Arthur. "I'm going to send Tump, she's a burden on us and she's the oldest. What do you think?"

Arthur never argued with Carrie. "Do what you want, she's your daughter," he said.

For Josephine, it was a double betrayal—her mother, as always, ready to forsake her, her stepfather too weak to say no. She was seven years old, and her childhood was over.

Chapter 4

—

CHILDHOOD IN ST. LOUIS

"There are no bastards in my family!"

*M*rs. Kaiser had no heart. She lived out in the country, and viewed her small scullery maid as a beast of burden. "She gave me cold potatoes and sent me to bed," Josephine said. "At 5 A.M., she got me up to work. At nine, I went to school because she was required by law to send me, but it made her furious. . . . After I returned . . . I had a dish of cold corn bread and molasses. Then the work began again.

"I was forced to carry coal for the night to each room, chop wood, clean and trim the lamps, wash the meal dishes and clean the kitchen. . . . I slept in the basement. . . . In the corner was a large box where the dog slept: he had to move over to make room for me."

Josephine shared her food with the dog; the dog shared his fleas with Josephine. But Mrs. Kaiser didn't like to see the child scratching herself in the house, "and she beat me terribly, completely naked, because she said that clothes cost too much and beatings wore them out."

Comfort came from the dog and Tiny Tim, a chicken Josephine fed until he got fat. Then Mrs. Kaiser ordered her to kill him. It's normal for a farm animal to be killed for food, but Josephine was traumatized by the terrified warm body between her knees, the squawking, the feathers drowned in blood when she cut Tiny Tim's throat. Still, in the face of Mrs. Kaiser's awful authority, what could she have done for the wretched chicken?

More and more she felt helpless against the adult world, Mrs. Kaiser's world, her mother's world, Aunt Caroline's world. Every slight became huge in her memory, every offense against her was magnified. She once told a fellow chorus girl her aunt had chained her to a bed. (Her brother remembered that she wasn't even good to herself, banging her head against the floor in violent tantrums.)

At Mrs. Kaiser's, worse was to come. According to Josephine, one day she left the dishwater boiling too long on the stove, and Mrs. Kaiser plunged her—Josephine's—hands into the pot. "I scream, I scream, Mother, Mother, help me. I escape to the next house screaming like a lunatic. I fall in front of the door. All my skin and my fingernails are boiled, ready to fall off. The blood is cooked. When I wake up, I'm in the hospital."

Richard didn't recall any of this; I think Josephine had been so agitated by hearing Elvira's accounts of slavery, of vinegar and salt poured on raw wounds, that these stories got mixed up with Mrs. Kaiser's cruelty in the susceptible child's head. In any case, Carrie was forced to take her daughter home again.

That winter, Josephine and Richard went to classes at Dumas. "The black schools," Richard said, "were down by the tracks. If you were out in the yard playin' at recess, and the train came by, all the smoke and cinders, you'd get that in your eyes. Our schools were only for blacks, and we would have to pass by the Catholic school, and the little white kids would be sitting on the fence, and they'd yell at us, 'Hey, Blue Gums,' and 'Where you goin', Shine?'

"I was small for my age, and the older boys tried to beat me up, and Tumpy would jump in and holler, 'Leave my brother alone!' One day a kid hollered back at her, 'He ain't your brother, he's a bastard!'

"When Mama came home from work, Tumpy grabbed her. 'Mama, Mama, the other kids say Richard is a bastard.' Mama looked so tired, but when Tumpy said that, Mama's eyes just got wild. She screamed, 'There are no bastards in my family, you all come from the same hole!' "

In Panama a great canal had been dug, joining the Pacific Ocean with the Caribbean Sea; across the Atlantic, World War I was raging, but President Wilson had proclaimed U.S. neutrality, and the paroxysms of Europe did not seem as real to the poor people of Gratiot Street as figuring out where their next meal was coming from.

Christmas was around the corner; Josephine wanted to make it festive for the younger children. "She'd bring home dolls without heads and arms that she found in garbage pails," Richard said, "and she'd make presents for us." Still, Josephine recalled, Christmas of 1914 was a disaster. "Mama had too much to drink, and each time she drank, she wanted to beat me and hurt me. . . . At one point she said she hated me and wished I were dead."

One week after Christmas, Jo Cooper found another job for Josephine. Through her laundry business, she knew what jobs were available in white people's houses. This time, Josephine would be sent to a couple named Mason.

The childless Mrs. Mason was kind. "She gives me a good warm bed and I eat well. . . . She lets me play with other children in the basement of her house, she sends me to school because she finds me gifted and intelligent . . . she gives me pretty dresses and shoes."

Dressed in Mrs. Mason's old clothes, including a hat "with an immense feather," Josephine resumed performing, singing and dancing for her schoolmates. "I was the star."

She ate with the Masons; she was made much of. Then Mr. Mason started giving her wet kisses, which she found repulsive, and one night, he appeared in her room. Thinking he might be a ghost, next morning she told Mrs. Mason.

Mrs. Mason said only, "Promise you'll call me if it happens again."

The next night, Mr. Mason reappeared. "He slid into my bed, and I screamed, 'Oh, it's the ghost, Mrs. Mason, please come quick!' " That was the end of that job.

When Mrs. Mason brought Josephine home, Carrie was furious. "Tumpy, how could you ruin such a wonderful chance?" And Arthur laughed at the story about the ghost. "What a fool you are, child."

In the next five years, as times got worse, the Martins used their horse and cart to move their belongings no less than ten times. When Arthur and Carrie could no longer afford Gratiot Street (a three-room apartment with stable cost $6.50 a month), they took an apartment on South

Fourteenth. After that came 2327 Walnut, 1537 Papin, and a couple of different addresses on Bernard Street. At Papin Street, they were closer than ever to the railroad yard, not even a fence separated the house from the tracks, and Josephine, lying in bed, listened to the train whistles and dreamed of escape from the bedbugs, from being poor and black. She would have settled for a coach seat to anyplace on any train chugging its way out of St. Louis.

It was the Booker Washington Theatre at Twenty-third and Market streets that fed her soul. Offering employment to black artists, it billed itself as the "Home of Mirth, Music and Merriment." Every Sunday, Josephine went there with Richard and Margaret. For ten cents apiece, they saw movies, musical comedies "direct from 9 weeks run in Chicago," and vaudeville acts, "15 all star performers 15."

Queen Dora, "the celebrated fire dancer" played the Booker. So did the Russell-Owens Company (headed by Bob Russell and Billy Owens), presenting *The Dope Fiend's Dream.* Josephine's favorite performers were the female impersonators. All her life she would love them. She also loved the animal acts like "Williams' Dogs and Monkeys," which featured a police dog in uniform and a patrol wagon pulled by a dog, with a monkey sitting in the driver's seat.

Once she discovered the theater, it became ever harder for her to stay in school. Albert Scott, the truant officer, would come to Gratiot Street, and the neighbors would laugh. "Try the Booker." After a while, he went directly to the theater, but Tumpy, the Phantom of the Booker, running like a mouse between the rows of seats, knew every nook and cranny that could hide a small body. And everyone—ushers, box office people, even performers—knew her and sheltered her.

The theater was on a cobblestoned street with trolley-car tracks running past it. Sometimes, Josephine performed for people out front, and they would throw coins at her feet while trolley passengers, riding by, applauded.

Once, her little sister Willie Mae got a splinter in her eye. "And our father," Richard said, "he tried to get it out by rubbing her eye with his big hands, and she lost it."

"That eye came out of her head and hung down," Helen Morris says. "And Mama said, 'Carrie, why don't you have that eye taken out?' And she kept after her and finally Aunt Carrie did have the eye taken out, and Baby Sis just had a socket there, and she went that way for many a year, until Tumpy sent a beautiful eye from France."

By 1916, Josephine's hooky-playing was out of bounds. School records show that she went to class for a grand total of sixty-seven days that year. She spent most of her time with a family named Jones that lived across the street. The Joneses were traveling musicians, and how could algebra or spelling compete with the sounds pouring from their house, horns wailing like human voices, sometimes a human voice wailing like a horn.

"It was a curious family," Josephine said. "Mrs. Jones was not married to Mr. Jones . . . he held her under hypnotism and she said she could do nothing against him. . . . He would cut locks of her hair, twist them around two nails that he would place in her side of the mattress. . . ."

The possessive Mr. Jones played saxophone, Dyer Jones played trumpet; their daughter Doll, the same age as Josephine, and their son Bill were in the band too. In years to come, Dyer's great talent would be recognized—"She was playin' before Louis Armstrong knew what a trumpet was," said the pianist Ikey Robinson—but back then, the Jones family was going around performing in coffee shops.

Dyer Jones coached Josephine on trombone ("The trombone was bigger than I was"), and then put her to work. "They asked my mother for me, promising clothes and food. My mother gave me away. While I learned the music, I carried the big heavy instruments because we walked many miles from one restaurant to the other. I used to carry the bass drum and arrive dead."

For Josephine, still grievance collecting, Carrie was again the villain, selling her child into servitude. But I think Josephine loved her life with the Joneses. She was in show business, no matter that it was more show than business, and except for the discipline of the music, she was free. It was what she had spent her whole short life waiting for. The Joneses traveled the Strawberry Road, a circuit so named because ripe strawberries don't grow in neat rows, you pick one here, another there, and during that summer, the Strawberry Road took the group from village to village, wherever they were offered cake and lodgings.

Sometimes the band would perform in a green-and-white-striped circus tent. Dyer Jones, Josephine at her side, would stand in a spotlight, doing a solo on her trumpet, a tiny woman who could blow like the archangel Gabriel. The tent would be pitched just outside of town, in a field, and audiences arrived by horse and buggy. There was a colored entrance and a white entrance; there were monkeys and a medicine man.

It was during these travels that Josephine first met Ethel Waters, then touring as one of a trio called the Hill Sisters. In her memoirs, Waters mentioned Josephine. "She was with one of those Negro kid gypsy bands they have down there." Waters described Josephine as "a mugger with a great comic sense. . . . She could dance and she could clown joy into you. She could also play the trombone."

That Dyer Jones was important to Josephine Baker becomes clear when you read *Une Vie de Toutes les Couleurs (My Life of Many Colors)*, another of her early autobiographies, this one in collaboration with André Rivollet. In 1935, at the height of her popularity in France, she ended this book by talking about "the woman with the trumpet, the one who belonged to the company of strolling musicians in which I found myself when I sang on the pavement of the coffee shops."

Dyer Jones had written to say that Josephine's success made her happy, Josephine reported. With the letter, Dyer had enclosed one of the nails around which Mr. Jones had twisted strands of her hair those many years ago.

"Is this nail on which one had to bang, bang in order to shape it, not a little bit the symbol of my life?" asks Josephine in her book. "When I think about the troubled days, I feel like crying: it is so far."

Chapter 5

—

RACE RIOTS, AND TUMPY LEAVES TOWN

"Oh God, why didn't you make us all one color?"

$\mathcal{I}$n 1917, race relations in St. Louis were worsening. A faltering economy set white men to worrying that blacks were being imported from the South to take their jobs, even though most whites were not eager to work for $2.35 a day at the sewer-pipe factory.

But to eleven-year-olds like Josephine, this was not a matter of great importance. The heat came early that summer, and on sultry nights, excursion boats offering the hope of cool air plied their way up and down the Mississippi. Sometimes the young Martins would go to the pier at the foot of Olive Street and watch the steamers set out in the moonlight. Departure time: 9 P.M. Admission: thirty-five cents. They could hear the music, and see people dancing on the lower deck. *The St. Louis Argus* touted a "Family Boat Excursion" to take place on Monday, July 2; it would feature entertainment by the Ragtime Steppers, and it promised to leave on schedule, "rain or shine."

As it turned out, rain or shine didn't signify. July 2, 1917, would be memorialized in blood.

RACE RIOTERS FIRE EAST ST. LOUIS AND SHOOT OR HANG MANY NEGROES. DEAD ESTIMATED AT FROM 20 TO 76 ran the headline in *The New York Times*. The details were ugly.

"A mob of more than 100 men, led by ten or fifteen young girls about 18 years old, chased a negro woman at the Relay depot about 5 P.M. The girls were brandishing clubs and calling upon the men to kill the woman. A lone negro man appeared in the railroad yards. The mob immediately gave up the charge of the woman and turned upon the man. He was shot to death. . . ."

Whites had attacked streetcars, taken blacks off them and beaten them, militiamen were helpless against the crowds, white men who tried to give blacks medical attention were prevented at gunpoint from doing so, policemen in patrol wagons were bombarded with bricks. Martial law was finally declared, and the killing stopped, but *The African American*, a Baltimore newspaper, compared the riots to "the ruthless, devastating German drive through Belgium."

Hundreds of blacks abandoned their burnt-out homes; they fled by way of the Eads Bridge and the Free Bridge to St. Louis proper, and many of them found refuge in the neighborhood where the Martins lived. "We kept a couple of families who came over cross the river, came over in St. Louis," Richard said. "We had two, three families; we got them on the street."

Josephine, of course, always claimed to have been smack in the heart of East St. Louis when it blew up, and insisted she remembered being shaken from sleep by her mother, who told the children, "It's the whites. Hurry!"

The reality was that she had learned about the riots by listening to people who had escaped them; it was from the safe side of the bridge that she and Richard watched the flames. "We could see the houses burning and the sky red with fire, smoke," he told me. "I was not afraid, because it was on the other side." Even so, years later, she would still be describing herself as an eyewitness. "I never forget my people screaming. . . . I see them running to get to the bridge. I have been running ever since." But the stories she told of escaping the mobs, her mother crossing the bridge like Marianne, symbol of France, pulling her children with her, were somebody else's stories.

It was a bloody time—thirty-eight lynchings were recorded in 1917—and it would get worse. (The following year would bring sixty-two lynchings; of these, fifty-eight victims were black, four were white.)

In New York City, under the auspices of the NAACP, thousands of black men and women and children responded to the East St. Louis riots by taking part in a "Silent Protest Parade" along Fifth Avenue. Children dressed in white marched in formation, one carrying a banner inscribed "Thou Shalt Not Kill," and on the sidelines, a little girl was holding a sign: MOTHER, DO LYNCHERS GO TO HEAVEN?

By fall, America was in the war. The black population of St. Louis, though offended by government questionnaires—each carried the words, "If person is of African descent, tear off left-hand corner"—was still willing to do its bit. In early November of 1917, twenty-five thousand people gathered at Union Station to cheer for 480 black draftees leaving for army camp. (Arthur Martin, having turned thirty-two, just escaped being drafted.) Living so close to the station, Josephine was in the midst of the excitement, watching men kiss their wives goodbye and mothers faint.

In 1918, pestilence was added to war. A flu epidemic—it would claim 550,000 victims across the United States—encircled the world, killing more people than any sickness since the Black Death in the fourteenth century. Theaters closed, and the Dumas school shut down for a short time too. This enforced vacation pleased Josephine; what did not please her were the endless confrontations with Carrie. Josephine's brown skin continued to be a tacit reproach to her black mother, living evidence of Carrie's dalliance with a white man; when they went out together, both felt they were being stared at, whispered about.

They tried, but they could not find common ground; Josephine longed to be loved, Carrie longed to understand her, but it just never worked. Josephine prayed for answers. "Oh, God, why didn't you make us all one color? It would have been so much simpler."

Her road trips with the Joneses had contributed to her dissatisfactions. It was hard to come back to the discipline, the poverty, of home. She had no pity for her mother, no respect for the stepfather who endured visits from Carrie's former lovers. Occasionally, Eddie Carson popped through the front door to check on Josephine, who didn't give a damn about him. Or Alexander Perkins came by to say hello to his biological son, Richard. "He was a nice man," Richard said.

Poor Weatherbird was now jobless, and Carrie was going off, sometimes for weeks, with other men. "Once in a while," Richard told me, "my father would get jealous and Mama would get a black eye."

Still, away from his wife, Arthur Martin was an easygoing person. On weekends, he would hitch up his old horse and cart and carry the children across the Eads Bridge. They would camp along the river and fish, and Arthur would make a fire and fry the catch—sometimes catfish, sometimes buffalo fish—in hot oil. "Tumpy would get so excited," Richard remembered.

Josephine still worked as a kitchen helper, a baby-sitter, one of the girls who delivered laundry for Aunt Jo Cooper. She loved handling the silky bedsheets of rich white people, the lingerie trimmed with hand-made lace, even though Aunt Jo was strict, and would make her wash her grimy paws before she touched a single handkerchief.

But relations between Carrie and her eldest had become so difficult that Josephine was once more living with Elvira and Aunt Caroline. "I think," Richard said, "it's because Josephine was a little lighter than the rest of us children—that's me and Margaret and Wilhelmina [Willie Mae]—I think that's why my mother just gave Josephine to my grandmother."

By now, both Elvira and Caroline were widows, and in addition to Josephine, they had taken in a boarder, a man who was seventy-two years old.

On the morning of March 22, 1918, Josephine was wakened by her grandmother, tears streaming down the old woman's face. Aunt Caroline, who had chronic endocarditis, was dying. "Run home and fetch your mother," Elvira said. Josephine ran home, but Carrie wasn't there. Arthur said she was at Aunt Emma's, Emma had gone into labor. "Once more, I set off through the darkness. 'Come quick, Mama. . . .' " Carrie refused. "I'll be along as soon as I can, Tumpy, I can't leave the baby, my place is here right now."

It was another lesson. Life took precedence over death. Back at Elvira's, Josephine found that Aunt Caroline had stopped breathing. Elvira said there was nothing to be scared of. "There's more to fear from the living than from the dead, child."

Now living with Elvira and the boarder, Josephine began to suspect that the man was stealing money. Elvira had inherited Caroline's little pension, and some life insurance, but it was disappearing fast. "Grandmother would have had enough for the rest of her life, but she couldn't count," Josephine said. "This man . . . became her secretary. He spent her money with other women." Josephine went to Carrie and reported that the boarder was a thief. Carrie "fired the man," and took her mother into the Martin household.

Naturally, Josephine came home too. According to her, Elvira still had some funds, "and with that small amount, the whole family was happy . . . as long as it lasted. Then life got hard again."

Especially for someone who was forced back to school by a mother weary of arguing with the truant officer. Carrie laid down the law: The choice was school or a correctional institution. But even in school, there were good days. Josephine didn't mind going to Sally Henderson's class, because Miss Henderson praised Josephine's imagination, her creativity. Miss Henderson also kept a turtle in a box.

Once a week, short, plump, sweet-natured Sally Henderson would read aloud to the class the latest news of black Americans fighting in France. The *Argus* printed the letters they wrote home. "The people here are good to us. They don't know anything about color prejudice." "Many places, the people met us with flowers." "No wooden houses here, all are made of stone, with beautiful lace curtains at the windows."

Josephine had heard of Joan of Arc, she knew there was a country where a girl dressed as a boy had saved her king, and even if she died in the fire, they made a movie about her, which almost made the sacrifice worthwhile, and now it turned out the people in this amazing land loved the colored people of America. (The Booker had advertised "*Joan of Arc*, a Wonderful Picture of the Historical French Revolution," so how do you expect Josephine Baker to know about history?)

Until she died, Sally Henderson talked about Josephine's ability to shake off the yoke of reality. "After the Thanksgiving holidays," Miss Henderson said, "the kids stood up and described what they had for Thanksgiving dinner. And Josephine Martin told about the fabulous meal at the Martin house, she described a feast fit for a king, and the other kids were young enough that some of them believed it. She never backed down. She said that's what they had."

At the age of thirteen, Josephine was tall and thin with a long face, light brown eyes that seemed to burn, and kinky hair that she hated to have to comb. It must have been just about that time that she encountered Mr. Dad. Her version of their relationship was filled with melodrama:

"There was a fifty-year-old man who liked to have little girls live with him. He was called Mr. Dad. . . . Mummy let me clean his house. . . . He clothed me, gave me money. Then one day he asked me to spend the night with him.

"I left. He was very upset and drank cider. He came to the house, spoke with Mama. Then she was upset and insisted I stay with Mr. Dad. I refused. She took off my clothes and beat me until the skin came off. . . . I ran in the street, naked. . . . Soon I came to the courtyard of a house and I went into the coal cellar. I hid.

"It was night. I prayed to God: 'Father, help me . . . let me die, I beg you! . . . I am so unhappy on earth.' "

Waking, Josephine says, she covered her nakedness with a "mouldy" coat she found in the coal cellar and took off for the Booker Washington. "When I arrived at the theatre . . . Mr. Bob Russell, the director of the company working there that week, came close to me, a very black man with white hair and very tall. He looked at me kindly and said, 'What do you want, my child?'

"I . . . begged him for work. . . . I said I had never danced but if I was allowed to, I would do my best. . . .

"Mr. Russell had me stand on the stage to observe. Seeing them prancing and jumping, I was impatient to do the same as the 'girls.' . . . I wished I could have leapt . . . to the beat of this music . . . for me, it was . . . a physical intoxication. . . . Is that what they call a vocation, what you do with joy as if you had fire in your heart, the devil in your body? . . . It was like if I had drunk gin. . . . Everybody was surprised to see how quickly I learned. . . .

"That same night, we left St. Louis. I was happy to travel and to work. I adored that life. I wished to work more. I was never tired."

Chapter 6

—

JOSEPHINE MARRIES
AT THIRTEEN

"She cut his head open with a beer bottle"

What went through your head, Mother, leaving St. Louis on one of the night trains you had listened to, lying in the crowded bed of your childhood? The way you recounted (in books, in interviews) the events leading up to your flight was not precisely accurate. For one thing, you erased two years of your life, and a husband; you forgot to mention Willie Wells. As for your brush with Mr. Dad, your brother told me the way it really happened.

"The man we called Mr. Dad worked in the steel foundry," Richard said. "And on the side he had an ice cream parlor. He made ice cream and candy and Josephine would sell it, and she went to live with him in his house, and people were talking about that."

Like Mr. Mason, Mr. Dad loved young girls. He bought them clothes, he fed them well, and Josephine was practical. In her dreams, she was a princess, but when she wasn't dreaming, she had few illusions. Already, she had learned there was a price for everything, and it was better to shut up about what you paid.

Because in the Martins' neighborhood—by now they were living on Bernard Street—everybody knew everybody else's business. And when Josephine, following in Carrie's footsteps, established her own independence, the neighbors were on Carrie's side. Her thirteen-year-old daughter playing house with Mr. Dad? It was a scandal, and everyone on Bernard Street concurred.

Carrie dragged Josephine home, and announced, one more time, "I'm going to send you to reform school." Even Elvira couldn't calm her. "Don't say a word, Mama! You just lost all your money to that old man, maybe we should put *you* in a home!"

Aunt Jo Cooper, who had always been a kind of fairy godmother to Josephine, saved the day. "The child is not a child anymore," she said to Carrie. "She wants to go with men? Let's find her a nice fellow, marry her off."

Thus did Willie Wells come into Josephine's life.

"He was a steelworker," Richard said. "He was too old for her. He was about twenty-five or thirty, she was thirteen, when she married."

In 1919, Josephine attended the L'Ouverture school for a grand total of thirty days. On December 22, she got married, and that was the end of her formal education.

On the day after Christmas, the wedding was noted in the *Argus:* "Willie Wells, 2617 Pine; Josephine Martin, 2632 Bernard." It was the first time Josephine would see her name in a newspaper, and it was on the same page with an editorial asking readers, "Have you been True, first to yourself, then to your friends and to your race?"

Carrie needed to consent in writing to Josephine's marriage because the bride was underage. (Even so, it wasn't legal, but neither Carrie nor the minister knew this. In 1919, the marriage laws of the state of Missouri stated that even with parental consent, "no marriage license shall be issued for any person under the age of 15 years unless authorized by an order of circuit or probate court for good cause and unusual conditions.") Aunt Jo Cooper gave the wedding party, serving roast pork and macaroni. "It was a very nice thing, very happy," Richard said.

The newlyweds spent the evening at the Booker, where Nettie Berry buck-danced, and some trained dogs waltzed. A female impersonator named Sammie Lewis opened the show.

At first, Josephine and Willie lived on their own in a furnished room on Laton Avenue. They paid $1.50 a week, gas and electricity included, and had kitchen privileges. After a while, Willie couldn't make the rent. He was still working, but Josephine spent every penny he brought home on dresses. Then, to assuage his anger, she produced some knitting, and announced that she was pregnant. The couple moved back to the Martin house, and Carrie melted. A new baby would be a joy to the family.

"They lived with us about two weeks," Richard said, "and after that, they were fightin' and she cut his head open with a beer bottle."

Why had they quarreled? Apparently, Willie had come home one night to discover Josephine was having her period, and had lied about a baby. For sympathy? For attention? Because she so much wanted a baby? All I know is she told every man she ever got involved with, "I love you, I want your baby," and there never was a baby. Her sister Margaret has told me, categorically, that Josephine was *never* pregnant.

Willie Wells took his bleeding head to a doctor, and never came back to Bernard Street. The marriage was over.

Now Josephine got a job in a restaurant called the Old Chauffeur's Club. "She worked serving tables and washing dishes," Richard said. "The place was on Fourteenth and Chestnut. She made three dollars a week." There was gossip that after hours, she made money a different way. "There was a woman told me Aunt Tumpy would be considered a fast girl," says her nephew, Richard, Jr. "That meant a girl who would take one or two dollars to go with a man. You can only believe half the bull people tell you, but Aunt Tumpy was like her mother, and my grandmaw, Carrie, was a humdinger."

Numbers of people deny these stories. In 1983, Blanche Felix wrote to assure me that her old Dumas schoolmate "never was a street woman, she was a respectful girl. . . ."

Blanche Felix recalled that she too had auditioned at the Booker for Bob Russell, who was hiring for a second road company, but that she didn't have Josephine's spark. "Josephine got onstage, and she made good, I guess she must have been cut out for it."

And she was ready. Over-ready.

If her attendance at school had been ridiculous, her attendance at the Booker had been fanatically faithful, and what she learned there, she could not have learned anyplace else. She had heard Bessie Smith sing blues before Bessie Smith had top billing. (There were four Smiths performing on the circuit then—Bessie, Mamie, Clara, and Trixie, none of them related.) Josephine had watched her favorites come and go, checked out their new tricks, recognized when one was having an off night.

She had spent eight years mimicking every line, every gesture she had observed onstage. She had studied the quick changes of the transvestites. She had fallen in love with their feather boas. And she had a nose for what worked. She watched Clara Smith pick out the ugliest man in the audience and sing a love song to him; later, she would work the same trick into her own act.

But there would be more to her relationship with Clara Smith than that. "It was Clara who asked Bob Russell to hire Josephine," Booth Marshall told me. Booth often toured with Russell ("I performed in drag, as an old mama, big bottom, big breasts, kerchief on my head, wearing big, big shoes and blackface, I was a killer with that number"), and he said Clara had spotted Josephine waiting tables at the Chauffeur's Club.

"Bob told me how he got stuck with Josephine in St. Louis. She had become Clara's protégée, you know, her lady lover as we called it in those days. Bob did not like that kind of hanky-panky, but Clara was a big draw, and anyhow, better a steady date than a fight in every city. Josephine had no real experience, you know, but Bob saw she had potential, and Clara did the rest."

Clara, who disliked publicity and all the fuss that went with it—this was not a dislike Josephine would ever share—was only twenty-six years old in 1920, with a voice Carl Van Vechten described as so powerful and melancholy "it tears the blood from one's heart." Josephine could not have found a better singing coach.

Besides Clara, billed as the South's "favorite coon shouter," the troupe, forty-five strong, featured Henry "Gang" Jones (a comedian), some bathing beauties, and a female baritone named Anna Belle Cook. No Russell company had played St. Louis in two years, but now the entertainers would be there for two months. The first show would open on Monday night, the twenty-ninth of November. Mr. Russell wanted it clearly understood "that he permits no smutty or suggestive words or action in any of his plays."

That her new boss wasn't thrilled with the relationship between his star and a chorus girl had not been lost on Josephine. "I thought I understood what was bothering Mr. Russell," she tells us, ingenuously. "He felt that his leading lady was monopolizing my time. He wasn't paying me to spend hours in Mama Smith's dressing room improving my penmanship."

Or massaging Mama Smith's feet, either.

St. Louis went wild over Clara, but Josephine didn't get to go onstage until the week of January 17, in *Twenty Minutes in Hell,* a melodrama "with a good moral." It told the story of a man who dreamed he had sold his soul to the devil. A scene in hell was replete with fairy costumes and electrical effects, Clara Smith sang "Someone Else May Be There While I'm Gone," and Josephine flew.

Literally. "I remember the first role they gave me. I was to be an angel. I wore pink tights and had big wings to flap. They expected me to swing around on a wire. But my wings kept getting tangled in the sets and my feet were dangling in every direction. After a while, I got so badly tangled up they fired me."

Nobody fired her, and another time, in another mood, she told what really happened. "I returned to the wings, to find Mr. Russell weeping with laughter. 'You're a real clown, Birdy. A born comic.' "

The Booker's stage manager remembered that Willie Mae showed up backstage every day after school. "That one-eyed girl had a whole lotta mouth, she wanted everybody to know she was Josephine's sister."

For the Russell company's final show, *Toby's Breeches,* Josephine danced in the chorus, which got several encores, and the *Argus* raved, "Nine weeks without a taint of smut or suggestiveness . . . The fastidious Mr. Russell has raised the standard of the stage here."

Even so, Mr. Russell's fastidiousness did not entice Carrie Martin to come out and see her daughter perform. In those days, show business gave a girl a worse reputation than going with men for money, or drinking homemade gin.

Sunday, January 30, the last show. A frenzy. Everyone packing, Josephine feeling—what? Sadness? Regret? Fear? She was detaching herself from Tumpy, like a butterfly breaking painfully from the cocoon, slowly unfolding its wings.

Now they are hurrying to Union Station to catch the last train to Memphis. It is just past midnight. The weather is fair and cold, thirty degrees, and Josephine runs along the platform, following Clara and a bunch of the bathing beauties.

As the train starts to move, Josephine recognizes the same excitement she had felt on top of the coal wagon. "I had never seen curtains as pretty as those in the Pullman-car windows. From my seat at Mrs. Russell's side, her cigar smoke pricking my nose, I peered nervously out the window, looking for Mama's angry face, Grandma's reproachful eyes or the stern gaze of Daddy or Aunt Jo. No, Daddy Arthur would already be in bed, so full of beer that nothing could wake him. I was safely on my way. Closing my eyes, I dreamed of sunlit cities, magnificent theatres, and me in the limelight."

What she could see through the window was like a silent movie at the Booker. A perfect picture, black and white, night all around, and in the darkness, pools of light from the windows she was passing. For a few seconds, it was clear—1537 Papin Street, which she could almost have touched if she had stretched out her arm, Chestnut Street, the Jefferson Barracks Bridge—and then it was gone.

On Bernard Street, Margaret was nervous because she had promised not to tell Carrie that Josephine was skipping town. Josephine had given Margaret reasons. She wanted to be famous, she wanted to be rich and help the family.

Loyally, Margaret followed the party line. She told me that the night the Russell company left St. Louis, Carrie asked where Josephine was. Margaret answered that she was staying over at Dyer Jones's house. Next morning, Margaret confessed that her sister was gone. Carrie seemed to take the news calmly. "To my surprise, Mama said, 'She has chosen her path. Let her be.' "

Chapter 7

—

LIFE ON THE
T.O.B.A. CIRCUIT

"It was going from one dinky theater to another"

n the map, the distance from St. Louis to Memphis looks to be about 250 miles, as the crow flies. But the journey is longer and prettier if you follow the curves and twists of the Mississippi, the river meandering south, dividing Missouri from Illinois and Kentucky, separating Arkansas and Tennessee.

It was one of the trains of the Illinois Central Railroad that carried Josephine on this first leg of her wanderings; Bob Russell had a private Pullman car for his large company, their costumes and scenery. Josephine was delighted to find that Andre Tribble, a female impersonator whom she had loved at the Booker (he carried celery as his bridal bouquet) was now part of the Russell entourage.

The Illinois Central prided itself on furnishing its dining cars with white linen tablecloths, bud vases holding fresh flowers, fine china; but black people weren't welcome in the dining cars, they ate in their seats.

Still, it was fun for Josephine. Bob Russell's wife (also named Josephine) had prepared hampers of food; there were sandwiches, ribs, hard-boiled eggs, cookies, bananas, and thermos bottles full of lemonade. The train slowly built up to speed—fifty miles an hour was its limit—and the tired company began to relax. It had been a long day, Josephine was to remember. "One by one the cast dozed off, their bodies rocking with the motion of the train." And if you couldn't sleep, all night long there was a show outside the windows, as passengers boarded at each new stop, some of them carrying frying pans and live chickens.

When the troupe got to Memphis, a city where the population was about 40 percent black, Josephine discovered there were three black theaters (the New Regent, the Palace, and the Venus, where Bob Russell's troupe would spend the next seven weeks) but it was difficult for black performers to find places to stay. There were few black hotels for the simple reason that there weren't enough well-to-do blacks who could afford to stay in hotels.

Booth Marshall recalled the boardinghouses of his youth. "Sometimes you had to pay extra for laying down during the day, because the lady would say the room had been rented for the night only! She would say, 'You didn't tell me you wanted to sleep during the day.' And some places, as soon as you put the light out, bedbugs by the thousand would come and bite you. I couldn't take that, I would go down to the railroad station and sit up until morning. Rooms were a dollar a night, the better ones were a dollar and a half. Clara Smith traveled with her own clean sheets; after a while on the road, so did I."

In Memphis, Josephine was taken to a boardinghouse "where Mr. Russell gave me a tiny room." That very afternoon, the troupe opened at the Venus, an opening Josephine described with gusto: "The show started. The heat was crushing. . . . Hundreds of black faces with yellow teeth died of laughter. They ate peanuts and threw the shells on the stage. The air was awful."

Again, she was cast as Cupid, flying with a bow and arrow over two lovers, until the lady's husband came on and tried to pull her from the arms of her boyfriend. Then a spectator tried to do the same. He hopped onstage, brandishing a razor and shouting, "Get your hands off that woman, trash!"

Some of the male dancers leaped to restrain him. "Everybody screamed, 'It's not the truth, it's only the play,' " Josephine recalled.

"Nothing helped. Mr. Russell was obliged to come and explain it was only a scene, and not true. Then the man put away his razor, smiled broadly and went back to his seat."

"You know, in them days," Booth Marshall said, "the colored people just talked back to the shows. Like a villain shoots somebody and hides behind the door, and the audience yells, 'There's that dirty rascal, behind the door, go get him!' Damnedest people I ever seen in my life."

The audiences were no more primitive than some of the playhouses with which the Theater Owners' Booking Association was affiliated. Black vaudevillians swore that T.O.B.A. stood for Tough on Black Asses. "Some of the theaters were so small," a female dancer told me, "you could not cross behind the stage to go to the toilet, you had to learn to pee in a bottle. Life on the T.O.B.A. was just going from one dinky theater to another, some of them blacksmith shops where they shoed horses. You worked hard, did four shows a day, and learned a lot."

Josephine was living proof of that. She learned from everything and everybody, including Mama Dinks, whose routine she had seen many times. And of course she continued to study the phenomenon that was Clara Smith. "Clara outdrew Bessie Smith in Nashville all the time," says trumpet player Doc Cheatham. "Because she was mean, and she sang mean. She would give everybody hell, give the men hell, give the women hell, in her blues singing. She was a mean woman but she was a great singer."

It wasn't only Clara's voice that Josephine loved, but the long silk handkerchief Clara used as a prop, and her blue feather boa. Blue was Josephine's favorite color, and I still keep, like a talisman, one of her headpieces, a satin turban out of which rises a three-foot-tall spray of blue feathers. When I'm in the room with it, it's as though Josephine is looking over my shoulder.

Though business was good there, Memphis wasn't memorable to Josephine, she never spoke or wrote much about it. New Orleans was different, New Orleans and the beautiful Lyric Theater where Bob Russell's troupe next landed. An ad in the *New Orleans Item* heralded their arrival: "Beginning Monday BOB RUSSELL and His 25 Hottest Coons in Dixie."

Two T.O.B.A. members, a Mr. Boudreaux and a Mr. Bennett, owned the Lyric. Bennett was a friend of the racing car driver Barney

Oldfield, who had given him a ring set with two three-carat diamonds, which he'd pawned for a thousand dollars to invest in the theater. A showplace that stood on a corner, the Lyric had arched windows, a white marble foyer, dressing rooms of marble and oak. The stage, which could be raised or lowered by hydraulic power, was thirty-eight feet deep; seven hundred patrons could sit on the lower floor, eight hundred in the balcony, and there were twelve boxes on each side.

Josephine wrote about this pleasure palace and the city that contained it. "There are the French and the Blacks. That is the origin of the creoles. Huge theatre with real orchestra, many musicians: happy! I thought I was coming into high society. . . . It's fashionable there to eat crabs with rice, corn cut in it, and a little green vegetable called okra. . . . And . . . I saw the Jones family again. . . ."

Hired by Mr. Russell for the New Orleans leg of the tour, the Joneses had shown up with instruments and prop trunk. "After we had fallen into each other's arms," Josephine said, "Mrs. Jones suggested that I move in with them and split the costs. It seemed like a good idea. . . ."

What seemed like a bad idea was Clara Smith's greedy consumption of sweet-potato pies. She ate too many, "and she made me eat them too. As I had a sweet tooth, I loved sugar . . . and I fell sick."

Sick, maybe, but not too tired to explore the city. "The piano player had told me that it was a musician's paradise and he was right. . . . I had never seen so many people, bars and dance halls. . . . 'This is nothing,' the piano player insisted. 'You can't imagine how it used to be. One parade after another; bands competing in the streets to prove they were the best. But Storyville's [Storyville, New Orleans's legalized red-light district, had thrived between 1897 and 1917.] been closed down since the war. It's simply not the same.' "

The ways Josephine remembered the rest of her tenure with Bob Russell were wonderfully creative. One variation went like this: She was fired in New Orleans, so she hid in a packing crate and was shipped on the train with the rest of the luggage, and after she was discovered, Mrs. Russell went to bat for her, and Mr. Russell agreed she could remain with the company until they got back to St. Louis. Then came a list of miseries endured. Fleabag hotels. A gas heater that rendered our heroine unconscious and caused the rest of the company to think she was suicidal. Work unending. It was Mrs. Kaiser's house all over again. "I sewed, brushed costumes, polished shoes, ironed, dressed hair, hooked and unhooked clothes, fastened, buttoned . . . hung up, laid out, packed, unpacked."

In a different story, when the Russell company came to St. Louis, Josephine found her mother in a basement apartment, "her lovely teeth completely yellow and destroyed by tobacco! My stepfather continued to lie down all day and spit on the floor. . . . In a corner there was a crate full of coal, the water used to wash is frozen. Dirty curtains . . . You can't take garbage out after six o'clock, it brings bad luck. So all the garbage is pushed under the bed."

This tale has Josephine going without a bath for a month in the Martins' hovel, and having to say no to her little sister ("she had only one eye and she was despised") when Willie Mae begged to be taken on the road.

The only difficulty with any of these marvelous fables is that the Russell company didn't go back to St. Louis, it went directly from New Orleans to Philadelphia, and even about Philadelphia, Josephine was not exactly candid. "I started in Philadelphia," she contended. "In a small theatre: the Standard Theatre, in a bad revue. I made ten dollars a week. In fact I earned nothing because they nearly never paid and I was always hungry. I was hollow, hollow enough to fall. Teeth came out of my mouth. I thought about New York, big money . . ."

I believe you thought about New York and big money, Mother, and I also believe your explanation of why you left home. "You cannot," you said, "do anything with your family on your back." But most of what you said about Philadelphia was nonsense. It was in Philadelphia that you became Josephine Baker.

Chapter 8

—

JOSEPHINE TRIES MARRIAGE FOR THE SECOND TIME

"She was a little snip, about fifteen years old"

*S*he met him in Philadelphia—Billy Baker, the pretty boy with fair skin, the one the Duchess called "trifling; he was lazy, half the time he didn't want to work."

The Duchess (remember the waitress who quit the Green Dragon speakeasy when the body count got too high?) was then employed by Billy's father in his restaurant. "Josephine," she said, "was nothing but a little snip, no more than about fifteen years old, and they eloped someplace."

The someplace was Camden, New Jersey, right across the river. In Camden, you could get married on the spot, no questions asked, so long as you brought two witnesses with you. These facts were verified by Billy Baker himself in 1934, after a reporter on the *Chicago Bee* tracked him down for a piece on "Forgotten Husbands of Famous Women."

Billy said he had first set eyes on Josephine when she was playing at the Standard. "I was living with my father at 1520 South Street. Because of her youth, Joe and I had difficulty securing a marriage license in Philadelphia but undaunted in our plans, we went to Camden."

Where the Reverend Orlando S. Watte united in wedlock William Howard Baker (twenty-three years of age; Colored; Birthplace, Gallatin, Tennessee; Father's name, Warren Baker; Mother's maiden name, Mattie Wilson) with Josephine Wells (nineteen years of age; Colored; Birthplace, St. Louis, Missouri; Father's name, Arthur Wells; Mother's maiden name, Carrie Martin). Each said it was a first marriage.

Mother, I love you! You are daring, you get what you want. You aged yourself four years, gave your father's name as Arthur Wells—poor Willie Wells, all that remained of him in your history was the temporary borrowing of his name—and covered your tracks. You were still doing the same thing fifty-two years later, when a journalist asked about your husbands. "I have been married thousands of times," you told him, "because every man I loved has been my husband."

I'm glad you said it yourself, Mother. Imagine if *I* had claimed you loved thousands of men!

It was on September 17, 1921, that Josephine vowed to love, honor, and obey Billy Baker. Indeed, Billy, not Willie Wells, would be Josephine's first legal husband, but she would die without knowing it. (In Camden in 1921, the fact that she was a minor did not invalidate her marriage, even though she had not produced evidence of parental consent.) Just five months earlier, on April 25, she had opened with Bob Russell's company at the Standard. They had a tough act to follow—the Billy King players had been thrilling Philadelphians with an onstage bullfight and "The Triumphant Return of the Shah of Persia on His Camel"—but Josephine wasn't intimidated, she was in paradise, dancing across the very stage where the Shah's camel had so recently galumphed.

"I had learned," she said, "that when I rolled my eyes and made the very faces that had earned me a scolding at school, the crowd would burst out laughing."

Appearing at the Standard on the same bill with Josephine was Maude Russell, the wife of Sam Russell. (They were not related to Bob Russell.) "Oh, Lord," says Maude, "everybody knew Sam Russell. He worked in blackface like all the comedians then. To be funny, you *had* to wear blackface. He and Sandy Burns had a comedy act called Bilo and Ashes."

Maude confirms that the fledgling Josephine was a crowd pleaser.

"She did her act, and I said, 'Where did they get *her* from?' She was a ugly little thing, but she was funny."

If Maude wondered where Bob Russell had got Josephine, she knew exactly where Josephine had got her act. "Mama Dinks. Dinks was never nothing but a chorus girl, but she was a *star* chorus girl. All her mouth was gold, she had funny legs, she could bend them way back, she did those antics, walkin' like a chicken, lookin' cross-eyed, and then she'd go offstage bowlegged with her butt stuck out. And Tumpy—she was introduced as Tumpy—copied Dinks.

"She was nothing but a kid, and the people was crazy about her. 'Tumpy! Ah, come on, Tumpy! Dance some more, Tumpy!' And those audiences were rough, if you wasn't any good, honey, they would boo you off the stage!"

It was no small accomplishment to draw bravos on a bill that blazed with so much talent: Butterbeans and Susie, who were popular comics; Alex Lovejoy, a much-admired actor; Maude herself, who could dance till she set the house to screaming. "I was featured!" she says. "I wasn't a chorus girl." Clara Smith had stayed behind—she never came north if she could help it—but Dyer Jones was still with the company, so Josephine still had a surrogate mother.

Dyer watched over *all* the chorus girls. "She would care for us children," Lilly Yuen says, "and look after us that we don't do foolish things." Lilly, half Chinese, half black, nicknamed "Pontop," reminds you how young they were. "We all used to play out in the alley between shows."

Most of the cast ate at a boardinghouse called Mom Charleston's. Mom set out good food—greens, fried fish, chicken, corn pudding, peach cobbler—all for seventy-five cents.

By 1921, Philadelphia was already a big city with more than 134,000 black residents. It boasted Independence Hall, and an interest in theater that dated back to the 1720s, when wandering players drew crowds to the outskirts of town. But for Josephine, its appeal lay in the fact that it was only eighty-three miles from New York City.

As it happened, *Shuffle Along,* playing the Dunbar, a few blocks from the Standard, was headed for New York City. Josephine heard from Wilsie Caldwell, a former Dumas classmate who was in the Broadway-bound show, that the management was looking for more dancers, and she asked Wilsie to help her get an audition.

Next thing she knew she was doing her routine for Noble Sissle and Eubie Blake. (Sissle and Blake were the elegant vaudeville team who had joined forces with Miller and Lyles, a comedy-dance act, and created *Shuffle Along,* the musical designed "to put the Negro back on Broadway.")

The way Josephine described her audition, Mr. Blake had said nothing, while Mr. Sissle had said she was too young, too small, too thin, too ugly. And too dark. " 'Can you even dance?' he asked me. 'No, but it doesn't matter . . . I watch, I dance without knowing . . . without dancing.' "

Whatever Noble Sissle may have said to Josephine, a letter he wrote to the dancer Willie Covan indicates clearly that it was only Josephine's age that had made him turn her away.

"I will always remember her," Sissle said, "leaving us without a word, her eyes full of tears. . . . The last we saw, she was walking in the street under heavy rain. Her clothes were all wet, so was her hair. She did not even open the big umbrella she was carrying. We felt so sad for her, but we were heading for Broadway, and the law was, you had to be sixteen to perform onstage there; on the road, nobody cared."

Josephine recovered fast. Next week, at the Standard, the sun was shining again. The Empress of the Blues, Bessie Smith, and her five Jazzoway Dandies, had come to play. The months flew by. Bob Russell and his troupe left town, but Josephine stayed behind and joined Sandy Burns's stock company. (In addition to the touring players who came and went, the Standard always featured a resident stock company.)

Sandy Burns bragged about the caliber of his people. "It's not every company that has girls in the chorus who can put over a number, or talk," he told the *Chicago Defender,* "and from the ovations my girls receive week in, week out, they must be pleasing and making good." Among those they pleased, of course, was Billy Baker.

Sketches changed weekly, guest artists appeared and disappeared. There were the Whitman Sisters, who played banjos and sang. "Sister Mae" headed the group, and had a low opinion of theater managers. Most of them, she said, "feel that any kind of show is good enough for a colored audience . . . their only desire is to have a comedian and a few half-naked girls on hand. . . . If these birds pay you a living wage, they want you to guarantee that it will not rain or snow during the week you are booked with them."

Once in a while, an exotic newcomer like Esther Bigeou, "The Singer with the Million Dollar Smile," would come along to entrance Josephine. Esther sang in French. *"Avez vous du boeuf rôti, de l'agneau, du porc, des petits pois, ou des pommes de terre?"* she would croon. "The words," said one reviewer, "flow from her lips so naturally that it seems like the careless warbling of a bird." A carnivorus bird. For those who do not speak my native tongue, permit me to translate. "Do you have roast beef, lamb, pork, peas, or potatoes?" is what Esther was inquiring of her audience.

Mildred Martien, who would become Josephine's lifelong friend, worked with her at the Standard. "I went in the chorus with Josephine, we were six girls, she was at the end, the comic one. Later on, she introduced me to Billy Baker. He and his parents were lovely people, they all looked like they were white. And their restaurant was so high-class, white tablecloths, waiters, everything. I went out with Josephine and Billy a few times."

Billy worked in his father's restaurant—"He was a good-looking thing," said the Duchess, but it was for Pa Baker that she reserved her highest praise. "If you had no money, he'd give you a meal. He did his own cooking, but he didn't serve no whiskey, didn't allow no cussing or nothing.

"The family lived upstairs over the restaurant. There were two sons, Billy and Edward, and after Billy married Josephine, she came to live there too, up on the third floor. I seen her at the Standard—oh my God, she broke the show up, how she could dance—and I seen her at home.

"I used to run upstairs from the restaurant and take the conk off her hair. She used to call me, 'Please come up and get it off my neck 'cause it's burning me.' She slept all day, then went to work, and as soon as the Standard would let out, she was right home, she didn't hang out with nobody. She was a loner."

Again and again we will hear this about Josephine. "She was all right in the theater," Maude Russell says, "but as soon as she hit that street, to hell with you, she's gone, she's on her own, whatever she was doing, you wouldn't be there to witness it. Not ever."

In Philadelphia, at least, there doesn't seem to have been much to witness; once she married Billy, for the first time in fifteen crowded years, she had a home. She called Mr. Baker "Pa," and the Duchess said this pleased him. "Her and her father-in-law was very close because he wanted a daughter, and she looked so much like the Bakers she could have been one of them, except she was darker. Mr. Baker called her 'Daughter,' he never called her Josephine. Yes, he sure did love her. He wanted everything for her."

But he never knew if she got it. After she left this country, the Bakers heard no more from her.

I couldn't find them, either. For more than fifteen years, I tracked Billy Baker, the man whose name I bear. My first attempts to locate him began in Philadelphia, where I had gone to interview Evelyn Anderson. (She was the chorus girl who came to Paris and fell in love with caviar "on those little pieces of toast.")

I went to the Free Library of Philadelphia, dug out a 1921 phone book, and there it was: "BAKER Warren Rest . . . 1520 South St.," confirming what Billy had said in that article in 1934. I ran out like a thief, grabbed a taxi, gave the address. The black driver looked at me. "I wouldn't advise you to go there alone." I told him I was hunting for the past, and nothing would happen to me. He dropped me on the corner of Fifteenth and South, and I started walking. I was on the street where she and Billy had lived, and it was deserted, houses empty, most of the ground-floor windows boarded up. But you could still see that the brownstones had been beautiful.

Here was the Royal Theatre, silent like the rest of the block, though I could imagine how grand it had once been. Now its sign was pitted with holes where lightbulbs used to burn, and the front of the marquee said, ALWAYS A GREA HOW; the missing letters had fallen on their sides.

The abandoned restaurant next door had no number over the entrance, but I looked down, and there it was on the floor, 1520, in mosaic tiles. It was just as the Duchess had described it to me, two big glass windows—now boarded-up—and a kind of Moorish arch connecting them. Debris was piled in the doorway, but I was seeing what wasn't there—lights, sounds of silverware and plates, a table for a wedding reception in the back, a young couple who looked like brother and sister celebrating their marriage.

I came to a corner, and went into a secondhand record shop. No customers, but a man behind racks of old records. I asked him about Josephine, and he said I should go down the street to Felix, the barber. "He lived his whole life on this block, he was a friend of Billy Baker's father."

Felix's barbershop smelled of age, and of the aftershave trapped in its walls. It was small and dark, with two barber chairs in front of a rusted mirror. Felix said he remembered when Mr. Baker opened the restaurant. "He was a good cook, and people from all over town—even white people—came to eat at his place. Mostly sports people, but I forget which sport. Billy came right here and got a shave on his wedding day."

As I left the shop, I noticed on a shelf the old straight razor and the strop used to sharpen it. It was exactly like the one the old man, Pepe Lombard, my friend in St. Symphorien, had used every Sunday. It made me smile, thinking how small the world is.

The way Josephine had Elvira to tell her stories of the old days, I'd had Pepe Lombard. He'd lived alone in a big old house across the unpaved road from us; you came into the front room, which was always very dark, warm in winter, cool in summer. He never talked to me like you talk to a child, but as a witness to his life. I can still see his wonderful face beaten by the years; you could tell the day of the week by looking at his beard, shaved only on Sunday, and his white mustache was like a big *M* under his nose. He always held up his pants with pieces of string, and his gestures were slow; he knew his strength was no longer what it had been, and he used it wisely, like a friend.

On that Saturday in 1921, Billy Baker had left Felix's barbershop, picked up his bride, and crossed the river to Camden. Then they came back to a party in the restaurant. Only ten or twelve people, the Duchess said; the big table had been set up in the corner. "My station."

For Josephine, the change in her fortunes was pleasant. Warren Baker took her to a tailor, and, the Duchess said, "She started dressing. She wore way-out clothes 'cause she could get away with them. When I first seen her with a long white astrakhan fur coat, and a muff, I kissed her. She looked beautiful."

Whatever Josephine told her in-laws about her family back in St. Louis, she was careful never to bring the two sets of parents together. Then, surprisingly, she took Billy home to St. Louis to meet the folks. "We honeymooned a while," Billy told the *Chicago Bee*. "We loved each other and were very happy."

Josephine's brother remembered the couple's staying at Bernard Street "one or two days. I don't know if she was in love, they weren't there long enough for me to find out."

And if Carrie—or anyone else who knew about Willie Wells—wondered how Josephine could have married Billy Baker, nobody said a word.

The bride spent most of that visit with Elvira, the grandmother who never questioned, never judged. Then, satisfied that familial duty had been done, Mr. and Mrs. Baker left St. Louis.

Back in Philadelphia, life resumed its usual shape. Mildred Martien was a bride too—she had married Johnny Hudgins, a young comedian touring the T.O.B.A. circuit—and she and Josephine liked to walk up and down South Street, window-shopping. Across from Mr. Baker's restaurant was Tryham's, a dry goods store with a shiny red door, and there were always pretty cars in front of the Royal Theatre. You could see movies at the Royal, and enjoy Fats Waller's piano-playing between features. Sometimes Mildred would come by to pick up Josephine and find her waiting outside, "leaning against the wall, kind of dreaming, not really there. But she would smile at the customers coming in."

Sunday in the City of Brotherly Love was referred to by actors as Doomsday, since blue laws kept the theaters closed. (They would reopen at one minute past midnight, offering a late-Sunday-night, or, more accurately, an early-Monday-morning show.) So sometimes on a Sunday, Pa Baker would round up Josephine, Mildred, and his friend, the composer and conductor Will Marion Cook. Then the foursome, two middle-aged men, two young girls, would take the train to New York, to 125th Street, the heart of Harlem.

Pa Baker admired Will Marion Cook and was honored to be in his company; as for Josephine, knowing Mr. Cook would turn out to be one of her luckiest breaks.

But I'm getting ahead of my story. Cook was a crotchety genius, a violin prodigy. He had studied for five years in Berlin with Joseph Joachim, and in New York with the popular Czech composer, Antonín Dvořák, at the National Conservatory of Music. As a young man, Cook had quit the Boston Symphony when he was told a black could not solo. "If I can't get fame," he said to a friend, "I'd like to make money." The gods were not listening. Fame came early to Will Marion, money gave him a wide berth.

So did a lot of musicians who found him difficult. He couldn't bear a false note, especially if the note had been written by him. He would stop conducting and, in front of the full audience, correct the sloppy player.

He had a lighter side too; he adored chorus girls, the more fair-skinned the better, and he enjoyed the Sunday excursions organized by Pa Baker.

Harlem was beautiful then. Seventh Avenue, its main artery, had trees and flowers planted on its center island. The buildings on either side of the boulevard were five and six stories tall, no skyscrapers to shut out the brightness. There were churches, nightclubs, theaters, photographers' studios, bookstores, beauty parlors, restaurants. Mr. Baker would take his guests to lunch at Dabney's on 132nd Street, and then to a matinee, because Josephine and Mildred had to be back in time for their own 12:01 show at the Standard.

The theaters were fun, the streets were fun. Looking for excitement and bootleg gin, whites came to Harlem in ermine and pearls and Duesenbergs and Pierce-Arrows. If you didn't have a Duesenberg, you could take the subway.

The nightlife, the music, the after-hours places, Josephine would not discover until she came to live there. But one magical afternoon, she got to see *Shuffle Along,* which wasn't in Harlem, but wasn't exactly in the theater district either. It was playing at the Sixty-third Street Theatre, a kind of run-down lecture hall; even so, white people came in droves, helping to make it the longest-running (504 performances) book musical ever coproduced, directed, written, and acted by black talent.

Shuffle Along was, Josephine knew, the show she needed to make her happy. The final curtain hadn't rung down before she was racing backstage, father-in-law by the hand, asking him to invite Wilsie Caldwell for a bite to eat. Chorus people hear all the gossip; Wilsie, who'd got her the Philadelphia audition, might be able to help again, she might have news of replacements, or touring companies.

Back in Philadelphia, business was so good at the Standard and the Dunbar that John T. Gibson, who owned both houses, put up new illuminated signs; a hundred lights made them so bright they could be seen from anywhere on South Broad Street. "Old Gibby kept them two theaters running," said Lily Yuen.

Josephine should have been happy. Christmas was coming, she had a handsome husband, a loving father-in-law, work she enjoyed. But what she wanted from Santa Claus was a job in *Shuffle Along.*

Have I said it was foolish to bet against her? Wilsie phoned one day to say a second company was being formed. The show, now in its sixth month on Sixty-third Street, was so popular that even the owners of white theaters out of town were clamoring for it. The road company was already scheduled to open on February 14 and play one-night stands through New England.

That was all Josephine needed to know. She took the train to New York, went to the theater, and was hired—at thirty dollars a week—by Al Mayer, one of the producers who didn't realize she'd ever auditioned before.

She went back to Philadelphia, packed, and bought a one-way ticket to New Haven. "It was the *Shuffle Along* No. 2 show that gave Josephine a new start in the theatrical profession of which she was very fond," Billy Baker recalled. Maude Russell put it more bluntly. "I don't think she stayed with her husband but a hot minute."

The way it turned out, Maude's was the first face Josephine saw when she reported to the theater in New Haven. Maude had been in the original New York cast of *Shuffle Along,* and had quit to go back to her on-again, off-again marriage, but when Sam Russell punched her, it was the end. "I stole a hundred dollars from him," she says gleefully, "and I left town so fast I blinded him with ass."

Now, having joined the second company of *Shuffle Along,* she was delighted to see Josephine, swathed in black sealskin and a silk turban, sweeping through the stage door.

"I ran over and threw my arms around her and said, 'Oh, Tumpy, how good you look, I'm so glad—' She cut me off. 'My name is not Tumpy anymore. My name is Josephine Baker.' And then she started to giggle. But I was impressed. I thought she was really grand out there, puttin' on the dog.'"

Chapter 9

—

ON THE ROAD WITH
SHUFFLE ALONG

"Some of those girls treated Joe like a dog"

From the moment the curtain went up on opening night in New Haven, the customers were captured by the surefire mix—the costumes, the fun, the girls—of *Shuffle Along*. There was no profanity, there was a foolish plot—three men running for mayor of Jimtown, two of them crooks—and there was a script that prefigured the dialogue Flournoy Miller would later write for the *Amos 'n' Andy* radio show.

There was also terrific music, supplied by Luckey Roberts. Luckey was not only the orchestra leader, but a pianist, his left hand so big that it could span two octaves. (One time at a private party in Palm Beach, Ignacy Jan Paderewski, an even more famous piano player, heard Luckey play, and approached him. "Oh God," said the future president of Poland, "if I had your hands, I would be greater."

Pictures of Josephine as a Happy Honeysuckle—she is made up with white powder—show her smiling and demure. She and eleven other Honeysuckles crouch onstage, half a dozen Jazz Jasmines posing behind them, while on the porch of the Jimtown Hotel a young groom sings to his bride about how "the preacher will be waiting when the knot am tied."

Things were going fine when Josephine made her move; she just broke loose. It was in the silence right after a number, the music had died away, the cast stood breathless, waiting for applause, and suddenly this imp was flying, mugging, strutting. Luckey tried to improvise an accompaniment for her while the other actors froze.

"Most of them were relieved," Maude Russell says, "when the stage manager told Tumpy to pack her things."

A phone call from Eubie Blake in New York: how had the opening gone? Great, said the stage manager, "except for Josephine Baker, who broke the line. I fired her."

"How did the audience react?" said Blake. The stage manager laughed. "The truth is, those crackers loved it."

"Put her back in," said Blake.

The reviews all mentioned her. "Unique sense of rhythm." "A born comic." "It's impossible to take your eyes off the little cross-eyed girl."

"Honey, the audience laughed so hard," Maude Russell says, "but the girls would whisper, 'That old Josephine Baker makes me sick.' "

This wasn't news to Josephine. "The other girls didn't like me," she said. " 'You act and dance like a monkey,' they shouted." Was their cruelty the result of simple jealousy? I think that was part of it, and color was part of it too. When I first came to America, I knew whites discriminated against blacks, but I didn't know that blacks discriminated against each other. "The high yallers [high yellows] had nothing to do with the blacks," Maude Russell told me. "And in between were the brown skins with their own circle. Listen, down South, if you weren't the color of the paint on the church door, which was yellow, you had no pew in that church.

"On the road, the girls who didn't like Joe would taunt her with 'God don't love ugly!' and she would just say, 'He's not crazy about beauty either, if it's not the right beauty!' " (In an *Amsterdam News* column, the songwriter Andy Razaf—a great lyricist who worked with Fats Waller—suggested "a 'get-together' movement . . . among our colored professionals with the object of checking the many jealousies and hatreds that exist within their group." Razaf decried the fact that musical producers hired the whitest black women they could find, and that black artists rushed to sign up with white producers. He felt it would be nice for "colored shows . . . to take a few colored girls, for a change.")

Josephine had been too light for her family, and now, for many of her colleagues, she was too dark. But while she envied the high-yellow girls their skin color, those ladylike stuck-up creatures were no threat to her. She had a talent to amuse, and tricks learned from old pros. She was a classical clown, hiding the anger that fueled her, turning that energy into a joy she shared with the audience.

The company was on a tight schedule, one-nighters, mostly. "You barely had time to catch your breath after a show," Maude remembers. "Fifty of us were running to get the train to the next town, we packed, we unpacked, we had our own railroad car—we didn't want those white theater people to think we weren't as grand as a white show."

In Stamford, they arrived in time to see "Anna Pavlova and her Ballet Russe with Symphonic Orchestra." Josephine was not impressed. "I never liked ballerinas on their toes. . . . They look like silly little birds . . . La Pavlova, you know, dreadful for me."

Massachusetts, Atlantic City, Brooklyn, as winter turned to spring.

On May 24, for the first time, Josephine performed on a stage in New York City. To celebrate its first anniversary at the Sixty-third Street Theatre, the Broadway company invited the road company, including Josephine, to come across the bridge from Brooklyn and join them. The cast of *Bandanaland*, another Sissle/Blake/Miller/Lyles revue, playing at the Paradise Garden, was also summoned. Altogether, 140 performers took part in that midnight show on Sixty-third Street. "I had a triumph, I must say," Josephine said. "The public applauded me so much nobody wanted to dance after me."

A couple of weeks later, Sissle, Blake, and partners decided to quit the Sixty-third Street Theatre and take the original company on tour. Several performers who didn't want to travel gave notice, making it necessary to hire replacements. The new people would spend a couple of weeks being assimilated into the Broadway cast.

Josephine and Maude were back on the road, in Atlantic City again, when they got the news. Sissle and Blake wanted them. They headed for Broadway.

So, from Paris, did Maurice Chevalier.

For more than two years, Chevalier had been playing in an operetta called *Dédé*, and now he had an offer to bring it to New York. He decided to spend his vacation checking out the Manhattan theater scene, and sailed from Le Havre with Mistinguett, his long-time music hall partner and lover. (Chevalier would remember as the highlight of this trip that he had seen "the sexually dynamic Josephine Baker.")

It was Americans coming to Paris, not Parisians headed the other way, that worried French musicians. They wanted, said one newspaper, "to eliminate American jazzers from France. . . . The French musicians . . . would gladly lay aside their violins and flutes and do the jazzing themselves . . . but their offers are scorned by dance hall managers who tell them: 'Call again when you have changed the color of your skin.' The musicians call it 'the black peril.'"

And they had good reason for jealousy; even the Prince of Wales was going home from Paris with "a collection of the latest popular music which he obtained from Negro jazz band musicians in various Montmartre dancing places." But the French public's interest in black musicians was not confined to those who played jazz. Roland Hayes, a black American tenor, found himself much in demand for his renditions of Southern spirituals translated into French. "Steal Away to Jesus" began, *"Fuyons, fuyons, fuyons vers Jésus, fuyons, fuyons vers notre patrie."*

Spirituals, however, were not on Josephine Baker's mind. In the brief time before she and her cohorts would once again hit the road, she was doing her best to light up Manhattan.

Among the new Happy Honeysuckles hired in New York was sixteen-year-old Fredi Washington, who went on to become famous in the 1934 movie version of *Imitation of Life.* "It wasn't that I wanted to get into show business," she said. "But somebody told me they were paying more to chorus girls than I was making as a bookkeeper."

Josephine, said Fredi, "wasn't just an ordinary somebody, she stood out like a sore thumb, the craziness was just a part of her."

"It was really a singing show," said Revella Hughes, who had signed on as vocal coach. "Eubie Blake wrote beautiful tunes. It was the first time a love theme was permitted in a musical with black people. A boy kissed a girl, told her he loved her." (Back at the beginning, Noble Sissle had worried about this, afraid that when Lottie Gee and Roger Mathews started to sing "Love Will Find a Way," they would be attacked, and Eubie, "stuck out in front, leading the orchestra—his bald head would get the brunt of the tomatoes and rotten eggs. Imagine our amazement when the song was not only beautifully received, but encored.")

Josephine took her first voice lessons from Revella Hughes. "She still lacked the ability to project a number," Hughes told me, "but she was just bubbling over with natural talent."

During their time in New York, Maude found Josephine a room at 126 West 129th Street, with a family named Sheppard. In 1985, Maude took me to have lunch with Ethel Sheppard, beautiful, feminine, and—at eighty—apologetic for being a bit overweight.

"We always had show people as tenants," Ethel said. "Sissle and Blake were good friends of my parents, and that's how my sister Evelyn—the one they called Little Shep—and my brother Bill and I got parts in *Shuffle Along*. Maude brought Josephine to us, and my mother loved her and so did my sister Evelyn. She and Joe were very close. Joe couldn't write very well, and every week she would give my mother half her salary, and Mother would send it to Joe's mother back in St. Louis."

There was still enough money left to buy Robert's Oriental Perfume, and cosmetics from Mrs. Lucille. Mrs. Lucille would also sell on credit, "but if you didn't pay," says Maude, "she would beat the living hell out of you. She was strong as a mule. She would blend powders to each one's complexion. Red on a dark cheek looked sexy, Josephine loved it."

Shuffle Along gave its final Broadway performance on July 15, 1922. Next stop, Boston. In Boston, no one had to stay in a crummy room with a buggy mattress. Citizens welcomed the girls of the chorus into their houses. Mamie Lewis, one of the Jazz Jasmines, gave me a picture of her and Josephine and Evelyn Sheppard outside the bay-windowed, ivy-covered brownstone where they roomed.

Some sixty years afterward, I found Mamie living in a ground-floor apartment in the south Bronx. There was no front door, and the fallen plaster from the walls was all over the floor.

She was very frail, and she was waiting for me, holding dozens of crumbling pages from an old photograph album. She hugged the pictures labeled "Summer, 1922" to her chest. She had nothing left, neither health nor family, everything gone except this handful of souvenirs, the snapshots yellowed, eaten away by the years. But for her it was proof that she had known another life, in a place where green things flourished. She had not always been on welfare, she had been pretty, and young men had come to call. On the backs of the pictures she had glued reviews of *Shuffle Along;* on the fronts, there were labels with arrows: "Josephine," "Little Shep," "Maude."

They looked like schoolgirls in their cotton dresses, and Mamie Lewis spoke of Boston, where she had won first prize in an essay contest. The essay, printed in a newspaper, had filled Josephine with awe for the way Mamie could use words to express herself.

Josephine had a lot to say, but no way to say it except by dancing. Always afraid someone would discover her lack of education, she trusted nobody. But occasionally, she would allow herself to ask for help. Once, backstage, she was writing Carrie a letter. "Dear Mother, much success," she muttered, then, struggling with the four words, turned to Mamie. "How do you spell 'much'?"

Opening night at the Selwyn Theater, Josephine again drew special notice. "One of the chorus girls is without question the most limber lady of whatever hue the stage has yet disclosed," wrote a rhapsodic critic. "Her name may be printed somewhere in the program—if it is, I can't find it—but it should be placed outside in lights. The knees of this phenomenon are without joints. . . . The eyes of this gazelle also defy all known laws as they play hide-and-seek with the lady's nose as goal. I've seen nothing funnier."

A day later, a reporter who thought he'd hit pay dirt told all. "That chorus girl who makes such a hit in *Shuffle Along,* that real jazz baby, is not mentioned in the Selwyn program, but if you can keep a little secret, we'll divulge her name. She is Josephine Baker. Washington, D.C., is her native city. Her father was a prominent Negro lawyer."

Mother, you made it, orchestrated it, pulled it off. Your talent recognized, your antecedents upgraded (from no known father to Arthur Martin, gravel hauler, to a prominent Negro lawyer), your secrets still safe.

If Josephine's name was not mentioned in that first Boston program, neither were the names of Maude Russell or Fredi Washington or Allegretta Andrews. One week later, the mistake was rectified. Josephine, Maude, Fredi, Allegretta, listed, validated, Happy Honeysuckles all.

Happy offstage as well. And looking good. "Josephine came in one day with a leather outfit," Maude says, "and she looked some kind of hot in it, she had those long legs and that red leather suit was fittin' her out of this world."

What was more, in Boston, once you got dressed up, there were places to go. "You know," Maude says, "once upon a time they looked down on show people, but when we went to Boston, black doctors, black lawyers gave parties for us, we were considered the society show-girls. But we had to be home by midnight. No later. That was the rule."

Rules are easier laid down than enforced. Some nights, Josephine spent alone in her bed, Vaseline all over her body ("How terrible it must feel," said Fredi. "I love it, it's good for my skin," said Josephine); some nights she wandered. "She was crazy about Evelyn Sheppard—Little Shep," Maude says. "I didn't think she was gay, she got around with too many men, but she didn't talk about those things. 'Hey, what you say, girl?' and she was gone."

Others, less guarded than Josephine, brought their troubles to Maude. She was experienced. She'd had an abortion early on because "babies wasn't in my mind. You know what all was in my mind? Show business and bein' a star. Abortions were done very crudely then, you went to some old lady or old man and took your chance on them killin' you, and you paid them ten or fifteen dollars. But I knew this little brown-skinned woman, and I told her I was pregnant, and she says, 'Honey, get yourself some carbolic acid and pour it in a pot of hot water and sit over it, the baby will dissolve.' And that's just what happened."

When one of the younger cast members got pregnant in Boston, Maude went out and bought the carbolic acid.

Booked for two weeks, *Shuffle Along* did such good business it stayed at the Selwyn three months. Josephine's troubles with the other girls continued. Once the loyal Fredi came to the theater and found they had moved Josephine out of the communal dressing room. "That's where I blew my top. All her stuff was in the hallway, and I knew exactly what had happened. All those girls thought they were a big deal, and looked down on Josephine, who was so much darker. I just decided to protect her. I went in and yelled, 'Who told you you own this dressing room? You go and get her stuff.' So they got it and brought it back."

"It seemed that Joe did not care," Ethel Sheppard said. "She was doing what she wanted."

There's a picture of the entire *Shuffle Along* company, some sixty-three people, under the marquee of the Selwyn. Josephine is sitting down front, in the same row as her bosses. (How had she managed that? Let me hazard a guess. Eubie Blake, an enthusiastic ladies' man, was very fond of her, and she may have been his lady of the moment. "Eubie," says one of his friends, "would pore over pictures of *Shuffle Along*, recalling the chorus girls he'd slept with. He would just point with his finger—'This one, this one, this one.' Josephine was no exception.")

The other women are dressed in the style of the season, simple shifts, a harbinger of flapper clothing to come. Only Josephine looks like a creature from another time. She is wearing taffeta, the skirt ruffled. A fringed bertha curves over her shoulders, her full sleeves are short enough to expose slender wrists and long fingers. Josephine liked her hands, and would often have them photographed. Under these photographs, she would write, "My hands."

She probably designed the dress herself. (Since her first road trip, she had passed time on the trains studying fashion magazines and sketching.) A big hat is on her lap, her hair is smooth, curved under, a single strand of pearls adorns her throat, her legs are crossed at the ankles. "I am the first black countess," she would say, after she claimed to have married Pepito; studying her likeness as she sat outside the Selwyn, anyone would have believed it.

I have another snapshot, more informal, in front of a *Shuffle Along* poster. It's of Little Shep, her brother Willie, and Willie's wife, Ruth Walker. I look at it and think of Maude's saying, "We all babied Evelyn, because she was the youngest, she wasn't even sixteen, and she stuttered." In my snapshot, Little Shep looks out at us shyly, huge brown eyes, little cat chin, as guileless a face as anyone has ever seen. Many—including Josephine—were charmed by her.

In Josephine's scheme of things, men were more important, or at least more necessary, than women. Not so much for sex as for power. Men had the money, they ran the banks and wrote the contracts. Still, once in a while—starting with Clara Smith—there would be a lady lover in Josephine's life. Little Shep was one of them.

I have talked to so many of those girls—by now respectable old ladies who have turned to Jesus.

"Often," Maude Russell says, "we girls would share a room because of the cost. (In the boardinghouses of that time, they wouldn't let an unmarried man and woman room together.) Well, many of us had been kind of abused by producers, directors, leading men—if they liked girls. In those days, men only wanted what they wanted, they didn't care about pleasing a girl.

"And girls needed tenderness, so we had girl friendships, the famous lady lovers, but lesbians weren't well accepted in show business, they were called bull dykers. I guess we were bisexual, is what you would call it today."

Little Shep was never very well known outside a small circle, but there were other girls in the chorus of *Shuffle Along* who did become famous. In the thirties, Katherine Yarborough would be the first black opera star to sing *Aida* with a white company, though *Shuffle Along* had offered her scant respect. "Talk about discrimination," she said. "I was put in the wings to sing. I had that beautiful voice, but I was too black to be onstage." Maude Russell backs up the story. "She was there in the wings, all by herself."

On November 11, 1922, the company finally closed in Boston, and traveled to Chicago. They had three sleeping cars, plus three baggage cars to carry scenery, draperies, costumes, and the many trunks filled with personal wardrobe.

Two days later, they opened at the Olympic Theatre, in the midst of a minor scandal. The *Chicago Star* had printed that the show "did not want colored patronage" (during the first week of the run, at any rate) and that the producers were not advertising "in Negro and Jewish newspapers."

But there was good news, too. It looked as though Charles B. Cochran—"Britain's Greatest Showman," known for the beauty of his chorus girls, who were called Mr. Cochran's Young Ladies—was going to invite *Shuffle Along* to London.

It didn't happen. Instead, Cochran signed Florence Mills to star in *Plantation Days.*

In Chicago, Josephine was reunited with her husband. Determined to try show business himself, Billy Baker had left Philadelphia with Booth Marshall. "I took him to Bob Russell," Booth said. "He could dance a little." (As a child, Billy had indeed been sent to dancing school—"I was the first Negro to give dancing lessons in Philadelphia," Walter Richardson told me—but the old teacher didn't remember much about his onetime student.)

In any event, by the time he and Josephine came together again, Billy's dancing career had tapped itself out, and he was waiting tables at the Grande Terrasse Café, the Cotton Club of Chicago. When he got off early, he could be found backstage at the Olympic, hanging around until Josephine was through. The other girls all thought he was terrifically handsome—though he was only a little taller than Josephine—and soon he had a temporary job with the company. According to Billy, "I was employed by Noble Sissle as his private secretary."

On the ninth of December, the *Chicago Defender* cautioned its readers, "Don't Go To Sleep and Miss the Greatest Breakfast Dance of the Season in Honor of the *Shuffle Along* Co."

The party would take place at the Eighth Regiment Armory; date: December 12, time: 4 A.M. There would be music by Wickliffe's Ginger Band of Dreamland, and Alberta Hunter would sing. (Alberta was the sweetheart of the town, appearing nightly at the Dreamland Café, where she sang what she liked, including numbers from *Shuffle Along,* the musical that hadn't hired her because Noble Sissle had said she was too black. In their book, *Alberta Hunter,* Frank C. Taylor and Gerald Cook say Alberta called Sissle "a dicty," and accused him of having "a color complex.") Admission to the Armory was fifty cents, and promoters promised that "No Expense Has Been Spared to Make This the Biggest Event in the History of Chicago."

Well, yes, except maybe for that night in 1871 when the whole city caught fire. It was the good life, especially for the creators and stars of *Shuffle Along.* They had earned a lot, and were busy spending it. Ashton Stevens, drama critic of the *Herald Examiner,* observed that "our colored brothers at the Olympic . . . have eleven limousines and their own chauffeurs. It is easy come, easy go with them. 'What's money for but to spend?' is their slogan, and they live up to it in union suits that cost $40."

But a number of the company's foot soldiers, less well paid and therefore less eager to work so hard, had begun to complain about the extra shows on Sundays. For no extra money. They were also chafing under the remorseless discipline of Sissle and Blake, who fined you if you moved wrong, hit a false note, came late to the theater.

Josephine didn't mind any of that. Josephine wanted to work more, she wanted to work harder, and in Chicago, she got her first chance to really step out. "There was a pretty girl who did a dance with a fellow," Fredi remembers. "She had a principal role, and she got sick.

"Josephine knew every step, she knew the whole thing. She was into the other girl's costume before the girl had left the theater. She was raving, she was telling everyone, 'I am going to dance tonight.' "

I am going to dance tonight. Not my partner and I. We see it beginning. Josephine is her own creation, and there is no place for a partner who is her equal. Throughout her career, many men will partner her, none will be remembered. Many choreographers will teach her, she will forget their steps and improvise her own.

But let Fredi get on with the story. "Josephine had to go up on a high platform backstage, and then come down on the stage and meet this guy. And she was on the platform and she was so excited she missed her cue. I felt so sorry because this was a big break for her.

"When she didn't come down, they didn't wait, they just moved on. The guy she was supposed to dance with, he just did a few steps and went on to his next routine. But that didn't hold her back, she had too much ambition. She knew where she wanted to go."

She knew where she didn't want to go, too, and that was home. In March of 1923, when the company left Chicago for St. Louis, Josephine and Billy were not with them.

Chapter 10

—

YOU CAN
GO HOME AGAIN,
IF YOU DON'T
STAY THERE

"My mother, poor woman, I was ashamed of her"

arrie came to the American Theatre in St. Louis, looking for her.

It was backstage after a performance, the girls rushing to get out, meet dates, taking no notice of the very dark woman who stood near the stage door. Too timid—though that was unlike Carrie—to approach anyone directly, she kept repeating into the air, "Excuse me, do you know where Josephine Baker is?"

Of all the performers, only Adelaide Hall stopped short, moved by the anxiety in the woman's voice. "Yes, ma'am, what do you want to know about Josephine Baker?"

"I'm her mother," Carrie said. "Do you know where she is?"

"She's doing fine," Adelaide said. "She just didn't come with us to St. Louis."

Carrie thanked her, invited her home "to have some food." Adelaide declined, but never forgot the encounter.

Why had Josephine refused to come to St. Louis that spring? It would have been a *coup de maître*, she could have won the city in a walk. But the victory over herself was not so easy. To forge the armor she hid behind, she had told too many lies. In Philadelphia, she was the daughter of Arthur Wells. In Boston, her father was "a famous lawyer." In neither place did anyone know different, or question her.

But St. Louis was dangerous territory, especially with the great public interest in *Shuffle Along*. Old friends from school, from the neighborhood, from the laundry, would surely come to see her, and maybe someone would tell Willie Wells that his wife was back in town. And what if he showed up one night to remind her that she had promised to spend her life with him, never mind that she was only thirteen years old when she said it?

Her fears cost her dear. Because the pattern was set; once she started running from her past, she couldn't stop. The best show that had ever happened for black people, and she was not part of its debut in her own hometown. We can presume that many of the other chorus girls enjoyed her absence, she wasn't around to take the attention away from them. They must have enjoyed too the fact that the American was a white theater; the only black performer who had played there before was Bert Williams, headlining in the 1920 *Ziegfeld Follies*. To dance on the stage where Bert Williams had walked, that was one of the things Josephine was denying herself.

When she rejoined the company, Billy wasn't with her anymore, he had gone back to Chicago, and nobody but Josephine knew why. In her absence, she found she had been promoted. She was now listed on a separate line in the program as "That Comedy Chorus Girl."

They played Atlantic City, opening in June at Nixon's Apollo Theatre on the boardwalk, and a few days later, Miller and Lyles broke up with Sissle and Blake. Though the four shared equally in the profits of *Shuffle Along*, the Sissle and Blake songs drew so much notice that Miller and Lyles had been feeling overlooked and undervalued.

Things fell apart, other things came together. Miller and Lyles went off to write a new show—it would become *Runnin' Wild*, another big hit—and took half the *Shuffle Along* cast with them.

Al Mayer stayed with Sissle and Blake, and the three produced *Plantation Days*, in a café at La Marne Hotel. *Plantation Days* was part *Shuffle Along* (the music, some of the performers, including Lottie Gee and Josephine), but it incorporated other acts too. Johnny Hudgins came in, so did his wife, Mildred, and a girl named Mildred Smallwood who danced on toe and played the violin.

Opening night, with Will Marion Cook conducting, *Plantation Days* was applauded through five encores, and Noble Sissle's grandmother was in the house to see it.

To work in Atlantic City in the summer was almost as good as a vacation. The ocean right outside the door, the salt spray you could taste on your lips. But the beaches were segregated—"Like everyplace else," Maude Russell says, "they had a white beach and a colored beach"—and fancy hotels posted signs: NO DOGS, NO JEWS.

"They didn't have to put NO NIGGERS, because we knew it," said Mildred Hudgins. "Josephine used to get up in the morning and put on evening clothes and stage makeup and walk up and down the boardwalk. People said she was crazy, but she wasn't, she just liked pretty clothes. She'd wear big picture hats with the evening dresses, and she'd walk, and everybody made fun of her. But Josephine just went about her business, she didn't humble to nobody."

It was Fredi Washington who suggested to me another reason why her fellow chorus girls "treated Josephine like a dog." Not only was she stealing the show, but she suffered from catarrh, which the dictionary describes as "an inflamed condition of a mucous membrane, usually that of the nose or throat, causing a discharge of mucus." In those days before antihistamines, newspaper ads promising cures asked, "What is Catarrh? . . . Is your breath foul? Is your voice husky? Is your nose stopped? Do you snore at night?"

Fredi had her own remedy for bad breath. "I told Josephine to swim in the sea every day, and after a few days, that salt water cured it, she never had it again."

Now Josephine was playing two shows a night, sleeping late, spending afternoons at the movies. She favored Pearl White and Rudolph Valentino—"Ah, in front of Rudolph Valentino, I have cried out my eyes and my heart"—and she had time left over for romance. It was rumored that she and Mildred Smallwood were lovers, and it was certainly Mildred from whom she learned to dance on toe. "Mildred was just an ordinary little pretentious toe dancer," says Maude. "She wasn't a great toe dancer, but she was a novelty because she was black. She and I had our picture in *Dance Magazine*, that was the first time colored girls had ever been in it."

When Josephine wasn't with Mildred, she was with Charlie Davis. She spent so many hours in the company of the tap-dancing Charlie that some of the cast believed they were married. They could believe what they liked, Josephine wasn't telling.

Backstage at *Plantation Days*, Johnny Hudgins spun stories. He had played with Helen Morgan—"the one that sits on top of the piano, she's a pain in the ass, God bless her"—and he had been encouraged by Fats Waller. "He'd talk to me from back of the curtain, 'Hold still, Banty, knock 'em dead.' " Johnny had seen Bert Williams on the stage of the Merlin Theater in Baltimore, "my hometown. His pictures were all over, and some of the people tore his picture and scratched it in the face. I guess they just didn't want no Negro in no white show like that."

Josephine listened raptly. She also liked to hear Lottie Gee tell about playing in France, England, Italy, and how she had found no race prejudice in those places. (Around the same time, the French press was reporting that France might expel Americans who were making rows in cafés where "management permits Negroes to dance with white girls.")

Toward the end of August, *Plantation Days* was converted back to *Shuffle Along*, and the company traveled to Toronto. It was Josephine's first trip out of the United States, and one reviewer said she "burlesqued jazz until the audience nearly fell out of their seats."

The show kept moving—Pittsburgh, Detroit, back to St. Louis. Eight months since it had played there without Josephine. This time she came, putting aside—for whatever reason—the anxieties that had made her avoid that earlier visit.

The American Theatre advertised that the "Entire CENTER and LEFT section in FIRST BALCONY Has Been Reserved For Colored Patrons," and Richard told me he and Willie Mae didn't mind having to go upstairs to watch their sister perform.

"Tumpy stayed with us," he said. "She was a big star, and she gave my mother seventy-five dollars."

Here is Josephine embroidering on that brief reunion. "I still can see that Christmas evening when after the theatre I found the whole family drinking whiskey. Grandmother, tipsier than the others, danced her great Indian dance."

Mother, you weren't there "that Christmas evening." On November 24, after the last show, you left for Philadelphia with the rest of the cast. This is the way you wrote of your retreat: "My mother insisted on taking me to the train. . . . Luckily she stopped in every bistro to see her friends. Poor woman, I was ashamed of her. . . . Quickly I went out through another door, left her and the train departed before anyone could see her. . . . Goodbye . . . that's life!"

This time in Philadelphia, they played the Forrest, and Josephine had her Thanksgiving dinner at Pa Baker's restaurant.

After that engagement at the Forrest, I lost her for a while. She disappeared. My research turned up the information that there were *Shuffle Along* companies touring all over America, but she wasn't with any of them. In a single line in one of her books, she dealt with this. "I left *Shuffle Along*."

Not much of a clue, but Alberta Hunter finally came up with a lead to Josephine's whereabouts at the end of 1923. "She was working with Buck and Bubbles, I think," Alberta said. "Yes, she was going with Buck."

Buck was dead, but I found Bubbles living in a nice house in Los Angeles. In 1967, he'd had a stroke that left him half paralyzed; it slowed him, but didn't break him.

Born John Sublett (he'd changed his name to John W. Bubbles), he was ten years old, and Ford Lee Washington (known as Buck) was six, when they formed their act. Buck played piano, Bubbles sang, and a scant ten years later, in 1922, they were playing the Palace. One wore pants that were too long, one wore pants that were too short, both wore shoes that were too big, both danced.

"Our costumes was our success," Bubbles said. "We looked poor, we talked like we didn't know nothing, and we danced like we didn't care. I'd tell Buck, 'Get out of that hole,' and he ain't in no hole, he's just so short. I say, 'Man, look at your feet, your feet sure big,' and he say, '*You* look at 'em, I'm sick of lookin' at 'em.' And he start playing, and I start dancing. We had a lovely act, ain't nobody can talk about this act not being the best act."

Josephine had met Buck and Bubbles in Philadelphia, when she was at the Standard, and they were on the same bill. "We both fell in love with her because she was so nice, and so different," Bubbles told me. "She had her own style, she'd dance ad lib, do whatever came into her mind. She came on the road with us, she had no agent, she booked herself. We went to Boston, to Chicago, to New York (we played the

Everglades Club on West Forty-eighth Street, Alberta Hunter was on the bill); I don't remember all the places we went."

Bubbles had been tall and slender, Buck small, not much to look at. "Why didn't she go out with you," I asked, "if Buck was so ugly?"

He thought that was funny. "We were famous," he said, "we were making fifteen hundred dollars a week, it didn't matter what we looked like."

Fine, I said. "Why didn't she and Buck get married?"

"Well," he said, "Buck wasn't thinking about getting married, you know. They were close, very close friends."

Bubbles recalled arriving in Rochester, New York, with Buck and Josephine. "And Sissle and Blake were already there rehearsing this new musical, *In Bamville*. They were going to open at the Lyceum, and I had a girlfriend who went to audition. She mentioned Buck and me and Josephine to Sissle and Blake. They said they'd been looking for Josephine. And they got her.

"*In Bamville* was a beautiful show, and Josephine was beautiful in it. She had such talent. What she did in Paris proved it, and they surrounded her there, they never surrounded nobody here like that, never."

The last time Bubbles ever saw Josephine was during the March on Washington, with Martin Luther King. Had they talked about the old days? "The old days spoke for themselves," he said. "We didn't have to talk about them, we only had to look at each other."

John Sublett, aka John W. Bubbles, died in May 1986; his companion of seventeen years, Wanda Michael, sent me a letter. "Don't be sad," she wrote, "just be happy that he had a long and many times splendid life."

Chapter 11

—

IN BAMVILLE,
OR *THE CHOCOLATE DANDIES*

"She'd be laughing, to her the work was joy"

Not only was she in the new Sissle and Blake show, but, Josephine boasted, "they had written a special part for me." (Later, she eliminated that bit of history, insisting that nothing good happened to her until she left the United States.)

Sumptuous was what Sissle and Blake had in mind for *In Bamville*. Determined to have sets and costumes as opulent as anything created by Ziegfeld or George White, they hired Ziegfeld veteran Julian Mitchell to stage the show, although he was by then so deaf he could hear the music only when he pressed his ear against the rehearsal piano. Charlie Davis choreographed, comedian Lew Payton played one of the leads and helped write the book.

The action centered on the last day of the Bamville Fair. There was a cast of 125, along with three live horses who ran a staged race on a treadmill. Three white men were hired to handle the horses. "Those horses were a lot of trouble," said Eubie Blake.

Opening week in Rochester went fine, but the second week, in Pittsburgh, was terrible. Al Mayer had died of cancer in New York. Sissle and Blake were devastated; Mayer had been not just a partner, but their friend. ("There has never been a piece of paper between us," Mayer had told the *Pittsburgh Courier,* describing his business deal with Miller and Lyles and Sissle and Blake. "The profits are split five ways.") Still, the show went on; Detroit was a big booking, so was Chicago.

In Chicago, another blow. "Too much white man," the critic Ashton Stevens grumbled. "Too much platitudinous refinement . . . too much 'art' and not enough Africa."

Eubie Blake had feared just such a response. At the beginning of the second act, a number called "Dixie Moon" featured girls in tiered white dresses with hoop skirts. Eubie went to B. C. Whitney, the producer. "I said, 'Mr. Whitney . . . the audience stops dead when they see the girls in the hoop skirts. The scene is too *beautiful* for a colored show.' . . . He answered, 'Eubie, this is *not* a colored show. This is Sissle and Blake's show for Broadway. . . .' "

Josephine spied an opportunity. Everyone else was pulling back from the old minstrel show buffoonery? She would embrace it. She begged Sissle to write her a blackface number. Few women—Mama Dinks was one of them—blacked up, but Josephine couldn't wait to get her fingers into the burnt cork packed in a can like shoe polish.

"I was in black with white lips, and I imitated the sound of a muted saxophone," she said, describing herself as "a grinning girl making all the silly faces I could think of." There is a photograph of her in full regalia—checked dress, black stockings, huge floppy shoes—sitting on a railing, her eyes crossed, her legs bent out like a frog's. One little push and she would have fallen. It was just another of the balancing acts that made up her life.

In that preciously almost-white show, she decided, she would explode, she would be black and funny-looking and funny and the audience would love her.

"She was very adventurous," Maude Russell says. "She was like a black Chaplin, and she would step on anybody's shoulders to get where she wanted to get; she didn't give a damn about me, you, or anybody else."

But Josephine was not only a comic, she was also an eighteen-year-old girl, and sometimes, an eighteen-year-old girl needs to be pretty. Having won the first round, she plagued Sissle and Blake afresh. "You think I can only make people laugh? I can be a vamp!" They gave her another scene. It was called "The Deserted Female"; in it, she got to wear a floor-length gold lamé gown, simple, elegant, draped up one side to expose a shapely leg. No critic raved over her prowess as a vamp, but that gown made her happy.

(Nobody objected to Josephine's experiments with blackface, but the casting of the black football hero/actor/singer Paul Robeson as the husband of a white actress, Mary Blair, in Eugene O'Neill's *All God's Chillun Got Wings* set off what *The Afro-American* called "a theatrical storm." It didn't matter that O'Neill had written the part of Robeson's wife with Miss Blair in mind; some critics believed it should have been given to a black actress with light skin. "Critics of both races are divided," reported the newspaper, pointing out that "the role of the wife requires her to kiss her Negro husband's hand.")

In Boston, *In Bamville* played twelve weeks, and Josephine discovered Revere Beach. There is a snapshot of her clowning on the sand with two of the boys in the band. The bags under her eyes seem especially pronounced, she is very slender, and her legs are long under the dark one-piece bathing suit. Her left hand is clenched, a wedding ring still visible on the third finger.

On September 1, 1924, after six months on the road, the company arrived in New York. The show had been renamed *The Chocolate Dandies,* and it opened at the Colonial, where, Johnny Hudgins discovered, Josephine was still stealing his bits. "I used to go up to the balcony and I'd watch her, and it was like seeing myself in a mirror. So the next night, I'd put in something new, and sure enough, she'd be doing the new thing the day after."

Josephine felt ready for the premiere. At the curtain call on opening night, she stood in her gold lamé dress, a sweet smile on her face, her head resting lightly on Johnny Hudgins's shoulder, listening to the audience cheer. She was the only female singled out by *The New York Times*. "As a freak Terpsichorean artist," wrote the reviewer, "Josephine Baker, with her imitation of Ben Turpin's eyes, made quite a hit."

Johnny Hudgins walked away with every other notice. It was a queer experience for Josephine, who had become accustomed to stealing the show, but she didn't have to compete with Johnny for long. Five days after the opening, he gave notice. He felt he deserved his name in lights, and a lot of people agreed with him. A true comic genius, he was making only $150 a week, while Josephine got $125. "All because I could cross my eyes," she bragged.

She knew she didn't have delicate features or fair skin like Maude, Mildred, Fredi, but she could—and did—improve her figure. Charles Walker, a dancer called Cornbread and one of her colleagues in *The Chocolate Dandies,* recalls Josephine's stationing herself in the wings, "going through the whole show, doing the numbers along with the performers onstage. She was always moving, doing headstands and stretches, we could see her muscles developing."

Josephine and some of the other girls were staying at 200 West 137th Street, in an apartment up over the Howell Funeral Parlor. She and Mildred Smallwood shared a room. In the 1980s, I went to Harlem to interview Lilly Yuen, who still lived in that fifth-floor walk-up apartment. She told me Mama Dinks had held the leases on a few places like this that she sublet to show people. "There was a bunch of us girls here, Josephine had the smallest of the four bedrooms."

She showed me the long narrow cubicle with a window at one end. I opened the window and leaned out, wanting to see the view Josephine had seen. "At first I was afraid to live over a funeral parlor," Lilly said. I wondered if Josephine too had thought about the dead people downstairs. It was strange to be there. Josephine had combed her hair in this room, and closed the door before she went to the theater at night. "People always say she was in the Cotton Club," Lilly complained. "Josephine wasn't in no Cotton Club. She was just a chorus girl, baby, we all was chorus girls."

What a long distance I had come from St. Symphorien to this place where I listened to stories of another world, told by these vital old women—Pontop, Maude Russell, Mildred Hudgins, the Duchess. At the end, I had been associated with someone they had known at the beginning. To strangers, she was the legendary Josephine Baker, but they still thought of her as a pushy, daring kid, a link to their pasts, when they had been young and the future glittered in front of them and they weren't afraid of anything.

Somewhere along the way, they had lost her. "I did not know anything about her after she left this country," one of them told me. And after she left this country, she did not know anything about most of them, either.

Leaving Lilly's building, I thought of that September in New York, the still-warm days when the city smiled at pretty girls of all shades. Josephine and the two Mildreds, Hudgins and Smallwood, would wander along Lenox Avenue, sometimes heading for a little shop above the *Amsterdam News* where they could try on the latest hats. And at night, Mildred Hudgins said, after the show, they would often go to Tillie's Chicken Shack on 133rd Street. "People would storm the place to get the hot biscuits and the fried chicken. White people and colored people would mingle there till all hours."

Three months at the Colonial, and *The Chocolate Dandies* closed. Despite its splendor, the lovely music and dances, the horses, it had not achieved the success of *Shuffle Along*. (Eventually, including its incarnation as *In Bamville*, its Broadway run, and the post-Broadway tour, the show would play sixty weeks and lose sixty thousand dollars.)

In Philadelphia, they came to the Dunbar. John T. Gibson had grown tired of seeing black shows that once would have been his booked into white theaters, and he outbid the Forrest to get *The Chocolate Dandies*.

"I saw Josephine in it," the Duchess said. "My God, she just got encores after encores, and Mr. Baker was so proud of her. He didn't care that Billy was gone, everything was 'Daughter.' "

By February 1925, Josephine and friends were in St. Louis, back at the American Theatre. ONE WEEK ONLY. OH, BOY, SOME SHOW! THRILLING KENTUCKY RACE SCENE. BRASS BAND ON STAGE. SYMPHONY ORCHESTRA IN THE PIT. 125—COUNT 'EM—CAST AND CHORUS. SEATS NOW ON SALE FOR ALL PERFORMANCES!

Who wouldn't have come up with fifty cents for all of that?

Carrie wouldn't. She could expose her concern about Josephine to a stranger, as she had done backstage with Adelaide Hall, but in the living presence of her oldest child, she was paralyzed, so the silence between them continued. "Me and Margaret and Willie Mae went," said Richard. "We went up in the section of the balcony reserved for colored. Tumpy had good numbers."

The Chocolate Dandies traveled to Canada, and from there to Pittsburgh, where Josephine held a press conference, setting reporters straight on manners and marriage. She was scheduled to bow to Pittsburgh society at the Cavalier's Reception, and, she said, "I will smile my introduction to friends. No shaking hands, it's terribly old-fashioned and quite a bore." As for being happy though married, "it can be done, I believe. The couple that looks for trouble usually finds it, the happily smiling pair goes merrily along forever after."

One week later, in Detroit, she began divorce proceedings against Billy Baker. (A decree was never granted. "This case was dismissed on October 25, 1928, for no progress," says the document furnished by the Wayne county clerk.)

"I never heard Josephine say one unkind word about anybody," said Clarissa Cumbo, who had recently joined the chorus. "Yes, she didn't speak good English, and had no education, but let me tell you, she had no complex about it. Why should she, with all the success she had with the public, black and white. We had mostly white audiences, you see. I remember she'd always come off the stage with this big split. When she got past the wings, she could hardly get up, she'd be so tired, and we'd put our hands out to help her. And she'd be laughing about what she'd done, to her the work was joy."

Had Josephine ever talked about Billy Baker? I asked Clarissa. Yes, she said. "She was not living with him, but she still used to send him some money when he needed it."

Clarissa's husband, Marion Cumbo, who played cello in the orchestra, had some memories of *The Chocolate Dandies* tour that were less than ecstatic. He recalled one early morning when the company had pulled into a new town. "We left the train to go have breakfast. Josephine, Clarissa, a couple of others, were walking together, and I was behind them. Two little white boys were crossing the street, and they looked over and saw these brown-skinned girls and I heard one of them say, 'Look at the niggers in the fur coats.' This was way out in the Midwest somewhere."

Marion Cumbo said he always felt there was something sad about Josephine. "Something missing. She was never completely happy. I think she never got what she was looking for, which was love."

In May, *The Chocolate Dandies*, dying on the road, barely managed to limp into the Werba Theatre in Brooklyn, where it was scheduled to play one week.

Lottie Gee, having read the handwriting on the wall, had already given notice. 43 COLORED PERFORMERS, HEADED BY MISS LOTTIE GEE, SAILING FOR EUROPE, announced the *Amsterdam News*. The forty-three were going off to Berlin to do a show called *Chocolate Kiddies*, with music by Duke Ellington, and Sam Wooding leading the band—and a good thing too, the paper observed, "as things have not been breaking as nicely in the theatrical game for some of our people as in the past."

Even without Miss Lottie Gee, the show made the front page of the *Amsterdam News*, and now it was Miss Josephine Baker getting all the attention. Over her picture was the legend "A Success Everywhere." She was called a "chocolate edition of Charlotte Greenwood" and "the bronze counterpart of a celebrated French eccentrique, Pasquerette." Miss Baker, reported the *Amsterdam News*, "has a sweet voice, loves jazz, but confesses that the sweetest music in the world is that of a burst of applause." The *Brooklyn Daily Eagle* also declared *The Chocolate Dandies* to be a "lot of fun," assuring readers it was "going back to Broadway." But the only place it was going was to court.

On Saturday, May 23, the curtain had to be held for twenty minutes because the performers, some of whom hadn't been paid for months, refused to start the show. A month later, Noble Sissle filed for bankruptcy, listing liabilities of more than $26,000. Among his creditors were two automobile companies and Josephine Baker, to whom he owed $1,235.

It was a bitter ending to a long and mostly successful adventure, but Josephine may have been looking forward to some vacation. What's more, she was carrying on her person a fair amount of hard cash, because, like Alberta Hunter and Mildred Hudgins, she was suspicious of banks.

"When we were on the road, I didn't even send money to my mother," Mildred said. "I didn't trust the white postman, and many of us colored people were afraid that banks would not give you your money back. Besides, most of us in show business could barely write our names, let alone make out a bank slip. I kept my money in a grouch bag sewn under the belt of my dress."

So Josephine had a pouch with money in it, and she had a place to go. Harlem was humming, Harlem was waiting.

Chapter 12

—

SUMMER OF '25: HEAT AND HARLEM NIGHTS

"She was hanging over Seventh Avenue, stark naked"

never was a Harlemite." That's what she said, years afterward, turning her back on the streets, the sounds, the tastes that had delighted her. Was it that remembering can make you too lonely in a foreign place? Or was it only that she had the gift of forgetting? Like the gypsy's daughter in Tennessee Williams's *Camino Real*, Josephine was reborn a virgin every time the moon rose.

It was the summer of 1925, and she was living at 2259 7th Avenue, in a solid corner house. On the 133rd Street side, under the stoop, more steps led down to an after-hours club. On the Seventh Avenue side, there was a drugstore where you could put a dollar on a number. Until May of 1924, when his life came to an abrupt end, a black entrepreneur named Barron Wilkins had owned number 2259—apartments, cabaret, drugstore, all.

Referred to in a Harlem newspaper as "the city's leading sporting man," Wilkins was killed by a fellow called Yellow Charleston. "Barron was shot right in front of the house, coming out of the drugstore," said

Sam Wooding, whose band played in Wilkins's club. "He died in a taxicab. He was going to the hospital but he never got there. St. Peter stepped in."

Mama Dinks was again Josephine's landlady, in the very apartment to which Barron Wilkins had brought his young bride. It was splendid, with floors made of Italian marble, and light pouring through large windows.

Harlem was filled with beauties like the brownstones on Striver's Row, left behind when the white people panicked and fled as the first blacks arrived.

Bessie Taliaferro recalled how marvelous the brownstone she lived in on 134th Street had looked to her youthful eyes. "The woodwork! The fireplaces! We had dumbwaiters, we had bells. We used to have more fun with the tubes, talking up to the top floor, you know, and the bells are ringing in the kitchen. People made jokes about those of us who lived in such a grand neighborhood. They said, 'Oh, those niggers up there just strivin' to pay the rent, and sleeping on the floor.' Striver's Row, they called it, and the name stuck."

It was about 1900 that the black trek from other parts of the city to Harlem had begun. Then, with World War I, Southern blacks came north to work. "A great migration," the playwright Wallace Thurman called it. "Southern Negroes, tired of moral and financial blue days, struck out . . . to seek adventure among factories, subways and skyscrapers. . . . New York to the Negro meant Harlem, and the great influx included not only thousands of Negroes from every state in the Union, but also thirty thousand immigrants from the West Indian Islands and the Caribbean regions. Harlem was the promised land."

Among its sadder promises were Ko-Verra ("Makes Skin So Light Would Hardly Know She Was Colored") and Bleacho ("Be more popular, earn more money. Lightens skin or money back"), to be found in every drugstore. Josephine bought it, along with Mary's Congolene, the same hair straightener that was to blight—or almost blight—her opening night in Paris.

Booth Marshall, then renting the apartment above hers, recalled a day when her water was turned off—for some reason, the little wheel that controlled it was in *his* bathroom—and he heard screaming from downstairs. Looking out of the window, he saw Josephine. "She had this white stuff on her head, and she was hanging over Seventh Avenue stark naked yelling, 'Booth! Booth! Turn the fucking water on!'

"We loved watching the people down on Seventh Avenue."

Anyone would have. Wallace Thurman described the Seventh Avenue of that time: "Adolescent boys and girls flaunting their youth. Street speakers on every corner. A Hindoo fakir here, a loud-voiced Socialist there, a medicine doctor ballyhooing, a corn doctor, a blind musician, serious people, gay people, philanderers and preachers. Seventh Avenue is filled with deep rhythmic laughter."

True, said Booth. "Joe and I were always laughing, oh, those were happy days."

And nights. All night long in Harlem, people danced. Even on the street corners, where pedestrians threw nickels to kids demonstrating the Charleston.

"You saw throngs on Lenox and 7th Avenue, ceaselessly moving from one pleasure resort to another," reported Lloyd Morris, another chronicler of the period. "The legend of Harlem by night—exhilarating and sensuous, throbbing to the beat of drums and the wailing of saxophones, cosmopolitan in its peculiar sophistications—crossed the continent and the ocean."

The queer thing is that Josephine, who would become part of that legend, credited with having put Harlem on the world map, never worked there until 1951. Courtesy of Will Marion Cook, she did get a job dancing, but downtown, at the Plantation, a supper club above the Winter Garden. The club had been a big success ever since producer Lew Leslie had lured Florence Mills to work there.

"Lew Leslie had the whole interior takened out and decorated as a plantation," said Florence's husband, the tap dancer U. S. Thompson. "Watermelons . . . and lights—little bulbs—in the melons. There was a well, where you could draw the water out, and statues of hogs and corn. The place was packed every night to see Florence. She had a peculiar high voice, and she was never a bighead woman, that's why everyone loved her."

That spring, Lew Leslie had decided to take Florence on the road, but first he'd booked her into the Palace for a week. She was the first black woman to headline there, and *Variety* reported that whites and blacks in the audience were equally enthusiastic. Blacks bought the eighty-five-cent tickets and sat upstairs, though some, like Ethel Waters, stayed away. "I didn't care to sit in the peanut gallery," she said. "Lincoln freed me too."

Josephine and Mildred Hudgins went, and were given a ride back to

Harlem in Florence's chauffeured car. "We were so proud," Mildred told me, "not just because a colored woman was headlining, but because she was our friend."

Me, I was looking for some indignation. In the 1980s, I wanted Mildred to tell me how insulted she and Josephine had been that they had to go up to the balcony to hear someone of their own race. But Mildred was not an angry person. "Times have changed," she said softly, "and we helped change them."

When Ethel Waters was first approached about following Florence Mills into the Plantation—in a show called *Tan Town Topics*—she had her doubts. "I felt Broadway and all downtown belonged to Florence Mills."

Tan Town Topics was set to open on June 5, with Bill Vodery's orchestra providing the music, but it was postponed for three weeks. The management (which included the Shuberts, in for 15 percent of the gross receipts) then asked Will Marion Cook to come in and help pull things together; that's when he chose Josephine to dance in the chorus.

"When anybody had a job to be filled, they went to Will Marion," said Bessie Taliaferro. "They'd say, 'We want a girl, Dad. You got a singer?' And he always had a string of talented girls around him, and he would recommend one."

In 1925, Will Marion Cook was fifty-six years old, a genius without a dime or a steady job, and he lived, like Bessie, in the Spiller house, a fairly clamorous environment, since the Spiller band rehearsed in the basement. "The neighbors never minded the noise," Bessie said. "It was good noise, you know. Will Marion could take a song and fix it. He could coach performers. He'd be stomping his feet, trying to get some spirit, some soul in them, and his eyes would be piercing. Ethel Waters wouldn't do anything unless he approved. I knew if Will Marion said Josephine had talent, she had it. Because that was one of his callings, to discover talent that other people couldn't see."

The heat was terrible that summer. People slept in parks or sprawled on subway steps, hoping for any gust of stale air pushed up by a passing train, and the owners of thirty-one Broadway theaters cut their ticket prices. It didn't help. According to *Variety* of July 15, "So far as business is concerned, there just ain't none."

But *Tan Town Topics* at the Plantation, with Ethel Waters singing "Dinah" fourteen times a week, was doing fine.

So was Louis Armstrong, a block away, at the Roseland dance hall. New in town, he blew his trumpet and astonished all who heard him. The Kentucky Club, on Forty-ninth and Broadway, was home to Duke Ellington. It was open all night, and other musicians would come there when they had finished working. Paul Whiteman always showed his appreciation, Duke said, "by laying a big fifty-dollar bill on us."

As for the Club Alabam', on West Forty-fourth Street, it boasted "a Colored Revue . . . combining the natural native talent of the Colored race with . . . refinement, lavishness and beauty. . . ." Talent did abound—Johnny Hudgins, Abbie Mitchell, Fredi Washington starred there—but the chorus girls of the Alabam', light-skinned, pretty, and not weighted down by too many clothes, were the club's big lure.

Uptown, Connie's Inn, the Nest, Small's Paradise, Club Bamville thrived too. And so did Sidney Bechet, playing New Orleans jazz at Club Basha. (Basha seems to have been an attempt to spell Bechet phonetically.) The club was fronted by a twenty-two-year-old, light-skinned showgirl named Bessie de Saussure. "I had this Jewish boyfriend—he was a kind of a gangster—and when I said, 'I want a nightclub of my own,' he financed the whole thing for me, but we called it after Bechet. My boyfriend said, 'Let's use his name because he has a following.' Sidney was the draw, he got the whites to come uptown."

Many of Josephine's friends and mentors were appearing in Harlem that summer. Sandy Burns and Sam Russell were playing the Lincoln Theater at 135th Street and Lenox Avenue, and at the Lafayette, on the corner of 132nd Street and Seventh, the names of Buck and Bubbles were up in lights.

It was at the Lafayette, one midnight in late July, that "A Big Monster Benefit" was held for Bob Russell, the "Father of Show Business." Russell, who had written the song "Open the Door, Richard," who had created more sketches than anyone could remember, who had given a hand up to any number of aspiring comics and singers and dancers—including Josephine Baker—was now aging and ill, and many black artists turned out to help him. Bill Robinson was on the bill that night; so was the dancer Willie Covan, but Josephine didn't show up.

Two weeks later, in St. Louis, Bob Russell died.

—

The newspapers didn't write much about *Tan Town Topics,* but I found a review in *The Afro-American.* Ethel Waters got one line, Josephine got three.

"Yeah, Josephine was with us at the Plantation," said Willie Covan. "She came back six, eight times a night with some new crazy step, she was the star of the thing." (Willie himself was no slouch at new steps. "I worked in show business since I was nine," he told me. "Me and my brother. My brother was taken to Russia with a pickaninny show, and my mother thought maybe he got killed or something, and she went to a detective. He said, 'You want your child back?' 'I ain't got no money,' she said. But the detective said he could do it, and to make a long story short, my brother came back to us in Chicago. Then he taught me the Russian dance. I did it without no hands, I was a sensation, just left my hands up and kept goin' like a coffee grinder.")

"Josephine was a natural, she never had dancin' lessons or nothing like that," said Dorothy Rhodes, another of the chorus girls. "And she did the darndest things. We had a big ledge outside the dressing room on Fiftieth Street, and one day, she said, 'I'm gonna walk that ledge,' and she got out and walked from one window to the next.

"We used to play two shows a night. Stars would come, Connie Bennett, all big-name theatrical people. Everyone asks me if white men made propositions to the girls in the show. How the hell were white men gonna get to the girls? We weren't allowed to go sit with the customers or nothin'."

Once, Ethel Waters was ordered by her doctor to spend two weeks in bed, and Josephine always claimed to have gone on for the star (singing "Dinah" and "Ukelele Lady" and bringing down the house). Actually, Waters stayed out only three days, and I asked Dorothy Rhodes, had Josephine really substituted for Ethel during those three days? No, said Dorothy. "Josephine never sang solo."

She was enough of a sensation without singing solo, but in years to come, she always played down the bliss of that summer, making herself the victim in story after story. Even in her very last book, *Josephine,* published in 1976 after her death, we find a pitiful chapter called "First Love," in which she recalls "Henry," a young white admirer, taking her to a "snooty" restaurant where people stare and mutter, "Where did he find her? In a zoo?"

Dorothy Rhodes remembered only good times. "We'd finish work about 4 A.M. and we'd come uptown in a taxi, go to a gin mill, and sit and drink. We didn't bother about no dancin', we'd been dancin' all night."

Once in a while, Booth Marshall would come down to the Plantation with his car and chauffeur to pick up Josephine. "She always dressed like an actress," he said. "In those days, you wouldn't catch a showgirl out there with jeans on. We would drive up in front of the Lafayette Theatre, across from where we lived, and young people would run over to our car. I would have the chauffeur open the door, and I would shout, 'Kiss my ass!' and Josephine and I would laugh."

Paul Bass, a singer and alto sax player, was another who provided wheels from time to time. (Like Willie Covan, Paul started in show business early—"when I was around five years old. I sang and I used to do a little cakewalk. I'm part Indian: my mother was half Cherokee, my father was half Indian and half Jewish.") Paul was courting Alice Allison. "Alice and her sister Bessie were both in the chorus with Joe Baker at the Plantation, and their show closed a little earlier than mine—I was at Connie's Inn—so I used to have a fellow by the name of Ralph Cooper that drove my car for me to go down and pick up Alice. And she would bring Josephine Baker with her.

"I had an Auburn Phaeton, a gray car with orange wire wheels, and we used to take long rides out into the country at five o'clock in the morning just to get fresh air. Then we would come back to Harlem, to Eva Branch's place." (Eva Branch, a onetime chorus girl, had converted her apartment into a "buffet flat," where you could get food and liquor at any hour of the day or night. Eva would also take your messages, hold your mail, store your valuables.)

"Eva would cook up pigs' feet," Paul Bass said, "and we'd eat and drink till 10 A.M. It was always dark in there, we'd hit the street all walleyed, go home, and sleep till 7 P.M. Most of us was working in nightclubs and the first show didn't go on till eleven o'clock or midnight."

Whether it was the Auburn Phaeton of Paul Bass or Booth Marshall's limousine, cars were symbols of success to performers. "They would have a car and no place to stay," Bessie Taliaferro said. "But everybody doesn't want a home. A room, a car, that's all they want."

Josephine wanted more. Most of all, she wanted to be free of the limitations of her own history. None of her books ever mentioned Ralph Cooper.

Ralph, who later became a movie star, wasn't entirely forthcoming, either. Maybe it embarrassed him to admit he had been working as a driver when he first crossed paths with Josephine. "I don't know how I met her that summer," he said, "but we became friends right away. It was so hot, we would rent a little boat and go rowing in Central Park Lake at 110th Street. We talked about show business, that was our only talk, how to do something new, how to improve an old routine. Joe was funny—funny onstage, funny in private."

It was during one of those boat rides that Josephine told Ralph Cooper how much she envied the girls with whom she worked. "She said to me, 'You know, Coop, they are so pretty.' I said, 'Joe, you're pretty too.' 'No,' she said, 'not like them. Their skin is so light.' I said, 'Joe, those girls are pretty to look at, but your prettiness comes from deep inside you, and on top of that you make people laugh.' She was always perfumed, always in the latest fashion, always smiling, in a good mood. She was so much fun, so happy."

Happy is the word that crops up time and again on the lips of Josephine's companions, but Josephine never admits, in print, anyway, that she lived one untroubled moment. Here is one of her reminiscences of life at the Plantation: "One day, a famous New York actress invited four of us cabaret girls to supper at her place and she promised them a lot of money. . . . I will never forget my reaction when we entered her suite at the Ritz Carlton. . . . The lady took us to the bathroom.

" 'Hurry up,' she said. 'Get undressed.' I undressed slowly because I did not know what she wanted. The others knew. When I entered the Carlton, I was still very naive.

" 'Quick, hurry up,' the actress said, entering the bathroom all the time. . . .

"All the while I was looking at the star's diamond bracelet. I had never seen one like it before. She seemed very nervous, almost hysterical. At last, I only had my undershirt on. . . . When I entered the room, she yelled, 'Get into bed.'

"In the bed, there were already three girls, and the lady dashed around like crazy. I was so scared. She was yelling. I started screaming: I had finally understood. . . . I was furious and created such a ruckus that I was thrown out without the money promised. The next day she telephoned the Plantation: 'You made me waste my evening. Do not ever send me this crazy Josephine again.' "

The truth about what went on at the Plantation probably lies somewhere between Dorothy Rhodes's assurance that no customer could get near one of the girls and Josephine's story of lesbians encouraged to phone in their orders.

Uptown, Joe Attles told me, white people would hang around the Harlem clubs till after the shows let out. "There were white men who wanted black boys, and white women who wanted them too, and there were white men who wanted black girls, and white women who wanted them too, and everyone had the time of his life in Harlem, in those crowded rooms with music and dancing and bad gin, and smoke, and sex.

"I wondered what was going on in those white people's heads, when they went back to their apartments, after they'd spent the night with the brothers or sisters of their maids. But it wasn't always nights without tomorrows; many true and deep love stories developed between white and black."

Wallace Thurman saw it differently, regretting that Harlem's clubs had become "sideshows for sensation seeking whites."

And every night and all day, Harlem blazed with music. On those summer afternoons, in the second-floor front room he rented on Striver's Row, James P. Johnson bent to his piano, arched fingers plucking at the keys, while passersby stopped in the street outside to listen. W. C. Handy, the father of the blues, lived a block away; so did Scott Joplin.

This was the world that Caroline Dudley Reagan came looking for. She was a small white woman, in love with blackness, with black music, black bodies, with what she called "the soul of the ebony chorus."

For Mrs. Reagan, climbing the stairs to the top of one of the Fifth Avenue Coach Company's double-decker buses on a sultry July morning, the heat was a matter of no consequence. She was wearing a dress that had been made for her in Paris by Paul Poiret, and she was on her way to Harlem, where she would change the course of Josephine Baker's life.

Chapter 13

—

MRS. REAGAN
COMES TO HARLEM

"I got off at Lenox Avenue. . . . I was happy"

osephine didn't know a thing about Caroline Reagan's crusade. Broadway babies don't sleep tight until the dawn, and in the shaded bedrooms of number 2259, nobody stirred.

There are dozens of stories about how Mrs. Reagan took Josephine back to Paris. Josephine's own recollections were, as always, fanciful. An impresario had offered her a part in an overseas tour, and the French waiters at the Plantation encouraged her to take it. " 'Go,' they said, 'you will feel better, you will be understood.' So I left."

Some variations on the theme:

U. S. Thompson: "The lady came to the Plantation lookin' for talent and right away, she could see Josephine had the makin's of a big star, all she need was a chance."

Ralph Cooper: "When she got the proposition to go to France, we talked a lot about it. She said, 'I don't know where it is, I don't speak the language, and you are not coming. I don't want to go.' I told her it was a good opportunity, and if she liked it, then she could arrange for me to come over; I guess that helped her decision."

Paul Bass: "This woman from the Folies-Bergère, she wanted Joe to go back and teach the Folies-Bergère chorus girls the Charleston. And Josephine told me, 'Well, I don't want to leave Ralph,' so I said, 'Look, Joe, this is an opportunity, you can go over to Paris and make the money and send back for Ralph,' and she laughed and said, 'Well, okay.' Then she went over and met this count, and she forgot about Ralph."

Dorothy Rhodes: "Our producers tried to scare Josephine from going to Europe, they were telling her they were gonna take her off the boat, and you know, if she go, they wouldn't let her into France, all that stuff. Well, she was a little leery, but the other girls got with her and we said, 'Go, don't let this chance pass you by.' "

Claude Hopkins: "Josephine was the end girl, last to leave the stage, she was doing some bits going off, and the house was coming down, hollerin' and whistlin'. And Mrs. Reagan noticed that. She wanted Ethel Waters, but Ethel wouldn't have been the star that Josephine was."

Ethel Waters: "I said I preferred to see America first. . . . Josephine ended up with a château, an Italian count and all Paris at her feet permanently . . . *Sacrebleu!*"

Few people ever got the story straight. Most of the ones I talked to called Mrs. Reagan the "little French woman."

She was actually a little American woman from Chicago. She had been the youngest of five children, four sisters and a brother, she the tiniest, "good to repair the electric wires under the dining room table." Her father, Emilius Clark Dudley, was a famous gynecologist. (At the age of seventy-one, he went to China to teach at the Hunan-Yale Medical College—known as Yale-in-China—and was "absent from home during most of 1922 and 1923.")

His daughters grew up interesting: One painted, one wrote, one was loved by Bertrand Russell. And Caroline, during the First World War, went to France and served coffee and doughnuts to soldiers.

She married Daniel Joseph Reagan, who would later be sent to Paris as a foreign service officer. The couple had one child, a girl they named Sophie, but Caroline did not settle easily into domesticity. She wanted to produce—in France—an all-black musical revue. The notion had come to her while she and her husband were still living in Washington, D.C., and she'd gone to a rehearsal at the Douglas, a small theater in a black neighborhood.

"Eight black girls in black tights, one more superb than the next, dancing, dancing, dancing. It was the Charleston. . . . I was overwhelmed, drawn by the invisible magnet, to produce a company, to show such artists, to amaze, flabbergast, dumbfound Paris . . . the elite, the masses, the artists from Picasso to the hippie painters of the streets . . . and there is where the seed for this *Revue Nègre* sprouted. The germ possessed me and began to grow."

Possessed as well of a certain sexual ambiguity—Gertrude Stein told her, "You are neither fish nor flesh nor fowl"—Caroline Reagan says she asked herself, "Was I a woman? A man? A spirit in every sense?" and decided it didn't matter. At the age of thirty, she had become obsessed with the élan vital of the American black.

In her efforts to bring a black revue to Paris, she solicited cooperation from the directors of all the big theaters, the Casino de Paris, the Folies-Bergère, the Odéon. The directors were respectful but firm. "Madame, we cannot," they said politely. Then the painter, Fernand Léger, came to her rescue. "Go see Rolf de Maré. He's got a white elephant of a theatre. Just the other day I told him, 'Get Negroes, they're dynamite, they're the only ones who will wake up your theatre. . . .' "

Rolf de Maré, a rich, Swedish-born patron of the arts who had brought Pavlova, Paderewski, Paul Robeson, *Les Ballets Suédois*—even Will Marion Cook and his Syncopated Orchestra—to Paris, listened to this possibly crazy woman. "I propose a black revue," she said. "Authentic, racial, the blacks so sure of themselves, it is their soul that sings, that dances without end."

De Maré gave her money to go to New York and put a show together. "That was the best day of my life. . . . I was flying. . . . I came home blinded by happiness."

Next stop, Harlem.

"Harlem," she writes, "a silken word. Harlem, land of banjos, piano and the mechanical victrola, gramophone, radio morning noon and night. . . . I got off the bus at Lenox Avenue."

She asked directions to the theater in which Will Marion Cook maintained a small office. "Young laughing boys led me, each holding slices of red watermelon, the seeds as black as their eyes . . . it was hot. I was happy."

Mrs. Reagan had been told Cook could help her choose the talent for her show, and he obliged. As male star and choreographer, he suggested his son-in-law, Louis Douglas. Douglas was famous in Europe; at the age of six, he'd been taken abroad by Belle Davis with a group called The Little Pickaninnies. (In 1898, Davis, a comedienne and singer, had starred in *Clorindy, or the Origin of the Cakewalk,* the first show written by Will Marion Cook.) Louis Douglas was newly returned to the United States after twenty-nine years away.

He came in and danced for Caroline. He had conquered Russia, Caroline said, and "he conquered me that morning."

He then proposed his wife Marion (daughter of Will Marion Cook) for the chorus. The casting had begun.

Florence Mills was Caroline's star of choice, and in fact, her picture appeared in the July 9 program of the Théâtre des Champs-Élysées as the fall's coming attraction. But Florence was a big name, and earned big money; Caroline couldn't afford her.

So Will Marion and Caroline still needed a female star, and a whole bunch of dancers. They couldn't check out the Cotton Club; it was closed for alcohol violations, forty-four of them. They could and did go to the Lafayette Theatre. This is the way Lilly Yuen described what took place there:

"We all was working at the Lafayette, and that French woman that took Josephine to Paris, she came there, and we were supposed to go. Mr. Miller signed the contract, and then this little French woman and Mr. Miller had a big run-in and he tore the contract up. Then this woman wanted to take us herself, and we was kids, you know, and we said, we can't leave Mr. Miller, he is like a father to us."

Irving C. Miller's company of forty had decided to dance with the guy what brung them, leaving Will Marion free to campaign for *Tan Town Topics,* the show he had doctored. He thought Mrs. Reagan should engage Ethel Waters.

Ethel Waters was marvelous, but she wanted $750 a week. Still, Reagan and Cook went back to the Plantation a second time to try to talk Ethel around, and that was one of the nights she was out. Watching Josephine clown, Caroline turned to Will Marion. "That's our star," she said.

The idea made Louis Douglas unhappy.

"He wanted no part of Josephine Baker," says Bessie Taliaferro. "He said, 'She'll never go over in Paris, they won't like her.' But you see, they did."

It was no easier to negotiate with Josephine than with Ethel Waters, Caroline discovered. She offered $150 a week and was rejected. "I was not Madame Ziegfeld, covered with jewels. (Even fake ones inspire confidence.) I was nobody important. I proposed, Josephine disposed. . . . She was happy where she was, free, the featured girl of eight girls."

Caroline persisted. " 'With me, you'll be the star of the Théâtre des Champs-Élysées.' In the end, it was yes. Above all, because she knew exactly what she wanted to do. She wanted to sing sweet pretty songs. She assured me that she knew them. 'All the better,' I said. 'That way, you won't have to come to rehearsals, you can continue at the Plantation.'

"My contract with de Maré gave me three months in which to wire him the name of the show and the names of the stars. I was partial to *Hotsy Totsy*. A friend told me, 'Stop, where is your tact?' So, quite without thinking, I wired: LA REVUE NEGRE, STARRING JOSEPHINE BAKER AND LOUIS DOUGLAS. God help me, the die was cast."

In Paris, Rolf de Maré had flyers printed, promising "Une Revue Nègre avec Josephine Baker et Louis Douglas," not to mention "Les 8 Charleston Babies," but two days after Josephine gave her word, she took it back again. Over the phone she told Caroline her bosses had doubled her pay. "I outbid them, saying, 'Wait for me, I'm coming,' " Caroline recalled. "Then I grabbed my extraordinarily beautiful mandarin coat, embroidered in gold. My father had brought it to me from China, as though he knew that I was going to need it for her. . . . A taxi, and there I was again at Josephine's. 'Quick, quick, Josephine, the taxi's waiting for us.' The mandarin coat worked its spell, and she followed me. 'We're going to see the great designer, Tappe, who's making a dress for you for Paris.'

"And here is how Tappe spoke to her, while draping her in the fabric beaded with pearls. 'Mademoiselle, what luck you've been chosen by Madame Reagan . . . she will make you famous, she's your lucky star.'

"Once she was put in her pearls, in that dress intended for the finale (later photographed in Paris by Man Ray), she kissed me. She was happy and beautiful, and she saw herself singing these sweet pretty songs. . . . I kept a hermetic silence, saying to myself, we shall see."

To the end of her days, Caroline Reagan mourned the loss of the glittering coat. But she had her star. At $250 a week.

She still had to get a good jazz band. She and Will Marion Cook auditioned forty groups before they went down to the Smile-A-While Inn in Asbury Park to hear Claude Hopkins, who was twenty-two, handsome, talented, a pianist as well as a bandleader. "When I learned she was there," Claude said, "I put up several novelty numbers that we used." One of them was a long comedy version of "The St. Louis Blues" set in a Baptist church, and, Claude said, "The act put the audience in stitches. Mrs. Reagan . . . was almost hysterical."

She had found her band. She also found several chorus girls, choosing them the way you choose ripe peaches, the ones with pretty color, the ones without bruise or blemish. Evelyn Anderson was eighteen years old, and working in the revue at the Smile-A-While. "After I did my Charleston for Mrs. Reagan, she asked me if I was interested in joining them to go to Europe. I said yes because I was likin' Joe Hayman then. He was playing alto sax in Claude's band.

"Claude's wife, Mabel, was working in a different cabaret in Asbury Park, and that's where Mrs. Reagan got her and Bea Foote and Marguerite Ricks. It was the end of August, and hot as hell when we came to New York."

Satisfied with the results of her foraging along the Jersey shore, Caroline's pleasure was capped when Sidney Bechet asked to join the band. Will Marion Cook told her the truth: Bechet drank, and maybe he'd miss a show once in a while, but every night he played, she would be grateful.

The real work began. Rehearsals for the Hopkins band in the Spiller basement, rehearsals for the chorus girls at Club Basha.

"My sister Dorothy's house on Twelfth Street had become a sweat shop," Caroline wrote. "It was hot, not work for the classic dressmakers of Broadway. . . . Dorothy had imagined corsets with red laces for the eight girls."

The girls loathed the corsets ("You want to dress us like monkeys") but liked the white organdy overcoats with real diamond buttons, and "the bras and panties, dyed separately to match their skin tones."

Caroline rejected a set design by her friend, the novelist John Dos Passos ("It was very nice, but I found it was a little bit too much the way whites thought of blacks, a street in the south with houses of all colors") and engaged Miguel Covarrubias to do the scenery. "I chose . . . sets from among the models. . . . My Mississippi steamboats, the Memphis and the Natchez . . . the skyscraper that leaned, while Bechet played. . . ."

In the midst of all this, a dispute broke out between Will Marion Cook and Louis Douglas. *Variety* of August 26 had carried the headline COLORED TAB FOR PARIS WITH WILL MARION COOK, along with the news that Cook would be leading the show's orchestra, but it turned out to be a false report. Something had gone wrong.

It was Bessie Taliaferro's view that quarreling with his son-in-law had soured Will Marion on the job. "He couldn't stand Louis Douglas, because Louis married his daughter, I guess." (Marion, in London with her father in 1919, had fallen in love with the young entertainer.) "And then Louis had been so nasty about Josephine, he had done everything he could to keep Will Marion from taking Josephine for the show. And then I think Mrs. Reagan and Will Marion fell out before she went across the seas."

Variety had got everything else right, reporting that "a chorus of eight girls and an orchestra of six pieces (males) will be included in the company of 20. Among the principals are Josephine Baker, Maud de Forrest, and Louis Douglas."

Will Marion was replaced by Spencer Williams (he would write the music, while Jack Palmer, a white man, did the lyrics), and Caroline signed Josephine as her star. "I needed a lawyer and a notary for each contract," she said, "but everyone assured me I risked nothing with Josephine, that with or without a contract, she would never leave me."

———

On September 10, the entire cast is milling around the passport office. It's a mess. Some of them can't read or write. Some who have never met before swear they are related because everyone needs a witness who has known him or her for ten years.

And you, Mother, you top them all. You deserve an award for your performance.

Six days before sailing, Mrs. Reagan has discovered you don't have your birth certificate. "What to do?" she asks herself. "Go to St. Louis and find her mother, a laundress, and have her make an authorization? There's no time."

She uses her diplomat husband's clout, and presto! the city of St. Louis sends her a copy of the missing document, and Booth Marshall drives you down to Wall and Nassau streets, along with your witness, Henry Sapan, a pianist. Caroline kisses you when you arrive, saying with relief, "My star is late."

She produces your birth certificate, the first time you have seen it. It must be a bit of a shock to read that you were born Freda J. McDonald, and that a man identified only as Edw. was your father.

You sit down at a heavy wooden desk to fill out the application form. You write "Freda J. McDonald." Then, on the line that gives you the choice of "father" or "husband," you cross out "husband." Your father, you declare, is named Edward McDonald. You don't know any Edward McDonald, but then, you didn't know the last father you invented—the Washington lawyer—either.

You're an actress, you're coming home in one year, you're five feet eight inches tall, colored, with a large mouth, a short chin, and an oval face. You take the application back to the clerk. He, one William Marshall, notes that you are going to France, and asks to see your contract of employment.

You present it proudly. He shakes his head. "What's this, Miss McDonald? The contract says Josephine Baker."

"Baker is my married name."

"But you wrote you are single."

"A mistake. I'm married."

McDonald is crossed out, Baker is written in; "single" is crossed out, "married" is written in. But there's no pleasing this Mr. Marshall. He wants to know where your husband lives. You don't have a clue to Billy's whereabouts, so you make you another correction. "Married" is crossed out, and in its place you write, "Divorced, April 15, 1925, in Detroit."

Mr. Marshall is showing definite signs of strain. He demands proof of your husband's citizenship. No passport can be issued until you, Freda Josephine McDonald Baker, single, married, divorced, "present satisfactory evidence of husband's American birth."

Quick as a flash, you see what you have to do. Kill the guy off. Cross out "divorced," write in "widowed." Only thing is, you do solemnly swear that your husband died September 14, 1924. Good work, Mother. He dies in 1924, and you divorce him in 1925. It's hard for Mr. Marshall to swallow your divorcing Billy Baker seven months after he's dead.

"You are crazy!" cries Mr. Marshall. Fortunately, Mrs. Reagan, who has been choking with laughter, jumps in and saves you. Now I understand why you said in one of your books that you were running around in circles in the passport office, afraid you might be put in jail.

You are Carrie's child, no question about it. When the census man came around, Carrie had the guts to look him in the eye, swear she'd been married to Arthur Martin for five years, and in one tidy sweep, legitimize all three of you children. You had the guts to go up against the passport man, daring him not to give you what you wanted. Your will be done. "Joe really got that clerk," Booth Marshall told me. Even so, he said, she was not excited to be going abroad. "She didn't know what was going to happen. She thought it was going to be like here, no future in it."

A year before, Bricktop had thought the same thing. "It wasn't unheard of for an entertainer to go to Europe," she said, "but not many did, and hardly any blacks did. . . . I wasn't excited. I wasn't nervous. I barely knew where Paris was and didn't know a word of French, but I'd traveled to a lot of cities in the United States, and it didn't seem to me that Paris would be much different."

On the eve of the *Berengaria*'s sailing, there was a farewell party for Josephine. Dorothy Rhodes was there. "It was at the Club Bamville on 129th Street and Lenox Avenue that was run by Broadway Jones, who had been in *Chocolate Dandies* with Josephine. And I can even tell you what Josephine had on. She had somebody to make her an outfit, pantaloons in gray, with suspenders. We had a good time."

Booth Marshall had been paid fifty dollars to deliver Josephine to the boat, but all he could remember later was being too drunk to get out of bed. In the end, a whole bunch of people saw Josephine up the gangplank: Will Marion Cook, Paul Bass, Alice and Bessie Allison, Ralph Cooper (Bessie and Ralph had been her most recent lovers), and Mildred Smallwood (a lover from the past). There is a picture of Josephine clutching a small violin, a going-away present from Mildred.

Right up till the last minute, Josephine considered not going. "As far back as I can remember," she wrote later, "I can only recall one single day of fear in my life. One day, which lasted only one hour, maybe one minute . . . one minute when fear grasped my brain, my heart, my guts with such force that everything seemed to come apart. It was September 15, 1925."

On September 16, the *Berengaria* sailed. The last cast member to make it aboard was Sidney Bechet. "He didn't show up for a long time," Claude Hopkins said. "And we couldn't move without him because Mrs. Reagan had his passport. He finally came. Later. Oh, he was something."

"A quarter of Harlem was on the docks," Caroline Reagan said.

" 'Bon voyage, have a good time, come back.' With little blue, white and red flags waving in the air. . . . On the boat, the orchestra played, and Harlem became farther and farther away."

The adventure had begun. Half the troupe wasn't sure where Paris was, and even the ship-to-shore phone was an astonishment. (On a different transatlantic voyage, Johnny Hudgins remembered getting a telegram from Louis Armstrong. "I said, 'A telegram? How can a telegram get way out through all this water?' I didn't see no land.")

Awake at last, Booth Marshall telephoned Josephine on the boat. She was summoned by a loudspeaker: "Miss Baker, Miss Josephine Baker, please come to the radio room."

Miss Josephine Baker hugged herself with excitement. It didn't matter that it was still mid-morning; true to form, she found reality too ordinary, and in one account of the sailing, she turned day into twilight. "The sea was calm, with a red glow from the setting sun. . . . Nobody paid any attention to me. Who would have looked at me? Who would have extended a hand or said a word? I was only a little girl, not even that, a little black girl.

"The Statue of Liberty disappeared on the horizon. It was over between America and me. . . . Goodbye, New York, goodbye, Philadelphia, goodbye, St. Louis. Goodbye the little girl with purple hands. Goodbye the rats of Bernard Street. Goodbye. . . .

"The secret in order to hold fast was not to move. . . . It was a game."

Chapter 14

—

A SHIPBOARD ROMANCE, AND HELLO, PARIS

"Men and women kissing in the streets!"

The *Berengaria,* Captain W.R.D. Irvine, loosened itself slowly from the berths of New York, drawn by four little tugboats," said Josephine. "The sea was quiet."

One day on City Island in the Bronx, I walked into a thrift shop and found an old booklet. It was a first-class passenger list (among the pampered voyagers were "Hon. John Cecil and valet, Mr. Ralph Curtis and governess") issued by the Cunard Steam Ship Company. On the booklet's front, covered with grease spots, a painting of the *Berengaria* being pulled out of New York harbor by four tugs, just as Josephine described it.

The French have a fairy tale called "Le Petit Poucet," about a little boy wandering through a dark forest and dropping small white pebbles to leave a trail so he can find his way back home. I have stumbled over so many pebbles marking Josephine's road through the world that I sometimes wonder if she is putting them out for me. The brochure I held in my hand was dated September 16, 1925, the very day that she had sailed.

My hands shook, but her name was not on the roster of "saloon" passengers because Caroline Reagan had booked all her people into second class. Herself, too. "I was not apart, like the other Broadway managers."

On board the *Berengaria*, Josephine fell in love with Claude Hopkins. He was tall, elegant, with a beautiful angular face. It was a *coup de foudre*; she was struck to the heart.

"We ran after each other," Claude told me. "She was different, she was something special, and I really was not cautious. I loved my wife, but . . ." His voice trailed off. "The chorus was with Mabel, they were on her side."

If there were sinners on the ship, there were also pilgrims praying for them. Josephine, who thought she had put her hometown behind her once and for all, was now surprised to find herself at sea with the Reverend John Thompson and forty-two of his flock on their way from St. Louis to Rome to celebrate Holy Year. We can assume they did not approve of the merrymakers who surrounded them.

"We played cards, did a little drinking," Claude said. "I won eight hundred or nine hundred dollars, we saw movies. Nobody could beat Sidney Bechet at cards, but he was miserable, got drunk, half the time he wouldn't show up for the game, and he didn't show up for the charity show either."

The charity show had been worked out with the Cunard Line; Mrs. Reagan was amenable to having her troupe perform for the benefit of children of sailors lost at sea. "I immediately volunteered to sing," Josephine remembered. "I decided on two sentimental numbers: 'Brown Eyes' and 'If You Hadn't Gone Away.' After one rehearsal, I was sure of my success. . . . I would soon be entertaining the first-class passengers. Yes, I would always remember . . . my first resounding flop.

"I couldn't seem to find the beat. Was that why no one listened? When they *did* listen, it was even worse. They clearly didn't like what they heard. My voice began to crack. In quick succession I produced three off-key notes, which the orchestra tried to drown out."

"She really insisted on doing those songs," Caroline Reagan said. "Beautiful in her Tappe dress, she sang those sweet songs that she cherished. Alas, or perhaps luckily for me, there was no response, no applause, absolute silence from these ladies and gentlemen in their black tie and their décolleté. In first class. I say luckily because I knew, and I had to make her know, but it was a mess."

The show was saved by a five-year-old. Into the chill following Josephine's performance, Louis Douglas threw his little daughter, Marion, sending her out in white socks and black patent-leather shoes to dance the Charleston. "I remember dancing until I saw stars," she told me. "I had an out-of-body experience. I danced, I danced, I danced, my legs kept going. And the audience was raving, people were screaming, and I was so excited I couldn't calm down afterwards. My father tried to take me downstairs, my mother tried to, but I wouldn't let anyone except Josephine put me to bed. That was my night."

Despite her kindness to young Marion, Josephine was seething with rage. "Before going to sleep," Caroline Reagan said, "I ran across her, grey with fury. 'You're fixing to kill me!' she cried. 'I'm going back to New York tomorrow morning.' 'As you wish, Josephine,' I said, 'but unfortunately, you'll have to wait till we get to Cherbourg. We are in the middle of the Atlantic Ocean.'

"What a child. What a star I had. . . . Next morning, she came knocking at my door quite timidly, asking me why I had chosen her. It was a nice way to be waked up. I answered, 'Meeting in our dining room at ten o'clock. Let Douglas and our composer, Spencer Williams, know.'

"When I arrived for the meeting, there was Josephine already. Worried. Louis Douglas and Spencer Williams were at the piano.

" 'All right,' I answered her question. 'Josephine, you know how to dance, you're beautiful, you have a chic that will amaze even Parisians, and you are a clown, don't forget that.' At that moment, Spencer Williams put his great black hands on the white piano keys and began to compose 'I Want to Yodel.' Josephine stayed with him to learn the song."

It would be a huge hit in *La Revue Nègre*.

Probably because of her affair with Claude, Josephine quickly recovered her high spirits. "She had a cabin by herself, her being the star, you know," Lydia Jones said. "But the other girls were really angry that she would take the man away from his wife. Some of them were actually plotting to throw Josephine overboard. Evelyn Anderson and I had to talk them out of it."

Evelyn vouches for Lydia's story. "When nobody knew where to find Claude, he was with Josephine."

At one point during the voyage, the ship stopped. In her first book,

Josephine told the story quite simply. "September 18. Everybody on deck. We put on life jackets, boats are unhooked, sailors work quietly. You can hear pulleys and small children scream. The ocean nevertheless is calmer than ever. . . . So what's the matter? There is a German mine in the area. Luckily, we didn't run into it."

In a later book, the tale was dramatically expanded. "There would probably be a boat for our deck if there were enough to go around, but we would be the last to leave ship. We could hear the first-class passengers shouting. Children were crying. Gathering by the railing, we began to sing. The same songs our ancestors had sung on the slave ships that carried them to America. A musician called Sidney picked up his clarinet. He played so softly and sweetly that tears came to my eyes."

Suddenly we have slave ships and spirituals. It's interesting to note how Josephine manipulates her souvenirs as the years pass. Yes, everyone did go on deck when the alarm sounded, and yes, Sidney Bechet was there, but he wasn't carrying a clarinet. Claude gave me a picture of some of the cast taken during that drill. The men are wearing jaunty peaked caps, everyone except Josephine is smiling. Life jackets are tied around their necks, the word FRONT spelled out across their chests. Only Josephine wears her jacket upside down. There are no tears in her eyes, she is squinting into the sun, lost in thought.

The *Berengaria* docked in Cherbourg at 8:30 A.M. on the morning of Tuesday, September 22. "When we arrived, it was raining," said Josephine. And cold.

The four-hour trip to Paris included lunch, which was a pleasant surprise. In the dining car, the whole company was welcome. Not like the dining car of the Illinois Central train with its white rosebuds and its white clientele.

The cooking in the restaurant car was a revelation too, "but not as much as that of my first dinner in Paris. Can you imagine, they gave me snails to eat. . . . And then oysters! What a strange business! They moved in the shells. So I wanted to have them killed before eating them because I was afraid they would stay alive inside me."

Josephine's impressions of Paris, when she arrived at the Gare Saint-Lazare: "What did I see first? Men and women kissing each other in the streets! In America, you were sent to prison for that! This freedom amused me. Yes, one could kiss in the street, and, in the theatres, women could show themselves without clothing. I could not believe it, so I bought dozens of pictures of nude women." She admired the train station, observed the people—"Everybody pushed, shoved without looking at each other"—and was charmed by the taxi horns. "It was a real orchestra. . . . I left at once for the Hôtel Fournet, boulevard des Batignolles. I thought I had settled in a palace. . . . What thrilled me was to have a private bathroom; it was the first time it happened to me. . . . In my little room, I walked like a queen. I strutted in front of the mirror."

Her sister Margaret said that Josephine "had set out to conquer the world." But that night in the Hôtel Fournet, her ambition was less grandiose and more specific. "I fell asleep with the idea of conquering Paris."

Chapter 15

—

JOSEPHINE CHECKS OUT POETS, PAINTERS, WAITERS

"I wanted to seduce the whole capital"

When the waiter arrived with breakfast, he nearly had a heart attack. It was Josephine's first morning in Paris, and, she said, "I definitely wanted to seduce the whole capital. Thus . . . I had half taken out my breasts from under my nightdress. A servant came in: it was a little old man . . . he only had one hair that he draped around his skull."

Out of breath from having carried a tray up three flights of stairs, the old man stood there in his long white apron, quivering. "He was so excited," says Lydia Jones, who had answered the knock at the door. "The poor fellow, I don't want to know what he thought about us colored people from America, but that was Josephine."

The waiter's name was Albert, and from then on, Josephine boasted, he would "steal a jar of jam from the owner and give it to me for my breakfast."

Albert got his reward for being the first Frenchman to gape in admiration at what Bricktop described as "the most beautiful bronze body in the world." The next year, when she opened Chez Joséphine, her club in Montmartre, Josephine hired him as headwaiter. She paid him further homage by naming her pig Albert, and lest you think that was an insult, bear in mind that she liked her pig better than she liked most people. Albert (the pig) waddled freely about the club until he got so fat he could no longer squeeze through the kitchen door, a problem Josephine solved by having the whole wall torn down.

Paris of the twenties was filled with tremors. Four years of *la Grande Guerre* had left France devastated. She had suffered 1,393,000 deaths and three million wounded, which represented 20 percent of her workforce. Women had been obliged to cultivate fields and work in factories, replacing their men, learning new ways to survive. But after the grieving, a madness set in. Young people longed to forget the gray days, they didn't want to be bound by their parents' values anymore. Lucky to be alive in the aftermath of so much carnage, they gave their appetites free rein, ushering in an era the French called *les Années Folles,* the crazy years. (Those years in America were known as the Roaring Twenties.)

Bricktop said it was a time when people with money but no talent helped people with talent but no money. "They used to take care of all the geniuses, the people who could write and paint and perform. . . . It was a beautiful thing."

Old games came back; in the summer of 1924, the Olympics (never held in wartime) took place in Paris; an American girl named Ethel Lackie won the one-hundred-meter freestyle swim, and track star Harold Abrahams of Great Britain won the one-hundred-meter dash. (His story would later be told in the movie *Chariots of Fire.*)

Traditionally a haven for painters, the city was by then also crowded with expatriate writers. They called themselves the Lost Generation, and were referred to as "literary pilgrims" by Sylvia Beach, founder of the bookstore Shakespeare and Company. Gertrude Stein gave dinner parties to which she invited her neighbor, Caroline Reagan, and Mrs. Reagan returned the favor, serving tea in her penthouse.

Stein, who lived at 27 rue de Fleurus, had found the Reagans their apartment at number 26, right across the street, and helped them hire workmen to install a new bathroom. "My mother wasn't going to put her husband and baby in an apartment without a bathroom," Sophie Reagan (then five years old) remembered. "She got me a governess, and disappeared from my life for a while; she went back to America to put together *La Revue Nègre*."

Paris was a city in which Ernest Hemingway took his little son to bistros and bought him drinks (they were made of grenadine), and everyone went to music bars, to gay bars, to transvestite bars. The autumn of 1925, wrote Noel Riley Fitch, was highlighted by "the rhythms of American jazz, the folk-singing of Paul Robeson, the Chaplin shuffle in his acclaimed film *The Gold Rush*, the erotic movements of Josephine Baker . . ." Women who looked like underfed boys, the Charleston, decadence in the arts—Jean Cocteau was said to have seduced a young man by giving him "his first whiff of opium in a kiss."

The country had always been fascinated by black people. After the Revolution, Robespierre's coachman dressed himself in feathers, painted on a ferocious face, and beat a drum in a place he had decorated like a cave. He called it Au Café du Sauvage. During World War I, black American soldiers came, bringing jazz. Lieutenant Jim Europe of the 369th U.S. Infantry organized a regimental orchestra (Noble Sissle was the drum major) and this "dusky band," boasted the *St. Louis Post-Dispatch*, was being celebrated all over France. (Lieutenant Europe wrote home to Eubie Blake: ". . . if the war does not end me first as sure as God made man I will be on top and so far on top that it will be impossible to pull me down.")

Jacques Charles, a god of the music halls who was also a wounded war hero, came home to discover a "cyclone of jazz" blowing over Paris. He proceeded to write and direct a show at the Casino de Paris that prefigured the opening scene of *La Revue Nègre*. When the curtain went up, the audience saw a Mississippi riverboat, and heard a black jazz band.

Jean Cocteau found it more noise than music. "The Negroes in the air, in a sort of cage, lash about, waddle, tossing to the crowd morsels of raw meat, to blows of trumpet and rattle," he wrote.

"Few thought of jazz as art," says dance critic Lynn Garafola. "But many felt, with Cocteau, that the 'savagery' and bold flouting of tradition associated with jazz could stimulate the imagination."

Even Picasso was influenced by African masks and sculpture, writers like Blaise Cendrars and Paul Morand were turning to black themes, Art Deco home furnishings and jewelry reflected the rage for black culture.

It was partly because of Jacques Charles's success with popular revues that, during the spring of 1925, Rolf de Maré decided to convert his beautiful Théâtre des Champs-Élysées—the one Fernand Léger called a white elephant—into the Music Hall des Champs-Élysées.

In 1920, de Maré had brought the Royal Swedish Ballet to Paris, and when he could not interest a single theater owner in his project, he had simply bought his own theater complex. In addition to the huge Théâtre des Champs-Élysées, it contained two smaller auditoriums, and boasted printing facilities in the basement, costume and sewing ateliers under the roof.

After his ballet company had disbanded, de Maré, hoping to attract a more general audience, tried various other entertainments. But even with its new name—and certainly, "Music Hall" had a more friendly, less intimidating sound than "Théâtre"—the house seemed too grand, too chic, to the working man who didn't want to have to dress in evening clothes to go out for a bit of entertainment.

Until, of course, *La Revue Nègre* came along and broke all the rules. Josephine recalled her first rehearsal in the huge house. "The theater is dark, the stage is lit. There are twenty people in the first row.

"Hello! Charleston. The stagehands watch, the two firemen are amazed. They are not used to receiving trombone blows in their stomach.

"At the end, behind the scenery, the younger ones try to imitate, they would like to dance the Charleston: they shake flannel legs, they kick their feet in the air like cows, they also kick their neighbors. . . . The Charleston already possesses them. 'Yes, sir, that's my baby.'

"The Charleston should be danced with necklaces of shells wriggling on the skin and making a dry music. . . . It is a way of dancing with your hips . . . to bring out the buttocks and shake your hands. We hide the buttocks too much. They exist. I don't see what reproach should be offered them."

It was still hot, that September, though the leaves of the chestnut trees had already fallen, covering the streets. At one point, because of the heat, it was decided to move rehearsals to the roof of the theater, and since nobody wanted to haul a piano up there, Bechet accompanied the dancers on his saxophone.

"Oh! What an intoxication to dance in the sun with practically nothing on," said Josephine. "But I have to say that I was more dressed up than on the stage . . . because of the neighbors. There were some at every window. The typists . . . the liftboys . . . All applauded. I was in a bathing suit: someone took a picture of me like that on that roof from where you can see the trees of the embankments and the Champs-Élysées. . . ."

"We had ten days before the opening," Caroline Reagan said. "Quick, quick to work. . . . It was now or never. I had to incorporate Josephine in the act, and pull the whole thing together. . . . And then to create Josephine's clothing. I'm not calling them costumes. First her dresses, her dances, her yodel, the play of her eyes."

Louis Douglas had different problems; he had to whip some excitement into this show that had been born of Caroline's infatuation with the "ebony chorus," and about which Rolf de Maré and André Daven seemed unenthusiastic.

Originally, the idea had appealed to de Maré because he knew that the black *Chocolate Kiddies* was already a huge success in Berlin. But he had given Caroline only enough money to go to New York and bring back a little *divertissement,* and when it arrived, it seemed *too* little. A few sketches, a few songs, some dancing, a star who wanted to sing though she wasn't very good at it, and on top of that the cast, whom de Maré had expected to be a collection of coal-black exotics, were not as dark as most sun-tanned Frenchmen. (In addition, André Daven told a friend, he and de Maré had "a lot of trouble stopping the black performers from using white-face makeup, which is very much the fashion in the Negro theater of New York.")

Caroline went to the flea market to piece out the costumes; she brought back "a strange hat and a pair of black and white laceup high boots, and also a wedding veil," along with assorted uniforms and headgear and medals and feathers, half of them from the Napoleonic era.

De Maré and Daven also hired a few very black African-born dancers (Joe Alex was one of them) and recruited some supernumeraries who couldn't dance at all. Mercer Cook, Will Marion's son, was studying at the Sorbonne (he would eventually become a diplomat) and he enjoyed the idea of moonlighting. "I just had to walk on the docks in front of the two big boats. It was easy money."

But after fleshing out the cast, Daven and de Maré were still unhappy. There was one man, they decided, who might save them. They would beg Jacques Charles for help, throw themselves on the mercy of the much-acclaimed director.

Caroline, however, was in no mood to acclaim some interloper hauled in at the last minute to shed his brilliance on her production. Bitterly, she recounted how de Maré had informed her "that *Mr. Casino de Paris* was supposed to come in two or three days before the dress rehearsal."

She felt humiliated. "A person of honor," she reflected, "would have said *adieu* and disappeared. . . . But I didn't know that sort of dignity. My mother taught me, 'You have two cheeks, turn the other one, my little one.' Since then, from time to time, both cheeks burn. What do you want?"

Until the day he died, Jacques Charles would insist that he created *La Revue Nègre*, rechoreographed *La Revue Nègre*, and plucked Josephine out of the chorus. "I invented her," he said.

—

Chapter 16

THE GOOD TIMES ROLL

"We need tits"

*I*t began one morning as he sat at his desk, Jacques Charles remembered. "Daven entered my office. . . . On the recommendation of an impresario, he had engaged a troupe of Negroes without seeing them. That revue had arrived in Paris, and the first rehearsal had been a catastrophe. 'My dear,' said Daven, 'they tap, tap tap for two hours and they are going to chase the audience away. You are the only one who can rescue us from this mess.' "

Charles agreed to take a look and determine if anything could be done in the forty-eight hours before the opening. "On the stage," he said, "I found the ladies and gentlemen with gray faces, because they could see the lack of enthusiasm from their managers for their talent."

I can believe that. For eight days, nobody had been strong enough to pull the show together. Louis Douglas was trying to direct two dozen black Americans who were far more strange to him than the girls at the Moulin Rouge would have been, and Caroline Reagan, passionate but inexperienced, was trying to be a producer. There was no real boss.

Jacques Charles watched a rehearsal and was agreeably surprised. "There was certainly too much tap, all was impossibly monotonous, but there were excellent elements in the troupe . . . remarkable intelligence and a rare good will. . . . The error was to have wanted to make it Parisian. You had to make it black. . . . I mixed everything. I put Louis XV hats with overalls, and big straw hats with fur costumes. I combined backdrops from one scene with designs from other scenes, and then I lit it all. Bizarre and multicolored.

"We cut, modified, inverted, reversed numbers, and mostly tried to make it what it was, a revue.

"But something was missing. I wanted a note a little bit more voluptuous, an erotic, sensual duet to give the audience some rest from all that jazz and tap. I talked about it with Joe Alex, who was a fine *porteur*. He could carry a partner onstage and make himself and her look good, an art that has little to do with strength. And Joe Alex suggested that his partner be Josephine Baker.

"I had already noticed her beautiful body, but to be honest, Josephine rejected my suggestion that she dance almost nude. In vain, did I leave Joe Alex alone with her to try and persuade her. When I came back, she was crying, and asked to go back on the boat.

" 'Very well,' I told her, 'but only after the premiere. Meanwhile, you will do as I'm asking you to do.' . . . Sobbing and sniffling, Josephine started to rehearse."

With all due respect to M. Charles, neither Evelyn Anderson nor Lydia Jones recalled any sniffling. "Josephine was for anything new," Evelyn said. "She thought she'd be the first black girl—they did it with white girls at the Folics-Bergère and the Moulin Rouge—to go naked onstage."

"I don't remember Josephine crying," said Lydia. "You know, she was always naked in the hotel, laughing and posing in front of the mirrors." (Despite the "delirium" created by the "Danse de Sauvage," Jacques Charles said later, "I'm still waiting for a simple thank-you letter.")

It was Jacques Charles who told Daven and de Maré, "We need tits. These French people, with their fantasies of black girls, we must give them *des nichons*."

In 1905, Mata Hari had danced at the Museum Guimet, bare-breasted except for two metallic shells, and shocked Parisians. Four years later Colette, that most sensual of writers, proved she was an equally uninhibited actress. In a melodrama called *The Flesh,* she played an unfaithful wife whose husband rips off her clothes. Audiences gasped as her breasts were exposed. Not even metallic shells to cushion the outrage. She left the stage to a storm of boos mixed with cheers from the more open-minded like Chevalier, who called her breasts "the most appetizing in the world."

Until Josephine's, if the response to *La Revue Nègre* is any gauge. But Josephine was not the only girl who appeared topless in the show; I have the Man Ray photographs that prove there were *six* bare-breasted beauties. In Ray's pictures they pose, sitting on the floor, naked except for straw skirts and necklaces made of shells. They are all looking out at the audience, smiling.

During breaks in rehearsal, the cast went sightseeing. "The streets surprised us with cobblestones," Evelyn says, "and on the boulevards, the *pissoirs* for men."

In Montmartre, they felt at home. The quarter, on a hill at the highest point of the city, was filled with *guinguettes,* the little cabarets where you could dance, and coffee bars where laborers and office workers stopped to have their morning café au lait.

Le Sacré-Coeur still looks down on the red chimneys, the crowded houses, the music clubs. Hundreds of steps lead up to the church, and far below, on rue Tardieu, is À l'Angélus, a little pastry shop that has been in the same place since 1912. I can imagine Josephine sitting in a white wire chair, holding a cup of hot chocolate, enjoying a respite from the tension of rehearsals.

At night, the cast flocked to rue Pigalle. Sidney Bechet remembered looking around a club and asking himself, "Why am I here?" But even as he posed the question, he knew the answer. "France, it's closer to Africa. . . . My grandfather, he was African . . . and I wanted to get back as far as I could . . . it's all so mixed up with the music."

When Bechet blew his horn on the opening night of *La Revue Nègre,* it was like the walls of Jericho, Caroline Reagan said. "The house came tumbling down."

While Caroline was generous with credit for others, everyone around her did not share this trait. For example, the famous poster of *La Revue Nègre*—there are only five known to be still in existence, each worth one hundred thousand dollars—was *not* created entirely in the brain of Paul Colin.

I discovered this by accident. From 1923 to 1925, Miguel Covarrubias had worked in New York for *Vogue* and *Vanity Fair*. In 1983, I was thumbing through a book that contained reproductions of sketches he had done in those years. They reflected the lives of artists in Harlem in a unique and powerful way. The book was called *Negro Drawings*, and I had bought a copy of it from an auction of Paul Colin's belongings sold when his family put him into a retirement home.

Suddenly I was brought up short. There they were, the three people of the poster of *La Revue Nègre:* a slender girl in a tight white dress, flanked by two men, one with a frieze of nappy hair, big red lips, the other with a hat tilted over one eye and a checked bow tie. The girl everyone believed to be Josephine, the one Paul Colin said he had sketched from life, had been drawn by Covarrubias before Colin ever set eyes on Josephine.

By then Paul Colin had died, and I went to call on Charles Kieffer, an artist known for his drawings of Chevalier. "Mr. Kieffer," I said, "I want you to help me. I strongly believe that Paul Colin did not create the poster of *La Revue Nègre*."

I told him what I knew, and also what I suspected. Colin had been an artist on Rolf de Maré's payroll. Every two weeks de Maré presented a new show, and Colin drew the posters for them. Since he was around the theater all the time, he had probably seen sketches by Covarrubias that Caroline Reagan had sent from New York and, impressed by their strength, had appropriated them.

A brief, Machiavellian smile crossed Kieffer's face. "How the devil did you find that out?" he said. "A few of us knew, but it was a secret."

A few of them knew, yet no art critic ever discovered it. Not even after Colin's *Le Tumulte Noir* appeared in 1927. *Le Tumulte Noir* is a gorgeously colored portfolio of pictures affectionately mocking the infatuation of Parisians with all things black—the Charleston, jazz, Josephine in her grass skirt—but it's easy to spot Covarrubias's influence behind the dazzling images.

Still, I don't mean to denigrate Paul Colin's great talent. I agree with his biographer, Jack Rennert, who said Colin's paintings captured "the essence of Josephine . . . of a sultry, sensuous performer . . . full of feral magnetism."

When I met Paul Colin, I hadn't yet stumbled across the Covarrubias sketches, and even if I'd known about them, I wouldn't have cross-examined the old man; by then he was ninety. I went to his birthday party at the Maison Nationale des Artistes, a château in Nogent-sur-Marne, where seventy venerable graphic artists lived in comfort, each with his own studio.

Asked about Josephine, Colin's face brightened. His strength was gone, but his eyes were fierce. *"C'est moi qui l'ai inventée!"* he cried. "I'm the one who invented her." I didn't tell him he was not the only man to make that boast.

He said *La Revue Nègre* had been a scandal, "but I found it very nice. Josephine invaded the stage, she was extraordinary. For the French people, there is always the lure of the sensual. They had this sexual fantasy, the women dreaming of black men, the men of black women."

His voice drifted off, returned. Again: "I'm the one who invented her. She didn't know how to sing. Many artists have something in their stomachs, but they don't have the opportunity to give birth."

He was clear and cold about having slept with Josephine—"She's not the first Negress I ever had"—but vague about how he had created the poster. He said he had taken Josephine to his studio, rather than sketching her at the theater, because he wanted to sleep with her. She posed for him, and yes, he captured her soul on paper, even after she had left him for other embraces. "For a few weeks," he said, "I took her everywhere, I introduced her."

In her own memoirs, she mentions going to his studio, but omits the sex. "Monsieur Colin . . . led me to a little washroom attached to the studio. I reappeared in my bra and panties. . . . I avoided Monsieur Colin's eyes. With a sudden gesture, he reached over and undid my hooks. Oh, *no!* I wanted to dash through the door and down the stairs, but was glued to the spot. Monsieur Colin calmly began to draw."

Josephine, Colin said, chattered away in English, which he did not speak. "Her expressions were exaggerated. She laughed too loudly, and then she would suddenly go dark. She was a born exhibitionist. And ambitious. Make no mistake."

———

"We haven't had this much sense of a bursting forth since the Ballets Russes," wrote Paul Achard of *La Revue Nègre*. Almost no one remembers now that *La Revue Nègre*, which made worldwide news, was only the second half of a two-part show, and ran less than an hour. The first half featured vaudeville—Ski Tayama (Japanese acrobats), the Klein family on trapeze, Saint-Granier (a tenor who impersonated Parisian stars), and strongman Louis Vasseur, who twirled on his head "a huge merry-go-round bearing six men suspended on trapezes."

The program for *La Revue Nègre* made no mention of Jacques Charles. It listed Caroline as producer, her husband, Daniel, as director, and Louis Douglas as assistant director.

The show moved fast, the numbers had names that made the audience laugh: "Shimmy Sha Wabble," "Boodle-Am."

Then suddenly, the stage was empty, and Louis Douglas, in blackface and tailcoat, a big white flower in his buttonhole, came on as Harlequin, and, tears running down his face, sang of his love for Columbine. Of those who had gone to the opening night, none I interviewed had ever forgotten the beauty and sadness of that number.

Louis Douglas's wife, Marion, danced, Maud de Forrest sang, Josephine did "I Want to Yodel" and her Charleston, and in front of a flat painted to look like a New York skyscraper, Bechet played alone.

But it took the "Danse de Sauvage" to conquer Paris, and even then, there were detractors. One critic couldn't make up his mind about Josephine ("She's horrible! She's wonderful! . . . Is that her hair I see or is her skull painted black?"), another complained that the revue was "not Negro enough," and Paul Robeson's wife, Essie, wrote friends that it was "rotten," that Josephine's voice couldn't be heard over the orchestra, and that the "Danse de Sauvage" was fine until the star did "this ridiculously vulgar . . . wiggling."

The French authorities got in a couple of low blows of their own. Despite the nudity at the Folies-Bergère and the Casino de Paris, a prefect of police was sent around to announce that more modesty was in order at *La Revue Nègre*. "The color black alone does not dress one," he said.

The press jumped on the story. "In one of the scenes," ran a newspaper account, "the ladies of the chorus appeared to be dressed in a few inches of lace and rows of glass beads. For the past few days, this costume has featured a piece of fabric between the lace and the skin. Why this modification? It was imposed by the prefecture of police, deciding that white dancers could complain if colored dancers were allowed to appear in such scant attire."

Evelyn Anderson still believes it was because the prefect's girlfriend was working in the chorus at the Casino de Paris. "The public," she says, "loved *La Revue Nègre*."

The public would, by and large, have preferred the cast to be more black, resembling Africans right off the boat. Because of this, the very light-colored Hazel Valentine was forced to apply black body makeup, an act she and the other high-yellow girls considered a supreme degradation. (Mother, were you laughing? These French people love you for your dancing, your singing—at that time, a high, quavery Florence Mills imitation—and also for the color of your skin. Nineteen years you have hated the color of your skin, now it is one of your glories.)

The day after *La Revue Nègre* opened, every journalist in Paris converged on the Hôtel Fournet to interview the new queen of the night. One of them asked her what it was like "when they all screamed at you, 'Bravo! Bravo!' "

"Nice," Josephine said. "It was nice."

"But what is your most vivid memory of last night?"

She thought a moment. "Well," she said, "last night after the show was over, the theater was turned into a big restaurant. . . . And for the first time in my life, I was invited to sit at a table and eat with white people."

She had tears in her eyes, a reporter observed. And why not? As Duke Ellington said, after his first trip to Europe, "You can go anywhere and talk to anybody and do anything you like. When you've eaten hot dogs all your life and you're suddenly offered caviar, it's hard to believe it's true."

Luck, of course, had something to do with Josephine's conquest of Paris. "It is necessary to say that she arrived exactly at the moment we needed her," wrote Jean Prasteau. "With her short hair, her free body, her colored skin and her American accent, she united the tendencies, tastes and aspirations of that epoque."

Josephine was even credited with bringing the Charleston to Paris, though Bee Jackson, a white American billed as Queen of the Charleston, had performed the dance on the stage of the Music-Hall des Champs-Élysées the previous July, warming up the audience for Paul Whiteman. (Ironically, in America, the Charleston was being called "the dance of death," because of a tragedy that had taken place in Boston. "The collapse of the dance floor in the Hotel Pickwick," *Variety* reported, "is attributed to the strenuous efforts of Charleston dancers.

Nearly 50 people are dead as a result . . . the off-beat rhythm of the Charleston, reinforced by the indulgence in things alcoholic, is said to have caused the building to sway so violently that it fell apart." It was then against the law to dance the Charleston on the sidewalks of New York.)

Besides being lucky, Josephine worked hard. Now, every night after the curtain rang down on *La Revue Nègre*, she and the band and a few of the dancers would go to Pigalle and double at Le Rat Mort. "We would strictly do our numbers," Evelyn says, "and then the band stayed after and played the dance music, but Mabel Hopkins and me, we would go to the dressing room and play blackjack. Because we couldn't leave until Claude and my boyfriend Joe left, you know.

"This used to tickle me because a fellow from the Vanderbilt family used to send champagne to me in the dressing room, and he always wanted to take me out, and I would say, 'No, Joe Hayman won't let me.' "

"Men sent us red roses and notes in French," says Lydia Jones. "And the white girls in Paris went mad for our boys, black men were the craze wherever we went. At the Dead Rat, we made a lot of tips, it was quite a naughty place."

Naughty wasn't the half of it. Le Rat Mort was owned by the Corsican Mafia. "We worked every joint in Pigalle, but not that one," says Stephane Grappelli, the jazz violinist who played with Django Reinhardt. "It was a tough place where a girl would come and grab a man and say, '*Chéri*, I'm thirsty,' and the man would buy a bottle of champagne and at the end of the night, the girl would go to the boss, take all the corks out of her bra where she'd hidden them, and turn them in for money."

A different girl might have been satisfied with the bravos of the two thousand people at the theater and the star salary Caroline was paying her, but Josephine had not refused the offer to perform at 2 A.M. in a decadent café. If her fans wanted to see her up close, she was pleased to oblige. Not even in Harlem had the white people abandoned themselves so shamelessly, and she got into the rhythm of it, flirting with lonely old roués, pushing champagne.

The Prince of Wales was at Le Rat Mort every night. "He liked to drum, and he'd get up on the stand and play," Claude Hopkins remembered. "He wasn't very good . . . but he was very popular . . . he'd give us a couple of hundred franc notes for letting him sit in for a couple of numbers."

Claude said the prince had to be taken out of the club "feet first every night—dead drunk and stoned." He was said to be grieving over the marriage of his cousin Mountbatten, with whom he was infatuated, but once he met Claude, he perked up. Claude claimed the prince was mad about him. It's funny to think of Josephine and H.R.H. waging a silent war for Claude's favors. (Johnny Hudgins, another favorite of the prince, had met him in London. "He come in to see my show. He married a woman from Baltimore, from my hometown; he didn't want to be no damn king.")

Moonlighting is easy when you're a teenager, because fatigue is not a concept you grasp. Josephine not only worked two jobs, she tried— briefly—to save some money. She kept on her body the first thousand- franc note she earned, even when she was dancing half naked—"I tacked it on my belt under my green feather"—until it grew tattered. Then she took it to the bank, where she was told that without its serial number, which had somehow got chewed off, the bill was worthless. "It is on that day I understood it was totally useless to save," she said. Spend, spend, spend, and keep moving.

She bought a little snake. "Around the neck, I twisted my snake. He kept very quiet, because he was warm, but when I started to dance, he woke up, and stuck out his tongue. My partner was frightened to death. Nobody wanted to dance with me anymore. Everybody was frightened. I had been noticed, that is what I wanted."

She also bought a small mean dog who ran away. "He wanted to be free," she said. "Free! The lovely word."

For a long time, I couldn't figure out why every black entertainer who came to Europe bought dogs. Fierce dogs, like wolves. Josephine had one so savage she had to board it in a kennel. Finally, a friend put it all together. "During slavery, blacks were hunted with dogs. In Europe, they could take a kind of revenge, they could own the same kinds of dogs that chased their ancestors. So there they were in little hotel rooms and they had these huge dogs."

Later, I read a book called *Bullwhip Days,* which confirmed for me that Southern whites had hunted down their runaway slaves with dogs. "Some slaves," testified John Crawford, "told me a sure way to keep the dogs from ketching you. They said if you put red pepper and turpentine in your shoes, they can't run you, 'cause they can't scent you."

In Germany, Sam Wooding said, the whole *Chocolate Kiddies* company bought German shepherds, and in Paris, Josephine, Claude Hopkins, Joe Alex, also had police dogs. Often Josephine moved, at the behest of a new lover, with her entire ménagerie. "I lived at Rue Henri-Rochefort, Rue Fromentin, and so on." In the tradition of the French, she was already being kept—and fought over—by rich and not so rich men. One of her first French suitors was a student of architecture. She told him she didn't love him, but let him buy her dinner at expensive restaurants. "One day he was imprudent enough to take out of his pocket a thousand-franc note. It was the amount his father sent him each month as allowance. I grabbed it. . . ."

" 'I won't have any more money to eat,' he said. I laughed. 'You want to go out with artists, you must pay.'

"Yes, when I think about this gesture, I believe I was not only crazy but a nasty girl. . . . I was like in love with myself. Paris had turned my head a little."

It's easy to see why. Every night at the theater, presents and love letters awaited her. Mercer Cook (the Sorbonne scholar) acted as big brother, translating the letters, and Josephine generously gave him a handful of francs each day.

Josephine was busy homemaking too. She bought fabric for a bedcover, and wood to build a platform for the bed. "I received in that bed," she said. "I was a coquette."

Bricktop, having missed the opening of *La Revue Nègre*—she was performing in Barcelona—came back to Paris to find everyone talking about Josephine. A light-skinned American black who dyed her hair red, Bricktop had played hostess at Barron Wilkins's club in Harlem, she'd been in the Panama Trio (with Florence Mills and Cora Green), and in 1924 she came to Paris to work at Chez Florence. A year later, she had her own club. She was a protégée of Cole Porter's; for her, he wrote "Miss Otis Regrets," about a woman who killed her lover. "Those bums," Bricktop said, "sometimes you have to kill 'em. Kill 'em before they kill you, baby."

Now she discovered Josephine had replaced her and Florence Jones as the most popular black female entertainers in Paris. "The French people, who loved all that chic, went out of their minds," Bricktop said. "Josephine was gorgeous. I mean naked or with clothes. She lived a bizarre thing, but what do you expect when you take a chorus girl and overnight she becomes a sensation? She had those legs that went from here to everywhere.

"All the great designers—Paul Poiret, Edward Molyneux, Jean Patou—were fighting to dress her. She had an apartment right around the corner from my nightclub, and one day I went there and the clothes were just piled high on the floor, and I said, 'Josephine, why don't you hang these clothes up?' 'Oh, no, Brickie,' she said, 'they are going to take them away tomorrow and bring another pile.' "

(I'd heard rumors of a long-ago affair between Josephine and Brick-top, and the rumors, it turned out, were true. Bricktop told me so herself, after Josephine's death.)

Caroline Reagan had introduced Josephine and Poiret at L'Exposition Internationale des Arts Décoratifs et Industriels Modernes, a cultural landmark of 1925. (Art Deco, the style, took its name from this exhibition.) Poiret had bought three barges—he called them *Loves, Organs,* and *Delights,* names representing "women, always women"—and moored them in the Seine at the entrance to the show. The boats were filled with textiles and furniture from his workshops; he considered this display his gift to the people of Paris, though he had to sell his painting collection—by Matisse, Picasso, Utrillo—to pay for it.

Poiret was a male counterpart of Josephine, rebellious, indifferent to criticism, wildly extravagant. As a teenager, he had made dresses that freed women from their corsets; in his heyday, he gave parties for three hundred guests, with peacocks and herons wandering on his lawn. How could Josephine not adore him, a man obsessed with rich colors, a man who ran a design school for talented poor children, and paid them to come?

Sadly, by the time she met him, Poiret's star was in decline (he refused to turn out chemises for scrawny flappers) and he was beset by money problems. Even so, he didn't charge Josephine for dresses. Christiane Otte, at that time assistant to Poiret's chief *vendeuse,* remembered Josephine's roaring into the salon, kissing everybody, then throwing open her fur coat. "It was November, and she was absolutely naked under it, laughing like a child."

But the first time she came—with Caroline—to look at Poiret's creations, she nearly gave the designer apoplexy. "All his models walked in front of us," Caroline recalled. "And Josephine was saying, 'No, not that, no, not that, no!' Poiret was starting to get worried. Suddenly,

Josephine asked for a piece of paper and a pencil; she drew, while laughing. She wanted fringe from the shoulders to the hem, light pink at the top, shading to dark at the bottom. 'American beauty, *voilà!*' she said, as she finished her sketch. Poiret was enthusiastic, he added the Josephine Baker dress to his collection."

In the streets, she was besieged for autographs, though Bricktop said she could scarcely write her name. "I said, 'Baby, get a stamp.' . . . I saw her on the Champs-Élysées, where you couldn't get within blocks of her."

No question but she had an air. A reporter described an evening at Caroline Reagan's, and Josephine's making an entrance in a "cherry-colored dress, small hat pulled low on her forehead, ermine-trimmed coat. 'Paris is marvelous,' she gushes. 'And your dressmakers are divine.' " (In her memoirs, she offered one final thought on fashion: "Love dresses you better than all the dressmakers.")

Ten glorious weeks *La Revue Nègre* played at the Music-Hall of the Champs-Élysées. Booked for a fortnight, it was extended and extended. Early in November, Josephine and company were still dancing there while the great Pavlova waited impatiently for the theater she had been promised.

On November 7, under the auspices of the president of the Republic, Gaston Doumergue, there was a dinner to mark the closing of the exposition. Pavlova danced (with M. Veron) during the appetizer, Josephine (with Honey Boy) during the main course. As though the great Russian were nothing but a warm-up act for the headliner.

At the end of the month, *La Revue Nègre* was finally forced to move to the Théâtre de l'Étoile, where Josephine added insult to injury by performing a wicked parody of Pavlova as the Black Swan.

Creative artists of the day—Milhaud, Van Dongen, Picabia, René Clair—lined up to meet the cast of *La Revue Nègre*. The composer Ravel wrote to a friend, "I must go and soak myself in this bouillon of culture." Princess Murat begged Caroline Reagan to bring Josephine to her house. And Josephine, who was crazy about automobiles, was given several of them even before she could drive. "One was a Bugatti worth thirty thousand dollars," Claude Hopkins said. "She used to throw her own money away, too, she played the horses."

But Paris is fickle, people were already looking for the next sensation; *La Revue Nègre* was winding down.

It didn't matter; Caroline had big plans. She and her troupe would tour Europe, seduce a whole new audience.

Josephine hated to go. "I had plotted to leave St. Louis," she said. "I had longed to leave New York; I yearned to remain in Paris. I loved everything about the city. It moved me as profoundly as a man moves a woman. Why must I take trains and boats that would carry me far from the friendly faces, the misty Seine . . ."

In spite of her reluctance, in mid-December, she and the rest of the company entrained for Brussels. But Josephine had a secret.

Chapter 17

—

JOSEPHINE
BETRAYS A FRIEND

"She had flown, she had been stolen from me"

The secret: three days after *La Revue Nègre* opened in Paris, Josephine heard a knock on her dressing-room door. "The man who entered spoke dreadful English, but his face was kind. 'I was told there was a girl at the Champs-Élysées who was setting the stage on fire. I see that it's true. I'm Paul Derval, director of the Folies-Bergère, Miss Baker. I'd like you to be in my next show.' "

There was irony in the offer. When Caroline Reagan had been running all over Paris trying to find a home for *La Revue Nègre,* she'd solicited help from anyone—including Paul Derval—who would listen.

Now Derval was preparing to steal Caroline's star, who was eager to be stolen. She signed a paper right then and there agreeing to come work at the Folies-Bèrgere in March, and afterward, kept her own counsel. During the entire Paris run of *La Revue Nègre,* she never said a word to a living soul about her intentions, but permitted Caroline to go on dreaming of new successes in Belgium, Germany, even Russia, where she had booked the company for six weeks.

They left Paris as they had come to it, by train. At the border between France and Belgium, Bechet disappeared, and, just as the *Berengaria* had been delayed for him in New York, now the train was held. It was three hours before he was found, dead drunk, and the troupe could proceed.

In Brussels for one week, they played the Cirque Royal; even though King Albert I of Belgium came to the show, the city appears to have made little impression on Josephine. "Germany is the first European country where I went after Paris," she declared.

La Revue Nègre opened at Berlin's Nelson Theatre on Kurfürsten-damm on New Year's Eve 1925, in a city where 120,000 workers were out of work. Two months later, the number of unemployed had risen to 227,500. In the wake of World War I, with Germany broke, Berlin was filled not only with starving people, but with people who no longer believed in the social contract. By the end of 1923, although the country's raging inflation had been brought under control, wrote Wolf Von Eckardt and Sander Gilman, "the German sense of values, the old propriety . . . were gone. . . . Hard work and thrift no longer meant salvation."

The city's fevered nightlife offered revues with naked girls, and clubs where men dressed as women danced together. The streets were home to young, pretty whores, and old, blind ones too. Criminal gangs roamed freely, morphine and cocaine were sold at hot dog stands, and pornographic films were easy to find. Despite its pride in its culture—it boasted three opera houses and a wealth of experimental theater—Berlin was the most decadent city in Europe.

Josephine adored it, and Berlin adored her in return. "It's madness. A triumph," she said. "They carry me on their shoulders. At a big dance, when I walk in, the musicians stop playing, get up and welcome me. Berlin is where I received the greatest number of gifts."

In her memoirs, she reeled them off. "I was given rings with fire as big as an egg; I was given a pair of ancient earrings which belonged to a duchess 150 years ago; I was given pearls like teeth: flowers that came in one day from Italy in moss and baskets . . . big peaches . . . perfume in a glass horse. One fur, two furs, three furs, four furs. Bracelets with red stones for my arms, my wrists, my legs."

Between the opening of presents and the trying on of bracelets, Josephine somehow found the time to pay a call on Sam Wooding. After touring Europe for eight months, *Chocolate Kiddies* had come back to

Berlin, and though some of the original cast—Lottie Gee, Adelaide Hall, Charlie Davis—had left, Gene Sedric was still there playing sax.

Gene and Josephine had gone to Dumas together; Gene's father and Eddie Carson had been fellow musicians on the Mississippi riverboats. The children used to walk the men down to the boats to try and cadge a ride.

Seeing Gene in Berlin, the secretive Josephine may have been brought face-to-face with more of her past than she liked. Sam told me she'd been cool to Gene. "She was a very fine artist, but in my estimation a very small person."

When *Chocolate Kiddies* had first played Berlin, many Berliners had been hostile, not only because the actors were black, but because it was thought they were blacks from French Colonial Africa.

A year earlier, France had sent a regiment of tall, black Senegalese soldiers to Bavaria, hoping this would intimidate Germany into paying its war debt. The Germans (who had heard stories about "savages" cutting ears off German soldiers and wearing them around their necks as charms) were already bitter at having lost the war, so to see Senegalese troops even after the Armistice was horrifying to them. It had to be made clear to the public that the *Chocolate Kiddies* company was American, before tensions were dispelled.

The same scenario was repeated with *La Revue Nègre*. On opening night at the Nelson, there was a sizable anti-black demonstration outside the theater. Again, the cast was not troubled because, as in France, they didn't understand the language. Even when Brownshirts distributed pamphlets calling Josephine subhuman (she was black *and* she went naked, both affronts to Aryan notions of perfection), she remained untroubled. "I'm not immoral," she said. "I'm only natural."

It is perhaps not surprising that Josephine, insulated by her fame and the powerful new friends who whisked her from pastry shops to bike races to dance halls to late-night suppers, did not observe signs of the storm that was coming. Sam Wooding, on the other hand, saw more than he wanted to.

Sam and the rest of the *Chocolate Kiddies* company stayed in a small hotel run by a Jewish couple, and one night, a few of the musicians were having a midnight snack when two Germans in hiking suits came in. "They walked over to where this Jewish lady was standing behind the bar and started a conversation," Sam said. "All of a sudden, one of the

Germans slapped the woman's face several times, and the other man broke some glasses. Then they walked out.

"My men and I jumped up and ran to her as she was crying. She said, 'They asked what right had we to have this hotel, why didn't we get out of Germany.'

"We felt very sorry for her; most of the men only wished they had understood enough German so they could have caught the bastards before they slapped this old lady.

"We didn't have long to wait. A couple of days later, in walks six of these same guys. They were drunk. The hotel had small rooms for private parties, and two of our people, Chick Horsey (one of The Three Eddies) and Bobby Martin from my band, were in one of these rooms eating with a couple of chorus girls, and these Germans came into the room. Chick told the girls to get lost, and after they left, one of the Germans locked the door and walked over and said something in German, and his friends laughed.

"But Chick Horsey was a master at gang fighting. He smashed this German and the German went down like a bull in a slaughterhouse, blood flying everywhere. Bobby picked him up and threw him out the window—it was on the ground floor—and from then on, as Chick would smash these bastards, Bobby would throw them out the window.

"Chick said every time he socked one of those guys, he saw the German that slapped that poor Jewish woman and he thought of how some of the white Southerners had treated black men and women in America, and this gave him strength.

"It seemed like a miracle, we didn't know Chick and Bobby was that good. Well, the Germans never came back."

German racism was, in fact, the reason some performers had quit *Chocolate Kiddies,* but Josephine didn't seem to notice it, she never spoke of trauma in Berlin, only of conquest. "Max Reinhardt, the famous director, comes to see me, he carries a contract: 'I hire you for three years at the Deutsches Theatre and believe me you will be the greatest star in Europe.'

"In the magazines and newspapers of Berlin, they wrote that I was a figure of the contemporary German 'expressionism,' of the German 'primitivism.' . . . Why not? And what does it mean?"

A review of *La Revue Nègre* appeared in the *Tageblatt.* The critic dismissed the show as noisy, but bowed to Josephine. "In her survives the untamed wildness of her forebears who were transplanted from the Congo basin to the Mississippi." Two days later, a Paris newspaper advised the French public to stop worrying about the rumor that Josephine was going back to live in America. "She will be one of the stars of the next revue at the Folies-Bergère."

From the embassy in Paris, Caroline's husband called to read her the paragraph. She didn't take it seriously; she had made a star of Josephine, she had a contract with Josephine, why should she listen to foolish gossip?

Especially since Josephine was working hard to make *La Revue Nègre* an international hit, doing what amounted to two shows a night. Because after each performance, the theater (it wasn't a huge house) was converted into a cabaret, and Berliners packed the place. Dolly Haas, who would become a German leading lady in the thirties (and later marry Al Hirschfeld, theater caricaturist for *The New York Times*), was only sixteen years old when she saw Josephine at the cabaret. "At the end of one number, she would sink to her knees, and finish the song like a prayer, her arms wide open. You did not know if she wanted to embrace the audience or wanted the audience to embrace her, but it moved everyone."

Never mind that half an hour later, Josephine would be absolutely naked, rolling around on the floor with another girl at a party, while Max Reinhardt watched.

The night of that frolic—it was February 13, 1926—Count Harry Kessler, a publisher and art collector who kept a diary, recorded the fact that Reinhardt had called him at 1 A.M. from the home of playwright Karl Vollmoeller and invited him to come over. Kessler went and found Reinhardt "surrounded by half a dozen nude girls including Miss Baker also naked except for a pink gauze loincloth, and the young Landshoff girl . . . dressed as a boy sporting black tie.

"Miss Baker danced with extreme grotesque artistry and pure style, like an Egyptian or archaic figure. . . . She does it for hours without any sign of fatigue. . . . She does not even perspire. . . . An enchanting creature, yet almost without sexuality. With her one thinks of sexuality as little as at the sight of a beautiful feral beast."

The party went on until 4 A.M. "Reinhardt, Vollmoeller, and I were standing around Miss Baker and Miss Landshoff, who were embracing like a pair of beautiful young lovers," Kessler wrote in his diary, leaving the reader to decide whether he was describing an orgy or simply youthful high spirits. Vollmoeller said he wanted to write a ballet for Josephine, Kessler said he would contribute a scene, a pantomime, and they should all meet for dinner at his house on February 24 for further discussion.

That time, the dinner was stag, except for Miss Landshoff, who at least *looked* like a boy, decked out in "horn-rimmed glasses and a touch of beard painted on with makeup."

After Josephine finished work, a couple of Kessler's other guests went to fetch her. "I had cleared the library for her to dance," Kessler said, but she "sat for hours in a corner sulking."

Until Kessler began to describe "the pantomime I was planning for her." It was to be a fantasy, the music half jazz, half Oriental. King Solomon buys a slave girl, a dancer, and has her brought to him naked, "to shower her with gifts, with his own gowns and jewels. The more he gives her, the more elusive she becomes. . . . In the end, it is the king who is naked, while the dancer disappears, ascending in a cloud composed of all the silks and jewels he has bestowed on her."

Josephine loved it, and became "an entirely different person who kept asking *when* she could dance."

In Kessler's library, he had a huge, powerful Maillol sculpture called *Crouching Woman.* Josephine studied the statue, leaning against her, "speaking to her, visibly startled by the overwhelming rigidity and impact of her expression. She danced around her in grotesquely grandiose movements resembling a priestess playfully making fun of herself and her goddess. One could see Maillol was more interesting and alive to her than the people watching." To Kessler, the scene was "one genius speaking to another."

You had to be very young and strong to live the life of Josephine. Kessler gives an account of her sitting on a couch at 3 A.M. "eating one bockwurst after another."

In Berlin, Josephine was in her element, diverted by the down and dirty action—the nightlife, she said, was of "an intensity Paris doesn't know"—and the streets blazing with lights that promised bawdy pleasures.

Between her numbers in the cabaret she would sit with customers, and they would issue invitations to further merriment. "There used to be a lot of high-society people around," Claude Hopkins said. "The

Krupp family, they were there almost every night. They really liked the music, and they really liked Josephine."

Once, she was asked to serve as a judge at a costume ball at the Neue Kunsthandlung. "A real can of sardines," she called it. "Women and men flattened against each other, Negroes in every corner."

She was actually beginning to think she might stay in Berlin. She endowed the thought with high moral purpose: She would study with Max Reinhardt, and become a respected actress. "He appeared to sense my feelings," she said. When a journalist friend of Paul Derval mentioned that he was looking forward to seeing her in the Folies, she shrugged. "Don't count on it, I may have changed my mind."

The journalist phoned Derval with this news, and Derval went into action, sending an envoy to Berlin to bring back his wavering star. The new show would have a supporting cast of three hundred, twelve hundred costumes, music by thirteen composers including Irving Berlin and Spencer Williams, sets by famous designers including Erté; she could *not* go back on her contract.

But the contract was never written that Josephine couldn't go back on. "Lawsuits, contracts," she said. "The less I knew about that kind of red tape, the better. . . . Anyway, who could make a decision when there was dancing every night and all that wonderful German beer to drink?"

She finally laid it on the line for Derval's agent. "If you want me to leave Berlin, it will cost an extra four hundred francs a show." Derval agreed. "What could I do? The show was too far advanced for us to cancel it."

So much for Kessler's pantomime, so much for Max Reinhardt's acting school, *au revoir, La Revue Nègre,* Josephine was going to star in the Folies-Bergère at a salary of more than five thousand dollars a month.

All sweet innocence in one of her autobiographies, she writes, "Mrs. Caroline had learned about my contract with the Folies and she was furious." What had she expected, congratulations? But Josephine saw herself as the abused one. "I felt like kicking everyone in sight. Why couldn't people leave me alone?"

Finally, poor Caroline was forced to face reality. "Louis Douglas came to me and he said, with what sadness, emotion, tact, that Josephine was leaving us in three days!

"Leaving us high and dry. . . . What to do? kill myself? . . . I called Josephine and we took a walk through Berlin, in the grey streets of melted, dirty, salty snow. What to say to her? What better than, 'Josephine, you are going to harm your soul.' 'But Missus, I'm feeling just fine,' whistled the red and black devil."

Louis Douglas was worried about cast reprisals against Josephine. "He was afraid of fights, razors, knives," Caroline said. "The troupe was right to be angry. . . . They found themselves empty-handed, and it was not their fault."

Mr. Nelson, the theater's owner, brought in two big policemen who patrolled backstage, and Caroline offered food and drink "to the survivors. We were like shipwrecks. No more Josephine. . . . Deep down, we were in mourning. . . ."

That Josephine's defection was the betrayal of Caroline's life there seems no doubt. "It was as though the Mississippi had lost its waters, after she left us, our boats could no longer navigate.

"Josephine had flown, she had been stolen from me. It was the end of the beautiful *Revue Nègre*. It didn't breathe any more."

Maud de Forrest took Josephine's place, but it was all over one week later. Not only had the star decamped, she had taken with her two of the most talented musicians, Henry Goodwin, who played trumpet, and Percy Johnson, the drummer.

Many of the cast were stranded. Caroline wired her brother on Wall Street for help, but couldn't raise enough money to pay everyone's fare back to America. "We had been having such a good time in the past five months, we had not saved a penny," Evelyn Anderson says. Everyone scrabbled for jobs. Joe Hayman signed on with some German brothers named Siegel ("They had a little combination, they played all around," Evelyn says), Claude Hopkins went out on his own, and Sam Wooding, who was taking *Chocolate Kiddies* to Russia, picked up Maud de Forrest and Sidney Bechet. The rest of the performers and musicians were left to get home as best they could.

In the end, Caroline forgave Josephine. "She had given me the best of herself, those three months in Paris, Berlin," she said. Even after a lawyer had convinced her to sue, she got as far as the courthouse but couldn't go through with the action. "Finding myself side by side with her, whom I loved and admired so much, I said, 'Tell your lawyer the suit is cancelled. Forever. Amen.'"

Years later, generously searching for virtues to attribute to her lost star, Caroline (whose own maternal instinct was fragile) praised Josephine's love of children. "I can still see how kindly she indulged my little Sophie in Berlin. . . ."

Sophie Reagan could see the same thing. "I remember a gilt and red plush hotel . . . and being taken upstairs to this beautiful salon, lots of gilt and flowery carpet, and having this marvelous young girl sink to her knees in the middle of the room, and I just flung myself on top of her, curled my arms around her and cried, *'Ma petite maman.'*

"My mother was standing looking at us. My mother didn't give me a very warm feeling, but this person who wasn't even a woman, she was an adolescent, I was calling this young girl my little mother, and I meant it. It was very strange, a very short but real love relationship.

"Later, it was explained to me that Josephine was one of the causes of the divorce between my parents because my father had lost his savings in *La Revue Nègre*."

Caroline used to make excuses for Josephine, Sophie says, because she was "a child who came from nothing. She had no morality because nobody had taught her morality. Mother said when she told Josephine she couldn't quit—'You have a contract'—Josephine laughed in her face. 'But Mrs. Reagan, I'm a minor, my signature isn't worth the ink I used to write it.' "

If Caroline had known what lay in store for Paul Derval, the star snatcher, she might have smiled. He wrote it in *Folies-Bergère*, his book: "The black pearl gave me a lot of white hairs."

Fifty years later, Josephine told a reporter that she had returned to Paris from Berlin with trepidation. "I never recognized my having taken Paris by storm. I have never recognized, felt nor understood that I was successful."

How was it possible? In her first weeks in Paris, she had achieved rapturous reviews; her career seemed assured, men vied for her favors, she had too many cars, too much champagne, but her insecurities drove her ceaselessly.

"I *had* to succeed," she said, ignoring the fact that success had already come to her. "I would never stop trying, never. A violinist had his violin, a painter his palette. All I had was myself. *I* was the instrument I must care for. . . . That's why I spent thirty minutes every morning rubbing my body with half a lemon to lighten my skin and just as long preparing a mixture for my hair. I couldn't afford to take chances."

Chapter 18

—

THE FOLIES-BERGÈRE: EVERYONE GOES BANANAS

"I was manicured, pedicured. . . ."

he Folies-Bergère is shabby these days, its red and gold look tired, though on any given night, you might still see girls dancing the cancan, or a topless reincarnation of Catherine the Great descending the high, shallow steps. (Never look down, that's the trick.) But the loin-cloth wearing performer stroking a half-naked woman's body does it as mechanically as if he were smoothing a tablecloth.

Once it was different. Opened in 1869, the Folies-Bergère was the first music hall in Paris. Over the years, it presented singers, dancers, acrobats, elephants. Yvette Guilbert, immortalized by Lautrec, appeared there; so did Chevalier, Mistinguett, and the young Charles Chaplin. But most of all, the Folies will be remembered for beautiful legs and breasts, for its glorification of the female body. Paul Derval, who became the boss in 1918, loved women.

In the old days, fashionable revelers strolled the great lobby filled with couches, potted palms, statues. To get to the dress circle, you made your way up winding staircases; to reach the downstairs seats, you passed through a "promenade" prowled by ladies of the evening.

Manet captured the hubbub in an 1882 painting called *Le Bar des Folies-Bergère;* the spectacle was also described by Camille Debans— "Men all smoking, drinking and joking . . . women . . . offering themselves as happily as you could wish."

Once Paul Derval took over, he cast out the happy hookers. "My work was to direct a theater," he said, "not a bordello." The great courtesans of *La Belle Époque* were not to be found in the promenade anyway, but on the stage.

Caroline Otero. Cleo de Merode. Liane de Pougy. Emilienne d'Alençon. They were beautiful, even talented, but it was liaisons with millionaires that made them famous. Of the four, Otero, a Spanish dancer, was greediest. A French duke built her a villa, Kaiser Wilhelm II contributed to her upkeep. She wore so many jewels, reported *Le Figaro,* that "when she ends her dance, the boards continue to glitter as if a crystal chandelier had been pulverized on them."

It was Otero who offered Colette advice from a platinum-plated heart. "Don't forget," she said, "there is always a moment in a man's life, even if he's a miser, when he opens his hand wide. . . ."

"The moment of passion?"

"No, the moment when you twist his wrist."

Josephine didn't need that kind of lesson. She once wheedled a diamond "as big as a frog's egg" from an admirer, but when he demanded she come to his place, she threw herself on the mercy of the cab driver—"I told him I didn't want to give in to the whims of the old man!"—and the driver sent the old man packing. If she took your baubles and broke your heart, was she not acting in the great tradition of *La Belle* Otero? Had she not come to the right country, at the right time?

Stories of Josephine's lovemaking were legion (in Berlin, someone called her "a beast for sex"), but in fact, she had many friendships with men where sex was no part of the equation. Even when she cavorted naked during the time she and Marcel Sauvage were working on her first book, he said her nudity was not provocative. "Sometimes when I would arrive and she was taking her bath, she would call out, 'Come in,' and I would go in and a little monkey would be on the rim of the tub. 'He doesn't like the telephone,' Josephine would say. 'When it rings, he jumps on it because he doesn't want me to answer.' "

The phone, a source of irritation to the monkey, gave pleasure to a young man named Henri Ruinet. Paul Derval had found his new star an elegant apartment near the Parc Monceau, and sure enough, when Ruinet, a country boy, was sent there to install the phone, he was admitted by a smiling Josephine, wearing her favorite covering, her skin. He cherished the memory till he died.

I know it's beginning to sound as if Josephine never greeted a visitor while dressed in anything more formal than a pleasant expression, but this is logical for a person who said, "I hate laces . . . I hope later we will live naked."

Contributing his bit to the Josephine-without-drawers legend, Ernest Hemingway told of meeting her in a club. "Very hot night but she was wearing a coat of black fur, her breasts handling the fur like it was silk." They danced. "She never took off her coat," he said. "Wasn't until the joint closed she told me she had nothing on underneath."

Josephine's first show for Paul Derval was called *La Folie du Jour*. It included seventeen "John Tiller Girls" (direct from England, and chaperoned by a minister) along with some fabulous Russian dancers. All grand dukes who fled the Russian Revolution did not open cabarets, some became taxi drivers; and some ballerinas who could not find work with Diaghilev were happy to dance at the Folies. Those once-privileged girls—Krasovaska, Komarova—who had spent evenings at the court of the czar were now reduced to making a living barely clothed, but their poses, their expressions, came direct from the Russian school. Josephine studied them, and learned.

There were thirteen letters in the show's title, because once, when Derval had deviated from the tradition, he'd had a flop. Josephine was as superstitious as her producer. Don't whistle in my dressing room, don't eat animals' heads if you don't want a headache, don't work with needles on Saturday afternoon.

She also prayed before she went onstage, and before she went to sleep. (In September of 1973, she and I were on Lexington Avenue in New York and she led me into a beautiful building. "What is this place?" I asked. She said it was a synagogue. "But we're not Jewish." "Jean-Claude," she said, "you can pray in any house of God.")

Whether or not Paul Derval was a believer, he didn't hold God responsible for getting Josephine to fittings on time. Whenever she failed to show up, he had her served with a subpoena.

Though her costumes should not have taken long to fit. "In this revue, they had the idea to dress me with a belt of bananas!" she wrote. "Oh! how people ridiculed this idea! And how many drawings and caricatures came out of it. Only the devil, supposedly, could have invented such a thing."

The credit for having dreamed up this costume was given at various times to various people; Christiane Otte, the *vendeuse* at Chez Poiret, insisted that the bananas had been the inspiration of Monsieur Poiret, while Josephine said Jean Cocteau was responsible. "It is Cocteau who gave me the idea for the banana belt. He said, 'On you, it will look very dressy.' "

Luckily, a section of the banana dance was filmed, but only the version made for the United States, in which she had to wear a bra, survives. Lost for sixty years, the footage was found in a box in Rochester. It is amazing to see. Josephine enters into a jungle setting at twilight and moves barefooted along the trunk of a fallen tree, her arms stretched back like the wings of a giant bird. And there on the riverbank, beside the sleeping body of a young white explorer, while his bearers beat drums, she dances. It's a Charleston, a belly dance, Mama Dinks's chicken, bumps, grinds, all in one number, with bananas flying. (Taylor Gordon, a black American singer who caught the show, remembered that "the vivacious Josephine Baker was flopping her bananas like cow-tails in fly time. I wished a lot of people who didn't like her at home could see her then.")

She was, said Marcel Sauvage, "a comic nudity of bronze . . . in tune with the sax, the banjo. . . . A little hate is mixed with it . . . quickly masked behind a grimace. . . ."

Some have suggested that she was being exploited, that white men had put onstage their fantasy of a nubile African girl, but it was not so easy to exploit Josephine; you couldn't make her do anything unless she was convinced the public wanted it. Besides, there was nothing prurient about all those swinging bananas, they were funny.

"The people were on the edge of their seats," the singer Suzy Solidor told me, adding that Josephine had "charm and youth. Always. When she talked, she was twenty years old right up until the end of her life."

Which almost came too soon. "It was four o'clock in the morning, a day or two before the dress rehearsal," said Paul Derval, "and we were going through the 'globe' scene. . . .

"An immense Easter egg, covered with flowers, was lowered from the ceiling. . . . The ball opened to reveal Josephine, nearly nude, nothing but a raffia skirt . . . on a mirror. She danced the Charleston, then the ball closed over her and steel cables pulled it slowly up again."

At least that was the plan. Halfway through rehearsal, the ball (thrown off-balance on its way back to the ceiling when some cables jammed) began to open. "In another second," Derval said, "Josephine would start sliding off the mirror and crash into the orchestra pit forty feet below." Somehow, she managed to hang onto the edge of the lid, and was lopsidedly hauled to safety. Two cast members fainted.

On opening night, all worked perfectly. "You could have heard a fly in that room," said Suzy Solidor, "when Josephine, reflected in the mirrors and the lights, stood up and danced a sensational Charleston. Mirrors multiplied the sight of her sublime body. All around us, we had thousands of Josephines, reflections and shadows, dancing."

E. E. Thompson's group was supposed to play for the number, but band member Bert Marshall later confessed they hadn't blown a lick. "If you were black in Paris, they thought you were great even if you were terrible. . . . The band was so lousy that when we went onstage . . . the pit orchestra played for us and we just mimed to it."

Following the mirror number came a parody of Josephine with the black actor, Benglia, got up to look like her. He wore a short grass skirt, and was partnered by the comic Dorville. (The year before, Benglia had caused a sensation at the Folies by dancing with a white girl. J. A. Rogers, visiting Paris for the *Amsterdam News,* reported that this sight—"of a magnificent Senegalese Negro nude, save for a loin cloth, dancing with an equally striking white woman, similarly dressed"—had caused "the crackers who are here in great numbers to gnash their teeth with rage. . . . In the dance, the woman sat on his knee and caressed him. It sure made the Mason-Dixon folks mad. . . .")

"Monsieur Derval couldn't do enough for his star," said Josephine. "He told me to buy anything I pleased and charge it to him. I spent hours at the dressmaker's. . . . I was manicured, pedicured. . . . 'Perfect,' I murmured, inspecting myself in the mirror. What a revenge for an ugly duckling!"

Other men were as openhanded as M. Derval. "M. Donnet gave me a cabriolet . . . totally upholstered in snakeskin. A dream of snakeskin, an indigestion of snakeskin.''

Once she had opened in the Folies, Josephine again began moonlighting, working two and three jobs. In the afternoons, she went to Le Jardin des Acacias, a club that featured tea dancing, and there she performed for gigolos and lonely ladies. At night, after the Folies, she entertained in a cabaret called L'Abbaye de Theleme, though she found it hard to dance "between tables in the midst of wild people who devour you with their eyes. After midnight, everybody is wild in Montmartre.''

She put in eighteen-hour days, and the stories she told depended on her mood at any given moment. Though she had remade her body through exercise, she denied being athletic. "I don't train, I never rehearse, I am no machine.''

She said, "I want neither to whiten myself nor to blacken myself,'' though she spent hours bleaching her skin.

"Joe wanted at any price to become white,'' said dancer Harry Watkins. "She would fill her bathtub with goat's milk, Eau de Javel (which is like Clorox), lemon, honey, and hot water, then plunge into it. In the process, she would burn her pussy.''

Observing his star growing paler before his eyes, Paul Derval screamed, but all he got for his trouble was a scratchy throat. Josephine delighted in torturing the boss. "How many times,'' he asked rhetorically, "did the conductor stand, baton poised, at the second when she should have made her entrance, while the stage manager yelled up the stairs, 'What the hell is she doing?'

" 'Dressing!'

" 'What do you mean, dressing? She doesn't wear a stitch in this scene!' ''

At that time, a man named Marcel Ballot was her favorite lover and "protector.'' Young and good-looking, he made cars, and he moved Josephine away from the Parc Monceau to number 77 Champs-Élysées. "He set me up in an apartment I called my marble palace. . . . In the middle of the apartment there was a marble swimming pool which took two months to build. It cost a fortune, this pool.'' Josephine advised everyone to swim every day. "Animals who live on the ground will never be as elegant as fishes.''

The "marble palace'' had interiors by Paul Poiret, the Venetian bed "of an ancient doge,'' Oriental tapestries. Lalique was commissioned to create sculptures of Josephine, one as tall as she. When Marcel Ballot came to visit, she said, "He always brought a surprise: white mice with tiny pink noses, parrots who ate the curtains, and finally a miniature monkey who loved to snuggle against my shoulder."

The story had a sad ending: Marcel died of appendicitis, and his death left Josephine lonely, but strange as it may sound, I think she was destined to be lonely in Paris. It wasn't that anyone was unkind to her, but during those first years abroad, she was always on the qui vive, feeling she had to pass tests in how to speak, how to eat, how to dress. Love seemed less of a problem, but when love was over, the loneliness came again.

Even the heady sensation of being the center of attention at parties began to pall. "People chattered or else crushed to stare at me: I was intimidated." She remembered behaving "nastily," drinking champagne and refusing to come into a garden where everyone was waiting for her. "I ran away after midnight, like Cinderella. . . . I got the reputation of being insufferable, surly."

Two months after she opened at the Folies-Bergère, Josephine's domination of the revue scene was threatened by Florence Mills's arrival as one of the stars—Johnny Hudgins was the other—of Lew Leslie's *Blackbirds of 1926; From Dixie to Paris.* Since the success in Europe of *Chocolate Kiddies* and *La Revue Nègre,* producers like Leslie had found a new market, and so had black American performers.

Edith Wilson, who sang jazz and blues in *Blackbirds,* was one of those performers. "Rhythm," she said. "That was it. Over there in Europe they didn't have that rhythm. . . . We had some boys that did all kinds of steps—taps, kicks, and all sorts of things. . . . The dancing always stopped the show. This was the show the Prince of Wales used to come to all the time. . . . I used to do a number onstage and he'd do it right along with me. He'd be in the box—they had curtains you could draw so you couldn't see in from the side—and he'd be dancing right along with the show. He used to have himself a ball!"

Blackbirds opened at the Théâtre-Restaurant des Ambassadeurs (in a roofed-over garden, with tables around the stage on three sides). The first night, a gala special was scheduled for 12 A.M., so the working show people of Paris could come. Josephine drifted in half an hour late, accompanied by eight white men in tails.

"We had to hold the curtain for her," Johnny Hudgins said. "She was wearing this white ermine floor-length coat, and a black velvet evening gown with a hood around her face, it made her look almost white. She got the best table, right down front, it was decorated with a model of a ship lighted by hundreds of little bulbs."

After the performance, Josephine went backstage. Florence Mills's dressing room was at the end of a corridor, Johnny's close by. He had opened his door and was waiting. Josephine glanced in but didn't stop, she went straight to Florence. "Ain't never asked for me," Johnny said, fifty years later. "To this day, it hurts my heart."

Back in St. Louis, the Martin family's hearts were hurting too. They hadn't heard a word from Josephine since she'd gone abroad. Then, "about six months after she left," her brother Richard said, "she wrote and told us she was in France and everything was going very good. Then she started sending money. Three hundred dollars a month for the next ten years. She would write, but she wouldn't send pictures, only money. Now we knew about her success, one newspaper said she was the richest Negro woman in the world. The family was proud. She bought a baby grand piano for my little sister, paid fifteen hundred dollars for it. She was a very good daughter and sister."

She could also be a very good friend. She loved Florence Mills, even when reviews comparing the two of them were not always favorable to her. "You take a coconut with its fiber, its crust, its lumps," said one critic, "and then you take an ivory ball with its paleness, its smoothness, its caress for the eyes. That's the difference between Josephine Baker and Florence Mills. One is a rat who kicks, with so much spirit! The other is an island bird."

A rat! A lumpy coconut! But it was only one man's opinion; Paris remained loyal to its lady of the bananas. And now Josephine had a playmate from home. Bessie de Saussure had abandoned the Club Basha ("Bechet was gone, so the business had dropped") and shown up in Paris. "When we came to Europe," she told me, "we didn't look at black men, and the black men didn't look at us anymore. We all went with the white people. You know, darling, I was too white to be black, and too black to be white. That was the problem of my life, and I must have had a lot of talent to have survived it."

Bessie stayed at Josephine's apartment, and the two tooled around the city "looking at babies. We wanted children so bad, and we went to doctor after doctor, but if something's wrong, you can't have a baby.

We'd say one day we're going to adopt some. Joe did, too. Believe me, she couldn't stop.

"One afternoon, we went to a club called Joe Zelli's Royal Box in Montmartre. They had gigolos there, and we danced with them. Zelli's is where Josephine met Pepito."

The French people wanted to learn the Charleston, the American girls wanted to learn the tango. "So we hired Pepito to give us private lessons. We liked him and Josephine invited him to escort us to a chic party given by some Rothschilds. Pepito said he did not have tails, so we gave him money to buy them. When we went to pick him up for the party, Joe and I looked at each other. This was not a new tailcoat, it was an old one, very worn. We said nothing, but we knew he had taken us for a ride."

Ride or not, Josephine was smitten. "And that's how it started," Bessie said.

Chapter 19

—

ENTER PEPITO

"He used to beat the hell out of her"

It's easy to forget how young they were. Josephine had just turned twenty around the time Pepito came into her life.

His real name was Giuseppe Abatino, he was born November 10, 1898, the fourth and last child of Sicilian parents. His father was an infantry colonel, his mother a well-educated woman whose family had some means. Pepito spoke not only Italian but good French, English, and German, and Josephine thought he looked like her idol, Adolphe Menjou, with "eyes at once gay and serious behind his monocle, his mouth ironic but tender." He had served as a second lieutenant in the Italian army, he had worked in Rome as a minor bureaucrat, and he was in Paris on holiday, visiting his cousin Zito, a gifted caricaturist and a friend of Josephine's.

When, after this vacation, he went home, Josephine pined. "Why couldn't I fall in love with an *orphan?*"

She threw herself into her work, and M. Derval complimented her on the new vigor of the banana dance. "It's good for an artist to suffer," he said.

Then, one night, Pepito reappeared. "I can't live without you, you're looking at your new manager."

She thought it was a terrific idea. "At last I had someone to help me fight my battles."

Opinions of the liaison varied. "Josephine died a lady who knew about books and paintings," Bricktop said. "Pepito taught her everything. And the first thing he taught her was that she shouldn't talk to me. Because the first time she came in my place with him, I said, 'Joe, what are you doing with that guy? He can't even buy a beer.'"

According to Christina Scotto, Pepito's sister, when Pepito met Josephine, "she was a little savage. She did not know how to behave at table, she ate with her hands." (Signora Scotto also confided to a friend that "in bed with Josephine, you can't promise, you have to deliver.")

Arthur Briggs, a black Grenada-born trumpet player, told me flatly that Pepito was "no good. He'd go to tea dances and dance with ladies and they'd tip him between fifty and one hundred francs. In those days, you could live two weeks on one hundred francs. We all knew what Pepito was, but Josephine fell in love with him, it was just one of those things."

A lady who didn't want to be identified except as "Mrs. G.," and who was well acquainted with Pepito, recalled that he dressed "with style, but in a showy way, bright colors, pomade, diamond rings. He spoke French with an Italian accent, and he most certainly came to Paris to seek his fortune by making love to aristocratic grandes dames.

"I do not know what kind of an interest he had in Josephine at first, whether romantic, physical, or material. In any case, he endeavored to educate her, and to teach her proper manners. This was not easy, since she lived by whims. She could be jealous, tender, passionate. She would scratch him, bite him, and beg forgiveness on her knees.

"Pepito managed her affairs in a sensible manner. He always appeared calm, and checked the outbursts of his protégée. They complemented each other."

Barely five foot six inches tall in his elevator shoes, Pepito understood the need for illusion. He hired a real countess, a down-on-her-luck blueblood, to give Josephine lessons in how to speak, how to behave at table (she drank from a finger bowl the first time one was set before her).

By October, *Blackbirds* had moved to London, and with Florence Mills no longer on the scene, Josephine was once again the biggest black star in Paris. She had switched her after-hours allegiance to a club called L'Impérial Souper, on rue Pigalle. The owners renamed it Josephine Baker's Impérial, and she signed a year's contract with them. Two months later, she and Pepito decided she should go into business for herself, and on December 10, she marched one block away, to rue Fontaine, and opened Chez Joséphine. It was financed by one of her protectors, a Dr. Gaston Prieur.

Since she took with her half the staff of the Impérial, and most of the customers, the owners sued. Already a veteran of legal skirmishes, Josephine was unfazed. "I get lawsuits occasionally, you understand?" (People like Caroline Reagan and Paul Poiret understood all too well. Once Josephine began to make big money, Poiret thought she should pay for the clothes he made her. She didn't agree, she said he was lucky to have her wearing his designs all over town. Deep in debt, Poiret took her to court and lost. It was not in Josephine's character to pay unless you sued her; even then, you could seldom collect.)

In any case, Chez Joséphine flourished, with Josephine dancing there from midnight till dawn "in front of a full room, before a brass band while the high-society ladies play tennis with racquets and paper balls above champagne bottles, and between dances Josephine feeds her goat, Toutoute."

"I never had so much fun," said Josephine. "I joke, I stroke the heads of bald men . . . I make fat ladies dance."

A correspondent for *Le Soir* painted a word picture of the club: "Midnight. Naked shoulders . . . Blue chandeliers pour a soft light . . . to the slow dying of the jazz. . . . The flesh is sad. . . . A world exhausted . . . Suddenly a shiver goes through the sold-out room . . . Josephine Baker has just made her entrance. Simple, quick, amiable, she slides between the tables . . . gives away confetti . . . she stops, pulls a beard, laughs. . . . Joy, absent until now, has returned. . . .

"She dances. . . . Then suddenly remembering she is the owner of a bistro, she forces a customer to dance with her, and then another, until everybody is on the floor. Then she goes to the kitchen to get her chef to dance."

The chef, Freddy, was as much a fixture of Chez Joséphine as Albert the pig. "I have an American chef six foot two who is a formidable

Negro," Josephine said, "with his white chef's hat and his Russian rabbit eyes."

It was a totem of a rich and careless age, this temple of the Black Venus, where businessmen mingled with the avant-garde, and an Indian maharanee won a Charleston contest dancing with the sixteen-year-old Aga Khan. "I want people to shake off their worries the way a dog shakes off his fleas," announced Josephine.

The place, Marcel Sauvage recalled, "was open twenty-four hours a day. Josephine asked me to help—'You will arrange everything during the day, because during the night I have given the job to Sim.' "

Neither Sauvage nor Georges Simenon (who signed his early writings "Sim") was paid for his efforts, and even so, Josephine was a demanding boss. "It took too much time from my work as a journalist, so I left," Marcel said. "Sim did too, but there was a flirt between him and Josephine."

Simenon's ex-wife Régine (nicknamed Tigy) put it more bluntly. "Of course Simenon was Josephine's lover. I have learnt it since but I was ignorant at the time."

Claiming, toward the end of his life, to have made love to ten thousand women, Simenon shared with Josephine a reputation for voracious sexual appetite. In 1984, during the course of a *New York Times* interview, the eighty-year-old Simenon said Josephine had been one of his great loves. "We were ready to marry, but I was very poor at this time . . . and I did not want to be Mr. Baker. So I went for six months to a small island . . . to forget."

He took his long-suffering wife with him. Simenon and Josephine remained friends; they understood each other. But I keep wondering about Pepito. What did *he* understand? Nobody faulted him as a manager, but friends found it hard to accept his hanging around while Josephine's other lovers came and went. It was as if, seeing he could not be the only man in her bed, he decided to be her alter ego, make her the most famous entertainer in the world.

As Christmas of 1926 drew near, her childhood was much on Josephine's mind. She had not forgotten Tumpy searching through the trash of rich white families to find a headless doll she could fix for her sisters. And now, amazingly, a Josephine Baker doll, the rage among children in France and Harlem that year, was sharing one of the Christmas windows of the Galeries Lafayette with Santa Claus and the Virgin Mary.

To celebrate the holiday, Josephine gave a party at the Folies-Bergère for the children of Paris policemen. "I had a fir tree in the theatre, tiny candles, glass eggs, cakes, toys. I had had this dream . . . to be a young black Christmas mother. That day, I had more joy than all those children."

She was doing too much. The Folies, the cabaret, the benefits, the lovers, the lessons in singing and walking and French conversation. "I was exhausted. They dunned taxes on me, I didn't understand anything."

Still, she couldn't stop. She loved being loved, she loved knowing accomplished people; it made her feel safe. "She was the one who introduced me to Pirandello," Marcel Sauvage said. "She called him Papa. Colette came to Chez Joséphine too." (Josephine saved a letter from Colette. It read in part, "Take my tender wishes on this old paper I have kept for so long it is yellow. Today these sentimental papers please only sensitive hearts, children, and poets. This is why I give it to you. . . .")

The night Josephine went to the Rothschild party with Bessie and Pepito, she had stared at the house, ablaze with lights, spotted dogs lying on the lawns, and asked, "Is it a hotel? Do you think they rent rooms here?"

Now she knew better.

Endlessly ambitious for his Galatea, Pepito was busy sending potential backers a prototype of *Josephine Baker's Magazine*. The publication never got off the ground, but if it had, Simenon was set to be editor, with Pepito and Josephine the "producers." They would print pictures of the famous at play, caricatures by Zito, pieces about art and cooking, and Josephine's opinions. She offered a sample column called *"J'aime."*

Among the things she loved: "Wives of gentlemen, because it is frightening to think that without them, I would be alone with all the men on earth," and dogs "because you cannot eat dogs, you cannot make furniture of dogs, or shoes of dogs or cigarette holders of dogs."

She loved money too, and was pleased when she got an offer to endorse Pernod. The man in charge of the liquor company's advertising treated her like a daughter, helped with her business affairs. He was rewarded with reprimands—"Monsieur Bondon, you are spending too much on stamps!"

On March 6, 1927, she not only signed her first movie contract—a script was to be written especially for her by the well-known novelist Maurice Dekobra—she also began rehearsing the new Derval revue, *Un Vent de Folie*. This show was no challenge for her; in fact, in a scene called "Plantation," she was dressed in overalls and white socks almost entirely copied from a *Revue Nègre* costume. In another sketch, she went bare-breasted, draped in a few ropes of pearls, a bunch of red feathers plastered to her backside. Again, in blackface, checked pants, and derby, she performed a bit of larceny, imitating Johnny Hudgins (though this time, she gave him credit in the program).

Josephine had asked Bessie Allison to come to Paris and be her companion, but Paul Bass (who was married to Bessie's sister Alice) said Bessie didn't stay long. "She could not stand the ménagerie of animals Joe kept, and she couldn't stand that pimp of hers, he used to beat the hell out of her."

Hadn't Josephine fought back? "I guess not," Paul said. "I guess she liked it. Joe had talent, but Pepito really made her do things."

"She just wanted to do what pleased her," said Marcel Sauvage, "but Pepito would lock her in her room until she had learned a song, or whatever he wanted her to learn."

Every afternoon, the impoverished countess came, and the pupil made progress. Now Josephine's French, still broken, was charming, her grammar improved, and she could offer her hand for a kiss in the properly blasé way.

On June 3, 1927, she turned twenty-one and, in rapid succession, committed two acts of recklessness. First she got her driver's license. How she passed the test is still a mystery, she was a nightmare of a driver, though that didn't prevent the driving school from using her in an ad. Once, motoring past the Grand Hôtel near the Opéra, she crashed into a lamppost, emerged nonchalantly from the car, signed a few autographs, got into a taxi, and went home.

But her driving was in no way so incautious as her announcement of a wedding to Pepito. She said they had been married on her birthday, at the American consulate, by Ambassador Herrick. She said Pepito was a count, and that made her a countess.

Would there be a honeymoon? Yes, as soon as her contract with the Folies ran out. "We will go to Italy. My in-laws are enchanted because they know I'm a serious woman."

Why had she got married? "To be happy, it's as simple as that." And why a secret ceremony? "I did not need a crowd around, and I thought it too theatrical to be coming out of a church in a white dress with a long train." Besides, "I'm only twenty-one, it's the first time I got married, and you see I really didn't know what to do." First time, second time, third time, who was counting?

Variety reported that Josephine's "tieup with the Count" was the sole topic of conversation in Harlem. Now, in a long *Amsterdam News* interview with J. A. Rogers, Josephine's words were sober. She declared she could never again live in America. She wanted to see her mother, but "I couldn't stand that dogging around we used to suffer when I was on the road, especially in the south.

"I'm glad of my success, and believe me I have worked hard for it. I'm glad because it makes it easier for colored people to get employment on the stage here. *La Revue Nègre* started a vogue for colored musicians in Europe. Of course many had been popular before I came. I do not for a moment wish to take any credit from them."

"The Countess," wrote J. A. Rogers, "admitted that she had made a fortune," but was looking forward to becoming even more famous than she was already. " 'The Count . . . is going to devote the rest of his life to perfecting me.' "

Then the sky fell in. Reporters who went to the American consulate and the Italian consulate could find no record of the wedding. The mayor of the *arrondissement* in which Pepito and Josephine lived didn't know anything about it either. A prefect of police showed up backstage at the Folies to explain that married people's taxes were different. He demanded to see some legal papers. A priest at Trinity Church found himself confronted by an American journalist who asked if he had married the couple. The priest could not believe the question. "Me? This stranger, this colored woman, this music hall artist that is shown naked in posters all over Paris, with bananas as her only covering? Monsieur, you are making a joke!"

Mildred Hudgins was in Paris at the time. (Josephine had sent a plane ticket to her in London, where Johnny was playing.) "And this one night," Mildred said, "after Josephine dropped me off at my hotel, she telephoned. 'Mildred, come right away, I need your help.' When I got to her place, she was pacing back and forth. 'What should I do? The police are after me.' I said, 'Deny everything, that will give you time to figure how to get out of it.' "

Now Josephine and Pepito tried to make a joke of the whole business. She was a countess, but only in the movie script written by Maurice Dekobra. She and Pepito were going to costar; he would play a nobleman who marries a girl played by Josephine.

But black Americans had taken Josephine's wedding seriously; they didn't know what to make of the fake story, the contradictory bulletins the couple kept issuing. The press rebelled too. Always before, Josephine had supplied reporters with fabulous copy, and they had dutifully printed her wildest tales: She had come to Paris from Argentina by accident. Somebody had put her on a boat, and when she woke up, too late, she was on her way to France. . . . Her father had inherited—from a crazy preacher who killed himself with an axe—a shop in which her mother and grandmother, both Indians, sold shawls. . . . In New York they called her the American Sarah Bernhardt but she could not judge how accurate this assessment was because "I haven't seen Sarah Bernhardt dance, or eat an egg, either."

Some journalists had adored her *because* she kept reinventing her life. "You tell your story," one wrote, "and every day there's a new version." But this time, they felt duped, foolish.

Three weeks later, more scandal. It began quietly enough, with a book party for *Les Mémoires de Josephine Baker*. She had invited friends for glass of champagne to celebrate the publication of the little volume. She greeted guests, signed books, spilled ink on one of her publisher's shoes. Many people praised Marcel Sauvage's artistry—"It is a book of poems for which Josephine is the Muse"—and the painter Maurice de Vlaminck admired every word. "She dances, eats what she likes, and ignores immorality. Life to her is an apple she bites with all her teeth."

Those teeth could bite a co-author like Marcel Sauvage, too. But I'm getting ahead of myself. It occurs to me that it may have been hard for the reader to reconcile an almost illiterate young Josephine with the Josephine of her early books: ". . . an indigestion of snakeskin" requires a command of language the teenager did not have.

But the two acclaimed French writers—Sauvage and André Rivollet—with whom she teamed up at different times were poets, and a poet is different from a historian. He doesn't sacrifice the emotional impact of a story on the altar of accuracy. Sauvage told me how he started to write Josephine's memoirs. "I told Paul Colin I wanted to do it, and he said, 'Go ahead, and I will do the drawings.' So I went to Josephine,

who found the idea funny. 'I'm too young, I haven't many memories.'
I said, 'I will give you some.' "

When he began spending time with her, Sauvage knew no English,
and Josephine no French "In the beginning, I was accompanied by an
interpreter," he confessed. Rivollet, because he collaborated with her
later, after she had learned his language, may have captured more of her
true voice. "She talked about her past," he said. "I took notes; her life
was the colors of the rainbow, so the title of our book was fitting. She
told me, 'I want these to be my only accurate and extensive memories.' " But again, history was less important to their book than were
flavor and style.

It was history, however, that caught up with Josephine and Marcel
Sauvage. In those earliest memoirs, Josephine said, "I heard a lot about
the war. Strange story. I admit I understand nothing but it disgusts me.
I am so frightened by men who have only one arm, one leg or one eye
left. I pity them with all my heart, but I feel physical repulsion for
everything that is crippled."

Vlaminck found that passage superb; to his mind nobody had "de-
fined war and its horrors with such frankness . . . A frankness deprived
of all hypocrisy." But when a delegation of war veterans came to Chez
Joséphine to protest, and her dressing room at the Folies-Bergère was
invaded by reporters who "barked questions concerning her 'insult' to
the veterans," she was scared.

"That book?" she said. "I don't know anything about my book. I
never wrote nor read a line of it!" She blamed Marcel Sauvage—"He
made me say something bad"—and declared that she was going to sue
him.

Marcel did not take this meekly. In a letter to the papers, he fought
back. "I don't know whether Josephine Baker will be so ill-advised as
to sue me on the score that I wrote her book without her, but if
she does, I shall take delight in publishing additional and very spicy
details. . . . I consider myself absolved of being gallant in this crisis, I shall
tell brutally what I learned about Miss Baker's private life from her own
lips "

Josephine did not sue; instead she danced at a benefit for crippled war
veterans. She needed to show she was as patriotic as the next big star,
especially when the next big star was Mistinguett, who was loved by the
soldiers she had entertained all through the Great War.

The Baker-Sauvage book, by the way, illustrated with thirty-five drawings by Paul Colin, was a big success. Marcel told me it was translated into eighteen languages.

Some of Josephine's friends wondered why she had not chosen as a collaborator her lover of that time, Georges Simenon. I think I know the answer. I believe Josephine felt that once you had slept with her, she had shared with you not only her body, but some part of her soul; when you left, you would take away with you a little bit of the truth.

Sauvage was never her lover—"Don't think I wasn't tempted," he told me, "but it would have shattered our collaboration, that's why I decided to remain a brother to her"—and as for André Rivollet, he was gay, and happy with his lover. With those two, Josephine felt free to create her legend, but with someone who had shared her bed, she had a certain modesty, a reserve; she would not have been able to lie to Simenon, not even to embellish the story of her life.

By September, Johnny Hudgins was in Paris appearing at the Moulin Rouge, and Fredi Washington was there performing at the Club Florida. "Paris was like Christmas every day," Mildred Hudgins said. "People so crazy about you, you forgot you were black." Fredi loved France too. She and her dance partner, Al Moiret, had just played Monte Carlo, where she'd had a hotel room with a terrace overlooking the sea. "It was as if someone had thrown a handful of diamonds into the water, it was so beautiful," she said. "And I was thinking of home, the boarding houses with no hot water, the bedbugs, the life we Negroes had to live, and how much had to be changed."

And so she sat under the stars, pretty little Fredi, smoking her Polish cigarettes that came in a box with a Picasso drawing of a dove of peace on its cover, living a dream, but still brooding about home.

On September 19, Johnny, Fredi, and Josephine were reunited on the stage of the Gaumont Palace Theatre in a benefit for the American Legion. It was like the Marne Hotel in Atlantic City, the three of them together again, and Johnny found himself forgiving Josephine for past slights; she was, he told Mildred, "good for the race."

Ah, the race. Even far from home, it was a problem. Mildred remembered white Americans insulting French girls walking down the boulevards arm in arm with black men. The men—from places like Martinique and the Congo—didn't understand English, but they understood an affront when they heard one, and fistfights would ensue, with the girls on the sidelines screaming, *"Gendarmes! Gendarmes!"*

Mildred, often mistaken for white, was sometimes vilified as a "nigger lover" when she was out with her husband. But Johnny, to use a French expression, was not a man to keep his tongue in his pocket. Or his feet either. He would chase the offending racists down the street. "The *gendarmes* got tired of it," he said. "They thought Americans were crazy to have fights because of color."

. Yet the conflicts went on. At one concert attended by a large number of Americans, black and white, there ensued a scene right out of the movie *Casablanca*. The concert over, a group of white Americans launched into a rendition of "The Star-Spangled Banner," while their black compatriots stood silent. Observing this, one of the whites exhorted the blacks to join in "your national anthem." The blacks conferred, then began to sing. Not "The Star-Spangled Banner," but the "Marseillaise." The French orchestra joined in, so did all the Parisian concertgoers; afterward, there was much cheering and celebration.

Even Josephine declared herself abused at every turn by white Americans. "I can't do it anymore," she told André Rivollet. "I cannot stand being snubbed in hotels anymore. An American woman barred me from the dining room at the Majestic! I am exhausted!"

But exhaustion didn't interfere with ambition. Now came *La Sirène des Tropiques,* a silent film, and Josephine's first attempt to be a movie star, if we don't count the footage of her dancing in the 1926 and 1927 Folies. She had not enjoyed those brief flings, the lights had burned her eyes, she had looked at the cameraman when she should have looked elsewhere, but she wanted to learn the new medium "because my greatest wish is to act in a great film, beautiful and true."

Wishing didn't make it so. She couldn't read the French script— "Nobody bothered to have it translated into English," she complained—and she grew to have contempt for the moviemakers. "I came, I acted in the tropics in a fur coat. . . . They did not understand anything. . . . They neglected to study, to take into account my nature."

At the studios in Épernay near Paris, African huts for *La Sirène* had been built right next to the stage where a movie about the French revolution was being shot. "Under brand new yellow straw huts we watched princesses led to the scaffold. . . . I danced the Charleston while they guillotined."

The plot starred Josephine as a girl who wants to leave her island "to teach a new dance to the Europeans," so she stows away on a ship. Once aboard, she lands in a coal bin and rises up black (an old lady thinks she is the devil), then she falls into a flour bin and rises up white (the same old lady thinks she's a ghost). When she reaches the "civilized" country that is the ship's destination (after a nude scene in the captain's bathtub where she is restored to her own color), she becomes a big success, falls in love with a white man but generously sends him back to his wife.

Josephine detested the finished film because, she said, "I loathe that which is badly done."

Was it badly done? Yes, but there are good things in it: Josephine's rubber body, the perfect timing. And when she is dancing, there is a candor, a sexiness that is at the same time pure and childlike; it is only when she switches to acting that one feels uneasy. Her stage gestures, the exaggerated way of rolling her eyes, which was fine when she had to reach the third balcony, were not suited to movies.

Pepito made frequent suggestions about the script (it echoed Josephine's own life, the poor little girl making good through dance), but, said Marcel Sauvage, "He and Josephine were impossible. Every day Josephine would impose a new story, or a part for a dog she had found on the street; her fantasies were costing the producers a fortune."

Luis Buñuel, at the beginning of his own brilliant career, was an assistant director on the picture. He quit because the whims of the star "appalled and disgusted me. Expected to be on the set at nine in the morning, she'd arrive at five in the afternoon, storm into her dressing room, slam the door, and begin smashing makeup bottles against the wall. When someone dared to ask what the matter was, he was told that her dog was sick."

But how could she be on the set at nine in the morning when she had been dancing at her club until five? And before that, at the Folies? Her schedule was not conducive to good temper.

That November, Florence Mills died after an appendix operation in a New York hospital. She was only thirty-five. "I belong to a race that sings and dances as it breathes," she had said. "I don't care where I am so long as I can sing and dance." She had made famous a song in which she confided to listeners that she was "a little blackbird looking for a bluebird." Now, as her funeral cortège left the Abyssinian Baptist Church and moved down Seventh Avenue, a plane flew overhead, dipped its wings, and released a flock of bluebirds. It was producer Lew Leslie's tribute to the star everyone loved.

In Paris, Josephine grieved for Florence, and found herself increasingly restless. "I was tired of always having to jig up and down. I was hoarse." She was disappointed in *La Sirène,* she was bored with what she was doing in the Folies, she thought longingly of a change.

Her contract with Derval was coming to an end in December, and Pepito had planned a long tour. They would go to all the capitals of Europe: Berlin was offering one thousand dollars a night, Copenhagen six hundred, and a producer in London sent them a blank check to fill in as they liked. But first there would be a big farewell, a *gala d'adieux* at the Salle Pleyel, a concert hall. Josephine invited the piano team of Wiener and Doucet to lend a touch of classical art to the evening.

Sold out. Extra chairs are set up in the aisles. The jazz musicians are already onstage when Josephine makes her entrance. Someone in the press describes her head as looking like freshly painted asphalt. She does the Charleston. The audience is indifferent, they have seen it before. "It is as sad as a waltz, without the grace," writes one critic. "Suddenly the audience seems to discover it too. 'It's ugly.' 'It's horrible.' 'This *négresse!*' Then Wiener and Doucet play, and are applauded wildly. 'What virtuosity, how ravishing.'"

Josephine comes back in a long red dress, sits on the piano like Helen Morgan, and sings. In French, for the first time. Now people are with her, they clap, they offer encouragement. She starts to thank everyone who helped with her success, her hairdresser, her shoemaker, a long list of names nobody wants to listen to, and can read in the program anyway.

Again, the listeners grow restless. During the intermission, she is supposed to auction off five signed souvenir programs designed by Jean Dunand (the proceeds to go to charity), and she does what she knows best. She picks a bald gentleman in the front row, jokes with him, but the jokes aren't funny, she is getting on the nerves of the elegant audience, and from the gallery, whistles are heard.

Josephine freezes. "Oh, this is not kind," she says. The whistles redouble, the insult puts steel in her spine. Her spirit returns. "Are you still French?" she asks.

She has won them back, they applaud her next song, partly to make up to her for the rudeness she has been shown. But Wiener and Doucet, coming on for their last number, are greeted with enthusiastic screams. Josephine can't fool herself, *her* welcome has not been so warm.

Pepito is right. It is time to leave Paris, before Paris leaves her.

But some in the press see Josephine's goodbye to Paris as a tragedy. "The black star without doubt will come back, but she will come back different," one devotee writes. "Even today, she is no longer herself. Those who saw her in 1925 at her arrival, the shy girl of the black revue, and saw her again at the Salle Pleyel, could not recognize her. She has lost a lot of weight, those beautiful round arms, hips . . . She seems to have lost too . . . a bit of her high color."

And Paul Reboux, in *Paris Soir,* begs her to remember in her wanderings that it was Paris that "nurtured your fantastic youthful glory . . . Paris that discovered in a little unknown chorus girl, the artist you have become."

In the end, it is Georges Simenon, writing in the newspaper *Le Merle Rose,* who offers the most heartfelt farewell. Not only to his lost love, but to "that *croupe.*" In French, *croupe* means a horse's hindquarters, a rump, hips. Josephine's *croupe,* Simenon tells his readers, is the sexiest in the world, "inspiring . . . collective fantasies that send a deep incense of desire wafting toward her in steamy waves." Why? "By God, it's obvious, that *croupe* has a sense of humor."

In fact, says Simenon, Josephine personifies humor "from her slyly slicked-down hair to her colt-like legs whose curves are blurred by perpetual motion. . . . Everyone everywhere rushes to see her. . . . When she is not the focus of thousands of opera glasses, she is the object of naked eyes or quivering fingers. How could she not laugh? . . . She shakes her pretty breasts, which are not large but softly contoured, and she explodes . . . but it is her eyes that laugh most."

He speaks of her upcoming tour. "They will talk about that *croupe* in Berlin, in Vienna, in Moscow. The incense of desire spreads. Three million, ten million, fifty, and when we get to a billion . . . ! All of this because of that *croupe* which laughs, in a woman who laughs . . . and who possesses at the same time a most voluptuous body, no matter how it is adorned—gold lamé, bananas, or pale-pink plumes."

Laughing *croupe* safely hidden under a traveling suit, the artist and her manager leave for Vienna with all the recordings (some twenty-four songs, including "Dinah" and "I Want to Yodel") that she has made since 1926. They also take along the Six Baker Boys (a white band), Pepito's mother, his cousin Zito, a secretary, a chauffeur, a maid, a typewriter, two dogs, 196 pairs of shoes, assorted dresses and furs, 64 kilos of face powder, and 30,000 publicity shots for the fans. It is the end of January 1928.

Chapter 20

—

CONDEMNED BY
CHURCH AND STATE

"They denounced me as the black devil!"

J had no talent," she said, looking back a long time after. "My body just did what the music told me to do."

As if that were not a gift. But in 1928, she no longer valued her genius for jazz dancing, she wanted to be respected as an actress, play Marie-Antoinette, do something as important as Lindbergh had done—"He was a real hero, what was a dancer draped in bananas beside him?" She was angry with the fickle French, with the critic who had said it would take a cyclone "to make Mademoiselle Baker stop wiggling in the same old way."

And though she herself was weary of wiggling, how could she stop, when huge sums were being offered her to continue? Indeed, on the first step of this "world tour" (in two years, it would cover twenty-five countries), when she and Pepito arrived at the Vienna train station they were met by journalists who told them of wild excitement in the city. "I found the capital flooded with leaflets denouncing me as the 'black devil.' "

Armed guards escorted her from the train to her hotel. (A week earlier, students had thrown tear-gas bombs in a theater playing the jazz opera *Jonny Spielt Auf,* because a black character bragged about his conquests of white women.) A petition to ban Josephine's "brazen-faced heathen dances" was circulating, and there ensued a debate in Parliament led by a man who said citizens were being asked "to pay 100,000 shillings to see nudity when 100,000 workmen are walking the streets of Vienna searching for employment and food."

None of this was exactly what it seemed to be. In the wake of World War I, Austria-Hungary's last emperor had been banished, his empire dismantled; a socialist government now ruled Austria, with workers and farmers—most of them fearful of a Marxist revolution—embracing the notion of union with Germany. The seeds of Hitler's idea that blacks were inferior to Aryans—in *Mein Kampf,* he called them "half-apes"—had found fertile ground.

Josephine was supposed to have opened at the Ronacher theater, but the city council said no. Apparently unconcerned, she traveled to the Alpine pass of Semmering, where she played in the snow and indulged in a bit of tea dancing because "I don't want to put on weight."

When she returned to the city, Catholic priests were still preaching against her. Ostentatiously, she began attending services every day, giving alms to the poor outside the church doors. But the authorities remained unconvinced of her fitness to entertain a population as moral as the Viennese; she still had to appear before a committee that would judge her act. (Pavlova had been dancing in the city, and offered her assessment of jazz dancers: "Do they need technique? No. Grace? No. Talent? Very little.") Diaghilev, who was also in Vienna, offered Josephine advice: She should audition by dancing on toe.

She did, and was granted a work permit. Meanwhile, Pepito had managed to book her into the Johann Strauss Theater, and on March 1, she opened. Across the street, the bells of St. Paul's clanged out to warn those sinners clutching tickets in their hands, as policemen escorted the star through the stage door. "An army of policemen," she said, "impassive and zealous, like a maître d'. They were expecting the revelation of the devil."

Pepito thought they were expecting something else. "They expect you to appear stark naked."

She came on in a long gown, buttoned to the neck, to a "second of total silence and surprise," and began to sing a blues song called "Pretty Little Baby." The applause that followed was wild; it seemed the theater would crumble. "Then I started to dance, the way I have always danced."

Next morning, a rude dose of reality. *Der Tag* compared her to Jezebel. Josephine laughed it off. The people who counted were those who bought tickets, and every night for a month, the sold-out theater had to turn some of them away. "What I like about success," she said, "is not so much the astonishment, but the love in it."

There were press conferences—one in the Grand Hotel so filled with flowers that she remembered the smell of white lilacs and mimosa long after she forgot how hard it had been to answer questions posed in a foreign language.

But there was a scene she would *not* forget. On a night when she came out of the Pavillon Cabaret, where she had been moonlighting, a young man ran up to her, pulled out a gun, and shot himself, falling dead at her feet. He was later identified as a Yugoslav singer named Gabor, but it couldn't be established whether he had died of love for Josephine or because he couldn't get a job in the theater. "I was haunted by the look in that young man's eyes," she said.

Still, the show went on. "The day I miss a performance will be the day I'm put in my grave." Those who couldn't get tickets to see her onstage could catch her driving through the streets of Vienna in a cart pulled by an ostrich. (A wit observed that ostriches had been more than kind to Josephine, since so many feathers had been plucked from their tails to decorate hers.)

In Prague, more mobs. Gathered to greet her at the railroad station, they stampeded, smashing windows, and she took refuge on top of a limousine. In the theater, she had never feared a crowd ("It is a duel between them and me . . . my heart becomes hard as my fist, it's a matter of winning") but she was afraid of this crowd, "its curiosity, its affection. . . . I was holding Pepito and . . . he disappeared, swept away and I was alone among hundreds of raised arms waving hats. . . . I was like a cork floating on the water."

It was the same in Budapest; she leaped onto an ox cart to get away from the citizens massed to welcome her. "They tore my dress apart, they wanted to see me naked."

And again she had to audition for government officials. "The once gay Hungarian capital is going through a prudish phase," said a press report. But Josephine, "wearing a few feathers, with one mad Charleston won a verdict in her favor."

Still, there were obstacles. Christian Nationalists, led by a man named Schayer, requested that the "indecent black devil" be prevented from exhibiting herself. In a burst of brilliance, Pepito invited Herr Schayer to monitor each performance, for which he would be paid 4,400 francs a night. After that, for a full month, Josephine was protected by her former adversary.

She loved Budapest, she loved the violins, and the sunset on the Danube. As homage to the country, she played a sketch in which she spoke Hungarian.

Then came a mishap which, for all her cleverness, she was not able to avoid. It began with a poetry-writing cavalry officer, Andrew Czlovoydi, whose attentions to her enraged Pepito and led to a duel. The men met at dawn in St. Stephen's Cemetery. Josephine, according to one report, "devoted herself to screaming," but after Pepito was nicked in the shoulder, everyone agreed that honor had been satisfied. The papers printed mocking headlines: REPUTED HUSBAND AND OFFICER FIGHT OVER HARLEM SINGER. BATTLE CALLED OFF WHEN COUNT GETS SCRATCH.

They sometimes doubled back to hit a good date again, never certain what lay in wait. In Zagreb, the show closed after people hurled missiles and screamed, "Long live Croatian culture!"

Holland was more restful. "The Dutch," Josephine said, "eat well, laugh a little and have very good hearts. . . . There are wonderful cheeses, tulips, chocolate. Can you imagine, I danced the Charleston in yellow wooden shoes?"

"Mrs. G." remembered coming back to Josephine's dressing room in Amsterdam. "The director of the theater walked in to discuss a matter of lighting. . . . He was a big solid Dutchman, rather solemn. . . . Their conversation moved . . . from *andante* to *furioso*. . . . It may be that the composure of the Dutchman roused the dark forces asleep in the volatile Josephine. . . . All hell let loose. A masterful slap landed on the plump pink cheek of the Dutchman. She finished off the job by making a terrifying face at him and sticking out the longest pink tongue. . . . Pepito managed to appease her wrath and convince her to go onstage.

"I was even more flabbergasted when half an hour later she came back beaming from her success and jumped to give a kiss to the very same director, who remained as stupefied as before."

Scandinavia, Josephine reported, was "very clean, very correct, though there was one unpleasantness." At the Swedish border, a guard told her she must abandon her two dogs. "Captain," she said, "I have never abandoned anybody, and certainly not a dog. My dogs come with me, or I don't enter your country."

A minister from the health department was called, and passports issued for the dogs, on condition that they never leave Josephine's room. She was up at five one morning, walking them in the street, when a policeman chased her back to her hotel. A few days before, the dog named Phyllis had given birth to two puppies, and all four animals were barking.

Josephine produced two dog passports. "What about these others?" asked the policeman. "Oh," said Josephine, "they're not dogs yet, they're only samples, and I hope you don't want me to put them back where they came from."

In Oslo, she marveled. "It is so strange, you enter the theater and it is still daylight, you come out and it is still daylight. I went fishing under the midnight sun."

In Stockholm, she played before the king. "But if you asked me how he looked, I couldn't tell you. When I dance, I dance, I don't look at anyone, not even a king."

This is vintage Josephine; she talks of playing for the king, but doesn't mention that Crown Prince Gustav-Adolf, then a young man of twenty-eight, was also present. I have heard how, after seeing her perform, the crown prince invited Josephine to the palace, and led her through a secret door into a room with a four-poster bed covered in precious furs. She lay down, naked, and the prince summoned a servant who came in with a silver tray heaped with jewels, and one by one, the prince covered Josephine's body with diamonds, emeralds, rubies. Every time I go to Stockholm, someone tells me this story; it is by now part of the country's folklore.

I'm laughing, because there's an old African saying: "To love the king is not bad, but a king who loves you is better."

It was in Copenhagen that she told an American reporter she was homesick for New York. "I wish I could fly over right now and see the lights of Broadway." But even if she went back to America, she would keep her home in Paris. "Anyway, I would have to return to Paris for new clothes."

Doesn't everybody?

Josephine says she is tired—"When I left Paris, I weighed 137 pounds, now I weigh 115, and I don't drink or smoke"—and she is hoping to get some rest in Berlin.

There is to be no rest for her in Berlin. She hires little black boys to hand out flyers proclaiming that she is the world's favorite actress. She studies German songs, and she opens a new Chez Joséphine at number 53 Behrenstrasse. In Paris, she says, there is no way to live anymore. "There is no money left."

There isn't that much money in Berlin, either. My friend Barney Josephson, who owned the New York club Café Society, was staying at the Adlon Hotel. He remembered the rates changed every day, as the value of the mark fell. "It was terrible on Friedrichstrasse, you would have twenty girls on each corner fighting for who would get the next client, people begging in front of the Adlon for food."

The American actress Louise Brooks, in Berlin to play Lulu for a movie version of playwright Frank Wedekind's *Pandora's Box,* also observed the number of women selling their bodies on the streets. "Sex was the business of the town," she said. She didn't blame economic conditions, but human nature. "Collective lust roared unashamed at the theatre. When Josephine Baker appeared naked except for a girdle of bananas, it was precisely as Lulu's stage entrance was described by Wedekind: 'They rage there as in a ménagerie when the meat appears at the cage.' "

"In Berlin," Josephine said, "two things left me with a dream-like impression. One was silent, the aquarium at the zoo, the other deafening, the colossal Vaterland where all the countries of the world have their echo."

Haus Vaterland was a palace of entertainment with many rooms. In one that could hold six hundred people, Barney Josephson said, "they had American shows, kind of burlesque acts, with dogs, chorus girls . . . Then there was a Spanish room with guitars and flamenco dancers and a Wild West bar with a black orchestra all dressed as cowboys, and a Turkish café that reproduced Istanbul, with belly dancers and strong sweet coffee . . . oh God, you can't describe it all."

By the time Josephine opened at the Theater des Westens in *Bitte Einsteigen,* it wasn't only "collective lust" that roared unashamed at the theater, it was Nazi sympathizers. Lea Seidl, a singer in the show, remembered the hoots and the catcalls on opening night. "I think they were not only against the Jewish management but against Josephine Baker too. You know, after the first night one of the Nazi critics wrote, 'How dare they put our beautiful blond Lea Seidl with a Negress on the stage.' It was already awful."

Three weeks into the run (which was scheduled to last six months), Josephine disappeared. "She had a very elegant chinchilla coat," Lea Seidl said, "and I saw her in her coat with a big sack on her back and she whispered, 'Don't say anything, I run away.' And she did."

(In that period of flux, Berlin audiences were hard to predict. Bessie de Saussure, playing at Haus Vaterland, was hooted off the stage not because she was too dark but because she was too light. "I'm singing, 'digadoo, digadoo, digadoo,' and they just carried on like niggers, they yelled, 'We want a *black* American.' The manager had to take me out the back door; those people wanted to hurt me, oh yes.")

Josephine quit Berlin, but her German tour continued.

Dresden. The citizens of Dresden "were scandalized," said one newspaper, "to see Germany's national dances parodied in the convulsions of the *'coloured girl.'*"

Munich. Worse than Dresden. "No, Mademoiselle, you will not dance in Munich, this city that respects itself."

Leipzig. The Crystal Palace, where she played on a bill with an animal trainer who worked with snakes, goats, and crocodiles. One day she found three of the crocs in her dressing room, "tap dancing with their teeth."

Hamburg. "My best memory of Germany. It's good American cooking, but a little more grease. I sang, in German, 'I Kiss Your Hand, Madame.'"

The photographs taken at that time show how much she had changed. We see her holding a saxophone in the Berlin Chez Joséphine; the pose isn't goofy like the old shots on Revere Beach or in *La Revue Nègre.* She's a well-dressed young woman in control, no longer a waif you want to take care of. Her eyes are sad, worldly. But she fascinates crowds wherever she goes. And where she and Pepito are going now is back to Paris, the city that isn't fun anymore because there's "no money left."

Many of the French still adore her, though they laugh at themselves for this fixation. "It was so easy for Josephine Baker to have us in the palm of her hand that she got tired of us," says an article in *Chronique du Pingouin.* "The good white Parisians are so dumb it was enough for her to wiggle her bottom, and they fell at her feet in adoration. The black idol got tired of humanity lying there like a rug, and left us to conquer new kingdoms . . . secretly hoping to encounter a resistance to match her talent."

Paris forgives her infidelity, she takes its love as her due. Now she wants to show how much progress she has made in French, she wants to play in French sketches. Unfortunately, the impresarios of Paris are not so constant as the public. News travels fast, they know that on the road Miss Baker has improved not only her French, but also her gift for being unreliable. No big theater offers are forthcoming.

No matter, there are friends to see, dresses to buy, and anyway, Josephine tells *Le Journal,* she has really hurried back to help Dr. Gaston Prieur, backer of the first Chez Joséphine. He is on trial for fraud, accused of presiding over a syndicate of fake doctors who treat 750 fake patients every day and split the insurance money with them.

"Poor Doctor Prieur," says Josephine, "what a fine fellow he is."

Despite Josephine's presence at his trial, Dr. Prieur drew a jail sentence, a fine, and was told he could not practice medicine for the next ten years.

Then Josephine got *herself* in hot water. She was riding in a taxi, one of three loaded with her luggage, when the first cab hit and knocked down a pedestrian. All three cabs stopped, but Josephine was unwilling to be held up by some stupid accident. She ordered her convoy to get moving. People surrounded her, indignant. A gentleman intervened on behalf of the wounded pedestrian, whose face was bloody. He got the victim into one of Josephine's cabs, and dispatched the driver to the hospital. Josephine grew more outrageous. "I'm Josephine Baker," she screamed at the crowd. "The one you applauded like imbeciles, in the show!"

The horrified listeners advanced as if to attack her, at which point, her driver accelerated and drove off. It is hard to know what to make of such a scene. Josephine was moody, she could be kind or unkind, you never got what you expected. "She was sick," Pepito declared, after the taxi mishap. "What she said was not what she meant."

In the spring of 1929, Josephine and Pepito went to Italy to visit his family, then boarded the ship *Comte Verde,* on their way to South America. Two weeks later, in Buenos Aires, they were again greeted by headlines: THE SCANDALOUS JOSEPHINE.

"My heart sank," she said. President Yrigoyen denounced her, and on opening night, the theater was filled with Josephine supporters fighting Josephine detractors. It made her angry to be used "as a banner waved by some in the name of free expression and by others in defense of public morality. . . . What did I care about Argentine politics?"

In her dressing room, hearing Pepito tell the theater manager he feared for her safety, she cried, "That stage is mine, no one can keep me off it!"

Demonstrators had put firecrackers under the seats; they exploded as Josephine came on. Hoping to appease the hotheads, the orchestra played all the tangos of the world. The show was, of course, a tremendous success. Two hundred performances, twenty-five hundred seats, sold out every day. "I have never made as much money," said the director. He should have thanked President Yrigoyen.

And so to Chile, by train, through the Andes. "The train goes up and down, women fainted. We were at an altitude of 3,200 meters, and stewards ran from one car to another to give oxygen to the fainting ladies. Through the window, I see we are in the clouds, I see an eagle, his scream more piercing than any siren I have heard.

"Maybe twenty thousand people were waiting for me in Santiago, it reminded me of my arrivals in Europe. I was rescued by the station chief who drove me away in his old Ford, like in the movies."

Brazil she found breathtaking, São Paulo where they spoke Italian, Rio, a city of "lights, hundreds of different orchids, thousands of monkeys playing. Ah! what beautiful films you could make here, my dream is to film in Rio."

She loved the food—"I recommend Feijoada, black beans with burned bread, sausages and smoked pork, a marvel"—she loved the Beira-Mar Casino where she played, her only complaint about Rio was "its one stupid skyscraper."

Thousands of miles to the north, New York, which had more than its share of stupid skyscrapers, was again talking about Josephine. Because on Sunday, September 20, *La Sirène des Tropiques* had its premiere at the Lafayette Theatre on Seventh Avenue. The crowds were huge; even His Honor, James J. Walker, the mayor, showed up. "The first time," said the *Amsterdam News,* "that such a high official of this city ever decided to enter one of the local playhouses."

Most people thought the mayor could have saved himself the trip. One columnist wrote that Josephine's performance was hard to describe. "The closest I can come to telling what it is like is to say that five minutes of her acting in an American studio would cause the director to hit her in the head with the camera." Her dancing was patronized too. "She is a spirited comic hoofer, but even in her hottest moments she isn't any hallelujah."

There was a hint that American blacks were starting to look at her more critically. She had been the pride of Harlem, *Shuffle Along* had made her a star, yet she had abandoned America and her language and her people. Even some who had lived vicariously through her triumphs were having second thoughts.

But what Josephine didn't know didn't hurt her. She was busy in South America, and anyway, she had already said that *La Sirène* was a rotten movie. (Even so, it was a big deal at the Booker in St. Louis. The *Argus* carried an ad heralding the arrival of "The Film Which Captured the Hearts of a Million Parisians," and urged customers to turn out for "The International Sweetheart of the Screen . . . See Josephine . . . With the Noted COUNT PEPITO D'ALBATINA [*sic*].")

Just before Christmas, Josephine and Pepito boarded the French liner *Lutetia,* sailing from Rio to France. I have a painting by Covarrubias of the star and her consort on deck in the moonlight; he made Pepito taller. The architect Le Corbusier was also aboard; Josephine seems to have had a penchant for famous architects. She was already friendly with Adolf Loos, whom she had taught to dance the Charleston, and who had designed a great house for her. The plans still exist; they show a façade of black and white marble, an interior that included a swimming pool lit by the sun coming through a glass roof, and a three-story-high cylindrical tower. The house was never built.

Once she met Le Corbusier, she went off in another direction. "She wanted," he said, "to build a little village with little houses, little trees, little roads for people to be happy. She was mad to do this project, the Josephine Baker–Le Corbusier project, near Paris."

That village wasn't built either, but Josephine found herself fascinated by the architect. "He was a modest, fun-loving man and we quickly struck up a friendship."

For friendship, read love affair. She came to his cabin and he sketched her, nude. She was, he wrote in his journal, "a small child, pure, simple, and limpid. . . . She has a good little heart. She is an admirable artist when she sings, and out of this world when she dances."

It was true, she sang well now. All the singing lessons, French lessons, German lessons, Spanish lessons, the lessons in table manners, all the steps Pepito had taken to turn a great clown into a lady had borne fruit. Though many were convinced he had moved in the wrong direction, it being easier to find a lady than a great clown.

She sang to Le Corbusier—"Her Negro songs were beautiful, what a dramatic sensibility"—while he drew. They were inseparable throughout the voyage. No longer inclined to fight duels, Pepito knew Josephine would go her own way, but he also knew he was necessary to her.

Was she still necessary to Paris, though, that was the question. In her absence, other black performers had put down roots there. Alberta Hunter was having success as a singer, but she wasn't flamboyant like Josephine, she could not be observed buying up half of the city on shopping sprees. "Alberta?" Arthur Briggs said. "She never spent anything but an evening."

You could hear Maud de Forrest (of *La Revue Nègre*) at the Melody Club, Florence Jones (of Chez Florence) and Bricktop still reigned in Montmartre, and Lew Leslie was back with *Blackbirds of 1929*, starring Adelaide Hall, whom he billed as "The New Josephine Baker."

The old Josephine Baker, sailing for France, walked the decks of the *Lutetia* "with a secret joy and a little fear. I'm going to find Paris again, I'm going, once again to try my luck in Paris."

Chapter 21

—

SEX AND THE (SORT OF) MARRIED WOMAN

"She saw him with his pants off, we didn't"

In New York, the stock market had crashed. No more checks arrived in the mail, so bohemians living in Paris went home. The tourists who had filled the hotels left too, and so did the expatriate artists. Hemingway headed for Spain, Ezra Pound for Italy. Robert McAlmon, a literary dilettante who had been the rage of a moment and had seen that moment pass, chose Mexico. "I knew all too well," he said, "that Paris is a bitch, and that one shouldn't become infatuated with bitches. . . ."

Although Parisians still went to the theater, live entertainment was being threatened by talking pictures. "For a long time, I did not believe in talking pictures," Josephine said. "It seemed to me impossible that one could speak sensibly, sing, shout at shadows . . . that this would be anything but gruel for cats around a screen. But in 1929, I witnessed in Vienna the filming of a boxing match. The public screamed. The people were barking. Everyone insulted everyone. It was funny. When the film was projected, there were the screams I had heard. I was dumbfounded, won over."

Al Jolson's two-year-old *The Jazz Singer* had finally made it across the ocean, and Maurice Chevalier could be seen—and heard—in *The Love Parade.* Audiences flocked to both, although French critics were wary. "*La nature est une grande dame dont la voix ne peut être rapportée,*" said one.

If the voice of the grande dame, nature, could not be reproduced, neither could the legs of the grande dame, Mistinguett. They were insured by Lloyd's of London for five hundred thousand francs, the price of a brownstone on the Champs-Élysées. When Pepito and Josephine came home, Miss was starring in *Paris-Miss* at the Casino de Paris, then being run by Henri Varna and Oscar Dufrenne. (Varna and Dufrenne, who were gay, put on splendid, over-opulent productions. The Casino women were put on pedestals, draped in silks and furs and feathers; even the nude scenes gave the impression that they were dressed.)

In January 1930, Pepito's mother died, within three months of his father's death. Josephine grieved with Pepito; the Abatinos had loved and accepted her. But his sadness did not deflect Pepito from his purpose, pushing Josephine to develop her gifts. "I needed to be constantly in motion," she said, "driving my roadster . . . running through the fields with my dogs. It was my way of expressing joy at being alive. What was the point of standing behind a piano practicing scales?"

Pepito told her the point. "Think of all the names that *used* to be in lights. The public is like a man. We're happy to stick with one woman as long as she keeps changing!" Bananas had served their purpose, it was time for "sensitivity, songs, feeling . . . I think you're ready."

By sheer accident, she got the chance to show she was ready. "Oscar Dufrenne used to pick up his newspapers in front of the Paramount Cinema," says Jean Sablon, the popular French singer. "And Dufrenne told me that one day he heard two people ask the paper seller, 'Do you still have the 1926 souvenir program of the Folies-Bèrgere with Josephine Baker?' The news dealer said no, 'I never have enough. As soon as I get some, they're gone.'

"Dufrenne went home and phoned Varna. 'We must engage Josephine.' And that's how she started all over again."

Once more, she was in the right place at the right time. The new revue, *Paris Qui Remue* (Bustling Paris), would be built around the forthcoming Exposition Coloniale, the purpose of which was to celebrate France's empire. Who better than Josephine, adopted daughter of the colonies, to represent the fever of the African jungle?

She followed Mistinguett into the Casino, a huge opportunity. Pierre Meyer, her new leading man, was very good-looking, Jean Sablon told me. "And his family was rich. He had a white Rolls, and a special piano Pleyel made for him in crystal."

Pierre Meyer opened in the show, "but he did not want to sleep with Josephine, so she had him fired."

She couldn't have the choreographer, Earl Leslie, fired, even though he was a boyfriend and dancing partner of Mistinguett, and Josephine considered him a spy in her camp. Mistinguett called Josephine "La Négresse," Josephine referred to Mistinguett as "La Vieille" (The Old One), but the irony is that, in other circumstances, they might have been friends. Both came from poverty, both endured on-the-job training, both had style and wit. Twenty years later, Josephine spoke of her rival as a role model. "When I am . . . on the point of dropping, ready to throw it all over . . . I think about Mistinguett. And I stand up straight again. I accept that one must go on, work hard . . . survive."

Survive, yes, surrender, never. Neither Josephine nor Mistinguett would permit anyone to compete with her onstage. Reviewing *Paris-Miss,* a critic had singled out the young American dancer Mona Lee, calling her "delicious." After that, says Mona Lee, "Miss was a royal pain. I was twenty-four, she was already in her sixties, she could barely kick her leg up past her knee, but the public was always on her side."

Josephine was equally combative. Bobby Mitchell, another American dancer, remembers Josephine trying to get a girl singer fired. "She raised hell, she wanted this girl out and her number struck. They didn't do it because they had a winner, but Josephine used to stand in the wings, and the girl's scene would come up, and you didn't need lighting, Josephine lit up the stage with her fury."

The French singer left to marry a South American millionaire, which didn't sit well with Josephine either. "I remember a Sunday morning," Bobby said, "a bunch of us chorus gypsies sitting around Josephine's apartment, and she's reading about the girl's wedding and she says, 'That motherfucker.' It was funny because the night before at somebody's party, she had been so elegant."

Though Oscar Dufrenne had suggested hiring Josephine, he confessed to his partner that he was worried. "Even if she sings, with that voice, what songs?" But Varna, watching the first rehearsal, as she took the stage and floated down the Casino's steep stairs (which were even trickier than the stairs at the Folies), exclaimed, "She can do anything!"

(Josephine did not entirely trust music hall audiences to recognize how much hard labor went into being able to do anything. "I'm afraid they don't really know," she said, "how a dancer must constantly work to keep her form, renew her repertoire . . . move from dancing to singing.")

The daughter of lyricist Geo Koger told me about the birth of the show's most famous song. "Vincent Scotto and my father were driving, and my father said, tentatively, 'Two loves have I, my country and Paris,' and Scotto said, 'What's that?' and they looked at each other and stopped the car. Scotto grabbed his guitar, they got out, ran under a *porte cochère* (it was raining), and wrote "J'ai Deux Amours."

"When Josephine sang 'J'ai Deux Amours,' " the actress Line Clevers told me, "it was the sun arriving onstage."

René Lefevre concurred. Himself a popular performer, he had known Josephine since *La Revue Nègre*. "I was half in love with her from the first day I saw her at rehearsal. Once, when I organized a charity in Montrouge, she agreed to participate, and she sang and sang, and had a triumph. The mayor said, 'Ah, Josephine, what pleasure you gave us, what can we give you in return?' At that moment, a couple was dancing on the stage, the man was very handsome, and Josephine pointed to him and said, 'I would like you to give me that!' The mayor was flabbergasted.

"People were crazy about Josephine, the women were not even jealous. How could you not like such a person? She was beauty itself." Pepito, on the other hand, got low marks from Lefevre. "He made her life hard, he was skinny, yellow, but Josephine, ah, she was a little island bird."

By this time, despite the disapproval of friends like Lefevre, Josephine had settled into a kind of domesticity with Pepito. Taking Varna's advice, they bought a house on avenue Bugeaud in the sixteenth *arrondissement,* rented out apartments for income, and kept the top floor for their personal use. They also bought the villa Le Beau Chêne in the suburb of Le Vésinet. It was a mansion surrounded by lawn and trees. A little river ran through the property, and the tub in Josephine's bathroom was covered in silver plate. But, she said, "I was forced to leave my green oasis daily and hurry to the rue de Clichy and Monsieur Varna's colorful, hectic world."

The world of *Paris Qui Remue*. When Varna showed her a sketch of the costume—two enormous white-feathered wings—for her first number, and a drawing of the set featuring a steep ramp, she was alarmed. "I'll never get down that wearing these wings." As soon as the choreographer agreed—"She's right, Henri"—Josephine changed her mind. "I looked at him coldly. How little he knew me! Precisely because he had said I couldn't navigate the steps, I would!"

In the number, Josephine played a bird pursued by hunters. They caught her, tore off her wings, and left her helpless on the ground. (Her crippled state would move theatergoers to tears.) There followed a scene about a Vietnamese girl, mistress of a Frenchman, and in it, Josephine sang "La Petite Tonkinoise" while wearing a gilded costume. "J'ai Deux Amours" then made its appearance in a sketch called "Ounawa" where Josephine, a native in an African forest, flirted with the white Pierre Meyer. Until Meyer got his walking papers, anyway. Josephine considered her real costar a cheetah.

The cheetah, called Chiquita (he was male, in spite of his name), had been ordered from Hamburg. "It will be marvelous publicity," Varna told Josephine. "You can take him everywhere with you." She did, she even took him home.

The poster made by Zig for *Paris Qui Remue* features a naked Josephine, bracelets up her left arm, an avalanche of feathers falling down her body, two strings of pearls curling across her hips. Chiquita sits on his hind legs like a tame dog, offering Josephine a bouquet.

Eugene Jenkins, an American musician, recalls seeing Josephine with Chiquita "about eleven o'clock one morning on the Champs-Élysées. And all of a sudden there were about a thousand people around her. Another time I saw her in Montmartre, she had been to a *boulangerie,* and she was standing in the street—she always had that kind of pouting thing, you know what I mean?—and all these people were saying, 'Madame Baker, Madame Baker.' She could just stand still and command, a loaf of bread under her arm."

The Casino's theater program was filled with ads for products endorsed by Josephine. Pepito had taken over all her business, everything was now in his name so she would be lawsuit-proof, and the money rolled in. The chocolates she ate were made by Marquise de Sévigné, she was dressed by Maison Jane, her liquor was supplied by Cherry Jacky, her car was a Delage, her radio a Vitus. The secret of her coiffure was Le Bakerfix, a pomade to slick down hair. Over time, lending her name to this cream would bring her more cash than anything but her stage appearances.

As opening night approached, she grew tense. The dress rehearsal was a mess—"One of the chorus girls sprained an ankle, a costume in the 'Electricity' number short-circuited, Chiquita chewed a hole in a dancer's trousers, and the wind machine broke down."

And then it was upon her, September 26, 1930, and her fears proved to have been groundless. "I could hear the drums of the applause, I cried, 'Thank you, thank you—' "

In the wings, Varna waited. "But no, my little one," he said as she came off. "You are not a street singer. . . . You don't thank people that way, you bow to the left, then to the right, with grace and dignity."

The critics were as thrilled as the civilians. "She left us a *négresse,* droll and primitive, she comes back a great artist." "The beautiful savage has learned to discipline her instincts. . . . Her singing, like a wounded bird, transported the crowd. . . ." (Over and over, we hear the bird comparison; it was to good effect that Josephine had studied Florence Mills and Yvonne Printemps, imitating their light, bright voices.)

Only Janet Flanner confessed regret at the pilgrim's progress. "She has, alas, almost become a little lady. Her caramel-colored body . . . has become thinned, trained, almost civilized. Her voice . . . is still a magic flute that hasn't yet heard of Mozart—though even that, one fears, will come with time. There is a rumor that she wants to sing refined ballads; one is surprised that she doesn't want to play Othello. On that lovely animal visage lies now a sad look, not of captivity, but of dawning intelligence."

That intelligence focused more and more on craft. "With a song," she said, "you can fill a big stage. It doesn't mean you have to wriggle like a frog. . . . I wanted to sing on my knees, alone, downstage, at the Casino de Paris. I won. But the pose must be true, nothing is good when it is artificial. The public asks to hear the beating of your heart between the notes."

Before the opening, Josephine had sent Varna her own good-luck charm, the nail with Dyer Jones's hair twisted around it. Varna, she said, "set me loose, but guided me, he gave me confidence."

He also fretted about her free-wheeling private life, and implored Marcel Sauvage to have a talk with her.

"I too was upset by her sexual adventures," Marcel told me. "I loved her like a brother, and I knew it was not good for her reputation to leave the theater, cross the street, and go to a cheap hotel with some man, in full view of everyone. Pepito was unhappy too, not only nursing his personal chagrin, but worrying about Josephine's image.

"Because she was often lonely in Le Beau Chêne, she would ask my wife, Paulette, and me to come and stay for a few days. The chauffeur would bring her home early in the morning, the maid would give her a bath, she would get into her beautiful bed and ask Paulette to hold her hand and tell her a fairy tale until she went to sleep. That beautiful bed, she told us, had belonged to Marie-Antoinette. 'Marie-Antoinette slept in it with Louis XIV!' Her enthusiasm was not matched by her knowledge of history. Louis XIV died in 1715, Marie-Antoinette, who married Louis XVI, was not born until 1755.

"One day at Beau Chêne, thinking about what Varna had requested of me, I decided to beg her to be more discreet.

"She listened. Then, in a firm voice, she said, 'Marcel, you may be the writer of my life, but my life belongs to me.' "

Sauvage recalled one afternoon at Le Beau Chêne when many invited guests—including the novelist Erich Maria Remarque—had arrived to find no sign of their hostess. "Everyone was waiting in the salon, and she was still in bed. I went to get her. 'I can't get up,' she said, 'I'm tired. They should wait, and if they're hungry, they should eat.' She had her childish caprices. She *was* a child."

Despite the warnings of Varna and Sauvage, Josephine continued to take her pleasure where she found it, often not bothering to go across the street at all. Bobby Mitchell said she and a handsome stage manager at the Casino used to have sex right in the wings. "She had a lot of time off in the last act, and she used to come down in a wrapper, and this English guy had four assistants to run things, so he and Josephine would stand there in the curve of the curtain, and nobody could see them, and afterward, she'd go upstairs and get all glamorous for her big entrance in the finale.

"She had a big thing with a friend of Chaliapin, the opera singer. It lasted about six weeks, then he went somewhere and that was the end of him. He was a big blond Russian, and Josephine took one look and that was that. She liked the big dick, she used to tell you that. Somebody said, 'Josephine, it isn't what you have, it's how you use it,' and she said, 'If you don't have it, you can't use it.' "

And Pepito? "Aside from his impeccable manners around women, there was nothing unique about him," Bobby said. "But you know, she saw him with his pants off, and we didn't. Maybe that's what it was all about."

———

When André Rivollet first came to Beau Chêne to interview Josephine for a newspaper, he did not know he would one day collaborate with her on yet another Baker autobiography. It was December 1930, and everything was white. "The Christmas tree is white, the floor is white . . . even the chandelier has snow." In the branches of the tree, a hidden phonograph plays a record, the words describe "Josephine, charming and divine," and Josephine dances. "Suddenly the door opens, and Monsieur Abatino, the star's manager, appears. He is dancing too, and on top of his jacket, he is wearing the famous banana belt. Josephine protests. 'Pepito, you should not mock the tools of my work.' "

On the dining room table there is lace, cut crystal, and Josephine is regaling Rivollet with lies about what a good cook she is. "Do you like turkey boiled with oysters?"

Then she opens the door, and in rush a lot of little dogs, and Chiquita. "Poor Chiquita," says Josephine, "he has to be happy with a pigeon, it is the closest he can come to the flesh of lovely chorus girls." (Chiquita also liked to go to the movies. "Especially," Josephine said, "those jungle pictures.")

Rivollet tells of the drawings and paintings on the walls, every one of Josephine, of the statues and dolls in her likeness, of "her pure line that inspires artists like Calder, whose first wire sculpture was of Josephine.

"She takes down a photograph and croons to it. It is a picture of her when she was a baby, she is moved, she whispers, 'Pretty little baby, I love you' . . . and Josephine rocks the black child she once was."

Meanwhile, Pepito tends to the bigger picture. Knowing that journalists like Rivollet have been instrumental in Josephine's rise, Pepito publishes a small book called *Josephine Baker As Seen by the French Press.*

It carries a dedication to the authors "who have made me what I have become," and contains 103 snippets of prose, pictures, and testimonials like that of Guido da Varona, who writes, "To the woman the color of night, with the eyes of dawn."

Pepito also launches into print with the novel *Mon Sang dans Tes Veines (My Blood in Your Veins),* written by him and a Monsieur de La Camara, and based on a story Josephine once heard and vows is true. It tells of Joan, a black girl who saves the dying white man she loves by giving him a transfusion of her blood. (A black girl's sacrificing for a white man is the plot of every movie Josephine made.) As soon as the man's fiancée learns of the transfusion, she abandons him, sneering, "You have become a white Negro."

The book didn't sell. "Nobody was interested in that story of mixed blood," Josephine admitted.

In May 1931, she was named Queen of the Exposition Coloniale Internationale. Protestors complained that she was American, not French, but nobody paid them any attention. I think of Carrie McDonald at that long ago World's Fair in St. Louis unable to buy a cup of water, and here was her daughter at another fair, pulling a cheetah on a solid-gold leash and being offered a conqueror's welcome.

If it was ironic that a black American had been chosen to represent the French colonial empire—Tunisia, Madagascar, the French Congo, Indochina, Morocco, Algeria, Senegal, Niger, Chad, spreading across some 4.84 million square miles, and inhabited by 100 million people—it seems equally incongruous to us today that a celebration of colonialism should have drawn enthusiastic crowds. There were pavilions dedicated to the glory of imperialist Holland, Belgium, Denmark, Italy, Portugal. Even the United States was represented, since it held sway over Alaska, the Panama Canal, Puerto Rico, Hawaii, and the Philippines; the American display was complete with a re-creation of George Washington's house at Mount Vernon. (Palestine also participated in the fair, but "unofficially," whatever that meant.)

The minister of the colonies, André Demanson, advised visitors to the exposition not to laugh "at things or people you do not understand at first sight," and told them they would leave the grounds better people for having "enriched your spirit, enlarged the knowledge of your human family . . . and magnificently enlarged your personality."

That same year, Miki Sawada, granddaughter of the founder of Mitsubishi, came into Josephine's life. Miki was married to a diplomat, but fascinated by artists. One day, at the home of a beautiful Russian émigrée whose salon was the talk of Paris, she overheard Josephine "standing in the midst of a group, telling about her visits to the poor quarters of Paris. She would go every two or three months to visit the underprivileged.

"I suddenly had the urge to tell her I wanted to go with her. She did not believe her ears. 'You will be shocked when you see how these poor people live. Why don't you keep the beautiful image of Paris as you know it?'

"I persisted. 'I want to know everything about this city, I want to see who inhabits the shadows.'

"Three weeks later, a call came from her house in the suburbs, and soon I was being driven by her through the streets of Paris to the slums. We arrived at this six story walkup. On every balcony and window, laundry was draped. Josephine parked and honked her horn several times. All of a sudden the windows were full of small faces, and then they came rushing down like bees out of a hive. Josephine unloaded the boxes in the back of the car, dividing them up among the women who had now appeared. Each package was tied with a different-colored ribbon to identify the contents—medicine, clothes, food, toys.

"The sight of Josephine picking up the little ones, stroking their heads, made tears come to my eyes. This was not done for effect, or for an audience."

After that, Miki often brought her small kimono-clad daughter Emi to Beau Chêne. "Josephine would kiss me and throw me in the air and let me play with the little monkeys," Emi says. "I remember all the lovely blond ladies on the terrace."

On these afternoons, Emi would make her way into the salon and overturn a big Lalique cup filled with colored stones. They were rubies, emeralds, sapphires (from what princes? what captains of industry?), but Josephine only laughed as the child scattered the jewels.

She had earned them, which didn't mean she had to take them seriously.

Paris Qui Remue ran thirteen months, and one night, Noble Sissle came backstage. He had been all over Europe and South America, he and Josephine just missing each other everywhere. Now he wondered if she'd be interested in doing a new version of *Shuffle Along*. She said no thanks.

After he left, Pepito sat, champagne untouched, "twisting his glass." He was, as usual, jealous. He said he wondered why Josephine hadn't married "a person of color." Josephine shrugged. "It's the person I care about, not the color." She knew how much she owed Pepito, but she was weary of his sulking (no matter how justified), and felt smothered by his refusal to distinguish between himself and her. "Pepito always says 'we.' *We* are going to sing at the gala, *we* caused a stir at the art show."

In October 1931, Mistinguett came back to the Casino with *Paris Qui Brille* (Paris that Shines), and Josephine and Pepito went to Brussels. Madame Buechels, who took care of their laundry, loved the star as an artist, but didn't care for her as a customer. "She was odious when it came to her laundry, especially the shirts she wore with her smoking jacket and her top hat." (Josephine often performed in a tuxedo.) "The girls had to re-starch and re-iron her shirts until they satisfied her, she was very demanding."

Was she making white people pay for the humiliations of her childhood, for the signs that had said WE WASH FOR WHITE PEOPLE ONLY?

Josephine was not only appearing onstage in Brussels, she and Pepito were negotiating a franchise for Bakerfix, building a business empire. The star was also doing a bit of personal business on the side. Albert de Raikem, whose family bought the hair-oil franchise for Belgium, told me it was well known that a night with Josephine cost thirty-three thousand Belgian francs, and the waiting list was long.

For a couple of years, Mistinguett and Josephine kept trading places on the stage of the Casino. Thirteen months after it opened, Miss's *Paris Qui Brille* closed, and Josephine came back in *La Joie de Paris*. The program named Josephine "the soul of jazz," promised "22 colored boys," and listed Joe Hayman, Evelyn Anderson's old flame, as one of the alto sax players. The poster for the new production, made by Paul Colin, showed three naked, dancing Josephines, one black, one green, one fuchsia.

She was feeling happy, in love again. His name was Jacques Pills; he had been "discovered" in Mistinguett's show and Varna asked him to stay on. Pills was a very good singer, dancer, lover. "Nature," Jean Sablon told me, "had given him a very dependable object."

Having heard of Pierre Meyer's impolitic refusal to sleep with the star, Jacques Pills was not going to make the same mistake. When he was invited across the street to the Hotel du Casino, he went; if he and

Josephine were more than thirty minutes late for work, Varna would send an emissary straight to the hotel.

In love or not, Josephine didn't put all her eggs in one basket. Jean Clement, the hairdresser who first worked with her during *La Joie de Paris,* saw the men come and go. "Backstage, the rich ones waited for her, and of course when she came in the next day, she would be wearing a fabulous new piece of jewelry."

And why not? "All men are businessmen," she said.

"But she was discreet," Jean Clement told me. "*Elle faisait ses coups en douce.* She conducted her business on the quiet."

As for Pepito, since he could not control Josephine's love life, he concentrated harder than ever on her career. "He was too proud and intelligent to allow his passion for me to become a defeat," she said. "He drove himself tirelessly, planning, plotting, manipulating. . . . He even set up a publishing operation to print my songs."

Pepito's name was mentioned seven times in the *Joie de Paris* program, along with a list of Josephine's hit records. She sang one of these—"If I Were White"—in the show, while wearing a blond wig. A portion of the lyrics, roughly translated, went: "As a child, I admired the pale complexion of blond dolls. . . . Crushed with grief, I said to myself, 'Ah, if I were white, what happiness, if my thighs and my hips would change color.' "

Still, by the end of the song, she was conceding that whiteness was not all. "Me, it is the flame of my heart that colors me."

This number enraged Nancy Cunard. The British aristocrat, who spent her adult life fighting for equality for blacks, blamed "ignorant" French critics for toning down Josephine's spirit and bringing it "into line with the revolting standard of national taste."

The blond wig didn't bother Josephine, it was her own hair that drove her crazy. "It was very curly," says Jean Clement. "This made her desperate. I used the Bakerfix. She wanted so much to have straight natural hair. She told me her father was Spanish, she would say, 'What a calamity that I have my mother's hair, if I'd had my father's hair it would have been marvelous.'

"I would say, 'Yes, Josephine, but then I would not have been able to do all your complications.' She always called my work her complications."

Before Christmas 1932, a giant tree was once again set up and decorated in the salon of Beau Chêne, and Josephine was busy sending presents home. (For a long time now, she had been indulging her family. A house for Carrie, a pair of Russian wolfhounds, Oriental rugs, the grand piano for Willie Mae.) But before that year's holiday largesse reached St. Louis, Willie Mae was dead. On the death certificate, under "Profession," it said *Domestic.*

"You know how she died?" asks Richard, Jr. "She had three abortions. I remember Dad took me to see her in her coffin. I was a little bitty baby and he picked me up so I could see his little sister, and I looked in her face. I will never forget it. She was very black-skinned, and had a white flower in her hair."

Baby Sister dead, with a flower in her hair.

"Tumpy was sending money over for her to go to nursing school after, you know, she got that artificial eye," Helen Morris says. "Willie Mae was very sweet, very quiet, very pretty. When she passed, Miss Carrie asked Mama to let me be her daughter, and she bought me a brand-new outfit, a brown and white linen suit and brown and white shoes, and that was in honor of Willie Mae."

In the Martin house, a light had gone out. For days, Margaret could not stop crying. "Mama would ask, 'Why are you crying?' and I would say, 'I don't know, Mama, I keep seeing Willie Mae.' "

Thousands of miles away, Josephine too kept seeing Willie Mae. "You play," she said to Marcel Sauvage, "you make jokes, and life is there, summoning you back to order. Death too. . . . It is hard."

Chapter 22

—

A STAR OF THE
ZIEGFELD FOLLIES

"I don't want to be refused in a hotel"

Duke Ellington made his first visit to Paris in 1933, and Josephine had him out to Le Beau Chêne, where "she heaped goodies on me as though I were really somebody."

She did the same for Evelyn and Ethel Sheppard when they arrived with a show from the Cotton Club. They hadn't let her know they were coming to France. "Just because she lived in our house when she was a kid," Ethel told me, "that don't mean that's she's our dear friend forever and ever, you know what I mean? And we were scared after what she did to those other girls."

Those other girls who had set out for Paris to become famous like Josephine Baker. The ones who had treated Josephine badly, but thought she would forget. "My sister and I laughed," Ethel said. "Honey, they packed their clothes and went, they thought Josephine was so dumb she was going to show them Paris and introduce them to all these white men, and she wouldn't even *see* them!

"So when we got to Paris, we stayed with Bricktop, and then Josephine heard we were in town, and she sent for us. We went to her gorgeous house, and she said, 'You mean to tell me you didn't write me a line and let me know you were coming?' And we told her, 'Listen, Joe, we heard what you did to those other girls.' Well, she just hollered. 'Damn,' she said. 'I knew something was wrong.'

"So then there was so much hugging and kissing and how is your mother, and oh, we had a time. She took us down to the basement. 'Come on,' she says, 'I got something to show you.' Well, I thought I was in the Bronx Zoo. I never saw so many cages with all kinds of animals looking at you. We screamed, and she said, 'They can't get out, they're locked in.' The place didn't smell at all.

"We were only in Paris for a couple of weeks, and she brightened our whole trip. I remember it like it was yesterday, the white, uniformed chauffeur, the car so shining you could see your face in it. Don't you know, honey, after that, everybody in that theater in Paris treated us like we were somebody."

The weather in the spring of 1933 was bad, but the Tour de France, Josephine presiding, took place anyway, with the race starting in Le Vésinet in front of Le Beau Chêne. "All the cyclists were there," said Madame Guignery, wife of the electrician at Beau Chêne. "And Josephine had brought flowers. We decorated the bicycles, and then she cut the ribbon, and they took off, and the officials came to her house for a cup of champagne."

When Josephine didn't have time to make a personal appearance for a good cause, she sent cash. Madame Guignery thought she sent too much. "My husband always told her, 'Josephine, one day you will finish on the straw.'

"As soon as she walked down the street, a monkey on her shoulder, all the children in the village would run after her, and she would take them to the candy store and buy them lollipops. She made Christmas for all the children of her servants, and the tradespeople. Her kindness was spontaneous, not calculated.

"She was loved here, she was integrated into the life of the village, so much that the priest would visit her once a week. She and I would go and distribute stew to needy people, and she would pick up a sick baby with no diaper on. She said, 'A baby is so beautiful, it is never dirty.'

"She kept three gardeners working all year long, in the park, the beautiful statues of naked women were lit by my husband. He devoted himself to Josephine as though she were our daughter. She loved to come and have dinner with us, on a plain table with oilcloth—'Do nothing special for me'—and one year at Easter she took out of her pockets two just-born yellow chicks, and set them on the table, and then took out little chocolate eggs. She was part of the family.''

Pepito was not so easy to adopt. "Monsieur Abatino, ah! He was a prince, arrogant. He was her manager, paying all the bills. He would examine them first, but no matter how much he argued with her, she could not save a penny."

Josephine, said Madame Guignery, "was always naked. At the beginning, my husband was very uncomfortable. And then you didn't notice, it didn't matter, God made us that way."

By fall of 1933, *Joie de Paris* had closed at the Casino, and Josephine went to London. During a four-week engagement at the Prince Edward Theatre, business was good, reviews were not. One critic called her "a brilliant fish out of water," another said the songs she sang were "trash."

There was no time to brood, Stockholm was waiting, and Alexandria, and Cairo, and Athens and Lyons and Rome. The American magazine *Vanity Fair* reported that Mussolini, "out of Fascist racial fanaticism," had banned Josephine from playing in Italy, and then had relented, "whereupon the entire royal family turned out to applaud her."

It was not until late spring 1935 that Josephine learned of the death of Arthur Martin. So far as I can tell, she didn't know anything that was going on in her family; she had no idea what had happened to the pink brick house she'd bought them on West Belle, that neat house with arched windows and trees out back.

"They'd been living high on the hog," says Richard, Jr. "They had to sell the house, and move to south St. Louis."

Helen Morris agrees that Carrie was not a wise guardian of her treasure. "Don's Pawn Shop on Jefferson got every diamond and fur coat Tumpy sent over here; Carrie pawned them, that's just the way she was. Later on when Tumpy came over here, she said, 'Mama, what did you do with the money?' and Carrie said, 'Spent it! That's what I did with it!'

"You know, Aunt Carrie opened a restaurant, and my mother cooked barbecue there. We children were little bitty things, and we would be up all night you know, sittin' on the steps sleepin', waitin' on Mama till she dragged herself on home. But what happened is some money came up missing at the restaurant, and Carrie accused Mama. Imagine that! Mama said, 'Carrie, I wouldn't steal from you,' and Carrie said, 'Oh yes, you did.' She was as bad as Tumpy in that way, when she got something in her head, it stayed there."

After Josephine's brother Richard married, and Richard, Jr., was born, that little family had hard times too. "Mom told me," Richard, Jr., says, "that Dad couldn't get work during the Depression, and he couldn't get relief, either, because he was related to Josephine. The city people said, 'You got a wealthy sister.' "

The younger Richard's recollection of Arthur Martin, his step-grandfather, is that he was "a crazy man" who used to beat Carrie for going out on dates.

"Weatherbird was simple," Helen says, "and Carrie took advantage of that. You know he lost his mind, and it wasn't funny. We called the police, I remember seven police, I counted 'em, and everyone of 'em would go up to the second floor, and he'd just pitch 'em down again. He was strong.

"They took him to the insane asylum, and he died mysteriously. Everybody said they gave him the black bottle. In those days, if you were difficult, they'd give you the black bottle, in other words, they'd kill you.

"Weatherbird just chewed cactus and glass, and Carrie had to put him in the insane asylum, and that's where he died. And that's where she got her next husband, the good-looking Mexican one. He was nuts. He'd stay on his knees all night praying, but she married him. His name was Tony Hudson, he was twenty-nine, a young man, and Carrie was old."

Poor Weatherbird, big, kind, not very smart, loving a pretty, slippery woman who confused him, giving her children his name, caring for them while she caroused. Through the hard St. Louis winters, he had fought a losing battle for jobs and food, but there had also been the summer nights when he'd taken the little ones across the Eads Bridge, and fried catfish for them on the riverbank. There is no record of Josephine's reaction to news of his death. Still, he was the only father she had known, and I wonder, did she sometimes think of him with affection, remembering soft twilights beside the river?

By 1934, the Depression had reached France, and a political crisis raged. Early in the year, during a march against Parliament organized by a right-wing group (the Croix de Feu), police shot into the crowd, killing twenty people and wounding one hundred. The government resigned.

But actors don't pay much attention to the real world, sellers of illusion have their own jobs to do, and Josephine was once again trying to be a movie star. She spent the summer in Paris and Toulon, filming *Zou Zou,* directed by Marc Allegret, with music by Spencer Williams, who was brought from New York.

Zou Zou was the movie of Josephine's that she liked best. It borrowed from her life, the tents she had sweltered in along the Strawberry Road, the laundry like Aunt Jo Cooper's, the young heroine's yearning for a life on the stage. She falls in love with a character played by Jean Gabin (in one of the few films where he sings). They have been brought up as brother and sister, and of course she loses him to her best friend, and of course she becomes a star, but the price she pays is loneliness, there is no one to share her life. (In the picture's big song, "*Haiti,*" a feathered Josephine sits on a swing in a giant birdcage, trilling like a wood thrush. Alone.)

Carlo Rim, artist, photographer, magazine editor, wrote the screenplay for *Zou Zou.* He had visited Beau Chêne to try and capture Josephine's essence. "Under a hot sun," he recalled, "the house was a folly in whipped cream, very Second Empire. The monkeys and parrots, eyelids heavy, contemplated a hose at the end of its strength, leaking big drops that evaporated into the warm air."

Making fun of Josephine's accent (she could not yet pronounce "Monsieur" properly), Rim claimed Josephine had greeted him with, "*Bonjour,* Missie Rim."

She wears a yellow bathing suit and is "built like a boy, long nervous legs, knees without fat, square shoulders, flat chest, concave stomach. Her head has the perfect shape of an egg, and when she smiles, her lips let you discover the whitest teeth you ever saw." Her hands are always moving, her voice like "the deep singing of a saxophone. She sweats, fans herself with a Vilmorin Catalogue. 'Missie Rim, take off your jacket, you are going to die in it.'

"I put my backside on a chair that breaks down.

"Josephine bursts into laughter and instantly becomes serious again, commiserating. 'You did not break your ass? Do you want iodine, or champagne?'"

Skillfully, she soft-soaps the visitor. He is so kind, (even if she knows you for two seconds, she will compliment you, especially if you are important). She says she has an allergy to caviar, but eats it anyway. She scratches herself "with nails more sharply pointed than household knives," and announces that she doesn't want to dance naked anymore, so she is working to improve herself.

Rim's script for *Zou Zou* made no mention of Josephine's color except in a throwaway line by a young sailor who says, "She is pretty, the little Creole."

And *La Créole*, as it happened, was her next venture, although when the idea of her starring in the Offenbach operetta was first broached, she balked. "What if Monsieur Offenbach doesn't think I'm right for the part?" Told that the composer had been dead for fifty years, she shrugged. "I prefer my playwrights living so we can discuss the role."

She did her homework. She went to Vienna to see an operetta (it was bad), she went to Brussels to see an operetta (it was good), and she wrote to Miki Sawada in New York (where her husband had been assigned to the Japanese consulate) that the music for *La Créole* was "simply splendid." She ended this note with a friendly bit of advice. "You mentioned in your letter you were trying to love America. Darling, forget it."

Every day now, Sacha Guitry, one of the most brilliant actors in France, came to Le Beau Chêne to give Josephine diction lessons. She was thrilled—"At last I would play to a family audience, without my feathers and spangles"—and terrified. "I'd never be able to memorize my part."

"Act onstage as you do in real life," Guitry said. "Keep the theater constantly in mind when you are *not* performing, and forget about the critics."

She insisted on wearing light stage makeup, and the director told her she looked like a clown. "Creoles are light-skinned," she argued. This time, color didn't matter. She was working in the "legitimate" theater, not a music hall, and she was good.

"It is dazzling, there is simply no one else today who possesses such radiance, spontaneity, and unique charm," said the composer Henri Sauget, and the composer/singer Reynaldo Hahn called her voice "true and supple throughout."

It had been ten years since *La Revue Nègre*. "Now I spoke French," she said. "I played in French at the side of strictly French actors."

The winter of 1934 was bitter cold. In her dressing room, Josephine sipped hot toddies and celebrated the fact that the theater was filled every night. Around Christmas, Eddie Cantor came backstage. It was time, the American comedian said, for her to tackle New York. "You've already conquered South America and most of Europe."

Josephine said she was tempted, "but suppose I got stranded there?" In print too, she voiced apprehension about going home. "They would make me sing mammy songs, and I cannot *feel* mammy songs."

The journalist to whom she said this had come to Beau Chêne to interview her, and had described the villa with its turrets and dormers, its monkeys, birds, ducks, geese, pigeons, pheasants, rabbits, turkeys. "When they all get to hissing and gobbling and barking and chattering at once, the chorus is superb. 'I do so love the quiet of the country,' booms Miss Baker passionately from the middle of the din."

At home, the interviewer said admiringly, Josephine dressed simply, wore no makeup, and sometimes went down to the grocery store "to buy champagne for guests. The shopkeeper curses her in French for a stingy American, and she curses him in fluent Harlem for a thieving bourgeois. Both understand each other perfectly, and have a fine time."

Josephine's show was selling out, but for some others, pickings were slim. Bricktop pronounced Christmas Eve the dullest she had experienced in years of operating a club, and said nothing would prevent her departure for America "save the complete destruction of all ships and planes."

Pepito, perhaps encouraged by Eddie Cantor, perhaps responding to inquiries from Lee Shubert, decided he should go to New York and check things out. While he was about it, he would pack a print of *Zou Zou* and see if he could find an American distributor.

On March 22, 1935, Josephine wrote Miki Sawada that Pepito would sail on the *Île de France,* leaving April 3. "I do wish you could meet him on his arrival because he doesn't know where to go. I mean the best hotel. And if you could get him a valet . . . You know how I feel being left alone, but we have offers to go to America next winter and Pepito wants to see for himself. . . . I do hope I am not asking too much, because you are my little sister, I take liberties." There was a postscript. "Do take care of my Pepito. Paris is splendid now that spring has come."

New York wasn't bad either. Lee Shubert wanted Josephine for the next *Ziegfeld Follies,* but he wasn't sure about the identity of this Italian gentleman. Josephine had to send a telegram: I AUTHORIZE JOSEPH ABATINO MY MANAGER TO SIGN ALL CONTRACTS IN MY BEHALF.

Two days later, there was an agreement. The *Follies* would open in October. Josephine would be assured of first-class passage on an ocean liner, she would be paid $1,500 a week, and if the show ran beyond June 1936, her salary would be raised to $1,750 a week. She had permission to double in any "smart east side cabaret," and would be given featured billing on a separate line, and a dressing room "equivalent in size and type to the usual #2 dressing room."

The #1 dressing room would go to Fanny Brice.

While Pepito labored in New York, Josephine was, as usual, titillating the French press. Here, a few remarks as they appeared in *Paris-Magazine*:

"If you ask me, how are you? I dance.

"Something enchants me, a dress, a play, a film, a cocktail, I dance.

"In dying, I will be dancing.

"I do not want to get married. I would be too black and him, he would be too white!

"Anyway, the day theatre is no longer my preoccupation, I will automatically become a widow.

"Widow of what? Of the theatre, of course, my only master, my only husband . . . I know only one God, the theatre.

"In matters of the heart, a white is worth—let's put it, a black and a half, and don't talk any more about it!

"Ooh la la . . . what are they going to say in my country if they read that. They are capable of not letting me get off the boat."

On May 12, *La Créole* closed.

On May 14, Josephine wrote to Miki Sawada that she had bought an airplane, and that after only six hours of instruction, "I fly myself, and I'm crazy with joy. They make a lot of stories each time there is a plane accident and they almost never speak about car accidents. That's why the public is afraid; it is ridiculous." Pepito was home—"Think how happy I am to see him, after a month and a half"—and soon they would leave for North Africa, where "I film my next movie before I come to America."

On May 19, she wrote again. Paris was cold, they slept with winter blankets, she was tired because they were going out so much. "Lily Pons had a great great success here. . . ." Again, she spoke of starting her next film "in four or five days, then I rest in Italy before sailing for New York."

On May 25, Josephine and Pepito left for Tunisia (and Tangier) to shoot *Princesse Tam-Tam,* based on an idea by Pepito. It is, in Josephine's words, "the story of an Arab urchin who is transformed into a social butterfly by a French nobleman."

Once again, she plays a free spirit. A famous French novelist, suffering from writer's block, comes to North Africa, where he finds her, and is so entranced he almost forgets he has a wife back home. He attempts to "civilize" Josephine, and next thing we know, she's in Paris attending the opera. She thinks she loves the writer, but she doesn't love having to use silverware, or to wear shoes. "Why do we have to put our feet in boxes? Why live in houses where they walk on your head . . . where the sun doesn't penetrate?"

She has two songs—the voice is beautiful, since *La Créole* it has grown even stronger—and dances the conga, but after a wise maharajah advises her, "When birds of the sky take food from the hands of men, they lose their freedom," she goes back to Africa. The generous novelist has left her a villa, she marries an Arab, has a baby, and welcomes a donkey into the parlor to eat a book called *Civilization.*

This last action is appropriate for Josephine, who in real life has told the world, "I have what I want now: A big dictionary in seven volumes, full of pictures. No, I do not open it, I do not have the time. I set down each volume and it makes me laugh. Everything makes me laugh. It is not my fault, but words do not weigh that much."

By early September, Pepito and Josephine were vacationing in Italy. They had been together for nine years; many people thought he was using her, but she knew better. "In the world of the theatre, each time a man manages his wife's business, people say he is a pimp. I think it's funny. . . . No, what is heavy for me is his jealousy. Meanwhile, I have the best manager in Paris."

From Paris, Josephine wrote Miki a last letter before sailing to New York. "I hope to leave on the *Normandie* the second of October . . dear Miki, I don't want to live in a hotel. If you know a good family . . . that would take me . . . naturally, I want to pay. I would rather live with friends, don't you think it's best? Pepito is going to live in a hotel, we are going to live apart because for my success, it is better that the American public think I am not married."

So far, all business, but here comes the cry of the heart. "Then too . . . I don't want to be refused in a hotel."

On the day she quit Paris, theaters were already playing *Princesse Tam-Tam,* and *Une Vie de Toutes les Couleurs,* her autobiography written with André Rivollet, was in the windows of every bookstore in France.

"In New York," the book says, "where I'm going to star in the *Ziegfeld Follies,* they ask me to sing and dance on top of a skyscraper. . . . I would love so much to be able to dance under the sky in the open air. It seems that all the kisses of the city are coming toward you."

And she is coming toward the city, traveling first class.

Chapter 23

—

BAD TIMES IN HARLEM

"She insisted on speaking only French"

$\mathcal{B}$efore she returned to her native land, Josephine might have found it instructive to consider the bitter experience of her old friend, Fredi Washington.

In 1934, playing a black who passed for white, Fredi had starred in *Imitation of Life*. Here, said historian Donald Bogle, "is a black woman who does not seek so much to be white as to have a chance at white opportunities. . . ." Not wanting to be a servant like her mother, she becomes a rebel "with a daring thirst for freedom."

Modern audiences see her as a rebel, black audiences of the thirties saw her as a thankless child. People were so naive, said the tap dancer Fayard Nicholas, that they confused Fredi with the part she played. "They believed she was a nasty girl. It compared to when Josephine came home in 1935. Most of the blacks said, 'Look at her, she thinks she's white, and she's acting like a white woman, a French white woman at that. . . .' "

The whites were even more snide. In *Vanity Fair,* George Davis wrote, "Does the Countess Pepito Abatino ever pause to dwell in memory on her pickaninny days in America . . . does Josephine Baker ever wonder what Sissle and Blake and all the other Harlem actors in her *Shuffle Along* days must be thinking about her?"

Exactly ten years after she had opened in *La Revue Nègre,* Josephine, with Pepito, his cousin Zito, a white French maid, and a white French secretary, sailed for New York on the maiden voyage of the SS *Norman-die.* It was October 2, 1935, the day Italy invaded Ethiopia. Before she left Paris, Josephine lauded Mussolini, telling reporters that the Ethiopian emperor was "really an enemy to the American Negro and keeps his people in bondage. . . . I will organize an army of colored soldiers and fight Selassie to the limit if Mussolini gives the word. . . . I am willing to travel all around the country and tell my people that if they line up against Il Duce, they will be making a great mistake."

Then she got on the boat.

Also aboard were several of her friends—the singer Lucienne Boyer, the writer Colette, Le Corbusier, and Antoine the hairdresser/savior to whom Caroline Reagan had first taken the burnt-haired Josephine. Antoine, now quite old, was accompanied by his cushioned glass coffin. "I do not travel with it for publicity," he said, "but just in case."

When the *Normandie* docked in New York, Josephine posed for the horde of photographers and reporters who had stormed aboard. She sat on a rail, her left hand holding down her long skirt against the wind. She wore no wedding band, but Pepito's signet ring was on her little finger. "I've had enough of Europe for the present," she told the press, addressing reporters as "confreres. I'm a writer too." She also said Pepito wasn't her husband. "Just my manager . . ." (In a rare moment of candor—or fear—she was telling the truth, as she'd done when she went to get her passport renewed. Then she'd confessed that she'd been married in 1921, that her husband had been born in the United States, and that her marital status had not been terminated.)

The *Amsterdam News* put it more bluntly. "It was well known to many persons that Miss Baker's original [*sic*] husband, Billy Baker, a tan-skinned waiter in Chicago, was still alive and going strong. Billy never seemed to have the urge to go to Paris to claim his wife, but he frankly admitted to friends in Chicago that there had been no divorce and that he expected to pick up relations where they dropped off ten years ago if Mrs. Baker ever returned."

The paper was also unkind about Josephine's lack of political acumen. She had, said a reporter, jumped "into something of which she knows so little it would take more than the public libraries of the country to contain the vast void of her ignorance on world affairs."

Married or not, politically dopey or not, Josephine made it off the ship, escaping into the Rolls-Royce of Miki Sawada. (The Rolls flew the Japanese flag.) With them rode Curt Riess, a German journalist who had first met Josephine in Berlin.

When I contacted him in 1991, Riess was eighty-nine years old, living near Zurich; he was a little deaf, but very sharp. In 1935, he had been in New York working for *Paris-Soir*, which commissioned him to ghost-write, under the byline of some prominent black person, a series of pieces on Harlem. Having read that Josephine was returning to America, Riess decided to ask her to be his "author."

She was delighted. "She clapped her hands like a happy child. She introduced me to her husband, an Italian count with small eyes and a little mustache. 'We live at the St. Moritz,' said the count, and we all drove to this hotel. But when people in the hotel saw the countess was a colored person, their faces froze. The concierge explained that the count was welcome, but not his wife. And this man that for years had lived off his wife moved in. Josephine, her maid, Mrs. Sawada, and I stood outside on the street."

"I took Josephine around in the consulate car," said Miki Sawada. "We went to several hotels, but were turned down. To top it off, the consulate chauffeur began to complain that he didn't want to be seen driving a black woman. In the end, I took her to my studio where I did my painting and told her she could stay there.

" 'America will not welcome home her own daughter,' she said in tears. I could not believe this could be the same woman I had seen in Europe, standing triumphant on the stage, showered with flowers. Here she was huddled before me on the floor, weeping."

Remembering the letter she had written Miki—"I don't want to be refused in a hotel"—you find yourself wondering why she had swept into the St. Moritz. Had she gone there intentionally to create a problem? Did she have too much faith in the power of celebrity? In Miki's being the wife of a diplomat? Did she feel immunized by her own fame, believing it would save her from the indignities other blacks had to endure?

It is possible that she was just being naive, trusting too much in

Pepito's ability to perform miracles. (Poor Pepito, he had dreamed with her, and with her he had become more than himself, a hustler transformed by his obsession. But how could a newcomer to America have known how deep racism ran, and in what genteel places? I think this was the first time he ever failed Josephine, and I also think it was the beginning of the breach between them.)

"Naturally," says Curt Riess, "she could have gone to Harlem and found a place to stay, but why should she have had to? In Paris, in all of Europe, she was a star, why here should she be a second-class woman?"

Her primary challenge was, of course, to reconquer the entire city of New York. And she lived in various places while she was making the effort. First, she left Miki's studio for Curt Riess's hotel, the Bedford, on East Forty-fourth Street. "It was a hotel of artists and actors and newspaper people," Riess says. "There she was admitted. She was by no means sad. She got a penthouse with a terrace, and spent a fortune on toys—dolls, electric trains, she played for hours on the floor. And she ate. I never saw anyone eat like that." (She may have been living at the Bedford, but she sent postcards from the St. Moritz as though she were staying there. Not being able to accept the rejection, she ignored it.) She did not ignore Curt Riess. "Yes, she had a romance in New York," he says. "With me."

Later, she was the houseguest of Sylvio Romano, an Italian movie star. A friend of Pepito's, he and his younger brother, Annio, lived on East Sixtieth Street. "She stayed with us for a month or two," Annio says. "I used to play guitar for her when she wanted to learn a song.

"She could read people's minds, and she had the softest skin. Once when she took a shower, she opened the door and asked me for a towel, and I saw that body. Mama mia! She was like an angel coming from the sky, she was beautiful."

To gather material for their *Paris-Soir* series, Curt Riess and Josephine went to Harlem. "Some friends held a nice welcome-home party for her," he says, "but the result was not nice. It was Josephine who made the mistake. To show the difference between her and the ladies and gentlemen of Harlem, she insisted on speaking only French, which few of them could understand. It was childish, but amusing. She was eager to make them realize she had outgrown Harlem."

While waiting for *Follies* rehearsals to begin—they were put off several times—there were diversions. Josephine went to the premiere of *Porgy and Bess,* and afterward to a party for its composer, George Gershwin, given by publisher Condé Nast in his Park Avenue apartment. One of the other guests, Gloria Braggiotti (then fashion editor of the *New York Post*), asked Josephine why she was wearing green fingernails. "To be different," she said.

Lucius Beebe, a chronicler of high society, was also present, and reported an exchange between Josephine and Beatrice Lillie, the comedienne then appearing with Ethel Waters in *At Home Abroad.* (One top white star, one top black star, Lillie and Waters mirrored the pairing of Fanny Brice and Josephine.)

Miss Lillie (who was Lady Peel, by virtue of marriage to an English lord) had listened, Beebe said, as Josephine "in a flood of French" went on about "how much pleasure she took in Miss Lillie's performances, how she envied her wit . . . and was overwhelmed at this so happy and providential concurrence of kindred spirits." When Josephine came to a stop, Lucius Beebe contended, "Miss Lillie looked up and said: 'Honeychile, yo' mighty good yo'self.' "

On October 13, Josephine flew home to St. Louis, stopping first in Chicago. SOCIALITES WELCOME FOREIGN NOBILITY, boasted the *Chicago Defender,* reporting that its editor, Robert S. Abbott, and Mrs. Abbott had entertained the Count and Countess Abatino at a reception attended by hundreds who "came to bask in the sunshine of the charm and the vivaciousness of the honoree."

Billy Baker was conspicuous by his absence.

If Josephine wasn't looking up old husbands, she and Pepito did manage to spend one evening with an old friend. They went to see Lydia Jones, who had been Josephine's first roommate in Paris.

Lydia had been working at the Cotton Club when she met Ed Jones. "He came in one night, said, 'I like you, would you have dinner with me?' and all the girls asked me, 'Don't you know who that is? He is one of the richest men in Chicago.' "

One of the three Jones brothers who had made a fortune in the numbers racket (they were so powerful that Al Capone bought them out, rather than starting a war with them), Edward Jones adored Lydia. He married her, making her Lydia Jones Jones, festooned her with diamonds, set her up in a mansion in Chicago.

"The time the *Defender* gave the big party for her," Lydia says, "that's when she and Pepito came to our house and had dinner. Our cook had prepared soul food, and Pepito couldn't get enough fried chicken."

Leaving Pepito in Chicago, Josephine flew to St. Louis. "She came alone," her brother Richard said. "She just slept and ate, that's all. She slept with our grandmother, who was surrounded by monkeys and parakeets. I was married then, and Margaret was married, and Willie Mae was already dead. I spent time with Josephine, and my wife was vexed, she was jealous, but I said, 'I'm just going to see my sister. I haven't spent time with her in fourteen years.'"

"I was not reared up with Aunt Tumpy, I did not know her," says Richard, Jr. "When I finally met her in 1935, I was very aware that she was famous, and I was very aware she looked so different from Sister— my Aunt Margaret—and so much lighter than my father. My father was proud that I could dance, and he took me in front of Aunt Tumpy, and I had to dance for her, between the living room and the kitchen of my grandmother's apartment. I did a split, I stood on my head, I did a kind of shuffle, but I didn't like it because they made me wash before I got to Aunt Tumpy.

"I was six years old, and she just looked at me with her aunt smile, no applause. You know, she was the star of the family, so nothing impressed her. But she was impressed with my father, she bought him a truck."

She was also impressed with Margaret's husband, handsome, light-skinned Elmo Wallace. Margaret told me that Josephine pulled her aside and said, "Oh, Sister, where did you find that good-looking man?"

Still, Richard, Jr., says, "I think Aunt Tumpy was absolutely flabber-gasted that the beautiful house she had bought them was gone. Now, my grandmother's apartment was on the second floor, and you had to go downstairs to the outdoor toilet. Josephine Baker had to go outside! She had to ask me to get her a basin of water so she could wash up, because there was no bathroom."

"She didn't appreciate it," says Helen Morris. Seventeen years old at the time, Helen remembers Josephine's entertaining the fire department. "My brother Virgil was a fireman, and one day she had all the firemen come over and eat dinner with her. She was wearing a long velvet gown, and as soon as one of those firemen would step on it, she'd stop dead till they got off. She would wear those costumes around that little apartment, she just dusted the floor with them."

In St. Louis, in 1990, Helen took me to meet Beredester Harvey, another Martin family friend. "When Josephine came home in 1935, it was Depression time," Beredester said, "and she would be sweeping around, coming in and out in these gorgeous robes, and everybody in the next houses would run outside. She'd just stand downstairs and talk with the neighbors, and she'd be wearing an evening dress. But you see, we wasn't accustomed to that, why, it was like having the queen of England to visit."

Beredester said Josephine had always been the talk of the neighborhood. "We would read about her accomplishments, she was a star in our life because we were so young, and it was just exciting. Helen and I tried to pattern after her. Helen's brother Ikey built us a stage in the yard, and we would dress up and be showgirls."

The St. Louis Argus reported that, on this brief trip, Josephine had "succeeded in eluding the watchful eyes of the press." She visited the site where the Booker Washington had stood, she went to a grammar school and spoke to little children in French and English, but she wouldn't talk to reporters, and neither would her relatives, who "declined to divulge anything about her visit or her past history." Then suddenly, she was gone. She flew back to Chicago, picked up Pepito, went to a football game, and returned to New York.

With Pepito, Zito, and the Sawadas, she went to the French Casino to see a revue imported from the Folies-Bergère, and staged by Jacques Charles. She also went to the Cotton Club, where the Nicholas Brothers were appearing. "Harold and I had heard she was the toast of Paris," Fayard Nicholas said. "And we were going to be in the *Follies* with her, so we went and introduced ourselves."

The Nicholas Brothers were fixtures at the Cotton Club, they had been there when Ethel Waters introduced "Stormy Weather," they had worked with Duke Ellington and Lena Horne and all those gorgeous showgirls. "Most of the showgirls," Fayard said, "were real tall, almost six feet, and light brown, teasin' brown, they called it."

But most of the audience was lily-white, especially the ones in the good seats. So when Fayard caught sight of Josephine up front, he was surprised. "It was the first time I had seen a black seated at ringside. This was one of the most famous clubs in America, and it was in Harlem, where mostly black people lived, but they couldn't come to see these shows. Except for maybe Bill Robinson, or the Jones brothers from Chicago. But even those people they would sit them on the side, see?

So when I saw Josephine Baker sittin' ringside, I said, 'Wow! it must be because she is a French citizen.' "

Josephine appeared as a guest star on *The Fleischmann's Yeast Hour,* was introduced to the radio audience by the crooner Rudy Vallee, and somewhere along the line, met Joe Louis, who invited her home for dinner. "His young wife is charming," she commented. "Joe is calm, silent. He gives an impression of strength that—I don't know why— reassures and comforts me."

October passed. Sixteen thousand Italians gathered in Madison Square Garden to rally for Mussolini, Haile Selassie was nominated for the Nobel peace prize, and Josephine found a photographer who made her happy. His name was Murray Korman, and he lit her so she looked white. She had hundreds of copies made to send to friends in France.

"My dear Carlos," she wrote to Carlo Rim (she continued to add an *s* to his name), "you see me as I am here. But be assured, if I want to make a telephone call in the street, I'm still a *négresse.*"

Rim said the pictures made him sad. In them, she sported "a light complexion. . . . You do not recognize her."

She promised she would be back when the show was over, "and I will find again my France, and my freedom."

Finally, rehearsals began. Through what Pepito called a curious twist of destiny, the *Follies* would be playing the Winter Garden, in the same building that had housed the Plantation, where Josephine had worked as a chorus girl.

Now her days were filled with new dances, new songs by Vernon Duke and Ira Gershwin. Vincente Minnelli (then twenty-eight years old and responsible for scenery and costumes) told me, "Josephine kept asking the count how she should express herself. She didn't like what we did with her. I made her a beautiful gold dress for the 'Maharanee' number, and Balanchine staged a great dance called '5 A.M.' for her.

"Everybody would come at the same time and ask for changes—'I can't dance in that dress,' 'The lighting is too strong'—and I don't know how I did not become crazy."

Josephine felt the same. In Paris, she had been able to call the shots, have her own way. She had come to New York with French gowns, furs, jewels, expecting to wear them in the show. The Shuberts said no.

"In Paris," she said, "rehearsing is a pleasure, in New York it is a matter of discipline. . . . People who do not have to work in the same scene have never seen each other. . . . I rehearsed without seeing anyone but the pianist and the dancing master. . . .

"Finally, one morning the director appeared in the auditorium. He was John Murray Anderson. . . . He watched me dance, then shook his head, saying, 'We must change everything.' I was in despair, then he explained, and I discovered he was paying me a compliment. . . .

" 'You are different, Josephine, you are from Paris—it's stupid to let you sing Harlem songs. You must give us something new, something Parisian.' "

Unhappy, she decided to give *herself* something Parisian. She wired Maurice Bataille, asking him to come to New York. The two had been friends—never lovers—since *La Revue Nègre,* though Maurice told me that the jealous Pepito had never liked him. "Once he came backstage when Josephine was appearing at the Casino de Paris, and he chased me down the hall waving a pair of scissors and yelling that he was going to put out my eyes!"

Now Maurice took a suite at the Ritz-Carlton, and his long-deferred affair with Josephine began. But not at the Carlton. "We spent our first night of love," he says, "in a room in Harlem that Josephine's friend Bessie Buchanan provided for us. While making love, we suddenly stopped and laughed at the silliness of the situation." (During his stay in New York, Maurice told me that Josephine said she still missed Marcel Ballot. "He was my greatest love.")

"But," Maurice said, "we had a fabulous time. We were guests of Father Divine (a black minister whose background was a mystery); Josephine knew every place in Harlem, even some very risqué ones.

"On Halloween, we went as the guests of Bessie Buchanan to a drag ball at the Savoy Ballroom." (By now, Bessie Allison, Josephine's friend since *Tan Town Topics,* was married to Charles Buchanan, one of the Savoy's owners.) There was a contest for best costume, and black men wearing crinolines and Madame Pompadour wigs paraded in front of the judges, some tripping over their long dresses. It was funny to go to the men's room, Maurice says, and see the "ladies" standing at the pissoirs holding up their gowns.

In the *Ziegfeld Follies,* Josephine had only three numbers to Fanny Brice's seven, and for the "Conga," which she insisted was "a real tribal dance," she was rigged out in a grotesque version of the banana belt, studded not with bananas but with sharp pointed cones that looked like porcupine quills. The matching bra also sported the ugly, menacing spikes. She had proved she could sing in *La Créole*, she had proved she could move audiences with "J'ai Deux Amours," she did not want to start all over again in a costume that might bring her ridicule. Even her body was different now, she was too thin; she had been ill and lost weight in Tunisia while filming *Princesse Tam-Tam*. But this time, the decisions were not hers to make.

"Maharanee," the sketch about a night at a Paris racetrack, frustrated her too. "She had on this beautiful white gown with furs," Fayard Nicholas said. "And she was singing and dancing with these white men in top hats and tails and masks, but they never touched her. One day, we were in the theater lobby, my brother and I, getting ready to go rehearse, and I saw her, and she was crying.

"I said, 'Josephine, what's wrong?' She said, 'These people here, they don't want black people to touch white people.' She said, 'They're trying to make me act like the people in those movies, like a maid or something.'

"And she couldn't do that. She was French now."

Josephine's old friend, the French-born soprano Lily Pons, then enjoying a professional triumph in New York, was upset. "I feel so bad the way they treat you in your own country," she told Josephine.

Still, some black people thought Josephine wasn't acting any better than the whites she was complaining about. She was accused of "going snooty," of having refused to receive Ethel Waters, who had called to pay her "professional respects." One reporter wrote that Harlem was "laughing up its collective sleeve at the rebuffs Josephine has received in her attempts to crash bigtime Manhattan society because of her countess title. Shoulders cold enough to freeze a polar bear are reputed to have been turned in her direction. While Josephine ritzes her own people, she in turn is being ritzed by those she most wants to accept her."

Maurice Bataille had gone home by December 30, when the *Ziegfeld Follies*, 1936 edition, finally opened at the Boston Opera House. The *Amsterdam News* said Harlem was waiting to see how Josephine would be received by the white public, because she had already got "some very unsavory notices about her arrival on these shores. Her appearance at the opera recently caused a mild furore. Those present contend she was the most bejeweled woman that evening."

She'd come a long way from St. Louis; La Belle Otero would have been proud of her disciple.

The scenery didn't make it to the theater in time for opening night, many of the sketches were cut at the last moment, and Josephine's notices were mixed. One critic said she "won" the audience, another found her hard to hear. "She wasn't a true hit," Fayard Nicholas said.

She wasn't a hit with her costars either. "To tell the truth, none of them were friendly with her," Fayard says. "Bob Hope was neutral, he never had much to say one way or the other about Josephine Baker. It was the women, catty and talkin' behind her back, sayin' who does she think she is? They forgot she was a bigger star than all of them."

The comedienne Eve Arden seems to have been an exception. She shared Josephine's love for animals, and spent time in Josephine's dressing room playing with "these beautiful little puppies. Josephine was darling to me. I used to watch the number she did with the boys in masks. It was fascinating, she was an exceptional dancer, and she sang pretty well, as I remember. But I guess she was ahead of her time."

The troupe moved from Boston to Philadelphia, opening at the Forrest on January 14. I wonder what Josephine thought, being back in the city where she had met Billy Baker. She certainly did not appear to be interested in rehashing old times. The *Philadelphia Tribune* put it in a headline—JOE BAKER HIDES FROM TOWN WHERE SHE MADE HER START—and went on to say, "Although the artist . . . got her start in Philadelphia in the colored district, no one would have known it from the way she very frigidly ignored the existence of such a place. Attempts to contact her were fruitless. . . ."

"About the same time as the *Ziegfeld Follies* arrived in Philadelphia, there appeared an interview in which Miss Baker said that her father was Spanish, and her mother half Indian, which left the other half colored. This she said in denying that she was colored, or anything near colored."

Still, the paper forgave her. "It might seem that in Europe where color isn't the handicap it is here, Miss Baker does not mind being known as a Negro, but over here it is something else again. And who can blame her?"

The *Tribune* also printed excerpts from the Curt Riess series "written" by Josephine for *Paris-Soir*. Her version of the past four months, headlined HARLEM, 1936, was not weighted down with facts. When she traveled in New York, she traveled in a Rolls, but never mind, she put herself in the subway for the sake of a good story. She got on at Times Square, wearing, she said, "an old dress, a poor little hat, almost the same clothes as I wore ten years ago, before I left America. Now, with a pounding heart, I find myself back again. This young girl that no one recognizes, who is being taken away by this river of human beings, it's me, Josephine Baker."

She tells us that by the time she gets to 110th Street, there are nothing but black faces around her, and that fifteen blocks farther on, 125th Street is "the entertainment center, the Montmartre of Harlem."

Even uptown, she can't get a room. "Harlem is against me. Why? I want to know."

Eventually, she finds a place willing to take her in, and she wants us to believe that she stays there for three days. "For three days, they have been looking for me. Manager, theater director, journalists, friends call everywhere. 'Where is Josephine?' "

She has rented "a modest room," she sings all day long, the land-lady hears her, suggests she head for the Apollo to try her luck on Amateur Night. She takes the advice. The theater is packed, and back-stage, the real amateurs wait their turns. "The audience is tough. If they don't like you in ten seconds, they start ringing cowbells and twirling noisemakers. . . . Suddenly, Ralph Cooper, the Master of Ceremonies, a young, good looking, charming black man, calls out in a strong voice, 'Gracie Walker.' Nobody answers. The audience starts to get restless. Ralph looks at his list, ready to call the next name, when suddenly I remember—Gracie Walker, it's me.

"I jump on stage shaking, that stagefright is ridiculous and I know it, after all, it's not the first time I've appeared in front of the public."

At last, a word of truth. The Ralph Cooper she describes as though she'd never seen him before is the boyfriend she left behind when she went to Paris, and now she sings a sad song and moves every heart. "My voice shook and strangled in my throat . . . a kind of miracle starts, people are listening to me. . . . I see myself 14 years old arriving in Harlem when I wanted to become a dancer."

She told in *Paris-Soir* about her recent rehearsals at the Winter Garden too, about running upstairs to the supper club that had been the Plantation when she had played there ten years ago. "Now coming back as a star, standing in the dark, I look at the little Josephine of those days, and ask myself, 'Have I ever been as happy as I was then?' "

No word in those articles of her cool reception in Boston. "The curtain rose. . . . I was acclaimed, but I don't want to think about it. I think already of Paris, of Le Vésinet, my animals . . . the boulevards so dear to me, the little cafés and restaurants where I will find my friends again . . . the very old man who sells the newspapers on the Place Clichy across from my dressing room at the Casino de Paris. The blue sky above the Champs-Élysées, the Seine, I cry a little. Just a little bit."

Josephine's effusions were romantic, but rehearsals were real, and the company had to keep rehearsing even while they were playing, because John Murray Anderson was not yet satisfied. "We were changing, always changing," says Fayard Nicholas, "my goodness, every town we went to."

One of the changes in Philadelphia had been the moving of the "Conga" number from the second act to the first. A newspaper columnist named Peter Stirling who went around to the Forrest found himself watching a rehearsal of this switch. He liked Josephine, her small true voice, her vitality, so he offered her some advice. "I mentioned that I thought it was a mistake for Miss Baker to use a fast jungle dance as her opening number. It was shooting the works before the audience had been won.

" 'I have been telling everyone that,' she moaned. 'But they won't listen to me. . . . Maybe if you mentioned it in your column, it would help.' "

It didn't. The "Conga" number remained in act one. But another piece of news came out of Stirling's interview with Josephine. She said she didn't want to discuss her husband. "That is something I feel need not be a part of professional life." This, about the man who had built and was still running the Josephine Baker empire, from Bakerfix on. The count, she told Stirling, "has gone back to France now." (Curt Reiss told me that Pepito left New York when Josephine refused to pay the hotel bill at the St. Moritz.)

Miki Sawada blamed the rift between Josephine and Pepito on "racial discrimination in the United States." It was clear that Josephine's dependence on Pepito had wound down, their connection—long, symbiotic, sometimes fond, sometimes violent—was coming apart.

"There was a rumor," said Miki Sawada, "that when they split up, Josephine gave him five hundred thousand dollars."

Chapter 24

—

TRASHED BY CRITICS, ENVIED BY PEERS

"My God, how does it feel to be a big star?"

The one in Philadelphia who would have been most proud of her, who had encouraged her from the start, was gone. Pa Baker had disappeared without a trace. Now Josephine had her name in lights, he wasn't there to see it.

In any event, the notices would have made him angry, they were even more harsh than they had been in Boston: "Josephine Baker seemed only ordinary, if agile. . . ." She had been transformed "into a French cabaret performer. Spotted in three numbers, she appears in an exotic dance, 'La Conga,' in the most abbreviated attire possible, poses as a wealthy woman at the races at Longchamp, and finally, in clinging cloth of gold sings, in a high, thin, reedy voice, a most lamentable song."

George Balanchine, her friend since the day he came calling at Beau Chêne, was sympathetic. "Thank God, when I first began to choreograph in Paris, I didn't speak French. Fifty years later, somebody read me my reviews. If I'd read them in the twenties, I would have gone back home to Russia."

As though the critical savagery weren't crushing enough, the *Philadelphia Tribune* ran a piece suggesting that Josephine might be "released from the current 'Ziegfeld Follies' because she failed to click. . . ."

That very same day, the *Tribune* had featured a front-page story about Marian Anderson, a native of south Philadelphia. Her concert at the Academy of Music marked Miss Anderson's "triumphal return" from abroad. And it could not have escaped Josephine's notice that while she was being scorned for her foreign airs and graces, Marian Anderson was being praised for hers. "Continental Europe has remodeled her in more delicate, more alluring lines, and has given her the high privilege of charm," said the *Trib*.

The newly married Donald Wyatt, then an official of the National Urban League, took his bride, Marian, to the Forrest to see Josephine (whom he would later meet in North Africa). "We had heard about her, so we went. In a number called '5 A.M.,' the Balanchine choreography was great, and Josephine was great. But the audience, mostly white, was unable to accept the public adoration of a black woman by four handsome young white men.

"Most blacks didn't like it any better, but as a sociologist, I felt this is where we needed to be going, to the point where there would be an interracial performance accepted by both sides for its artistic value.

"At the end of the number, the boys lifted her into the air and ran off the stage with her, and there was total silence. Nobody clapped. Then the tempo of the music picked up, and the Nicholas brothers made their entrance tap-dancing like mad, and everybody was relieved, and burst into a tremendous wave of applause."

Josephine returned to New York unhappy. Gossip was rife that a feud between her and Fanny Brice was the reason. Despite its temperamental leading ladies, the show pulled itself together and opened on January 30. New York critics Percy Hammond, John Mason Brown, Burns Mantle, and Brooks Atkinson were stylish writers who loved the theater, but weren't shy about panning performers who disappointed them. Josephine was so riddled with their arrows she could have posed as Saint Sebastian.

Atkinson: "After her cyclonic career abroad, Josephine Baker has become a celebrity who offers her presence instead of her talent . . . her singing voice is only a squeak in the dark and her dancing is only the pain of an artist. Miss Baker has refined her art until there is nothing left of it."

Hammond: "The most prominent Negress since Eliza in 'Uncle Tom's Cabin' . . . exhibits herself and her person . . . in African displays too exotic for me to talk about."

Mantle: ". . . Josephine sings unusual songs. I suspect they are descriptive songs, but I could not catch the words, so I cannot tell you as to that. . . . It just goes to prove that fifty million French press agents can be over-enthusiastic."

Brown: "Josephine Baker, whose voice sounds gnome-like in the vast spaces of the Winter Garden, is on hand. . . ."

There were others. The nameless reviewer for *Time* magazine sneered, "In sex appeal to jaded Europeans of the jazz-loving type, a Negro wench always has a head start, but to Manhattan theatregoers last week she was just a slightly buck-toothed young Negro woman whose figure might be matched in any nightclub show, whose dancing and singing could be topped practically anywhere outside France."

Variety weighed in with a left-handed compliment. "Miss Baker cannot sing but sure can wear clothes and roll those eyes."

Compliments like that could give a star a headache.

If she hadn't already got one from reading the accolades accorded Fanny Brice. "Fanny is marvellous. . . ." "It is her evening. . . ." "Miss Brice . . . is given many a chance to bring her delicious mimicry, her occasionally crossing eyes . . . and her knees that often are not on speaking terms with one another to skits and songs which gain enormously because of her ever-hilarious presence."

Josephine had once got such raves for *her* crossed eyes and *her* rubber knees; she must have wondered if God was playing a joke on her.

The *Amsterdam News* reported that Josephine had told friends she regretted having come back to the States "because of the hostile attitude of the white public here." And not just the white public, either. "Harlem observers feel the French star's style of work is outmoded," the paper added, noting that Josephine *had* opened in the *Follies,* "despite the rumor that she had been dropped from the cast."

It came close to being more than a rumor. Maude Russell was working with Fats Waller's band at the Loew's State Theater when representatives of the Shubert office approached her. "They wanted a replacement for Josephine because she wasn't going over," Maude says, "and I had opened on a Monday and got a beautiful write-up in the paper, so they came looking for me on Tuesday.

"I said, 'What happened to Miss Baker?' They said she was acting up and they were fixing to get rid of her. At that time, nobody wanted to see a colored girl being twirled around with four white boys and dressed up like a queen. All those people were saying, 'She's black, trying to be white, why don't she go on and be her original self like she was in *Shuffle Along,* when she was stickin' her fanny out and looking ugly?' But that same day, they had a conference with her and patched things up. I don't know whether she ever knew they had talked to me. I never told her."

Fanny Brice denied that she had threatened to resign if Josephine stayed in the cast. "I have never snubbed a performer in my whole life," she said. Maybe so, but Balanchine witnessed one unpleasant scene. "We were sitting at a run-through, Larry Hart, Josephine, Gertrude Niesen, Fanny Brice—she really didn't like Josephine—and Josephine said something in French. 'Ah, you nigger,' Fanny Brice said, 'why don't you talk the way your mouth was born?' "

Fred de Cordova, the movie director who would in time become producer of *The Tonight Show Starring Johnny Carson,* stage-managed the *Follies.* "I have the belief," he told me, choosing his words with tact, "that there was no particular cordiality between Fanny and your mother."

Offstage, Josephine retreated to the safety of her lavish dressing room, where walls and ceiling were draped with sky-blue satin (the beloved blue of Clara Smith's feather boa) and her feet rested on a white fur rug. "Next time my brother and I worked the Cotton Club," Fayard Nicholas says, "we made *our* room all blue."

One night, after finishing her own show at Loew's State, Maude Russell went to see Josephine in her dressing room. "She had changed into a beautiful blue outfit with a chiffon bottom, real frilly, and she sat there like a madonna, and when I walked in, she smiled sweetly.

"I said, 'Girl, you are something else.' She said, 'You liked it? They don't seem to be taking to it here.' I said, 'If you had come here and they'd said you was a Moroccan or somebody, they would have accepted you to the hilt. But everybody in the world knows who Josephine Baker is now. My God, how does it feel to be a big star?' And she said, 'You get used to it.'

"She was so different from the days when she was giggly, and falling over, now she was so elegant. She shook my hand, no hug, and I tried to talk about the old days, but she just cut that right off, she said, 'France is very beautiful and fascinating,' but she didn't really make any conversation, and she didn't offer me nothing, so I didn't stay but a minute."

Pepito was gone now, and Josephine blamed him for her troubles. Why hadn't he negotiated a better contract? Why hadn't he let her quit this disaster of a show before it was too late?

Maybe he just got tired of sailing against the wind. He couldn't protect Josephine from her own hardheadedness, and he couldn't protect either one of them from snide comments in the tabloids. For a proud man, it was hard to read, "Her major diversion is heckling the dapper and harried pencil-mustached fellow who says he is an Italian count and to whom she is married."

Jo Bouillon, Josephine's last husband, insisted that she left "no further written account of this period of her life, nor would she talk about it. This was typical of her wish to suppress anything that wasn't a personal victory. . . . Her failure to conquer New York in the *Follies* . . . barred her from a future in Hollywood."

Indeed, when Josephine came to New York, Hollywood was very much on her mind. And she was on Hollywood's mind. The buzz was everywhere. She had been offered a major role in *The Green Pastures,* she had been offered a starring role in a movie with Paul Robeson. But after her reviews came out, the movie people's courtship of her ceased. (Fortunately for her *amour-propre,* producers of stage musicals were less fickle. Ichizo Kobayashi, known as the Ziegfeld of Japan, was wild to have her do a production in one of his theaters—he said she was the best musical comedy actress he had ever seen—and though Josephine wouldn't commit herself, she did say she thought Japan would be a nice place to work.)

When Pepito came back to Paris, his friend Arys Nissotti (who had produced *Zou Zou*) was shocked by his appearance; he was jaundiced and seemed fragile. Nissotti attributed this to heartbreak. "Instead of returning to Le Vésinet," he said, "Abatino moved into a hotel room on the rue de Marignan. I persuaded him to see my doctor because he complained of constant stomach pains. Immediately after the consultation, I received a call from my physician. 'Your friend is dying of cancer.' "

Nissotti never told Pepito; neither did the doctor.

Upon returning from America, Pepito had sent a postcard to Miki Sawada, by then back in Tokyo. "The business between Josephine and me will be liquidated through common accord," he wrote, "and each of us will go his new road in life. A thousand kisses to Emi. Pepito." The postcard had a picture of the Place de la Concorde taken in the early morning before the traffic starts; the obelisk stands lonely in the square beside the Seine. Did he choose it because it reflected his own sadness, or am I only being fanciful?

Stanley Rayburn, one of the Shubert officials who had signed Josephine's contract, was now acting as her manager, though she scarcely knew him. He stood beside her when she announced that she was opening a nightclub on the site of Barbara Hutton's old town house at 125 East Fifty-fourth Street. During the day, the place was a restaurant called Le Mirage; late at night it would become Chez Joséphine.

Frank Cerutti owned Le Mirage. "I was eleven years old when Josephine came to the club," his daughter Doris says. "On the opening night, a friend of hers gave her a baby pig. We kept him in the basement, and Josephine took him back with her to France.

"To me, she was a fascinating woman. I remember one night my father came home and said that an admirer had given her a brand-new Rolls-Royce! It was parked right outside!

"At each table in the club, there was a glass figurine of Josephine in her famous bananas costume. She was wonderful with children, but she kept telling me, 'You cannot come to see me, you cannot come.' "

Doris's sister, Anita, almost sneaked a look. "I was thirteen, and my father seated me at his table and said, 'I want you to be very quiet, at any moment Josephine will come and perform.' The room went dark, Josephine came upstairs from the kitchen carrying the white baby pig and wearing this gown that had to have cost a few thousand dollars, even in those days. Magnificent. She said hello to everyone and introduced the pig, and then came back to my father's table and said I had to leave the room. 'Frank, I will not perform in front of the children.' So that's as close as I came to seeing her nightclub act."

And no wonder. At Chez Joséphine, the star danced (in a number staged by Balanchine) the way she wasn't permitted to dance at the Winter Garden. She worked almost naked, flanked by two white men who maneuvered around her in a wildly suggestive adagio. And the press, which had seemed to turn on her, was beguiled again. "The Baker bumps got going," wrote journalist Cecilia Ager, "in a costume which amazed even her press agent."

Snippets from other nightclub columns:

"She works at high tension from midnight until past 3.A.M. . . ."

"She, if anyone, was the personification of that mad, pre-depression night life which put the gay in Paree for most Americans. . . . You who are homesick for Babylon, vintage 1928, may find an echo in East Fifty-fourth Street."

"In the right setting, Miss Baker is a bewitching performer, and the informality of a supper club is just the setting she wants."

These were reviews a girl could paper her room with. Now she was able to show what she could do when she was in charge, she could even wear the fabulous gowns she had brought from France.

She was once again working two shows a night, this time hating the theater, enjoying the club, and the presence of celebrities at the front tables. The Count de Gramont came, and Cole Porter and Fred Astaire, and Paul Robeson. Years later, Stanley Rayburn said Josephine had not wanted "colored patronage." "What few colored people did come were seated as far back in the rear as possible. She never mixed with them. . . . She wanted to be among white people."

The singer Dick Campbell disagrees. Campbell played in *Hot Chocolates on Broadway,* he played the Savoy Ballroom, and when I interviewed him, he was eighty-eight years old. "Colored people just didn't have the money," he says. "I went there once, it was costly. And except for Birdland, black people didn't go to downtown clubs much. They stayed in Harlem, they went to Small's, and the Nest."

In May 1936, Haile Selassie lost his throne, Mussolini was decorated by his king for service to the "Fascist Fatherland," Robert E. Sherwood's antiwar play, *Idiot's Delight* (on Broadway with the Lunts), won the Pulitzer Prize, and Paul Derval of the *Folies-Bergère* showed up in Josephine's dressing room at the Winter Garden. He had been out front. "They don't give you much of a break, do they?" he said.

He asked if she wanted to be in his next show, to open in October. "I threw my arms around his neck," she said.

"I sat down in a white satin chair," he recalled, "whereupon Josephine began to scream. . . . I assumed that she was just getting worked up for her usual outrageous salary demands. . . . As it turned out, she was having a fit because I had sat on top of her chihuahua."

They worked out the deal at Chez Joséphine, in the wee hours of the morning. The star made her own contract. (When she returned to Paris, she told Maurice Bataille how proud she was. "It's a good deal, a fortune.")

Since one of the stipulations in the new contract was that she could choose the people she wanted to work with, she chose the dancer Paul Meeres (with whom she was also sleeping) to costar in the Folies-Bergère. A light-skinned West Indian, Meeres, like Jacques Pills, was famous for his "dependable object." Before going onstage, chorus girls used to run into his dressing room and touch it for good luck. Meeres was married, but that had never stopped Josephine, and Meeres's wife, Thelma, left behind, felt apprehensive. "The French women will go mad over my Paul," she said.

Paul Meeres and Josephine sailed on the *Normandie* on May 26, immediately after the *Ziegfeld Follies* closed. (The closing was blamed on Fanny Brice's neuritis, but several people in the cast assured me that Josephine had given Fanny a nervous breakdown.) The minute she hit the deck of the French ship, Josephine felt lighter. In the beauty salon, she found Jean Clement, her old friend and hairdresser; every night she dined at the captain's table, restored to her royal position. Her reckless mother's loss of the family house, Fanny Brice, the cruel theater critics— it had been a bad dream and it was already receding.

Chapter 25

—

ANOTHER HUSBAND, MORE LOVERS, AND SEX, SEX, SEX

"She knew I was gay but she had to possess you"

$\mathcal{B}$ack in her beloved Paris, she was surprised to find herself lonely. "Without Pepito," she observed, "Le Beau Chêne was an empty shell."

"He had been so much part of her life," says Maurice Bataille. "Like a shadow. She asked me to come and stay at Beau Chêne. In the day, she kept herself busy going to the Folies-Bergère, getting on with the rehearsals for the new show, but at night, she could not be alone.

"She went to call on my mother, dressed in a sober dark-blue suit, and carrying a large bouquet of red roses. She knelt in front of my mother and said, 'Madame, I have the honor to ask you for the hand of your son Maurice.'

"My mother helped her to her feet. 'My little Josephine, it is Maurice you should ask.' And can you imagine? That scenario was repeated four times."

Why hadn't Maurice married Josephine? I put the question, and he shrugged. "I was in no rush, that's all."

While Josephine was begging Madame Bataille for her son, Carrie Martin took a husband without asking anyone's permission. On June 17, 1936, Josephine's mother became Mrs. Tony Hudson in St. Louis. She hadn't even confided her plan to the daughter with whom she shared a house. "My husband went upstairs where Mama lived," Margaret told me, "and she was all dressed up, and she said, 'I'm getting married.' Elmo came back downstairs, astonished. 'Your mother's getting married today!' So then *I* rushed up and she told me, 'It's none of your business.' "

A month after Carrie's latest wedding, Elvira died of old age. Another door had closed. Elvira, the little slave girl with the long silky hair, was gone, and with her, the secrets of her blood. "Maybe there was some Blackhawk Indian in my grandmother," Richard told me. "But she always said her family had struggled on the desert, and from that I thought she was African."

Beau Chêne without Pepito, St. Louis without Elvira, neither place would ever again be the same for Josephine.

She now became even more obsessed with having a baby. "Doctor after doctor had told her she could not," says Maurice Bataille, "and my mother finally sent her to a famous gynecologist, Professor Alexandre Couvelaire."

By the time I started researching this book, Alexandre Couvelaire was dead, but I was able to speak with his son, René, a professor of urology. "I met Josephine," he said, "when my father went on vacation and left her my phone number. She called me to Beau Chêne. My father had told me she had a congenital malformation of the uterus and could not conceive a child. He took care of her until the war started, then he destroyed his dossiers because he did not want them to fall into German hands."

She went, says Maurice Bataille, from one medical man to another, some reputable, some quacks. I once said that Josephine had a fairy godmother watching over her cradle. Really, there were two of them, and they could never agree. One said, "You are going to be black"; the other said, "Yes, but I'm going to put some milk in your coffee." One said, "You are going to be a great sex symbol"; the other said, "Yes, but you are not going to be able to bear children."

The sets and costumes for *En Super Folies* were being designed by Michel Gyarmathy, and Josephine told him he could do whatever he liked, as long as she was center stage at all times. And as long as everything was white.

"Michel, you understand, in the North Pole number, I want white snow, white furs, white sled dogs; in the circus number, there should be a white parade; in *The Fairy Dream*, I will be queen of the white country . . ."

He understood. Gyarmathy, a young Hungarian, had first met Josephine in Budapest in 1928. "I was a student at the Beaux-Arts, and she was playing two shows a day, doing some sketches in Hungarian, and doubling every night at the Moulin Rouge cabaret. The Moulin Rouge held a contest for the best poster to announce Josephine, and I won first prize.

"She impressed me very much. She impressed all the Hungarians, because of her hairdo—all glued back, black, polished—and her music and the way she held herself. Women imitated her, they used the Bakerfix. When I met her again eight years later at the Folies-Bergère, she was just back from the *Ziegfeld Follies*, where she had not done well.

"She was beautiful and wanted to forget that she was a woman of color. She did her hair like the Parisian women, long and curly, wore light makeup. . . . She wanted to be married to a white man . . . she did not want to know that her color played a great part in her success at that time."

Josephine worked hard in rehearsals, but she also threw her weight around. No other artist could have his name printed as large as hers in programs or on posters for *En Super Folies*, all publicity would revolve around her, and she could fire whom she liked.

"By now," Gyarmathy says, "Josephine's talent was not disputable, she shone in the sky of international stars. She no longer thanked . . . her audience with words, she threw kisses with those admirable hands, long, narrow, supple, capable, and she was good to everyone she worked with—except the too talented ones and the ones with no talent. There she was exactly like all the other stars, including Mistinguett. For Miss, the ideal partner was the partner who served her well but wasn't noticed."

For some reason, Josephine took Gyarmathy for a soulmate, confessing her deepest anxieties. "You see, Michel, I do not like myself deep inside. And you will understand me because you are Jewish, and the skin of a Jew is as easy to recognize as the skin of a black, so I know you hate your skin, and at the same time want to claim justice for your brothers."

This was news to Michel. That there were black Jews, white Jews, brown and yellow Jews, and their skins were not colored by their religious beliefs had never dawned on Josephine, who was convinced of what she was saying. Again, she told him her father was a Spanish Jew—this was a story she came back to with great regularity—so there was double persecution in her history. "I would like to be white," she said, "and go to crusade for those who are black. Michel, I'm talking to you, Michel . . ."

Weary of these intense and sometimes lunatic confidences, Michel would try to steer the talk in another direction. "Josephine, I have a beautiful white fox cape for you to wear in the North Pole sketch . . ."

En Super Folies provided Josephine with two fine dancing partners—not only Paul Meeres, but Frédéric Rey, a young man who had been smuggled out of Vienna without a passport when Mistinguett hid him in a wardrobe trunk.

Fred Rey, Gyarmathy recalled, "was making all the girls lovesick, but they despaired. He was not eating that kind of meat."

"Josephine knew I was gay," Rey says, "but she did not care: I had to sleep with her. Since we were dancing together almost in the nude, I guess it made her feel better. She had to possess you. When we danced, she let herself go with total abandon, so she had to know her partner well. Once I slept with her, we were good friends, and it never happened again. She was half that way herself, or at least she had the soul of a gay person."

On September 21, two weeks after the opening, Pepito died.

"The last time I saw him," said André Rivollet, "was in the pink of a spring morning, near the Parc Monceau. He was gaunt, coughing, shabby-looking, no brilliantine in his hair . . . ruined, perhaps, after a difficult tour in America. Racial laws had kept them apart; she stayed in Harlem while he strutted about in a classy hotel on Fifth Avenue. They became estranged and he tried to cash in.

"As her ex-manager, he claimed damages, demanding the larger part of the fortune she had made with his unselfish help! No talk of love or friendship now. But she showed her gratitude after his death. She asked me to escort her to his funeral service in Neuilly. He had lived there with a beautiful redhead from the Folies. Flanked by two lines of chorus girls in mourning, I walked behind the widow-in-title, carrying a huge heart of red roses that I laid on the coffin.

"Josephine mourned with dignity. She glanced with pity across the wreaths at her white-skinned substitute. Being romantic and possessive, she decided she wanted his body and would have a marble mausoleum built for him in his native Sicily. It would be as large as a Renaissance palace, it would be sparkling as a show at the Casino! Meanwhile, the coffin stayed in a drawer of the crypt of the church in Neuilly. A temporary resting place that almost became eternal."

For some months after Pepito's funeral, Maurice Bataille told me, if he happened to be driving Josephine within three blocks of the church at Neuilly, she would start to scream. "I don't want to go so near Pepito, he has the evil eye on me."

Anna Sosenko, musician, producer, and manager of the singer Hildegarde ("I created Hildegarde!") knew Josephine and Pepito in the thirties. "He was the brain," she says. "He did the dirty work, and the minute she thought she didn't need him anymore, kaput. I don't think she felt the loss of Pepito until she had to fight on her own, until she had managers to whom she was just another act.

"These people always think everything came to them naturally, but nothing comes naturally. The talent is there, but you have to get somebody who can nourish it. That happens once in a lifetime if you're lucky. When Josephine had problems at the end of her career, nobody could really help her out. She was shrewd, but she did not have vision, this came from him. She was impulsive, first she did it, then she thought about it. I think she had as much understanding as you *can* have when the whole wide world is telling you how great you are, but I think a good part of her died when Pepito died."

It wasn't until April 1937 that Josephine wrote to Miki Sawada in Japan to say she was at the Folies, having an "enormous success," and adding that Pepito had "passed away. No need to tell you I was much distressed, you know he was only 37. . . . He had a liver cancer. You see that in any case we are not a big thing on this earth, and it is useless to grieve oneself or complicate one's existence as we do. But let's not talk about it anymore, the subject is so sad."

In the next sentence, she was on to other matters. Beau Chêne was marvelous, she was going to make another film, and right this minute, "while I'm writing to you, I have a little rabbit on my knees. . . . Here, everybody is getting ready for the Exposition."

The Exposition Internationale opened in May, foreshadowing things to come. Albert Speer had designed the German Pavilion, over which a

Nazi flag billowed. Parisians could not have guessed that within three years, all public buildings in the city would be flying the swastika.

Josephine's association with Pepito had not, as it developed, ended cleanly; all her possessions were still in his name, and it took a while for her to regain houses, jewels, the Bakerfix royalties, the music publishing company. She had a good lawyer, but even so, she had to give a portion of her fortune to Pepito's sister. Oddly, she harbored no resentment. After Pepito died, she wrote to Christina Scotto saying, "You are the only family I have."

That she had no sense of money had been proven beyond a doubt in New York, when she signed the contract with Paul Derval and told herself how clever she had been. She was to get half the box office take, true enough, but out of that, she had to pay salaries for cast and musicians, along with various other production costs that would have left her next to nothing. Mortified and incensed when she discovered this, she told Derval she would not appear, the services of the good lawyer were once again called into play, and a new contract for *En Super Folies* was negotiated.

A love letter from Josephine to her public was printed in the program. It said she had often sung of her two loves, "My country and Paris," but now she wanted the audience to understand, "My country, it is Paris, and Paris, it is my country."

She had cut the United States out of the equation.

But she was still proud of the accomplishments of fellow Americans. When Leslie Gaines, a dancer who was one of The Three Dukes, opened (with Chevalier) at the Casino de Paris, Josephine not only attended the premiere, she climbed up to the Dukes' dressing room. "Here comes this gorgeous lady," said Gaines (nicknamed Bubber). "And she said, 'I'm Josephine Baker, I'm at the Folies-Bergère, and you'll never know how you thrilled me.'

"We're looking at her, we don't know what to say except, 'Oh thank you, Miss Baker,' and she says, 'I want you to come around to the Folies-Bergère.'

"She was so warm and human, and my God, there was nobody in France the people loved more than her. Josephine was the Frenchmen's mistress."

An unpunctual mistress, who was always late for her own show.

"Sometimes she had a new love or something else on her mind," says Michel Gyarmathy.

In the second half of *En Super Folies,* she appeared in a number called "The Marvelous Jungle," seated on a papier-mâché elephant painted jade and gold. Once the applause faded, she got off the elephant and drifted down the stairs. There always had to be a reason to use those stairs. "But one day," Gyarmathy recalls, "she was so late that she jumped on the elephant in her street clothes. After dismounting, she came down the staircase very dignified, starting to undress, and handing her clothes to chorus kids all the way down. They would run off and bring her costume back to her piece by piece. It was so beautiful I wanted to keep it in the show, have her do it every day.

"Derval said no. 'Or she will *never* show up on time.' "

During the run, Mistinguett would sometimes visit Derval's office. "How is the show doing?" she would ask. "How is—I forget her name—that colored girl, my substitute?" Josephine retaliated with innocent sarcasm, always referring publicly to Mistinguett's "long" career and her brave beginnings "back in 1895."

Josephine was then singing at the top of her form—her records were selling well—and since she never liked to go right home after the show, she agreed to open another club. Jean Merlin, director of Paris's Hôtel Château Frontenac, had made her the offer; the club—called Gerny's Cabaret—was in the basement of the hotel. It had been run by a man named Louis Leplée, who discovered Edith Piaf singing in the street and, moved by the scrawny young girl's voice, hired her. He also changed her name from Edith Gassion to Edith Piaf—"like the Paris sparrow."

For her opening at Gerny's, Piaf had worn a black dress knitted by her sister, and stared out nervously at the chic audience as Louis Leplée introduced her. "From the street to the cabaret, here is La Môme Piaf."

The audience didn't know whether to laugh or cry, said Piaf's biographer, Simone Berteaut. "Her poor hair looked like a bad wig, her lipstick so red, her face so white, her hands shaking, the badly made black dress on her small body."

After she finished her first song, there was a long silence. "It was painful," Piaf remembered, "it grabbed me by the throat. At that moment, people started to applaud, it was like everything breaking, like rain on a drum. In my corner, I started to cry. . . . I heard the voice of Louis saying, 'You've got them, La Môme.' "

But Piaf's world was the streets—pimps, gangsters, soldiers, sailors—and it came to Louis Leplée's door and ended his life. "Leplée was gay, and both he and Edith had the same taste for rough-looking men," says Jean Merlin's wife, Odette, "and they killed him."

Gerny's Cabaret closed. But Jean Merlin had started thinking about the tourists who would be coming from all over the world to the Expo, and that's when the club became the latest Chez Joséphine.

Its star was more skittish than ever. "Some nights," Odette Merlin says, "she would just come and take a look at the room, always very crowded, and if she did not like the people, she would have Jean call Chez O'dett, and ask Piaf to come and sing in her stead. Can you imagine how surprised all those chic people were when Edith showed up with her stained little dress? And when, at the end, she would take off her black beret and go from table to table passing the hat?"

The night the journalist Pierre de Regnier visited, Josephine was on, and he loved it. "Everything is pink, the mirrors, the leather, the glasses, the lighting." Josephine sang and distributed funny hats. "It amuses the guests. . . . At 4 A.M. when a few customers start to leave . . . you can find Josephine doing washing in her dressing room."

"She would wash Jacques Constant's dirty laundry, his socks, underwear, shirts, in the sink of her bathroom at Chez Joséphine," says Manouche (a beauty who became the mistress of Paul Carbone, the Al Capone of France, and bore him a son).

A successful stage director, Jacques Constant was, according to Manouche, "a Don Juan with a nice tail. He had slept with our Josephine Nationale, as we called her, and she was in love with him. When she was doing his laundry, she was a very big star, but she never fully understood that. At the same time, she was flirting with Jean Lion, the good-looking, blond, blue-eyed one that she would marry later on. Josephine loved to do *partouzes*, orgies."

I've thought a lot about Josephine and her sexual conquests. Sleep with me, show me you accept me, and after that, maybe we can be friends. She used her body as a weapon against the world because it was the only thing she trusted, it had got her where she was. But scrub the makeup off the mythical Josephine of the stage, daring, modern, free, the one feminists claim as their own, and underneath, you find the little girl from St. Louis who had so much to prove. They can say what they like about her voracious carnal appetites; I think the primary object of the game was power.

She played a different—nonsexual—power game with poor Paul Derval, and he always lost. Once, she canceled a Sunday matinee, using illness as an excuse. "She was with me in her apartment at avenue Bugeaud," says Maurice Bataille. "That apartment she kept for herself." Like her first hotel room in Montmartre, the ceiling was mirrored; so were the walls. "That Sunday," Maurice told me, half embarrassed, half amazed, "we had sex nine times."

A week later, Josephine again failed to show up at the theater. She phoned Derval to say she was in the country, had shot a fox, and would send the fur to Madame Derval. "I hope she'll like it." She also said she would return in two days. For another five thousand francs.

"She came back," Michel Gyarmathy said, "with her ménagerie of monkeys, goats, dogs, and said, 'On top of all this, I have a zebra.' We were relieved to see she'd had him flattened before bringing him into her dressing room."

Made into rugs, or living and breathing, she adored animals "the way humans adore them," says Gyarmathy, "making them prisoners of our caresses.

"One night, we couldn't find the most malicious of her monkeys. As the curtain rose, Josephine, all in feathers, walked out onto the apron of the stage to explain to the theatergoers that the show could not start until we had found her baby ouistiti. Then we saw the orchestra fall to their knees, searching under their seats, calling *'Petit, petit, petit.'* It looked like a gathering of Muslims at prayer in the mosque. When at last the darling was found, hanging onto the neck of a terrified lady in the audience, the revue began in a thunderous atmosphere."

The company didn't have to put up with Josephine's animals for long; during one of her disappearances, she had signed a contract to appear in London in December.

Derval couldn't believe his ears. "My dear Josephine, you have no right to leave me, I have a contract, you owe me two more months of work—to be exact, nine weeks."

She was the injured one. Did he want her to break her word to the people in London? He gave up.

Jean Lion, the flame with whom Maurice Bataille was then sharing her, rode horses, flew planes, hunted. But he was not, as reports had it, a millionaire. His company, begun in 1935, consisted of three partners: Maurice Sachou, Albert Ribac, and himself. They were sugar brokers.

"We were the three of us childhood friends," Albert Ribac says. "We each put in five thousand francs to begin the business, and we made good money. We had a plane, we had American cars, but that's all. Jean was not a rich industrialist. We met Josephine at her cabaret in the Hôtel Château Frontenac, Josephine and Jean liked each other, and it flattered Jean.

"One day, the three of us partners were in our office on avenue Matignon, and Jean said, 'What would you say if I married Josephine Baker?' 'You would be a fool,' we said. 'What's the need? You already sleep with her.'

"But Jean had political ambitions, and he thought Josephine's popularity could help him."

On November 30, 1937, they were married. Only a week before, Josephine had spent the night with Maurice Bataille, and in the morning, he confronted her. "I've heard you are going to marry Jean, is it true?" She laughed. "Oh no, that's gossip for the journalists."

She had dissembled as well with André Rivollet. He and his mother had spent many hours "as a family" at Beau Chêne, where "poplars, privets, spindle-trees shadowed white statues. . . . I can see Josephine running to her bedroom. She hummed from her balcony, and one day roses landed at my feet. They smelled of musk, cedar, and ambergris. She had sprayed them with Oriental scents! Josephine caressed my mother, signed her letters, 'Your black daughter.'

"One day a friend said, 'Congratulations, I heard of your forthcoming marriage. At a cocktail party yesterday, Josephine Baker announced, "I marry Rivollet." ' I thought he was kidding me. A few days later, my mother asked me to take her to the Folies for the first time in her life. During intermission, we went to Josephine's dressing room. Josephine was peeling off her false eyelashes, and she invited my mother to sit. A bell sounded. Time to change costumes. I moved discreetly into the corridor. My mother stayed in the dressing room, making small talk.

"I'm a few steps away from the stage, naked women brushing past me with fragrant thighs. Suddenly Josephine appeared beside me, a goddess with huge eyes, tiara, gold nipples. 'Wait!' she said. 'I am going to ask your mother for your hand right now.'

" 'Look, Joe,' I said, 'you'll miss your entrance, we'll talk later.' I tried to break free, but she held me with her gold nails until the stage manager pulled her away. . . . The discipline of the music hall put a stop to her attack.

"Where had that proposal come from? I had the explanation a few weeks later. An anonymous phone call, a woman's voice saying, 'Josephine Baker gets married tomorrow!' And the voice adding that I should use my influence to stop the madness, saying the future groom's only virtue was his good looks.

"I was puzzled, and ran to the Folies that evening."

Rivollet asked Josephine about the rumor, and she denied it. "She pulls her kimono around her body . . . tears fill her eyes. 'You know all about my life, how could you believe . . . if I were to marry anyone, it would be you.' "

The next day, at lunch in Neuilly, he heard the news from Jean Prouvost, the owner of *Paris-Soir*. "Josephine Baker got married!"

"I was hurt in my pride," Rivollet admitted, but gave himself reasons for Josephine's action. "She had searched high and low for a white husband. Too many potential lovers, not one potential husband. Eventually I realized that she believed she would be legitimized if she married a white man."

On their wedding day, Josephine and Lion arrived in his village of Crèvecoeur-le-Grand to traditional sounds of greeting—hunters firing shotguns, percussion caps being thrown under the feet of horses and cows and geese, not to mention the more modern sounds of photographers' shutters clicking and reporters yelling out questions.

Jean Lion's parents were Jewish, they were bourgeois, they had not harbored dreams of their beloved son's marrying a black woman, but they were dutifully present for the ceremony, and the entire population of the village cheered the couple as they made their way into the city hall.

He was twenty-seven, she was thirty-one; Paul Derval and Georges Lion (Jean's brother) were the principal witnesses. On the wedding license, Josephine gave her parents' names as Arthur Baker and Carrie McDonald. The mayor of the village, Benjamin Schmidt, pronounced himself delighted by the goings-on. "Heretofore, the prominence of our village has been confined to a fifteenth-century château and our famous black chicken hatcheries," he said. "Hereafter, it will be known as the village La Belle Baker chose for her wedding."

In a sable coat, she became a French bride, and a French citizen. (Or so it seemed. Since, as far as anybody knows, she was still legally married to Billy Baker, this latest "wedding" to a Frenchman did *not* confer on her the nationality she would claim—and flaunt—from that day forward.) She later told the press that she would be leaving show business, after the upcoming English date. "I have finished with the exotic," she said, "you won't see me dashing around with my pet cheetah any more. Home, children . . . those are the things I am looking forward to now. . . . I lived for my public, for the excitement of show life. Now I am a little bit tired, perhaps the time has come for me to say goodbye. Then I shall not be Josephine Baker, just plain Madame Lion."

Not so plain. Jean had exquisite taste, and he brought elegance to Beau Chêne. It had already been furnished expensively, but with flamboyance, Josephine and Pepito being, after all, show people. Now the newlyweds had linens embroidered with gold thread from the house of Noel, and eighteenth-century crystal chandeliers from Baccarat, and servants in white gloves waiting table in the grand dining room where sixty-four people could be seated.

What they did not have was a marriage.

"Jean was the type," Albert Ribac says, "who would get bored with a woman—before Josephine, and *during* Josephine, he was going out with girls, and he would ask me to join them. I would tell him, 'Two is a couple, three is a crowd,' but to be honest, I didn't complain that much because I picked up his crumbs.

"It was not a *grand amour* on Josephine's part either. She was impossible, so was he. He was a *tombeur,* a lady killer, but it was involuntary, I must say, women just fell for him. The atmosphere around them was dreadful, fights, screams, you had to leave."

Maurice Bataille liked Jean Lion, but believes that he spent—in one year—five million francs of Josephine's money. Even the four-carat diamond he gave her on their wedding day had been cut down from a thirty-carat heirloom presented by one of her protectors. Jean said the thirty-carat ring was old-fashioned.

Four days after the wedding, Josephine received her French passport; by December 18, she was performing in London on the first leg of her "farewell" tour. She told one reporter her new husband sent her two letters a day and phoned every afternoon. She told another reporter, "I feel we might be divorced in the next three months." Score one for Albert Ribac.

A macho Frenchman, Jean wanted to make the rules. He kept his own apartment on avenue Victor-Emmanuel, but he moved to Beau Chêne. Now Josephine came home from England to discover her house was often filled with his relatives. She played at domesticity, sitting with

Jean's mother, knitting little garments, Mrs. Willie Wells all over again. She let everyone believe she was pregnant, the girl of the Roaring Twenties tamed at last. Then: "I lost my baby. . . . Mama Lion did her best to comfort me. . . . I wanted to flee, like an animal that hides in the forest to nurse his grief."

"She was never pregnant," says Ribac. "I saw Jean every day, and I would have known it." Even so, newspapers ran with the story. INTERNATIONALLY FAMED DANCER BEARS CHILD FOR WEALTHY WHITE HUSBAND IN PARIS announced the *Amsterdam News*. Josephine never denied that she was a new mother any more than she had denied—until trapped—that she was a new countess; all publicity was good publicity. And anyway, there *was* a baby lion (lowercase *l*) in her life; she had recently christened him at the zoo. Now things would be fine as soon as she could move some of the two-legged Lions out of her house.

She used to come to Blanche Guignery with her woes. "She had lost her gaiety," says Madame Guignery. "She could no longer go around naked, that made her a prisoner in her own house, and she couldn't run things because Jean's mother was in charge. There were sometimes twenty people, mostly Jean's family, living at Beau Chêne." One of them, Jean's brother Georges, became Josephine's financial adviser. "He would tell me, 'She's impossible,' " Albert Ribac says.

Nonetheless, for a short time, Jean and Josephine were seen everywhere together, this amazingly good-looking couple at the races and at supper clubs, entertained and entertaining. Lydia Jones, then living in Paris with her husband, Ed, and their two children, remembers Jean Lion as "very elegant. Josephine took him away from the actress Simone Simon. But she kept pestering him all the time, I think she really drove him away by pestering him."

In her unhappiness with her new family, Josephine escaped the only way she knew, to her old family, the public. She went back on the road. So much for a farewell tour. Tony Clyde, a dancer who had been with her in *En Super Folies,* was in her troupe. "We were out for fifteen months, and they were very agreeable. She wanted all of us to sound very French, so she changed my name to Gaston Lefort, which I did not like, but agreed to.

"I was her *porteur,* and with her high heels and feathers, she was taller than me. We were sold out every night, and Josephine got not only a big salary but a percentage of the box office.

"In Norway, we couldn't play—someone from the royal family had died, and some of our numbers were too daring. In one, Josephine and I were almost nude, and her gold G-string was minimal, but in my whole artistic life, I never saw a body as fabulous as hers."

For South America, Josephine auditioned potential dance partners on the stage of the Folies-Bergère. (The long-suffering Derval gave her the use of the hall.) "It was like a slave auction," said a dancer who used the stage name Chalin. "We had to show our muscles, she came onstage and poked our bodies like you examine a cow in a livestock auction."

She hired Chalin, but refused to give his dancer girlfriend a part in the show. The troupe's departure from the Gare d'Orsay was marked by an army of journalists, and Jean Lion presented Josephine with a wreath of violets as tall as she was. Then the train took the performers to Bordeaux, from which port they sailed on the *Massillia*.

Chalin proved indifferent to Josephine's sexual advances, even after she summoned him to her cabin, where she was lying naked on the floor. "Look at my body," she said, "all the world is in love with that body, why are you so arrogant?" Spurned, she was "very nasty. But she still wanted me to teach her some new steps. She was not a good student, she danced her own way.

"We played in three casinos in Brazil with a lot of success. Then Jean Lion came to visit her, and they had a big fight. Josephine had her household statements sent from France, and she discovered that Jean had charged her account for the wreath of violets at the Gare d'Orsay. She called him a thief, and he left."

On February 1, still in Brazil, Josephine filed for divorce.

Chapter 26

—

JOSEPHINE GOES TO WAR

"I am ready to give the Parisians my life"

She came home to Paris in July 1939, and found change everywhere. Posters appeared on the walls: "Because of the aggressive attitude of the German government, the government of the Republic has declared a general mobilization. You will answer with courage, discipline, and composure the call of the fatherland in danger."

With the situation in Europe deteriorating, Henri Varna's plans to put on a Brazilian extravaganza—for which Josephine had brought him two new South American dances—were abandoned. On September 1, the German army (having annexed Austria and—with the help of Hungary—dismembered Czechoslovakia) marched into Poland. Two days later, Britain and France declared war against Germany. France believed it was protected by the Maginot line, a system of fortifications that included underground bunkers, munitions dumps, power stations, and stretched along the country's northeastern frontier, from Switzerland to Montmédy.

Hitler's generals, who had not put their faith in fixed defenses, but moved armies and matériel with lightning speed, would eventually run around the Maginot line, but for nine months of the *drôle de guerre* (the phony war), they made no move to do so. Their blitzkrieg roared through Norway and Denmark, lulling France into a false sense of security. The French, says historian Louis L. Snyder, "apparently anesthetized by Hitler's war of nerves, even demobilized some of their troops and sent them home."

It was during this period that Chevalier and Josephine first went to the Maginot line to entertain the troops. For him, who had done all this before, in the *Grande Guerre*, it was déjà vu, but to Josephine it was new and intoxicating.

Chevalier, claiming to be the bigger star, wanted to sing last, so Josephine agreed to take the stage first. The problem was that, having taken it, she seemed determined to keep it. She sang on and on, the soldiers cheering raucously. Many of them had never been to Paris, they were from villages that didn't have electricity—there was no electricity in my village in 1943—and even if they had heard of Josephine Baker, they had never seen her. So while his co-star hogged the glory, Chevalier (at fifty-one, a father figure to that audience) waited his turn. When he finally got it, he muttered, "Josephine, you too will age."

Toward the end of October, Henri Varna, Josephine, Chevalier, and Nita Raya (Chevalier's lady friend, a Jewish singer of Rumanian birth) put together a new show at the Casino de Paris. It was called, aptly, *Paris-London*. Blackouts, curfews, rationing were already in effect, and Varna wanted to do something cheerful for the boys—English as well as French—who would be coming to Paris on forty-eight-hours' leave.

The theater was always full. Josephine's final song, "Mon Coeur Est un Oiseau des Îles," was the prettiest Vincent Scotto had ever given her. (He wrote it for *Fausse Alerte*, the movie she was shooting during the hours when she wasn't at the theater. Though *Fausse Alerte* was set during the phony war, it was a comedy.)

When Josephine sang that her heart was an island bird, she could make a soldier believe she was singing only to him, believe he would go back to the front with the kiss of Josephine on his lips. That was her magic. She had seen East St. Louis burning, but from across the river; now she was in the thick of the action, France was at war, and she was ready to go all the way for her adopted country.

The country itself seemed more ambivalent. It was a strange time; except for the soldiers in the street, you could have pretended everything was normal. "In 1914," Louis Snyder wrote, "the French had gone to war in an outburst of patriotic enthusiasm. In 1939, they answered the call to arms like somnambulists, without spirit. . . . Sit it out. Nothing would happen. We French won't be bled again . . . that vulgar madman across the Rhine would stop his nonsense sooner or later."

Much of France lived with illusions, but Jacques Abtey had lost his. As an officer working in the Deuxième Bureau, the French military intelligence service at the beginning of the war, his job was to enlist patriots he wouldn't have to pay, since he had no budget to hire professionals. The newcomers would be working for *la gloire et la patrie,* not le cash.

"It was a delicate situation," he says. "We needed people—we called them Honorable Correspondents—who could travel around without attracting attention, and who would be able to report what they saw. One of them, Daniel Marouani, the most successful theatrical agent in France, was a Tunisian Jew, and he is the one who suggested Josephine Baker. He said, 'She is more French than the French.' "

The French secret service rarely recruited women, but Abtey and Marouani (who knew Josephine, and set up the meeting) went to Beau Chêne. They walked up the winding driveway, and heard somebody call hello. "Then she appeared above the bushes," Abtey remembered, "a banged-up old hat on her head, one hand holding a rusted can full of snails, which she was collecting to feed her ducks. . . .

"A maître d' in white jacket led us toward the salon, where a fire was burning and a bottle of champagne was waiting . . . I found myself in front of a real patriot. 'France made me what I am,' she said. 'The Parisians gave me their hearts, and I am ready to give them my life. . . .' "

For her part, Josephine was delighted to find Abtey young, blond, blue-eyed, the Nordic type she fancied. "She walked us to the door two hours later," he said. "Night had fallen, it was cool, and the open can was now empty of the snails, who had gone back to their bushes."

Soon, Josephine informed Abtey that she had available to her two promising sources of information. Renzo Sawada was by now the Japanese ambassador to France, and she knew the family very well. Not only that, but she had good connections with Italian diplomats. (Her support for Mussolini had guaranteed such connections, though she didn't feel called upon to mention this small error in judgment.) She could go to receptions at the Japanese and Italian embassies, and report back what had been said. Poor Miki Sawada. Sisterly devotion was swallowed up in Josephine's zeal to prove herself a patriot.

"Sometimes," Abtey said, "she would write along her arms, and in the palm of her hand, the things she heard. I told her this was dangerous, but she laughed. 'Oh, nobody would think I'm a spy.' "

Almost at once, she had become Abtey's lover, as well as his student. "She was not a crazy sex-obsessed person," he says. "We could go one or two weeks without having sex." At first, he worried about whether she was calm enough for intelligence work. Once, out driving, she was trying to tell him something she had heard at the Italian embassy, and she got so nervous she lost control of the car.

As 1939 wound down, she was frantically busy. She had her assignments from the Deuxième Bureau, she was filming *Fausse Alerte*, every night she played at the Casino, and every Saturday afternoon she did a radio show, singing in French and English for the soldiers at the front.

Then it was Christmas again. Josephine had a secretary come to Beau Chêne to send records and pictures to her four thousand "godsons of war," and to help answer mail. One letter arrived from Maurice Blech, the blond boy who had seen *La Revue Nègre* every night of its first week (the boy she had taken to bed), and she answered it. "You are the last person I was expecting to hear from," she wrote, going on to tell about her broadcasts, her Red Cross duties ("I'm Chief of Entertainment for Aviators"), her new animals. "Two little white mice that each gave birth to five baby mice . . . they look exactly like miniature little pigs. Thank you for asking me to be godmother of your unit, I accept with joy. Unfortunately, I cannot come and visit you for the moment because our revue at the Casino will last until the end of May. After that, I think I will start again a tour of army bases. . . . I kiss you all affectionately. Your godmother who loves you."

Jean Lion was now at the front, and Josephine had a new lover, Jean Menier, heir to a chocolate fortune. Their engagement made the front pages, though Josephine's divorce from Lion would not become final until April 1941. Menier gave her a ring, and went off join his regiment.

Early in 1940, Jean Lion was seriously wounded, and Josephine asked Albert Ribac to take her to see him. "She cried all during the trip," Ribac says. "Both ways. She was screaming, 'My hero!' As with all great actresses, she was fantastic, capricious, and a pain in the neck."

On May 10, the Germans hit the Low Countries all along the western front. The Dutch capitulated in less than a week, the Belgians held out for eighteen days, until King Leopold III ordered his troops to surrender. (In the Cartier shop on rue de la Paix, Leopold's picture was taken out of the window and English Queen Mary's put in its place.) Leopold's decision saved Belgian lives, but put British and French soldiers in jeopardy. "The thunder burst," says Jacques Abtey. "Thunder in Belgium, thunder over the Dutch. It was the end of the funny war on the terraces of Paris cafés."

Paris was filled with refugees fleeing before the Germans. Every night after finishing at the Casino, Josephine ran to a homeless shelter on rue du Chevaleret, and did what she could to comfort new arrivals. In times of crisis she was magnificent; petty selfishness abandoned, she made beds, bathed old people, whispered words of comfort, and kept her eyes and ears open.

Abtey had warned her that vermin—an enemy fifth column—always preceded an invading army, and she took the warning to heart. "One night," said Dominique Gianviti, then one of Abtey's coworkers, "Josephine called us from the shelter and urgently asked us to come. Twenty minutes later, we arrive and find her washing the swollen feet of an old man. 'Monsieur Gianviti,' says Josephine, excusing herself from the old man, 'I regret that I'm not a policeman. There are a lot of suspicious people here. Look at that strong guy, twenty-seven, twenty-eight years old. He should be fighting. And there are two other young ones you should have a look at.'

"A fast examination revealed nothing special. The young men were Belgians who had escaped before the Germans."

Abtey, knowing that worse days were coming, finally told Josephine she had to quit the Casino. "Pack your things and go to the south of France."

She shared this advice with the Guignerys. "She came to see us and said we should get ready to move, the Germans were going to invade and occupy Paris," Blanche Guignery remembers. "My husband was laughing, 'But my dear Josephine, *c'est impossible.*' She asked us to come and help her move everything out of Le Beau Chêne. 'Stones I can replace,' she said, 'a house can be rebuilt, but my souvenirs are irreplaceable.' "

Trucks were loaded. "Armor from the Middle Ages," André Rivollet said. "The gold piano, Japanese ivories, Marie-Antoinette's bed, feather pillows, furniture and linens, everything was piled into vans. Especially linens. Feminine instinct, love for whiteness, a wish for bourgeois security. She was always ecstatic about towels and sheets." (The Guignerys, following her instructions, would send her belongings after her.) Then Josephine, carrying a cage full of parakeets, got a lift to Paris with a young man driving by. All her life, in peace or war, someone would recognize her, stop to pick her up, and take her where she wanted to go.

She stayed a few days at her apartment on avenue Bugeaud. The life of the city seemed still quite civilized. Theaters were operating—there was a comedy by Jean Cocteau at the Bouffes, and the Comédie Française was playing *Cyrano de Bergerac*—and though there were meatless days, and cakeless days, supper clubs were open. The news that French soldiers were dying in the north and the east was terrible, but also made people proud.

Josephine now transferred her business—the affairs she had been trying to conduct by herself since Pepito died—into the hands of faithful old Monsieur Bondon, who was still with Pernod. Then she went to Jean Lion's office, picked up his Packard, and left the city.

It was the first week in June. "I had told Josephine to go south," Jacques says, "but she went southeast." Looking for a house, she eventually reached the village of Cenac. It was château country, three hundred miles from Paris, the farmland of Périgord, where the river Dordogne runs and the earth is rich and black with truffles. The old castles hang over the river, the centuries seem to have passed without touching fields, rocks, forests.

There was even tobacco growing there, like the tobacco of Elvira's youth. She stopped in the shop of the butcher, Guinot, and asked if any of the nearby places was for rent. Madame Guinot said yes, five miles from here. You went along a tortuous little byway, took a bridge across the river, and there in the old stone village of Castelnaud-Fayrac, on top of a hill, was the château Les Mirandes. (Josephine, who couldn't pronounce "r" in the French way, decided to call it the château Les Milandes, which had been its name before the Revolution.)

Driving slowly up the hill along a dirt road, Josephine passed a wood and a little cemetery, so peaceful in the sun that for once she was not frightened by the gravestones. It was like a secret garden, almost welcoming her. She stopped in front of the castle, and Eli Mercier, twenty years old, son of farmers who had been at Les Milandes since 1912, opened the great iron gate for her. It was the seventh of June, 1940, he says. I asked him how he could be so sure, more than fifty years after the fact. Simple, he told me. "Because on the ninth, I was going to war."

The place belonged to a French doctor named Males. He was happy to rent it to Josephine (his American-born wife had already taken their son back to the United States), so the deal was made.

On June 3, the Germans had bombed the outskirts of Paris, damaging the Renault and Peugeot factories, and on June 14, without firing a shot, they entered the city. It was queerly still. Two-thirds of the people had fled.

"Hundreds of thousands of refugees . . . jammed the roads south to Bordeaux for a distance of 400 miles," wrote Louis Snyder. "They used everything that could move—carts, bicycles, taxicabs, trucks, bakery vans, roadsters, even hearses. . . . German pilots in speedy Heinkels roared up and down at tree level over the roads where civilian refugees were trapped and helpless in the traffic jams. Bombs and bullets burst among the automobiles, carts, farm wagons and bicycles, catching humans and horses in a deadly melange of flame and smoke. . . ."

All this Josephine had avoided, thanks to Jacques Abtey. That was the good side of being an Honorable Correspondent.

But Les Milandes grew crowded. Among the cast of characters were Josephine's maid, Paulette, her twenty-two-year-old Polish valet, François (he was later shot by the Germans while carrying messages for the Resistance), an old Belgian couple, Mr. and Mrs. Jacobs, who had met Josephine in the homeless shelter, and any number of Lions. Jean, convalescing from his war wounds, and all his relatives had shown up at the château. Only Albert Ribac, whom they considered a member of the family, was missing. "They were worried," he told me, laughing. "I had foolishly gone off to the war."

The irritated Josephine hauled a mattress up to the attic, and slept on the floor. To further escape her in-laws, she often took the Malaury children, Georges and Georgette, whose father ran the blacksmith shop across the road, to the nearby village of Sarlat. "She spoiled us," says Georgette. "It pleased her to see how ecstatic it made us to climb into her beautiful car. She would do her marketing in Sarlat, and buy us cakes from the *patisserie*."

Josephine, who had lost touch with both Maurice Bataille and Jacques

Abtey, now miraculously found them both again. First, Maurice. Back from the army, he was a guest of his former employees at their house in Beynac, a few miles from Les Milandes. "My mother had gone to stay with Yvonne and Joseph Robin, who had been our cook and butler," he says. "The minute I arrived, Yvonne said, 'You see the château on the hill? Josephine Baker is now living there.' I couldn't believe it. Joseph went up to the château on a bicycle to tell Josephine I was there, and she came right down.

"She said Les Milandes was just like Beau Chêne, Jean Lion and his family had taken over the place. Often, she spent the day with my mother, knitting scarves for soldiers and complaining."

During the second week in June, the French government had moved from Paris to Tours to Bordeaux. (It would settle finally in Vichy.) While the new premier, the eighty-four-year-old Marshal Pétain (who had been the hero of Verdun in World War I), was preparing to sign an armistice with Germany, General Charles de Gaulle, then undersecretary of war, fled to England to head up a government in exile. Condemned as a traitor, he was sentenced to death in absentia, but on June 18, from London, he addressed his countrymen over the radio.

"Whatever happens," he said, "the flame of French resistance must not and shall not die." It was a message many humiliated citizens had longed to hear. De Gaulle was asking them to redeem the country's honor, to fight on from North Africa, and among those who listened, thrilled, was Jacques Abtey. He was at La Courtine—a military camp near the city of Agen—with the archives of the Deuxième Bureau, trying to save not only documents, but also the lives of hundreds of patriots and Honorable Correspondents whose names were in those papers, people "who had risked their skins so France would live."

Unfortunately, de Gaulle's message had not reached all of the French for whom it was intended. "It passed almost unnoticed among most of the population," Abtey says. In mid-July, he learned that Josephine was at Les Milandes, only ninety miles away from him. "I sent a courier to her, and she came to see me in her Packard. I told her about de Gaulle's call—she had not heard it, either—and how I was going to join him if I could find a way to get to England."

Abtey and Josephine spent a few days together at the convent of Bonencontre, near his military base. The nuns had fled, but "we found hospitality there. Three monks and their superior lived with us, their heads in prayer books. And Josephine asked me to obtain exit visas for Jean, his family and friends."

Jean had handed Josephine the passports—twenty of them, her own not among them—with a request that she use her influence to get the visas, and this had made her furious. "I will never forgive him," she told Abtey. "It is a shame for him to be so preoccupied with all those people, and not his wife."

When she came back to Les Milandes with the visas, she hurled them at her husband, threw his suitcase from a second-story window, and showed his family the door.

Toward the end of summer, Jacques Abtey and two fellow officers, a navy man named Emmanuel Bayonne and Joseph Boue, a flier from Brittany, came to hide out at Les Milandes. Josephine was ecstatic. Taking Abtey by the arm, she whispered, "When are we going to join de Gaulle?"

Her question was about to be answered, though Abtey, at that point a frustrated man, didn't know it. "Everywhere," he recalled later, "the Nazis were watched by our agents, their formations identified, their movements noted . . . but none of this information had reached London, our Underground had been cut off from that city since the surrender. We needed to find a means of reestablishing contact with the British Intelligence Service."

This problem was solved when an agent of the Deuxième Bureau arrived at Les Milandes, and asked Abtey if he still wanted "to go to the English. We will get you a false passport, then you will go to Lisbon, and from there you're on your own." (The best way to get in touch with the British was through Portugal, where they had representatives.)

"I had the idea that Josephine Baker should accompany me on this mission," Abtey says. "She would be an excellent cover. Nobody would suspect an officer of the Deuxième Bureau to be associated with Josephine Baker. But I told her if she came with me, there would be no secrets between us, no flirtations with foreigners who might be spies. She pledged herself to the cause, I never saw anyone with such fire."

It was all of a piece with the rest of Josephine's life. Being a French citizen, and black, she could have ended in a concentration camp but for having met Jacques Abtey. It was like the opening night of the road company of *Shuffle Along,* when the music stopped, and she jumped out of the line and did her little dance and got the applause. Now the war has brought the world to a stop, and here she is jumping out onto another stage.

While waiting for orders, Josephine, Abtey, Bayonne, and Boue went boating, hunting, fishing, and en route to the river or the forest, they would pass Monsieur Malaury bent over his anvil. Every time he brought his hammer down, he snarled, *"Un Boche!"*

Living in the country, even in wartime, Abtey said, Josephine achieved a kind of tranquillity she had not known before. "I think it brought her closer to real things . . . away from the factitious life of the theater and the music hall. . . . She told me she did not like her profession, that dog-eat-dog world. . . ." (What had happened to "the stage is my God, the theater my life"? The same thing that always happened with Josephine: Whatever role she was thrust into, she acted it with brio.)

In the evenings, the friends sat, their hands on a three-legged table, attempting to communicate with the spirit world. "Josephine did not believe in it," Jacques says. "When one of us would ask, 'Spirit, are you here?' she would burst into laughter, and we would say, 'If you won't be quiet, we'll throw you out.' "

That October, with German bombs falling all around London, Winston Churchill spoke to the people of France—*"C'est moi,* Churchill, *qui parle!"*—vowing that England would never give up. And he spoke of a morning that was sure to come. "Brightly will it shine on the brave and true, kindly upon all who suffer for the cause, glorious upon the tombs of heroes. Thus will shine the dawn. *Vive la France."*

It was as inspiring as the speeches broadcast by General de Gaulle, speeches the Germans tried to jam. "We surrounded the radio," Abtey says, "and listened to that voice . . . calling us to arms in the name of a Free France, an immortal France. The voice warmed us in the darkness."

In Paris, there were those who believed the darkness had been exaggerated. Many who had fled the city returned. German soldiers on leave walked the boulevards with their French girlfriends; you could smell the chestnut trees instead of gas fumes, because there were so few cars on the streets—and those few belonged to German officials.

Some Parisians who had connections, influence, gold bars buried in their gardens, sat in cafés sipping champagne with German officers. Jean Cocteau drank his Dom Pérignon at Maxim's, right next to the table that had been Josephine's favorite, and, lifting his glass, offered a mocking toast: *"Vive la paix honteuse!"* ("Long live the shameful peace!")

By August 1940, the Nazis had banned Negroes and Jews from the French theater—"No longer does Josephine Baker, American singer and dancer, headline Paris cabaret revues," said an AP press release—and the Vichy government was said to be planning a "purge" of French movies and radio. Sacha Guitry had just completed a revival of his play *Pasteur;* he was the only first-rate French actor to have appeared since the German occupation. Soon, however, he would be followed by hundreds of his fellows.

"Among the French film performers wholly free of the collaborationist taint," wrote Roger Peyrefitte, "there seemed to be only two genuine stars: Jean Gabin and Michèle Morgan, both of whom had earlier escaped to Hollywood. . . ."

Chevalier was singing over German-controlled Radio-Paris (the main radio medium for Nazi propaganda), and Mistinguett was back at the Casino de Paris; at every curtain call she begged the audience to send food and coal around to her house, and her concierge was almost buried under the avalanche of contributions.

When Paul Derval, who had closed the Folies-Bergère and left Paris in the exodus, decided to come back, he found a sign nailed to the theater door. Reading it, he called out a warning to Michel Gyarmathy, whom he'd left in the car: "Michel, don't come!" But it was too late. Gyarmathy was standing right behind him. The sign said, ACCESS FORBIDDEN TO DOGS AND JEWS, and Gyarmathy made a joke. "Don't worry for me, boss, I'm not a nude dancer. My religion will not jump out and hit the Germans in the eye." But he was shocked, he admitted later. "I turned to stone." (In his book, *The Good Frenchman,* Edward Behr wrote, "Jacques Copeau, the famous theater director and chief administrator of the Comédie Française, insisted that the male *sociétaires* display the proof of their noncircumcision to him.")

I think of Mildred Hudgins, of Atlantic City, and the signs on the fancy hotels there: NO DOGS, NO JEWS. And Mildred saying, "They didn't have to put NO NIGGERS, because we knew it."

One day in October, a courier came to Les Milandes from Captain Paillole (who was in Vichy reconstructing the Deuxième Bureau right under the noses of the Germans). Paillole had agreed that, under the pretext of embarking on a South American tour, Josephine and Abtey, posing as her *maître de ballet,* would get to England by way of Lisbon.

But first, Josephine and Jacques were to come to Vichy. There, Paillole and his colleagues gave a dinner to thank Josephine for her previous services in the cause of freedom, and Jacques got his new fake passport. He became Jacques-Francois Hébert, born 1899. (No man under forty was permitted to leave France, and Jacques was thirty-five.)

Then Paillole gave Abtey and Josephine papers and pictures—"all the information that had been gathered concerning the German army in France." The photographs, Abtey says, were pinned under Josephine's dress, and as for the written material, "Using invisible ink, we transcribed all fifty-two pieces of information onto Josephine's sheet music."

"You look good together," Paillole said. "Good luck."

"To get to Lisbon," Abtey says, "we would have to cross Spain. To cross Spain, you had to have a transit visa. Josephine convinced the Spanish consul in Toulouse to grant me one, alleging that she could not leave for Brazil without her ballet master. (Prior to this, she had also pried visas for me from the consuls of Brazil and Portugal.)

"To make myself look older, I sported spectacles and a heavy mustache. Josephine was enveloped in an immense fur coat, her face grave, but shining, as we got on the train that would take us through the Pyrénées. It was November 23, 1940.

"At the Spanish frontier, nobody paid any attention to me . . . the Spanish police and the German plainclothesmen were infinitely more interested in the star Josephine Baker than in the shabby little man carrying her suitcase.

"In Madrid, we were lucky enough to get the last two seats in a plane leaving for Lisbon. When we were alone on the plane, Josephine laughed. 'You see what a good cover I am?' Then she slept, disappearing into her fur.

"Let me try to explain the importance of what she had just done. If the Spanish or German authorities had discovered my true identity and arrested me, if they had found the information on the music sheets, they would have realized that the French Secret Service had reorganized covertly and was working against them, that we were not respecting the terms of the armistice, and as to the fate that would have been meted out to Josephine and myself, I would rather not dwell on it.

"This woman had undertaken, of her own volition, to cover me to the very end, closing the door behind her and binding her fate to mine. I call that courage.

"Luck was still with us in Lisbon, for the major who had been head of British Intelligence in Paris opened to us the doors of his headquarters in Portugal."

Portugal being neutral territory, Lisbon was full of life, light, spies. It was a set for a James Bond movie—beautiful women, war profiteers, people offering jewels, paintings, gold, to get berths on ships going to America. In the streets, Abtey recognized German agents, but they didn't exchange words. At the Hotel Aviz, Josephine was mobbed by journalists (she charmed them) and within one week, there was word that London was pleased with the information Abtey had sent, but that he and Josephine were not to come to England. He was to stay in Portugal awaiting further orders, Josephine was to return to France.

She flew to Marseille, a city in the Free Zone, on December 1. Paillole was waiting to debrief her. Also, quite by accident, she met Frédéric Rey, and together, they decided to put on a revival of *La Créole* at the Opéra.

The Opéra management was blissful, and in the space of two weeks, she and Rey mounted a production.

Meanwhile, in Portugal, Jacques Abtey requested of his British contact that he and Josephine not be considered spies, but members of the Free French forces. Josephine didn't want to be paid, Jacques would accept reimbursement for his travel expenses. "One month later," he says, "the British put me in charge of setting up—with Josephine—a permanent liaison and transmission center in Casablanca." (In Casablanca, they would receive information from Paillole, and periodically, Abtey would take that information by boat to Portugal, whence it would be forwarded to London.)

It was Christmas Eve, opening night of *La Créole*, when Jacques rejoined Josephine in Marseille. On the fifteenth of January, 1941, Paillole told them they must leave sooner than they'd expected. "I believe the Germans are going to take over the Free Zone, only the bad weather conditions have stopped them." (Actually, his belief was unfounded; it would be many months before the Germans finally took over all of France.) In any case, a boat was leaving for Algeria in two days. "It may be the last one. I don't want you to be stuck here."

Abtey canceled Josephine's last two shows. "The director of the Opéra asked me for a doctor's certificate. . . . The doctor said Josephine had a shadow on her lungs, and should leave this cold country as soon as possible.

"But Josephine did not want to go without her animals. She sent our associate, Bayonne, to Les Milandes to get them. At a time when it was almost impossible to move around a defeated France!"

Bayonne came back with a crowd. "Bonzo, a Great Dane," Jacques said. "And Glug Glug, a malicious female monkey, Mica, a suave lion-monkey, Gugusse, a tiny monkey, nasty as the plague, and Curler and Question Mark, two white mice. As soon as she freed them from their cages, it was madness in the room, Josephine laughing, trying to catch one or another. We finally left Marseille on the boat, the *Governor General Guyedon*."

"Poor darlings," Josephine said, surrounded by her chattering, squeaking, barking loved ones. "For them, too, it is a great adventure. *Allez*, we all go together."

"She moved," observed André Rivollet, "from her Creole yelling to singing the 'Marseillaise,' then bravely to the songs of the Resistance."

Chapter 27

—

ARABIAN NIGHTS

"As a mistress, she wanted the whole treatment"

*S*he didn't travel light, like a refugee with two emeralds sewn in her underwear; twenty-eight pieces of luggage went with Josephine to North Africa.

The crossing was a misery, the Mediterranean wild and choppy, the animals panicked as they ran between wardrobe trunks waltzing around the cabin.

And in Algiers, more aggravation. A policeman armed with a subpoena met the boat. The Marseille Opéra was suing Josephine for having "scandalously abandoned *La Créole*."

She couldn't believe it—"I would have to pay 400,000 francs in damages before I could enter Morocco!"—but had to stay behind while Jacques went on to Casablanca.

Happily, she discovered the Merlins were in Algiers. Jean was running the St. George Hotel (which would become General Eisenhower's headquarters after the Americans landed), and Odette was trying to become pregnant. Wanting a second—or fiftieth—opinion about whether or not she could conceive a child, Josephine visited Odette's gynecologist. As usual, the answer was no.

By the time she reached Casablanca, on January 28, there was more bad news. The consulate of Portugal would give Josephine Baker a visa, but refused one to her ballet master.

Abtey and Josephine wondered if his cover had been blown. "We decided," she said, "that I would have to travel to Lisbon alone. Taking my sheet music, of course." A month later, she boarded a train from Casablanca to Tangier, first stop of her journey. Tangier was neutral, an international zone, filled with spies and money, and there Josephine spent a few days with Abderahman Menebhi.

During earlier times in North Africa—*Princesse Tam-Tam* had been shot in Tunisia and Tangier, and she had given concerts everywhere— she had made many highborn friends, most of them related by blood or marriage to Mohammed V, sultan of French Morocco. Abderahman Menebhi was one of these. And in his palace on a hill overlooking the sea, she found herself reunited with some of the others, including Ahmed Ben Bachir, court chamberlain to the caliph of Spanish Morocco.

His son, Bachir Ben Bachir, says the feeling between Josephine and his father, whom she had met in 1935, "developed into a physical relationship" during the war. "My father could not speak French, but she could speak Spanish. She often spent time with him at his palace in Tetouan, where she met Spanish government officials. She taught the high commissioner the merengue and also passed information from the Americans to my father, and my father tried to convince Franco to let the Americans use the Spanish Sahara as a military base."

But that would come later. Now, even as Josephine arrived in Lisbon with her music scores for Captain Paillole, General Rommel's troops were marching into Libya.

"The pro-Germans were jubilant," she said, "the rest of us heart-sick." From Lisbon, says Bachir Ben Bachir, "she contacted my father and told him she needed a safe-conduct pass to give her more flexibility She got the document, and with it, could go all over the world, even to America."

Where she went with it was to Les Milandes, still in the Free Zone. Henri Chapin, who had escaped the Germans and come home to Beynac, was now working at the château as an electrician, along with his friend Coudert, a stonemason. "From time to time during the war," Chapin says, "Josephine would arrive to see what we had finished, and tell us what else she wanted done.

"In the kitchen of the château was a big table, and she would come with a suitcase full of money, bills of all different currencies, and she would dump it out on the table and say, 'What do I owe you? Pay yourselves, and keep the accounts straight.' And she would be walking around totally naked. At the beginning, we were very surprised, you know, we were young men, but then we got used to it."

Even on a flying visit, she managed the odd escapade. "One of her lovers would come on a motorcycle," Georges Malaury remembers. "And he would hide it in a wooden shack down the road. But there was no gasoline during the war, so while he was with Josephine, the local guys would go siphon off the gas. What's he going to say? 'While I was having sex with Josephine, somebody stole my gasoline'? And he was doing black market, so nobody felt sorry for him.

"My father was in the underground, he had a radio transmitter in the tower of the château and he transmitted to England. One time the Germans came—Josephine had just arrived—and she greeted them in German, saying, 'There's no maquis here, I'm Josephine Baker, let me entertain you.'

"They later killed the *chef de gare* of the railroad station, poor man. He said, 'I was in the first war against your country, I have a wooden leg, fuck you,' so they shot him."

In Lisbon again, Josephine found that posters advertising her concerts were plastered everywhere. She stayed in the city through March, gathering documents by day, and by night singing to sellout crowds that provided her with much-needed cash. (She couldn't get funds from Monsieur Bondon in Paris; it had become as difficult to move money as it was to move human beings.)

Then she returned to Morocco, messages from Paillole fastened in her bra with safety pins.

Although she came close to death there, I think the years in Morocco were among the happiest of her life. It was a country that had always been, in the words of the British writer Gavin Maxwell, "xenophobic and mysterious, guarding splendors and horrors that the wildest travellers' tales could not exaggerate." (Among those tales were accounts of salted human heads displayed in public.)

By 1912, most of Morocco (except for a few Spanish enclaves, including the ports on the Mediterranean) had become a French protectorate, but it remained a land out of the Arabian Nights. And wasn't it queer that Josephine, who had spent her childhood dreaming of kings in golden slippers, should find herself there? In a place where, even more amazingly, racial discrimination did not exist? Thami el Glaoui, pasha of Marrakesh and the most powerful tribal chieftain in French Morocco at that time, was himself black.

"Most harems in Morocco had women of all colors," says Bachir Ben Bachir, "and their children were recognized by their fathers, with full inheritance rights."

Yet I wonder what Josephine thought about the rights of those Moroccan women confined, no matter what their color, to seraglios? For that matter, what did those women think of her, a female sitting down to dinner with the men? A female untrainable as a wild bird in the art of subservience?

In Marrakesh, she could not stay with her old friend, El Glaoui, though he had offered her his hospitality many times before the war. Mohamed Hedidech, now chief concierge of the Hôtel Minzah, still remembers how, sixty years ago, Josephine's arrival would thrill the whole city. "She was so beautiful," he says. "She would come by boat to Tangier and stay overnight at the Minzah, and next day, two Rolls-Royces would be waiting outside, one for Madame, the other for her trunks. El Glaoui liked pretty women, and he was generous."

That was all Josephine required of a man, but in 1941, the pasha was in the thick of political intrigue. The French were asking for his allegiance, the Germans pushing for revolution. It was no time to renew romance with such a famous—and outspoken—partisan of France. Nor to have her as a live-in guest. Instead, El Glaoui sent her to the palace of his brother-in-law, Moulay Larbi, which proved to be embarrassing for that gentleman. Because every morning, as soon as the birds started singing, Josephine was up and running around in the buff, going to the kitchen to help the servants cook.

A very old lady named Mabrouka (still employed by Moulay Larbi's daughter Kenza) told me that Josephine loved chicken feet, and her laugh was "crystal clear, like a little child's."

But for Moulay Larbi, a religious Muslim, it was a danger to have this bare-skinned houri flying through the halls. (Even in the fifties, after the sultan had converted the state to a constitutional monarchy and changed his title from sultan to king, there were riots when one of his daughters appeared on a beach in a bathing suit.) So Moulay Larbi begged Mohamed Menebhi, yet another of his brothers-in-law, to rescue him. And Mohamed Menebhi offered Josephine the use of a little house he owned in the medina.

Of all the Moroccan aristocrats who lavished favors on her, Mohamed Menebhi is probably the only one Josephine didn't sleep with. And probably the one who loved her most. She had affairs with his brother Abderahman (she had even wanted to marry him), with El Glaoui, with Ahmed Ben Bachir, with Moulay Larbi. But not with Mohamed Menebhi.

"Magnificent," Jacques Abtey calls him. "Not good-looking, he was small, with an ungrateful face, but noble in his way of behaving, and he gave all his heart to the Gaullist cause."

Or most of it. He reserved some part for Josephine.

Forty years later, accompanied by Mohamed Menebhi's eldest grandson, Aziz, I visited that little house in the medina. For me, it was like walking up to the front door of Pa Baker's restaurant in Philadelphia, I was convinced I was feeling what Josephine must have felt.

The medina is the heart of the old city, and in its narrow alleyways, women passed silently, their faces masked except for eyes that burned through us like X rays. Aziz led me through a wooden door into a patio open to the sky, water splashing in a white marble fountain. Four rooms surrounded the courtyard; one still held Josephine's big brass bed from France.

It was here she had settled in with Jacques Abtey, and adopted Arab customs. She liked eating with her hands, wearing the loose djellaba, going with her maids to the *hammam,* the Turkish baths, once a week.

"There were three orange trees perfuming this oasis," Jacques Abtey recalled. "We found there the serenity that detached soul from body."

But a little serenity went a long way with Josephine. At the beginning of May, Moulay Larbi came by with the news that Morocco might be invaded by German troops. Abtey remembers that Josephine's pet monkeys were jumping from one orange tree to another when she announced, "I should go to Spain and perform there."

She toured Seville, Madrid, Barcelona, deluged with invitations wherever she landed. "Embassies, consulates, full of interesting people. Coming back to my hotel room, I made careful notes." As before, the notes were pinned to her underwear. "Who," she asked rhetorically, "would dare search Josephine Baker?"

Before returning to Marrakesh, she stopped again in Tetouan to see Ahmed Ben Bachir. "Every time she could get away, she came," says Bachir Ben Bachir. "She liked to have a tent pitched by the seaside, and drink tea, while musicians played and cooks barbecued lamb. She would swim, run back into her tent, and my father would entertain her. She was a courtly mistress, and she wanted the whole treatment. She asked my father to have his soldiers turn their backs the minute she stepped out of the house. Until she got into the car and dashed off with him.

"He was a bachelor then, about five years younger than she. He put a private Turkish bath in his house because she loved Turkish baths. She used to drink raw eggs after the bath, it was Moroccan tradition. She lived her fantasies there, and always, she had the urge—you can tell from her letters—to get back to my father because he made her feel like a woman, and for a time she could be divorced from the war."

She wrote to him when they were apart, asking favors, giving instructions. "Could you send me a visa for my maid, Paulette, still in France? . . . and do not forget to feed the horses, those poor animals could starve to death."

Amused by that particular note, he wrote back that the horses had got an extra pail of oats in her name, and that he was sorry not to have been with her at a recent concert "to admire your delicious temper."

But, his son recalls, Ahmed Ben Bachir was also very useful to Josephine in her other life. "She developed a network by which she secured Spanish Moroccan passports for Jews who were coming into the Spanish zone; my father used to go to the high commissioner and say they were Moroccan Jews, but they were really Eastern Europeans who would get passports and go to Latin America. Josephine helped a Rothschild lady in Tangier."

Once, on her way home from Tetouan and a rendezvous with Ahmed Ben Bachir, Josephine stopped in Casablanca for a consultation with yet another gynecologist. I have been told by Dr. Georges Burou (who attended the royal family of French Morocco) that this man was a charlatan. "He performed a procedure which consisted of blowing air into Josephine's fallopian tubes. He also gave her an injection of Ipedol, a very debilitating drug. After that, he should have prescribed a total rest;

instead, he sent her back to Marrakesh, a 350-mile journey, on the very poor roads of that time. And she developed peritonitis."

Not knowing how sick she was, she returned to find that she and Jacques had a houseguest, Bayonne, their colleague in the underground. He was still there two days later when Josephine was seized with terrible pains in her belly. Bayonne fetched ice, Jacques held her hands, but it was clear that she needed to be in a hospital. Not in Marrakesh, but in Casablanca, which had better facilities.

"I went out," Jacques said, "and borrowed a station wagon for Josephine to lie down in. At the Municipal Hospital in Casablanca, the head nurse insisted that Josephine get out of the car and walk. 'You are crazy!' I screamed at her, and asked our chauffeur if there were another place. He said yes, the private clinic of Doctor Henri Comte, two streets away."

It was the end of June 1941, and she would not be released from the Comte clinic until December 1, 1942. Her fanatic determination to have a child had driven her to consult so many quacks, to try so many risky treatments, that finally the poor body had rebelled.

"I assisted my friend Comte with that first operation," says Dr. François Bolot. "Josephine had an abscess between the bladder and the genitals. Comte lanced the abscess, and put in a drain. A few days later, Comte had to go to France, and I supervised Josephine's postoperative care.

"The French captain Abtey often slept on a cot in her room, and when her fever would rise, he would run to get me. He was blond, he had a nose shaped like a saber blade, and I always distrusted him, because in time of war you distrusted everyone, and I was always wondering if he had been put there by the Gestapo or the French police.

"Josephine told us that her ancestors had lived in Louisiana and that after Napoleon sold that province to the Americans, they had moved to the Antilles so they could stay French."

Josephine wrote to Ahmed Ben Bachir, saying she could not come to him for the August vacation they had planned. "I'm heart-broken. Today, with fever and being in bed, I'm skinny like a skeleton, and it is better that you don't see me like that. When I come out of the clinic, I will go to rest at Les Milandes." At the time she scrawled these lines, she expected to be sent home in a couple of weeks.

"During those long days," Jacques Abtey says, "Josephine read a lot.

She was very impressed by the lives of Louis XIV and Napoléon. When someone compared Napoléon's armies to Hitler's, she would get furious. "I like great monarchs! Napoléon was a genius, Hitler is a crazy person."

Right across from the Comte clinic was the Parc Murdoch, filled with flowers and shadows and palm trees, but Josephine was still too fragile to venture out. "They operated on her so many times," Jacques Abtey says. "Once she asked the doctor, 'Why don't you just put a zipper in? It would be so much easier.' "

She never lost her humor; when a priest came to give her last rites, placing his crucifix across her chest, she laughed. "Not yet, Father." Doctors, nurses, strangers, were always stopping by to see her. (I often wonder if her many relapses were due to the fact that she was seldom quiet except when she was unconscious.) Even her ex-husband, Jean Lion, appeared. He had been fighting in Tunisia with the French army— he would eventually receive the Croix de Guerre—and Josephine put on jewels and makeup to look beautiful for him.

The sickroom served as a perfect cover. What could be more natural than for American diplomats to come pay their respects to an American-born artist? And to meet, at her bedside, Moroccan leaders? And to discuss German intentions toward Morocco? And the Free French invasion of Syria? And when the Americans might land in North Africa?

On December 7, Japan attacked Pearl Harbor, crippling the American fleet. On December 10, Germany and Italy declared war on the United States. On December 13, Hungary and Bulgaria did the same.

Christmas 1941 was not festive, but Jacques tried to spread cheer, bringing to Josephine's room a tiny tree and dressing it with little candles, red, yellow, green.

She was beginning to feel stronger, and one day he took her for a carriage ride. Muffled in a fur blanket, only her hands outside, she put one of them on his. "Look how beautiful your color is," she said. It distressed him, as it had distressed Ralph Cooper on that long-ago summer afternoon. "She hated the color of her skin so much, it made me feel terrible for her."

But even as Josephine continued to suffer over her blackness, her life, as compared to the lives of some of her old acquaintances, was charmed. In occupied Holland, Evelyn Anderson was interned by the Nazis, then sent to Germany. "I was dancing with my partner Harry Watkins at the

Zuid," Evelyn recalls. "It was a cabaret in the Hague, and when the Germans came, Harry said, 'If you see a dark cloud passing by, you'll know it's me running.' "

He couldn't run fast enough. He was deported. "And the man that used to own the Zuid, he was Jewish, and they sent him away, and Papa Toby that ran the pension where I lived, they took him away too, and then they came and got my friend Ida Johnson and her two children and myself."

Ida's husband, Freddy, an American pianist, had been taken first. "The Germans told him they were picking up all American men regardless, black or white," Ida said, "and all he could take was a toothbrush."

Marilyn Johnson, Ida's then sixteen-year-old daughter, remembers saying goodbye to her father at the train station. "We were crying, he was very calm, but he was frightened. He said, 'I don't know whether I'm going to see you all again, but keep a stiff upper lip, and if I get a chance, I'll write.' "

"When the Germans first occupied Holland," Ida says, "we would lie in bed at night and hear the footsteps of the soldiers taking the Jewish people away. They came in the middle of the night. The only reason they tolerated us was because a lot of Germans had never seen any black people. They'd rub you to see if the color came off you."

Ida, her daughters, and Evelyn were soon removed to another camp in Holland. "They were killing Jews there," Marilyn says. "I saw men kicked to death by German boots with the metal spikes. They did not fight back, and I couldn't understand. My mother used to worry because I believed in speaking my mind. If I saw an old man, a skeleton with cheeks and eyes sunken, and the Germans were kicking him, I would yell, 'Stop it!' and my mother would grab me and pull me aside with a hand over my mouth.

"I'll never forget it. Kicking an old person until he died. And these were young, most of the German soldiers, fourteen, fifteen. I talked to one of them once, he was crying and saying, 'I miss my mother, I'm afraid.' "

Later, in Germany, Evelyn and the Johnsons were held in a convent in Liebenhau.

In 1942, the world was exploding. Americans fought at Bataan, Midway, Guadalcanal; Germans slogged through Russia, reaching all the way to Stalingrad; the British beat Rommel at El Alamein.

But all continued calm at the Comte clinic. On the arm of her devoted nurse, Marie Rochas, Josephine was now able to walk in Parc Murdoch. Mohamed Menebhi brought her lemon chicken. Jean Gabriel Domergue (who had painted her portrait for the cover of the Folies-Bergère program in 1936) came to visit and was horrified to see she had lost fifty pounds. "Ah," he said, "your beautiful buttocks have disappeared." A crowd of locusts flew in through the window, and when Marie tried to stamp on them, Josephine screamed and called her a murderess. An American vice-consul named Bartlett stopped by to say how happy Washington was with the material Captain Abtey had been supplying.

In August, Maurice Chevalier appeared, but Josephine refused to see him. "He is a great artist," she said, "but a very small man." (She would later accuse him publicly of being a Nazi collaborator.)

Back in Paris, Chevalier, his pride wounded, made up a story that spread like a brushfire: the dying Josephine had clung to him, saying, "Maurice, do not abandon me." The German-controlled French press printed that she had syphilis, and Josephine wrote to the Guignerys at Le Vésinet. "Thank God all those reports are big lies, I ask myself why people amuse themselves with such ugly stories, and I beg you to tell our friends not to pay any attention to them."

She wrote to the Rivollets as well. "She sent us postcards telling us alarming news," said André, "with gynecological details and a total lack of modesty. The post-office employee blushed."

In October, she found a stray cat, for whom she knit a sweater. "It is God who sent him to me," she said. Vice-Consul Bartlett was called home, but before he left, he told Jacques and Josephine, "It won't be long now, we are coming in considerable strength."

They came on November 8, a huge force of Americans and British disembarking in Casablanca, Oran, Algiers, from five hundred warships and cargo ships under air support from Gibraltar. Once the Allied troops landed, Hitler and Mussolini hastened to occupy all of France, there was no Free Zone anymore.

Because the political situation was so bizarre—"Marshal Pétain," wrote Louis Snyder, "immediately ordered resistance and broke off relations with the United States"—French troops fought Americans in the streets of Casablanca.

"The Americans arrived on land where the French flag was flying," said Jacques Abtey bitterly, "and they were welcomed by machine-gun fire." Abtey resolved to report to American headquarters—he hoped to be received by General Patton, but this did not happen—and Josephine wanted to go with him, but he said no. He drove from the French sector to the American sector in a borrowed ambulance, flying the flag of the Red Cross, and all along the roads, he passed dead soldiers. "The first I found was Senegalese, he died as a servant of Hitler, not knowing the French had used him. After that, two Frenchmen . . . then the first American. Death had not disfigured his adolescent face. He was lying with his arms crossed over his chest. . . . I turned my head away, I was ashamed to be French."

Three days later, all was sunny again, there was a military parade with troops—American, French, Moroccan—marching through Casablanca. "A reconciliation," Jacques called it. Later, he and members of Paillole's group went to Josephine's room and drank champagne. "We raised our glasses to America, to England, and to our eternal France."

Nineteen months after she had arrived there, Josephine was discharged from the clinic (Dr. Comte never gave her a bill) and returned to Marrakesh. This time, Mohamed Menebhi took her into his own palace, where she could be better cared for.

Now rumors of her dying turned into rumors of her death. The *Chicago Defender* had her breathing her last "in the city hospital at Casablanca, Portugal [*sic*]. . . . By her side . . . was her estranged Italian husband."

And in an obituary written by the black American poet Langston Hughes, Josephine was called "as much a victim of Hitler as the soldiers who fall today in Africa fighting his armies. The Aryans drove Josephine away from her beloved Paris. At her death, she was again just a little colored girl from St. Louis who didn't rate in Fascist Europe."

"When I saw in a newspaper that my sister had died," Margaret told me, "I ran home and tore upstairs to Mama's place. She was sitting in a chair, staring out the window. 'Mama,' I said, 'Tumpy's dead.' "

Slowly, Carrie turned and shook her head. "Tumpy ain't dead," she said.

Freda J. McDonald?
The only baby
picture of Josephine
Baker. But is it
authentic? "Is that
you, Mother?"
*(Courtesy Jacques
Abtey)*

Eddie Carson, one of Carrie's lovers
and believed by some to be
Josephine's father—but she knew
better. *(Courtesy Richard Martin, Jr.)*

This sign was typical in Josephine's youth and
she saw it when she helped out at the
Cooper's laundry in St. Louis. It would fuel
her rage. *(John Vachon, Schomburg Center for
Research in Black Culture, NYPL)*

A wistful Josephine McDonald Martin Wells before she left St. Louis in 1921—with her lady lover, Clara Smith.

Clara Smith, billed as the South's "favorite coon shouter." Josephine could not have found a better singing coach.
(Courtesy Frank Driggs)

Booker Washington Theatre: the incubator of Josephine's dreams. What she learned there, she could not have learned anyplace else.

August 1922, in Boston with *Shuffle Along,* looking like schoolgirls in their cotton dresses: second from left is Josephine; next to her are Ruth Walker, Mamie Lewis, Evelyn Sheppard ("Little Shep"), and her brother, Willie. No one remembers the identity of the man at left or the little girl.

The Honeysuckles on bended knee in *Shuffle Along:* "The preacher will be waiting when the knot am tied." A smiling Josephine is fifth from left.
(Courtesy Robert Kimball, Sissle-Blake Archives)

A sartorially splendid Josephine, long before Paris fashion claimed her. This photo was inscribed to Mr. and Mrs. Eubie Blake. *(Courtesy Robert Kimball)*

The entire company of *Shuffle Along:* Josephine is down front, second from right, a standout in taffeta and ruffled skirts—always a scene-stealer.

AL. MAYER

Presents

PLANTATION DAYS

1/3/2 1923

Produced by

SISSLE & BLAKE

Composers of

"SHUFFLE ALONG"

LeRoy Smith'

1. Opening C
   Virginia ...
   Carolina ...
   Georgia ....
   Alabama ....
   Kentucky ...
   Tennessee ....
   Mississippi ...
   Louisiana ......

2.   A Few Mon
   HARMON
   First Tenor, Ivan H. Browi
   H. Berry; First Bass,
   Second Bass, W

3.   "I Am Running V
   MAY HUDG.

4.   **CHARLES DAV**
   in "The Land of Dancing F
   Assisted by
   DIXIE SHUFFLER:

5.   **MISS LOTTIE GEE**
"Shuffle Along Song Bird"
—IN—
"BIRD OF PARADISE"
AND
"KING TUT"
Introducing
MILDRED SMALLWOOD
Watch **JOSEPHINE BAKER**
The Comedy Girl of "Shuffle Along"

JOHNNIE HUDGINS
in a Class by Himself

IVAN H. BROWNING
Presents His
"HARLEM VAMPS"

A Few Shuffling Taps by
CHARLES DAVIS

SS BLANCHE CALLOWAY
lues Singer of "Shuffle Along"

d Finale by Entire Company,
by the Premier Strutter
OHNNIE HUDGINS
AND HIS
COLATE DANDYS"

Staged by Elida Webb
by Brooks Mahieu Co.
ngs by Minnie Allen's Orchid
Shoe Salon
nged by Caldwell & Johnson,
Along" Orchestra

NIGHTLY, 11.30 AND 1.00
Charges, 1.00
Holidays, $1.50

Plantation Cafe

(LA MARNE HOTEL)

BOARDWALK AT OCEAN AVE.
ATLANTIC CITY, N. J.

Plantation Cafe,
on the boardwalk,
Atlantic City.
(Courtesy Johnny Hudgins)

Program from the
Plantation Cafe.
Inset: Josephine
clowns at Revere
Beach, 1924, with
Howard Nelson
(center), violin, and
Edgar Campbell,
clarinet.
(Courtesy Marion Cumbo)

At the curtain call of *Chocolate Dandies* (1924), in the arms of Johnny Hudgins while Lew Payton looks on. "To be funny then, colored comedians had to cork up," said Hudgins. *(Courtesy Robert Kimball)*

The great Florence Mills, the first black to headline the New York Palace Theatre, 1925. Josephine loved her, even when reviewers compared them— to her disadvantage: Josephine ". . . is a rat who kicks with so much spirit! The other is an island bird." *(Courtesy Joe Attles)*

Maude Russell, the "slim princess" of the T.O.B.A. (Tough on Black Asses) circuit. Beautiful, talented, and unfailingly honest. "You learned a lot in those days, baby." *(Courtesy Maude Russell)*

CUNARD

A random search in an old thrift shop brought this precious discovery: the *Berengaria* passenger list of Wednesday, September 16, 1925. The very date of Josephine's departure for Paris—and destiny.

Josephine *(foreground)* looking like an urchin on the deck of the *Berengaria* during a mine alert, September 18.
1) Mabel Hopkins
2) Josephine Baker
3)"Jack," an actor on his way to England
4) Spencer Williams
5) Maud de Forrest
6) Bea Foote
7) Marguerite Ricks
(Courtesy Claude Hopkins)

mabel (1)
Joe (2)
Jack (3)
Spencer (4)
maud (5)
Bea (6)
marg. (7)
on old
" Berengaria"

September 22, 1925. "Bonjour, Paris!" *La Revue Nègre* in all its elegance at the Gare Saint-Lazare. *(Courtesy Claude Hopkins)*

The calm before the storm. Josephine and Joe Alex rehearsing "La Danse de Sauvage." "Barbaric . . . naughty . . . a return to the customs of the dark ages," a critic would say.
(Courtesy Claude Hopkins)

The famous banana costume from the 1926 Folies-Bergère. Many will claim to have invented it, but only Josephine would dare to strategically fashion herself a substitute phallus.
(Roger-Viollet)

Imitating Johnny Hudgins in blackface, Folies-Bergère, 1927.

In the 1926 Folies-Bergère after emerging from her famous Crystal Ball. She never tired of looking at herself in a mirror. *(Courtesy Shubert Archive)*

A rare photo of Josephine flashing. The tigress is in her element, but who is she stalking this time? *(Roger-Viollet)*

Parodying the great Pavlova. She never liked ballerinas on point. "They look like silly little birds . . . dreadful." *(Studio Piaz)*

In 1932 at the Casino de Paris, singing "Si J'Etais Blanche" ("If I Were White"). She hated being black, but she never forgave whites for the racial injustices she had suffered at home. *(Studio Piaz)*

Do you have a light? Cross-dressing at the Casino de Paris. *(Studio Piaz)*

The "Electric" Fairy: Celebrating the modern convenience of electricity, Casino de Paris, 1930. *(Roger-Viollet)*

A 1927 Folies-Bergère pose inscribed to her friend Mildred Hudgins, whom she had first met in Philadelphia in 1921. Not all memories of home were bad. *(Walery-Paris)*

In Offenbach's *La Creole*, 1934. Her introduction to the "legitimate" theater. "Now I spoke French," she claimed, "at the side of strictly French actors." *(Studio Piaz)*

First flying lesson with instructor Demay, 1935.

On her twenty-first birthday, she got her driver's license.

Infectious joie de vivre draws a crowd on the streets of Paris, 1926.

chez Joséphine BAKER - PARIS 1927

From left to right, Mildred Hudgins, "Count" Pepito, and a friend celebrate with a pensive Josephine at Chez Josephine, her boîte in Montmartre.

On St. Catherine's Day, when unmarried French girls don hats and search for husbands, she played the innocent virgin with designer Paul Poiret and his models. *(Courtesy Christiane Otte)*

A blooming Josephine, inscribed to her friend Miki Sawada. *(Courtesy Emi Sawada-Kamiya)*

A prickly version of the banana costume in the *Ziegfeld Follies* of 1935. Her return home was less than triumphant.

Josephine and her pet baby pig. She had a lifelong love of animals, from the exotic to the domestic.

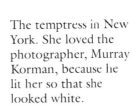

The temptress in New York. She loved the photographer, Murray Korman, because he lit her so that she looked white.

On the train to
Bordeaux, 1939, with
husband, Jean Lion,
and secretary.
Josephine, chic and
radiant, plays to her
adoring crowd.

The star in war-torn
France, knitting scarves for
the soldiers at Les Milandes
with Madame Bataille and
her niece, July 1940.
(Maurice Bataille)

Arriving in Paris from a
South American tour,
1939, with friends and
a menagerie of
chattering souvenirs.

PALACE FRIENDS . . .

Thami el Glaoui,
pasha of Marrakesh.
*(Courtesy Abdessadeq
el Glaoui)*

Ahmed Ben Bachir.
(Courtesy Bachir Ben Bachir)

Mohamed Menebhi.
*(Courtesy Medhi
Lamghari-Menebhi)*

Casablanca, 1943,
with Jacques Abtey
and a friend.
(Donald Wyatt)

Rehearsing before the
opening of the Liberty
Club, a Red Cross facility
for black soldiers.
Casablanca, February 1943.
(Donald Wyatt)

With Major Donald Wyatt and friend.
(Courtesy Donald Wyatt)

Richard Alexander Martin, who looked
much like his half sister, Josephine, on duty
during the war, in Great Lakes, Illinois.
(Courtesy Richard Martin, Sr.)

Sublieutenant Josephine Baker on her way back from North Africa to a newly liberated Paris on a Liberty ship, October 2, 1944. Air Force officer Catherine Egger snapped the photo.

SOIRÉE DE GALA du 30 Avril 1943

DONNÉE AU PROFIT DE LA

CROIX-ROUGE FRANÇAISE

SUR L'INITIATIVE DE

JOSEPHINE BAKER

et de la DIRECTION du CINÉMA-THEATRE le

"RIALTO"

Madame BOUVIER, Présidente de la Croix-Rouge Française de Casablanca, remercie M. Oswald M. Wyatt de bien vouloir honorer de sa présence, le Gala du 30 Avril 1943

Place N° 9 2

LA TENUE DE SOIRÉE N'EST PAS OBLIGATOIRE   Rideau à 19 heures 30 précises

An invitation to the Rialto, Casablanca.

Soirée de Gala, starring Josephine and Frederic Rey.

Programme des Soirées de Gala

DONNÉE AU PROFIT DE L'AIDE

A LA RÉSISTANCE FRANÇAISE

PLACÉE SOUS LE HAUT PATRONNAGE DU

GÉNÉRAL DE GAULLE

ET ORGANISÉES PAR LE

COMITÉ DE LA FRANCE COMBATTANTE D'EGYPTE

LES 26-27-28 ET 29 OCTOBRE 1943

AU THEATRE DE L'EZBEKIEH

DU CAIRE

Le programme est vendu au bénéfice de l'aide à la Résistance Française

PRIX P.T. 5

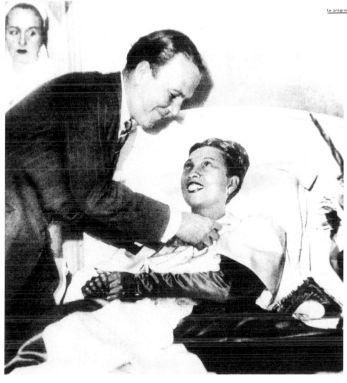

Josephine is decorated with the Medal of Resistance on her sickbed in Paris. De Gaulle himself wrote to congratulate her and wish her a speedy recovery. "I would like to be upright to receive a medal from France," she said. (France-Dimanche)

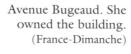

Avenue Bugeaud. She
owned the building.
(France-Dimanche)

Le Beau Chêne,
Josephine's villa
at Le Vésinet.

Les Milandes in all its imposing splendor. (Paris Match)

At Place Josephine, the star in stone
as the Virgin Mary blessing
the tourists. *(Arthur Prevost)*

A tableau from the Jorama, a wax
museum at Les Milandes: "Saint"
Josephine with her husband,
Jo Bouillon, being blessed by
Pope Pius XII. *(Courtesy Arthur
Prevost)*

Josephine with her glittering friends—Jean Cocteau, Mistinguett, Katherine Dunham, Jean Marais, and a dancer—at the opening of Dunham's dance company, Paris, 1949. *(Courtesy Katherine Dunham)*

Josephine charming students at Fisk University in Nashville, 1947. *(Courtesy Donald Wyatt)*

Creating a furor in 1951 Havana with yet another new look with the help of hairdresser Jean Clement. *(Courtesy Jean Clement)*

Coccinelle, the most famous transsexual of France, with Marlene Dietrich. To Josephine, Coccinelle was always "my daughter" and Dietrich was always "that German cow." *(Courtesy Coccinelle)*

Powdering her legs backstage in Cuba, a rare private moment getting ready for the public. *(Courtesy Julio Sendin)*

"Thank God for making men like Perón," said Josephine, here pictured in Buenos Aires, 1952, with her hero. *(Courtesy Koffi and Diane Bouillon)*

Members of the Rainbow Tribe with "Uncle Fidel," Havana, 1966. *(Courtesy Jarry Bouillon-Baker)*

Newly decorated with the Legion of Honor and the Croix de Guerre with palm, Josephine stands at attention with Commandant Cournal at Les Milandes, August 1961. (France-Dimanche)

Josephine and daughter Stellina with Golda Meir in Israel, 1974. *(UPI)*

Carrie McDonald Martin Hudson gets a kiss from her first-born child backstage at the Folies-Bergère, 1949. *(Courtesy Maryse Bouillon)*

The self-crowned Universal Mother choreographing her dance of world brotherhood. Josephine holds in her arms Brahim and Marianne while looking down on Moise, Luis, Jean-Claude, Akio, Jari, and Janot. *(Reporters Associés)*

The Rainbow Tribe "protected" from the outside world but still on display at Les Milandes, the "Capital of Universal Brotherhood."
(Courtesy Arthur Prevost)

Lunch, *en famille,* in the kitchen of the château with the two "uncles," Monsieur Marc and Monsieur Rey. Aunt Margaret is seated in front of the large American refrigerator.
(France-Dimanche)

"A poor old lady alone in the rain." A dream comes to an end.
(Paris Match)

Luce Tronville, my natural mother. The virginal convent girl with the perpetually sad face and full heart.

Eleven-year-old "Yan-Yan" with my sisters, Marie-Jo, Marie-Annick, and Martine in St. Symphorien, 1954.

Josephine loved this faunlike portrait of me—and my natural mother was ashamed of it.

Bal à Tout Coeur, Cannes, 1973. At far left, that's me in mod dress, Rama (Margaret's daughter), a beaming mother, Marianne, Luis, and Janot.
(*Courtesy* Hörzu)

I can almost hear her say once again, "Il faut, il faut!" "One must always do better!" *(Ludwig Binder)*

Josephine with her benefactors, Prince Rainier and Princess Grace of Monaco. *(Robert de Hoe, courtesy Photo Archive of S.A.S., the Prince of Monaco)*

Escorting "Maman" backstage at the Pimm's Club, my discotheque in Berlin, 1970. *(Erika Rabau)*

Au revoir,
but not adieu!
At La Madeleine, France
mourns—but Josephine is
still the Queen of Paris.
*(Above: Pellepam—SIPA Press;
right: UPI)*

Chapter 28

—

REDISCOVERING
HER RACE

"My people, my people, I have abandoned them!"

The first time Josephine read a report of her own death, she was more than five thousand miles from St. Louis, lying on a chaise among the flowering trees that perfumed the roof of Mohamed Menebhi's palace. It made her laugh. In an interview for *The Afro-American*, she told Ollie Stewart, "There has been a slight error, I'm much too busy to die." She said this, he reported, with "a gay smile and a French accent . . . her face uplifted toward the eternal snows of the nearby Atlas peaks." She also asked Stewart to help her find Carrie, through his newspaper. She said she hadn't been able to reach her since the outbreak of the war. "I cannot locate my mother. I know she still lives in St. Louis, but where?"

(Josephine hadn't been in touch with Richard, either, but then, he himself had been gone from St. Louis. "My father was drafted into the U.S. Navy," his son Artie says. "He went to Great Lakes, Illinois, and I hate to say it, but with six kids in the family, that was the best thing that happened to us, when the money started coming in. The war did quite a lot for black people.")

Two weeks after Josephine talked to Ollie Stewart, her appeal was answered; his newspaper ran the headline AFRO FINDS JO BAKER'S MOTHER. It hadn't been all that hard. "Mrs. Carrie Hudson-Martin" [*sic*], said the story, was "living at 4324 Garfield Avenue rear, this city."

All was well, and Josephine spent the last weeks of her convalescence not only enjoying the luxuries provided by Mohamed, but beguiling his three daughters.

"I was Josephine's favorite," says Hagdousch, who was then sixteen years old. "I loved her like a big sister. She had her own quarters, and my father invited her every day to his table. She lived in a different world from the other women, my father's wives and concubines.

"She would play with the children of the house, help feed them, put them to bed. Once she wanted to adopt a little child of one of the servants, but she had a relapse of her intestinal problem, and had to be transported to the hospital at two o'clock in the morning. My mother said, 'Thank God that happened,' and went right away to get the child so Josephine wouldn't take her.

"In the beginning, she used to take us with her to visit the *souk*, but afterwards, she liked to go by herself."

At the market of Djemaa el Fna, Josephine, dressed Moroccan-style, except for a face veil, wandered among snake charmers with their flat-headed cobras, and mingled with crowds listening to storytellers. Vendors hawked snails and oranges, there were baby falcons for sale, and rugs and leather, and everywhere the smells of curry, lemon, mint. She was Cinderella, with a clock that never struck midnight.

In 1990, I visited Fadila Menebhi, the eldest of Mohamed's daughters. She was living with a cot, a lamp, a radio, no flush toilet, in the ruins of what had been Josephine's wing of Mohamed's palace. But Fadila was merry, her eyes that had seen so much of splendor still danced in these dilapidated surroundings. "Tata Joe," she said, offering a photograph of Josephine covered in white fox and feathers. "We called her Tata—it means Auntie—because she was part of our family."

In January 1943, the Allied chiefs were holding meetings in a suburb of Casablanca, at the Anfa Hotel, but General de Gaulle was not happy, because Prime Minister Churchill and President Roosevelt wanted him to merge his Free French forces (fighting the Battle of North Africa, even as the politicians wrangled) with the forces of the Imperial Council, another Resistance group headed by General Henri Giraud.

Roosevelt asked if de Gaulle would be willing to shake Giraud's hand "before the camera" (the photo op is older than we think) and de Gaulle answered, "I shall do that for you." It was the only time during the entire conference that he permitted himself to speak English.

A scant month later, Josephine found herself in the Anfa Hotel. It happened when Sidney Williams, a black American Red Cross official, having heard she was in Marrakesh, phoned and asked for her help. He was in charge of opening a service club—the Liberty Club—for blacks; the army at that time still practiced segregation. ("For me, as for many French and Moroccan men," said Jacques Abtey, "it was a surprise to find that skin color continued to be so important in the country of freedom and equality. We had thought racial prejudice existed only on the other side of the Siegfried line." President Harry Truman was to desegregate the armed forces in 1948.)

Josephine entertained at the opening of the Liberty Club. "She was sick," said Donald Wyatt, an associate of Sidney Williams, "but she came." Black himself, Major Wyatt met Josephine for the first time that night.

It was twenty years since she had performed for an all-black audience. Seeing those boys out front, time fell away, she was in Philadelphia at the Standard. Makeup could not disguise the gauntness of her face, her skinny legs shook under her long dress, but when she sang, the response of the black soldiers was so wild that she cried.

After her performances at the Liberty Club, General Mark Clark invited her to a reception at the Anfa Hotel. Flanked by Mohamed Menebhi and Moulay Larbi, she made a grand entrance into a room filled with top brass, American and English, including generals Patton, Anderson, Alexander, and Cunningham. "That night Josephine was reborn to life," Jacques Abtey said. "Her life as a star." But the day's activities took their toll; on being introduced to General Patton, she fainted in his arms.

Next evening, having been invited by Mohamed, Donald Wyatt came to dinner at the Menebhi palace. He remembers every detail of his first Moroccan meal. The old female servant bringing basin, soap, and water to guests seated on pillows around a low table, the women of the household gathered on the balcony, hidden by shadows, "looking down on us. Mohamed explained to me that in this society, women's purpose was to serve and give men pleasure and children. But Josephine did not come under these restrictions."

Wyatt was fascinated by his host. "Mohamed's father had served as ambassador to the Court of St. James, Mohamed's mother was a black concubine. Mohamed was darker than Josephine or I, witty and well-educated; I think he put himself in debt to win Josephine's affections, building a costly addition to his palace for her."

In time, Donald Wyatt, Jacques Abtey, and Mohamed Menebhi became such fast friends that they referred to themselves as the Three Musketeers, and, during the same period, Donald forged a brother-sister connection with Josephine.

"Having seen the almost miraculous impact she'd made on the audience," he says, "it occurred to me she might be willing to help in my work with black soldiers. She now believed she had been allowed to continue to live because she was destined to be the instrument of change in international affairs. Her doctor still wanted her to take it easy, but even if she didn't sing, I realized she would be wonderful just talking to groups of men. A lot of the black troops were angry because they'd been trained to fight and then when they got to Casablanca, they'd been sent to unload ships along with the Moroccan stevedores.

"She agreed to go with me. VD was rampant in our camps, the medics lectured on the risk of syphilis if the soldiers kept patronizing prostitutes, the chaplains preached abstinence, but it took Josephine to get through to the men. 'I want you to look at me,' she said, 'as your mother, your sister, your sweetheart. I'm your family. You are going around exposing yourselves to these diseased girls and you can't miss getting sick. As for getting mad because of race prejudice, wait till the war is over. I will come back to the States and join in the fight to break down segregation, but let's win the war first.'

"They cheered. Even Josephine wasn't enough of a hypnotist to keep them celibate for the duration of their stay in Morocco, but the VD rate did go down."

Meeting those boys from home was a shock to Josephine. "In order to further her own ambitions, she had pushed out of her mind the lot of black people," Donald says. "Now she was being very dramatic—'My people, oh! my people, I have abandoned them!' "

She, who had been accused by so many blacks of turning her back on

them, was suddenly reborn. A life of service beckoned, Georges Guignery's prediction that she would wind up broke seemed to charm her.
"This time, I'm really on the straw," she said. "But isn't it magnificent?"

To be sure, her idea of destitution included life in a palace, forty-eight
trunks full of clothes (twenty-eight had grown to forty-eight because
every time she came back from Spain or Portugal or Les Milandes, more
clothes came with her), and any number of precious stones stashed with
Ahmed Ben Bashir in Spanish Morocco. ("She entrusted my father with
a significant amount of high-quality jewelry," says Bachir Ben Bachir,
"including a big collection of gold and diamond men's pocket watches
on gold chains. She was shrewd enough to know it was better to have
it on neutral ground during the war.")

At Mohamed's palace, old theatrical costumes were taken out of
garment bags and remade; it wasn't just that Josephine was thinner, but
moths had eaten holes in some of her finery. By May, she began to tour
American military camps with Fred Rey. Fred had been interned in
Morocco (bounced from the Foreign Legion because he was Austrian-
born, and so considered an enemy of France) but Jacques Abtey pulled
strings, and Josephine had her dancing partner restored to her. Although
now she too appeared to consider him an enemy. "That little bastard,"
she said, "he oils his body before we go on, and I slip all over him."

Sometimes, en route from one concert to another, she made it back
to Algiers for a day or two. During one of these breathers, she fell in love
with the infant son of Odette and Jean Merlin. Holding him, Josephine
wept, then marched off to a lawyer's office, where she named mother
and child the beneficiaries of her will.

It made Odette uncomfortable. "In time of war, you never knew
what might happen, and I barely knew Josephine, certainly not well
enough to be her beneficiary."

Back on the road in Oran, Jacques Abtey says, "Josephine had a good
black orchestra backing her up, and at the end of every show, she would
sing three anthems, the 'Marseillaise,' 'God Save the Queen,' and 'The
Star-Spangled Banner,' in which she would be joined by the audience.

"This one night, German planes flew over and started shooting.
There was a crackling and sputtering, and the theater—it was just a stage
set up outside—was plunged into darkness. Josephine used the unex-
pected intermission to help herself to the supper the American army had

set out in a tent. The sky was lighted by fire, everyone flat on the ground, and finally, things became so violent she was obliged to throw herself down like everyone else."

Later, thinking about it, she laughed. "Me, belly down, among soldiers from Texas, Missouri, and Ohio in my 1900 Paris dress, must have been an irresistibly funny sight. Mostly because I kept on eating my ice cream."

A week later, in Marrakesh, Josephine, Moulay Larbi, and Mohamed were dinner guests at the American consulate, and Josephine was given the seat of honor, at the right hand of Robert Murphy, President Roosevelt's official envoy. Subsequently, Mohamed decided to give a party in his palace to promote racial harmony. There would be French, English, and American intelligence officers, and Donald Wyatt was asked if he could produce some army brass who were black.

"It seemed," Wyatt said, "that Mohamed had some misgivings about an affair where he and the Berber musicians and dancers would be the only persons of color. I had about a week to get together this black contingent, which was no small feat, as black officers were scarce as hens' teeth in Casablanca. In the end, there were five of us, including Sidney Williams, the Liberty Club director, and Ollie Stewart, a newspaper correspondent."

Jacques remembers that the party included many diplomats, Donald remembers something worse. "Drinks were served by barmen from the Mamounia Hôtel, and by the time we sat down for dinner, a couple of the younger American officers were a bit tipsy. Suddenly one of them said, 'I never sat at a table with niggers before.'

"Mohamed jumped up and seemed about to eject the man, but Josephine took him aside, begging him to be diplomatic. Later on, Mohamed got even. When the dancing girls came out, he handed each of them over to a black man, and finally the six of us, including Mohamed, were sandwiched between the girls, snaking round the fountain in a conga line in the center of the room, while the white officers stood looking on. The slight to them was obvious, and Josephine thought it was the cleverest thing she had ever witnessed."

On May 30, General de Gaulle arrived in Algiers, and in June, Josephine asked French officials if they would send her to Tunisia, where eleven thousand soldiers had been reported killed and five thousand wounded. Word came from headquarters: "They don't need entertainment."

Stung by the rebuff of her adopted country, she accepted an invitation from the British. "I was asked to secure her services for the British army, that's how I got to know her," said Harry Hurford-Janes. "I was a second lieutenant, and I traveled throughout North Africa with her. She had been insulted by some British South Africans who were very anti-color, and she said unless I could go with her to keep those people in their place, she wouldn't give any more performances. I found that very attractive."

In three weeks, they covered fifteen thousand kilometers (nine thousand miles), ranging across Tunis, Lybia, Egypt, and Josephine was moved by her encounters with the men. "They did not know that the Sicilian landing was to come so soon," she said. "I knew it. And to see them full of enthusiasm, when so many were already marked by the sign of death . . ."

Beirut, Damascus, Cairo. She was working with Laurence Olivier, Vivien Leigh, and Noël Coward. ("She is doing a wonderful job for the troops," Coward wrote in his diary, "and refuses to appear anywhere where admission is charged or where civilians are present.") All went well until she clashed in a Cairo nightclub with Egypt's King Farouk. The director of the club came to the table where Josephine sat with her date, an Englishman, and said His Majesty would like her to sing. Josephine declined. Farouk sent another minion: "It is an order, you do not refuse a king."

Josephine got up to dance with the Englishman. The king ordered the orchestra to stop playing. The music was finished, Josephine was not. "His Majesty should have understood," she said sweetly, "that if I broke rules, it was only to be happy."

A few days later, in the name of Franco-Egyptian friendship, she participated in a royal evening. Still, she had faced down a king. He was fat, but she was tough.

It was not only Farouk with whom Josephine locked horns in Cairo; she and Jacques Abtey also fought. "I had told her," he says, "if she had an adventure with anyone else, she couldn't work with me anymore. Because a woman talks when she has her head on a pillow. But she had an affair with this English guy, I could smell it." (Despite the fact that they were allies, the French, the English, and the Americans all spied on each other.)

Jacques describes Josephine's Englishman as tall, handsome, and attached to the British embassy. "We were staying at Shepheard's Hotel, and she didn't want me to come to her room, she said 'I have a headache.' I went and knocked at the door. She opened it a crack—'I don't want to see you!'—and closed the door on my nose. I put my foot in, pushed past her, and she said, 'You get out!'

"The tall guy was standing next to her. She repeated, 'Get out!' I hit her. Pom! She fell on the floor. I said to the guy, 'You can come here too if you're interested.' He didn't move. I would not let a woman be treated that way in front of me. He left, and now Josephine was angry he had not come to her defense. She sulked for three days, but she never saw the guy again."

She sang in Tripoli, Tobruk, Alexandria. On July 14 (four days after the Allies invaded Sicily) Algiers, now the capital of wartime France, celebrated Bastille Day for the first time since 1939.

After reviewing a military and civilian parade, General de Gaulle addressed the crowd. "For one thousand five hundred years, we have been France, and for one thousand five hundred years, the fatherland has stayed alive in her pain and in her glory. The present trial is not over, but now, from far away, the worst drama of our history is drawing to a close."

Friday, August 13, there was a great gala at L'Opéra d'Alger. "Everyone knew de Gaulle would attend, and Giraud too," said Raymond Boucher, then an officer in the French navy. "It promised tension. Many artists would be present, some who had escaped occupied France. Josephine Baker was expected, and it was the first I had heard about her since the reports of her death. I was part of General de Gaulle's guard, and it was a thunderous coup for us to have Josephine Baker to draw the people.

"Sometime during the show, a list of French artists who were considered collaborators was read aloud. I remember the names of Chevalier and Danielle Darrieux being disparaged, and it made me sad about Danielle, I have to confess I was a little bit in love with her. You could feel hatred in the theater, but when Josephine appeared, everybody stood up, people were crying; she was a symbol.

"The high-ranking Americans supported Giraud, but when they saw Josephine on the side of de Gaulle, she authenticated, a little bit, the Free French.

"Giraud did not show up that night."

Five hours before the performance, Jacques Abtey says, "Josephine got the idea to have a great tricolor flag falling from the ceiling of the Opéra, with an immense cross of Lorraine sewn on it. Odette Merlin helped her find fabric, and Josephine took it to the mother superior of a convent, who mobilized the nuns to sew the flag.''

She made her first entrance dressed in a long white gown, sang "J'ai Deux Amours," and halfway through strangled on the words. "I can't," she said, pointing toward the box where de Gaulle was seated. "*He* is there."

Soon, she was there too. During the intermission, she was invited to join the general. "He introduced me to Madame de Gaulle," she wrote later. "He seated me next to her, in his own seat. I can still see Madame de Gaulle . . . discreet and simple, in her grey lisle stockings, her little flat shoes. She called me, so kindly, 'Nasty little Gaulliste.' General de Gaulle is a great, tall man. . . . I like when you have to raise your head to look at a man. . . ."

"He gave her," says Jacques Abtey, "a tiny cross of Lorraine, gold, very beautiful, designed by Cartier." He laughs, because this story brings back another memory. "When Josephine and I first worked together, she gave me a military I.D. bracelet in pure silver, with my name on it. Misspelled. Inside, she'd had engraved *PFQA: Plus fort que l'amour.* Stronger than love. I told her, 'Listen, you cannot want me to wear that with my name on it, I'm a spy.' She took it back and said she would have Cartier erase the name. I never saw it again."

When the "Marseillaise" was played, ending the evening, the huge flag and its red cross of Lorraine was unfurled; it fell eighteen feet, while the audience screamed.

It took the United States and Britain until August 24 to recognize the French Committee for National Liberation, and five days later, General de Gaulle was finally acknowledged by the British, the Americans, and the Russians as "Chief of the Resistance."

The rest of the year, Josephine was back on the road, driving herself relentlessly for the troops. "I wanted them to take away a vision of Paris, a breath of France." With her on this tour went Jacques, Fred Rey, and Mohamed, who was recruited because his name could open doors in the Arab world. The four traveled the Middle East in two jeeps.

Rey recalled driving along while Josephine, in her army overcoat and helmet, bent over her knitting. "The blazing heat of day, the cold nights, sand fleas . . . the desert strewn with the twisted remains of tanks

. . . In that cruel landscape we took turns keeping watch at night to ward off the scavengers who preyed on corpses and would have preyed on us as well."

In Jerusalem, the troupe checked into the King David Hotel. Josephine was thrilled by the city. "Here you breathe God's presence," she said. She went to the Wailing Wall, and keened along with the old men. "Before leaving Judea," she said, "the last thing I saw was the house of Mary Magdalene, the great sinner."

"We were vagabonds of the road in the service of France," Jacques says, and indeed, Josephine not only entertained, she preached the word of de Gaulle. At the Grand Hotel in Beirut, she auctioned off her gold cross of Lorraine and raised three hundred thousand francs for the Resistance.

But when the tour was done, Josephine, back in Algiers, found she was in trouble. She had gone from pillar to army post reproaching ambassadors and generals who—she felt—were not ardent enough in their support of de Gaulle, warning them if they weren't sensitive to the aspirations of native populations, France would lose its influence.

Her outspokenness—"Sometimes we struck, we never retreated," says Jacques—had resulted in complaints to the Foreign Ministry that she was playing politics instead of sticking to show business. (Truthfully, she didn't see much difference, both were dog-eat-dog enterprises.)

Even some Free French thought she did their cause more harm than good. They called her and Jacques adventurers and their "intelligence mission in the Middle East" ridiculous. "Are you really arrogant enough to think you can do better than the professionals we have in those places?"

Taken aback, Josephine still had no regrets. "I have had several close calls in enemy air raids," she told a correspondent for an American newspaper, "and sometimes I'm bone tired, sometimes I don't feel well, but whenever I'm tempted to chuck it all and hie myself off to some quiet nook, I remember France, my race and my resolve and I gain fresh strength to carry on."

She said this resolve had been born on the day she read how the Germans were welcoming all visitors to Paris "with the exception of Jews and dark-skinned people." After that, she would sometimes wake from a dream that "crowds of Germans and other prejudiced nationalities were breaking down my door to grab me. . . . When soldiers applaud me, I like to believe they will never acquire a hatred for colored people because of the cheer I have brought them. I may be foolish, but it's the way I feel."

While she was singing, Paul Poiret was dying. The man who had changed the history of fashion, interior design, theatrical costuming, who had been one of Josephine's first French friends, was now old, poor, largely forgotten, yet his spirit still blazed.

"The winter of 1943–4 in wartime Paris was dire," wrote Palmer White. "But Poiret had work to do. . . . Rain, snow, sleet or shine, he would be painting outside in the city he loved, grey, hushed and invaded though it might be. He did not see the Nazi flags, the soldiers of the Occupation, and the German signs in the car-less streets."

Ankles swollen, suffering from Parkinson's disease, his heart failed; he gave up the struggle on April 28. The funeral took place May 1. Once, Palmer White said, "fifty articles would have been written about him, in May 1944 only two appeared. In *Beaux-Arts* the reporter wrote: 'On that May morning, in the sun-drenched, ravaged capital, I would have liked to see, weeping over his grave, one beautiful young woman, a passerby, a Parisienne.' "

General René Bouscat, commander in chief of the French Air Forces, had invited Josephine to stay with him and his family in Algiers, and though Jean and Odette had offered a suite at the St. George, Josephine knew it was better to live with the big boss who could protect her from her enemies. Like Miki Sawada before her, Bouscat's wife, Blanche, became "my little sister."

D day arrived in June, and under the aegis of Bouscat, Josephine flew to Corsica to sing in the service of Free France. As her plane approached the coast, its motors died, and the pilot had to land in the sea. Nothing suffered but Josephine's costumes, soaked in salt water.

Josephine and Jacques were surprised to be welcomed to the island by Gianviti, their old friend from the homeless shelter on rue du Cheval-eret. He was now director of the Corsican police force, appointed by de Gaulle. (Everybody but Josephine and Jacques seemed to be reaping rewards for their loyalty to Le Grand Charles.) Gianviti showed the visitors two antiaircraft guns named "Josephine" and "J'ai Deux Amours." They had shot down six German planes.

After June 6, it seemed as if every French person in Algeria had been a fervent Gaullist from the beginning, and all of them were claiming victory and trying to snag seats on the first plane to Paris. Jacques, who had been gone for a short time, returned to Algiers to find Josephine "absolutely changed. 'I think I'm going to give up show business,' she said. 'I'm going to retire to a convent.' 'Bravo,' I said. She looked at me; she was not amused."

"For a full week, Josephine went around Algiers dressed as a nun," says Odette. "She was tired of sickness, travel, performing, and political intrigue. Also, Jacques was no longer the great flame he had been when they arrived in 1941, and she had been forced to accept the fact that she could not bear children."

"I believe she sincerely thought of entering the order," Jacques says. "We were sad for her, it showed she was not happy in her skin, but one week was enough. She exchanged her nun's robes for her fatigue uniform; she had been made a sublieutenant, and was very proud."

On August 25, Paris was liberated, and on October 2, along with a whole unit of air force women, Josephine left Algeria for France on a Liberty ship. She came aboard hiding a new dog in her coat; it was forbidden to take pets with you. The dog's name was Mitraillette (French for machine gun; when it peed, it made a staccato sound, *ra-ta-ta-ra-ta-ta*).

One day on deck, air force officer Catherine Egger, struck by a whiff of some half-remembered fragrance, looked around, and recognized Josephine. "I went to her and asked what perfume she was wearing. 'Arpège from Lanvin,' she said. We fell into each other's arms; before the war, it had been my perfume too. We were soul sisters."

Catherine Egger took a picture of her soul sister, and in 1982, after watching a TV tribute to Josephine that I had presented on cable television, she sent me the photograph.

Trembling, I hold the snapshot. Josephine is laughing, and again, I can hear her saying, "You! You always want to know about me, and when I am no longer here, you will discover the truth and write my book." And I see myself shaking my head. "Ah, Mother, you are crazy."

Chapter 29

—

JOSEPHINE, HEROINE OF THE RESISTANCE

"That German cow in my blue satin sheets!"

*I*f Hitler hadn't cast out blacks along with Jews, might Josephine have stayed on in Paris entertaining the conquerors throughout the occupation?

It's possible, but history doesn't disclose its alternatives, and anyway, some have greatness thrust upon them. She came back a heroine of the Resistance, untainted. Few who had remained behind could claim as much. During the four years she was gone, Pétain's "collaboration with honor" had been seized on by many who were willing to accommodate the Nazis, so long as they could continue their own lives.

On August 17, 1944, German forces were retreating before the Allied armies. "In the rue Lafayette," wrote a journalist, ". . . monocled generals sped past like shining torpedoes, accompanied by elegantly dressed blondes."

On the nineteenth, the insurrection had begun. Posters exhorted citizens to revolt, people sang the "Marseillaise," hidden guns were dug up, barricades built. To redeem their honor, citizens fought (behind ramparts made of dug-up cobblestones, old cars, sandbags, and trunks of chopped-down chestnut trees) in support of General Philippe Leclerc's Second Free French Armored Division. General Leclerc had also asked for—and got—help from two American battalions of field artillery as he moved through Paris.

After six days, the fighting ended. Germans were coming up out of the subways with their hands in the air, and General von Choltitz, the German military governor of Paris (who had ignored Hitler's orders to blow up bridges and monuments), signed a cease-fire agreement.

Three months later, François Mauriac wrote that the city's deliverance by the Parisians was "the thing in the world we had least imagined. . . . A too cruel contrast existed between the . . . risks of the small number who led the underground fighting, and the apparent indifference of the man on the street, the tradespeople, the sharks of the black market. . . . The resistance was a deaf struggle, carried on in the darkness where men suffered and died alone. . . ."

A new struggle posed new questions. "What was to be done about the searing shame of it all?" asked David Pryce-Jones in *Paris in the Third Reich,* ". . . about the damage to the nation by its loyal serving of foreign interests and its complicity in genocide as well?"

Through an accident of fate—"I didn't choose this moment, moments always choose me"—Josephine had escaped the violence that accompanied the liberation. And when she returned from North Africa, she was, according to Alain Romans (a fellow worker for de Gaulle), "more French than Louis XVI. I said to her, 'It was very nice of you to save France for us, Josephine.' "

Traveling to Paris from Marseille in an old Cadillac, she observed that half the windows of a passing train had been blown away, replaced by wood, and all along the route were bombed-out villages.

I was a tiny child during the war, and I still remember a night when the Germans rode motorcycles around our house while my mother shook and held me and my little sister Marie Jo close to her in her big bed. As I grew up, my love for my mother was mixed with a kind of contempt because I thought she was so passive, so unlike the bold Josephine. It was only after her death that I learned how she had traveled between the occupied and unoccupied zones, smuggling messages for the underground, defiantly wearing a yellow Star of David on her coat, though she wasn't Jewish.

I wonder if she'd ever met Jean Moulin, a legendary leader of the underground who fell into the hands of Klaus Barbie, the Butcher of Lyon.

Christian Pineau, another Resistance fighter, recalled the day a German officer brought a man from his cell to the prison courtyard. "To my horror, I recognized Moulin. . . . There was a bad bluish wound on his left temple. A light rattle escaped his swollen lips. . . . Barbie gave him a piece of paper to write down the names of other resistants. Weak and bleeding, Moulin took it, and after a few seconds gave it back. . . . On the paper . . . was a caricature of Barbie. Jean Moulin died of torture, but never gave a name."

Long afterward, in front of the Panthéon, André Malraux, then French minister of culture, paid homage to this hero. "More than twenty years have passed," he said, "since Jean Moulin became leader of the people of the night. . . . Young people, think of this man, of the poor misshapen face of his last day, of his lips that never talked. That day, his was the face of France."

In October of 1944, Josephine arrived in Paris. "She stopped traffic," Buddy Smith told me. Smith, a black American soldier and musician, said there were "a million people up and down the Champs to see her when she came in. It was a glorious day, as big as the day they liberated Paris. She was in a big Daumier, and that car could only crawl about three miles an hour, so many people were out there. She was in the back, with all the flowers—people were throwing these flowers."

Despite her triumphant return, Josephine's satisfaction at being back in France was mixed with irritation. Le Beau Chêne, though still in good condition, had been occupied first by Germans, and now by Americans, while her apartment on avenue Bugeaud had been allocated to Jean Gabin, who was sharing it with his current lover, Marlene Dietrich. Josephine felt possessive not only about the apartment, but about Gabin, who had played her brother in *Zou Zou.* "When I think that German cow is sleeping in my blue satin sheets!" she raved.

Many stars who had fought a less honorable war than Gabin or Josephine were having to face the consequences of their behavior. Women accused of nothing worse than sleeping with German soldiers—"horizontal collaboration"—had their heads shaved and their foreheads marked with swastikas before they were marched through the streets.

Brought up before a Governmental Commission for the Purge of

Entertainment, the actress Arletty was asked how a great French artist could have had a German lover. "With your talent!" said the judge.

"My talent belongs to France," said Arletty, "my ass is international." She received a reprimand.

In the case of Chevalier, he was able to show he had sung only once in Germany, at a prison camp, on condition that ten French prisoners of war be set free. His name was cleared.

Josephine, her own wartime conduct above reproach, had different problems. On Christmas leave, Jacques Abtey arrived in Paris and was informed by the concierge at the Carlton Hotel that Miss Baker had left for the market at 4 A.M. (Not being able to move the "German cow" out of her apartment, she was billeted at the Carlton, which had been requisitioned by the military.)

"The concierge told me," Jacques says, "that for the past two days, she'd been buying meat and vegetables. I thought, I'll be damned, has she become a chef? Indeed, I found her at Les Halles, laced tightly into her big blue uniform coat—she had replaced the French air force buttons with English ones, don't ask me why—and she was gesticulating among the butchers.

" 'Jacques,' she screamed as soon as she saw me, 'you came at the right moment,' and she put at least ten bulky packages in my arms. 'Take these to that gray Citroën.'

"She had gathered two hundred kilos of veal for needy old people, one ton of vegetables, and one ton of coal. The coal she had discovered in the basement of her building on avenue Bugeaud, and taken away under the strong protest of her tenants. 'You are rich,' she had said to them. 'You can buy some more on the black market. This coal belongs to me, my super bought it with rent money.' "

At each stop, Josephine would announce to the recipients of her largesse, "You see, the Free French and General de Gaulle are not forgetting you."

"What I did not know then," Jacques says, "is that she had put her jewels in pawn to be able to do all that."

Though sometimes she got a little of her own back. When Jacques told her he'd been given one hundred thousand francs to establish a mission in Morocco, Josephine seemed pleased. " 'For once,' she said, 'they have been a little bit generous. Listen, would you be kind enough to lend me that money for forty-eight hours?'

"I said of course, but after two or three days, I was going crazy, I barely knew the colonel who had advanced me the money. Then Josephine said she was not going to return it. 'I have done enough for France. She can do this much for me.' "

"With the winding down of the war, and the restoration of Josephine's health," says Donald Wyatt, "came an overriding ambition to fight her way back to the top."

"Poor brave girl," said André Malraux. "She was saying it is easier to make a comeback than to become a star in the first place."

But her ambition did not make her turn away from the soldiers who loved her. The War Ministry had been pleased to issue an order for Josephine and a troupe of forty to follow the French First Army through the liberated countries, and she was preparing for the adventure. "She came direct to my salon," Jean Clement reported. " 'You have to do my hair, *chéri.*' "

Clement's shop on rue Clement-Marot was flourishing. In 1942, in the midst of an electricity shortage, Mistinguett had taken him to the flea market, and they had bought three generators and put them in his basement. "We had six bicyclists (two shifts of three) with their wheels attached to the generators, pedaling to make electricity for the hair dryers. I paid them good money, they had been racers in the Tour de France, and the chic women would go down to the basement and thank them and give them champagne, rare bottles the pedalers would sell on the black market. La Miss and the pedalers, they gave me my start."

Once Josephine was properly coiffed, Odette Merlin took her to Balenciaga to order gowns. Then Josephine turned her attention to finding a musical conductor to tour with her. A *good* one, she told Jacques, because "I can't take risks anymore, I have been too sick, it's too hard on me."

Enter Jo Bouillon, handsome, a prodigy in a family of prodigies. He had won first prize in violin at the Paris Conservatory, but fell in love with jazz, turning from classical music to show business. Before the war, he'd had his own orchestra.

"In 1940," Pierre Guillermin told me, laughing, "Jo and I were sent south with the 255th Infantry, and courageously, we defended the French Riviera! I was musical director of our regiment, Jo played violin, we did free concerts for the boys. Then Jo started his orchestra again, and I was the pianist. By the end of the occupation, we had to work for the Germans or they would have sent us to a labor camp."

Part of that work consisted of a daily broadcast over the Nazi-controlled Radio-Paris. (The French laughed behind their hands, and said, *"Radio-Paris ment, Radio-Paris est allemand,"* which translates as "Radio-Paris lies, Radio-Paris is German.")

Result: Jo, accused of having been a collaborator, was facing "purification" at the hands of a purge committee. He was also facing a challenge from Josephine, who indicated that, through association with her, he could be shriven.

She found him rehearsing for a radio show. "I told him it was a matter of his dropping everything and following me. . . . I was facing my responsibilities, he should face his." She said he would be donating his services.

Complications arose at once. Besides performing, Sublieutenant Baker was producing the show, and while she and Bouillon and the other singers and comedians might be willing to work free, Jo's musicians were not.

Josephine was undaunted. To pay their salaries, she pawned jewels and mortgaged the building on avenue Bugeaud. The tour went forward. "She was a woman with a human intelligence, and an animal instinct," says Pierre Guillermin. "Traveling, she always wore her uniform. Paris was liberated, but the war was not over."

Jo Bouillon was amazed by her fortitude throughout a bitter winter. "The barracks in which we put on our show were sometimes too small to contain all the troops, and Josephine wanted to sing for *everyone.* 'Throw up a stage outside,' she'd order. 'But it's too cold, Madame, the men are hardened to this kind of weather, they're soldiers, but it's not fair to you.' 'I'm a soldier too,' she'd retort, and sing outdoors for an hour at a time."

According to the autobiography published in 1949, she even performed in Germany at the end of the war, in a camp where typhoid raged. She described the scene. "Deportees from the four corners of the world were wearing armbands with the croix de Lorraine around their thin arms. . . . I had to smile, I had to sing. Yes, songs have a soul. But the soul of songs sometimes can strangle you." After her death, Jo Bouillon said the camp was Buchenwald, which surprised me. Josephine never named the place, or mentioned the presence of any Jewish prisoners.

Earlier, she and Jo had done fund-raisers in Monte Carlo, Nice, Cannes, Toulon, collecting two million francs for war victims, and everywhere they had gone, Josephine knew all the generals. French, British, American, and Canadian generals. "I knew Churchill too," she told a reporter in 1973. "Just before he died, I sent him a telegram and said, I HOPE YOU WILL HAVE A HUNDRED MORE BIRTHDAYS, and he sent a telegram back saying, DON'T BE SO CRUEL, JOSEPHINE."

On March 28, 1945, she was in Paris, appearing in a "festival of French song and dance" at the Théâtre des Champs-Élysées, where *La Revue Nègre* had begun. The 18th of June Club (named for the day in 1940 when de Gaulle first broadcast to his countrymen over the BBC) had organized this benefit for the Free French forces.

The general was in the audience, and reprinted in the theater program was a letter he had written commending "the few" who had listened to their hearts. "It is the heart that was right," the letter said. "My companions, my friends of the 18th of June, '40 . . . we have done something."

It was as though the general were speaking directly to Josephine. For this show, no titillating burlesque bumps, all was elegance; the star changed costumes nine times.

The weeks flew past, she went to London (at Churchill's request) to appear in a victory show, and, on May 9, the war in Europe ended. Half an hour before midnight, the Germans signed an unconditional surrender.

Now Josephine resolved to give a lecture about *her* war. She went to the Folies-Bergère to enlist the aid of Michel Gyarmathy. "She told me again that her father was Jewish. 'Like yours,' she said. She asked me for a big green piece of fabric. She had decided to perform in a Paris auditorium, for free. 'Alone?' I said. She said, 'Yes, I have a lot to tell.'

"I went, and I could not believe it. On the bare stage, she had a long table covered with that green fabric, and a glass and a carafe of water, and a pile of notes. She came on in her blue air force uniform, wearing glasses, and when the audience applauded, she stopped them. 'Please, we are not in a music hall, you can applaud me at the end if what I tell you pleases you.' Then: '*Voilà*, on the day the Germans occupied that, I did this,' and for two hours, she talked to two thousand people, and she had a triumph.

"I asked her afterward how she had been able to make all those notes. 'You barely know how to write.' She said, 'During the night, I heard a voice, as though I were Joan of Arc, and it dictated to me, and I wrote.'

I looked at her, wondering, is she talking seriously, or is she dreaming?"

Now, with the weather softening, the trees in bud, Josephine's thoughts turned to the Dordogne valley. She phoned Donald Wyatt. "Through the Red Cross, I had a Hillman truck at my disposal," he says, "and she wanted to pick up things she had hidden in the farms and villages around Les Milandes at the time she left France."

Before the trip, Jacques Abtey, who would be coming along, told Donald that he and Josephine were no longer lovers, and would not marry. "I am an officer, I don't want to be Monsieur Baker."

"It was a shock to me," Donald said. Then the trio set out for a weekend in Les Milandes, the Hillman piled with linens bought on the black market in Paris.

After unloading these at the château, they went off to collect Josephine's belongings. "In one farmhouse," Donald reports, "we gathered up two dozen gold-rimmed goblets—given to her by the king of Denmark, she said—that had been stored in a dry well. In another, there was a set of Limoges china buried underneath floorboards. We got gold place settings from attics and secret places in walls.

"Whenever we arrived at a new house, people would run to Josephine and kiss her, tears coursing down their cheeks. It was so strange for me to see white people bowing in front of a black person. By afternoon, the Hillman was packed to the top with articles that had been entrusted to the custody of Josephine's faithful neighbors over the past five years."

Late in June, she invited Jo Bouillon to Beau Chêne. (Jacques had reclaimed it for her.) Jo was totally unprepared to find the house "flooded with light and a party in full swing. Dressed in a clinging white gown that molded her marvelous body, Josephine moved among her guests . . . Allied dignitaries, officers sporting multiple stars . . . I drew her aside. 'Why didn't you tell me you were having a big reception?' 'I wanted to surprise you, Jo'. . . . She thrived on intrigue. That night she had floodlit the statues in her garden to make them stand out in the darkness; looking at them I realized that part of Josephine would always remain in the shadows."

The party was for Josephine's erstwhile lover, El Glaoui, who had come to Paris on an official visit. At that time he was the Moroccan official with the closest ties to the French government, and he had paid a heavy price for this, having lost a son in the battle of Monte Cassino.

"Josephine had sent Jacques and me to pick up girls from the Lido and the Folies-Bergère," Donald Wyatt remembers. "At dawn, you could see couples coming out of the bushes in the park, tenderly, arm in arm. It was a big success."

And why not? Josephine knew how to entertain men, the men, including the Glaoui, were pleased to be entertained, the prefect of police was pleased to close off the traffic around Beau Chêne for the night, and Monsieur Guignery was pleased to do all the electrical work in the park. "It was the beginning of electric guitars, and Josephine wanted them," says Madame Guignery. "We were not used to that sound, to the effect of loudspeakers in the trees. It was formidable."

Josephine in the vanguard, one more time.

Summer came, and with it, a longing on her part to spend more time at Les Milandes. She invited Claude Menier and his mother to the château for a fortnight. (It was Claude's older brother Jean to whom Josephine had been engaged when he was killed at the front.) "Claude had been afflicted with polio," says Donald Wyatt, "and during the war, he developed a lung ailment. He was thin, almost emaciated."

"Claude Menier was a rich man, a millionaire," says Georges Malaury's wife, Yvette, who still lives at Les Milandes, and guides tourists through the château. "He was an artist, he held his palette in his teeth, because one arm was no good."

A generous suitor, Claude showered Josephine with expensive presents, and followed her to Switzerland when September came. She had decided on Switzerland as the scene of her comeback tour—in real theaters, not army camps—because while most of Europe was still bleeding, the Swiss were rich enough to buy theater tickets.

"Since 1940," says Jacques Abtey, "she had dedicated herself to France, now she had to think of her own future."

She also had to prove that she was still alive. "In Switzerland," she said, "the newspapers were saying, 'It is not Josephine, but a double. This one is thinner. She is not bad, but she doesn't have the shape of Josephine.' "

"She had been away all that time," Jacques says. "She was not getting any younger, she had witnessed at first hand the games politicians played. The only positive thing in the past few months had been her association with Jo Bouillon's orchestra. She could rely on him and his pianist, Pierre Guillermin, to make her sound good."

In Zurich, a theater critic wrote that reports of Josephine's death had been premature, but the information "had some truth in it. . . . The banana dancer . . . is no more. . . . The elegant Parisienne has elegantly eliminated the Negress in herself."

In Lucerne, Lausanne, Berne, she held press conferences, talked of her war years, and "told us," said one reporter, "the lessons she has learned. 'The contact with the troops makes you more human. . . . In the old days, I studied attitudes, effects, today I try to be myself.' " She said she was surprised by the warm welcome of the public. "I thought they would have forgotten me."

Nobody forgot her. In January 1946, the French government sent her to Berlin to perform in a gala for all Allied soldiers. "I had the honor," she said, "to represent France with Jo Bouillon and Colette Mars . . . a friend."

By now, Josephine had convinced herself she was in love with Jo Bouillon. The fact that he was bisexual—homosexual by preference— was of small moment to her; she had always found the difficult conquests more interesting than the easy ones. She was also very fond of Colette Mars, a talented singer, very blond, very white-skinned—the kind of looks that always attracted Josephine.

"I too had left France in 1941," Colette told me. "Like Josephine, I was a fervent Gaullist. I knew her when she was in Dr. Comte's clinic; one day she was so bad off we had already ordered the floral arrangement. Then I served under her in the air force. She had done a very beautiful war. When she talked about representing France, she lit up.

"That 1946 trip from Paris to Berlin took three days, because much of the track had been blown up; every so often, we would be switched from one train to another. Josephine insisted I travel in the compartment with her and Jo Bouillon and his lover. He was charming, with clear eyes, and Jo was having a serious relationship with him, and Josephine was jealous.

"One afternoon, she and I were sitting in the compartment while Jo and his lover talked in the corridor outside. Through the glass door, we saw Jo take his lover's hands. Then he came back into our cabin, bent over Josephine, and kissed her on the head. Suddenly, I saw before me a fury. She got up and started kicking him—she was wearing heavy combat boots, though the war was over, she loved the game—with such energy that I huddled in a corner, holding on to the luggage rack, and poor Jo was completely petrified.

"There were four sleeping berths in our compartment. On one side, Jo Bouillon had the top berth, his lover the lower. On the other side, Josephine was up and I was below. That night, we got into our beds, and suddenly Josephine said, 'I'm so cold, I want to go down with Colette.' And she scrambled down, exactly like a monkey, and lay next to me, very close. So now Jo was jealous. It is very difficult to explain everybody's feelings. He aimed a flashlight at us and said, 'What are you doing?'

"I was trembling, I was very young, and Jo Bouillon's poor friend didn't move, and then Josephine said, 'Enough, I want to sleep.' It was dark, I made myself as small as possible, when suddenly Josephine took my hand and put it on her superb breast. I have to say it was very agreeable, but I did not dare to go further."

Upon their arrival in Berlin, Josephine took Colette on a tour. "Here was the train station, nothing left but this field. And here was the Hotel Adlon.' Half the buildings she remembered had been razed; the gala was held in the old Palace of Justice, which was still standing."

For the gala, Josephine loaned Colette a white ermine cape, a diamond necklace and earrings, and a dress by Jean Dessès. "She told me, 'I want you to be beautiful for France.' "

A party raged—that's the right word—in the stately rooms of the former palace, before, during, and after the show. France had sent champagne and cognac, and the Russians got drunk.

It was, says Donald Wyatt, "the most exclusive party I had ever attended, and the most boisterous, especially on the part of the Soviet generals who set the pace. They were big men, they guzzled tumblers of vodka, and during the dancing, they cut in whenever they saw an attractive woman. Some of them, inebriated, played a game of sliding down the long and curving balustrades of marble to the floor below.

"The party ended in a spirit of fraternity; everyone—even the great Russian generals, Marshal Zhukov among them, who were sitting in the first row—joined Josephine in singing the 'Marseillaise.' "

The rest of the week, Josephine and her troupe worked in the quartier Napoléon, the sector of Berlin that housed the French army. "She had us perform without stopping from 10 A.M. to 5 P.M.," says Colette. "When I wanted to eat ice cream, she took it away from me. 'You have a fragile voice, and it is very bad for your throat.' But I never saw anyone eat ice cream like Josephine."

Things change, things stay the same. I think of Josephine in Mr. Dad's shop, making a trade. Her child's body for ice cream.

More resonance from the past: The quartier Napoléon had been Hitler's Olympic Village. In 1936, when the American track and field star Jesse Owens won four gold medals, Adolf Hitler refused to recognize this stupendous achievement by a black athlete. Now in the same place, young French soldiers were enjoying the songs of a black American-born artist.

And helping her to bathe. "We traveled with a zinc tub," Colette says, "and when she was fatigued, she would just put herself naked in that tub and the soldiers would bring warm water and pour it over her head. After that, she could start again. Soldiers asked for autographs, God only knows how many she signed. She always pushed me to the front, but nobody was asking me for autographs."

After Berlin, the company headed for Brussels, where they found Noble Sissle and Flournoy Miller staging a wartime version of *Shuffle Along* for restless American troops awaiting transport home. Sissle and Josephine had a friendly reunion. She had been fifteen years old when he rejected her, sent her weeping from the theater in Philadelphia. Now she was forty. No one had seen her cry in a long time.

Chapter 30

—

JOSEPHINE DUMPS A MILLIONAIRE FOR A BANDLEADER

"I can't marry Claude, he's much too jealous"

They played Brussels, Copenhagen, and by late June, Josephine was again on the road to Morocco to entertain air force troops. And again, she landed in the hospital. Odette Merlin came from Paris on an army plane dispatched by General Bouscat to bring the patient home.

"When I arrived," Odette says, "the rumor was that Josephine had received the *bouillon d'onze heures,* a poisoned soup fed her by the Glaoui's women." Was it possible? Had the Glaoui's women—or the women of some other Moroccan nobleman whom Josephine had dazzled—thought, with the war over, they were finally rid of her, the veil-less one? And here she was back again, so they had tried to kill her with eleventh hour soup?

Four days later, she was delivered to the Clinique Ambroise Pare in Paris. "She was cold and gray," Odette says. "A doctor opened her up, then did nothing. He was afraid. Jacques and I were desperate, we did not sleep for three days."

By now, Jacques was engaged to Jacqueline Ceiller de la Barre, a girl from Sarlat, who joined him and Odette in their vigil. "I knew he and Josephine had been lovers," Jacqueline says. "She could barely speak, but she dissected me with her eyes."

At two o'clock one morning, Jacques found Josephine covered with sweat "like a dead body. There was a doctor in Paris who was famous for blood transfusions, and we called him."

An hour later, accompanied by a donor (a burly young policeman), the transfusion expert showed up. Isn't it odd that, in 1931, in *Mon Sang dans Tes Veines,* Josephine wrote about a black American girl giving her blood to save the white boy she loved, and in 1946, a white French policeman came out of the night and gave his blood to save Josephine, yet she never spoke of him to anyone?

A few weeks later, the recuperating invalid wrote to Donald Wyatt (home at last in Nashville, Tennessee, and teaching at Fisk University) that she was engaged to Claude Menier. "He is in Switzerland, also quite sick. As soon as I am in good health, and he as well, we are going to be married."

Claude wrote to Donald too. "Josephine is now much better, thank God. She was decorated with the Medal of the Resistance and had a reception at her nursing home."

It happened on October 8, and made the papers. SECRET AGENT OF FREE FRANCE DECORATED! At Josephine's bedside were Blanche Bouscat, Colette Mars, Colonel Guy de Boissoudy, and General de Gaulle's daughter, Madame de Boissieu. De Gaulle himself had written to congratulate her. "I knew of and much valued the great services you rendered not long ago . . . the enthusiasm with which you put your magnificent talent at the disposal of our cause . . . My wife and I send ardent wishes for your quick and complete recovery."

"Josephine was weak, but she looked radiant," Colette says. "She asked me to help her pull on long white satin gloves, and to put some pillows behind her. 'I would like to be upright, to receive a medal from France.'

"During the speech of Colonel de Boissoudy, I cried all the tears in my body. You could see the emotion Josephine felt as the colonel pinned the medal to her hospital gown."

From Claude to Donald on October 12: "I have not seen her for five months now, but I write her very often. I hope to have some news, and that it will be very good."

From Josephine to Donald on October 29: "I do not think I will marry Claude, for he is much too jealous and wishes me to leave the theater. It is a lot to ask, for there is no woman in Paris who can star in a large theater. Mistinguett is too old, so that leaves me alone. I cannot stop now, Donald, and I am sorry for Claude and myself, but alas, there is nothing that can be done about it."

That same month, Josephine emerged from the hospital and insisted on giving Jacques and Jacqueline Abtey their wedding party. Ninety-three people attended the reception at Beau Chêne, though many were surprised by the arrangement. (Josephine's liaison with Jacques was widely known.) Artists, the wedding guests told each other, are different.

"Josephine came down the grand staircase supported by Jacques and me," Jacqueline says. "She was wearing a long gown from Balenciaga, one side white, the other ruby red. I hadn't been able to find anything but a plain gray dress—Josephine's closet was full of beautiful outfits, but she never offered me one—and Jacques was in uniform.

"For about ten minutes, Josephine stayed downstairs and was charming with our guests. Then she asked to go back to her room. The maid and I undressed her and put her to bed, and she told me, 'The only man in my life I should have married is Jacques.' Then she crossed herself. It's unbelievable, but true."

On New Year's Eve, Josephine checked into the Clinique Bizet for more surgery. This time, the operation—which should have been performed earlier—was a success, maybe because Josephine had asked the priest of Le Vésinet to celebrate a Mass for her prior to the operation. She said heaven had sent Dr. Thiroloix and Dr. Funck-Brentano "to whom I owe my life."

She asked Odette and Jacqueline to go and prepare for her homecoming. "She wanted her bed made up with Swiss linen," Jacqueline says, "embroidered with forget-me-nots."

By now Jo Bouillon was staying at Beau Chêne off and on, and Odette, who had been delegated to supervise the help there, stumbled into his private life. "There was an Alsatian war orphan, blond, very good-looking, helping the gardeners, and I was surprised to see him wearing expensive leather shoes—we had no leather after the war—and an English jacket. I asked the servants where the boy got his clothes, and they told me they were gifts from Jo Bouillon. 'And you don't know the worst,' they said. 'He made that boy wear Mademoiselle Josephine's gowns.' "

Jacqueline, who knew nothing of this, was startled when she entered the master bedroom. "The bed was unmade, sheets stained with blood, men's underwear on the floor. I had to tell Josephine. It was very unpleasant, and the next time Jo Bouillon arrived, she yelled at him, 'Go away, faggot!' "

Six months later, to the consternation of her friends, she announced that she and Jo were going to be married. Then she told the Guignerys that she was going to have to sell Beau Chêne. Georges tried to dissuade her—"Such a superb property so close to Paris will be very valuable in a few years"—but the owner of Les Milandes was pressing, threatening that if she didn't buy the château, he would sell it to someone else. Afraid of losing Les Milandes, she sacrificed Beau Chêne, though she could not bear to supervise its dismantling, or, for that matter, its sale.

The Guignerys also tried to dissuade her from marrying Jo Bouillon.

Madame Guignery: "When Georges went to her and asked, 'Josephine, why? You know what he is,' she answered, 'I need an orchestra and I'm going to cure him of his habits.' "

I believe she *was* in love, or at least infatuated, with Jo Bouillon, and for a while, at least, they were certainly lovers. In French, we have a saying, *tout feu, tout flamme.* All fire, all flame. Too hot not to cool down.

Jacqueline Abtey remembers receiving the wedding invitation in Morocco. "We were very surprised. We got to Les Milandes a few days early—Jacques and I stayed in a room under the roof, to have peace, and Josephine gave Mohamed Menebhi the Louis XVI room on the second floor. Most of the guests hadn't arrived yet."

The afternoon before her wedding, Josephine decided to exercise the female equivalent of *droit de seigneur.* "I was walking in the park," says Georges Malaury, "when suddenly I see Josephine having sex with Jacques Abtey. I had been an altar boy, I was twelve years old, at first it gives you ideas. At the same time, it seemed shocking. But Josephine was very amorous, she had such a temperament."

At four the following morning, her temperament exploded. "In a nightgown, she erupted into our room like a tigress," Jacqueline says. "She was brandishing a knife and calling me names, blaming me because she was going to marry a queer. It was frightful.

"I said to Jacques, 'I'm leaving,' and Mohamed, hearing voices raised in anger, came into the room as Josephine was chasing me with the knife, and he stopped her. He said, 'Josephine, I will never forgive you that as a host you betrayed your duty. Never as a guest of mine did you witness such a scene. I'm sorry, but since Jacqueline is leaving, I'm going with her.'

"Jacques, Mohamed, and I went to the hotel in Beynac. We could not believe what had happened, we wanted to think she was delirious, or walking in her sleep."

Early on her wedding day, Josephine was out haranguing the German workmen who were weeding and cutting the grass. "The war was over," Georges Malaury says, "but we still called them prisoners of war. About ten of them had stayed behind after Germany was defeated; they rented themselves out to the surrounding farms, and Josephine sometimes employed them.

"She was very harsh with them. I think she was trying, a little bit, to show them the other side of the coin, that things had changed. She was paying them back. But she was harsh with everyone. Guy Hutin was French, and acted as gardener, barman, chauffeur, whatever Madame needed, and still Josephine put him in his place. She instructed him that she wanted everything very clean for her wedding, and he said he knew it. " 'Madame,' I told her, 'Monsieur Bouillon told me that already.' She answered me, 'Guy, after God, I'm the only master here!' "

When one of the protagonists is extremely ill, French law permits a marriage to be performed away from city hall. In the case of Josephine, the mayor of Castelnaud Fayrac thought he would be officiating at ceremonies for a dying woman, until Josephine appeared, all smiles. She was dressed in blue, with a plunging neckline, a feathered hat, a corsage of white orchids, and a gold belt, a present from Mohamed. (Bachir Ben Bachir had sent seven gold bracelets encrusted with diamonds.)

At the civil ceremony, held in a salon of the château, she again claimed—for the record—to be the daughter of Arthur Baker.

In the chapel for the religious ceremony (and not wanting to look like an orphan), she had Pepito's sister and brother-in-law, Christina and Philippe Scotto, act as her family. During the Mass, they sat on her left. Many Bouillons were also in attendance; Jo's parents had come, and his two brothers with their wives and children, including Jo's favorite niece, the then seventeen-year-old Maryse. (What none of them knew was that, under French law, this marriage was no more legal than the one to Jean Lion had been. The bride was still Mrs. William Baker.) It was Josephine's forty-first birthday.

"Famous Negro songstress puts on clothes and marries a bandleader," said *Life* magazine, adding that the wedding had been "gay but genteel." No pun was intended.

"We musicians were surprised by the wedding," said Pierre Guillermin. "We knew that women were not Jo's strength. A few days later, we left on a tour of South America."

But first, Josephine bought Les Milandes; it was her wedding gift to herself. In a contract witnessed by Jo's brother Gabriel, she stipulated that it was bought with her own funds, and would remain her exclusive property.

There were a couple of reasons why she was once again leaving France. The country was still divided politically, and even though Josephine was a die-hard Gaullist, she sympathized with the disgraced Marshal Pétain. In 1945, he had been condemned to death, but his sentence was commuted to life imprisonment in the fortress jail on the Île d'Yeu. Josephine felt the marshal should be freed, that "the drama of the great old military man, whatever his weaknesses have been, hides a last secret: the possibility of once again forging in France a union of all men of good will."

Moreover, Europe was now a sad continent, short of food, houses, jobs, money. The thought of the crazy years between the wars, the years when Josephine had reigned, made people uncomfortable. So did Josephine's marriage. Odette Merlin says that high-ranking military men were disgusted. "*Their* Josephine marrying a homosexual seemed an insult to their manhood. Jo Bouillon's crime was not the worst committed during those shameful years, but many friends turned away from Josephine. I asked her to take me out of her will. I was sad, but I could not understand."

Jacques Abtey concurs. "From the day she married Jo Bouillon, it was as though Joan of Arc had become small, had cut off her legs, so to speak. The generals and the great French families, they did not come to her anymore."

But the Argentinians came to her in throngs, as she toured their cities, and the Chileans, and the Mexicans. In Mexico, she found her old friends the Joneses. Lydia and Ed had fled Europe at the beginning of the war. "We went back to Chicago," Lydia told me, "but we couldn't take it no more the way our people were treated, and we moved to Mexico."

In Mexico, Lydia said, Josephine fell "absolutely madly in love" with the composer Augustin Lara, who was married to the actress Maria Felix. "To affirm herself, Josephine still needed that attention from men, to sleep with them, to possess them, and one night when Jo was not around she said, 'Let's go have dinner with Lara,' but he was crazy about the beautiful Maria, he did not want to be with Josephine, she did not get him."

If Josephine could not get the man she wanted, she could still go to a bullfight and upstage the bull. The Joneses took her to a *corrida,* and their son George, then fifteen, recalled, "When the *banderillero* stuck the dart in the bull, Josephine just cried and yelled until everybody in the place got nervous."

"That winter," says Lydia, "Josephine was having an enormous success in Mexico, packing them in every night, and she begged my husband to bring her back to America. To present her in America. He said okay, and he advanced her fifty thousand dollars, and an IOU to sign, but she never paid him back.

"She was going to open in Boston, but first we stopped off in Chicago for a few days. We were traveling by train, and Josephine insisted on going to the dining car and talking to everyone about the injustice of racism. I told her, 'You are going to get us lynched.' "

The Joneses' place in Chicago—they had held on to it even in their self-imposed exile—was as pleasant as Josephine had remembered it from her visit there with Pepito: a ten-acre estate, a pond, a tennis court. "My sister-in-law Jean Starr—she was a great blues singer—invited Josephine to dinner," Lydia says. "She thought to please Josephine by cooking cornbread and chitlins. Josephine stared at the chitlins. 'What is this?'

"Jean Starr said, 'Oh, girl, get out of my face, you know what hog guts are!' "

In Boston, where Ed Jones had booked a hotel suite, Josephine assigned him and Lydia the maid's room. "Can you imagine?" says Lydia. "She was in the master bedroom with Jo Bouillon, and we were in this hole, and it was our money we were spending presenting her to America!"

For her part, Josephine was determined to present Jo Bouillon to America—from the stage of Boston's Majestic Theatre. "Ed told her not to do it," says Lydia. "He said, 'Just let Jo come on and play, you didn't introduce him in Mexico, so don't be a fool here. This country is not ready to see a black woman introduce her white husband.' 'Oh yes,' she says, 'I have to introduce my Jo.'"

Before the Boston opening on Christmas Eve, almost as an after-thought, Josephine had wired the French singer Roland Gerbeau in Paris and asked him to join her in *Paris Sings Again,* which he was happy to do. But the real excitement in the press centered around Josephine's costumes by Schiaparelli, Balenciaga, and Jean Dessès—no star since Gertrude Lawrence had appeared with such a huge wardrobe, said the *Boston Post.* As for her jewels, they were so valuable, Josephine would be "under police guard while on the stage of the Majestic."

There was a thirty-three-carat emerald, a sixteen-carat sapphire, and a black diamond that gave off "glints of red fire." The black diamond got better notices than the show.

"The theater was empty," says Lydia. "We lost our money, and she never even said thanks."

"The war had just ended," Roland Gerbeau says, "and with Josephine's halo as an angel of the liberation, she thought it was the right moment for her American comeback. But the show was not what the Americans wanted from her, she was a French chanteuse, nothing left of her American roots."

Was the party over? She sent an S.O.S. to Donald Wyatt in Nashville asking him to come north and talk to the Negro press. "She was aware," he says, "that some black people were still complaining that while they had continued to suffer the effects of segregation, she had escaped to Paris and lived a life of gaiety and luxury.

"When I arrived in Boston, Jo Bouillon was cordial but cool. I don't think he took kindly to my occupying an adjoining room, especially when Josephine came in every night to get my dirty socks to wash in the basin with his."

Pierre Guillermin: "She was afraid of nothing. She would sing oper-etta with little trills, *cocoricos* like a rooster, and sometimes the mouth would open and the note did not come out, but she would go on. She was conscious of having been one of the first blacks to come out of the ghetto, proud of it, but she acted superior to white people, as if she wanted to make you pay for what she had been through. You could feel it, it was her complex.

"We went to New York because she was still hoping to perform there. We had difficulty finding a place where she could stay; it was against the law to refuse her, but we tried all the grand hotels, and when we would say it was for Josephine Baker, they would say, 'Excuse us, we made a mistake, we are fully booked.' "

It was the same scenario as when she had come to do the *Ziegfeld Follies,* with the additional humiliation that no one was offering her work. So she decided to play reporter again, to reveal America through the eyes of a simple black woman. That she was not a simple black woman didn't deter her for an instant.

She suggested a series of pieces to *France-Soir* (the biggest afternoon paper in France) which agreed to print them. But for this job, "I cannot be Josephine Baker, star of the music hall. . . . I will be Miss Brown . . . the name seems to me amusing, given the circumstances."

First she would go to Fisk (at Donald Wyatt's invitation) to speak to the students—"I want to give them courage." Jo asked to come along. "I said no, I don't want to be with a white. You will stay in New York . . . someone has to come help me if they put me in jail."

"Miss Brown" would be accompanied by a black journalist friend, Jeff Smith, who had orders not to intervene if she got in trouble. At one stop, the train sat in the station for an hour, Josephine got off, and instead of going into the coffee shop with a sign that said COLORED, went into the one with a sign that said WHITE, bought a couple of apples, and came out to be greeted by scowls from nervous blacks.

"I found only two friendly eyes," she told Jeff Smith. "They belonged to a poor hairless dirty dog." She asked him to explain the strange attitude of the blacks. "You make them afraid," he said. "Afraid? Because I bought apples?"

By the time they got to Nashville, Josephine's blood was up. When Donald Wyatt met her at the station, she couldn't wait to tell him her newly hatched plan. She would get on a bus in Nashville, and sit up front. "And the bus driver," says Donald, "would have to stop the bus, and then she was going to protest, and be pushed around, arrested. She would take a photographer and a writer from *Ebony* with her, so people could see what a martyr she'd been. But when she got to the jail, she would pull out her French passport, and then the president of America would have to apologize to the president of France for doing this to a French citizen."

Josephine never thought small. It was no police chief or governor but the president of the United States himself who would have to eat crow. Jim crow.

"I told her I thought it would be counterproductive," Donald says mildly. "I said black people had been sitting in the back of the bus all their lives. 'And you come here too good to sit where we sit.' I said the ending would be bad, because her being French gave her protection she would not have if she was just an ordinary black person living in Tennessee. She thought about it, and she didn't do it."

"At Fisk, though she was not highly educated," Donald says, "she could discuss any topic with the students."

She told the young people that in France, marriage between blacks and whites was not frowned on. The students were astonished.

From Nashville, she went home to St. Louis, spent one weekend there, and announced to Carrie, Richard, and Margaret that they must come live with her at the château. "At first my husband, Elmo, said no," Margaret told me, "but then he changed his mind."

Richard refused. "I couldn't leave. In 1936, Josephine had bought me my first truck, now I had four, I transported coal, I was a contractor, with employees."

Surprisingly, Carrie agreed to emigrate as long as Margaret came with her. "She was willing to leave that good-looking husband, Tony Hudson, behind," says Helen Morris. "Tumpy said he was too young for Carrie, he looked like a white man." The reunion in France was set for the fall, giving everyone time to make arrangements, and Josephine returned to New York.

Where there were still no job offers, but there were lots of old friends. Sometimes, in the afternoons, she went to have tea with Coco Chanel, Edith Piaf, Lucienne Boyer (both Piaf and Boyer were enjoying successful singing engagements in New York clubs). Sometimes Lucienne's husband, Jacques Pills, would join the ladies. Lucienne knew he had been one of Josephine's lovers, but wasn't jealous. ("*All* the women were crazy about him," she told me. "They ran at him with their bare breasts." Jacques, she said, used to tease their small daughter, Jacqueline, telling her, "You know, you could have been a little Baker.")

Another of Josephine's former lovers, Ralph Cooper, was now running the amateur nights at the Apollo Theatre, and one Friday, Josephine and Jo went up to Harlem to take a look. Ralph ensconced them like royalty, in a box, and at one point during the show, he introduced the legend to the audience. They didn't stop applauding until Josephine came down to the stage to receive her ovation.

She returned to France with enough money—mostly from South America—to get the rest of her jewels out of hock. (Boston hadn't seen the whole array by any means.) In March, eleven thousand copies of Jacques Abtey's book, *The Secret War of Josephine Baker*, were shipped to bookstores, and in April, Josephine opened at the Club des Champs-Élysées.

Bernard Hilda, the club's owner, found himself awed by her continuing ability to seduce the public. "I watched her many times, and I asked myself, why? Why does she get applause at the exact moment when she needs to catch a breath? And one day I understood. First of all, she looked at the people way in the back, in a cabaret. Then slowly, she raised both arms, and everyone was hypnotized, they applauded. And when she had got what she wanted, she slowly lowered her arms, and bent her head. She had obtained that second which was absolutely necessary to her."

"I sang again at the Club des Champs-Élysées with a big white feather fan to chase away the bad memories," she wrote. "The King and Queen of Belgium came to see me, incognito, which means that everybody recognized them. . . .

"Ali Khan and Rita Hayworth, sitting near the orchestra, very nice . . .

"Emperor Bao Dai, his hair as black as mine. He froze, listening to me, holding a matchbox in his delicate fingers. . . ."

It was during this engagement that Maryse Bouillon turned eighteen, and Josephine gave her a birthday party. "She bought me my first evening dress, by Dior. The next day, she tore it to shreds. I still don't know what I had done.

"From an artistic point of view, Josephine was a very great lady, but in life, she was jealous, mean. I think she had been too spoiled by what she had done, by the people surrounding her, and absolutely deformed by her own success.

"I think she loved herself, but I wonder if, deep inside, she ever loved anyone else. Even Pepito, who had been her Pygamlion—I don't know if she loved that man.

"My uncle Jo dropped everything to take care of the Milandes. The

Milandes was my childhood, I knew it without plumbing, no central heating, still a medieval castle. And I witnessed its transformation. Josephine was never around, the children did as they pleased. Margaret was elderly, overwhelmed by them, and they talked back, they were awful to her. Jo faced all that, and also managed to collect some money to leave to the children. He tried to bring some sense to the Milandes, he tried to slow Josephine down."

It wasn't possible. She had too many reasons to keep moving. After all, wouldn't the date in Milan pay for a soccer field? She was possessed by the notion of modernizing Les Milandes, building an amusement park that tourists would pay to visit. In 1940, a wandering dog had discovered a cave at Lascaux dating back to Cro-Magnon man, its walls painted with pictures of cows, bison, horses; that this nearby wonder could attract two thousand visitors a day convinced Josephine she could lure equal numbers to her kingdom. If she built it, they would come.

"When she bought the château, it was in terrible shape," Georges Malaury agrees, echoing Maryse. "Barely water, barely light. She wanted to do a casino and a *guinguette*, which is a little bar-discothèque, and a swimming pool in the shape of a J, but there was no water here. There is the Dordogne, the river down there, but the people didn't want to let her go through their land, so to make a well, she had to buy everything. She bought a big farm of a Monsieur Dartin, who never wanted to sell to her because she was black, and because she was show business. Then one day he fell off his bicycle and died, and the family sold to Josephine."

In the end, she got five of the seven houses that surrounded the château, and was in the throes of designing her own little Monte Carlo when Carrie, Margaret, and Elmo arrived in Le Havre.

On November 3, Jo went to the pier to pick up his wife's family, whom he later described as "three round-eyed gaping figures without a word of French." (Helen Morris remembered that Carrie and Margaret had their teeth pulled "and new teeth put in because they wanted to look good for the French people. I saw poor Tony Hudson a couple of times after that. He was very sad. He thought she would come back, but she never did.")

Jo drove the newcomers directly to Les Milandes, where "they fell into Josephine's arms. . . . The important thing was to get everyone settled down in the château as quickly as possible."

Josephine, to help to pay for all the reconstruction going on, was still working nights in Paris at the Club des Champs-Élysées, a cabaret the American dancer Katherine Dunham remembers well.

"This little man," Dunham says, "he was prince of one of those African states, took me to the club to see Josephine. She came over to our table, but seemed upset. I got up and danced with the prince, and then I realized why she was glaring at us. He had tennis shoes on, and she was trying to make that club go on a snob level."

Bobby Mitchell once witnessed the rivalry between the two prima donnas. "It was on the Riviera. Dunham was there with the then Aga Khan, the big fat guy. And she showed up at the Casino in Monte Carlo wearing these emeralds, earrings, necklace, bracelet, all matching. Then Josephine swept in (she always made a big entrance), took one look at these emeralds, and sparks flew from her eyes.

"So she disappears up to that hotel, the elegant one, the Hôtel de Paris. And she comes down, and she's got these diamonds on that she wasn't wearing before, and she makes sure she sits next to Dunham at the table, and every time she reaches for anything, there are these diamonds glittering. And Dunham sits back with this marvelous posture of hers and keeps adjusting the bloody emeralds. It was so funny, those two out-bitching each other."

By March of 1949, Josephine was rehearsing for *Féeries et Folies* (Derval had broken his rule—this title had fifteen letters) at the Folies-Bergère. France was still recovering from the traumas of war, the tourists were returning, there was an exhibition of sixty-four Picassos at the Maison de La Pensée Français, but Josephine was a nervous wreck. She had been, she said, "dreaming for months about the show, then . . . seeing the scenes we have conceived taking form, starting to live—it's wonderful. . . . But one day, the doors will open, the public will come and judge . . . and I worry, I have stagefright. Was I right to change a formula that had proved itself? I tremble, I feel my heart pound. . . ."

She wanted to offer Paris a new Folies-Bergère; there would still be naked girls, but Josephine the war heroine would cover her body with thirty different costumes, and play many famous women of history—most of them French. She would start with Eve (nationality unknown), mate to Fred Rey's Adam, go on to the Empress Josephine, and finally she would personify the unfortunate Mary, Queen of Scots. But she demanded a lot of reinforcement from her director. "Michel, I'm too old. First, there was an infatuation with me, then I did the war, but I'm forgotten now."

Gyarmathy told her what she craved to hear, that she was fabulous, and she returned the compliment. "You are to me like Max Reinhardt," she said, "and the things you propose to me are things I have never done—to dance with bananas doesn't interest me anymore."

"She was an angel during rehearsals," Michel says, "first to arrive, last to leave. She rehearsed in Jo Bouillon's underwear, with a towel around her hair, which she had burnt off one more time."

First to arrive? Last to leave? Here was a new Josephine, except for the burnt-off hair, and this time it was Jean Clement, not Antoine, who was called to the rescue. "Before the Folies rehearsals began, she asked me for some *défrisant*, a kind of French Congolene. I warned her not to leave it on too long, but she did her hair, started to read, and fell asleep. She phoned me, hysterical. '*Chéri*, a catastrophe, I'm shorn like a woman collaborator, I can't do the Folies-Bergère.'

"The next day, she came into my salon. Arletty, Edwige Feuillère, la Comtesse de Toulouse-Lautrec, they were all there. Josephine twirled around, said, '*Changement de décors*,' whipped off her turban, and laughed like a crazy person. She had only little tufts of hair left. I got the idea to do her the way they do flower arrangements, build a wire foundation with two crowns of hair woven on it for Mary Stuart, and a ponytail for her next number.

"On opening night, I was shaking. I was afraid it would come loose. I had used long pins and turned the few poor hairs around them; it was very painful for Josephine but she never complained."

The hair didn't come loose.

"I told Josephine, 'They will cut off your head,' " Gyarmathy says. "She loved it. She walked up the big black staircase, her back to the public, and at the top the executioner was waiting. I used some Beethoven, I forget what, and she knelt and put her head on the block on the last beat, and the executioner raised his hand with the axe, and *pang*—blackout!

"Then her soul rose to heaven, and the glass windows were lit by blue light, and she sang 'Ave Maria.' "

The voice, wrote Janet Flanner, was still "as sweet . . . as a woodwind instrument." (What Flanner gave with one hand, she took back with the other, saying that at the beginning of her Paris career, Josephine had "looked Harlem; then she graduated to Creole; she has now been transmuted into Tonkinese, or something Eastern, with pagoda head-dresses beneath which her oval face looks like temple sculpture. Her show consists principally of her changing her costumes, which are magnificent." Flanner also pointed out that Josephine, as the headless Mary, went on to sing Schubert's "Ave Maria," though it hadn't been written until two hundred years after Mary's death. What's more, she sang it in Latin.)

No nit-picking from Noël Coward, though. He confided to his diary that Josephine was "wonderful as Mary Stuart in a miles long white satin train." Carrie, too, finally saw her hardheaded firstborn child, Freda J. McDonald, on the stage. Carrie was so agitated she had a nosebleed.

She came backstage wearing gold-rimmed glasses and a black feathered hat, and the photographers were waiting to shoot mother and daughter kissing. Carrie was more unpredictable than that. "It was good," she said to Josephine, wiping tears from her eyes. "But you're lucky I didn't have a cane. I would have come around and smacked you and all those young girls who don't have enough clothes on!"

In New York, the powerful newspaper columnist Walter Winchell wrote of Josephine's most recent triumph. "Fans report that she is again the toast of Paree, where a new type of lighting makes her decades younger."

But it wasn't her youth anymore, now it was her art that pleased the customers. Her pure sweet voice rising to heaven so moved people that they began to applaud before she was done singing. Again, she had gambled and won.

She wrote to Donald Wyatt that Mohamed and Moulay Larbi were in Paris. "We talk for hours, hurry and come so we can be together as a big family. I'm still packing them in every night. Marian Anderson, Katherine Dunham, great, great success here, really our people are *adored* in France, what a contrast from America."

In May, there were posters all over Paris advertising *Les Mémoires de Josephine Baker,* Josephine's third—and final—collaboration with Marcel Sauvage. This volume not only brought her life up to date, but reprinted the six articles she had done for *France-Soir.* In these pieces, she had once again been hard on her native country, insisting that most Americans would like to see signs on their houses saying, NO JEWS, NO DOGS, NO NIGGERS.

She said Americans had killed their souls, theirs was "a world of lost people, it is only money that counts."

She said, "You know I do not like what makes life theatrical, I'm not a novelist, it's hard for me to invent, I don't know how to lie." Four lies in a row.

Her resentment of light-skinned blacks, the high yellows she had envied and hated when she started out, was here in print. "Twelve thousand white Negroes with blue eyes are born every year in the USA, they are the most terrible adversaries of the blacks. I am on the side of the 'niggers.' I take no glory from it . . . I didn't choose it."

In this book, she also permitted herself a diatribe against American Jews. Interspersed with lines like "I have been married to a Jew, I have nothing to reproach him with," and her expressed admiration for Israelis in Jerusalem "looking like prophets with long curls" was her complaint that "blacks cannot work on Broadway without the intervention of Jews." As for boxers managed by Jews, "many of them don't receive a tenth of what they make for their broken noses."

But *Les Mémoires de Josephine Baker* was in French; what American was going to read it? And anyhow, Josephine was a fabulist, you couldn't hold her to strict account as you could a tailor who measured slipcovers.

The Folies closed for the month of August—it was traditional—but Josephine and Jo didn't stop working, they began another tour. They didn't stop fighting, either. Jean Clement, who went along to do Josephine's hair, had a ringside seat. "She was jealous of the boys around him. They had a big battle in Switzerland, and Jo left, and Pierre Spiers, a respected conductor, came to replace him."

Josephine and Pierre Spiers became friends right away—he was the one who brought her voice down, he said, "You are too old now for that little bird voice"—and to surprise him, she sent for his wife and three-year-old son, Gérard.

"The night we arrived," says Marie Spiers, "little Gérard walked onstage with a big bouquet for Josephine. Pierre, in the orchestra pit, could not believe his eyes. And then Josephine picked up Gérard and threw him to his father. 'Pierre, here is your son.' I almost fainted, seeing my baby flying through the air.

"Josephine adored Gérard; she even asked Pierre if she could adopt him. 'I will be a good mother to him,' she said, 'and you and Marie can come to visit.' 'You are crazy,' Pierre said."

"On the tour," says Jean Clement, "Josephine had taken a little basset hound because the dog could bark 'J'ai Deux Amours.' So here we go with that dog, and Josephine made him sing the song all the time and people were laughing in Italy, Spain, Turkey, Egypt."

That fall, Josephine was back in the Folies, and reunited with Jo. "I have," she said, "the husband I love who understands that existence is not an operetta."

But at Les Milandes, it *was* an operetta. "I remember she had just bought a Peugeot from a garage owner in Sarlat," Georges Malaury says, "and she promised to pay him, and he came one day, she was not there, the next day she had no money, the third day he came screaming. So she told her maid to let him come up. She was in her bath, and here came that old man—the village still talks about it—and she stood up, dripping, while the maid held the checkbook, and Josephine signed a check. When he came out, he said to my father, 'I got my money with interest—I saw that fabulous body, bless God.' And in those days, the check was good."

The mad preparations for the grand opening on September 4 spared no one. Michel Gyarmathy, summoned to Les Milandes to "get some rest, you need it," was roused by Josephine's "ringing a bell at 5 A.M. and waking everybody, including the hens. I don't know where she found the energy. We went to Bordeaux and bought fishermen's nets, she wanted the *guinguette* decorated like a boat."

Madame Carrier, owner of the Grand Café in Sarlat, loaned Josephine trays and glasses. "I must say," she told me, "things were moving. You never know with show people, but we thought it might be good for the region. Jo Bouillon had formed a committee of neighborhood men to help open the park. The officials, the press, the bishops, church choruses, had been invited for a hundred miles around. There were to be banquets for three different sets of people, the most important would have dinner at the château, the others in the fields or the *guinguette*. A parade had been planned, people came by bus, car, bicycle, and foot. My son Alain had done a poster of her for the opening of the park—he was a student of Paul Colin—but she turned it down. She thought she looked too Negroid."

"She was expecting four hundred," says Michel Gyarmathy. "Over two thousand came. They almost broke the place down, there was not enough food for everyone, and at the end, Josephine went to hide in her bedroom. I was afraid because when you have people who come from miles away, they expect something, and the prices were exorbitant for the country."

Despite the mob scene, Josephine was elated. There had been card games, footraces, dancing, drinking, volleyball. "Can you believe it?" she said to Jo. "They managed to get here without a proper road . . . without a train. It proves they'll come . . . we'll move ahead with the soccer field. . . ."

At home in Beynac, Henri Chapin, the carpenter, was also reflecting on the events of the day; he and his wife felt sick. "Josephine had put a dancer from the Folies at the cash register," he says. "And we watched him. For every thousand francs he took in, he would put seven hundred francs in his pocket, and we could say nothing, he was Josephine's friend and she had confidence in him."

Worse was to follow. Josephine's nightly decapitation as Mary Stuart was painless, an illusion. Her illusion that she could turn Les Milandes into a business that would pay for itself was something else again. Financially, she was already beginning to bleed to death.

Chapter 31

—

BREAKING
THE COLOR BAR
IN MIAMI

"She wanted to go down in history, like Lincoln"

*L*es Milandes devoured francs the way its fireplaces devoured wood. (The fireplaces figured prominently in booklets calculated to lure tourists.) "Winter has come," Josephine wrote for public consumption. "I'm in the big salon, in front of the high chimney with its coat of arms, and clear flames dance around black oak logs. Curled in an armchair . . . in my half sleep, I perceive a whisper. . . . The walls around me . . . my old stones are speaking."

The old stones could have told a thousand stories, going back to the Lord of Castelnaud, François de Caumont, who in the year 1489 abandoned his family's twelfth-century château and built a new one to please his young bride.

Now Josephine, the most recent lady of the manor, was planning to add to its legends. There would be a museum tracing her beginnings from a basement in St. Louis. Her sister Margaret would run an "exotic" bakery on the premises. There would be a modern farm, and above each stall, the resident cow's name would be written in blue neon. Pigs would happily sun themselves right up until they were killed and eaten. At which point, Josephine would shed no tears. An old fighter, she knew what life was.

She also knew she would need great infusions of money in order to realize her ambitions. It would be profitable for everyone, she assured her neighbors, if she could turn Les Milandes into a Deauville or a Cannes complete with casino. The problem was, she couldn't get a casino license. ("We were afraid of the risks for our young people," says Leon Burg, president of Sarlat's Court of Commerce.) With fallible human beings thwarting her will, Josephine took her case to Pope Pius XII, bringing away from the Vatican a papal blessing for her project.

It still didn't get her a casino license.

So she went back on the road, and mailed home instructions to Jo: "Plant geraniums along the terrace."

By mid-October, the season over (Les Milandes would close until Easter), Jo could join his wife on a major tour, which would start in Mexico. En route, they stopped in St. Louis to try to convince Josephine's brother Richard that he was needed in France. "Tumpy told me, 'If you come, I will give you this and that,' " Richard said, "but I wanted to wait a little bit, and see what Mama and Sister had to tell."

A St. Louis paper ran an interview that featured Josephine groping for words in English. "What's wonderful about my public is that they're *fidèle*. You know, loyal."

In Mexico, six months of success, "and after that, we went to Cuba," says Roland Gerbeau, who was once again singing in the act. "Josephine adored white mice, and in her dressing room, she would have five or six of them under her bathrobe. The robe would be tied at the waist over her naked body, and she would let the mice run free between her breasts, and she would catch one in her hands and play with it, then put it back on her breast. I found that bizarre. The Castro brothers came to see us, they were unconditional admirers of Josephine."

Fidèle, Fidel; it was fated.

At Havana's chic Hotel Nacional, Josephine found herself turned away (management was afraid to lose the business of rich white Americans), and oddly, she did not protest. "There are other places where I will be welcome," she told Roland, and moved to a hotel owned by a friend.

She repaid the Castro brothers' admiration by giving two free concerts to raise money for their cause.

Ninety miles away, in Miami, Willard Alexander, a big-band agent, was making arrangements to bring Josephine across the Straits of Florida to work in a club called Copa City that handled very big acts. This turned out to be good for Josephine, but bad for Alexander, because Ned Schuyler, the owner of the Copa City, took over Josephine's career. "He stole her from me," said Alexander. "I think he was 'connected,' involved with the big boys."

"Ned flipped over Josephine," says Shirley Woolf, Schuyler's lawyer. "He promised her the world. He even signed a contract agreeing that patrons were to be admitted to his club regardless of color or creed. He figured no blacks would come anyway." This was at a time when Negroes couldn't go to a restaurant or a movie in Miami Beach; if they were stopped by a policeman after 6 P.M., they had to produce identity cards and explain why they were out.

Not Josephine. In Miami Beach, she lived in the white-occupied Arlington Hotel, owned by Ned Schuyler's family, and was supplied with a car and a white chauffeur. Shirley Modell-Rinehold (Ned's girlfriend, not to be confused with Shirley Woolf) believed that Schuyler, "being Jewish, felt an outsider in the South and was sympathetic to integration. 'Baby,' he told me, 'it's time.' "

Ginette Renaudin, Josephine's wardrobe mistress, was with her at the Arlington. "It was the first time they had a black person," she says. "Nothing extraordinary happened, she was accepted. But people would ask me, doesn't it bother you to work for a black? I said, 'Why? She is a woman like any other, I'm French, and in any case, I'm not a racist. On top of that, I like her very much.' "

"Eleven black people, including Joe Louis and the singer Thelma Carpenter, showed up at Josephine's opening," says Shirley Woolf. "And Sophie Tucker introduced Josephine."

Thelma Carpenter: "Sophie Tucker said, 'Well, if they come to blow up the place, they'll blow me up,' and wasn't nobody going to mess with Sophie Tucker. Then when Josephine came on singing 'J'ai Deux Amours,' and drug that fur across the stage, she was just electrifying.

"And how do we know that some of those dyed-in-the-wool crackers hadn't seen her in Paris at the Folies-Bergère? Think how many Southerners were in the army, and over there they didn't fit in with the

Frenchmen, so they had a certain bond with colored people. At home, they would lynch you, in Europe you couldn't get rid of them. In Copa City, this one man turned to me and said, 'You're real proud of her, aren't you?' and I said, 'No, she's proud of herself.' "

Shirley Woolf agrees that Josephine got a wild reception. "The audience didn't know what the hell she was doing—she sang in French, she sang in Portuguese, she sang in Spanish—but they were fascinated. They had never seen an actress who changed clothes so much." (The clothes, incidentally, were by Balmain and Dior. Ginette, who was not similarly apparelled, had to come onstage too. "She called me out to take a bow. I was all dirty, working in my old blue jeans, but she insisted.")

Rita Charisse, one of the show dancers, was awed to find herself on the same bill with Josephine. "Walter Winchell brought her roses, and for the whole week she played there, he was outside her dressing-room door, like a watchdog."

Or a lovesick puppy. Clearly, Winchell adored Josephine; he told the readers of his column in the *New York Mirror* that she had "magic and big time zing."

"She was more thrilled about Winchell," Shirley Woolf says, "than about the colored people who came in."

The audience wept as she told them she considered this her first appearance in her native land in twenty-six years. "The other times didn't count. . . . I am happy to be here in this city when my people can be here to see me . . . and when I say my people, I mean my race." (Earlier, at a reception given by Miami's Negro community, she had said, "We should not be ashamed to use the word 'Negro.' It is a beautiful word.")

With Ned Schuyler beside her, Josephine was finally set to conquer the United States. As Ahmed Ben Bachir had known how to make her feel like a woman, Ned knew how to make her feel like a star. Even better, her agreement with him specified that she work in America for nine months of each year, but left her free to return to Les Milandes for the other three months.

Her next booking would be at the Strand Theatre in New York. Ned asked Shirley Woolf to hire the band. "I picked Buddy Rich because he and I were from Brooklyn," she says. "I didn't know he was the greatest drummer in the world."

Before leaving Miami Beach, Josephine fired off a telegram to President Truman: MY HUSBAND AND I THANK THE AMERICAN PEOPLE THROUGH YOU FOR YOUR MAGNIFICENT RECEPTION HERE AND FOR THE OPPORTUNITY TO ADVANCE THE CAUSE OF CIVIL RIGHTS WHICH I KNOW IS SO IMPORTANT TO YOU. She also wired Winchell: THANK YOU FOR YOUR WONDERFUL WORDS OF PRAISE AU REVOIR FOR A LITTLE WHILE GOOD HEALTH TO YOU AND YOURS.

On March 2, 1951, she opened at the Strand, with Jo Bouillon—the band called him Jo Soup—helping to make her musical arrangements. She did her act between showings of *Storm Warning*, a Warner Brothers movie starring Ginger Rogers and Ronald Reagan and, oddly enough, about the Ku Klux Klan. That first day, the line of people waiting to see her stretched for a block.

One critic said the star's gowns "clung to her shapely body like a frightened baby to its mother," and *Variety's* review was a rave. Even though Josephine managed to "fracture" half a dozen languages as she moved from song to song, "she could just as well have sung 'em in Braille the way the customers ate it up."

For the *Chicago Defender*, Fredi Washington, Josephine's friend since *Shuffle Along*, wrote a loving piece. "You find your chest swelling with pride because Miss Baker is a Negro. . . . She manages to get 3,000 people, four times a day, to act as though they all know each other and her in particular."

Phillip Leshing, then twenty-three years old, was playing bass in the Buddy Rich orchestra. "Josephine did not have a great voice," he told me. "I mean she was not a Sarah Vaughan or an Ella Fitzgerald or even a Judy Garland, but it did not matter, there is a certain magic certain performers have, they completely take over, people become hypnotized. Nobody wanted her to get off the stage, and it was difficult, because there were more people waiting to get in.

"I remember once Josephine invited several of us to come to her dressing room and try some very good reefer. I went down with Harry 'Sweets' Edison, the trumpet player, and Buddy Rich, and we smoked pot with Josephine Baker. She was funny, she was cute, she sat on the floor, and it was like talking to one of the kids in the band, like the girl singer. We smoked and nibbled on fruit—there was always fruit in her dressing room—but the marijuana didn't affect her performance. Never.

"She had this gorgeous gold loving cup made for Buddy and the band, a trophy, like an Academy Award, with our names engraved on it.

And it was filled with marijuana. She gave it to us after the last performance at the Strand."

I wonder, had she smoked her first joint in Paris, with the Prince of Wales? Or with Simenon, who used to mix a little hashish into the tobacco in his pipe?

"Eleanor Roosevelt was staying in the same hotel where we were staying in New York," says Shirley Woolf, "and she had sent flowers with a note—'Would you please have lunch with me this week?' We had lunch in her room, and Josephine was charming, she was flattered.

"Ethel Barrymore came backstage to see her, too. Josephine could have been the Martin Luther King of her time, but she wouldn't listen to anyone, even about things she didn't know. I'm not talking about her show, she did that pretty good all by herself. But in other ways, she was stupid. Once I came into her dressing room at the Strand, and she was being interviewed by a man from the Communist party newspaper, the *Daily Worker,* and that paper was poisonous to everybody. So here was this nice Communist intellectual asking her questions, and she's being very cooperative, and he's writing away. And I said, 'Why don't you tell him about your good friend, the one you call your sister?' 'Oh!' she said. 'Evita.'

"How could a woman who believed in freedom turn around and say, my sister, Evita Perón. She was smart, but she was ignorant."

Insatiable, too. Enchanting twelve thousand people a day was not enough; Josephine had also agreed to play a late show every night at Monte Proser's Theater Café. At that point, it wasn't money (she was already making over ten thousand dollars a week), it was an animal thing; she loved to be close to her audience.

But not always. "For her opening night at the Theater Café," says Shirley Woolf, "Ned had people from *Time* magazine and *The New York Times* coming, it was unbelieveable the interest she generated. When we got to the club, the big fat comedian Jackie Gleason had just ended his show. Sweating like a pig, he was walking toward his dressing room, and Josephine was standing there, followed by Ginette with all the clothes over her arm. Josephine said to Jackie Gleason, 'Excuse me, do you know where my dressing room is?' and he said, 'Git out of my way, I don't even know who *you* are,' and Josephine said, 'That's it, come, Ginette, we'll go.'

"She went back to the hotel. I had been friends for many years with

Hazel Scott, the pianist who was at that time married to Adam Clayton Powell, and I thought maybe a congressman and a preacher, a big man, could move Josephine. So I called Hazel, and Adam came over and explained that if she didn't go on, she wouldn't be able to work again in any club in the United States. 'So what?' she said. 'I'll go back to Paris.'

"You know how many times she said that during our tour? Hundreds. 'Good, I'll go back to Paris.' But she wouldn't be making forty thousand dollars a month in Paris, would she? And you know she used to send all that money to Switzerland, under the name of Mrs. Kaiser. I had to do it for her, she gave me all kinds of account numbers."

Still, Josephine won. Because of "laryngitis," her doctor ordered her to give up all "extra-theater" performances, and that settled that.

On April 6, she was in Philadelphia, at the Earle Theatre. Backstage, she welcomed Evelyn Anderson. "I went up to her," Evelyn remembers, "and I said, 'Oh, Miss Baker,' and she said, 'Oh, Evelyn!' and threw her arms around me."

Josephine who, during the *Ziegfeld Follies*, had refused interviews to black newspapers, was making amends. Now she went—unannounced—to visit the Standard Theatre on South Street, and talked to the stagehands about the days when Old Gibby had run the place. The *Courier* reported that she "insisted on colored stagehands and musicians" wherever she worked. (The *Courier* did *not* report that, for this particular tour, Sweets Edison was the only black musician who had been hired.)

Josephine also paid a call at a New Jersey jail to comfort the Trenton Six (six black men indicted—though many believed they were framed—for the robbery-killing of a shopkeeper). "Have confidence," she urged, "that justice will prevail." Two of the defendants were veterans who had been entertained by Josephine in army camps abroad. "They were so moved by her remarks," reported the *Philadelphia Inquirer*, "that they broke down in tears."

On May 20, Josephine Baker Day was celebrated in Harlem. A motorcade carried the honoree, blowing kisses, past thousands of cheering bystanders wearing buttons (courtesy of the New York branch of the NAACP) that said WELCOME JOSEPHINE BAKER. Little kids ran alongside her open limousine, and, sitting beside Bessie Buchanan, Josephine smiled.

Other old friends—Maude Russell, Alberta Hunter—were in the caravan too, but Bessie was the one acting proprietary. "Like she was Josephine's mother," says Maude. "I mean, we all came up together, Bessie Allison was dancing for ten cents with anybody at the Savoy, and then honey, as soon as the owner married her, her butt went up on her back."

At the Golden Gate Ballroom, Ralph Bunche, a recent Nobel peace prize–winner, presented Josephine with an award for her work against prejudice in the theater, and the French consul was so impressed he went home and wrote a long letter back to the Foreign Ministry. He said Josephine was a heroine. Not only had she broken the color bar in Miami ("a colored artist dared, and the whites surrendered"), but she had reminded people that she was a French citizen, and "in our country racial problems do not exist."

During Dr. Bunche's tribute to her, Josephine sat on the stage wearing a yellow chiffon Dior dress. In spite of the heat, she looked, Maude says, "cool as a cucumber. We acted as hostesses, Fredi Washington and me and Little Shep, and then all of the *Shuffle Along* girls came up to the stage and Noble Sissle introduced us, and they played 'Bandana Days,' and we did a little step and got off. Then Josephine got up and said, 'Oh, I'm so happy to be back in my native America, I wish my mother, a poor washwoman from St. Louis, could see this,' and I thought to myself, she's lying."

The brass bands, the handshakes, the luncheon, the cocktail party, the ball, Josephine sailed through the whole day, stopping only to change clothes from time to time.

The night ended at the Savoy Ballroom. Bessie had invited a few friends to her husband's place, and Charlie Buchanan told me that at one point a bouncer came in looking alarmed. A black man at the door was waving a piece of paper and claiming to be Josephine's husband. "If you don't believe me, here is our marriage license."

"I felt sorry for him," Charlie said, "but I sent the guard to chase him away." Was it Willie Wells, surfacing after so many years? Was it the elusive Billy Baker?

By June, Josephine was playing Hartford, Connecticut. (It was the very week General de Gaulle chose to visit Les Milandes. He was out of government for the moment—he would call those years away from politics his "crossing of the desert"—and his trip to the château was noted only by the neighbors. "He came on June 3," Georges Malaury remembers. "And everybody was asking, 'Who is that tall guy?' ")

Georges Simenon traveled to Hartford from nearby Lakeville, where he was then living with his second wife, Denise, and later, Josephine and Jo paid the Simenons a return visit. "She came after a show on Saturday and she left on Sunday," says Dolores James, then seventeen, and nanny to Simenon's children. "He told me, 'You must be here to meet this person, she's very famous and you look just like her,' and he went on to explain how this lady went to Europe and was accepted, and color made no difference. And I said, 'Well, it does here.' In Lakeville, there are black families, but we are of no importance.

"He was giving me a chance, he was saying, 'Here is someone you can be like,' and when I finally saw her, when she walked into the living room and started speaking French, I said, 'I don't believe this lady.' At nineteen, she had gone to France, and at seventeen, I was afraid to leave Lakeville. She had complete control over people, she could snap her fingers and everybody jumped. I loved it, because most of my own people were the opposite. White people snapped their fingers and we jumped. And Josephine wasn't light-skinned, she wasn't passing. She was *black*."

If the young girl harbored any reservations about her new idol, they sprang from the way Josephine dealt with Jo Bouillon. "He was a delightful man," Dolores says, "but he seemed to be so small next to her. I was confused, here I was, a young black girl, wanting to idolize this powerful black image, yet resenting the way she treated her husband. Like at the dinner table, all the emotion and the eye contact was between her and Simenon. Like Jo Bouillon and Mrs. Simenon did not exist. Are you supposed to treat someone like that because you're a star? I don't know, I'm not a star. But why? He was a human being.

"That Sunday, I went upstairs, and she was standing in her bedroom, nude. It's nice when you're close to fifty and you can say, 'Look at me, I look better than you, and you're seventeen.' She was not at all ashamed, I was the one that went, 'Oh, excuse me!' Jo Bouillon was there too, and it was strange. I always felt as a black person, you're there, but you're not noticed. Here's a white person, and it's reversed, *he's* not there. I was trying to take it in, trying to understand how an individual as big as she was could step on someone she slept with, who made love to her."

"Foolishly," says Shirley Woolf, "Ned had given Josephine a contract where she agreed to work twenty-eight days a month if he had the work for her. But even if he didn't, she got eighty-five hundred dollars a week. Ned was a sporty man. He thought nothing of chartering a plane to go somewhere, but on the road, Josephine didn't want to fly."

She was forty-five years old, and there were days when she was bone weary. On June 10, she wrote to Donald Wyatt that "the four and five shows a day are too much for me," and reproached him for not having been to see her. "Why don't you like me any more?"

Donald was not the most important person in Josephine's life, but he was her conscience. He had brought her together with the black soldiers for whom she was a lodestone, comforted her when she mourned that, for twenty years, she had turned her back on her people. "I think," he says, "she had come to realize that a performer's acclaim fades when the curtain falls, and she wanted to go down in history among immortals like Lincoln and Gandhi. She wanted to convince the black community that she had not deserted the fight for equality, even though she had lived so long outside the arena."

One can make the case that Josephine was no Sojourner Truth, slave-born, God-driven ("Children, I talk to God and God talks to me!"), traveling the country, braving the fury of mobs to preach abolition and women's rights. But who was? One can make the case that Josephine had grabbed at the chance to live in a country that offered her honors and rewards. But who would not have? And though the civil rights movement began without her, she came to it fairly early. After all, it wasn't until 1958 that Arkansas schools were desegregated, and here she was pushing for integration in 1951.

Josephine was a public person, and she made public scenes, in hotel lobbies and restaurants and trains and waiting rooms and sometimes, even, from the stage. When Willie McGee, convicted of rape in Mississippi, was executed, she paid for his funeral, and talked to her audience about his death. "They have killed one of my people," she said, adding that a part of every American Negro "died a little with him."

"We were in the Paradise Theatre in Detroit that day," says Stanley Kay, who was playing drums for her on the road. "And she came down from her dressing room and said, 'Good morning, Mr. Sweets,' to Sweets Edison, but she never said anything to the rest of us. Finally, I went up and knocked at her door and said, 'Josephine, I'm white, but

I didn't execute Willie McGee.' 'You're right,' she said. 'I was upset, please forgive me.'

"Between shows, she liked to watch the movie, so she would put a robe on, and go to a box—from backstage, you can get to the boxes—and sometimes when we were traveling by train, I would get off in a station and buy hot dogs or ribs or ham hocks and a six-pack of beer, and we'd have supper together, and we'd talk. I asked her about being with royalty, talking with kings; it was like she was telling me about Cinderella, and I was eight years old.

"I didn't think she was the best singer in the world, or the best dancer, she was what we call a shake dancer, but she could put it all together, she knew how to get the audience to come to her."

On that tour, a gangster friend of Ned Schuyler's was traveling with the company. "His name was Tony," says Shirley Woolf. "He was avoiding the police. Somewhere between Evanston and Chicago, I was talking to him in the train corridor when a dining-car waiter came up and said, 'Excuse me, ma'am, I was married to Josephine Baker.' Tony opened the door to Josephine's compartment and shouted, 'Hey, Joe, one of your husbands is outside.'

"She refused to come out. She could see him through the glass panel, and she said, 'I don't know that man.' He meant as much to Josephine as a grain of sand. When she said goodbye to someone, she meant goodbye, not *à bientôt*."

By this time, Shirley was managing every detail of Josephine's daily life, so it was inevitable that they would clash. It happened in Washington, D.C. "On the first of July," says Shirley, "she was working in an armory, seventy-five hundred seats, and we were sold out. That afternoon, she went off with some people from the NAACP, and I said, 'Joe, you have to be at the armory by seven,' and she said, 'Oh, I'll meet you back at the hotel at six.' Well, she marched in at quarter to eight, and I said, 'Where've you been?' and she said, 'Darling, one of your people insulted me.'

"One of *my* people? Some NAACP members had convinced her to go into a segregated dining room and order a Coca-Cola, and the waiter had said, 'We don't serve Negroes at the tables,' and she said, 'I want to speak to your boss.'

"The boss's name was Schwartz, and she said to him, 'Mr. Schwartz, I fought for your people in Israel, and you won't serve me a Coca-Cola,'

She told me this story, and announced, 'I'm not going on tonight.' I said, 'There's a bus strike and a cab strike in Washington, and there are seventy-five hundred people waiting for you who had to double up in cars, and you're not going to show up at the armory?' She said, 'No, I'm not, darling.' In the end, she went and she played, but she was horrible to the audience. 'Here we are in the capital of your country, and you wouldn't serve me a Coca-Cola,' she told them, and she went on like that.

"Next morning, we get up. We have to catch a plane. She's opening in California July 4. She's sitting in the bathtub and she says, 'I don't fly.' I say, 'You have to fly. The Fourth of July is a very important holiday, it's like Bastille Day in France.' She says, 'I don't care, I'm not an American.' I say, 'Please, you promised, get dry,' and I give her a robe, and she takes her hand and slaps me across the face.

"When I get up off the floor, I say, 'How dare you?' and she says, 'Darling, I love you like a mother.' Of course she got on the plane, but not until she ate my heart out."

She had canceled an appearance in Atlanta after being turned down by three hotels there and warned that she couldn't bring Ginette— "People told her I would have to black up. 'If you want to keep your wardrobe mistress, she will have to dye her skin' "—and now there was a backlash against her new activism. She'd had threatening letters, and at the RKO Hillstreet Theater in Los Angeles, she was greeted by a man shouting, "Why don't you go back where you came from?" The audience froze as Josephine walked to the stage apron and looked out. "I *am* back where I came from," she said. "And you—where do you come from?" She got an ovation.

Encouraged, she went out and made a citizen's arrest in a country where she was no longer a citizen. She challenged a Dallas corset salesman who had uttered insults "directed not at me as a person but at my race."

"I was having dinner in the Biltmore Grill with Frankie Laine," says Shirley Woolf. "Josephine had just walked in, and this Dallas character said, 'I didn't know they allowed niggers in here.' So we all went down to the police station, and she filed a complaint.

"They kept the corset salesman in jail overnight, and the judge fined him a hundred dollars and made him apologize, so she got great satisfaction. I didn't see anything so great about it, but listen, I was the one who had to get up at six o'clock in the morning to go to court at eight."

"We played a big benefit in California," says Stanley Kay, "and all the Hollywood stars came out, and they talked, they were rude. I said, 'Gee, Joe, I feel bad,' and she said, 'They didn't come to see me, they came to see one another, it's all right, I don't care.' "

While in Los Angeles, Josephine came face-to-face with a bit of her youth. "I'd just got married," says Caroline Reagan's daughter, Sophie Reagan-Herr, "and I was living in Santa Monica, and these beautiful announcements had been in all the papers that Josephine was coming to Los Angeles.

"I didn't know whether she had bad memories of me because of my mother, but one morning I phoned her hotel and woke her up. 'Oh, my little Sophie,' she said, 'why don't you come to the show?' The warmth coming across the telephone was wonderful, so we went to the theater— my husband, my little stepson, and I—and she had left us seats in the front row. She had an act that, I see now, looking at pictures of *La Revue Nègre*, was a sort of remembrance. She had a wheelbarrow full of vegetables, and she picked up a small cabbage and threw it to me. It was a pun—in France, my little cabbage, *mon petit chou*, is a love name."

In San Francisco, where she played the Golden Gate Theater, Josephine had a reunion with Thelma Carpenter. "She had noticed," says Thelma, "the city didn't have any colored bus drivers, so one morning, she drags me down to the bus depot, and finds the man in charge of hiring. Why, she wants to know, could so many Negroes qualify to drive trucks in the army, 'but cannot qualify to drive your city buses?' He denies there's any policy of discrimination. So here stands Madame Bakaire, red scarf tied around her head, ain't got the makeup on, ain't got the ponytail on, and after he gets through talking, she says, 'Monsieur, you're a nasty little man,' and we walk out.

"Only a queen would do that. I used to call her the biggest gyp on the Nile, because who was the gyp on the Nile but Cleopatra?

"Ned and Shirley nurtured her, babied her, took care of her, there was nothing she wanted that wasn't given to her. She was appreciated, she got her money, pay or play, she never had to worry with Ned Schuyler."

Had Josephine dallied with her handsome, free-spending manager? No, says Shirley Woolf. "She flirted, but Ned was on the needle, he was pretty far gone. It was an interesting time, and I have no regrets. Toward the end of that summer, we went to Paris with Josephine. Ned bought me a ten-thousand-dollar wardrobe, and we stayed at the Crillon. It was all very nice for a kid from Brooklyn.

"Josephine took us to the Dervals' house, she took me to the Folies, and introduced me as her attorney, we met the duke and duchess of Windsor. I had thought Josephine was popular in Cuba, but not like in France."

Ned fell in love with Les Milandes, and in their heads, he and Josephine built empires, as the grand renovation continued. Under Jo Bouillon's command, six young gardeners dressed as American sailors bent to their work. (Jo had bought the uniforms from a surplus store in Harlem.) The musical comedy spectacle of the hapless growers stooping for potatoes and lettuces, backsides in the air, straining the seams of their tight pants, had the villagers screaming with laughter. But not in front of Jo.

As always, Josephine was everywhere, challenging her guests, leading forced marches over as much of the six hundred acres as her captives were willing to slog through, pointing out wonders present and to come. "Here, we'll have the first-class hotel, there the African huts . . ."

She couldn't get a gambling license? Never mind, there would be gardens and bars, there would be a gas station and a heliport. "I think she was guided by her *bonne étoile*, her good star," says Georgette Malaury. "I believe the souvenirs of her youth—the way black people were treated in America, her success in France—marked her. They made her strong, gave her plenty of cheek. But here at Les Milandes, she found calm, she was at the right age, she needed that stop in her life, and again, it was her *bonne étoile*, she always arrived at the right moment in the right place."

Josephine, however, was not quite ready to settle down. She was like Saint Augustine imploring God for chastity, "but not yet." After the humiliations of the *Ziegfeld Follies* and *Paris Sings Again*, she had finally seduced America. Copa City, the Strand, the tour—she who was a star all over the world had been recognized at last in the country of her birth. And now she was going back there for some more applause. Ned had arranged for her to open at the Roxy.

She had it in her hands, everything she wanted. And she blew it.

Chapter 32

—

THE FEUD WITH
WALTER WINCHELL

"She broke my heart, I am a finished man"

*S*he came to the Roxy like a hero," says Shirley Woolf.

"Extraordinary Limited Engagement!" boasted the ads. "Ned Schuyler Presents The Exotic Rage of Paris . . . in her only New York theatre appearance this season." It was a long way from Bob Russell's "25 Hottest Coons in Dixie."

For the finale at the Roxy, Jo Méhu (he staged the show) recalled that Josephine wore "a cloak made of sixty-six feet of satin, trimmed with fifty-five pounds of pink fox." And a headdress trembling with pink bird-of-paradise feathers.

Then the feathers hit the fan.

It took a few days. At first, the audiences were perfect, the notices were perfect, Josephine was so buoyed by her reception on opening night that she announced she wasn't going to sing "J'ai Deux Amours" anymore—"I don't need to"—and was scolded by Sophie Tucker: "You put that song back in!" Josephine put that song back in.

On Tuesday night, October 16, along with Bessie Buchanan, Roger Rico and his wife, Solange, Josephine went to the Stork Club.

Here are the bare bones of the plot. The four arrived around midnight, and were shown into the long narrow Cub Room (reserved for VIPs) where owner Sherman Billingsley fed and flattered the famous. On the way to their table, they passed Walter Winchell, who was having supper with Jack O'Brian, the *Journal-American* columnist, and Mrs. O'Brian.

"Josephine stopped and said hello," O'Brian remembers. "Winchell told her he liked her ponytail." She and her friends were seated, drinks were served, but no food arrived. After an hour or so, a furious Josephine went to the phone and called Walter White, then executive secretary of the NAACP, to charge that the Stork Club was practicing racial discrimination.

Here are the fleshed-out bones of the plot. Roger Rico, a bass with the Paris Opéra, had come to this country to take over the role of the French planter, Emil de Becque, when Ezio Pinza left *South Pacific*. Rico was offended by suggestions that, since his parents had owned plantations in Algeria, this was typecasting. He felt he was being called a colonialist, and was sensitive to charges of racial exploitation. He wanted to take Josephine—they had known each other for years—to the Stork Club, but asked a friend if it could be done without incident. The friend laughed. "She is an actress, you can perfectly well take her."

Bessie Buchanan—the one-time chorus girl who would become the first black woman elected to the New York State Assembly—also insisted there would be no problem. "You are French, Josephine." But Thelma Carpenter, stopping by the Roxy that night, suspected Bessie's motives. "Josephine had done her last show, she was sitting with a hat on her head, naked except for a Hermès scarf tied around her belly like an apron (it covered the scars from her operations) and she said she was going to the Stork Club. I told her not to take Bessie, I said, 'It's trouble.' "

Charlie Buchanan thought so too, he blamed Bessie for all that followed. "She plotted everything," he told me, after Bessie's death. "I spent over four hundred thousand dollars on my wife's political ambitions, just so I could have some peace."

Paul Bass: "Yes, my sister-in-law Bessie was ambitious. She used Joe and her fame to get where she wanted, up in politics."

Hycie Curtis (a dancer and longtime friend of Bessie's): "Bessie could sell herself. Even in show business, she couldn't do a damn thing, but she always got a spot. I figure Bessie gave Josephine bad advice. She knew what would happen."

Jo Attles: "Josephine shouldn't have done what she did because she just came here to visit, make some money, get out. She shouldn't have come back here and get treated like a secondhand somebody. But her one dream after the war was maybe to come and make a slight dent in America. 'Let me put my foot in Hollywood. Or my face.' "

The singer Dick Campbell was a Bessie loyalist. Acknowledging that she might have used Josephine to further her own goals, he still admired her. "I think Bessie wanted to go to the Stork Club and break down the discrimination there. Josephine gave her the opportunity."

"We were at Walter's table, number fifty, a banquette," says Yvonne O'Brian. "Josephine was more in the middle of the room. She had on a blue satin dress, and she looked beautiful. She and her friends were drinking champagne, there was no incident. In a place like that—crowded after theater—it takes a while to get food orders on the table. Perhaps there was a delay but I don't think it was on purpose, because Sherman Billingsley wouldn't discriminate against a celebrity. Celebrities were his life."

Right, says her husband. "Josephine Baker was the star of a show on Broadway, and Winchell liked her. Billingsley would never have done anything against her in front of Walter."

Be that as it may, says Solange Rico, "When my husband called the waiters, they acted as if they didn't hear him. Finally, he obliged a waiter to come, and the waiter said, 'There is no steak left.' Then my husband asked for crab cakes. None of them were left either. 'Very well,' said my husband, 'we are going to order something else.' But the waiter was already gone."

This was when Josephine got up and went to the phone. Roger Rico went with her. Again, they passed Winchell's table. "How nice," Winchell said to the O'Brians. "They're going to dance." (You couldn't dance in the Cub Room, you had to go to the big room next door where a rumba band alternated with a more conventional orchestra.)

Winchell and the O'Brians left the club to go to work—they were bound for a special late screening of *The Desert Fox* at the Rivoli—while Josephine was calling Walter White. "When she came back to the table," Mrs. Rico says, "the waiter was serving the steak, but she didn't want it anymore, she wanted to go."

Bill Harbach, a television director who was in the Cub Room that night, remembers hearing loud voices coming from Josephine's table. "Mr. Rico was screaming, 'This is outrageous,' and a big discussion was going on."

Upon demanding the check, Rico was told that Mr. Billingsley never permitted celebrities to pay. "Until tonight, you have always taken my money," cried Rico, throwing thirty dollars on the table and stalking away.

As for Josephine, French citizen, she had become Marianne, the symbol of *liberté, égalité, fraternité*. When she was done phoning Walter White, she phoned Billy Rowe, a black deputy police commissioner. Then she and Bessie made straight for Walter White's apartment, where they recited their grievances—not only had Josephine been barbarously handled, but Walter Winchell had sat by and let it happen. (Interestingly, there was no mention of an insult to Bessie, who chose not to make her own African heritage an issue. It was like the old joke "Let's you and him fight.")

Still steaming when they left the Whites, Bessie propelled Josephine to Chandler's restaurant, from which Barry Gray, known as a liberal, broadcast a late-night radio talk-and-music show. The women arrived too late to get on the air—Gray signed off at 3 A.M.—but he offered them a rain check. "Come back another time, and bring your lawyer."

By then, Josephine was out of control. "She came into my room at the hotel," says Shirley Woolf, "and she was yelling about Winchell. I said, 'Look how much good he has done for you, did you want him to hit his friend Billingsley in the head?' I said I wouldn't go to a place where my people weren't wanted, and she said, 'Darling, *your* people would buy the place.'

"While I had always disliked Winchell, I explained that the worst thing she could do was attack him. I said, 'He writes every day, he's on the air every week.' 'Oh, but darling,' she said, 'I am much bigger than he is.' Her ego by this time was beyond belief. You could not hold her back!"

Winchell was still sleeping when his phone rang at noon the next day. It was his secretary in a tizzy. People were calling from all over town to find out what had happened at the Stork Club. Had Josephine Baker been treated shamefully? A telegram from Walter White inquired why Winchell hadn't come to Josephine's rescue. Winchell was horrified. More feared than loved, he was entirely capable of nasty behavior, but this time, he was innocent. He had not even been in the room when the big scene played out. "I am appalled," he later wrote, "at the agony and embarrassment caused Josephine Baker and her friends at the Stork Club. But I am equally appalled at the efforts to involve me in an incident in which I had no part."

There was also a rumor that Grace Kelly had been in the Stork Club that night, and had failed to champion Josephine. As he had defended Winchell, O'Brian defended Kelly. "If she'd been there, I would have seen her. I was a kind of godfather to Grace."

Now a council of war took place in Josephine's dressing room between shows at the Roxy. Present were Josephine, Curt Weinberg (Josephine's press agent), Bessie Buchanan, Solange Rico, Ted Poston (a black reporter for the *New York Post*), Henry Lee Moon from the NAACP, Ned Schuyler, Shirley Woolf, and a second lawyer Schuyler had called in.

Bessie wanted to picket the Stork Club. The lawyers said if Josephine picketed, she could be sued and her salary attached. Moon phoned Thurgood Marshall (then special counsel to the NAACP) who said yes, Josephine was liable to a suit, but he wished she would picket anyway.

Solange Rico was asked by Moon if Winchell had tried to ease Josephine's humiliation. She confessed that Winchell hadn't known about it. "He left before we did."

Moon didn't care. "It's time we got after him anyhow."

The drama grew uglier, bad for everyone it touched. Billingsley was threatened with the revocation of his liquor license; state and city examiners were all over him like a rash. True, the ex-bootlegger who screamed at employees, "If I catch you bastards stealing a cup of coffee, you can get your asses out of here," was not a sweetheart. And besides that, he was nosey. "Under every table in the Cub Room was a mike," said Tony Butrico, one of the bartenders. "What you said could be heard in the offices upstairs."

(I wonder if everything Josephine said at the table that night was taped by Mr. Billingsley and passed on to Walter Winchell and J. Edgar Hoover. In any case, it appears that the FBI chief was not interested in *Baker* v. *Stork Club*. When Walter White wired him to ask if he would make public a statement of disapproval "regarding gratuitous refusal of service to Miss Josephine Baker," Hoover scribbled across the wire, "No answer required, I don't consider this to be any of my business.")

No matter how unlovely Billingsley's habits, many believed the Stork Club was being unfairly singled out. In 1951, most New York establishments practiced discrimination, although the great Pierre Franey says Le Pavillon, where he was chef, put out the red carpet for Josephine. "My boss, Henri Soulé, was honored by her visit, she got the best table and we prepared special dishes."

After the incident at the Stork Club, the prizefighter Sugar Ray Robinson came to the Roxy to talk to Josephine. He was Winchell's friend, and, according to Stanley Kay, "Josephine asked him, 'Why are you here?' He said, 'Because I love you, and I don't want you to make trouble. Walter is too powerful, he can kill your career.' "

In 1991, reading that Winchell's private papers were going to be auctioned, I phoned in a bid. I bought his files on Josephine for $648.86, surprised there was so little interest in what had been a cause célèbre.

I have also seen Josephine Baker files supplied to Winchell by the FBI, and some of the material seemed to me so childish I began to wonder about the agency's ability to protect America. Josephine had performed during May Day demonstrations in Paris. She had said she hated the United States "except for the money she can earn here." It was rumored of her early years in France that she had been "promiscuous in her sex relations with both men and women" and "would do anything to further her career."

Among Winchell's personal papers, there are memos expressing his outrage. "After all I did for her!" was scrawled across one scrap of paper.

To Herman Klurfeld, one of his ghostwriters, he expressed bafflement. "If she was discriminated against, why didn't she tell me? She knows I'm one of her fans, and I thought she was one of my friends."

No more. Now he would show her she had chosen the wrong enemy. He swung into action, digging up a sixteen-year-old story from the Associated Press quoting Josephine's praise for Mussolini in his war against Ethiopia. "I am willing to recruit a Negro army to help Italy . . . to travel around the world to convince my brothers Mussolini is their friend."

Astonishingly, though Josephine had indeed offered to raise an army for the Italian dictator, she took herself to Lucien le Lievre, a French-born lawyer with a respected Wall Street firm, and told him she wanted to sue Walter Winchell. "She was in a fighting mood," says le Lievre.

"I thought she might have a good case for defamation, and I sent her to Arthur Garfield Hays, a great litigator and author in the field of civil rights."

But a woman screaming "Shame on America!" while brandishing a French passport alarmed and embarrassed the French government, which sent an envoy from its embassy in Washington to baby-sit Josephine. His mission was not easy. "Josephine was dangerous," he said, "because she was sharp, personally ambitious, and she did not know the difference between what could be done and what could not be done."

She announced that she was going to continue to fight "this horrible thing," even if she were deported.

Winchell, who by then thought she *ought* to be deported, went on with his campaign to reestablish his liberal credentials and tarnish hers. His column was filled with tributes to himself. A man named Larry Steele wrote to say, "The vast majority of Negroes know that in you we have a friend." And Valaida Snow, the Sissle and Blake star of Josephine's early days, wrote to thank Winchell for the part he'd played in making her recent engagement at Café Society a success. "It was the most important step in my career."

People seeking Winchell's favor and people who just enjoyed a good feud offered observations. George Schuyler, New York editor of the black *Pittsburgh Courier,* denounced Josephine for "successfully horn-swoggling the colored brethren into accepting her as a group heroine and champion." He said she was being used by "fellow travelers and crypto Communists," and had repudiated them only once, "when she protested that she had been fleeced by the Reds on Willie McGee's funeral expenses."

Winchell's attacks redoubled. He reprinted some of the poison Josephine had spewed in her last book with Marcel Sauvage, including the observation that the Negroes of Harlem were "victims of the Jews."

By now, Winchell was feeling so aggrieved that he couldn't walk away from the battle. Josephine also was in too deep to drop it. Her show had closed at the Roxy, but before she left town, she called on Katherine Yarborough, whom she'd known since *Shuffle Along.* "I was living on Fifth Avenue," Yarborough says, "and Bessie Buchanan had told her I had powerful Jewish friends. She wanted me to bring my friends to her defense. She seemed destroyed."

In late November, Josephine appeared in Montreal, and, attempting to salvage what she could, gave an interview to *Le Petit Journal.* "You know I have a tough skin," she said. "To discourage me, they are nasty, they dig up my past, they falsify it. . . . I'm convinced that millions of people are thinking like me, even if they can't say it out loud for fear of being martyred. I will keep on being a missionary of peace, I will keep on fighting for Americans because I don't want them separated by prejudice."

Then she sent an S.O.S. to Jacques Abtey in Morocco. It was the first word he had got from her in four years: "My lawyer and I are going to attack Walter Winchell who protects the director of the Stork Club where I had my incident of discrimination. . . . Try to get the Moroccan, Algerian, Tunisian, Egyptian and Palestinian newspapers to write about it, to publish something so you can come here with it. . . . You must bring a lot of documents about how I have fought injustice at any cost. You will say you are coming from North Africa because you have learned in the press of the insults of Winchell and Billingsley. . . ."

At the very end of the letter, she stopped giving orders and was suddenly, unexpectedly touching. "Jo is panicked that something could happen to me. You must understand him, Jacques, if by chance the thing turns sour, Jo is no fighter like us." In a follow-up note, she told him all businesses in New York were "in the hands of Jews. . . . It's the same as it was in Berlin before the war, but you can't say that. . . . When you arrive, I'll give you a lesson."

December 10: Through Arthur Garfield Hays, Josephine issued a statement to the press. She was not anti-Semitic ("I married a Jew"), she had never been a fan of Mussolini ("so ridiculous it does not require comment"), and her services to the Allies had been outstanding ("My former commander, Colonel Abtey, is coming from his home in Casablanca to protest against these reflections on my war record"). In this statement, Josephine promoted Jacques from commandant to colonel.

Almost hidden in two pages of self-justification was the line "Miss Baker accepts Walter Winchell's statement that he was not present at the time of any discourtesy." But, said Mr. Hays, "this is beside the point."

If there *was* a point, it was beginning to get lost.

December 17: Josephine was in Chicago addressing a breakfast meeting of the Chicago Women's Division of the American Jewish Congress. She did not tell them all the businesses were in the hands of Jews; she told them, "We are working for the same ideal: a world without hate."

December 19: Josephine opened in Harlem at the Apollo for a nine-day engagement. (It was the first time she'd played an uptown theater.) She asked Jacques to come one night, and at the theater, her new secretary, Carolyn Carruthers (a light-skinned black woman and a friend of Bessie Buchanan), led him to his seat. "Suddenly," he recalls, "a black giant gets up, takes me in his arms, and says, 'Thank you for what you are doing for Josephine.' It was Paul Robeson, and he too had a lot of troubles in America."

December 20: The Mayor's Committee on Unity sent His Honor, Vincent Impellitteri, its final report on the incident at the Stork Club. The committee said it had found "nothing to substantiate a charge of racial discrimination."

December 21: Josephine sued Winchell, the Hearst Corporation, and King Features for four hundred thousand dollars, charging defamation of character and claiming her profession and earning capacity had been impaired. That night, she and her cadre—Arthur Garfield Hays, Bessie Buchanan, Walter White, and Jacques Abtey (with an interpreter)—finally appeared on Barry Gray's radio show. Jacques said he had traveled over three thousand miles to "defend the honor of a war heroine," and read aloud laudatory letters from two French generals.

In days to come, Sugar Ray Robinson would show up on Gray's show to say Winchell was an ally of black people, and Ed Sullivan (a *Daily News* columnist and host of a popular Sunday-night television show) would argue that Winchell was *nobody's* ally. As for Gray himself, the affair almost put him out of business. "Sponsors were intimidated by the pressure of Winchell's friends, guests that used to come on the program were no longer appearing, I was physically attacked twice."

December 26: The *Chicago Daily News* quoted Edith Sampson, "noted Negro attorney of Chicago." Miss Sampson had pronounced herself weary of Josephine's bad-mouthing the United States and extolling the great race relations in France while "French colonialism is a blot on the world's conscience." Miss Sampson said the forty-five million blacks in France's African colonies "suffer much more than does Miss Baker in Atlanta or New York."

December 31: Josephine was in her dressing room at the Earle Theatre in Philadelphia with Jacques Abtey and Donald Wyatt (whom she had also summoned in the wake of the Winchell crisis). They were icing champagne for a midnight toast to the new year when the telegrams of cancellation began pouring in from theaters across the country.

"Jacques and I were devastated for her," Donald says. "But her face showed nothing. She was strong."

Not quite strong enough, though. "Anyone following her tactics had to be someone without a stake in the system," Donald observes, "someone willing to lose what he or she had. W.E.B. Du Bois, Paul Robeson, Dick Gregory, Martin Luther King made such sacrifices. Josephine wanted badly to emulate the actions of these leaders, to win the admiration of black Americans, and to denounce their oppressors. But at the same time, she needed to earn millions to support her projects at Les Milandes, millions that had to come through the establishment against which she was protesting. She failed to see that it had to be one or the other, not both.

"I admire her courage and am inclined to forgive her lack of judgment. I think she was guilty at having taken so long to speak out. The 1950s were difficult. Black veterans wanted to win for themselves the democracy they had fought for abroad, but the Ku Klux Klan and the White Citizens Councils had mobilized to keep us in our place."

Fighting for the oppressed when she wasn't buttering up their oppressors—Mussolini, Juan Perón—Josephine was a paradox, but Donald always gave her the benefit of the doubt. Jacques's eye was colder. "She was caught up in the game," he says. "The sacred fire of the stage was no longer enough for her, she was now deep in politics, writing to de Gaulle, to Malraux, to Eva Perón. But what was the goal she wanted to reach? I don't know if she herself knew. Her black friends were almost white: Bessie Buchanan, Walter White, the big man in the NAACP, he was absolutely white. I could not understand America."

Like everyone who cared for Josephine, Jacques hung around long enough to be badly treated. "I said, 'Since I'm here now, let me try my luck.' I wanted to see if I could sell my book, *The Secret War of Josephine Baker,* to a New York publisher, but she said no.

" 'You will never get a book contract, you don't know Americans. You come with me.' She still had a few dates to play—not everyone had canceled—and she wanted me with her. She had told me to bring no money when I came from Morocco—'I will advance it to you and you can reimburse me in France'—so I was at her mercy. I asked her to let me have my freedom, and she started to count out, 'Two dollars for a room, one dollar for a movie, this much for food, a few extra dollars for the weekend,' and it came to a total of $130 for fifteen days, and that's all she gave me. After what I had done for her against Winchell!

"We were in her dressing room in Philadelphia, and I looked at her in the mirror and I wanted to punch her face. But I had only two dollars in my pocket. I took the $130 and said, *'Salut!'* I went to New York and a Jewish friend—I had saved her mother during the war—found me a room. I was happy there, and you know, I met Winchell. The meeting took place at his barber's. It was quite amusing. Winchell was in the chair being groomed, and he said, 'Major Abtey, *ça va?*'

" 'For a sick man,' I said to his assistant, 'he looks good.' I had been told he was very sick.

"The guy translated, and Winchell smiled. 'I'm good-looking? Yes, I'm good-looking. Please, wait five minutes.' Afterward, we got into a taxi, and he said he was going to his doctor because Josephine had broken his heart. 'I'm finished.'

"It was sad, that powerful man. I said to him, 'Yes, but you have been asking for it a little. You said she did nothing during the war, that she was with the Italians in 1935 and against the French and the Americans.'

" 'But it's true,' he cried. 'I have the newspaper clippings.'

"I said, 'Listen, Winchell, I don't know about 1935, but during the last war, she was remarkable!'

" 'She broke me,' he said, 'she broke my heart. I, who have done so much for the black cause—'

"I said, 'Listen, since I'm involved in the story, I'm going to see Josephine and arrange a reconciliation.'

"He said, 'Yes, you could.' Then, suddenly, 'No, I don't want it. I have the translation of her book, I have the newspaper articles, I was not at the Stork Club when it happened—'

"It was fantastic, he was like a child, I had to console him. I will always see him in the taxi crying, 'She broke my heart, I'm a finished man.' "

Chapter 33

—

A CAREER COLLAPSES, A UNIVERSAL MOTHER IS BORN

"I want to adopt five little two-year-old boys"

*A*lso finished, at least on Broadway, was Roger Rico, fired from *South Pacific*, another casualty of Josephine's night on the town. But she didn't hang around to offer condolences, she was off to Chicago and St. Louis.

In Chicago, Richard, Jr., and his brother Clifford, then teenagers, showed up to see their famous aunt. (Their father, having yielded at last to her persuasion, had already left America to begin a new life at Les Milandes.)

"With Clifford and me," says Richard, Jr., "she did all this family bullshit—'Why don't you write your father?' So Clifford said, 'Don't act all holy, Aunt, you haven't done a damn thing for us,' and Aunt Tumpy, being the great queen, says, 'How dare you? I'll call the police,' and Clifford says, 'I'll kick your butt and throw you out the window.' I stayed quiet and let Clifford be the big fighter because I wanted to get next to that glamour, all right? I wanted to get on the stage with Aunt Tumpy at that Chicago theater."

Faced by these two young nephews, one confrontational, the other starstruck, Josephine may have decided a little family went a long way; when she returned to her hometown, she stayed with a lawyer, David Grant, and his wife.

The Kiehl Auditorium in St. Louis was a big barn of a place with ten thousand seats. "She had come back," says Richard, Jr. "They had rolled out the red carpet, but the house was only half full."

Helen Morris and her husband were there. "It was really good," Helen says. "Tumpy had those beautiful French gowns and feathers and she pranced on, she was the star. After the show, she made a speech. She told everybody to stand up, and she got carried away; it was over an hour everybody standing there waiting for her to finish. She was talking about segregation and all that crap."

It was a good speech, if too long for a crowd whose feet hurt. Josephine said her heart swelled at the sight of the beautiful "salt and pepper" audience. "I mean by that colored and white brothers mingling." And she talked about black soldiers fighting in Korea. "These men want to love America . . . they also want to love the white race, but want to be respected . . . they want their wives, their mothers, their children to be happy and at peace here while they are giving their blood over there.

"My people have a country of their own to go to if they choose, Africa, but America belongs to them as much as it does to the white race, in some ways even more because they gave their sweat and their blood in slavery. . . ."

That day, she finally told the truth about her role in the East St. Louis race riot, confessing to having been an observer, rather than a participant. "I was very tiny," she said, "but . . . I can still see myself standing on the west bank of the Mississippi looking over into East St. Louis and watching the glow of the burning Negro homes lighting the sky."

At the end, she laid it on a little thick, contending that she had never enjoyed her European success because she could not stop thinking "of the suffering of my people here in America. . . . I was haunted until I finally understood that I was marked by God to try to fight for the freedom of my people. It was then I heard of the atrocities going on in Germany against the Jews . . . so when war was declared, I went into it with all my heart. . . ."

After exhorting her listeners to love one another, she retreated to her dressing room and refused to see her almost-sister, Helen Morris. "I was pregnant with Lena, my second child," Helen remembers. "I was very big, very tired. When we went backstage, we asked the lawyer man to tell Josephine I was there, and he went away and came back and said she was not receiving. 'But we're family,' I said. 'Tell her it's little Hemmen. She'll receive us.' But no, she didn't. She didn't come by the house either. Maybe her being so famous in France affected her, she could not think rational, like the average person. I didn't hold it against her, that's the way she was."

Maybe, Helen suggests, it was easier for Josephine to deal with people she didn't know intimately, who demanded no emotional response of her. "She came here one time, and she heard about some woman in Mississippi whose child died, and she paid the whole funeral, bought the family clothes."

Before she left St. Louis, Josephine sent Jacques a prospectus. "She had cooked up the idea of a nonprofit organization 'to perpetuate the work and the ideals of Josephine Baker by fostering goodwill and harmonious relationships among all mankind.' She said, 'Just look, there are seventy-five million blacks in America, if one out of two signs up at a dollar per person, do you see the money we can make?' In return, she was willing to give one free concert a year. I laughed."

Floating in front of Josephine's eyes were $37,500,000, some for the fund, some perhaps in "Mrs. Kaiser's" Swiss bank account. Right from the beginning, the numbers were skewed—in 1952, there were only 16,749,000 blacks in the United States—but that didn't prevent a meeting of the Josephine Baker World Cultural Society from taking place in New York City on April 7. The star was not present.

Around this time, says Shirley Woolf, "Josephine and I decided to part. Ned was very sick, so it was over. Still, I gave her a nice going-away present. The United States had a treaty with France under the terms of which French scientists and researchers did not have to pay American taxes. Josephine had asked me to apply for it, even though it wasn't for show people. Would you believe she got it? Because she was so 'unique'! She got a free pass on her taxes!"

Now she signed with Bill Taub, a wheeler-dealer who claimed to have been a confidant of Richard Nixon, Howard Hughes, Madame Mao, and Aristotle Onassis. He had first met Josephine in Paris, and while he thought she might find it difficult to make a comeback in her present circumstances—"She was no longer regarded as an entertainer but as a troublemaker"—he decided to see what he could do.

Which was considerable. "In February 1952, I booked Josephine into El Patio in Mexico City and took a full-page ad in *Variety* announcing the show was sold out."

El Patio turned customers away. Sweet news for a headliner taking home 20 percent of the gross. In her spare time, Josephine made speeches about how she had "personally seen a number of lynchings of entire Negro families." (This greatly irritated the CIA and the U.S. State Department.)

Then Taub got her a job in Las Vegas—four weeks, $12,500 a week at the Last Frontier; she would open there on April 18—so, after the Mexican engagement, the star, her secretary, maid, two musicians (one of them Sweets Edison), and twenty-four suitcases traveled to the Nevada desert.

"They had a red carpet all the way from the airplane to the inside of the airport," says Sweets, "and a big sign that said WELCOME JOSEPHINE BAKER.

"At that time, blacks were not welcome on the Strip, but she was staying right there at the Last Frontier, and when we came to rehearsal, she asked me how did I like my room. I said, 'Well, I don't stay in the hotel, they sent me around the west side, you know, in the black neighborhood.' So she says, 'Oh, no, that can't happen, Mr. Sweets,' and she right away informed the owner of the Frontier that the show would not go on until I had a room. And right before the show, they had me a room, right there on the Strip, you know, yes, yes. And she had a table there in front of the stage every night, in case they would say the joint was full, blacks could have her table. She was a fighter, very much for her people."

In Las Vegas, Josephine also lined up several experts willing to come to Les Milandes and teach her how to run a gambling palace. By June, she had left for South America; Taub was not with her.

Brazil. "Its name touches my heart because it sounds so soft to the ear," said Josephine.

Uruguay. Singing and dancing and, when her "artistic schedule" permitted, lecturing. Speaking in English, which most of her listeners didn't understand, she told an audience that most Negroes in the United States were unhappy.

Argentina. She announced she would campaign against racial discrimination, although the country had only five thousand blacks out of a population of eighteen million. The Argentines were baffled, but polite.

Juan Perón received her on October 3 at Government House in Buenos Aires. The general and his late wife (Evita had died in July) had received so many letters from Josephine that they had thought of her as an old friend.

For obvious reasons, Josephine identified with Evita, her "dear sister." A bit player in movies, Eva Maria Duarte de Perón had risen from "her first soiled love affair . . . to marry Juan Domingo Perón, the strong man of the Argentine government!" confided a blurb on the back cover of a book called *Eva, Evita*. She also "built the most beautiful orphanage in the world, gave her countrywomen the vote, fed the poor, and died at the height of her glory with $20 million in stolen funds nestled in Swiss bank accounts!"

Now the heavily embalmed "Martyr of Labor, Protector of the Forsaken, Defender of the Worker, Guiding Light of the Children" lay in state, holding a rosary blessed by the pope.

Carolyn Carruthers was acting as Josephine's companion and assistant. She remembered kneeling with Josephine in front of Evita's glass-covered coffin. "General Perón had received us just like officials. He and Josephine decided she would carry on Evita's fight for the poor people. He even had the government vote her a special position, we went everywhere in the name of Evita and the general. It was very strange."

"I cannot conceive of Heaven without General Perón," Evita had said.

"Thank God for making men like Perón," said Josephine, calling her new buddy the man who had "set the pattern for brotherhood . . ." (If Cain was your brother. Or if you could put out of mind the cattle prods used in his jails, the labor unions and newspapers smashed by his orders.)

So delighted was the general with his new acolyte that he assigned her to "oversee the chain of failing hospitals Eva had founded. The nightclub singer spent two days touring psychiatric and maternity hospitals . . . health-care centers, and a leper colony. Everywhere she went she was appalled by the lack of equipment and the miserable living conditions of the patients."

Never shy, she turned the sharp edge of her tongue against Ramón Carillo, the minister of health, who wrote Perón in despair: "It is true the Señora Eva Perón called me often to make me aware of deficiencies in our services . . . but she never treated me like the Señora Baker did."

For three months, Josephine threw her weight around, ordering a brand-new ambulance to "give" to the people, and almost having a breakdown when it was delivered to her hotel. (She certainly didn't intend to pay for it.) But it wasn't her good works that got her in trouble, it was her big mouth. Interviewed by Perónist newspapers—there was a five-part series in the evening daily, *Critica*—she assured reporters the United States was the only country where Negroes were "treated like dogs."

"She and I were fussing all the time now," Carolyn Carruthers told me, "about the terrible things she said to the press."

And the terrible things she said in three lectures she gave at Buenos Aires theaters. Offering her own revisionist view of World War II, she announced that "we Free French" had liberated France without any help from England or America, then took a swipe at the newly elected president of the United States, Dwight Eisenhower, predicting that under him, "the colored people will suffer as never before." She also wrote an open letter to Herbert Clark, who had done an unflattering piece about her in the New York *Daily News,* calling him "a typical scandal monger," and assuring him that "North American democracy is a farce."

Suddenly, Winchell had company. American journalists who had been keeping their own counsel erupted into print. Robert Ruark liked Josephine's legs, but didn't like her saying that persecutions in the United States were now "more shocking than before World War II, with lynchings, condemnations without trials and electrocutions. . . ."

How would she know about pre–World War II conditions, Ruark wondered, "since she lived abroad and was wed to a series of Frenchmen."

Baker: "White men prate of democracy and send the Negro to die in Korea."

Ruark: "I could have sworn a few white boys were listed on the casualty reports."

Warming to his task, Ruark said that on her most recent trip to New York, Miss Baker had lived in a lavish hotel suite "and never met Jim Crow socially. She traveled in drawing rooms with her white maid. . . . She hasn't seen any lynchings, nobody treated her mean."

The columnist called Josephine "an abject liar," the *New York Post* (more in sorrow than in anger) called her "the pin-up girl of Argentine fascism," and the Justice Department said it was studying ways to bar her from the United States. In Argentina, Josephine sniffed, "I shall count it an honor to be barred."

Even her old friend Adam Clayton Powell charged her with presenting "her own wild imaginings as facts." Powell spoke of civil rights won in "an unrelenting fight waged by Negro and white leaders during the twenty years when Miss Baker was not in the United States. She never helped us by word or deed." Neither had she, proud citizen of France, ever protested "the sorry plight of African colonials" under French rule.

Her anti-USA, pro-Perón rhetoric was beginning to have dire consequences in Latin America as well. "At the Opera Theatre in Buenos Aires," *Variety* reported, "the gross declined noticeably throughout the past week."

A projected tour fell apart. The Uruguayans didn't want her because of her Perónist views, the Peruvians didn't want her because she "planned to carry out racial propaganda against the United States." Moreover, Argentina was beginning to pall, she was growing tired of playing understudy to the memory of Evita, and tired of the general, who spent his leisure chasing thirteen-year-old girls.

February 1953 found her again in Havana. Three times she had postponed her arrival there, and now her contracts with Montmartre Cabaret, the National Casino, and CMQ-Television (which had signed her for two weeks at fourteen thousand dollars) were canceled. "We can't be at the mercy of her whims," said one producer, but the truth was that her campaign against North America was making potential employers uneasy.

She settled for a couple of weeks' work in a small neighborhood movie theater (a run-down former burlesque house), which thrilled Walter Winchell. By appearing at this "emporium of bump and grind," he wrote, "Miss Baker has publicly acknowledged that her professional day is done."

An audience with President Batista went badly, he refused to enroll in her crusade against America, and the next day, she was arrested. Military intelligence officers seized books and pamphlets from her rooms, took her to headquarters, and interrogated her about her Communist leanings. She said she didn't have any. Like a criminal, she was fingerprinted and photographed with a number across her chest. She never forgot the number, 0000492, one more thorn in her martyr's crown.

It was time to go. Spring was coming back to France, and so was Josephine, tired, angry, and empty of pocket. With creditors prowling around, Jo was getting cold feet about the transformation of Les Milandes, but the iron-willed Josephine simply hit the road again. Switzerland, Rome, then Paris for the annual Bal des Petits Lits Blancs, a charity ball to raise money for sick children. She performed with Lily Pons and came down into the audience to kiss Charlie Chaplin. Had not she and Charlie both been thrown to the lions by a wicked United States where the dollar was king?

In June, Josephine came to London for the coronation of Queen Elizabeth II. "She and my wife and I walked from Trafalgar Square to Buckingham Palace, down the Mall," said Harry Hurford-Janes. "And she turned to us and said, 'All this will be swept away one day.' You know, the queen and everything. Well, it probably will, but it was strange how she admired and yet envied the royal family. For years, she sent them Christmas cards, and they were all acknowledged, and then she used to put these acknowledgments out in her apartment."

Harry remembered going to the House of Lords with Josephine, and passing a black speaker, a Communist, haranguing the crowd in front of Hyde Park. "She went up to him and said, 'My friend is white, I am black and white, why are you Red?' Then she invited him to come to Les Milandes; she wanted to de-Communize him."

Toward the end of October, in an uncharacteristic show of selflessness, she wrote to Colette Mars, who was sailing for New York to play the Persian Room of the Plaza Hotel.

"Do not paralyze yourself with fear which doesn't serve you but takes away your talent," she advised, confessing that only the night before, she herself had been fearful, opening at the Drap d'Or, a small cabaret near the Champs-Élysées. (It was the best she could get now, she was considered to be washed up.) Stage fright, she told Colette, "is allowed to me because I'm much older than you."

Thelma Carpenter was working in a club not far from the Drap d'Or, and she saw Josephine often. "She didn't know how to be happy," Thelma says, "but I could make her laugh, I entertained her. Before Christmas, she took me to the Galeries Lafayette. She wanted to buy Jo something.

"Now, she'd had husbands before, but Jo was gay, every queen in town knew him. And he was in the country, at Les Milandes, with his lover. When you'd call on the phone, the lover would answer and say he was "Madame Bakaire."

"We go in the men's department, and we're trying on dressing gowns, trying to decide what would look best on Jo, and she says, 'What should we give my wife-in-law?' and I say I would give him poison, and she laughs. I think she saw she was in a ludicrous situation, but she came from that old school that said a woman's gotta have a man, any kind of man. And maybe a regular man would have wanted too much of her, I don't think she cared that much about sex. Anyway, she had done so much for herself, she *was* a man.

"I remember asking her about Germany because I knew she'd been in Berlin in the twenties. 'We worked with no clothes on,' she said, 'so to keep us warm, they gave us cocaine. It was wide open in Berlin, it was a wicked city.' "

Suddenly, it added up. Everything Count Harry Kessler had confided to his diary: Josephine rolling naked on a floor, Josephine dancing for hours "without any sign of fatigue."

"Pebbles to make my tired body gay." It's a line from the old melodrama *The Shanghai Gesture,* uttered by a character called Mother Goddamn. She is recounting the sufferings inflicted on her as a young girl in a brothel. "But," she says, "I survived."

White powder to make cold blood run hot. But Josephine survived. Long enough to grow tired of men. They were deceivers ever; the older they got, the more they used young girls as shields against age, and dropped them without pity. She had collected many grievances against the male sex, starting with her abandonment by the man who had fathered her and left her a child of bad luck.

I can identify with that, because I too was conceived as a child of bad luck. I can hear the villagers whispering behind my mother's back, *"Pauvre Luce, elle a pas eu de chance."*

Josephine could no longer conquer with the laughter of her *croupe,* nor as a war hero either. Her uniform had been consigned to the closets of Time, the soldiers who had dreamed of her had gone home to their sweethearts.

Her growing distrust and contempt for men—with the possible exception of Charles de Gaulle—caused her to offer ever more insults to her hapless husband. Because it was in the fifties—nobody can remember the exact year—that she took as her companion a gorilla.

Maryse Bouillon: "She called him Bubu. He was as tall as a thirteen-year-old boy, it was frightful, everyone feared him."

Yvette Malaury: "She dressed him like a man, with trousers, a shirt, and tie. Yes, like a man. And she and the gorilla would walk down the street together, occasionally making appearances at the *guinguette*. People would say, 'It's a scandal!' She had become fond of that gorilla. When Jo Bouillon came back and tried to enter her bedroom, she told him, 'I don't need you anymore.' "

Georges Malaury: "He was a beautiful animal but people were afraid of him. And let me tell you, man to man, he had a big tool."

Georgette Malaury (Georges's sister): "Josephine did not treat him like an animal, but like a human being. He was jealous of anyone approaching her. In the end, she had to have him shot. She could have given him to a zoo, but she was always hasty."

Eli Mercier: "He became wild, and escaped in the park. They killed him in the park."

Incidentally, Bubu was the name of one of Josephine's partners in the 1930s casino show *Paris Qui Remue*. An M. Maccio, dressed as a gorilla, stood next to Josephine as she sang "J'ai Deux Amours."

In February 1954, Josephine went to Denmark and played a second-rate Copenhagen nightclub called the Harlem. She also lectured in the National Museum, under the auspices of a French organization called LICA (Ligue Internationale Contre le Racisme et l'Antisémitisme), in the National Museum on "Why I Fight Racial Discrimination."

"There is good and evil in all people," she told her audience, adding that they must wonder why she was "joining the crusade for the freedom of humanity, instead of satisfying myself with my theater life, where doors are opened freely, where people are always friendly, and where there are few disappointments and obstacles."

A definition of theater life not recognizable to most performers, but let it go. She talked about South Africa, Japan (where, she claimed, whites discriminated against the Japanese), Germany, where the "innocent babies of colored American soldiers who had been stationed there and white German girls . . . had already created a problem." It was against the background of this problem, she said, that she had decided "to adopt my five little boys." (Nowhere else have I found any record of Josephine's giving this reason for going into the Mother business.)

But mostly, she talked about the United States: how the actor Canada Lee was hounded to his death, how a Burmese judge was turned away by a restaurant in Washington, D.C., how two colored people in the South were killed because they used a toilet reserved for whites.

She said three-quarters of the world was composed of colored people, "and these peoples are uniting. . . . I am afraid of revenge, because nothing is more horrible than revenge which has its roots in hatred."

On the face of it, there wasn't much in the lecture that a human being with an ordinary amount of goodwill could fault, but the Danish foreign minister, a Mr. Hansen, was taken to task by the American ambassador for having extended formal hospitality to someone promoting "anti-Americanism in Denmark."

Mr. Hansen said he didn't think Josephine wanted to injure the United States, though he had, in fact, asked her why she hadn't included "any mention of racial discrimination in the Soviet Union," and she'd said she preferred to talk about places she had personal knowledge of. The American ambassador replied that he doubted Josephine had personal knowledge of South Africa or Japan, both of which she had mentioned in her speech.

At least part of that would be changing very soon. Josephine was going to Japan. She had decided to seize the moment. No big contracts were coming her way, the Casino and the Folies no longer fought over her, she felt vulnerable to the future. But she always had a new plan. Enter Josephine, the Universal Mother. If young men no longer wanted her, a brood of abandoned babies would make her feel needed again. She was going to turn the world into a better place, not only by fighting from public platforms, but in her private demesne.

In the spring of 1953 she had written to Miki Sawada (who was by then running an orphanage) and ordered a child, as you would a take-out dinner. "I would like you to find for me a Japanese baby of pure race, a healthy one, two years old. I want to adopt five little two-year-old boys, a Japanese, a black from South Africa, an Indian from Peru, a Nordic child, and an Israelite; they will live together like brothers."

No more dolls out of the garbage can for Tumpy, she would have unbroken ones, healthy, perfect. She asked for the Japanese baby's papers to be prepared at once. "Because I want to take him away with me. I will need a little kimono, because I would like him to live in his national costume so he will not forget his ancestors and his motherland. He will, of course, be raised in France. I would also like his first name to be Japanese."

She left Paris for Tokyo with Ginette, her wardrobe mistress, and trunkfuls of new dresses by Christian Dior.

Chapter 34

—

LIFE IS A CABARET
AT LES MILANDES

"Jo [Bouillon] would seduce young men"

Except for fallen petals under the trees, the cherry blossoms were finished, but the azaleas, pink, white, orange, red, were coming into bloom when Miki Sawada fetched Josephine from Haneda Airport.

They drove to Oiso, a town forty miles outside of Tokyo, to the Elizabeth Sanders Home (named for an Englishwoman whose money helped start the place). It was in this villa near the sea that Miki had begun to save abandoned babies of American soldiers and Japanese girls.

Although she was born a child of privilege, Miki's comfortable life had been shattered by the war—a son killed, her husband stigmatized as a criminal by the American army. "My father could take no job," says Emi Sawada, "our possessions were confiscated. When we lost the war, we lost everything."

Including the villa in Oiso. But Miki got it back. First, she won permission from occupation authorities to set up an orphanage, then she started raising money to rescue Eurasian infants.

It began, Emi told me, on a train. A package fell from an overhead luggage rack onto Miki's head. "My mother opened it, and discovered a newborn baby boy wrapped in newspapers. He was black, a child of the occupation."

After that, Miki Sawada started taking in children nobody wanted. The first was found in the Imperial Palace plaza in the dead of winter. "The mothers used to leave them at the door," Emi says. "There was no help from the Japanese public, these were impure children, children of the enemy still occupying our country."

Between 1948 and 1954, Miki welcomed more than a thousand foundlings, and struggled to find money for milk, medicine, clothing, rice. When Josephine came in 1954, it was not only to adopt a child, but to give a series of free performances for the Home. Informed by an American officer that her friend was a Communist, Miki was stunned. "I had never heard of anything so ridiculous. She owned a castle!"

Because of American displeasure with Josephine, even her costumes were held hostage. Instead of arriving in Haneda, they had been unloaded in Hong Kong. She performed her first shows in Japan wearing one of Emi's kimonos. (Forty years later, a woman named Laura Flannery told me there had indeed been a cabal against Josephine. While a CIA employee in Tokyo, Flannery had found a file describing a scheme to destroy Josephine's reputation. "I asked why the agency would lie about a woman trying to adopt babies, and was told she was a leftist who went around the world talking down the United States.")

In Hiroshima, Josephine visited a peace monument. "She stopped," Miki recalled, "at the little store in front of the Atomic Bomb Memorial Hall, and put her hand on the shoulder of an old man. It was covered with raw-looking red keloids. . . . Tears ran down her face. 'This is unforgivable,' she said. 'The countries that think they have won the war have lost something precious in the process.' "

After twenty-three concerts, she left Japan with two orphans. "First she had a Shinto ceremony performed for them," Emi says. "I think she wanted to show her sincerity by putting these children in the care of the old gods."

At the ceremony, M. Martin, director of the Air Force, stood proxy for the children's father. (Jo did not yet know he had become the lucky daddy of *two* little boys.)

The older child, Yamamoto Akio (who would be called Akio), had been born on July 7, 1952; the younger, Kimura Teruya Seiji (who would be called Janot), had been born on July 15, 1953. They wouldn't be legally adopted until 1957.

"When Josephine went with Mrs. Sawada to the orphanage," Ginette says, "I stayed in our hotel in Tokyo. When she came back, she said, 'Look, Ginette, look at the two beautiful children I have, my first two children, I'm so happy.' Then we started to take care of them, give them bottles, all of that. It was a new part for her. I went to the Shinto ceremony; Josephine made me the godmother of Akio."

Both Akio and Janot had been born of white fathers, though Miki Sawada said that, during her visit to the orphanage, Josephine had spoken with—and comforted—two young women with babies fathered by blacks. "One of the mothers spent a long time with Josephine under the trees in our garden . . . and returned home looking considerably happier and with renewed courage."

Still, Josephine had not selected for herself a baby with a black father. I don't really know why, except that maybe, in choosing abandoned children born of white men, she was choosing the little Josephine to nurture and make whole. (She would in time adopt black children, but never an American one.)

"On our way back to France," Ginette says, "we spent five days in Saigon. It was an eleven-hour flight from Tokyo. Josephine sang in a cabaret, and also went to military camps to entertain the French soldiers who had been wounded fighting in the infamous battle of Dien Bien Phu."

Then it was time to go home.

A stewardess aboard the Air France Constellation remembered Josephine's asking to have the babies' bottles warmed in the galley. "She came there to change the children. She seemed satisfied, soft."

On May 12, the beaming new mother deplaned at Orly, a baby in each arm. What had she come back to? Les Milandes going full tilt. "Sometimes," said Leon Burg, "a truck would be unloaded in front of the château, and its contents loaded onto smaller trucks and driven away and sold somewhere else. But Josephine would get the bill. She helped put Périgord on the world map of tourism, three hundred thousand people came that spring and summer, but the owners of restaurants and hotels in the neighboring villages worried she was going to take all their business. More than once, she had her tires slashed, until they saw there was enough for everyone."

The place had grown without, it seemed, any rational planning at all.

"You can't believe what went on here," says the electrician, Henri Chapin. "Josephine had an architect who made no blueprints, he drew on raw walls, and then he would leave, and when he came back, the wall had been painted or papered, and the drawings would be gone. At the Chartreuse, the chic restaurant-hotel, they had done the upstairs rooms, but forgot to allow for the pitched roof; with the roof in place, you had to crawl on hands and knees to get from one room to another. It had to be redone.

"When her employees weren't ruining her, Josephine was ruining herself. I worked three months to build her a water pump, new motors, copper pipes from Limoges, electric cables, and then Jo Bouillon comes to me and says, 'Stop, we are going to do something else, a water tank.'

"I quit. I said, 'Josephine, I like you, but I don't like what's going on here.' If we had been near Paris or Marseilles, we could have catered banquets, weddings, but here we were lost. La Chartreuse was too beautiful, too fragile for the country, people broke everything."

"When she gave a dinner in the grand salon," says Jacqueline Abtey, "she would go and take the chalice and the monstrance and other consecrated articles from the chapel and decorate the long table with them. I was shocked. And guests would sit under large silver chandeliers, and eat off blue porcelain encrusted with roses. Only four sets of that Bohemian china had ever been made, for the duke of Windsor, the king of Italy, the queen of Holland, and Josephine.

"Her bathroom was covered with gold-leafed tiles; when she needed money, she would have them taken off the walls and sent to the bank as collateral."

She thought she was achieving what she had first plotted with Le Corbusier, her "little village with little houses, little trees, little roads for people to be happy," but when she was in residence, not everyone was happy. Subconsciously, she re-created the conditions of her childhood, turning herself into Mrs. Kaiser of dreaded memory, rousing her victims at dawn.

"During the day, a twelve-year-old girl from the neighborhood tended Josephine's sheep," says Georges Malaury. "Evenings, she worked in the kitchen, washing dishes, cleaning the stove. Josephine would keep her till 11 P.M., midnight, it was dark, we had no lighted roads, and the child's mother worried. Every night, she would come to pick up her daughter, and wait outside.

"Josephine didn't like that, so one night she goes out and says to the mother, 'What are you doing here?' and the mother says, 'I came to pick up my daughter,' and Josephine hits her. They fought, rolling on the ground, Josephine screaming. It was unpleasant, we heard it across the road."

"Josephine was terrible," says Henri Chapin. "She left us independent contractors in peace, but her maids ran when they saw her coming. She would have them carry things from the basement to the roof, from the roof to the basement, just to keep them busy. And she didn't sleep, day and night she kept running, she had a terrible vitality.

"When she started the adoptions, Jo Bouillon would tell me, '*Dis donc,* I'm a father again of I don't know what.' She used those adoptions as weapons for her racial fight. At the beginning, she put billboards along the road saying COME SEE LES MILANDES AND ITS RAINBOW TRIBE. The people all around protested, 'You don't show little children like monkeys,' so she had the billboards taken down."

Even the children's nurses were driven mercilessly. Here are excerpts of a letter to a touring Josephine from one nanny: "I have been eight days at Les Milandes, and have not yet found time to unpack. . . . On top of my duties as nurse-assistant, I am a maid of all trades, washing, cleaning, scouring, cooking. Is this included in the job description, and if so, what is the pay? And when during twenty-four hours is the time permitted for rest?"

"The personnel went filing past for years," says Jacqueline Abtey. "Josephine engaged them like musical acts, wherever she was, and months later, when she was back for a short visit at Les Milandes, she would have forgotten she'd hired them, or she would discover they were no good for the job. It was turmoil, in one year I counted over two hundred nurses. This was bad for the children, they would get attached to a girl and cry when she left, but you could not reason with Josephine. The nursery was badly kept, the odor of *pipi* on the mattresses was almost as bad as the monkey house."

"People in the village were worried for their children," Georges Malaury told me. "And they were worried for these children of Josephine when she was away, because Josephine's life had become their life, Josephine's worries became their worries. Jo would seduce young men, and a few families blackmailed Josephine. Most of these boys were working at the château, and suddenly their pay would be a bit higher. For young kids, that place was a sex palace."

Like the rampant ivy on the château walls, sex ran amok at Les

Milandes. "Josephine's brother-in-law, Elmo, would say he was going to get some grass for the rabbits," Georges says, "and he would be with a girl, and suddenly he would see his wife, Margaret, running, looking for him. He would jump over a wall and be working next to my father at the anvil when Margaret arrived breathless, a revolver in her hand."

Richard Martin behaved even more recklessly than Elmo. He loved France, loved "bein' able to walk down the street with a white woman and not bein' scared of gettin' hanged." When he wasn't working on the farm, or running Les Milandes' gas station, he was chasing girls. He impregnated one—Josephine sent her to Switzerland for an abortion—and he also fathered a baby boy by a sweetheart in Bordeaux.

"Phone calls would come to the château," Jacqueline Abtey says. "Richard was drunk, in delirium, there would be knives, fistfights with the local farmers, running after women until somebody called the police. It was a circus.

"Can you imagine what the local people had to endure? Elmo was kind; Margaret was different. She despised the local people, found them dirty. She really practiced racism against the Dordogne people—she, who to them was an intruder!

"As for Josephine's mother, she mostly stayed in her room. She had a profile like an eagle, she was very black, tall, slim, and her eyes could flash lightning. The poor woman did not speak French—she was the only one of Josephine's family to live at the château, the others had their own little houses. There was a tension between Josephine and her mother. Carrie would never come to the table for dinner, you saw her nowhere, and at the end she was bedridden."

Richard too spoke of the tension between Josephine and Carrie. "My mother said, 'I don't know what's going to happen, Josephine doesn't seem to love us anymore. Everything she do is contrary.' Mama told me Josephine said, 'I don't understand you people.' Oh, that turned me against Josephine. 'You people.' Like we were animals."

Even so, in any fight between Josephine and Jo, Carrie took her daughter's side. One night, husband and wife were battling so noisily that Carrie came to investigate. Jo was up against the wall, his eyes puffy, and he yelled, "Look what your daughter did to me, I'm going to kill myself, I'm going to jump out the window." Carrie walked to the window, opened it, and shouted, "Jump."

It was in September 1954 that Josephine brought Jari home from

Finland, the third member of the Rainbow Tribe. ("He was very cute," says Ginette. "Again, she just appeared at the hotel with him. I don't know how or where she got him.") Six months after that, she found Luis in Colombia. She'd given Luis's parents money, but when she got back to France, she discovered they were demanding another thirty-five hundred dollars to let her keep him. "Josephine," said her lawyer, "you are not adopting him, you are buying him."

Luis was the first of the children to be baptized a Catholic, and the first black child. Now Jo felt it was time to call a halt, complaining to his wife that their financial situation was precarious. "Josephine's eyes blazed. Surely one more mouth to feed couldn't matter."

"All those children were her biggest mistake," says Jacqueline Abtey. "To make her point, she could have taken a black and a white and been done with it. But she always needed a big scene, and when she reached menopause, and she had no real man around her, she went totally into politics, and adopting children, she became the Universal Mother. I think the menopause worked on her psyche; some women pass through it calmly, some are unhinged."

Still, until the whole operation unraveled some years later, Josephine seemed to be the only one who didn't worry. She kept hiring and firing, ordering and reordering, going her imperious way.

"She had a chauffeur named Maurice whom she used shamefully," Jacqueline says. "He would go pick up the trout, the chicken, the vegetables for the restaurant. He would make fifty trips a day, and at 2 A.M., she would decide to go to Paris. It is a six- or seven-hour trip from Les Milandes to Paris, and when they got there, he would wait around while she bought some gloves, some perfume, and then bring her back again. He would see the madness, but he loved her and she knew it, and she could squeeze him, exploit him."

The question of whether or not she exploited the children is still being argued among those who knew her. When the youngsters were indoors, they could be observed through a picture window. They were washed, reprimanded, fed in full view of anyone willing to pay an extra five francs for the spectacle, and the cameras never stopped. Josephine told her lawyer not to report this income. (While she cheated the government, her accountants cheated her. They were keeping two sets of books at Les Milandes, and Josephine knew it, Richard said, "but she didn't do nothing.")

Her most steadfast defender, Yvette Malaury, denies that Josephine "pushed" her brood in front of the public. "It was just that some people had traveled ten hours to get here, and if Josephine wasn't home—she was away so much—they wanted to see the children."

But Richard thought the tourists—even the bad-mannered ones—were being swindled by his sister. "Josephine overcharged, she just wanted them to come with their pocketbooks."

"To visit the château," Jari remembers, "the people would come through the big iron gate, and in the courtyard there was a chain with a sign that said FORBIDDEN TO PASS, and we would be on the château side and the visitors on the other, and Maman would push us out a little, so the people could see us. Never during the week, only on Sundays.

"We could not understand her spirit of brotherhood. She would tell us, 'You have clothes, other poor little children need some,' and she would send money to buy new clothes to those poor children. Sometimes we would tell her, 'But my trousers are too tight'—we were outgrowing everything—but she made us keep wearing our too-short pants with the let-down cuffs. We liked her spirit of helping others, but we resented the way she was doing it. Still, we could say nothing, she would have accused us of being selfish."

Eli Mercier doesn't blame Josephine for what she did to the children or the tourists, but for what she did to the farm. Eli, the boy who had first opened the château gate to her, had come back from the war to work at Les Milandes as a tenant farmer. "We had been there forever, we knew the land, the seasons, what the earth could take and what she could give, but Josephine wanted it her way. You know, there are no miracles with farming. And in those days we came out better than today. The oxen, the horses, were better than the machines. With the animals you had the compost, the fertilizer, you were closer to nature and happier. Josephine wanted to revolutionize all that with modern techniques. It was pure madness.

"At 5 A.M., she would get up to show the farmers and the gardeners she could work better than they. She had them plant vegetables in October. They warned that a frost would arrive in a couple of weeks and kill everything, but she didn't listen, and when the frost came, she shrugged and said, 'You would have been happy if we'd had fresh tomatoes for Christmas.' She was half crazy most of the time, and often tipsy because she would eat a jar full of cherries in alcohol; once she started, she could not stop.

"My wife and I couldn't take it, we decided to leave. I told Jo and Josephine, 'Don't worry for me, one day I will be the rich one, and you will be poor.' "

To replace Eli, Georges Malaury says, "Josephine had someone come from Alsace to be head farmer. She paid him four hundred thousand francs a year, when she could have had any good farmer from here for eighty thousand."

"She was no administrator," Leon Burg concurred. "And she had lost all sense of money. She would sign a contract for rose trees, and then refuse to pay the nurserymen because they had used her name for publicity. When a package arrived COD from Paris—it contained a coat of feathers, a stage costume—she screamed that the mailman was trying to rob her, and she locked the Abbé Tournebise out of the chapel when he asked for the money she had taken from the poor box. He said, 'The money belongs to the priest of the village.' Josephine answered, 'The priest, *c'est moi!*' "

Josephine and Jo, says Eli Mercier, used to fight in the streets of Castelnaud. "She would scream, 'Faggot!' he would yell, 'Dyke!' They weren't hiding anything. Jo would come to our house with another man, their arms linked, Josephine would find happiness with a girl from a Paris ballet company.

"During the big tourist season, they had *corridas* with cows, they had dog races, they put on wonderful cabaret shows. Jo was capable, but he could do nothing, she put sticks in his wheels. But can you imagine, in the good times, two thousand cars would come in a day?"

Even the American consul general in Bordeaux appeared to be impressed with what Josephine was trying to do at Les Milandes. "It seems that Josephine and Jo set themselves up as idealists in that they pursue an effort to destroy racial hatred and prejudice," he reported to the State Department in Washington. "They are highly considered throughout the country, and Josephine herself allegedly plays the role of a fairy queen with great success."

In the summer of 1955, beginning to sense at last that it was not prudent of her to keep expressing her contempt for the United States government, Josephine wrote the French consul in New York, assuring him that she was not a Communist, but a victim of the cold war, and asked him to help her win an audience with President Eisenhower. Despite her dire predictions of what would happen if Eisenhower were elected, she wished "to present him in person with my respects." (She did meet him, but not until later.)

Her four-year-old damage suit against Walter Winchell had recently been dismissed—she'd skipped a court appearance—but by November, she was once again embroiled in a legal fight far from home. She was arrested in Quebec, and her costumes seized, at the behest of William Taub, who had been waiting to nab her ever since 1952, when, he charged, she had run out on her contract with him. Frantic, Jo Bouillon borrowed the five thousand dollars for bail money from friends.

Two more children, both French-born, arrived right befor Christmas. "We drove to a foster home near Paris," Ginette says. "First we picked up Philippe, a two-year-old boy, and then in a nearby village we picked up Alain Jean-Claude, fourteen months old." Again, Josephine renamed them according to her whim; Philippe became Jean-Claude, Alain Jean-Claude became Moïse. Having failed in an attempt to adopt a baby in Israel, she decided to fabricate her own Jewish child. She announced that Moïse would be fed only kosher food, and plunked a tiny skullcap on his head.

"She wanted all races, all religions," Ginette told me, "and she would give them the religion she wanted on the spot."

So then there were six.

And Josephine, about to turn fifty, telephoned Bruno Coquatrix at the Olympia. "I've decided to give my farewell at your theater," she told him. "I want to say goodbye to my public while I still have the physical strength."

Marthe Mercadier saw the show early in its two-week run. A comedienne, Marthe was shooting a picture called *Jésus La Caille* with Jeanne Moreau. "The press was full of Josephine's farewell, and one night, after we finished shooting, Jeanne and I dressed up and went. We were going to be picked up afterward and taken to an elegant dinner.

"The evening began well—when Josephine arrived onstage, a wave of warmth filled the sold-out house, we were very moved. Guards were down in front to stop people if they tried to approach her. Suddenly, a very young black man pushed through the guards, and arrived at Josephine's feet, his clothes a bit disheveled from the struggle. He was holding a little bouquet, and he threw himself at her feet, crying, '*Merci.*'

"The show stopped, everyone in the house was paralyzed with astonishment, and Josephine, touched at proof of such love, kept the boy with her, and sang a song to him, holding his hand. The house was in tears, the boy looked ready to faint, and Jeanne and I sobbed, mascara falling on our beautiful dresses. We didn't care. We were in such a state by the end, our eyes swollen, no mascara left, except on our faces, that when we came out, our boyfriends were furious. They said, 'Listen, we're taking you home.'

"Next day, we told everyone at the studio what we had seen, and four days later, the cameraman came to us laughing. 'About your evening with Josephine, this boy escaped and went onstage and stopped the show?' We said yes, it was intense, so unpredictable. Not quite, said the cameraman. 'I went last night, and that boy is paid, he comes up at every performance with his little bouquet.'

"Jeanne and I looked at each other, the ceiling falling on us! We had believed, and we were hurt. Then admiration took over. What an extraordinary piece of choreography! A ballet between the guards, the kid, it was fabulous. What cheek to dare to do it every night, to be able to summon up the emotion every night. It was a little hard to swallow, but I bought it."

That farewell engagement in mid-April (Josephine lived to say goodbye as often as Sarah Bernhardt) was one of her most spectacular. "She had asked all the big Paris theaters to do a number in her honor, an homage to her," says Paulette Coquatrix, wife of the Olympia's owner. "The top French performers came from the Lido, the Casino, the Folies, they were fighting to be part of it. On closing night, after Josephine finished her last show, they went on.

"You couldn't move backstage, just the cancan number from the Moulin Rouge involved fifty people, the same for the other theaters, they sent scenery, costumes, everything. And Josephine had the two center seats taken out of the first row and replaced them with a big armchair, and there she sat, in a long black velvet gown, bare-shouldered, wearing a rhinestone tiara fringed with brilliants, and long glittery earrings. On her right was her dear friend General Vallin, on her left, Jo Bouillon. Everyone wore black tie.

"The show was fabulous, no theatre owner in the world could have afforded what was offered to Josephine that night. And they all played for free."

Marthe Mercadier, who described Josephine to me as "a great professional," was less impressed with her as the Universal Mother. "I found extraordinary this idea of adopting children from all over the world, trying to establish a mini United Nations around baby food. I thought maybe it could have been a solution for all of us, so one day I went to Les Milandes to see how this woman was organizing herself with that family, that litter, as they were called.

"There were great numbers of tourists, you had to wait on line as though you were visiting Fontainebleau, and we saw the children behind a large window. It was like the monkey rock at the Vincennes Zoo, with the children staring back at us from the other side of the window.

"The atmosphere was bad. You felt it. If it had been sincere, authentic, good for the children, I think the people all around would have said, 'Did you see how they live together, all the races, how wonderful it is?' But people were outraged.

"I am an artist, I don't pay attention to critics. When you innovate, you always have critics, but those children were totally uprooted, used for photos, articles, their private lives compromised.

"Les Milandes was like her farewell performance at the Olympia. At first you cry, *Bravo!* Then you scratch a little, and find hidden motives. When children were at stake—and not all of them were orphans, she adopted children who still had parents—then I was turned off, and she could not take me for a ride anymore."

Josephine continued to act out the drama of a star going out of business. She had, Jo reported, piled her old wardrobe trunks in front of the château "along with the costumes she knew she would never wear again. 'Take whatever you want,' she urged the villagers who picked through what had been such an intimate part of her life. The clothes that remained, my Josephine, always thirsty for symbols, set on fire. Then, joining hands with our sons and the village children, she led them through the steps of a farandole."

Good thing she held a few gowns back, because the very next month, she was touring Italy.

———

In June 1956, Princess Grace and Prince Rainier came home to Monaco after their honeymoon. The same issue of *Paris Match* that carried pictures of their return also featured snapshots of Josephine and Jo Bouillon and their six tiny sons arriving at the wedding of Josephine's brother Richard to the postmistress of Les Milandes. "In marrying a man of color," said the bride, Marie-Louise Daziniere, "I am making myself happy, but I also think I am helping Madame Josephine, who does so much to bring races together."

Five minutes before the wedding, Richard was baptized. "I said to myself, 'To be safe in the eyes of God, I'm going to baptize him,' " Abbé Tournebise told the Malaurys. "Because with Josephine you never know what to believe."

Wise priest.

As one of the witnesses at the wedding, Josephine signed her name "Josephine Baker, ex-artist." Next thing anyone knew, the ex-artist was off again. Or on again, depending on how you looked at it. Flying from Paris to Rome, she took three of her little boys with her. On the same flight, Line Renaud, the music-hall headliner, observed that Josephine could use even an airplane as a stage.

"She suddenly marched through the cabin like the Olympic flame bearer, holding in her hands a chamber pot, and headed for the toilet. The other passengers' mouths fell open. She reappeared carrying the now-empty pot at the end of her fingers, like an old wig, and smiling, wanting everyone to approve her dedication as a mother. People didn't know whether to laugh or to give her an ovation."

By December, Josephine was back in North Africa, where she had once been so happy, and so sick. Now wars of independence raged there. In Algeria, the entire population of a town called Palestro was massacred, but two babies—a boy and a girl—were found alive, hidden behind some bushes. Josephine got permission from the authorities to adopt the infants, both six months old.

Jo was beside himself. She had promised to stop gathering children, she had promised they would not adopt a girl—"Our children have no blood relationship," he had said, "if we add a daughter to our collection of sons, we'll be asking for trouble"—and here she was, both vows broken.

The girl, Jeanne, renamed Marianne, was decreed a Catholic.

The boy, Jacques, renamed Brahim, was decreed a Muslim.

In June 1957, all eight children were finally—and legally—adopted in a judgment handed down by a civil court in Sarlat. All name changes requested by Josephine were granted. "Since it seems that the return of the children to their parents is not foreseen," said the court, "the adoption is recommended."

At the time, the oldest was not yet five.

Koffi was the ninth baby, born in Senegal. Josephine had visited an Ivory Coast village and been presented with this infant. She claimed that he—as the thirteenth child in his family—would have been sacrificed if she hadn't taken him. She asked President Houphouet-Boigny to act as godfather.

According to her nephew Artie, Josephine brought Koffi home "in a shoebox. Without the cover." (While serving in the American army in Germany, Artie—one of Richard's sons by his first wife—had married a girl named Janie, and the couple was then living and working at Les Milandes.)

Janie Martin remembers Koffi's being kidnapped by Josephine's guenon, a long-tailed female monkey. "She took Koffi from his cradle—he was still a little baby—and ran away with him, to the park, and the nurses were searching everywhere for him."

(Sometimes, there were as many as thirty monkeys at Les Milandes, and they were often trouble. Some were rabid and died in their cages, some escaped. Once, Yvette Malaury says, "a monkey stole a six-week-old baby, the daughter of an employee. He had rabies, and the little one died, and the monkey had to be killed, and, can you believe, the police were not even called.")

Now Arthur Prevost, Josephine's journalist friend from Canada, arrived to view with his own eyes the mecca of world brotherhood. "I went to the nursery on the top floor, and Josephine was holding Koffi in her arms, I was carrying Marianne, and a nurse was playing with a third child. How crazy to have little children barely able to walk using those stairs, they could fall and be badly hurt. For food, for play, they had to go up and down, it was not practical."

Prevost walked in the rain with Josephine and the children in yellow slickers, and when they came back, "Josephine took us into a room. A woman was lying in bed. I said, 'Oh, excuse me,' and Josephine said, 'It doesn't matter. That's my mother. We always have the children undress in front of her.' "

I think this was just another scene in the love-hate play acted out by Josephine and Carrie, Josephine showing her mother, "Look how good I am with my children, you were never there when we went to bed cold and hungry."

Even though Josephine repeated Carrie's pattern of neglect (Carrie had gone off with lovers, Josephine went on the road), it troubled her, "because my babies are growing up and will forget me." Once, coming home at night after a long absence, she rushed to the nursery, turned on the lights, woke the sleeping children, and, arms outstretched, cried, "My little darlings, where is Mother?" As one, the children stood up in their beds, turned their backs on Josephine, and pointed to the wall where a large picture of her in full makeup and theater regalia was hanging. "There is Mother!" they chorused.

"In adopting all those children and taking them from their natural environments," Arthur Prevost said, "Josephine had done something dangerous. . . . Even animals—like the bears in Canada, or the poor wild animals in zoos—are disoriented when you take them from their natural places. But Josephine thought her love could cure everything.

"She took me around her kingdom, I visited the museum of her life, the Jorama—there were fourteen stations like the stations of the cross. All the figures had faces and hands of wax, and were life-size. There was a worried little girl wandering along the Mississippi, there was Josephine dancing for her sisters and brother in the basement, Josephine kneeling to be blessed by the pope, Josephine as a sublieutenant in the war, Josephine and Jo at their wedding, Josephine and the children walking up a hill toward a giant cross. [This one could also be bought as a plate in the gift shop.]

"I asked Jo Bouillon what Les Milandes would be in fifty years. He said, 'It may be the last island of peace in a jungle where everyone will devour everyone.'

" 'What about your careers?' I asked.

" 'Me,' Jo said, 'I have no career left, and I'm happy that way.'

" 'Me,' said Josephine, 'I now sing only for my children.' "

One week later, Jo was served with legal papers. Josephine didn't want to be Mrs. Bouillon anymore.

Chapter 35

—

MORE COMEBACKS, MORE BABIES, MORE LOSSES

"In 1959, Josephine Baker was a has-been"

THE HEART-RENDING DRAMA OF JOE AND JO, THOSE 50-YEAR-OLDS WITH BIG HEARTS, trumpeted one headline. The divorce announcement made worldwide news. From Japan, Miki Sawada urged Josephine to go slowly. "I remember your husband took such tender care of the children, and they had confidence in him. Abandoned by their natural parents, if they lose a second time, it is too cruel."

Arthur Prevost also begged for reassurance—"Tell me it is not true"—and Jo Bouillon wrote back, deploring "the disarray in which I find myself. I have worked for eight years to try to realize my wife's dream."

In her own letter to Arthur, Josephine described herself and Jo as "only two spokes in the immense turning wheel that is life; the axle is the children. To ensure their happiness and their future, I must say nothing."

But when it came to her divorce suit, she found her tongue. Some crimes of which she accused her husband:

- He had manifested no affection for her.
- He had not fulfilled his marital duties.
- He thought she was good only for earning money.

Still, she was afraid the divorce might cost her the children. Pierre Dop, her lawyer, assured her the adoptions would stand up in court, but she continued to be anxious. If she died, "Jo would certainly get the children . . . and my fortune, and Les Milandes would find itself with all that gang and their immoral behavior. I want the children to bear my name as well as his. . . . He never wanted those children, that's why at first he didn't want to legalize the situation. . . ."

In the beginning, Jo had sent Abbé Tournebise to Josephine to argue against the divorce, but she stood firm. "I'm doing what God tells me to do."

She talked directly to her Maker, giving herself absolution. The abbé had grown used to it. "In my head, I used to ask God to forgive me when I saw Josephine walking up to the altar to take Communion on Sunday," he said. "She hadn't been to confession, but there she was, head bent under a black lace mantilla, as if in a trance."

Once, in an act of generosity to her fellow worshipers, she had replaced the old statues in the chapel, and asked the abbé to bless the new ones. He walked from one stone figure to another until he found himself confronting an unfamiliar saint. Suddenly he recognized her—it was Josephine gazing down on the earth below with a beatific smile. Screaming "Blasphemy!" the abbé threw the châtelaine out of her chapel. She retaliated by complaining about him to her friend the pope, but had her statue moved into the open air. (*Time* magazine reported the "fabrication of a startling memorial to herself," and described a statuary group "depicting La Baker in ancient saintly wraps, arms outstretched in benediction over kneeling figures of seven kiddies of various races. . . .")

Observation by Josephine to lawyer Dop, after she met Jo wandering the halls: "He seemed to avoid me."

Why not, considering that she had cast him out? But it worried her that he would sign no papers. Although she owned the land, all commercial enterprises on that land were listed as belonging to the Société Jo Bouillon & Co.; Josephine could not operate them without his permission.

Now bank directors arrived. "If I renounce the divorce," Josephine wrote Dop, "they are willing to wait for the twenty-nine million I owe them, if not, they want the money now."

Wait three months, suggested the judge before whom Jo and Josephine appeared. Think about reconciliation.

So they must muddle through the summer, and try to keep everything running, even if it wasn't running well. On the one hand, Josephine trusted no one—after a party at the château, she would wash the priceless gold knives and forks, the china, and store them in a cupboard to which she had the only key. On the other hand, her suspicious nature did not prevent her being fleeced; she was not as shrewd as the peasants around her.

From the start, the union of Joe and Jo had been a strange one: Josephine out to prove she could ensnare any man she chose, no matter that his appetite led him down another path; Jo up against a tornado.

"Jo was good to Josephine's family," says Janie Martin, Artie's German-born bride. "Jo is the one who suggested putting the little house where Margaret lived in Margaret's name, 'so if you die, your sister will have something.' " (In fact, says Jacqueline Abtey, "Jo Bouillon is the one who had wanted her family to come over. Josephine told Jacques and me, 'I would never have invited them, they should have stayed in America.' " Once in France, it turned out they had to sing for their supper; Josephine put them to work as soon as they arrived. Margaret opened a pastry shop—the tourists loved her pies; Elmo rented out canoes on the Dordogne; and Richard took charge of the Esso station at the entrance to the park.)

During her war with her husband, Josephine buried lawyer Dop in details. "The situation is becoming more and more difficult. A waiter came and asked me for glasses with the "Joe and Jo" engraving on them for the hotels and restaurants. When I refused, he was extremely vulgar toward me. Another worker told me his boss was Monsieur Bouillon, not me. . . . How can people treat me with so little respect?"

I was exhausted just working my way through the blizzard of papers. Where did she find the strength? Running around the world performing, coming back to this or that hotel room and firing off ten, twenty letters a night, sinking herself in potatoes, tobacco, cows, nurses, children, paintings, contracts. Even for a woman who never slept, the output was prodigious. Why didn't she make herself sick with all those fulminations? Maybe because she only wrote them, she didn't have to read them.

"She attacks me on all sides," Jo told a friend. "She has no confidence in me, but she wants me to stay. Even if I was the big boss, I could not live in a desert; I would want to put in the personnel I thought would be good for the place, but she claims my people are thieves . . . pederasts."

Josephine pawned her jewels (one more time), sold the avenue Bugeaud house in Paris, and wrote a fairy tale. *The Rainbow Tribe*, illustrated by Piet Worm, is beautiful. The cover shows a little black one-eyed hen looking up at eight children sitting in a tree. On the title page are the words "This book was made in Les Milandes, where Kott-Kott found her happiness." Kott-Kott, the hen, travels the world searching for her lost eye, and comes to rest in a place where no one laughs at her anymore; this was Josephine's tribute to Willie Mae. She was convinced that some rich producer would want to make a movie of it, and her money worries would be over.

It never happened.

Part of the problem was Josephine's own inconsistency. When a respected Austrian producer offered her a picture deal, she said no, she could not permit her children to be exploited. (The producer was too polite to mention the gaping tourists outside the windows.)

No sooner had she got off her high horse than she was writing to the cultural attaché at the American embassy in Paris. Could he put her in touch with "an American film company like Walt Disney"? A movie about Les Milandes and the children and universal brotherhood was crying to be made, but it must be made "by a very big company with a lot of authority. . . . I will give the world rights to this company, but of course they have to pay me. . . ."

Broke though she was, Josephine could not stop spending. She ordered ten walk-in refrigerators from America, and was shocked to find one of them being used as a chicken coop. Told they couldn't be made to work on French electrical current, she was appalled. "There is racism even in kitchen equipment, it has to stop. The Japanese are much more intelligent, you will see, they will inundate markets all over the world with machines that can run without discrimination."

She was right, but how did she know?

September 24, 1957: With school desegregation being threatened by white mobs, President Eisenhower sent federal troops to Little Rock, Arkansas, to protect nine black students on their way to Central High.

Shortly thereafter, Arthur Prevost wrote a newspaper piece headlined NO LITTLE ROCK IN DORDOGNE. There were pictures of Luis and Akio in class in Castelnaud, along with a statement from Josephine: "No incidents when my little ones went to school for the first time, no matter what the color of their skins."

Her little ones may not have been discriminated against, but they were certainly confused by the life they led. Between club dates, a speech on brotherhood, and a visit to a doctor, Josephine would squeeze in a few days at Les Milandes, where she fought with, fired, cajoled her employees, then turned her ferocious attentions on the children. Guilty for having been gone so much, jealous of whatever affection they might have developed for anyone but her, she focused like a laser.

"Sometimes when she arrived home from the road," Jari says, "there would be a reunion around the kitchen table. She would take us, one by one, on her knees. But we were in a hurry to get down, it was embarrassing, too much love, a bit exaggerated. What she could not give us while she was away, she wanted to give us all at once. It was *tout ou rien,* then she would leave, and our normal life would start again. Our father would go away too, but when he came back, it was more normal. He cared about our work at school, he was there to answer questions."

Still, during Josephine's short stays at Les Milandes, the public was fed a picture of domestic bliss. On a Sunday afternoon, Josephine, Carrie, and the children could be seen in the front row of the audience as Jo conducted the grand orchestra of Sarlat, or there might be a conference about racism led by Josephine, while movie cameras rolled and flashbulbs exploded. "It was terrible," says my brother Jean-Claude, "because we always had to keep our eyes open while the lights were blazing into them."

October 18: Since Jo and Josephine could agree on almost nothing, the court made several decisions for them. Jo would be permitted to stay in the Maury house, personal souvenirs would be divided, and the children awarded to Josephine. Jo could visit them on Thursdays (not a school day in France) and two Sundays a month, but in Josephine's absence, Carrie was named their guardian. If you enjoy paradox, consider this woman who, in order to follow a pair of laughing eyes, had, time after time, forsaken her own maternal duties. Now she was being appointed by law to cluck over chicks who weren't even hers.

The day the bank sent a sheriff to attach the furniture, Josephine met him at the front door and slapped his face. With the imprint of her fingers on his cheek, he struggled for control. "Madame Baker, one day you will pay dearly for that."

She slapped strangers, and she slapped people she knew. Once, when the melons in the fields were overripe—customers in her restaurants were not ordering melon—she told the head gardener that he and his men should eat the fruit before it rotted. Two days later, she came into the kitchen where the grounds crew was having lunch, shrieked, "What! You are eating my melons!" and slapped the head gardener in the face. To the delight of his assistants, he rose and slapped her back.

Artie Martin says his imperious aunt thought of herself as a monarch. "She liked me because I had been a military man. 'You know how to rule people,' she kept telling me. She didn't say manage, she said rule."

Somehow, even after her scene with the sheriff, her lawyers were able to reassure the bank, as they would several more times before the end, but the situation remained ugly.

Jo's inquiring about Carrie's failing health evoked a diatribe from Josephine. "He is like a murderer drawn to the scene of his crime." He had, she said, created "a kingdom of immorality, only a red light is missing."

Sweden, Germany, Holland, Denmark. Crowds everywhere, and Dop commended her on refilling Les Milandes' coffers. "We were able to pay November expenses and salaries, and even a million francs of our debt to the bank." But he was concerned about her health. "Take care of yourself."

She was as concerned as he. "I'm everywhere but at home, and daily in a situation that makes me tremble, my mother sick, my children separated from me."

Still, she hatched grandiose schemes. To tap into the pilgrim trade (Lourdes would be memorializing its hundredth anniversary in 1959), Josephine was already planning a huge celebration of her own. She would have a monument to many gods built on a hill; there would be a Christ, a Buddha, a Moses, a Mohammed, and a voodoo god, each thirty-five feet tall.

From Berlin, she wrote Dop that her opening was sold out. "I had been afraid because some newspapers carried terrible stories. They said that since the separation, we had divided the children, the white stayed with Monsieur Bouillon, and the black with me."

She also said she was recording a song for a film in Berlin, and would get one million francs for it. "I'm deeply grateful to God. . . . I'm going on stage now, it is the last show, I'm tired. Good night. Kiss my little ones."

Two weeks later, she sent Dop an obituary of Jean Lion, holder of the Légion d'Honneur, the Croix de Guerre, the Croix de la Libération, dead in Paris of the Asian flu. Dop would see, she predicted, that Lion "is quite a different personality from Monsieur Bouillon." She spoke of the fallen hero in the present tense. "The dead," she said, "are always part of the family."

On December 18, great joy. She had been informed that she too would be given the Légion d'Honneur. "It is moral support to think that France loves me so much." On the same line, she wrote, "Save electricity."

And she kept on making speeches. In a church in Frankfurt, she talked about her children. "They belong to you just as much as they belong to me. You have the same responsibility as I have to take care of them."

Listen up, world. Josephine is willing to share her burden with you.

Christmas Eve in Germany, she went to midnight Mass and wondered if somewhere Jo was praying. "And begging God to forgive him all the bad he has done." A theater director in Stockholm paid for airline tickets so the children and a nurse could come spend January with her. She told the authorities she was removing the children from school for health reasons. "The snow is very good for them."

And while on the subject of health, she was going to send some polio vaccine for Dop's children—"It is very safe." She thanked the lawyer for news that Carrie's morale had improved—"As you say so well, we have only one mother"—and then got down to business. "I cannot believe that we cannot have peace at Les Milandes when the staff have no worries but to eat well, sleep, and do their work. . . . I have to close my eyes for now but I will get rid of all of them."

In mid-January, she received a letter from Mohamed Menebhi. He had loved her, sheltered her, and now he was in trouble. (Liberation had brought changes in the fortunes of many powerful Moroccan families. Palaces and lands were taken from those known to have sided with the French.) "I hope you have not forgotten our friendship," Mohamed wrote, "and the bad hour that comes to everyone as it has to me. I have no friends but you and Jacques. Could you lend me the sum of three hundred thousand francs for a year?"

Josephine forwarded the request to Jacques. "This is from Mohammed, begging for money. I didn't give it to him, but I invited him and his family to come to Les Milandes. . . . Write him if you wish."

Jacques sent Mohamed five hundred thousand francs. It was a debt he and Josephine owed.

Pressures mounted on Josephine. Not only must she tour to make money, but she must also go back to Les Milandes at least once a month, she told Dop, "because of Jo's accusations that I have abandoned the children for a new career. So this month, I lost 3,250,000 francs in bookings." Besides money, the children were costing her peace of mind. There had been rumors of child abuse inflicted by various nurses, and Jo was talking of suing for custody. But she had heard he was planning to return to his old job as musical director at Le Boeuf sur le Toit, and since "this place is known for catering to homosexuals, it will be a help in our fight to keep the children."

She also decreed that none of her brood were to spend time in Paris with their father because "Monsieur Bouillon does not have the necessary female personnel to take good care of the children." (Jo fought back, contending that he, at least, had not put the children on show for the public to gape at.)

The war accelerated.

Dop was instructed to get rid of the "Joe and Jo" ashtrays and order others: ten children in native costumes holding hands in a circle. "We must add the tenth, because when I go to South America, I will get a little Indian."

But the situation had become impossible to sustain. She was on the road, Carrie was sick, and finally, Josephine announced a reconciliation with Jo. For the second time, she gave a wedding banquet. This one was held at the Chartreuse.

"I was invited," Eli Mercier says. "There were famous people from Paris, Josephine was dressed in blue, the wine was extraordinary, a king could not have done it better. She had the gold glasses, gold plates, gold tablecloths."

It was the end of April, plans for the summer had to be firmed up. She wrote Arthur Prevost telling him that "for religious reasons," she had called off the divorce, and imploring him to give Les Milandes some publicity in his paper. "We are near Lourdes, Lascaux, Bordeaux . . . we are in the center of pre-history, the Middle Ages, Cro-Magnon man."

Then she went off to tour Poland with a young Norwegian pianist named Tor Hultin. (If the Western world was tiring of Josephine, a new market had opened for her behind the Iron Curtain.) Tor Hultin remembers that every night before her last song, she made a speech. "She spoke of human values, respect for liberty, and the whole theater, four thousand people, would stand up and scream.

"She and I visited the Nazi concentration camp at Auschwitz, and later, during lunch with the minister of culture, Josephine was asked her impressions of the camp. She said it was the most inhuman thing that ever existed in the world. Then she bent to the minister across the table and said in a loud voice, 'And where are your camps today, Monsieur le Ministre?' I almost choked. Back at the hotel, I said, 'Josephine, I want to see my wife and children again, you are going to have us arrested.' Don't forget we were there in 1958, the worst time in Polish history.

"She turned to me with that special look of hers, strange, half laughing, half serious. 'There is no one who dares to touch me!' "

How many times we have heard that.

"Josephine was interested in everything," Tor said. "At one press conference, she told foreign journalists that the biggest problem with black people in America was their lack of confidence. 'They pity themselves,' she said. 'That will not help them.' She was also concerned about South Africa ('The white man there doesn't understand he is sitting on a bomb') and the Indians in South America.

"I was with her in Caracas when she adopted—or I should say, kidnapped—little Mara. We met a wonderful Indian woman who was in the government, and Josephine said she wanted to adopt an Indian child, and this woman took us to Maracaibo. It was a one-hour flight, and then we went with a jeep for three days visiting Indian camps, sleeping in tents. The Indians were poor, a lot of sick people and children.

"In one camp, we saw a little boy, maybe eighteen months old. They had made a hole in the sand, and he was lying in it. He looked like those pictures of concentration-camp children, big belly, skin and bones, he couldn't walk.

"Josephine wanted to take him, and the parents were happy, they had nine or ten other children, so she gave them some money and we left. I carried the little boy on the plane, and suddenly Josephine said to me, 'His name shall be Mara, for a big Indian chief.'

"When we got back to the airport in Caracas, a man in uniform came walking toward us, he looked like a general, and he seemed angry. I said to Josephine, 'That man speaks a lot, but I do not understand Spanish.'

" 'He wants my autograph,' she said.

" 'No,' I said, 'I think he's a policeman.'

"Suddenly a car came, and we were taken to jail. Josephine screamed for the French ambassador, but we were held for twenty-four hours. The French ambassador was there when we were released, and the 'general' came to apologize, and would you believe it, Josephine spat in his face. He didn't move. He spoke bad English but he kept saying, 'Excuse me, it was a mistake.' They thought we had stolen an Indian baby."

Arriving at the airport in Paris, Josephine was met by Paulette Coquatrix. Mara, the chosen descendant of Chief Maracaibo, was not happy, he was screeching. "Take care of him," Josephine begged Paulette, "I can't stop him."

Paulette accepted the baby and, leaving Josephine behind to deal with the press, whisked him off to the Coquatrix apartment. "He still hadn't stopped screaming, so I decided to change him. To my stupefaction, his skin came off with the diaper. Josephine had forgotten to change him, his poor bottom was absolutely raw. Josephine loved children, but did not know how to take care of them."

Aside from Mara's bottom, things were looking good. Preparations for *Paris Mes Amours* were already in the works (Josephine would make her Paris comeback at the Olympia, the same theater where she had made her farewell appearance), and Jo was home again. When he walked in, Josephine accosted him. "Do you know what Akio wants for Christmas?" "Yes," he said, "a violin." "No," she said. "He told me he wanted for Daddy and Mommy to be more together."

It was like the old days, an immense tree glittering next to the chimney in the salon, a mountain of toys in front of it. The whole family, Margaret, Elmo, Richard and Artie and their wives, shared a Christmas feast of oysters, turkey and chestnuts, *bûche de Noël*. Tor Hultin, his wife, and two young daughters joined them. "It was fantastic," Tor says. "Josephine had invited all the children of the village and her employees and their families. There were presents for everyone. The children were playing with Gigolo, Margaret's chimpanzee, tall as a four-year-old child and dressed in a sailor uniform, and I played Christmas songs on the beautiful grand piano that once belonged to Franz Liszt."

Carrie did not leave her bed. There is a picture of her taken that day, lying against white pillows, her eyes far away. Is she homesick? Does she think of Arthur Martin? Tony Hudson? Willie Mae? Does she have a premonition that this will be her last Christmas?

After the holidays, Josephine took to the road again. On January 8, Charles de Gaulle became president of the Republic. On January 12, Carrie died. Josephine was in Istanbul, but did not come home. Dop had wired condolences, and she responded, "Your telegram did me good. . . . I'm completely upset." Maybe she was, at that. Once she had told Jo, "You're never sure about your father, but you know you came out of your mother's belly."

At first, Carrie's body rested in a borrowed niche in the Malaury family's vault, to the disapproval of Georges's grandmother. "I do not want to spend eternity next to a *négresse*," the old lady kept saying. "If you do not remove her from my vault, I will curse you from the beyond."

In time, the removal was accomplished.

André Rivollet said Carrie had quit her home in America "for truffle country; now she rests forever next to an Italian count she never knew." (Or, rather, next to his heart. According to Maryse Bouillon, it was Jo who had suggested that Pepito's body, after having lain in the basement of a church for twelve years, should be moved to Les Milandes for a proper burial. But this was not dramatic enough for Josephine; she decided that she would bring back only his heart. Which she had put into a heart-shaped coffin and consigned to a grave, while the servants crossed themselves and remarked on how kind she was.)

Carrie left her son Richard her Bible. In its pages, he found a small picture of Tony Hudson.

"Josephine's mother was lonely," says Leon Burg. "She is buried here in the little cemetery of Les Milandes, with Jo Bouillon's father, Pepito's heart, and the little girl of Arthur and Janie Martin. My wife and I go sometimes to put some flowers on the right side of the cemetery where they lie. We put white flowers for the baby. The wood crosses fell long ago, you have to look under the leaves to find them."

The children missed Carrie. "I know she adored us," Jari says. "When Mother got angry and sent us upstairs without dinner, Granny would sneak us food."

As a member of the family, Jo's niece, Maryse Bouillon, had seen some of the darker side of life in the château. She was on the scene when

Carrie, Margaret, and Elmo arrived from St. Louis, and describes Carrie as "imposing, a grande dame. She and my grandparents used to take long walks together, and they talked, she in American, they in French, and they understood each other perfectly."

Maryse says she never saw any affection between Josephine and Carrie—"Carrie was a kind of prisoner there"—and she wasn't surprised that Josephine was away when Carrie died. "She was always away when people died, she was away for my grandfather, for my grandmother, for her own mother, for the little girl, Artie's little girl. Josephine was never there, never."

Margaret was the person most crushed by the loss of Carrie—"I had lived with Mama all my life"—and the next time Josephine came home, she brought her sister a child, her own answer to any life crisis. Born in Belgium, the little girl's name was Anna Balla Rama Castelluccio. Margaret called her Rama.

Paris Mes Amours, Jo Bouillon said, was going to be billed "as a rescue operation." In fact, Bruno Coquatrix was spending a fortune on new costumes, and Paulette had brought in André Levasseur, a talented young designer, to work with Josephine. "She would stand for three hours having fittings, and not complain," Paulette says. "Once, I stood in for her, and the clothes were so heavy they made me giddy. I had not realized you could walk in anything that heavy.

"For us, and for Josephine, this show was a very big risk." (George Reich, who choreographed *Paris Mes Amours,* puts it more bluntly. "In 1959, Josephine Baker was a has-been, Coquatrix took a big chance.")

For the run of the show, Josephine had rented a little studio at 4 rue Saint-Roch. Harold Nicholas was in Paris, and she asked Bruno to hire him. "I did a Caribbean number with her," Nicholas says. "We had fun, I will always cherish the memory."

George Reich's memories of Josephine were less sweet. Reich not only choreographed *Paris Mes Amours,* he used dancers from his own company—Ballets Ho!—to support, as he put it, "the old star in a new sauce."

A handsome blond American, he was just back from Hollywood, where he had worked on *Daddy Long Legs* with Leslie Caron and Fred Astaire. "I was thrilled to meet Josephine, but she asked me to partner her in a piece—'Antinea's Snack'—and I couldn't find the time. I was already dancing in four numbers, besides choreographing the show, and working in TV. I explained the situation, and Coquatrix understood, but Josephine took my explanation as an insult, and used it for publicity. She dragged out the old story—Reich is white, he refused to dance with a black lady.

"She finally did the number with one of my dancers, he was a beautiful boy, it was a very sexy scene. After the reviews came in, and it was a triumph for everyone, she apologized.

"She was so tired by then with all her problems. She would arrive ten minutes before the show, and everything would be ready. False lashes, wigs, makeup, the wardrobe mistress waiting with the costume in her hands. Josephine would take three steps to the right, and the costume had to be there, three steps to the left, and Ginette would slap the wig on her head. She was like a doll, you wound her up and she went. If there was any change, she was screwed up. She would make her entrance with not a second to spare.

"Each day was a miracle. Between numbers, she would put her head on her makeup table and fall asleep for a minute or two, and they would wake her up for the next number, and she would crawl backstage, still asleep, but when the music started, she would go on and be incredible.

"She never missed a performance, she never missed an entrance, she was a workaholic. Josephine, Marlene, Edith—I have known them all. They were beasts, beasts of the stage, that's all. It doesn't exist anymore. They were the last of the last, they knew how to walk onstage and give you shivers.

"*Paris Mes Amours* was supposed to run three months, but Josephine was such a success we stayed for eight, and then left the Olympia to go on tour."

The theater program carried ads for Les Milandes, ("Capital of World Brotherhood") and ads showing the Rainbow Tribe drinking Pschitt, an orangeade ("now my nine children have adopted Pschitt, making it a world drink"), and ads showing them wearing "soft, non-shrinkable, color-fast" terry-cloth robes by Boussac, a company that promised SATISFACTION OR YOUR MONEY BACK. There were also pictures of a glittering Josephine bending to the rhinestone-covered mike in her right hand. She changed with the times. Borrowing from the art of Clara Smith, she had worked with a handkerchief, and she had worked with an electric guitar before electric guitars were common. Now she had mastered the microphone, using it as a weapon of seduction, voice and machine fusing into a single instrument.

Bill Taub was impressed all over again. Throughout the summer, Josephine held meetings with the producer who had once tried to put her in jail. It was a recurring pattern, she would sue you or you would sue her, but all would be forgiven the minute there was some mutual advantage in a new deal.

No other American producer was willing to touch her, but Taub believed a smart man could still make money presenting Josephine Baker back home. Although, visiting Les Milandes in September, he may have had second thoughts, because she had also invited Premier Khrushchev to be a houseguest. Fortunately, the premier couldn't make it. Despite her apparent tolerance for godless communists, Taub signed her to two "exclusive" contracts.

Oddly enough, I got to meet Khrushchev that same year. But more important, I got to see Josephine onstage for the first time. I had been in Paris for twenty months when the headlines announced that she was coming back to the Olympia in *Paris Mes Amours*. It was thrilling. I had loved her voice on the radio, I had poured out my soul to her while she sat with a towel around her head in the Hôtel Scribe, and ever after, I was sure that when she sang, it was for me, to give me courage and bring me luck at work, so I could get big tips and be able to send money to my mother.

Now I bought a ticket to go and see my very first stage show at the Olympia, one block from the Scribe.

I didn't know you were supposed to tip the usher, and when I sat down, she said, very loud, "Still a farmer, that one!" which embarrassed me. But once the lights went down and the music started, I was lost. I remember nothing but the number where Josephine, dressed like a gypsy, sang "Give Me Your Hand." I thought of my village, and the gypsies coming, women brightly dressed, barefooted children, dark-haired men; they would park their caravans at the edge of the fields, and make fires in the grass, and cook, and we would smell the strange odors. At night, I dreamed they would take me away with them.

Wearing her fortune-teller's costume, Josephine took me—and the rest of the audience—away with her. Coming down into the first row, capturing a man's hand, she teasingly told his future: "Monsieur, I see you have lost your hair, but Madame is happy because I also see love in your heart, and big success will come to you."

In my trance, it was my hand she was holding. She was my heroine; I had seen the headlines about her fight for human dignity, her fight for her children, she represented everything I wished my real mother was. I wanted my mother to be assertive, not quiet or embarrassed, I wanted her to fight my father, curse, rather than stand there with her pain written on her face.

Josephine was different. And when she sang, I knew I would follow wherever she led. I wanted to go backstage; after all, less than two years ago, this woman had promised to be my second mother, but there were so many people around that I grew shy, and left.

Now about Khrushchev. The day he came to Paris, I was working as a parking boy at a chic restaurant, Pavillon Dauphine, where the Soviet leader was to lunch with four hundred businessmen. We all had to go through metal detectors and get badges, there were cops with guns in the trees on the Bois de Boulogne, it was exciting.

Suddenly, a motorcade arrived, and I, in my dark trousers and white jacket, opened a car door and bowed, tipping my cap. Khrushchev stepped out, smiling. He kissed me, and turned me toward the reporters. "Oh, my little one, what a shame you are a servant in this capitalist country, if you were in my country you would be at school." A translator dutifully repeated this for the press; the premier had turned me into a prop.

His arm around me, he led me into the dining room, sat me down, asked me what I wanted to eat. When he'd had enough of me and turned to talk to the businessmen, I ran back outside. I was a star. Reporters weren't allowed inside, and one of them offered me a hundred new francs to go back, listen, "and come out and tell me what he says."

I moved back through the guards, Khrushchev spoke, I listened to as much as I thought I could remember, then ran outside and told the guy. Other reporters cornered me and I did the same for them. I made five hundred dollars that day, and was on the evening news, but I had to work, and I didn't see myself.

With the success of *Paris Mes Amours* came new business for Les Milandes. Not only tourists but performers and politicians showed up, and everyone who appeared on the premises was invited to join Les Amis des Milandes and pay yearly dues for the privilege of helping World Brotherhood. "Josephine," Leon Burg told me, "was now attracting more visitors than the stone cave at Lascaux with its drawings by Cro-Magnon man."

And she was once again happy with a lady lover. "Josephine and a famous and flamboyant Mexican actress were inseparable during the run of *Paris Mes Amours*," says Maryse Bouillon.

Sunday nights, after her last show, Josephine left for the country. "Maurice, her chauffeur, would be waiting," says Paulette Coquatrix, "and sometimes I would go with her. At the château, the first thing she would do is clean. Poor Jo would be trying to sleep, but she would check behind everything! Me, I was always wondering what would happen to all those children. It made me sick. Josephine thought she was a good mother, she would go away and work for them, so they had all the comforts, but they needed something else.

"My feeling is, if she had adopted two or three, she could have made them happy, but she had so many. One you can take into your arms, or two, but you cannot take twelve.

"Josephine was a superb bird, and she had plenty of heart, but she went wrong all her life because she wanted to compensate for what she had missed, give it to others. And nobody could explain to her that it was not possible.

"All day long at Les Milandes, she ran everywhere giving orders. She insisted that the electric lines be buried underground, so as not to destroy the look of the countryside with ugly poles, she worked out themes for each of the rooms at the Chartreuse (one was the Revolution Room, all in red, white, and blue), I never saw her go to bed.

"It is not attacking her to say she used people. Most artists do that. Maybe it's not only the law of show business but the law of all people with talent."

One night during the run of *Paris Mes Amours*—it was in November, and cold—a tramp on the street found a live baby boy in a garbage can and took him to the police.

"As soon as we saw that story in the newspapers," Paulette says, "we decided not to say a word to Josephine. But after the show, she was in the restaurant of the Eiffel Tower, and a journalist ran up and said, 'Josephine, what do you think about that poor little boy?'

"Well, she couldn't be stopped. She insisted on going to the hospital, she fell in love with the little boy, and he became her eleventh child. Since it was so close to Christmas, she called him Noël, though the nurses had given him the name of André."

In January, Noël was christened by Abbé Tournebise; Josephine looked happy, Jo did not. He felt hopeless. "My attempts to salvage Les Milandes and our marriage had clearly failed."

He decided to return to Paris. "Since we can't seem to agree," he said, "I think it's best I leave, Josephine. I wish you luck . . . but I refuse to divorce until all the children are of age."

Despite her renascence at the Olympia, Josephine was losing ground. One by one, the people she depended on—except for Margaret—had left her. Carrie was gone, Jo was gone (again), Richard was gone, and Artie had taken his family home to America.

"Les Milandes could have been a big success," Artie says. "Jo Bouillon was good for the place. But my aunt would reproach him if he bought a magazine for two francs, while she was buying feathered costumes for millions. She was brutal with the help, not paying them for two or three months, screaming at them, so how could you expect them to love her? And that's what she wanted, to be loved.

"She wanted me to call her 'Mother'; I said no, 'You are my aunt, not my mother.' If she arrived home at 5 A.M., she still expected people to line up along the streets to greet her. It didn't matter that they were sleeping, they had to show thankfulness for all she was providing. She should have stuck to show business, everything she did was theater.

"She had lured my father from St. Louis promising him everything. 'You will have a gas station, a house, you will be happy.' By the time I went home, he had already left."

Josephine's estrangement from Richard was her own doing. His marriage to the postmistress had been unhappy, and he'd fallen in love with a young woman of Sarlat named Marie-Louise Yvonne Marchive. The first Marie-Louise refused to give him a divorce, the second Marie-Louise was pregnant with his child. Josephine disapproved. She who had never cared what anybody said, who had lived exactly as she liked, lectured him about the immorality of his situation. She drove him away, her handsome, merry brother. Her only brother.

Chapter 36

—

TWENTY LAWSUITS
AND THE LEGION
OF HONOR

"I can't take care of six hundred acres and eleven children"

*J*n February 1960, Josephine wrote to Dwight Eisenhower:

MR. PRESIDENT OF THE
UNITED STATES OF AMERICA
MAISON BLANCHE
WASHINGTON (U.S.A.)

Mister PRESIDENT,

Very soon I will be coming back home and a thought keeps coming back to my memory (you can take a man out the country [sic] *but you canot* [sic] *take the country out of the man); so here I come and happy I am to come!*

My husband Jo Bouillon and our tribe of eleven children from the four corners of the world greet you and Mrs. EISENHOWER.

She signed this effusion Josephine Baker Bouillon, and someone on the Eisenhower staff filed it with a notation that no reply was necessary.

Josephine also tried to make amends to America through Art Buchwald's column in Paris. "I was misquoted in South America," she said. "I never said anything down there that I didn't say in the United States. I did say America wasn't a free country because of the way they treated Negroes, but I think things have improved a lot since then. . . . I'm not mad at Winchell, I believe in love and brotherhood." So much did she long to be recognized as a pillar of world brotherhood that she had become involved in Freemasonry—the name of the lodge she joined was New Jerusalem—even though, according to one of her fellow Masons, "She was too busy to regularly attend our meetings." ("Josephine was very Catholic," says Jacques Abtey, "and the Masons were often denounced by the Catholic church. When I told her that, she said, 'Oh, I didn't know.' ")

Bill Taub, as good as his word, came through, booking *The Fabulous Josephine Baker* (an English-language version of *Paris Mes Amours*) into Chicago's Regal Theatre. It opened there in March, but the Regal was not Josephine's idea of a proper milieu. She objected, said Taub, "to appearing in a colored theater." And business was bad. "Perhaps due to freezing weather."

Don Dellair (he sang in the show, his partner, Tommy Wonder, danced) remembers it differently. "Josephine couldn't finish a song, the predominantly black audiences stomped and screamed and yelled until she had to tell them, 'Wait, there's more, I assure you.'

"Every time we came out of the stage entrance, there were fans waiting, they gave us fried chicken—'Please take this, I cooked it especially for you'—and I thought, gee, that's never happened to us before. The adoration they gave to Josephine was something to behold. I was thrilled."

In April, *The Fabulous Josephine Baker* was to play the Huntington Hartford Theatre in Los Angeles, but the star still had time enough to fly east for a couple of personal appearances. She went to a ball given by the National Urban League at New York's Roosevelt Hotel, and pressed the singer Charles Aznavour into service as her escort. He was staying at the Roosevelt anyway. "I'm this little white guy," he says. "She's the queen. I had never seen such an elegant black gathering." Marian Anderson was there and Josephine knelt to kiss her hand, while everyone applauded.

Then came a reception for President de Gaulle at the French embassy in Washington (the general and his wife were enjoying an eight-day tour of the United States), and at the embassy party, Josephine finally met President Eisenhower. She wore her military uniform, partly hidden under a mink jacket. "She borrowed it on consignment from Revillon," said Bill Taub, "and never returned it."

(Taub was as exotic a figure as Josephine. In 1979, he wrote a book called *Forces of Power*, and he described himself as a man who had lived "in the shadows of some of the most extraordinary dramas of recent history." Among his assertions: President Eisenhower had told him he didn't want to die and leave the presidency to Richard Nixon. JFK had discussed Marilyn Monroe's death with him. He'd raised bail for Jimmy Hoffa. In his spare time, he managed some stage and movie stars.)

Variety's response to the Los Angeles production of *The Fabulous Josephine Baker* was lukewarm. The show business paper praised Josephine's figure, clothes, and choice of music (she opened and closed with a song called "Oh Say, I Love the USA") but added, "Some of her confidences to spectators are inclined to be tiresome."

No matter. Movie stars turned out in impressive numbers. One theatergoer told me he watched Yves Montand and Marilyn Monroe emerge from a limousine, the wet red imprint of Marilyn's lipstick all over Montand's neck. (Eight years earlier, Josephine, the aging sex goddess who was playing Ciro's on Hollywood's Sunset Strip, had first met Marilyn, the eager sex goddess in training. Taub claimed he'd introduced them, and that Marilyn had dreamed of going to Paris to become "a woman of culture and sophistication under Josephine's tutelage.")

Having gone ten rounds with Josephine—and lost—in the fifties, it is hard to understand why Bill Taub came back for more of the same in the sixties, but he did. With the same result. In Paris, he had advanced Josephine fifty thousand dollars; she never gave him a receipt. Then she had demanded another eight thousand dollars before she would come to the United States at all.

Later, she denied that Taub had done anything for her. Stephen Papich, who directed the show at the Hartford, knew better. Taub, he says, had fought to get Josephine entry permits: "He opened the doors of the United States to her."

Even so, Bill Taub and Josephine Baker were not destined to make beautiful music together. By the middle of the second week in Los

Angeles, it was all over, Josephine had walked out on her contract, and Taub had filed yet another suit against her. He said she owed him $157,000. Miss Baker was not cowed. "This is nothing," she told reporters. "I was in the Resistance."

She, along with Stephen Papich and the rest of the company, had fled to San Francisco, where they were playing the Alcazar. A rumor spread that Taub was sending someone to attach her costumes, so every night after the final curtain, Josephine's wardrobe, even headdresses, were put on ropes and pulled into the fly space high over the Alcazar stage. A search party invading her dressing room wouldn't be able to find so much as a paillette.

Fearful of Taub's long arm, Josephine requested an interview with the FBI. During that session, "she volunteered that she had never been a Communist and was pleased by the treatment she had received in the United States." Except for the treatment she had got from William Taub. She was in San Francisco "to publicize her château in France for the tourist trade."

Then she and the cast took off for Montreal and a club called the Faisan Bleu. There a bunch of French-speaking detectives grabbed her and Papich and took them to jail.

"The owner of the Faisan Bleu gave us seventy-five hundred dollars to ransom Josephine," Don Dellair remembers. "When we got to the jail, there were paparazzi all over, *click, click, click,* and Josephine was furious because she had been searched. 'The trouble here is that they don't understand perfect French,' she said, 'so they don't know what I'm saying.'

"When we get back to the club, it's way past the appointed showtime, and Josephine goes directly onto the stage, and says, 'I have just come from jail, sorry I'm late, thank you for waiting.' And she does the show in her street clothes. They adored her, they screamed, 'Josephine! Josephine!' "

Josephine had told her friend Arthur Prevost, the Montreal newspaperman, that she wanted to go to High Mass at 10 A.M. on Sunday, and he took her to St. Martin's Church. "After the Mass," he recalled, "people went to get autographs, and would you believe it, she signed their prayer books."

When she finally appeared in a Montreal courtroom, she denounced producer Taub as "a bad man" and was so convincing that the judge issued a warrant for Taub's arrest. "I heard it with my own ears," says Don Dellair. "The judge said, 'If this man ever steps foot into Canada, he will be arrested.' Then Josephine told Tommy and me, 'I have had it with this place, you are coming to France.'

"In Paris, she took us in a limousine to Madame Arthur's place, famous for its female impersonators. We sat down and then Marlene Dietrich walks out of one door, Mistinguett walks out of another door, Josephine out of a third. I had to keep checking to see she was still sitting with us, that's how much that man looked like her, sounded like her, held the microphone the way she held it.

"Later, she took us to stay at Les Milandes. We saw it all, the animals, the grounds, the beautiful château. We met the children, we sat in the bakery/ice cream place where Josephine's sister worked, and just talked. I mean, what can you do in Les Milandes except talk? But Josephine kept traveling back and forth to Paris and leaving us there to swim or play checkers or watch the children being tutored."

(In his book, *Remembering Josephine*, Stephen Papich wrote that the tutors hired by Madame "usually fled in a few weeks." A tutor brought in to teach Hebrew to Moïse took off after commenting to Stephen, "Mr. Papich, I think that woman is mad, don't you?")

"She was fixated on getting an artificial snow maker so she could make money all year round," says Don Dellair, "she was trying to convince the people around her that it would be formidable. There were tourists that summer, but not many."

And some of those were not entirely pleased. In August, Josephine got a letter from a countess who had been staying at the Chartreuse for two weeks. "Many times," this lady complained, "I could not sit in the drawing room because all the armchairs were occupied by a cook or a dishwasher or a waiter."

Josephine's bombardment of lawyer Dop continued apace. In August, she had "just learned from a trustworthy source" that Jo Bouillon was in Cannes spending a fortune "on hustlers." She enclosed a check for five hundred francs, explaining, "I could not do better this month."

I'm sad, reading that. It's high season on the Riviera, in Deauville, all the places where once they would have crowded into clubs to see her, now few came, her husband preferred other company, "and as you know, I do real acrobatics to be able to pay for it all."

By September, she was beginning to face the truth, Les Milandes was falling apart. "One employee called me a liar and threw me out of the place, and I *own* it."

From a cabaret in Milan, she fumed about fines levied against her ("I don't need more fines!") and about the fact that five of her calves were missing ("I want them back!"). It turned out the calves had been sold—three of them were tubercular—and she became a philosopher. "Like all women in my case, I ask nothing. I accept life as it is."

For twenty minutes. By November, she was demanding "support for myself and the children. . . . if Jo Bouillon refuses to be reasonable, I am ready for war with open knives. . . ."

In December, she came to final terms with Jo. For fourteen million francs, he sold the Maury house and land back to her, dissolved the Jo Bouillon company, turned over all papers and powers. He would get a down payment, and the rest sent to him in monthly installments. "I bought all of it," Josephine mourned. "Now I have to buy it all again."

Two months later, in her diary, another wail of anguish. "I don't know how or where I'm going. . . . I have only a few thousand francs left. . . . I feel so alone and think of the way Christ was abandoned. But I also realize how hard it must be to live with people like me."

Marc Vromet-Buchet, a family friend who was acting as Josephine's secretary, said local merchants, "tired of IOUs, had slammed their doors in her face. Since she had few visitors now, the family lived in her office and the kitchen, where a log fire burned. We roasted chestnuts in the ashes. It was an incredibly rustic life."

She could no longer pay insurance for employees on the farm or in the restaurants, and there were twenty lawsuits pending against her. No big contracts were forthcoming either, though in many countries, cabaret and theater owners would book her for a week or two between bigger attractions. They felt sorry for her; pity that she had solicited—and yet despised—had replaced professional respect.

Booked to play Nice for two weeks, she showed up at the apartment of the Abteys, who spent six months a year on the Riviera. "She came in a cab with two of the kids," Jacqueline says, "and she told me, 'You pay the taxi.' By the time I got back to the apartment, she and the kids had raided the fridge, it was absolutely empty, they had not eaten for days.

"When there was no money, she would open cans to feed them, and she could not buy bananas anymore for the monkeys. There were sometimes thirty monkeys, some as tall as people, they cost a fortune, and they were starving."

"When people read in the newspapers that Josephine needed money," says Yvette Malaury, "they would come and give it to some employee, and most of the time it ended up in that employee's pocket."

On August 18, 1961, she got a boost; she was awarded the Légion d'Honneur, which had been a long time in coming. Sixteen years earlier, she had written Donald Wyatt that she expected to be decorated at Les Invalides "when I am stronger"; now it was finally coming to pass.

But it wasn't as grand as her fantasies had suggested. For one thing, it didn't take place at Les Invalides; for another, General de Gaulle was not there (she had asked him, but he said he did not personally decorate anyone) and neither were any of the other top diplomats or military men of France. From Bordeaux had come the consuls of Spain, Morocco, the United States, Italy, and Finland; there were a baroness, a French actress (Gaby Morlay), a few colonels and commandants, but except for General Vallin, none of her old brothers in arms were at her side.

At exactly 12:15 P.M., General Vallin and various other officials dropped out of the sky over Les Milandes in two helicopters. One of the officials was a black man. Seeing him, the four-and-a-half-year-old Koffi ran up to Commandant Cournal. "Are you my Daddy?" he asked. A band played the "Marseillaise," and Josephine, in her threadbare uniform (she had filled in the worn places with ink, proving that an old show business horse knows how to improvise), stood at attention.

The courtyard of the château teemed with press, tourists, neighbors, dignitaries from the Dordogne, a few friends from Paris, the children in their best clothes, holding bouquets. (Jo Bouillon was not there. Tracked down by reporters, he was diplomatic; he said he'd had a previous engagement.) General Vallin pinned to Josephine's jacket the Légion d'Honneur and the Croix de Guerre with palm, and spoke of her wartime services to France and her peacetime role as "moral educator."

Tears streaming down her face, Josephine responded: "I am happy that this ceremony could take place here at Les Milandes because this is where I first heard the general say all was not lost. . . . I am proud to be French because this is the only place in the world where I can realize my dream."

Holding in one hand a message sent by de Gaulle, she circulated among the guests. "You will see, everything will go well now," she said.

"I will keep Les Milandes. No one can do anything against me, I have the *baraka*." She had learned the word in Morocco; it meant she had an angel sitting on her shoulder.

Her euphoria was brief. When lawyer Dop had the temerity to ask payment for his faithful service, she gave him the gate. "I don't know how I can keep working with you, since one always has debts to his lawyer, as business keeps going." Six months later, she begged him to come back. "Only the old friends like you can I trust."

In the summer of 1962, she decided to put on a production of *L'Arlésienne,* the Bizet opera, in her backyard. Seeking encouragement, she paid a surprise call on Jo Bouillon in his new apartment near Paris. For all the world as though they were still the best of friends and she had not accused him of every crime but serial murder, she cross-examined him. Did he think her plan could work? He said of course. The heroine of *L'Arlésienne* was a dedicated mother, just like Josephine. The tourists would love it.

She had already made up her mind to do it in any case, not with an orchestra, which cost money, but in playback. "But suppose my lips move when they shouldn't?"

After the first performance, she wrote to Jo that the audience had been wild about it, some had wept.

Now Bruno Coquatrix, a normally wily man, in an apparent lapse of sanity, agreed to move the production to the Olympia. There the cast—except for Josephine—would do their songs and dialogue live.

"But Josephine could not remember her lines," says Paulette Coquatrix. "Since she was incapable of staying in sync with the record, her performance was one of the most comic things I have ever seen on the stage. The public as always adored her, they laughed and at the same time made excuses. 'It must be the man who's running the machine.' Even the press was kind."

But she knew. The blow of another failure, one she could ill afford, was compounded by her increasing sense that the center was not holding. While the younger children were still at home, attending the local public school, Akio, Jari, Luis, and Jean-Claude were now at boarding school in Switzerland. It was the right thing, but she missed them.

When she got the phone call with the worst news of all—Les Milandes had been seized by creditors, and would be sold at auction on June 7, 1963—she was playing in Copenhagen. "I thought I was going to faint," she said. "Fifteen years of fight, hope, and suffering."

As usual, a miracle happened. A group of Danish hotel men paid off her most importunate creditors. The headlines read, SAVED FROM RUIN. The hotel men had come, had seen, and had pronounced Les Milandes wonderful, it simply needed reorganizing. Josephine agreed. "I know I'm not a businesswoman, I can't run six hundred acres of land, a château, hotels, restaurants and take care of eleven children. When those Danish men left, I had their promise that in a few weeks they would tell me what to do."

Truthfully, many people in France were growing tired of the auctions, the farewells, the tin-cup approach to child rearing, they didn't see why Josephine and her family needed to live in a castle with servants when their own families didn't live that way. Besides, Josephine's vow to be led by the conservative Danish gentlemen died with their departure. Like mad King Ludwig, her schemes grew wilder. She didn't want local visitors, she wanted rich Americans. Next year, she would fix it so tourists weighed down with dollars could fly into Bordeaux, transfer to helicopters, and be set down in Les Milandes. She would build them a 130-room hotel. "I can die in peace," she said. "I have won."

It was not clear just what.

The Wyatts, who hadn't seen her in years, came to visit with their daughter Linda, Josephine's godchild. (Josephine had hundreds of un-official godchildren all over the world, in addition to honorary brothers, sisters, uncles. If she liked you, you would become a member of her extended—and extended and extended—family.) She put the Wyatts in the Marie-Antoinette suite at the Chartreuse.

"At the restaurant," Donald says, "there were waiters in tuxedos, but the place was almost empty. I remembered sadly when we first came back to reopen Les Milandes after the war, and the people were bowing, so happy 'Madame Josephine has returned.' Now, like the hotel, the cabaret was almost empty, though it was the high season."

Marian Wyatt, being a mother, thought more about the children. "It was not a family. They had people to take care of them, but they did not have the love and understanding of a mother and father who were there. Oh yes, I felt sorry for them."

Only Linda Wyatt, seventeen and on her first European trip, found no snake in the garden. To her journal, she confided, "I could stay here a lifetime . . . children of all races and nationalities being brought up as brother and sister, a famous star who is a fabulous person, a castle, two night clubs, pool, tennis court, what more could one want?"

Moulay Larbi's daughter Kenza was another guest that summer. Not much older than Linda Wyatt, she saw Les Milandes in a less romantic light. "For Josephine, it was an abyss. De Gaulle wrote to her. 'The Dordogne is the worst place for you to be, so come back to Paris where the people love you.'

"It's funny, when she died, I thought about that letter. When I saw the whole Paris in the streets and crying, I thought how right he was. It's a pity she was so stubborn and stayed in that place.

"She would tell me when someone exploited her, lied to her, but with the children, it was different, a deeper disappointment. She was not going to tell me, 'I failed.' She didn't want to realize it didn't work.

"You know, she was an artist, and it's very difficult for these people to be constant, because their own natures are not disciplined. Children need order, security, they are not made for artists. And these children from all sorts of backgrounds, abandoned in earthquakes, abandoned in a garbage can, they were traumatized children to begin with."

Josephine was fifty-six years old, she couldn't remember her lines anymore, or see without her glasses; every few months, angry creditors threatened to throw her into the street, her children were without ambition (or at least the kind of ambition she understood), but she was not finished. Again she was about to rise from the ashes, and this time, the rebirth was midwifed by a young man named Jack Jordan. Back in the United States, Jack Jordan had been working to bring Josephine home for the March on Washington.

Louis Douglas's daughter Marion remembers meeting Jordan in New York in about 1950. (Her family had migrated back to the United States in 1937.) "I was fascinated by Jack, he was stagestruck, he wanted to be somebody. He used to go to the Plaza Hotel, and this was when black people couldn't even sneeze at the front door. Jack would get himself invited, and take me.

"At the time I'm talking about, he was very poor, but he would bring a piece of feather or some lace, and put it over my poor little clothes, and we would make the grand entrance at the Plaza. When we walked in, I wasn't getting very loving looks, so I told him I didn't want to go anymore. He said, 'You're never going to be anybody, because you don't like the Plaza.'

"In 1963, he called and told me he was bringing Josephine Baker back. The March on Washington had been talked about for months before it happened. Everyone was very frightened that there was going to be bloodshed. When Jack said Josephine was coming, I forgot all about the troubles between her and my father, I forgot I wasn't interested in Josephine, I was very excited.

"Jack had assembled a group. There was Charles Burney, chairman of 'The Friends of Josephine Baker,' who taught school in Harlem, and he had said, 'We must have Josephine, this is too important, she has to be part of it.' And there were Juanita Poitier, Sidney's wife, and a young black woman producer named Billie Allen. These were the people who put up the money to bring Josephine over. I was just there for nostalgia. I was the link, Louis Douglas's daughter, part of Josephine's roots.

"We all went to the airport to meet her."

Chapter 37

—

THE MARCH ON WASHINGTON, AND THE DEATH OF JFK

"I'm not the star, just another sister"

ob Bach, a television producer, remembers flying into Washington and looking down at some of the two hundred thousand people beginning to gather. "It was August 8, muggy, with a haze hanging over the city. The plane banked over the Potomac River and the Washington Monument, and we could see crowds coming from all directions, like ants swarming toward honey. I thought, this is going to be tremendous.

"In the VIP lounge of the airport, there were a lot of big stars, and then I saw this woman in uniform, and I said, 'My God, that's Josephine Baker.' And very quietly, she joined us on the bus to the Washington Monument."

"Josephine was wearing her uniform with all her decorations," says Marion Douglas. "She had on the Médaille de la Résistance with rosette, the Médaille de la France Libre, the Croix de Chevalier de la Légion d'Honneur, and the Croix de Guerre. Everything. But she said, 'I'm not the star, just another sister.' She was so sincere that she was insincere, but I didn't know it then.

"When we got to the place where everyone was assembling, there was a lot of anxiety, because the word was out that the toughs were going to beat the shit out of anybody who marched. It took guts for those actors like Charlton Heston and Burt Lancaster and Marlon Brando to be there, they were perfectly aware that what they were doing by their presence was protecting black people. It took courage for Josephine—for anyone—to be there.

"Jack Jordan was rushing ahead of everybody yelling, 'Make way for a star, make way for a star,' and I heard people turn around and say, 'I don't see any star, where's the star?' Nobody recognized Josephine. But when she got up to the platform where the cultural contingent were already sitting, Sammy Davis and Sidney Poitier, they paid obeisance. They were trying to speak this poor sad French, calling her Madame la Bakaire, trying so hard, and she knew she was back, a queen had come home. And when they called on her to speak, she was fantastic."

"You are here on the eve of a complete victory," Josephine told the crowd. "You can't go wrong. The world is behind you. I've been following this movement for thirty years. Now that the fruit is ripe, I want to be here. You can't put liberty at the tip of the lips and expect people not to drink it. This is the happiest day of my life."

It was very simple, Marion says, very moving. "She spoke just a couple of minutes, that's all anybody did, because it was all building up to Martin Luther King. But the fact is, the moment Josephine hit that podium, you knew she was a superstar. She didn't have to work at it.

"After Martin's speech, there was a big crunch, there were no taxis, nothing. Sammy Davis had a limo, and he told Josephine she could join him, but so many people were running after him, trying to get his autograph, he had to leave her and flee in his car. And that's when Josephine changed. When she couldn't get into that car with Sammy.

"Now she's stuck with me, Jack Jordan, Billie Allen. We all went to the Sheraton to get dressed, and then we met at Mercer Cook's house. My uncle Mercer was not yet an ambassador, and Billie Allen was with a guy in the State Department, but he still wasn't a star, and Josephine, in the middle of the night, gets livid. 'What am I doing at this second-rate party?' she says. 'I can't hang out with Jack, he doesn't even know how to get to a decent party!' "

Back home again, in a better—or at least a more high-minded—mood, she wrote to Martin Luther King:

Dear Doctor,

I was so happy to have been united with all of you on our great historical day.

I repeat that you are really a great, great leader and if you need me I will always be at your disposition because we have come a long way but still have a way to go that will take unite—unite—[*sic*] so don't forget I will always be one of your sincere boosters.

Your great admirer and sister in battle, Josephine.

Earlier that summer, Jo Bouillon had left France. He told *France Dimanche* he was going to open a restaurant in Buenos Aires. "It is hard to tear apart one's heart and start again at fifty-six, but I hold nothing against Josephine."

"She broke his career," says the pianist Freddy Daniel. "He never walked by her side, always behind her."

When Josephine returned from the March on Washington, Freddy was already working at Les Milandes. At Josephine's insistence, he had been in residence since June 15. "The personnel in her office were dazed when I showed up. I asked, 'Where is Madame?' but they weren't sure, they thought maybe Copenhagen. A few rare clients were boring themselves at the Chartreuse, and I asked the staff to help me get the piano from the *guinguette* to the salon of the Chartreuse so I could entertain. Then I asked them to help me fix the roof of the *guinguette*—it was straw, and during the winter, rats had nested in it, half of it was falling on the floor—and to clean up the kitchen, where I discovered dirty dishes that had been there since New Year's Eve. They refused.

"As soon as Josephine arrived, she started to scream because I had had the piano brought up to the salon. Then she said, 'Ah, but I'm happy you're here.'

"I told her the staff had refused to do anything I'd asked. 'They said, Madame did not give the orders.'

" 'They were right,' she said. 'If Madame did not give the orders, they did not have to do it.'

"Then she told me, 'Come, *we* are going to do the cleaning.' I said no. 'Josephine, I came here to supervise your cabaret, play the piano, watch over the bar so they don't steal too much from you, but I do not do dishes.'

" 'Well,' she says, 'if Monsieur feels he's too big to do the dishes, I, Josephine Baker, will do them.' And she spent the whole day, alone, cleaning up. Nobody on the staff came to help her, it made me sick.' "

Four years earlier, when Josephine's success at the Olympia with *Paris Mes Amours* had brought record crowds to Les Milandes, Freddy had spent a happier summer there. The shows he and Jo had put on then were good—"We had Louis Armstrong, Jacques Brel, as well as Les Petits Rats of the Paris Opéra in the open-air theater. But when I came back in 1963, Jo had left, and Josephine still had 105 people on her payroll. We were always waiting for money coming from Stockholm, Munich, or Berlin, wherever she could get a booking to try to cover the expenses at Les Milandes. We had a very poor season, only on weekends we had a few customers.

"The staff didn't care anymore, they stole from her, they had sex everywhere. There were a few nurses trying to take care of the children, I must say without great competence. Those children needed affection, and they would ask me to tuck them in at night. 'Uncle Freddy, Uncle Freddy, come put us to bed . . .'

"Sometimes Josephine would go to Paris and buy things at the Galeries Lafayette or Le Printemps. Then the chauffeur drove her home—they drove most of the night—and she would arrive at Les Milandes around 6 or 7 A.M. All the children had to be waked up and dressed in their best, waiting for her at the bottom of the château's staircase.

"But most of the time she would go directly to the *guinguette* or the Chartreuse with new sets of tablecloths and napkins and matching candles. She would have the tables changed three times—not one or two tables, no, she wanted to see the effect in the whole place—with each different-colored set, and then she would exclaim, 'But it is adorable!' or, 'No, it doesn't work, put the blue here and light the candle.'

"Meanwhile, it was 10 A.M., and the children were still waiting up at the château, so they rolled in the dust, fighting each other. They got so filthy you wouldn't want to touch them with a barge pole. Quick, we would try to clean them up so Josephine would not see them in that state.

"Life was chaotic, full of ups and downs. Josephine wanted me to teach the children piano, all together in the same room; she had no idea how you learn to play piano.

"It was the same as with the Hebrew lessons. Once, while Josephine was away, a young woman arrived from Jerusalem to teach Hebrew to the children. I told her, 'Some of them are eleven years old, some are one, they cannot all learn Hebrew at the same time.' It did not last long; when Josephine got home, she put a mop in the girl's hand and asked her to clean the big stone staircase of the château. The girl refused, and was fired."

It was not just their education that was chaotic, the children's medical care was eccentric too. "When one of us caught a childhood disease— measles, mumps," says Jari, "Mother would put us all in the same room so we would all catch it, and be done with it."

That was the year—1963—that Josephine, who was fifty-seven, told everyone she was sixty-four. "It is good that I make myself older," she explained to Line Renaud, who followed her into the Tivoli Gardens in Copenhagen. "Then they find me formidable for my age." She also gave Renaud a piece of advice. "Don't get involved in politics, it cost me too much."

On the rare occasions when she was home, she was beginning to avoid her fans. "One day," Freddy says, "two buses arrived, full of schoolteachers. They had paid in advance—Josephine gave them a group price—and it was understood that she would welcome them at 4 P.M., and sing. As always, I was the buffer between her and her guests. When she did not appear, I called the château. After thirty minutes, she came to the phone. 'What do you want?'

"I told her, 'Listen, Josephine, if you do not come down, I will come up and get you and drag you here by the skin of your backside. I don't want to get screamed at for what you're doing.' Then I sent the barmaid's husband to pick her up. Ten minutes later, she arrived. From far away, I could see her sitting next to the driver in his open jeep, her face the face of her worst days, looking 112 years old. But as she came closer, she put on a wide smile, and by the time she arrived in front of the cabaret, she looked ecstatic. 'Oh, my dear friends, you came, how happy I am that you made this detour to visit me, come, you will see the children, *venez, venez* . . .'

"The children were down by the pool, and a little girl, not a member of the Rainbow Tribe, had just come out of the water. It was a very hot day, but Josephine hurled herself toward the child, wrapped her in a towel, and screamed, 'Who is the assassin who wants to kill this infant? Can't you see she is going to catch a cold because her hair is wet?' And she dried that child in the sun, while the teachers murmured, 'She is a saint.'

"By now she would travel with old suitcases and cartons held together with pieces of string. I would take her to the airport and ask the porters to take care of her bags, and they would say, '*That* is Josephine Baker's luggage?'

"At Les Milandes, she wore dirty work clothes and didn't try to hide that she had almost no hair. Not only had she burnt it off too many times, but wearing those heavy wigs that the hair cannot breathe under also makes you bald. Mistinguett was the same."

—

October 11, 1963. Edith Piaf died at seven o'clock in the morning. Jean Cocteau, who heard the news at noon, suffered a heart attack and died an hour later. From New York, where she had come to do a benefit performance at Carnegie Hall (proceeds to go to the NAACP, CORE, SNCC, SCLS, and "Miss Baker's International Children's Camp"), Josephine paid her old friends tribute. "Now that they are gone, there is a kind of emptiness that cannot be filled."

That night, she conquered Carnegie Hall. Her press representative had wired Walter Winchell an invitation, saying Josephine held "no animosity, hopes you don't either, and feels that perhaps her past views were premature." Winchell wrote across the telegram, "After all the lies she told! Wow," and gave it to his secretary to file.

At that benefit performance, she showed it all, furs, jewels, feathers, the great heavy wigs. Her quick wit was also in evidence. When a woman in the audience put opera glasses to her eyes, Josephine stopped singing. "Madame," she cried, "don't peer at me through those silly things! Hold on to your illusions!"

Pierre Spiers, who conducted the orchestra, said the real show took place later, at a supper party given by Duke Ellington's sister Ruth, when Josephine sang "a series of touching Negro spirituals . . . far removed from such show business bravura as the feather headdresses. . . ."

"I asked her what kind of food she would like," Ruth Ellington told me. "She said soul food, so my cousin Bernice fixed greens, sweet potatoes, chitlins, ham, fried chicken, peach cobbler. Josephine was wonderful. If you are black and told from the day you are born that you are inferior to the majority of people in your country, that's enough to make you pathologically ill. But she had risen above it. That was what Duke always said, 'Rise above it.' "

At Les Milandes, in November, Josephine received a communication to warm her heart. It read:

Dear Miss Baker,
    This is just a brief note to express my deep gratitude to you for all of your kind expressions of support. We were all inspired by your presence at the March on Washington. I am deeply moved by the fact that you would fly such a long distance to participate in that momentous event. We were further inspired that you returned to the States to do a benefit concert for the civil rights organizations. I only regret that a long standing previous commitment made it impossible for me to come to New York to witness the Carnegie Hall affair. I was pleased to learn that it was a great success.
    You are certainly doing a most dedicated service for mankind. Your genuine good will, your deep humanitarian concern, and your unswerving devotion to the cause of freedom and human dignity will remain an inspiration to generations yet unborn.

The letter was signed, Martin Luther King, Jr.

Almost every month now, Josephine flew back and forth across the ocean, planning a tour of America for the following spring. She was grabbing for the brass ring one more time; it took a catastrophe to slow her down.

It slowed everyone down. I was living in Germany when President Kennedy was killed. I walked the ten blocks from my room to my job, and the Kurfürstendamm was deserted, like the streets you see in an American western when the bad boys come to town. Behind every window, a candle burned. The man who had claimed, *"Ich bin ein Berliner!"* was dead, and we in West Berlin felt the world had stopped.

"I was not two days in New York when the assassination of the president happened," Josephine wrote Jacques Abtey (who was attempting to manage Les Milandes now that Jo was gone). She proceeded to review the obsequies as though they were a Broadway spectacle. "Big success of notables who came for the funeral," she reported, awarding first place to President de Gaulle, and second to the medal-bedecked emperor of Ethiopia. (She forgot she had once wanted to raise an army against him.) "Of course I went to Washington. There is one month's mourning, and in any case I could not have played before because we need time to get out my publicity. . . . I'm bored, everything has stopped. . . . It is very unfortunate, this national *malheur*, one can do nothing against it."

Then: "Ask the Spanish maid to make me an embroidered belt, and see that she does it well."

During her engagement at the Strand twelve years before, she and Florence Dixon had become friends. It was Florence—along with a nineteen-year-old acquaintance, Elizabeth Patton—who had accompanied Josephine on the train to Washington to pay their respects to the slain president.

"At the Union Station," says Elizabeth Patton, "we asked a porter which way to the rotunda, and he said not to worry, if we walked across the street, we would see the people.

"There were thousands waiting on the line, it was a crisp day, and Josephine kept saying, 'Look at all the different kinds of people!' There were blacks, whites, Asians, people from all over.

"It started to get a little nippy, and there was a delicatessen nearby, so Florence stayed in line to keep our places, while Josephine and I went to get coffee. As we waited in the delicatessen, we watched a television set overhead; the police in Dallas were taking Lee Harvey Oswald from one prison to another, and as they moved him, Jack Ruby walked up and pulled out a gun and killed him. We could not believe we were standing there watching this while waiting to go and view President Kennedy's body.

"Josephine was distraught. 'This is what I'm talking about, all this violence.' Everybody in the delicatessen said the same. 'It's horrible, why didn't they have more police guarding him, now we will never know if this is the man who actually killed Kennedy—' We took the coffee and left the shop, and as we got closer to the rotunda, we saw Jacqueline Kennedy and the children coming down the steps, and they had little blue coats on, and she was all in black, and Josephine said, 'How tragic for her, she is such a young woman to have to go through this.'

"It was about four in the afternoon by the time we were allowed to go in. '*Mon dieu,*' Josephine said, 'look how small the casket is.' Because the rotunda is so high-ceilinged everything beneath it looks minuscule."

A quick Christmas trip to France, then back to the States to rehearse *Josephine Baker and Her Company*. This time Josephine brought Kenza with her. "I was in Paris," Kenza says, "and she said, 'Come, it will be all new for you.'

"The opening at the Brooks Atkinson was fabulous."

It was her first Broadway appearance in twelve years, if you didn't count the evening at Carnegie Hall. And she was the biggest draw in town, if you didn't count the Beatles.

She told a reporter for *The National Observer* that before the March on Washington, she had always been afraid of white Americans. "I didn't want to be around them. But now that little gnawing feeling is gone, for the first time in my life I feel free. . . . I came back wearing my Resistance uniform for the March."

Some, commented the interviewer, would argue that she had come back "as a beneficiary of others' pain and blood. She returned when the hard part of the battle was over, and this is why many cannot forgive Josephine Baker. . . ."

Many could, however. She still drew crowds. "She never had any money, and she owed money, right?" says Shirley Herz, then her press agent. "We were to open in Philadelphia, and the sheriff or somebody decided to impound her costumes, so she had Florence Dixon and me pack as many as we could in suitcases, and we went out the revolving door of the hotel just as the sheriff or whoever it was came in.

"Her producer got the thing settled, but it was exciting, she was always one step ahead of the law. One day she called me—'I need somebody else for the show'—and I suggested the dancers Geoffrey Holder and his wife, Carmen de Lavallade, and that's how they got involved. When she went back to Paris, she took them with her.

"In New York, she was living at the Navarro, and she was always having stomach pains, all she'd want was these hot towels. She was involved in politics because it was the start of the civil rights movement. The fact that she was being accepted on Broadway meant nothing, she wanted to achieve more than that.

"She was so complex a person that nobody really knew her. She didn't want to belong to the black world, and she didn't really belong in the white world. Florence Dixon and Bessie Buchanan, who were around her all the time, were both very light-skinned. If Josephine had been Florence's color, if she could have passed, she would have. Yet her fame came with being this wonderful exotic black woman.

"She used men to achieve what she wanted—in a way, she castrated men—but she was only comfortable with women, she was surrounded by women."

Carmen de Lavallade says Josephine could be incredibly generous. "Geoffrey and I were added into the show in New York, and when we got to Paris, we reopened at the Olympia. Josephine was always pushing me forward, telling me to take longer bows. She was so secure, so proud in what she did, a younger woman didn't worry her. She knew who she was.

"Once we went to her château right after the show. We rode for hours, got there early in the morning. She was so tired, but then all the children came in, and I will never forget Josephine, her arms around Moïse, talking to him, and sleeping at the same time. Just sort of hugging each other at the kitchen table, tired as she was, it was beautiful."

By the end of May 1964, Josephine was in West Germany trying to borrow four hundred thousand dollars from German banks in order to save Les Milandes. "Periodically," said a news story, "Josephine goes back to work, but despite recent engagements in the United States and at the Olympia, which netted $60,000, she just can't seem to make ends meet."

"Ideals cost a lot of money," said Josephine. Not *our* money, muttered her neighbors. She had slapped one too many mailman, fought with one too many worker, she had even taken on the new priest who had replaced Abbé Tournebise when he retired. To be sure, the new priest had started the fight. When she'd popped into the Les Milandes chapel to ask if he'd like any help, he had answered abruptly, "I don't need help from a woman when I don't know where she got her money." A major brawl ensued, the priest ringing the church bell for assistance as Josephine attempted to haul away a statue of Christ she had bought and paid for.

"Every night now," *France Dimanche* informed its readers, "eleven children pray to God to save their house and their mother."

Jari says it wasn't so. "We never read those newspapers, Mother did not show them to us. But we knew something was happening, because now she wanted us to sleep in her room with her. Marianne would share her bed and we boys would bring our mattresses and sleep on the floor.

"She tried to reassure us that everything was fine. If the king of Morocco had invited her to visit, she would say, 'We are going to move to Morocco. Or to Algeria. We will live in the desert and start all over again.' To her, the desert meant purity, no contact with materialistic society.

"She liked to see us playing in her costumes, she directed us as if we were performing in a serious show. We swam in the dresses, walked like ducks in her shoes, and laughed, we were all clowns, it was such fun."

In Paris, a committee formed by Bruno Coquatrix and full of famous Baker enthusiasts—François Mauriac, André Maurois, Gilbert Becaud, Brigitte Bardot—tried to convince Josephine she should sell her castle, "house her children more modestly," and put any money from well-wishers into a trust fund.

She was not ready to give up. On June 1, she called a press conference. She sat at a big table on which there were four lighted candles, because, she said, the lights had been cut off. The rest of the grand salon was dim, and Josephine, wearing her by now famous heavy horn-rimmed glasses, looked serious. Begging the reporters to help, she blamed everyone but herself for her plight. "If everyone had done what was needed, I would not be in the situation I am in today."

She attacked:

• *The media.* Hadn't some journalists suggested that she was a publicity hound? And left her (even though she had created a village of brotherhood) to fight alone?

• *The husband.* "When I married Jo Bouillon it was to have a family . . . and one day he told me, since I'm the one who wanted those children, I had to keep them." Though *he* had sold his private life to the press, *she* had too much dignity to do the same. "I keep my humiliation for myself."

• *The neighbors.* "They try to hurt me in a thousand ways." Shop owners and contractors charged her too much, jealous people took down the signs to Les Milandes, refused to give tourists directions, telling them "we were closed," and subjected Josephine to insults and dirty words.

• *The utility companies.* "We have been without light or telephone for the past ten days, although I am the one who twenty years ago brought

light and running water to Les Milandes. Now only the two houses that
do not belong to me have light, all the rest of my village is dark."
• *The people who brought lawsuits against her.* "Every time I'm sued, it
costs me so much, and as soon as I'm finished with one suit, the next
one is waiting. I know I'm making the lawyers of Sarlat rich."

Now she asked for money to save Les Milandes "once and for all. But
this time, I scream, *Help me!*" She ended with a sigh. "In two days, my
son Brahim will be eight. The same day, I will be fifty-eight. I think of
my eleven children, the littlest one is four. I would not like them to lose
their home."

Who could condemn such a woman? And if anyone dared, would he
not be speaking against brotherhood and a better world? Josephine's
powers of persuasion were so compelling that not one of those ordinarily
cynical journalists had thought to test her story by flicking a light switch.

In fact, the director of the electric company, fearing that Josephine
would use the press conference to make him look bad, had restored her
electricity at two that afternoon. Everyone spent the afternoon in the
dark, while the poor aging star who had given so much to so many
convinced them she was being ill-used by heartless tycoons. "To her it
was a game," said Leon Burg.

But now the game was a race against time. In less than a week, by
court order, all the furnishings—from the pots and pans to the farm
implements—of Les Milandes were to be auctioned off. Josephine remained sanguine. "There are plenty of kindhearted people in France.
They're the ones who will save me, not the businessmen."

In the end, it was Brigitte Bardot who saved her. On Friday, June 5,
Bardot went on television and made an impassioned appeal for Josephine
Baker, whom she had never met. "I'm asking you to help," she said.
"You know that Tuesday, Les Milandes will be sold and this woman and
her eleven children will be homeless."

Listening in a café in Castelnaud, Josephine wept.

After Bardot's plea, money poured in. Akio told me that Pope
Paul VI sent money from his personal account, and Zsa Zsa Gabor
contributed twenty thousand dollars. ("I had met Josephine on a TV
show," Zsa Zsa says. "She was an old lady then, but still fabulous.
We had dinner and she talked about the castle and the children, and
explained to me her ideal, and I was very moved. I thought, 'This is

wonderful, children all mixed, not just one race.' When Stephen Papich called and told me how bad off she was financially, I was happy to be able to help her.")

Even the porters at Kennedy Airport took up a collection. After the phones at Les Milandes were reconnected, wire services flashed the news as though, one reporter said, "it were a national emergency." The auction was postponed. (From Buenos Aires, Jo offered the press his view of the situation. "Unfortunately, I'm not able to give my wife a large gift like Brigitte Bardot. I lost my personal fortune in Les Milandes. . . .")

Now Josephine's spirits were lifted not only by the rescue of her property, but by the arrival of a baby girl. Born June 18, 1964, at a clinic in Paris, the child of a Moroccan mother, Stellina became the twelfth member of the Rainbow Tribe.

But since the personnel at Les Milandes had been drastically reduced—no longer could Josephine afford to hire and fire nurses at will—Margaret took the baby to her house. For the next four years, Rama would have a little sister.

Chapter 38
—
UNCLE FIDEL,
AND LAST GASPS AT
LES MILANDES

"I know God will not abandon me"

*L*ife is over for me, now I give myself totally to the children," Josephine told Marie Spiers. And certainly she believed it when she said it.

Years later, Marie, who loved her, and forgave her her trespasses, was still living in the chic Trocadéro section of Paris in an apartment filled with Baker memorabilia. There were exquisite Art Deco silver statuettes of Josephine in many poses, and there were photographs: Josephine in the Folies-Bergère, with the bananas, the picture she would never show the children . . . Josephine with Pepito, looking happy on the boat to Brazil . . . Josephine and a Cambridge rowing machine. She beat the health craze by generations. "Now I have three loves," she said in the ad, "my country, Paris, and my Cambridge."

On a clothing dummy, there was even an old costume, red velvet with wide cuffs of black fox and a black fox muff, the velvet so heavy with jewels you could sense the weight without picking it up. "Her stage clothes were like the armor of soldiers in the Middle Ages," Marie says.

It was after Josephine hit the downward slope that she and Marie became really close. When Josephine's older children were sent off to various schools, Marie was asked to take them in on weekends. "She sent me so many they had to sleep in my hallway, I had them from Saturday to Sunday evening. I have spent a lot of sleepless nights.

"When I first went to Les Milandes, I thought Josephine was bringing them up very well. It's just that with her, everything was overdone, the punishment was overdone, the love was overdone, the makeup was overdone. I think Marianne was the most difficult, she was very rebellious."

Marianne had been placed in a boarding school surrounded by a high brick wall, lost in the forest of St. Germain. Children whose parents held the Legion of Honor could go there free, and on Sundays, the mothers—many of them widows of military officers—would visit, dressed in black. But most Sundays, Josephine was not available, and then Marie Spiers or Blanche Guignery would play Maman.

With three of the boys also away (at St. Nicholas school), weekending in Paris or a suburb like Le Vésinet was more practical than trying to get home to Les Milandes, all those hours away.

"We had the house full of them," says Madame Guignery. "Once we even had the princess from Morocco." (She's talking about Kenza.) "They had to sleep on mattresses on the floor, Josephine said it would be good for their backs."

Marianne was the one who told Marie Spiers, "I hate my mother!" "Can you imagine that?" asks the shocked Marie. "And it was Marianne who would come to my boutique and steal a skirt. One time she escaped me with a boyfriend, and next day, a lady brought her back to my apartment. Being one month older than Josephine, I wasn't getting any younger—and it was hard on me, trying to watch over those children. One day, one of the boys stole my radio and went to sell it in the subway. Later, he came back furious, and threw the radio on the floor. 'I could not find anyone to buy it!' To tell the truth, sometimes I was afraid of them.

"And I couldn't tell Josephine any of this, she was somewhere around the world, we didn't know where. The children resented that, too, but she was working to pay all those bills."

She was somewhere around the world, they didn't know where. Africa was one of the places she went in 1965: Guinea, Mali, Ghana, with Kenza as her companion. (Kenza had become a little sister to Josephine and a big sister to the children. She remembers being with them and watching western movies on TV. "When the cowboys attacked, only Mara would scream and support the Indians. At the end, he would be in tears. 'It is always the same, the cowboys win and my people are the losers.' "

Josephine had been asked to Africa, Kenza says, "by all these presidents. She was preparing some speech to explain what she was doing—the children, the peace of the world, whatever—and the heat was so unbearable the first place we landed that she couldn't talk.

"We were a couple of days in the capital of Guinea, and then the president invited us up to the mountains where the climate was fantastic. He arranged a flight for us.

"We went to the airport and there was a German plane, with the swastika on it. Josephine was shocked. 'Look at that!' The Africans didn't know what she was talking about, I think maybe Germany had sold them some old planes, and this one had not been painted over. She refused to get on it. 'I can't believe they wanted to put me in a Nazi plane!' We had to wait three hours before another plane came."

A quick trip to Kenza's homeland brought an audience with King Hassan II. "It was in Fez," Kenza says. "The king was very nice to her, he gave her a piece of property outside Marrakesh, and money for Les Milandes."

The check was large enough so she could forestall the next foreclosure, which was slated to take place on November 5. The king also promised her twenty thousand dollars a year to take care of the children, and arranged for her to do a singing tour of Morocco. He offered not the dry crust of pity, but a chance to shine again as an artist.

With the blessings of His Majesty, and Pierre Spiers conducting the orchestra, she played Rabat and Casablanca, blooming under the applause. The king had known that for a star the bravas were as necessary as the dollars. After a performance in Marrakesh, she went off with Mohamed Menebhi to relive the war years. When she came back to the Hôtel Mamounia at 6 A.M., Pierre Spiers was frantic. "It's all right," she told him gently, "I was with an old friend."

On August 30, 1965, Eddie Carson died. His obituary in *The St. Louis Argus* called him the father of "entertainer Josephine Baker." If the old man—he was seventy-nine—knew the secret of Josephine's real parentage, he took it to his grave.

Josephine did not send flowers.

She welcomed in the new year with Fidel Castro. He had invited her to the first Tricontinental Conference celebrating "the solidarity of the peoples of Africa, Asia, and Latin America and Cuba," and Josephine pronounced herself ready to sing and dance for the delegates. "I wanted to see the Cuban revolution with my own eyes," she said. "Generally I don't believe what newspapermen say."

Her comments made their way into her FBI file (which would eventually grow to almost a thousand pages).

Home again, she told the children she had a wonderful surprise. "Uncle Fidel has invited us all to spend a month's vacation in Cuba next summer."

First a wonderful surprise, then a bad one. Josephine was rushed to the hospital for emergency surgery. Intestinal blockage again. Kenza remembers putting cold compresses on her stomach. "It was better than the hot-water bottles she used before."

Jo Bouillon flew back from Argentina, and Akio, Jari, and Luis were given a day off from school to go and meet him. Akio asked Jo to stay in France. "Nothing's gone right since you left, Papa."

The newspapers loved it, Josephine and Jo together again, twelve children had got their father back; only Josephine, gazing at the family crowding around her hospital bed, was half amused. "How sweet of you to come," she said, "but I'm not dying yet."

Two weeks later, Jo paid Josephine's hospital bill, and went back to his restaurant in Buenos Aires.

In April, Josephine was well enough to travel to Dakar for the first International Festival of Negro Arts. Mercer Cook, by then American ambassador to Senegal, gave a small dinner party that included among the guests Katherine Dunham and Langston Hughes. (The writer Arna Bontemps had suggested to Hughes that he was "the ideal person" to do a biography of Josephine. ". . . The warm element of controversy combined with the warm element of sex and no strings and the French flavor! This could be your first best seller. . . .")

"Josephine was quiet during dinner," Mercer Cook told me. "And when she left, in that beautiful voice of hers, she just said, '*Au revoir*, Monsieur l'Ambassadeur.' I kissed her hand, tears in my eyes. I felt she was so proud of what I had achieved. We both knew the long way we had come from *La Revue Nègre*, when I was spending my nights at the theater translating her love letters."

Josephine's brother Richard had also come back into her life. He now had three children—Patrick, Guylaine, and Alain, all born out of wedlock, whom Josephine had never seen. "I was three years old when my father married my mother," Guylaine says. "Before that, we were never invited to Les Milandes. Afterward, Aunt Josephine relented.

"Sometimes my mother would dress us in our Sunday clothes, and Aunt Josephine would come pick us up in her big car, and we would be so excited, we would jump all over the upholstery while my mother was telling us to sit properly.

" 'Let them be, let them be,' Aunt Josephine would say. 'This is my blood, these are my children.' '*Non*, Madame Josephine,' my mother would say, 'these are *my* children.'

"We loved the ride up to the château, and we played in the park at Les Milandes with our cousins. There were fights and kisses—I remember Marianne was very haughty—and at four o'clock, we had delicious ice cream and cake in the kitchen. Otherwise, we were never allowed inside.

"At some point, Aunt Josephine told my parents they had to give her one of their children. 'It doesn't matter which one.' She said she had adopted many children, but it was not the same. 'My brother's children have my blood.'

"My father refused, and my mother said, 'Even if I had fifty, I would not give one away.' Aunt Josephine said, 'You can have more children, me, I cannot have any, and you would not miss one.' From that day forward, she wanted nothing to do with my family, we didn't exist for her. Only once, she sent my father a signed picture of her with her long ponytail, not even a note with it. We children did not miss her, we barely knew her, but when she appeared on TV, my father would ask us not to make noise. That was the way he followed his sister's life, through newspaper articles and her TV appearances. He would be sad after he saw her like that, he would say absolutely nothing.

"From Sarlat, we went to live at Baillargues, four hundred miles from Les Milandes. We never saw Aunt Josephine again.

"Of my grandmother Carrie's three children, my father is the only one who found happiness; he was generous, amusing, he liked to have a good time. He would invite us to play cards with him, and the winner could have a sip of beer. He would dance with us, we played horse on his back.

"We were lucky children, we had the love of two parents, my father was good in his skin, he never spoke about color or discrimination. In his half-French, half-English, he used to tell us about Tumpy—that's what they called Aunt Josephine back home. He said once he and she and Aunt Margaret stole a pack of cigarettes and sneaked under a bed and lit up and Grandma smelled the smoke and found them. She made them smoke the whole pack. 'We were sick for the whole day,' my father said. He still laughed when he told us that story.

"He said the family was poor, but never missed a meal. He was upset with Josephine that she wrote books telling how they were starving. 'I don't know why she does that, it's not the truth, we had good food.' He always told us about the chicken my grandmother Carrie would cook.

"Everyone adored my father. He would walk through the town, and you would hear, '*Bonjour,* Richard,' '*Bonjour,* Monsieur Martin,' from everyone. My father was not famous, but on the day of his death, we did not know where to put the flowers."

In July 1966, Josephine and the Rainbow Tribe set out for Cuba, and a visit with Uncle Fidel. Before they left, Stephane Grappelli paid a call at Les Milandes. Grappelli, who had played in the thirties with Django Reinhardt at Bricktop's, was a friend of Jo Bouillon. "We both played the violin," he explains simply. "Josephine took me all over the property, and when we came back to a salon on the second floor, we had a bottle of champagne. We started to talk, and I could feel she was trying to pump me about Jo, what he was doing and so forth.

"For an hour, we spoke of him. The bottle was empty when I left. She said she hoped the next time we met, it would be with Jo. Her eyes were filled with tears, she was incredibly quiet for a woman so vibrant onstage.

"She accompanied me to my car, and I must have turned back fifteen times to wave goodbye. Then I had to face front because the road was winding, and my last look was through the rearview mirror. She was still standing there. Suddenly, I saw her raise her arms like an eagle unfolding his wings."

Raise your arms in triumph like de Gaulle, it will chase the blues away, it will win cheers from an audience, even an audience of one.

Fidel Castro was celebrating the thirteenth anniversary of his revolution, and the Baker-Bouillons spent several weeks as his guests. "Mother gave three concerts for Castro," Jari says.

Jean-Claude pieces out his brother's memories. "First we arrived in a splendid villa on the ocean. And I remember enormous insects like tarantulas, even inside the house. There was strong sentiment against Yankees. Everywhere in Havana you could see huge posters, some one hundred and fifty feet high, showing Americans torturing the Cuban people. But there were only American cars, or the remains of American cars. Not one was whole.

"We saw Castro three times. He indulged in speeches that flowed like a river, running on for four, five, six hours under the glaring sun. And we would be under the presidential dais listening. But we understood next to nothing—he spoke in Spanish—so we sat there stoically, sweat dripping."

"Without anything to drink, not even a glass of water," Jari adds.

The night before the Baker-Bouillon family left Cuba, Castro came to the beach house he had loaned them. "He kissed us," Jean-Claude says. "We had to call him 'Tio Fidel,' Uncle Fidel. All of Mother's friends were 'Uncle.' Like Claude Menier, the son of the chocolate family—he was an elderly gentleman, very soft-spoken, one of his arms paralyzed, stiff, twisted, like a tree branch, with snakes coiled around it. He had pythons, boas, and we called him 'Uncle Petit.' He had white hair, Castro had black hair, a black beard, and he always wore a military uniform. He was very impressive."

"The children were thrilled," said Josephine, "they knew him from television."

At the end of August, the family left for Argentina. "We went to our father," Jari says. "We hadn't seen him for a long time. It was *la recherche du père*, we wanted to see how he lived, worked. Mother left us with him and again went back to perform."

Josephine herself had avoided the press during her brief stopover in Buenos Aires, though one reporter had cornered her long enough to ask why she had gone to Cuba. "Please forgive me for not discussing my trip to Havana," she said. "I have a tremendous headache."

She continued to need more help than anyone could supply, even though big businessmen with heavy pockets and soft hearts went on trying to rescue her. Early in 1967, the owner of the famed Club Méditerranée, who had fallen in love with Josephine's "inner radiance," came up with a solution. "We proposed," says Gilbert Trigano, "that Josephine keep the château for her personal use, and we would manage the rest of the property and deal with the people who came from all over the world. But she wanted to do it her way, and that was impossible."

Still, if you had chanced to visit her *en famille* in the summer of '67, you would not have believed there was anything amiss in her world. Harry Hurford-Janes, who hadn't been to Les Milandes in twenty-one years, spent several days there during that August, and made notes.

"I entered the château by the side door leading directly into a large kitchen boasting an enormous refrigerator with glass doors, a dingy little sink, an armoire painted cream and yellow. A long table was laid for about eighteen (for breakfast it seemed).

"I was glancing around when a door burst open and a little lady of about sixty darts in, hair scraped up on top, in a woollen dressing gown. She greets me warmly . . . reveals that she was a journalist for thirty years, and had taken a domestic job at Les Milandes two weeks ago but did not think she would last much longer. Throughout my stay she was in a state of exhaustion. '*Très fatiguée*, M'sieur,' she would say, putting her palm to her forehead every time we met."

Harry was also greeted by Moïse ("dark and good-looking"), who said Josephine was expected home from Copenhagen late that night, and by Jari ("fair and Finnish") who took his bags upstairs.

Passing Josephine's bedroom, with the bed once owned by Marie-Antoinette, gilded and hung with curtains of blue silk, he felt himself flooded with memories of a cold winter night in 1946 when he had sat by the fire in this house "while Josephine knitted and we talked of her possible marriage to the Menier chocolate heir, who was delicate and whose family disapproved of his infatuation. In her mind then, it was a toss-up between the invalid and Jo Bouillon. It all came back to me vividly, the long conversations, 'You are my brother, you are like a rock. But you see' (as if that explained it) 'you are an Englishman.' "

During that week, Harry was not the only guest. There was another Englishman known as Monsieur Jack. And a Spanish lady. And a German author who photographed the monkeys and drew Josephine's wrath. "It is like a studio!" she shouted. Belgians, Swiss, French people arrived and departed. Josephine cooked lunch, and monitored lunch.

"There were cries from her," said Harry, "of 'Sit up straight, Brahim!' . . . 'Don't bolt your food!' all in French, with despairing glances at her guests ('You see what a handful I have!')."

Also present at this chaotic repast was an unfortunate tutor newly arrived from Lebanon to teach the children Arabic. "The older boys asked if they could swim after lunch," Harry recalled, "and Josephine said they would have to wait. 'Five children in France have died through bathing too soon after meals!' At this point, the Lebanese professor said it was perfectly in order for the children to bathe as soon as they wished after the meal—it was fish, being Friday—as they would have digested their food by the time they reached the pool.

"Josephine, furious at this reversal of her orders . . . reminded Monsieur that he had been engaged as a schoolmaster, not a doctor. I knew he was doomed, and this was shortly confirmed to me by J. B., who told me he would never have done, as he was 'playing with himself,' with his hands in his pockets. . . . He would leave first thing in the morning."

The Spanish lady was concerned about the turnover in staff, she said Margaret was the only one with any authority, "that J. B. was always flying off for engagements and the children ran riot." This the children were happy to demonstrate by fusing the lights, slamming the doors, seizing Ping-Pong paddles from each other, hitting at the monkeys as they jumped from branch to branch of a tree. But they redeemed themselves by putting on a pantomime that enchanted their mother. "She covered her mouth to stifle her laugh," observed Harry. "She slapped people on the shoulder as if to say, 'Isn't it killing?' Between times, she was adjusting costumes, controlling the volume of the amplifier, falling into her seat beside Margaret, convulsed with laughter."

—

Every family in France received a monthly stipend for each child; Josephine, with twelve children, got 1,305 francs. In addition, large families got a 75 percent deduction on railroad fares, so when Josephine traveled now, she took the train. And one of the places she traveled to was Le Vésinet. She wanted to buy a house and live there again, she told the mayor, "because there I have known happiness."

She thought going back would change her luck, but Blanche Guignery says nobody in the village wanted to help. "They were avoiding her. Poor Josephine, here she was on the straw, just as my husband had sadly predicted."

Still, you aren't on the straw if you don't know it. Josephine continued making plans. Her latest idea was for a College of Brotherhood to be built at Les Milandes. "We can save Les Milandes and help the world at the same time! . . . Students will learn that all creeds, like all people, are essentially one. And when they have mastered that lesson, they'll go home and preach it to their people."

Drunk with grandiosity, she solicited blueprints from architects, and never paid a penny for any of them.

In January 1968, the American consulate in Paris refused her a four-day visa to come to New York. She believed it was because she had joined the March on Washington and visited Cuba. She wrote to Bobby Kennedy, and he called the State Department, which put her papers through. Kennedy also sent her a wire saying, I AM HAPPY TO INFORM YOU THAT YOUR REQUEST FOR A VISA HAS BEEN GRANTED AND YOU WILL HAVE IT ON MONDAY. (His office *did* mention that the delay had had nothing to do with Cuba, or civil rights, it was just that Josephine hadn't filled out the forms correctly.)

Now in possession of a visa, she went to Chicago to speak at a meeting of the West Side Organization on behalf of Martin Luther King (who didn't appear), then came right back to France, where the roof was leaking all over her Oriental rugs. Les Milandes was still in jeopardy, and once again, a powerful tycoon tried to save Josephine.

Sylvain Floirat, a kind of French William Paley, owner of the powerful radio station Europe 1, made her an offer she should not have refused. He said he would pay all her debts, 146 million francs, and then, though she would no longer own Les Milandes, she could stay there as long as she lived. She said she had to think about it, and never got in touch with him again.

On February 16, her creditors finally forced the sale of the estate for ninety-nine million francs, but one dissatisfied lender—he thought Les Milandes should have brought more—used a loophole in the law to have the sale annulled, and rescheduled. Another auction would take place on May 3.

It was a reprieve for Josephine, who was working more than ever, mostly in cabarets. They were perfect for someone who wanted to avoid paying taxes, since the owners were often willing to give a performer money under the table. In St. Moritz, jet-setters, expecting a beaten-down creature, were shocked by her confidence as she took possession of the stage. Now there were no new designer clothes, but only Marie Spiers making miracles with sleeves from an old Dior, a skirt from an old Balenciaga.

Though Josephine begged for sympathy from the press and in her speeches, onstage she laughed, reminisced about past splendors, looked like a winner. The empress of Iran, Farrah Diba, vacationing with her children, was so moved she sent a gift of money and a beautiful carpet.

The newspapers followed Josephine's every move. From *France-Soir:* "She will once again run through the world trying to find before May 3 the millions she needs. The children will go back to school, little Stellina will stay with Aunt Margaret, and only the screams of the peacocks will disturb the silence of Les Milandes. The storm passes over the children's heads, they don't know what is at risk."

Josephine said she realized people might wonder what she had done "with all the money they gave me, especially in 1963, after the plea from Brigitte Bardot. . . . Well, my employees have stolen from me, and suppliers abused my confidence. And then I was not always there, I was singing, working. . . . In my absence, not nice things happened. . . . People said all my sheep had died, but we never found the bodies. . . . I have been abused. . . ."

If the French press was sympathetic, some foreign publications were not. *Constanze,* a West German weekly, sent a reporter to the château, and he accused Josephine of having degraded the idea of brotherhood. " 'They don't give me milk for my children,' she will cry to the world, and she expects the world to come to her rescue. . . . For years, her farewells only prepared you for her comebacks. Of course she comes back because she needs money for her children and wants you to admire this poor good hard-working mother who allows herself no rest. . . .

"I was there when Josephine received her mail. She went to her desk and with a letter opener, she opened them, took out the money, the bills of ten francs, fifty marks, and did not even read the letters, she just counted the money.

"I dared to ask her one question: What will happen to all those letters? She said they would be given to her lawyer. . . . 'Les Milandes must not die! Here my children should find a secure existence.' "

The reporter was not swayed. "The grass," he said, "is already growing over Les Milandes."

The grass may have been growing, but the water was not flowing. The day it was cut off, Josephine came to Paris, and that night, she and Marie Spiers went to a movie. "As soon as it started," Marie says, "Josephine fell asleep and began to snore. The people around us were upset, but I didn't wake her, I knew she needed the rest.

"Afterward, she wanted to go eat something at the Café de la Paix. She told me how in the old days her suitors would take her there, how glamorous it was, but we could not afford the second-floor dining room, so we ate downstairs. Curious, I asked her, 'How do you all wash with no water?' She laughed. 'We fill a basin with water from the Malaurys,' and then she went through the whole process, miming everyone's washing.

"I felt uncomfortable, heads were turning, they had read the news in the morning paper about her water being turned off, and here she's laughing at the Café de la Paix!"

Laughter turned to tears on April 4, when Martin Luther King was killed. That spring of 1968 was terrible. Two months after King's death, Bobby Kennedy would be assassinated, and student unrest (which would lead to riots in the streets of Paris) was already building when Bruno Coquatrix, Josephine's own Don Quixote of the Olympia, grabbed his lance and went into battle. First, he booked the lady into his theater for a fortnight in early April, then, with the record company Pathé-Marconi, he produced a record called *S.O.S. The World's Children*.

He also sent the photographer Hugues Vassal and the journalist Yves Le Roux to get new pictures of Josephine's children, since the S.O.S. crusade was for them. "She would be paid," Vassal says. "It was a decent way for our newspaper to help them." "She was happy to see us. She was panicked by what was happening at Les Milandes, but she knew the number of readers she could reach through *France-Dimanche*, and that lifted her morale."

At the Olympia, the house sold out every night, and the S.O.S. record moved briskly. On it, Josephine sang "J'ai Deux Amours," "Dans Mon Village," a new hit, "Merci pour Les Milandes," and also "Hello, Dolly," because she intended to do the show with Bruno next year. "I realize I'm sixty-two, but Dolly was no spring chicken either," she told reporters. One of them, throwing journalistic objectivity to the winds, ended his piece with a rallying cry: "One can find the S.O.S. record at the Olympia or any record shop. *If you love Josephine, you know what you have to do!*"

They did it. They did it all over Europe. "It's the little people who are helping to see me through," Josephine told the journalist Jacqueline Cartier. Bruno Coquatrix also bought newspaper space for an open letter to his star. "It is pure chance," he said, "but once more at a critical moment in your life we find you at the Olympia. . . . And once more, it is formidable! You never sang so well, you never were so dynamic! . . . One had to have been twenty years old several times in one's life in order to be able to express such youth and humanity!"

He ended this loving testimonial by thanking her "for being what you are: the greatest. I kiss you."

The French press could not get enough of Josephine stories. *France-Dimanche* ran a shot of the star emerging from a faint, and said her friends were worried about her being back on the Paris stage, "a hard test for a sixty-two-year-old." The headline posed a question: WILL HER HEART STILL HOLD?

It did, along with her voice and her legs.

She finished her fortnight at the Olympia (she'd be back soon; when Coquatrix realized two weeks could not accommodate all the people who wanted to see her, he arranged for her return on May 15) and set out for Scandinavia. Before she left, she went to Paulette Coquatrix. "All goes well," she said. "Thanks to you and Bruno, Les Milandes are saved." "Careful, Josephine," said the more realistic Paulette. "You think you are the queen there, but you will never be a queen to those farmers."

"We went to talk to the people Josephine owed money," Vassal said. "There were two kinds. Some were like creditors since Molière's time, grumpy, wanting to dispossess her because her property was valuable; well run, it could have made a lot of money. Then there were the others who were tender toward her, unhappy to see that no one could really help her, half admiring what she had done, even though there was more than a touch of folly in it."

That made me think of something Eli Mercier had told me. "Here we do not have bad memories of her," he said. "She made all of us a lot of money, and the unpaid bills—grocery bills, gasoline bills—are past, it is not serious. When the children were hungry, the poor ones, we had pity."

From Sweden, Pierre Spiers wrote to Marie. "Every night, I take the money from Josephine. Tell the Fetiveaus they will be reimbursed when we return." (Dr. Fétiveau, owner of a private clinic near Paris, had helped out with a loan.)

On May 3, Pierre and Josephine were killing time in her hotel room in Göteborg. "Josephine was not too worried," Pierre said. "She kept saying, 'I know God will not abandon me.' "

She had been able to convince herself that the Bergerac tribunal, sitting that day in the Sarlat courthouse, would not put Les Milandes up for sale at 2 P.M., that Bruno Coquatrix would be there and in some way be able to stave off her creditors. Every hour that passed made her more confident.

The phone rang at last. She picked up the receiver and heard the voice of a stranger. "I'm really sorry," the man said, "but my paper wants to do a big piece on the sad news. What was your first reaction to the sale of Les Milandes?"

It was finally over. She had lost.

Chapter 39

—

DOWN AND ALMOST
OUT IN PARIS

"What happened to all that money?"

abriel Bureau, the lawyer in charge of the sale, says there was nothing irregular about the proceedings. "Bruno Coquatrix was there, checkbook in hand; his funds were insufficient. He begged the creditors to give Josephine one more extension. But she had received a lot of donations. What happened to all that money? I didn't see it come, I didn't see it go. The afternoon of the auction, few people showed up."

So many times, at the last second, Josephine had been saved. So many times, she had used the press, Leon Burg recalled, "to make her creditors look like the bad guys. Men who had been patient for years saw their names and faces dragged through the papers as if they were murderers, when the truth was they could have bankrupted her long ago.

"Les Milandes was sold legally, for very little, because the few friends of Josephine who were there did not dare to bid it up. My cousin and I had enough money, but we were afraid of gossip, of people's saying, 'They claim to be Josephine's friends, and they profit from her misery.'

"We should have bought it and given it back to her, I still regret that we didn't. But the reason not many people came was that we all thought Josephine had been saved, that was the impression we had got from the press, and from Bruno Coquatrix's S.O.S. campaign."

The château, the farm, the hotels and restaurants, the amusement park, the forest, a second run-down château on the grounds where Josephine kept her sheep—everything went. Only Margaret's house and the Maury house (which couldn't be sold until the last Bouillon child came of age), and the chapel which belonged to the community of Castelnaud, were exempted. The land and the buildings—sold in twenty lots—brought 125 million francs, less than a fifth of their assessed value. A man named Jean-Marc Joly bought the château.

Sent by Josephine, Akio was the only family member to witness the auction. "It reminded me of wild beasts attacking a defenseless animal," he said. "I've never seen such unfeeling faces."

André Rivollet found Josephine's defeat inevitable, the logical end to her *folie des grandeurs.* "She went bankrupt with Les Milandes, its moat, its travelers' inns (one for the rich, one for the poor), its housing with showers and radios for the workers, its zoo of wild beasts, its dance hall in the middle of nowhere. The dream collapsed, her megalomania, her generosity, turned her into a victim." Her attempts to be the Universal Mother seemed to Rivollet equally quixotic. "Disappointed by the men she had chosen, she adopted children as a prism for her ego, children she exposed to green pastures, not life."

"They had been like on death row for too long," said Georges Malaury's mother, Henriette. "Now peace had come at last."

Still in shock, Josephine spoke to Hans Vangkilde, a Danish radio interviewer. "To me, money has never been very important," she said. "I suppose that's the reason Les Milandes is lost. But I had such hope. . . . I have found many people throughout the world interested in brotherhood. Maybe not enough of them to unite . . . but it will happen one of these days. . . . It's a question of time, that's all. . . . Will I go on? How can I stop? If I could stop, I wouldn't."

On the very afternoon of the auction at Les Milandes, the student revolt began in Paris, after the rector of the Sorbonne called in police to break up a noisy meeting of undergraduates. The rector's act, said Janet Flanner, "violated the sanctuary of the university, maintained over centuries." Trouble spread, teenagers burning automobiles, digging up paving stones and piling them into barricades, occupying public buildings (like the Odéon Théâtre, because classic plays were "dated"). Tear gas, clubs, arrests were the response of government security forces. A general strike would follow.

This was the situation when Josephine returned to Paris and the Olympia on May 14. The streets were on fire? Josephine would burn brighter. "She was unique, the only one, every day, she got standing ovations," said Sy Oliver, the American trumpet player and arranger who was working with her. "I had seen *Shuffle Along* in Zanesville, Ohio, and I still remembered her at the end of the chorus line. When I told her that, she was amused. She didn't seem depressed, she was preoccupied with what we were doing, with the music."

On May 13, there had been an antigovernment parade, almost a million people marching. Cries of "De Gaulle, assassin!" and "Charlie, resign!" rang through streets the general had once entered as a liberator.

Gaullists may have suffered the odd pang of guilt—the educational system did need renovation, ten million union workers were seriously underpaid—but on May 30, they counterattacked, holding their own march. Bruno advised Josephine not to go. "Cool down, or you will lose one million people who will not come to see you."

"She did not want to hear him," says Paulette.

She walked at the head of the line, again in her army uniform, Akio at her side.

"It is hard to believe that those born in foreign countries are more French than those who had the luck to be born here," wrote Marcel Brandin to a friend. Brandin, Culture Minister André Malraux's chief of staff, said de Gaulle loved Josephine, and had often helped her. Even so, she was "without a *sou* or a roof . . . because she is a good girl and trusts everyone. Artists make bad accountants."

Now, because of the riots, business was so bad at the Olympia that no accountants were needed; the theater closed its doors until feelings settled. During this time, Robert Kennedy was killed, and Josephine set out again for the United States. ("I thought the most beautiful homage I could pay to that family and to the country that I was born in," she said, "was to go back and take five of my adopted children. . . . Robert Kennedy knew that the way to freedom for the entire world was through youth.")

Bruno Coquatrix couldn't believe she'd bought six round-trip plane tickets. "There go her earnings from the show!"

"They stayed at the Hilton Hotel," says Florence Dixon. "The funeral was at St. Patrick's Cathedral. Then I brought Josephine and all those boys up to Harlem and gave them dinner. They sat on the floor around the coffee table and they ate. Luckily, I had a big leg of lamb, and some ham, they cleaned it up. There were boys everywhere, they ate everything but the bones."

Josephine closed for good at the Olympia on June 29, and headed to Les Milandes, where she would endure a long, hard summer. On the Fourth of July, she was taken to a hospital in Périgueux with a minor heart attack. And always, there was the struggle over the home, which she no longer owned but refused to give up. The new owner had got an eviction order for October 7. This did not worry her; in France, a family with children can't be evicted in the winter. She had six months' grace, if she could hang on.

She continued to try to reverse the sale of her castle. "Everyone's out to get me," she wrote de Gaulle.

"The son of the new owner would come and harass us," Brahim says. "We ran to the top of the château and threw stones at him. He left, calling us scoundrels and saying he would have the law respected."

At the end of vacation, the children started back to school, most of them believing—despite Josephine's protests to the contrary—that they would never again live at Les Milandes. Brahim describes their last lunch in the château. "My mother, my aunt Margaret, Uncle Elmo, and Rama were there. And our two 'uncles,' Monsieur Marc and Monsieur Rey— we could see that for them it was very dramatic."

"When we first came into the kitchen," Brahim continues, "my mother was not yet present, and Monsieur Rey told us this was like the last supper of Christ and his disciples. He was crying, and he said, 'Children, never forget what you have known here with your mother.'

"Now Uncle Elmo was crying, and we were not used to seeing men cry. Then my mother arrived and she was crying too, but we boys looked at each other, thinking, 'Is it that serious?' We went out and knocked down a wooden cabin we had built so the new owners' kids wouldn't have it."

Marianne wanted to say goodbye to the trees. "I'll never forget her," Moïse said, "standing there, arms tight around a scratchy trunk."

There were to be no more exclusive Swiss academies for any of the children; they were enrolled in less expensive schools around Paris. "It was the same with food," Brahim recalls, "depending on whether or not my mother had money. When she was poor, she would say, 'Well, children, it is Sunday, would you rather do a big breakfast?' Because it wouldn't cost much, bread, butter, jam, chocolate. Sometimes, she would suggest a cafeteria. 'Self service, children, is it okay with you?' We younger ones would say, 'Yes, the self-service is much more fun,' but some of my brothers—like Jari or Jean-Claude—with grand tastes would say, 'It is not comparable to a steak at the Café de la Paix.'

"There were weekends when she *would* take us to the Café de la Paix with the maître d' and the waiters. For the first two school semesters, we swung between those two lives, and then Marie Spiers found us a little apartment on avenue MacMahon and everything became a bit more normal."

"I signed the apartment lease in my own name," Marie says. "The landlord did not want children or animals, and when he discovered that Josephine and all those children—sixteen people, including Elmo, Margaret, and Rama, plus cats and dogs—were living there, he was furious with me.

"There were not enough beds, and one more time, my friend Doctor Fétiveau came to the rescue, sending some mattresses from his clinic. The apartment had two bedrooms and a living room, there were mattresses everywhere.

"Every morning, Josephine would send her sister to my shop to pick up the money I had taken in the day before, so she could feed all those people at avenue MacMahon. It was hard times for her, but she never complained. She spent hours in my shop phoning the whole world; when I got the bills, it was terrible."

Josephine's casual way with money—other people's or her own—was no surprise to Marie. "One Christmas Eve, I picked her up at the Hôtel Scribe, and the doorman said, 'Good evening, Mademoiselle Baker, Happy Christmas,' and she turned to me and whispered, 'Give me a hundred francs.'

"I gave it to her, but I said, 'Josephine, you are crazy, we have no money and you give a hundred francs to a doorman.' She said, 'He has children, it's Christmas, so what?' She didn't know if he was married, she didn't know if he had children, the only thing was, it was Christmas.

"Maguy Chauvin was trying to book her as much as possible, and Josephine would sometimes arrive at my shop between planes, so tired she would lie down on the dressing-room floor and fall asleep. My customers were astonished to see two legs stretching out from under the curtain. I would tell them to be quiet, and not wake the famous Josephine."

Tired or not, in work she found salvation. "I always worked, even as a little girl," she said that year, on a Canadian television show. "And this has been my good luck. Because today, I'm still working."

She didn't tell the Canadian viewers that her world had crumbled, but harked back to the past that warmed her, the early days in Paris. "Cocteau was a friend, Paul Colin, Fujita, we were young together. . . . I posed at the Beaux-Arts, they wanted to see me naked, so they saw me. What is wrong about admiring what nature and God have created? . . . . Colette loved me very much, I used to visit her after work on summer nights when I lived at Le Vésinet. . . ."

The night of November 6, 1968, was the only time, Marie Spiers says, that she ever saw Josephine "absolutely drunk on whiskey. Because Nixon had won the American election. Josephine felt Humphrey's ideals were close to hers."

Have you been wondering why she had not sold her fabled jewels in order to keep her castle? I don't have the answer. She hung on to the rings, the brooches, the necklaces and tiaras—"I am keeping them for my future daughters-in-law," she said—but put everything in Marie's name, in order to escape the creditors still hounding her.

Most of the time, the jewels lay in the vaults of the Crédit Municipal, a state-run pawnshop on rue Pierre Charon in Paris. This was big time, people pawned their Picassos at the Crédit Municipal, and if you missed an interest payment—which rolled around every six months—your belongings were sold the very next day.

"Each six months, as the deadline came close, I would shake," Marie says, "but she would do a gala here, a concert there, and we would save her jewels."

In some magic-thinking part of her brain, she still believed she would save Les Milandes too. She kept going back and forth to the ghost château, where only a few faithful guards and some animals remained. But writing to Miki Sawada in Tokyo, she did not mention her travail.

"After these long years of silence," she said, "here I am again." She wanted to send Akio and Janot to college in Japan. She said she would like Miki to make sure the boys learned the Japanese language and manners. (Indeed, Akio and Janot spent a year in Japan, where Janot found it hard to adjust. "When I asked for bread in a restaurant, they would bring me a cup of rice! And you are not supposed to put sugar in the tea; when I did, everyone looked at me.")

Babies she cherished, babies were easy, but Josephine was finding it harder to cope with her children's growing up, so many of them beginning to rebel, despising the rigidity of teachers and classrooms—"No fun, no girls," Brahim says of his school—all but the littlest ones, Noël and Stellina, testing the boundaries of their universe.

Josephine had no patience and too much responsibility, committed as she was to the grandiose plans she had made for my brothers and sisters when they were babies. This one must be a doctor, this one a lawyer, it didn't matter in the slightest whether they were interested in medicine or law. I, on the other hand, needed nothing from her, I was twenty-five years old, with my own nightclub in West Berlin; she was about to rediscover me, the perfect son.

Chapter 40

—

PRINCESS GRACE
TO THE RESCUE

"I want to be buried in the nightgown of my agony"

Tepe Lombard would have been proud of me.

For five years, I had survived in the big capital of Paris, I had learned to give my seat on the subway to old ladies and pregnant women, I had learned how to dress, work hard, get along. I was smart, I could see the power of languages—I had been amazed by Khrushchev's translator—and the sound of English, which meant big tips, was music to my ears.

I went to Liverpool to learn it, waited tables in the old Adelphi Hotel, discovered kippered herring, met Peter Brown and Brian Epstein, who liked a band called the Beatles. Often, we went to the Cavern, a basement club, to hear them, but I was bored; to tell the truth, I preferred the alternative band. Then I had to go home, I had been called up for military service. It was a few weeks until my induction, and my cousin Nadette, who was studying at the Goethe Institute in West Berlin, suggested we hitchhike to Germany. We caught a ride in a milk truck.

Nadette found me a job as busboy at the elegant Maison de France on the Kurfürstendamm, the Champs-Élysées of Berlin. West Berlin was a kind of Las Vegas then, an in-your-face capitalist insult to the Communist empire.

On my twentieth birthday, walking in the street, I felt such pain I fell down, and woke up in a hospital (I had appendicitis, and developed jaundice), where I stayed for three months. I was excused from military duty because I had to be on a diet the French army could not provide.

Now I got a job in a famous gay bar, the Kleist Casino. Four years later, I had my own place, the Pimm's Club, with a varied clientele, not all gay, not all straight. I did not want any sexual discrimination because I myself was AC/DC, I could tango or I could waltz.

Our Russian neighbors did what they could to destroy our morale, their MiGs flew over, creating sonic booms, families were still separated by the wall of shame, but in the Pimm's Club, there was always a party. Now I wore custom-made shirts, and entertained the rich, the successful, the stars.

Errol Garner, Mahalia Jackson, Rudolf Nureyev, Margot Fonteyn, Leonard Bernstein, Jessye Norman were my friends. I called the mix of patrons my cocktail of human beings. Mick Jagger propositioned all the women customers, while I tried to appease their husbands and boyfriends. I remember Orson Welles autographing the bare arms of pretty girls; I remember being introduced to Pierre Spiers for the first time. He was on tour with a singer, and we talked about Josephine. I said I had met her when I was a boy.

As Christmas of 1968 approached, the spirits of West Berliners, walled off and surrounded by East Germany, were sagging. City fathers, looking to give the town a lift, organized a fair, and a beer company called Schultheiss hired Josephine Baker to come and perform.

I was thrilled. For ten years, since our first meeting at the Scribe, I had followed her adventures. I suffered when she lost her house. In my head, I talked to her. But was the relationship between her and me real, or had I fantasized it? Would she even remember me?

When she and Pierre Spiers got to town, he phoned me, and I headed for the Schultheiss beer tent. It stood in a bombed-out lot across the street from the war-ruined Church of Remembrance on the Kurfürstendamm. Inside the tent, there were rows of wooden benches, a beer bar, and at the back, a little platform for Pierre and five musicians. Josephine's dressing room was improvised from a couple of sheets of canvas behind which were a dress rack on wheels, a mirror on wheels, and a small electric heater.

I found her seated at a collapsible metal table that held her makeup. It was pitiful, what I was seeing. She seemed so fragile in a faded pink negligee, she was heavily made up and wearing a cheap wig. She was talking to Artur "Atze" Brauner, head of CCC Studio. I kissed her, said, "*Bonsoir*, Maman," and noted that Artur looked surprised at my calling her Maman, but I never called her anything else. He told her I was the darling of Berlin, and I assured her that everything was going to go well. "The whole city is talking about your being here!" We both knew I was lying. It was freezing, and I helped her dress. Her costume was grotesque, a kind of Cossack tunic, seven-league boots, two rows of fake pearls.

When Pierre introduced her, I handed her the mike, and crouched on my knees behind the makeshift curtain, feeding her the long cable as she needed it. She had already started talking to the audience before she came on—"Ooh la la, I'm not ready, in the old days it was easier, only a few bananas, but today my children have eaten those bananas"—and then she walked through the curtain, stumbled as she tried to step up on the band platform, and fell back.

I jumped up as if on a spring, and holding out my hands, touched her back and pushed her forward. It looked very easy, almost a ballet step, part of the act. The audience, which had gasped, now sighed with relief, and Josephine, still talking—she might lose her balance, but never her aplomb—turned around and gave me a wink. It was a sign that cemented our liaison.

Trying to reach the people, she went to material she thought would be surefire, telling how she had brought the Charleston to Berlin in the twenties. As Pierre started "Yes Sir, That's My Baby," she began to move her head, her pearls swinging around and around until suddenly they broke, and flew all over, *ploup, ploup, ploup.* People laughed derisively, but she finished the show. Then I helped her pack the cardboard suitcase, and since nobody came for an autograph, we headed for my 280SL Mercedes coupe, brand-new and smelling of leather. "How do you like it?" I said. "Oh, I like the Mercedes," she said airily. "When I was here the first time, they gave me one *free*—the seats were snakeskin, and I had ermine covers put on them."

I loved that. She was saying, "Okay, kid, you made it, but I did it before you, and I didn't even have to pay for it." (How different from my birth mother, who had refused to get into my car, telling me I could have bought two houses in our village for the price of "that German automobile.")

My friend Heinz Holl owned a chic restaurant; I took Josephine and Pierre there, people recognized her, and she was happy. The pain of a few minutes ago was not even mentioned. We tried to catch up on the last ten years, but her real enthusiasm was, as always, for the future. She said she needed only to be represented in the right way, and there was no limit to the money that could be made in this rich Germany. Pierre backed her up. "If a good producer could be found, Josephine could once again move big crowds."

At the Pimm's later, Josephine took over, telling Rex, my disc jockey, to play faster music so people would sweat, and drink more. "Look at that energy," Pierre said. "In France, nobody wants her, she is unreasonable, but try to see if some of your German friends can do something."

I took her to her hotel at 2 A.M., but she wanted to go on talking about the children. She had a brown manila envelope full of scribbled notes about her finances—money to pay grocery bills, boarding schools, her account with Marie Spiers—and pending lawsuits. The envelope was also stuffed with money; she had just been paid in cash by Schultheiss, and she was trying to translate deutsche marks into new francs.

She was also full of plans for "our German tour." I was dumbstruck. Did she believe what she was saying? At five, I went home, put five thousand marks in an envelope, grabbed two black leather suitcases, and went back to meet her for breakfast. She hadn't slept, she was still carrying on about how I should arrange the tour. "Don't trust anyone, all producers are crooks." She accepted my leather suitcases and the envelope full of money—"*Merci, mon chéri*"—and I took her and Pierre to the airport.

She was counting on me to change her life, and I was happy to have the assignment. Later, I looked in the Pimm's Club guest book. She had written, "For my little Jean-Claude the second, with a kiss from your second mother, Josephine. 1968, Happy New Year."

Now Josephine, coming back to France, was once again faced with hard reality. The furniture at Les Milandes was auctioned off on January 19, 1969. (The first auction had been real estate, the second, the contents of the houses.) All the beautiful things bought with Pepito, all the presents from the great of the world. "They even sold my wedding jewels," she complained.

It was a heartrending story, but not entirely true. During the weeks before the furniture auction, Josephine, Margaret, and a few friends had managed to spirit away sixty packed containers, some of them, says Marie Spiers, "as big as a room." Again, everything was put in Marie's name, and she was left to pay the monthly storage costs.

Even without furniture, Josephine had continued to camp out part-time at Les Milandes. At night, there were phone calls threatening to kill her cats. On March 7, she left the château with Margaret, Stellina, and Noël to join the rest of the children for the weekend in Paris.

As soon as they had gone, the new owner changed the locks. "I have been patient long enough," Monsieur Joly said.

Josephine alerted the press and rushed back, arriving at nine Sunday morning to play out the last act. She got in through a window, and before Joly's guards knew what had happened, she was barricaded in the kitchen with the devoted Madame Boudoir and a little cat. From there, she talked to the journalists staked out in the courtyard.

"I will not leave," she said. The journalists were thrilled, they passed her food through the window. All day Sunday and Monday, she stayed in the kitchen, resting on a cot. The nights were hideous with racket, the new owner had his men make noise so she could not sleep.

On Tuesday morning, the water having been cut off, Josephine headed out of the house toward an auxiliary tank. Eight of Joly's henchmen caught her, but she broke away, ran back to the kitchen, grabbed the iron bar across the front of the stove, and hung on. Her enemies followed, wrestled with her, and threw her out into the rain, hurling a doll of Stellina's and some canned goods after her. They handled her, a reporter said, like a bundle of dirty laundry.

Across the road, Henriette Malaury had been arguing with her husband and her son. Elois and Georges had got their hunting guns and wanted to go to Josephine's rescue, but Henriette, afraid of what might happen, stopped them. "I did not want to have to cry over them in jail for the rest of their lives. We called the police.

"It was very cold, the rain didn't stop. My husband and I walked over and asked Josephine to take refuge in our house. She refused. She said she wanted to stay on her property."

Which she did. She sat at the top of the stone steps leading to the kitchen. Even on that raw gray day, there were signs of spring; the vines that arched around the door were putting out new leaves. Josephine wore an old nightgown, a nightcap, and heavy glasses, the little cat sat on her knees, her feet were bare. Around her were the cans of food and some bottled water. For four hours, she stayed there in the driving rain.

Did she think of Tumpy, rummaging through the garbage pails of rich white people? What a ride that little girl had taken; even now, she could look around and know she had created her own Shangri-la, and wasn't that a victory for Elvira's scrappy grandchild?

"I went and got a bowl of warm milk and a blanket," says Henriette Malaury, who was Jean-Claude's godmother. "I forgot that a few months before, in the press, she had accused us of refusing to sell milk to her. We always gave her the milk free, but Josephine would say anything as long as she looked good in the story.

"I put the blanket on her legs to give her a little warmth until Monsieur Dumont came."

Dumont, the public prosecutor, took Josephine back into the château, and they were sitting in the kitchen discussing options—she could sue Joly for illegal entry, assault and battery, duress—when she began to feel sick. Her arms were numb, she was flooded with nausea, they were the same symptoms she had suffered with the last heart attack. An ambulance was called, and she was taken to the Périgueux hospital. "If I die tonight," she said, "I want to be buried in the pink nightgown of my agony."

She didn't die; instead, she was once again propelled onto the front pages of newspapers around the world. Over the years, the two most famous pictures of her have been the one with the girdle of bananas and the one sitting on those stone steps, a poor old lady alone in the rain.

It was Pierre Spiers who'd insisted Josephine be moved from Périgueux to Dr. Fetiveau's clinic near Paris. "When the ambulance got to the clinic," Marie says, "reporters were already there. I was shocked when I first saw Josephine. Her hands were swollen, her skin was gray. I thought it was the end of her. Then the doctors gave her an electrocardiogram and a blood transfusion, and later on, she laughed and told me she felt like a superwoman. 'They gave me *electricity*!' "

She had agreed to open in a Paris club called La Goulue on March 27, and she intended to be ready.

La Goulue had been a restaurant that the movie and theater star Jean-Claude Brialy decided to turn into a supper club. "I had seen Josephine in her farewell show at the Olympia," says Brialy, "and I contacted her with an offer. She accepted, and said she could sing ten new songs, some old hits, but I would have to help her with music and dresses. I asked all the grand couturiers, but they said, 'She is too old, she is forgotten.' Then Jany Six, who had a boutique on rue Godot de Mauroy, a street of prostitutes, said she was willing to dress Josephine free.

"We called a press conference, and that was the day Josephine heard the new owner of Les Milandes had changed the locks, and she left Paris. Wednesday night, her picture was in all the papers, in the rain with her little cat. The heart attack followed. But at the Fetiveau clinic, she was getting better every day, asking to have the dress rehearsals there! She still had the IV in her arm, and she was telling us, 'In two days, I will be up!' "

She told me the same thing when I called her from Berlin.

"It was all free publicity," says Jacques Collard, the manager of La Goulue. "Before then, we had tried a few acts, an opera singer, an all-woman orchestra, but nobody came. We racked our brains to think who might be able to make this place work, and someone suggested Josephine Baker. The night of her opening, *le tout Paris* was there.

"During the dessert, she made her entrance on the arm of Jean-Claude Brialy to resounding applause. Josephine went to the mike, thanked everyone, but said she was too tired to sing, she had got out of her bed just to be with her friends.

"The next night, she did her act. I have to tell you it did not work at all. Again, no one came. Even Josephine could not bring people into that club. But while the main room was empty, the bar was packed, mostly with gay people—Josephine was very much loved by the gay world—and she would talk with them, push champagne. She got excited every time she sold a new bottle. She liked to talk to those boys, she always said, 'They are my children.'

"During her stay with us, she learned of the death of Henri Varna. I believe she was sincerely moved, it was a part of her youth that went with him."

In Germany, I heard that my friend Gert Pempelfort was leaving for Paris, and being concerned about Josephine's most recent illness, I asked him to go see her.

He went. "She had become an old lady trying to hide the years with all that makeup and powder," he told me later, "but she had such a big personality it did not matter, there was a family feeling in that room."

"When she was at La Goulue," says Georges Debot, a journalist and gossip columnist who covered the nightclub scene, "I was living across from her on avenue MacMahon in a ground-floor apartment, and evenings she would come and knock at my window, and we would share a taxi to the club. My concierge asked me, 'Who is that old black woman who comes and knocks on your window every night?' and I told her it was Josephine Baker, but she did not believe me. Josephine would say, 'Ah, *chéri*, it is my liver and my head, I will not be able to sing tonight; with all the children and the noise, I have to sleep with earplugs.' But she would come on stage all smiles, singing; it was extraordinary.

"Once we left the club together at about 2 A.M., and a little girl was standing outside selling lilies of the valley. Josephine was appalled. A nine-year-old on the street at 2 A.M.! She gave the child some money and said, 'Go to your mother and tell her Josephine cried.' Then, turning to me, she said she would like to adopt the little girl 'but I already have twelve, I don't know what to do anymore.'

"Business at La Goulue was so terrible, I did some free publicity during the last two weeks of Josephine's run, hoping it would bring in more people. She took it very badly. I was no longer '*mon petit* Georges.' She came to me and said, 'Thank you, Monsieur, for your kindness in announcing our closing, thank you for the sorrow you have given me.' "

"Jean-Claude Brialy was very good to this old lady," says Jacques Collard. "But Paris was just acting sulky." Once again, however, Josephine's good fairy came to her rescue. Grace Kelly dropped by La Goulue with André Levasseur, who had designed her wedding gown, as well as Josephine's costumes for *Paris Mes Amours*.

Grace and Josephine had never met before, but they were like a photograph and its negative image, white daughter of a bricklayer, black daughter of a washerwoman. Both had shaken off the dust of home to become royalty abroad—Josephine, queen of the music halls; Grace, princess of Monaco. Both had been promiscuous—and ambitious—in their youth; one had married into a castle, the other had bought her own. Both had cried over their fathers; Grace couldn't please hers, Josephine couldn't find hers.

Both enchanted Charles de Gaulle.

It was inevitable that they become friends. "The princess had a great admiration for Josephine Baker as a fabulous talent," says Georgette Armita, then secretary of Monaco's Red Cross. "And she was very moved by her situation with so many children."

Besides, Grace had already heard good reports of Josephine from Miki Sawada's daughter.

Emi Sawada-Kamiya: "My father had been restored to favor, and in 1952 he was Japanese ambassador to the United Nations. We lived at 988 Fifth Avenue, and Grace Kelly lived in the same building. I used to meet her in the elevator with Oliver, her black poodle, and we became friends.

"In 1958, she invited me to spend several months in the palace with her. I was there for the birth of Albert, it was a great joy to everyone. During that time, I was corresponding with Josephine, and she wrote that she admired Princess Grace, and she sent me *La Tribu Arc-en-Ciel*, the fairy-tale book about the Rainbow Tribe. I showed it to Grace and to Princess Antoinette, Rainier's sister. They became very interested in Josephine's work."

Emi describes the princess's life in Monaco as difficult, constrained by protocol and a lack of privacy. Eventually, the princess bought an apartment in Paris, and it was in Paris that she recruited Josephine to star in Monaco's Red Cross gala. ("It was the princess of Monaco," says Madame Armita, "always in accordance with His Highness the Sovereign Prince, who made the choice of the principal artist each year.") Josephine not only agreed to perform, she refused a salary—"It's for charity." (Still, she could keep all the clothes being made for her.)

A few days before the gala, there was a screening of *Zou Zou*. Pepito's old friend, Arys Nissotti, supplied the print. "It was to be an evening to help Josephine Baker and her children, who no longer had anything," says Georgette Armita. "The princess personally organized it. It was difficult, because Josephine was a little forgotten, but the princess called her friends, and the entire evening's receipts were given to Madame Baker."

"The screening was in an open-air theater," Jari says. "And Mother was complaining: 'It is such an old film, I do not like to see myself in it.' But since it was organized by the princess, we all had to go. It was funny because Mother would always fall asleep during a movie, and that night, one of us had to give her a little poke every time we saw her head falling, since she was seated next to the princess."

"Josephine's great joy during our stay in Monte Carlo was not the gala," says Marie Spiers, "nor the shows during the rest of the week—for which she *was* paid—nor playing to millionaires and movie stars, it was that we had been invited to spend an afternoon at the palace.

"The boys wore white trousers, blue blazers, white gloves, and Marianne and Stellina were in white dresses. We were led into the gardens, and the prince went to his zoo and picked up a little lion for the children to play with.

"Josephine was a big success in Monte Carlo, and the children were a tourist attraction on the beach, but we had no money, so she went off to do a gala in Venice. When I joined her there, I found she had taken a splendid suite in the Royal Danieli. The minute I saw her, I said, 'You are not being serious, I warn you, I have no money left.' 'Ah, Marie,' she said, 'everyone was so charming to me, I was obliged to take an exclusive suite.'

"That night, as she went onstage, the producers of the gala came to me. 'Madame, we would like to do something for Josephine, but we are afraid to offend her, can you help us?' I could not believe my ears. I said, 'Well, I know she will object, but why don't you pay the hotel bill?'

"After the show, I told her what had happened. She said, 'You see, Marie, you should not have worried.' "

Feeling welcome in Monte Carlo, Josephine started to look around on her own for a little house. She found a villa in Roquebrune, on the French side of the border between France and Monaco; it was a modest place, but since she didn't have the money to buy even a modest place, she called the Red Cross.

"She got me on the phone," says Georgette Armita. "She told me her problem, I told the princess, and the princess decided to help Madame Baker." She made the down payment, and then had the house put in the name of a Real Estate property company, to be administered by the Red Cross. Josephine would never again be evicted.

She left Monaco knowing she had a home to come back to, and indeed, when she and the children returned in the fall, the Villa Maryvonne was in perfect readiness. "The princess was president of the Red Cross," Madame Armita says, "and we had furnished the house. Beds, dishes, whatever was needed. We even took care of finding new schools for the children."

Stellina would go to class with Princess Stephanie, all was right with the world.

Chapter 41

—

MAMAN IS
TOUGH ON THE KIDS . . .
AND HERSELF

"At a certain age, one should stop having sex"

The way Josephine seduced people was to make them think she owed everything in her life to them.

She did it with me, she did it with the Grimaldis. Her Christmas card for the year 1969 was a fairy tale about three "adorable" children living in a castle not far from "twelve tiny tots who were blown together by a soft wind as a symbol of universal brotherhood. . . ."

It was part inspirational and part boot-licking, as she attempted to bind herself and her family ever more tightly to the rulers of Monaco.

The little villa in Roquebrune that looked out over the bay of Cap Martin was far from the paradise that she proclaimed it. With four bedrooms, two baths, twelve children, it was crowded, and the mostly adolescent tribe was no longer manageable.

Perhaps it never had been. The children grew up with chaos the only thing they could be sure of. "Life was somewhat more normal when we moved from Les Milandes to Paris," Brahim recalls, "and Roquebrune was even better. There were palm trees and the swimming pool at the Sporting Club (as guests of the princess), but it was the beginning of another time; the older boys were growing up and there were unbelievable fights. That was when my mother started to say, 'No long hair, no bell-bottoms, no flowered shirts.' "

It wasn't easy to assert one's individuality in the teeth of Josephine's decrees. "Bell-bottoms are for homosexuals," she would announce. "Most of her friends were homosexual," Brahim says, "but if we opposed her, her reaction was to slap us or scold us. 'One does not argue with parents, one respects them.'

"One time we called her because she was on TV, she was dancing the Charleston, half naked, and she came and turned off the set. She was furious. We thought we could make a point that she had broken all the fashion rules so why couldn't we be a little bit free. 'What about you, Mother, in the days when you greased your hair and wore bananas?'

"Luis was the first to rebel. He refused to get rid of his flowered shirts, and she did not know what to do. Luis was one of the taller ones, one of the stronger ones, and while he did not quite put it that way, what he meant was, 'Try and force me, I am no longer a kid.'

"That's when my mother called Maguy Chauvin's husband, and asked him to come over and play the father role. Later on, she would ask Brialy to do the same. Even you, Jean-Claude, had to go through it. But we were too much to handle, ten rowdy boys in two bedrooms, it stank in there.

"Actually, it was eight boys, because Akio slept downstairs, and Jari had already moved to Argentina. The reason for Jari's being sent away was that my mother had found him and a friend in a bathtub, fondling each other.

"She sent him straight to our father. She told Uncle and Auntie she was afraid he would 'contaminate' us, and we would all become homosexuals."

"I remember the scene very well," says Jean-Claude. "It was the night [Neil] Armstrong walked on the moon. Mother gathered us together, Aunt Margaret and Uncle Elmo were there too, and it was like a court-martial.

"She said, 'Here it is. Your brother is not like you.' She had always told us we were all the same, all equal, now she was saying the opposite, and we did not understand.

"She rendered justice her way, there was nothing you could say. And poor Jari was there with his head bent."

Jari, that most amiable of boys, says he never felt betrayed or rejected. "I am what I am, I thought it would be easier to grow up around Daddy. He was rational, we were friends. He taught me to be careful; he said in the gay community relationships are short, men are always after novelty. He helped me, and so did my brothers and sisters. They never reproached me for being homosexual."

"With her own friends," says Brahim, "my mother gave the impression of having a good time, laughing, but with us, she did not want to appear frivolous. When we played her records, she would say, 'Children, you can listen to them when I am not around.' She tried to hide her artistic side from us. She wanted us to remember her as a respectable mother."

I thought of what Kenza had said, that it was a shame the children never knew the real Josephine. They found Jo Bouillon more "normal," which further upset her. Jo had come for the family's first Christmas at Roquebrune. "He asked us what we wanted," Brahim says, "and we wanted bicycles or mopeds, which my mother refused to give us—she was afraid we would hurt ourselves—and he bought them.

"She did not say anything on Christmas day, but five or six days later, Luis did not give her a kiss before breakfast, and she slapped his face.

"My father said, 'Josephine, this is Christmas vacation, do not start a fight,' but they argued, and he left two days later. As soon as he was gone, she took all the bikes and mopeds back to the store.

"My father came back two or three times, but my mother was afraid we would become more attached to him, since he was rational, sensible, very French, Cartesian, whereas one could say that she was very American and extreme. At Les Milandes, she had given us an allowance, and when the public school principal told her we had more money than the other children and that wasn't good, overnight we had no allowance at all. We couldn't even buy chewing gum, and if you tried to beg or borrow, people would say, 'You're the son of Josephine Baker, you have a castle,' so some of us started to steal.

"We all did our share, and so we were all punished. You can't imagine how many times, since almost every day, someone would break a window, and we would be asked, 'Who did it?' and no one would say. In a way, this impressed my mother. 'They are so united they will not give each other up,' she told a friend. 'That pleases me even if their upbringing is not an absolute success.'

"I think she must have had mixed feelings toward us when we became teenagers, and the older ones started telling her, 'No one can hit us anymore, especially not your male friends.' She was losing ground, she stood in front of us in her robe, like a grandmother confronting seventeen-year-old boys. One day, she just gave up. Overnight, we were given total freedom, even Noël, who was only twelve or thirteen."

Josephine was plagued not only by her inability to control the children, but by the bills that followed her to Villa Maryvonne. She still owed social security for the employees at Les Milandes, she still owed taxes, she had to keep working. That spring, she wrote Harry Hurford-Janes and his wife, Peggy, asking them to take some of the boys for the summer. "Be careful before you answer," she warned, "because they eat a lot."

Josephine said she wanted her "four devils"—Akio, Jean-Claude, Luis, Mara—to become "real English gentlemen." (Moïse, another troublemaker, had already been sent to Israel to work on a kibbutz.)

In August, an AP reporter came to Villa Maryvonne to interview Josephine, and she confessed to having reservations about the Black Power movement.

"I suppose," she said, "if I go back to the States, they'll say I'm an Uncle Tom. But I would ask the young boys and girls of color what they would do with the white boys and girls who believe in the right ideals. . . . The last time I was in Chicago, a Negro boy told me he wanted to kill all the white people. . . ."

The reporter went away and filed his piece. The star declared afterward that she had not intended to denigrate Black Power, it was just that those words gave her "an impression of separation among human beings instead of unity . . . for years we of another generation felt humiliated when our brothers were called black or nigger. . . ."

She wrote this in a letter that included her most recent—troubled—musings on children. "Very few of us understand our children," she said. "We . . . have perhaps made great mistakes in bringing them up. . . . Neglect, bad teaching at home, bad manners, the wrong influences, too much freedom, too much money, drugs, too many fine clothes, cars . . . Many parents are . . . slowly realizing that they should say, 'It's my fault. . . .' "

On November 11, 1970, Charles de Gaulle died.

"France has become a widow," President Pompidou declared, and Josephine, weeping, asked Marie Spiers to send a heart-shaped wreath of white roses with a banner saying "From Josephine and her Tribe."

"All that concerns the Resistance and General de Gaulle is like a sword that pierces my heart," she said, in a letter to the conservator of the Jean Moulin Centre. "When we refer to those years, 1939–45, we evoke a name . . . joined to that era the way the links of a chain are welded together."

In Berlin, I had been calling friends, asking them to help get Josephine work. All advised me to forget it. "She's playing dates in little bars, how do you expect anyone to present her in a leading theater?"

It was true, she was taking any kind of job. A summer tour in Italy had gone well? She would call me, reproach in her voice that I had not been able to stimulate the same enthusiasm for her in Germany, while neglecting to say the producer of the Italian tour hadn't paid her.

But then she would have Stellina send me a drawing—it was addressed to "janclode de berlin" and bore the legend "I love you very much"—or have Marianne write, saying, "Dear Big Brother, Maman tells us how kind you are." How could I turn away?

Early in December, the Pimm's Club would celebrate its third anniversary, and I was going to put on a charity show to help orphans in Berlin and Israel. I decided to star Josephine, who expressed her delight on paper. "My dear little Jean-Claude No. 2, thank you for what you are doing for me . . . And for abandoned children in Berlin and Israel. You know my little Moïse has been in a kibbutz there for the past six months, but I'm going to have him come back because there is an epidemic of cholera. . . ."

I built a tent over the parking lot, put down red carpet, installed gold chairs and an antique sofa for the mayor and his wife; I knew the mayor's presence would appeal to Josephine, she was crazy about titles, even if the title holder was an ex-dictator or an unfrocked priest.

I met her at the airport, still accompanied by her cardboard satchels. Why didn't she use the leather cases I had given her? Because a saint who lived for brotherhood did not require such ostentatious luggage.

But she didn't mind getting into my Mercedes.

My cousin Jacqueline Angonin (Nadette's sister) had offered to act as Josephine's dresser. "She was double my age, but marvelous," Jacqueline says. "Oh, that body. I will never forget her arms. I tied her into a wide rubber cinch that laced in back; she kept saying, 'Tighter, tighter.'

"She needed that show life, she lived off it, when she hit the stage, she exploded."

The night of the gala, Josephine waited in the Pimm's Club kitchen while I introduced "the Universal Mother, my mother, our mother." On her way to the stage, people grabbed at her hands. Her dress was daring, a kind of fishnet in gold, loosely draped, and she had glued sequins under her eyes to cover the bags; it was, I thought, a gorgeous act of bravado.

After the cheers died down, she told the audience she had overheard two girls talking in the kitchen. "One said, 'You know, Jean-Claude's mother is here.'

" 'Oh? Who is that?'

" 'Josephine Baker.'

" 'Well yes, but who is that?'

" 'I don't know. I can only tell you my parents always talk about *their* parents' honeymoon trip to Paris when they went to the Folies-Bergère, where Josephine Baker was dancing naked with a girdle of bananas. . . .' "

She paused. "Well, little girls, it is already three generations . . . but during all those years, I have been happy . . . because I love people . . . because I need people . . ."

Behind her, the violins began as she started to sing "People." She brought the room to tears.

I was almost in tears for quite a different reason. Right before her entrance, noting the TV camera and lights, she had stopped short. "What is that?" I told her it was the crew from the TV news show, she had rehearsed for them that afternoon, and even asked that they bring lavender gels through which to shoot her. Her face set in hard lines. "If they want to film me, I want five hundred marks before I go on."

I was panicked, she was balking, and the TV people were leaving, outraged. (They refused to let me pay her out of my own pocket.) It was beginning to be clear to me why no big producers were fighting to present the famous Josephine Baker. And yet, she was wonderful. At the end of the show, she called me onstage to take a bow with her. Later, we held a press conference at my apartment, and Josephine talked about her children. She produced an old wallet full of pictures; to my dismay, she had to peer at the back of each photograph to remind herself of the child's name and age. As she spoke to the reporters, she held on her lap Marcel-Roger Cicero, the two-year-old son of Eugene Cicero, the show's pianist. "Children are the most wonderful gift on earth," she said.

She also told us that Marshal Tito had given her an island in the Adriatic. Not long ago, it had housed criminals, but soon it would be the site of the College of Brotherhood. (Some of the children had gone with her to check it out. "It was only rocks," Brahim says, "nothing but rocks. She began climbing around, pointing—'This will be the sports center, here the club, here the office . . .' When we left, Tito gave each of us a watch.")

Recently, I interviewed Rajko Medenica, Tito's doctor, who had given the Yugoslav leader cellular therapy shots believed to slow the aging process. "Tito was a bon vivant," the doctor said, "and for him, your mother was one of the greatest figures of the artistic world. She visited him on Brioni, his favorite island, and he asked me to come there. He said, 'I would like for this lady to stay exactly as she is now.' I can't remember how many times I gave her injections."

Maybe cellular therapy supplied her with strength for the demon housekeeping she practiced. Her last night in Berlin in my apartment, she redecorated. When I got up in the morning, I found my house-keeper sitting speechless on the sofa. The living room had been remod-eled. Josephine had managed to move a couch, a big TV set, even a Biedermeier secretary. On top of the secretary, she had set a blue crystal vase holding a red plastic rose that an admirer had given her the night before. I was in shock. Still, I managed to say thanks and go to comfort the housekeeper, because Josephine had also cleaned the kitchen, which the housekeeper took as a tacit reproach.

After breakfast, she suddenly announced that she was going to go to the market because, she said, "I want to buy meat, butter, and eggs. You know, Jean-Claude, they are much better here than in France."

"Mother, that's crazy," I said with a laugh. "By the time you arrive home, you will have an omelet."

Not liking my answer, Josephine went across the hallway and woke my neighbor, Eugene Cicero (she had already fallen in love with his son). To his astonishment, she enlisted him to accompany her and off they went on a mad food-buying spree—which he ended up paying for, of course.

When they returned, I greeted her at the door dressed in a crazy new outfit I had recently bought on a trip to Carnaby Street, then the fashion center of "mod, swinging London." I had hoped for a "bravo" from her. Instead, she sneered. "My poor darling," she said. "Don't you know that fashion, like life, is an endless cycle?" Then, inexplicably, she added, "Oh my God, I hope you're not doing drugs."

I was puzzled by her remark because I had never done drugs. I wondered if it wasn't my outfit that had caused her snap judgment. I didn't have much time to reflect on that, however, because suddenly she was off on one of her reveries.

"When I was with Picasso and Jeannot [Jean Cocteau], I would go to that whorehouse, and on the third floor, there was an opium tent, and poor Jean would succumb to drugs," she recalled.

Her amazing story set off all kinds of questions in my mind. "What was the saintly Josephine doing in a whorehouse?" I wondered. And though I knew Cocteau was gay, I was dying to ask her, "Mother, did you f. . . Picasso?" But I knew that if I'd broached that subject, she would never again open up her past to me.

Rushing for the plane, she continued her lessons. "Your introduction last night was very nice," she told me in the car. "But, don't forget, when you are in a foreign country, you always do two things: You praise the blue sky above and the most famous person of that moment." Then another lesson. "Jean-Claude, never be ashamed of what you are doing. But do the best. Even if you are a street cleaner, be proud of having the best-cleaned streets in the city."

At the door of the plane, she kissed me. "You have to come and meet your brothers and sisters. I know that you will love them very much."

With ten thousand marks and still another new set of luggage (again, gifts from me), she left for Monte Carlo, from which she wrote to Willy Brandt, chancellor of the Federal Republic of Germany, explaining that she would be playing Berlin, Munich, Frankfort, Düsseldorf, and Hamburg in January, and that she and I had made this plan together.

"These five great performances are to be given to help poor children of each city and Israel, and to help me pay the rest due on my house. I do not wish another shock like the one that happened to me at the Milandes. We will need your help, tax-wise, organization-wise, publicity-wise, etc. Jean-Claude will certainly contact you either by telephone or by correspondence. Please do try to help us."

The projected German tour was entirely in her head—it was never going to happen—which didn't stop her from suggesting that I should contact not only Willy Brandt, but also the the jet-setting Krupp munitions heir, who lived on an allowance of nine hundred thousand dollars a year. "He is very interesting and very generous," she said. (She had not forgotten the largesse of his father and his grandfather when she had first come to Berlin with *La Revue Nègre*.)

In March 1971, she was in Berlin again to perform at a gay ball. She had to work with a strange pianist who didn't know her routine, the show was terrible, and she was angry with herself. "Next time, *mon chéri*, you will be in charge," she told me as we fled the place.

Again, we talked till all hours. She was planning a tour of Brazil, but was concerned lest the Brazilian producer go broke as the Italian one had done the year before. I advised her to have the money put in escrow in Paris before she left.

Then I showed her the phonograph record I had just made. It was my first, and for the liner notes, in the time-honored tradition of show business, I had lied about everything. I claimed to have gone to Paris (after the death of my father) to study acting with Michel Simon and dancing with Roland Petit. "Do not go into show business," said Josephine. "The artist's life is very difficult and ugly."

This was strange, coming from someone who looked so happy onstage. I hadn't yet read her early memoirs, in which she had talked about the disillusion of "this artificial life . . . The work of a star disgusts me now. . . . What this star has to do, what she has to bear . . . disgusts me. Bad things, sad things. I want to work another three or four years, and then I will leave the stage. . . . I will have children . . . but if one of my children one day wants to go on the stage, I will strangle him with these two hands, I swear it."

On April 12, she wrote to thank me for a check of one thousand dollars. "I am sending it off right away to the Foundation for the future school. . . . A thousand million kisses from your second Mama. . . . See you in Rio." (She had invited me to be her companion in Brazil, and I'd said yes.)

I was at the Rio airport to meet her, but she was in a foul mood. I said the city was magnificent, she snarled, "You know nothing!" She hadn't set foot in Brazil for twenty years, but had already made up her mind about it. "Nothing has changed, the skyscrapers may have got taller, but the misery of the people has only dug deeper into the earth!"

Her Brazilian producer had spread a red carpet on the tarmac, there was French champagne in a VIP welcome room where she was to meet the press, but she wouldn't move toward the red carpet or the journalists. A pretty young girl with long black hair came up to her and explained that she was the assistant of Flavio Cavalcanti, on whose live television show Josephine was booked to appear. "It's the most popular show in Brazil," said the girl.

Josephine grabbed her by the arm, said, "Let's go to the hotel," and left me to take care of the producer.

We followed her to the Savoy, where she spoke a few words—"I'm an old woman now, but still fighting for human rights"—and begged to be excused. "My oldest son, Jean-Claude, will stay with you." Then, to me: "You know what to say, but don't talk too much." I was brilliant; I gave the "I'm happy to be under the skies of Brazil" speech, and asked everyone to understand that Josephine was exhausted, a brave old lady fighting with so much courage for brotherhood. When I joined her in her suite, she was drinking fresh sugar-cane juice. "It's good for the body."

My birthday was the next day. I woke to find her standing beside me with a little box; it held a gold tie clip from H. Stern. "As soon as I'm rich again," she said, "I will put a diamond in it." That night, we were among twenty people invited to dine with the owner of *Manchete*, Brazil's most important weekly magazine, and I dressed in hot colors to match the hot music, the hot sun of Brazil. Josephine took one look and redecorated me, choosing a blue suit and a white shirt. "We are representing France, we must be elegant."

The restaurant was on the beach; Josephine wore a long multicolored caftan and went barefoot, we ate lobsters and drank champagne. At that time of the evening, beggar women carrying babies sauntered along the sidewalks of Copacabana. There were stories that they rented the babies in order to evoke sympathy and bigger tips. One of the women came right up to our table, whereupon Josephine yelped, dropped a lobster claw, plucked a naked child from the stunned woman's arms, and demanded that a waiter bring her warm water. He fetched a lobster steamer in which she proceeded to immerse the filthy infant. Then, forgetting the baby, she wheeled on the journalists in our party.

"You want to interview me about fashion? About life in France? What you should write about is your own people's misery!" She lectured them, and she lectured the rich ladies, decrying their Diors, their jewels—"You think I don't recognize Cartier?" Some who were insulted left the table, as Josephine turned back to the half-drowned baby. Lifting him out of his bath, she held him on her hip as she went around collecting money from those still seated at our table. Then she presented the money and the damp baby to his mother. Or his renter.

Happy with her performance, she expected applause. When none was forthcoming, she cried, "Shame on you!" and ran into the street. "Happy birthday!" she yelled back at me as she got into a taxi. I apologized for her—"Her weakness is children"—but the remaining guests were cool. "It must be very difficult to live with her," said one lady.

Flavio Cavalcanti's show was broadcast live every Sunday; it came out of the old Beira-Mar Casino, where Josephine had worked in its glory days. Now it was a sad, run-down place with dressing rooms like jail cells, all dirty walls and peeling plaster.

Josephine got into a black lace jumpsuit, added a curly wig, glitter under the eyes, and when she was finished she stood studying herself in a big mirror. The last time she was here, she had been twenty-three, drunk with success. Forty-two years had passed, countries had disappeared, others had been born, but she could still look into that mirror and be proud.

"Come on," she said, "let's go to rehearsal." By the time we found the rehearsal room, a young singer was already working with the orchestra. We had been due at five, and it was five past. Upset that people wouldn't wait for her more than five minutes, she led me outside into an open courtyard filled with garbage cans. The smell was terrible, the sun pitiless, but we leaned against the cans, and she talked. Not really to me, to herself.

It was like Sidney Bechet returning to a theater in Montmartre thirty years after he had first played there. "You come in the door," he said, "and you're in the same place and nothing seems to be changed. . . . But all the time you know how much has changed. . . . You don't believe you can go back. . . ."

For four hours and thirty minutes under that killing sun, she talked. About 1929, and Pepito and how she had been attacked as immoral by the president of Argentina, and the fights in the streets, and the theaters selling out every night, and the madness and the music—"How beautiful is the tango in Argentina.

"And Brazil! I was so powerful that the president killed himself because I told him he had sold his country to America. He shot himself with a gun, and the people carried me on their shoulders through the streets, I could have led a revolution, but I left, it was not my country." (Later, I discovered that a Brazilian president, Getulio Vargas, had indeed killed himself in Rio, though Josephine wasn't there when it happened.)

I could hear Alvero, the pianist, calling, "Miss Baker, Miss Baker," and gratefully, I got off my garbage can. "Stay here!" she ordered. Then she sent me to fetch some toilet paper. "It's the only way to blot your makeup without leaving spots." Well, at least I was learning some show business tricks.

I came back with the toilet paper. "Did you know," she said, "that the dark-haired girl is Flavio's mistress?"

"No, but it doesn't surprise me, she is good-looking."

"Well, I'm not going to talk to her anymore."

She must have sensed my growing apprehension. "In difficult moments, you should pray," she advised. "It helps kill time."

"Mother," I said, "it's almost a quarter to nine."

"So let's go." A last patting of her face with toilet paper, and we're on our way.

In the studio, there is frenzy. "Where have you been?"

"Never mind where I've been," says Josephine. "I'm here on time."

Twenty musicians await her cue, they don't know what she's going to do first, and neither does she, but she knows Alvero will save her. She says a few words to the audience, they applaud, as Flavio's girlfriend walks onstage with a bunch of roses. "Miss Baker, would you answer a few questions?"

"Go away, dirty girl!" says Miss Baker.

The girl, near tears, tries again. Josephine turns her back, and stamps her foot angrily; her high heel comes down on the girl's instep. The girl screams and falls, clutching her bleeding foot. A cameraman moves quickly to Josephine's face; she produces a smile and launches into a ballad.

Backstage, a priest stands with twenty young children dressed in white, each holding a white rose. "They're orphans," the stage manager tells me, "they're supposed to bring the flowers to Josephine, but it may be better not to send them out there after what she just did to that girl."

I say, "Send them out right now." One by one, the children walk on and hand Josephine the roses. She stops singing, seats the little ones in a half circle around her, sits down with them, her back to the audience, and says, "You are not alone anymore because I am your mother and I love you very much."

After several moments of discourse (on brotherhood, freedom, the Rainbow Children), with blood still on the stage, she begins to sing, "People, people who need people, are the luckiest people in the world . . ."

The audience gives her a standing ovation, but Flavio refuses to acknowledge her when she comes off, he is too busy screaming, "Never again will I have her on my show, I don't give a damn about Josephine Baker, that fucking bitch, and her fucking Rainbow Children." His English is perfect.

Afterward, I ask her why she behaved so badly. "I don't like young girls with old men," she says. "At a certain age, one should stop having sex; your brothers and sisters will never be able to say they have seen me with a man since Jo left me. Never."

I tell her Flavio isn't that old, she says, "Be quiet!"

(Jacqueline Abtey confirms that in Josephine's later years, there were no more adventures with men. "She surrounded herself with women, nurses, secretaries. A lot of young girls were in her entourage, so people talked, but by then they had seen so much that nothing could surprise them.")

Before leaving Rio, Josephine insisted we go to a Macumba church in the hills beyond the city. Long ago, she said, she had been made a goddess of the Macumba. We took a cab through terrible slums, the driver trying to maneuver according to the goddess's instructions—"It's around here, take a left, no, a right." We were lost, it was getting dark, and she was explaining to me that in the old days the Macumba had offered human sacrifices to their gods. "Today"—a note of disdain— "they use chicken or goats!"

We finally gave up and came back to the hotel, Josephine disappointed but glad she had tried.

Next on the tour, Pôrto Alegre. The producer and Alvero flew there direct, but Josephine and I took a puddle jumper that made four stops. Why? Because Madame wished to meet the press at every landing.

On our way to the airport, we passed a pet shop, and she spied three monkeys in the window. "We can't leave them in that terrible place, they'll die."

"But Mother, we will miss the plane."

"Jean-Claude, don't be so cruel, they are crying for help! Driver, *momento, por favor*—" and we were out of the cab, and into the store. Josephine chatted up the owner—how much were the monkeys? how was his mother?—though the poor man was easily sixty-five and had surely lost his mother long ago. Down on the floor in the back of the shop was another bunch of monkeys in a cage, tiny ouistitis, no bigger than Parisian sparrows, with tails twice as long as their bodies. There were twelve of them, some going bald. Once Josephine discovered them, new negotiations over price ensued.

After an incredible amount of bargaining, she got the monkeys—I paid for them—and the two largest birdcages in the store. We put the twelve ouistitis in one, the three larger monkeys in the other, and we left, me with a cage under each arm. A mob had gathered outside, faithful viewers who had seen Josephine on Flavio's show. There were requests for autographs, children to be kissed, before we could leave.

On the plane, another circus. She didn't want the air conditioning, it would be bad for the monkeys. She was feeding them mashed bananas through the bars, talking softly to them. "My little darlings, you are so beautiful, don't be afraid anymore." After a while, she fell asleep.

When she awoke, she wanted to discuss—again—the Rainbow Tribe. "You have to come home to your brothers and sisters, they are growing up, and it's so hard for me alone. Am I a good mother, Jean-Claude? Do I give them what they need?" (These were questions I was not equipped to answer, never having seen her and her children together.) "They miss a father," she said, "we need a father at home."

She talked about Jo Bouillon. "On our wedding night, he came to our bed crying, and confessed he was gay. He said he had married me because I was a myth."

Not knowing what I know today, I grieved for her. But I wasn't the only one. Dear Maman, I swear *you* believed—100 percent—that you were reciting the facts.

If Josephine was pouring her heart out to me, so was I to her. I told her how upset I was with my own mother. I wanted to buy her a chic apartment in Dijon, but my mother wouldn't hear of it. She wanted a more "humble" place. In fact, she'd found one already and had fallen in love with its draperies.

"Jean-Claude, you want to make her happy?" asked Josephine. "Buy her the place she wants."

It was a direct answer—and a good one. My mother was the happiest and proudest after she moved into that apartment.

From Rio, she had wired the French consul in Pôrto Alegre, telling him what time we would be getting in, orchestrating her arrival. Still, she worried. "Will he be there?"

When we landed, we could see from the windows that there was a welcoming committee, a group that included the consul and an accordion player. Josephine told me to sit still while everyone else deplaned. Let those who were waiting for her wonder, "Is she coming?"

She would create a little suspense, hang back just long enough, then, at the right moment, appear in the doorway, start down the stairs. When she hit the bottom step, I was to follow. Her descent was simple, dignified, accompanied by the "Marseillaise" on the accordion.

"We are so proud to have you here, Madame," said the consul. "You bring us a breath of France."

She was thanking those gathered to honor "a poor old woman like me," as I finally appeared with the monkeys. "My son, Jean-Claude" was introduced. I can still see her, happy, tired, charming everyone with that velvet voice.

At the hotel, we had a big suite; she gave the smaller room over to the monkeys, and hung a DO NOT DISTURB sign on the door. Under the words DO NOT DISTURB she wrote "the monkeys."

The rehearsal in Pôrto Alegre was a disaster. The musicians couldn't read the charts, Josephine forgot words, missed cues, lost the beat, and the theater was only half sold out, an embarrassment, because the French consul and his wife were coming.

I helped Josephine dress: red velvet gown with black fox hem and sleeves, and over this, an embroidered coat so tight she couldn't peel it off by herself.

The music started, "Paris Mes Amours." Josephine talked to the people: "How do you like me? . . . I love you . . ." But one by one, musicians were putting down their instruments and shuffling off the stage. She was too hard to follow, so *adiós*. Only Alvero remained at his piano. Momentarily stunned, Josephine called for me. "Jean-Claude, come quickly, help Mother do her striptease!"

The audience laughed, as she introduced me. "This is Jean-Claude, the thirteenth of my twelve adopted children, the oldest." Polite applause. I began to wrestle her out of the coat—it took all my strength to undo the hooks and eyes—while, for the benefit of the audience, she caroled to me, "Turn your head, you're too young to see me strip!" Then, in a fierce whisper, "What are you doing? Why does it take you so long? Hurry, you good-for-nothing!" In time, the coat was separated from the wearer, and she sent me off with it. "Go now, let Mother work," she said, to more laughter and applause.

She made it through the rest of the show. Alvero didn't fail her and she didn't fail herself; she was never better than when she faced a challenge. The finale was corny but effective: rudimentary drawings of her (dancing naked with bananas; in an air force uniform; with twelve children) dropped down from the flies in a traveling version of the Jorama. As the last picture descended, Josephine fell to her knees and, gazing skyward, bawled, "IIIIII did it MYYYYYY WAYYYYYY . . ." The audience clapped till their hands must have hurt.

On her way to the dressing room, worn but victorious, she said, "You see? They love me, it's just bad organization, we should have been sold out!"

She seemed to enjoy the havoc she created, like a pyromaniac who starts a fire, turns in the alarm, and then is first on the scene to try to put out the blaze. She was a sorceress and a mischief-maker and she could always make me laugh. On a night when an elderly gentleman in Pôrto Alegre invited me to visit some old ruins, she muttered to me, "Be careful, he wants to show you *his* old ruin." How could I be irritable with such a woman?

The next day she was flying to Buenos Aires. She had asked me to come with her. Much as she missed Jari, it was almost as though she was afraid to see Jo by herself. But the two weeks' tour through Brazil had almost killed me. I said I was going back to Rio for a week's vacation. She understood, and gave me motherly advice. "You're a good-looking boy, so be careful, there is a lot of syphilis in Rio."

At the last minute, somebody had told her she couldn't take monkeys out of the country without a permit from the Board of Health. She went mad. One monkey she could have hidden under her coat, but not fifteen. She called the French consul, who called a colonel in the cavalry who was also a veterinarian, and willing to help. He came to the hotel, and she served him tea and apologies. "Monsieur le Colonel, I'm so sorry to disturb you, but Monsieur le Consul was kind enough to tell you of my little problem. It's really nothing, just a few monkeys . . ."

She wrote to me when she got back to Roquebrune to say that Pelé (I had named one of the ouistitis Pelé in honor of his famous country-man) was doing nicely. "You should see him, he looks very Parisian in the little pink sweater I knitted for him."

By mid-May, there was bad news. "Little Pelé is dead."

In short order, fourteen of the fifteen monkeys went to the big ménagerie in the sky. Josephine had carried the last survivor to Prince Rainier and begged him to care for it in his zoo, but even there, it didn't live. To save fifteen monkeys from the place where God had put them, my second mother, filled with goodwill and ignorance, took them away and killed every one of them.

"When Pelé died," my brother Noël says, "Maman kept him in her arms for hours, cradling him as if she could bring him back to life."

Chapter 42

—

A PLAN
TO MAKE THREE
MILLION DOLLARS
IN AMERICA

"She knew how to profit from her friends"

lfred Biolek, a Munich-based producer, recalls her appearance on his television show, *Nightclub*.

"When she started her second song, she walked among the tables, and there was a young man sitting at one of them, and she leaned toward him and touched his shoulder while she was singing. And he started swinging his body to the rhythm of the song, so she kind of had to swing with him. And when there was a little pause in her song, she just looked at him, and said, 'Too late.' He was a young blond boy, and the swinging was like flirting, you know. And she said, 'Too late.' It was wonderful."

In many ways, it was too late for the family as well. Their closeness was an illusion. Moïse had come back from Israel an outsider who didn't know where he belonged. He now had "complexes," as Josephine put it in a heartbroken letter to Harry Hurford-Janes.

Worse still, she told Harry, Jean-Claude No. 1 had become a bigot, talking like Adolf Hitler. Even in Africa, he instructed his black mother, he would know that he was superior, "for the blacks are lazy, dirty . . . without any intelligence. . . ."

The shock had been terrible, Josephine confided to Harry. "Jean-Claude is racist."

I asked Jean-Claude about this episode. Had he really made such an ugly speech? "I don't remember," he said. "But if I said it, it must have been out of spite. I knew I could push that button, I knew how to provoke her."

That was the year, Akio says, "that my mother went to see the pope to demonstrate that what she had accomplished was a success. Not only had she gathered races together, but religions, that was what we children represented. She had asked for an audience in order to show that she had been ecumenical before the Church had.

"We had a private audience with the Holy Father, and as we left, he gave us key rings with the Vatican seal."

All through 1971, Josephine was scrabbling for bookings; there was never enough money. If you had given her one million dollars at 9 A.M. by 4 P.M., she would have been in front of the *métro* entrance, begging for a token—and getting it from somebody.

"I met her again in Spain," says George Reich (with whom she'd had her differences in *Paris Mes Amours*). "She was broken down, but she still had the magic, because she was a *monstre sacré*. The owner of the theater where my company was playing took pity on her and asked me to put her in our show for a week. I had to lend her costumes, wigs, her music scores were terrible, it was sad. She was trying to do the Charleston, all that bullshit. She came and asked me, 'Do you have any feathers?' She and Mistinguett had been the queens of feathers, and now nothing was left, she was like a bag lady, it was a shame."

Some who loved her didn't see the shame of it. "Her makeup then was as outrageous as a drag queen's," says Coccinelle, the most famous transsexual in France. "She did not care, it was funny, marvelous. Once, knowing I was in the audience, she stopped the orchestra. 'Ah, my daughter is here among us, big applause for my daughter Coccinelle.' On her day off, she would cook couscous for our company, we were her children *du spectacle*."

Her phone calls to me in Berlin were incessant. I knew she wanted me, like a kind of minor-league Pepito, to travel with her, take care of her. She would send pathetic notes from all over: "If you could come and see me in Eindhoven, it would give me great pleasure," and sign them, "Your little Mother and your brothers and sisters."

I hatched a plan. First, I took a wonderful theater, the Hochschule für Musik, for one night only. Under the patronage of Mayor Schutz, I would organize another benefit for my orphans and the Rainbow Tribe. It would be an all-star event, Josephine backed up by the singing and dancing Kessler twins, Alice and Ellen, the pride of Germany.

Georges Debot, covering the event for the French press, came to rehearsal. The director said he'd told the Kesslers that Madame Baker would like to rehearse, but they'd said, 'We are not yet finished.' Josephine smiled. 'Leave them alone, the little ones, they still *need* rehearsals.' "

To introduce my two mothers, I had no rehearsal. My mother and my sister Marie Jo had come for the big show, and were staying at my apartment. Entering with Josephine, I said with a flourish, "Mother, this is Mother." My birth mother was diffident—"Oh, *merci*, Madame, for what you are doing for my Jean-Claude." Josephine poured on the snake oil—"*Mais non*, you gave me an angel, call me Sister . . ."

I left them, and went back to the theater.

"Josephine was marvelous," Marie Jo told me later. "She talked about the troubles she was having with Marianne and her oldest boys. We talked about my two-year-old, Agathe, and we discussed giving birth. She asked me to squeeze six lemons in warm water for her, she said it was full of vitamins, and that's why she had such a figure."

She was sharing a dressing room with Romy Haag, a beautiful transvestite stripper. "I was embarrassed to undress in front of her," Romy said. " 'Don't be,' she said. 'When I started in Paris, I was naked on the stage.'

"To me, she looked like a nice old lady, she just undressed and started putting on some stockings. I finished my makeup, looked at her again, and would you believe it? She was still putting on stockings. I don't know, she must have pulled on something like ten pairs."

I hadn't had time to go back and see her until just before the Kesslers wound up their routine. I couldn't believe my eyes. She was in a tiny miniskirt. "Oh, sainted Mary," I said, "that's shorter than the skirts the Kesslers are wearing. Where did you find it?" "In the bottom of my suitcase," she said. Alvero and the orchestra were already playing her introduction, and when she sailed out, and the audience saw those legs, they went wild. She was telling them, you thought the old one couldn't follow those beautiful girls, that youth is everything, well, friends, that's your problem. Watch this.

They did. A reporter from *Die Welt* swore he heard somebody say, "She's the greatest medical wonder since Adenauer." She toyed with the spectators—"My right leg is thirty-three, and my left leg is thirty-three, if you want to know my age, you do the addition, I'm too tired"—and when it was time for her to go down into the house, she called, "Jean-Claude, come help Mother, I'm too old to do the stairs alone."

At the end, there was a magic moment. Remember now that people trying to escape from East Berlin were still being shot to death, and here was Josephine, down among the elegant audience, saying how terrible it was for brothers to be separated. Then, flattening her back against a side wall of the theater, she began to sing.

I ran to the electrician and had him turn off all the lights except for the pink one on her face; in the darkness, the wall behind her disappeared, as the Berlin wall would not do for another eighteen years. The song over, she sank to her knees, imploring, "Oh God, give peace to the world."

Does it sound hackneyed, sentimental, old-fashioned? It was all of those. It was also theatrically effective, thrilling everyone but the Kessler twins.

"The Kesslers were spectacular too," says Georges Debot, "but she overshadowed them."

"Our mother was crying," says Marie Jo, "when Josephine asked you to come and take a bow with her, and said to the people, 'A big round of applause for my Jean-Claude!' The theater became a big living room, the people members of a family, you felt good in your soul."

"Your own mother was a good mother," said my cousin Jacqueline, "but she loved you in silence, she was missing that warmth Josephine had so much of. Josephine had to touch, to express her feelings. I'm sure that even in sad moments she knew how to find a little bit of happiness, enough to let her start again."

At the reception afterward—we had it in the Pimm's Club—Georges Debot found the scene amusing. "I saw Françoise Sagan totally drunk, but then, she never said that she disliked alcohol. I went to say hello. She answered me, 'What are you doing in Moscow?'

"She was looking with her gloomy eyes at Josephine, surrounded by the most beautiful men offering her little gifts, like the Virgin at Lourdes. Josephine, with a glass of beer in her hands, was not displeased."

Next day, we had a party at my place because Josephine wanted to follow the German elections. "I will always keep in my memory," says Georges, "the picture of that extraordinary personage down on all fours, ass in the air, in front of the TV set. She drove everyone crazy, no one could talk, and she was drinking that dreadful concoction of lemon, sugar, and warm water."

At 4 P.M., she demanded that I call Willy Brandt in Bonn. I didn't get through, but an assistant promised to relay her message—"Don't worry, you'll be reelected!" Still, she insisted on sending a telegram.

That night, I took Josephine to my old workplace, the Kleist Casino. She entered the packed gay club like a queen visiting her subjects. We sat by the dance floor and every couple that passed threw kisses, and Josephine, with a motherly smile, would throw kisses back. Suddenly, two burly moustached guys stopped in front of us and gave each other a French kiss. "Oh!" exclaimed Josephine, "Look at the little darlings, how adorable they are!"

Her Berlin notices were raves. "The Black Venus is back," said *Der Abend.* "Rainstorm of applause for Josephine," said *Die Welt.* I made the papers too, billed as "Josephine Baker's thirteenth child, a well-kept secret."

Josephine went home happy, but a few weeks later, was again in the hospital. She blamed this on sixteen-year-old Marianne, who had fallen "headlong in love" with a nineteen-year-old boy. Marianne had been staying out, Josephine wrote Harry Hurford-Janes, "until five o'clock in the morning. . . . The shock was so hard I had a heart attack. . . ."

A month later, she felt well enough to take Mara to Venezuela, where he met his grandparents. "His grandfather is an Indian chief," Josephine told Marie Spiers. "That was a wonderful experience for him and me."

It's possible it wasn't such a wonderful experience for the fourteen-year-old Mara. Josephine led him into a swarm of strangers who badgered her for money, and who spoke in a dialect Mara did not understand. Then she asked him, "Do you want to remain with your people?"

"I looked her square in the eye," Mara recalled. " 'When you brought me to France, I was sick, wasn't I? Thanks to you I'm alive. Why would I want to leave you?' "

Meanwhile, Jack Jordan had come back into her life. He and his partner, Howard Sanders, were convinced they could bring Josephine in triumph again to Carnegie Hall. Josephine, always willing to forgive the shortcomings of a producer so long as she didn't have a more important producer lined up, finally said yes.

In New York, having won his heart's desire, Jack panicked—what if nobody came to the show?—and hired an army of boys to hand out flyers in gay bars and restaurants all over the city. Jack was a man like Willy Loman, "out there in the blue, riding on a smile and a shoeshine." Already, he had borrowed seven thousand dollars from Bricktop to bring Josephine over.

Before the opening at Carnegie Hall, on Josephine's sixty-seventh birthday, there was a press conference at the Plaza, and a reporter brought up the idea of Josephine's playing herself in a movie. She laughed. "Josephine Baker is too old to play Josephine Baker."

On Tuesday, June 5, the audience—among them, Eubie Blake and Miki Sawada—stirred in their seats as an old lady wearing house slippers crept onstage from the wings. She moved painfully on her arthritic feet toward a standing mike. Some people were stunned. *This* was the famous Josephine Baker?

The old lady reached the mike. "My name is Bricktop," she said, going on to give Josephine a lovely introduction. ("Much too long," Josephine told me later.)

"And when I said, 'Now here she is,' " Bricktop recalled, "I saw a theater shake."

Yvonne Stoney had first worked as a dresser for Josephine at Carnegie Hall ten years before. "It was one of the most fascinating jobs I ever had, because she made most of her changes in front of the audience's eyes, and they were not aware of it. She would be talking to them, and have one arm behind the proscenium, and I am pulling off her glove, and I am under her dress taking off one shoe and putting another shoe on, and she never left the stage."

Now Yvonne was helping Josephine again, on an opening night when the stage was covered with roses thrown by admirers. "I would say six inches deep, I had never seen anything like it. And when Josephine walked on, they would not let her open her mouth, every time she started, the applause rolled in. I was standing in the wings waiting for her to come and get the top part of her headdress taken off, and as she leaned against the piano, I could see her trembling. I went and got Jack.

"She came off after the first segment, and we got her into the dressing room, and she was turning blue. The last pill she was supposed to have taken was still there in the ashtray, and I gave it to her. It was like a metamorphosis. When she went back onstage, she was fine."

She looked ageless, people said, in the skin-colored sequined body stocking, a huge headdress of pink ostrich plumes on her head. "How do you like my Eiffel Tower?" she asked, patting the feathers. They liked her Eiffel Tower, and they liked her. At the end, each person in the theater lit a match, and sang "Happy birthday, dear Josephine."

Somebody once said that Josephine spent the last two years of her life in redemption. Certainly during that brief stay in New York, she tried to mend some fences. Caroline Reagan's grandson Arthur remembers his family's being invited to Carnegie Hall.

"Out of the clear blue. I was eleven years old, and sitting in the front row, and this woman is dedicating the show to my grandmother and my mother, and we all have to get up and go onstage with her."

In another spate of reconciliation, Josephine invited herself to stay at her nephew's house on Long Island. "I need some peace, the old arm is getting tired." Artie drove her to the theater each night and picked her up after the show. "She'd come home and fix her famous spaghetti," Janie Martin says. "Two o'clock in the morning, she'd eat a plate of spaghetti."

"She let me know I was her blood," says Vertel, the daughter of Artie and Janie, who was sixteen at the time. "She didn't act like a big shot."

Donald Wyatt came to the opening-night party. "I was shocked when Josephine walked into the Plaza," he told me. "I could see how much she'd aged."

The New York critics didn't agree. "A body any thirty-year-old could proudly take to a beach resort," said the *Post*'s man, Edmund Newton, while Howard Kissel, of *Women's Wear Daily*, called her voice warm "and, when she wants it to be, velvety, and always bright and joyful." Booked for four days, she could have played for four years, to judge from the crowds mobbing the box office. This was not lost on Jack Jordan and Howard Sanders, who were already planning for next fall—a sixteen-city tour and a movie.

She phoned me the minute she got home to Roquebrune. "I'm so happy," she said, "I'm sorry you weren't there, but we go back in September, and you will come with me. I'm taking the children to Copenhagen, why don't you join us?"

I went sooner than I'd planned, because in Copenhagen, she suffered a stroke. At Rigshospitalet, I was directed to the ninth floor. On the black and white plastic tiles, a little girl was playing hopscotch. Nearby, some big boys and a teenaged girl leaned against the wall.

From talking to them on the phone, reading their letters, seeing their pictures, I felt I knew them. I went to Stellina, who had stopped jumping in order to check on who was getting off the elevator. "I'm Jean-Claude, your brother from Berlin," I said, and we kissed. I was meeting the children at last, but my happiness was shadowed.

None of them had been allowed into Josephine's room, and when I saw her, I understood why. She lay in a large white metal-framed bed, looking small and lifeless. The left side of her face was twisted, her head was bald except for a few curly white hairs. Her eyes were closed, and she breathed with difficulty; there were so many tubes in her nose, arms, chest, it was like a science fiction movie.

The staff were relieved I had arrived, the children were without supervision and reporters had been hounding them. I said I would take them with me, and a nurse promised to call if Josephine's condition worsened during the night. As we left, I spoke to the reporters who were waiting outside; I told them Miss Baker was doing well.

I took the children to a restaurant. We were almost in mourning, certainly in shock, trying to reassure each other, when out of the blue, flashbulbs erupted, bombarding and blinding us. I was shocked. This is what it is to be the children of someone famous, I thought. The children were *not* shocked, they were used to it.

Next morning, astonishingly, I found Josephine awake and reading telegrams. She smiled when she saw me, and handed me one of them: DEAR JOSEPHINE, WE ARE PRAYING FOR YOUR RECOVERY. It was from some Jehovah's Witnesses. "When I was fighting with God, who wanted me back, I told him I still have so much to accomplish here on earth, and the prayers of the Witnesses were added to mine, and God listened to them. That's why I'm still here today."

She was weak, and spoke slowly. "You've met your brothers and sisters?" "Yes, Mother, I love them." "I knew you would," she said. Suddenly, she turned practical. "How did you hear I was in the hospital?"

I said it was on the news. "Oh my God," she said, "the Americans are going to cancel the fall tour, no one will book me if they know I have had a stroke, you must call a press conference and deny it, say I fell on some stairs."

I said I would. By now, she was off on another tack. "Look, Jean-Claude, look at all the people who worry about me." She waved telegrams from Princess Grace, Jean-Claude Brialy, Golda Meir, the queen of Denmark.

A report to her doctor in Paris from Ole Thage, the consultant neurologist at the hospital, said she had made "a speedy recovery from what we consider a cerebral thrombosis of the right hemisphere." She had been admitted on July 17 "with a paresis of the left side of the face and the left arm." She'd had trouble speaking, the left side of her face drooped, her heart rhythm was irregular.

Ten days later, she was sent home with digoxin and an anticoagulant, and I made my first visit to the Villa Maryvonne. I had decided to leave Berlin, join Josephine in her world, since she wanted and needed me with her. I'd achieved success, money, friends, lovers of both sexes, but her idea of universal brotherhood brought me back to my fascination with Abbé Poulot, the wonderfully eccentric religious mentor of my childhood village. I was once again happy to be an altar boy, to serve a cause bigger than myself.

I left everything behind but my new Mercedes 350SL coupe.

The villa at Roquebrune was built on two levels, with a stone terrace that looked over the sea. Josephine called the upstairs, shared by the boys, the pigsty. Broken doors, floors covered with dirty underwear, metal lockers, bunk beds. Downstairs, the only full bathroom was across from Josephine's bedroom. Marianne and Stellina slept in a converted pantry, and Akio had a small room that Josephine asked him to give up for me. I said nothing, but felt odd about displacing him. These kids had enough problems.

One of which was Josephine's flash tempers. Only recently she had expelled Moïse from the house, and he was working as a waiter in a restaurant in Monte Carlo. The older boys and I went down to see him. He had cut his hand very badly, and was just back from the hospital. I found him very nice, good-looking, apparently well-balanced. When we told Josephine that he had been in the hospital, she did not respond. It was as if he did not exist.

Dinner was meager. Pasta with margarine—"Butter is too expensive," she told me—and for water glasses we used empty mustard jars.

The next day, I went out and bought meat, groceries, and colored plastic tumblers to give a little color to our lunch. Josephine, seated at the head of the table, made an announcement. "Your brother, Jean-

Claude, will read you a letter from Dr. Thiroloix." Then she handed me the letter.

I started to read, and could barely keep from laughing. "You are murderers, and you are killing your mother," Dr. Thiroloix had written. When I had finished, Josephine stood up and ran to her bedroom, slamming the door behind her.

Stellina was sobbing, "Maman is going to die." "Idiot, it's a game," said one of the boys. The others just looked at me as if to say, "You see the circus we live in?"

I followed the distraught Stellina to Josephine's room. I was stunned by the way she brought order into her home. "They don't care about my health," she said. Now that Moïse was gone, Jean-Claude had become her obsession. "He's a drug addict, you have to talk to him before it's too late."

I took Jean-Claude to the Café de Paris for a conversation over a couple of beers. "You know she means well," I said. "She is difficult, and not very logical, but she loves you so much."

"She is mad," he said bitterly. "You see how she traumatized Stellina. She can't do that number with me. I never asked to be adopted, I would have been happier in an orphanage, with an ID bracelet, at least I would have known who I am. And I wouldn't have been an object of curiosity, like we all are with her."

I let him talk. He spoke with the passion of an unhappy twenty-year-old. "She chose pretty babies, none of us are ugly or mutilated. At home, she plays the poor old black mother, and when we open the newspapers, here she is half naked at close to seventy, laughing, drinking champagne with actors, presidents. And always dropping a word about her children, her ideals, human dignity. If she had dignity, she would not treat us as she does. She has used us for her career; if she wants us to live like a normal family, then she must act normal too!"

His outburst floored me. I said I understood, but that she too had endured a hard youth, and didn't know how to show love. "Even with me, she is tough, and I take it."

He didn't want to take it. "Look at her. She's even too old to be my grandmother, how could I feel like she's my mother?"

I went home and told Josephine that Jean-Claude was not a drug addict, and that I found him very bright. It made her angry. "I knew you would fall under his spell, you're against me like everyone else, why are you here?"

There was so much that could not be fixed that I turned my energies to matters over which I might exercise some control. The house was dirty, the Italian maid was not doing a good job. Josephine said she knew it. "But she is young and pretty, and the boys sleep with her, so they don't have to go out of the house for sex. It's safer like that."

Next day, as though we'd never had this bizarre conversation, Josephine brought up the subject of one of the boys (who shall remain nameless). "You have to take X to a girl, because he is very shy, but his body is ready."

Flabbergasted, I stared at her. Yesterday, everyone was having sex with the maid; today, she wants X to lose his virginity to a stranger, and she doesn't even know if he's interested. It reminded me of farmers in my village taking a cow to the bull when they decided it was the right moment.

"Here are two hundred francs," she said. "Take him to Nice and find him a nice young girl."

I didn't know where in Nice one went for nice young girls, but I told X the good news, and two of the other boys and Marianne resolved to come with us. We parked in front of a little hotel—it was the right part of Nice, a few girls were already walking the streets at 3 P.M.—and I got out and went to a young blonde and told her the story. "Be nice to him," I said. Then I gave X the two hundred francs, and we all wished him luck.

He was back five minutes later. "We went to a room," he said, "I sat on the end of the bed, she asked me for the money, I gave it to her, then she said I could go."

Even Josephine laughed. Then she blamed me for having chosen the wrong girl.

Seeing that many admirers still beat a path to her door fired Josephine's fantasies. "Princess Grace, that filthy American," she burst out one day. Shocked by this denunciation of her benefactor, I waited for an explanation. It was not long in coming. The prince and princess had decided Monte Carlo needed a new discothèque, the better to lure tourists, and Josephine had thought she was the logical person to front it. "Instead, the prince and princess took Régine, the fat one from Paris.

So, Jean-Claude, here at the Villa Maryvonne, we will build a new Chez Joséphine, and you will manage it.

"And we will kill Régine, the princess will be sorry she did not take me. We will have shops where guests will buy postcards of me, and dolls, and on the top floor there will be the cabaret with glass walls, the only decoration will be the splendid view over Monte Carlo, people will come from all over."

It never occurred to her that the villa wasn't zoned for commercial use, or that she might be perceived as too old, too sick, too unreliable to run a club. Especially as she didn't plan to entertain. "If I start, I am obliged to continue. Once or twice a year, I'll do a special show, but I'm tired, that is why my United States tour will be my last one. It will bring us three million dollars."

"Three million?" I say. "Are you sure?"

She's sure. The tour, the selling—one more time—of her story. There will be a movie, and three more books, one about her career ("not my sex life"), one about the famous people she has known, and one about the war. Then, when we come home again, the new club. "You'll be boss, but give some of your brothers little jobs, teach them."

She is exhilarated rather than exhausted by all this planning. She can't stop. She is going to build a tower of thirteen floors, a floor for each child. With two apartments on a floor. "The second apartment can be rented out for income. You will have your own floors because your sisters-in-law will cause disputes, so privacy is necessary."

She thinks of everything. "Come on, let's go," she says. "I want to show you that piece of land we are going to buy."

There are good days and bad days. When she wants to talk privately, she asks me to come to her bedroom. There she opens a big armoire— she travels with the key—and shows me files. "I have kept a file on each child. You will not believe it, but as they grow up, they develop the characteristics and faults of their race. Look at Akio. Like the Japanese, he'll smile at you and knife you in the back. And Luis, have you noticed what a beautiful black boy he is? He will drive the girls crazy, and in the end, he will fall in love with one who drags him around by the nose."

She was like a mad scientist documenting lab specimens, a little frightening, and certainly racist.

But other times, we were almost like an ordinary family. She would be happy with her children. One night I took everyone—including Rama—to a restaurant called The Pirate. Preparing to go was like getting ready for a big wedding, people washing in the bathroom full of Josephine's wigs hanging like dead birds after a shooting spree, and the suffocating smell of Madame Rochas (always perfume, never cologne) seeping from the large crystal bottles with the initials J.B. in gold.

Josephine was dressed in tight white pants, a pretty shirt, and she looked young and proud as we made our entrance into the restaurant. She was greeted by flashbulbs and applause, the orchestra struck up "J'ai Deux Amours," and we drank champagne and danced and laughed till morning.

Vertel Martin came from America for vacation that summer, and stayed with Margaret. When she was introduced to Josephine's brood, she was bewildered. "I had grown up with Aunt Josephine's records, I had seen the pictures of the Rainbow children, but meeting them was just strange. I thought, how can this white guy be my cousin?

"I saw Aunt Margaret in a very subservient position, the children were very cruel to her, called her la bête noire. I'll never forget her going up the hill every morning to serve those children. She used to scream about those kids, but she did it every day. It was hard to see family treat family like that.

"But Aunt Margaret found solace in Rama: Rama was clean, Rama went to school, Rama loved her mother."

Aunt Margaret, says Vertel, "would tell me I couldn't wear red. Black people were not supposed to wear red, it was too flamboyant. She was living in the past, and so was Aunt Josephine. My whole black family in France lived in the past. I told them there had been a lot of changes in the United States, but they were afraid of changes."

At Margaret's house, Vertel met her grandfather again. Richard had brought his French family to Monte Carlo, hoping for a reconciliation with Josephine. He came to the Villa Maryvonne, and one of my brothers of the Rainbow Tribe ran up to the house with the news. "Maman, Uncle Richard is at the gate, he would like to see you."

Josephine turned to me. "But Jean-Claude, you know I can't see him. I adopt orphans and he *makes* orphans."

I'm not proud of myself, I could have fought with her, but I didn't. Because Richard had many children by many women, she, the queen, was refusing to receive him, and I was the messenger who delivered the bad word. "Sorry, dear Richard," I said, "Maman loves you, but she is too busy now." He understood. More than I wanted him to.

Among the people Josephine did *not* turn away from her door during that August was the seventy-eight-year-old Michel Simon. The French actor and his German lady friend paid a call, and Josephine received them in bed. She asked Akio and me to bring chairs for her guests and then go away. Intrigued, we listened at the door, and were rewarded for our nastiness. Turning to the German lady, Michel said, "Tell Josephine I still get a hard-on, tell her—"

And Josephine whispered, "*Mais oui*, Michel, I have heard." It was wonderful. Forty-eight years had passed since their first encounter— Michel was never a handsome man, he and Josephine had been called Beauty and the Beast—but their youth still burned in them.

Now Josephine accepted an invitation to go to Jerusalem for the state of Israel's twenty-fifth anniversary. I disapproved; the doctors had told her to rest. When I refused to make the trip, she was amazed. "But Jean-Claude, the whole world will be there, Pablo Casals will perform." She took Stellina and went.

A lot of the world—the world she valued—*was* there. "Four hundred and fifty international guests," wrote Terence Smith in *The New York Times,* "sang 'Hello, Golda, well hello, Golda . . . ' to Israel's premier at a torchlit party. . . ."

Bricktop got a wire from Josephine. HERE I AM IN THE HOLY LAND THINKING OF YOU . . . I HAVE AS USUAL WHEN I AM HERE FOUND PEACE IN MY HEART AND MIND.

Peace was quickly dissipated when she returned to Roquebrune. One night, she gave me permission to take the oldest children to a disco-thèque in Monte Carlo. They loved to dance, we went in two cars, had a good time, nobody got drunk, and at 2 A.M., I decided we should leave. Marianne and one of the boys got into the family Fiat, I took Rama and the others with me. After we dropped Rama, we went home and crept into the house so we would not disturb Josephine or Stellina.

I had just turned out my light when a fury burst through my door. Josephine was screaming, "Where is Marianne? Where is your sister?" (She always brandished the words brother and sister like weapons against us.) Now she continued to yell: "You broke my trust, get up, we are going to go find her!" She was in nightgown and bare feet.

"Mother," I said, "this is not good for your health—"

"Forget my health! You are the one who is killing me!"

She sat beside me as we took the little road behind the house to go to Margaret's. There, Rama corroborated my story that Marianne had been right behind us. By the time we got back to the villa, Marianne was in bed.

Josephine went to her bedroom and I to mine. Again, I was in shock. It was impossible to live here in any normal way. Next day, Josephine wrote Harry Hurford-Janes: "Marianne is still impossible, I have suggested she go to Jo Bouillon."

Still, we made plans for our trip to America. I was going to be the master of ceremonies, and sing in Josephine's act, so I must have a tuxedo to match each of her dresses. "Go to Pierre Cardin," she said, "but tell him he should give you a big discount."

I went to Berlin to wind up my business there. Soon I would be off to America as Josephine's nurse, secretary, son, agent, buffer between her and the world—not to mention spokesperson for the Rainbow Tribe. My second mother and I would next meet in Paris, where she was to have costume fittings.

In the station waiting for the train to take her to the city, she told a young American reporter that racism was alive in France. At Les Milandes, she said, people had wanted her gone from the neighborhood "because they could not accept a black woman living in a castle."

The reporter, Henry Louis Gates, Jr., now a distinguished professor at Harvard, was then twenty-two years old, and working for *Time* magazine. He asked Josephine if she had ever felt guilty for having left the United States, for "not being there to participate, particularly during the civil rights era."

She said she'd often thought about that question, "about running away from the problem. At first I wondered if it was cowardice, wondered whether I should have stayed to fight. But I couldn't have done anything. I would have been thwarted . . . I probably would have been killed."

In Paris, she stayed at Marie Spiers's apartment, and went for her fittings to the costume house of Raymonde and Catherine. "She had asked for black fox from Revillon, though we could have used dyed rabbit and got the same effect onstage," Catherine says. "But that was not good enough for Josephine. As soon as she had a generous producer, she would demand splendor.

"We made her a corset dyed in the color of her skin, it gave the impression that she was naked, and on top of that she wore a body stocking of nylon tulle, very strong, and again the color of her skin, embroidered where it had to be to reinforce the illusion of that fabulous body. (Marlene Dietrich did the same.) The wigs and feathers came from Madame Février, the shoes—size 7—from Capobianco, the money to pay for all of it from the embassy of Morocco, the embassy of Sweden, the Red Cross. She could always get somebody to pay.

"She was what she was. She knew how to profit from everything, from everyone who loved her."

The night before we left Paris, we—Josephine, Marie, my sister Marie Jo, and I—went to Chez Michou, a famous transvestite club, for dinner. (Michou had started in the female impersonator business by transforming himself into Brigitte Bardot, but he didn't need to put on drag anymore, he was the boss. "I'm the greatest impresario in the world," he likes to say, "who else can present Josephine Baker, Diana Ross, Liza Minnelli in one show?")

Next morning, I was at Marie's place with two taxis, to pick up Josephine and her luggage. We were on our way to America to make three million dollars.

Chapter 43

—

JOSEPHINE MARRIES "IN SPIRIT," AND WRECKS A TOUR

"Once men get what they want, they keep walking"

ince we had some time before our plane left, Josephine led me to Orly's duty-free shops. She was like a child in front of the perfumes, scarves, belts, the fake jewelry. Catching her excitement, I offered to buy her pearls and rubies. "Look at that one, and that one and that one!"

She cooled me down. "Too big, too flashy. If we choose simple ones, they will pass for real."

I bought her a handful of glass diamonds and emeralds, and learned a lesson. Thanks to her legendary past, she could lend even phony jewels credibility; other women, seeing them on her, would feel admiration and desire.

Air France always treated Josephine not as a VIP but as a marvelous old aunt. We were baby-sat by the flight attendants, and it was like Brazil all over again. With her feet off the ground, Josephine became another person. "*Mon* Jean-Claude, I'm happy you're with me," she said, "and that you will be discovering America. It is a great country with great people." I couldn't believe my ears, I had thought she hated the United States, and here she was sounding like a lovesick girl.

Strictly speaking, we didn't go straight to America, we went to Cuernavaca, where Josephine's friend Bob Brady had been living since 1961. "When you wake up in the morning," she said, "a servant will be at your bedside with fresh-squeezed juice on a silver tray."

Bob Brady was a painter and tapestry designer; his house was splendid and simple at once, but Josephine found it hard to breathe in the high altitude. We got her an oxygen tank.

No sooner had we arrived than Stephen Papich flew down from Los Angeles. He was the one who had managed to get her booked into the Ahmanson Theatre. She was to open in two weeks, but the tickets were not moving, and Stephen wanted to discuss ways in which she might help save the show.

He needn't have wasted his breath. "It's not my problem," she said of the poor advance sales, and though her contract promised her eighty-five hundred dollars per performance, she now wanted ten thousand dollars, and twenty thousand dollars on a matinee day. This ensured that her producers would go broke.

Being determined not to go broke herself, however, she took a step she thought would guarantee her future. In Mexico, she married Bob Brady. Not formally. Often, she gave herself absolution without the interference of a priest; why not marry the same way? It was Brady, a handsome homosexual (Josephine believed he was also very wealthy), who is said to have suggested the union. The idea suited Josephine. No sex, but plenty of money, at a time when she didn't want the one, and craved the other.

"You are my good husband in spirit . . . without any ties," she told Brady. "It would not work otherwise because I am a nomad from the desert . . . it will be a pure marriage without sex because sex spoils everything." She suggested exchanging their vows "before God, and not man—in church Sunday morning alone. . . . No one must know about this . . . even we . . . must not speak about it again."

We did indeed go to church that Sunday morning. The Mass was celebrated by Sergio Mendez Arceo, known as "The Red Bishop." (He was a friend of Fidel Castro, and brought animals and mariachi bands into the cathedral to make the farmers feel at home.) After the service, Josephine bawled him out. "I talked about you with the Holy Father," she said. "He wants you to stop all that nastiness." The bishop just smiled and gave her his blessing, as she knelt to kiss his ring.

Next day, she sent me back to Los Angeles with Stephen, requesting that I keep the reporters happy until she got there. I gave interviews according to her instructions—though it wasn't me reporters wanted to talk to. I also met Ivan Harold Browning, who had been with her in *Shuffle Along* and who told me about her great success in that show; he was the first of many—Bricktop, Lydia Jones, Bessie Buchanan, Alberta Hunter, Sam Wooding—whom I would find in America who would help me discover those first nineteen years of Josephine's life, the years she had tried so hard to erase.

When she arrived from Mexico, Jack Jordan and Howard Sanders came to our suite in the Beverly Hills Hotel to see the costumes. Without changing from her slacks, she put on black satin shoes, a black fox muff, and paraded, describing the gown that went with the shoes and the muff. "Red velvet, with a train . . ."

Next, she slipped into white shoes and a white fur hat. In a trembling voice, Jack said, "Josephine, this is wonderful, but where are the dresses?"

The show was to open in four days. "Don't worry," she said, "they're in Paris; it's just that Raymonde and Catherine are waiting for their money."

Close to apoplexy, Jack tried again. "Josephine, when you left New York last June, we gave you a check for forty thousand dollars to pay for costumes, you signed a contract."

"Oh," she said sweetly, "I'm so sorry. I thought it was an advance on my salary and I spent it."

Checkmate. Jack and Howard had no funds left, and Raymonde and Catherine were not inclined to part with the clothes until they saw some dollars.

"Call your friend Michou," Josephine instructed me. "His place is full every night, he must have lots of money."

At that point, Michou had met Josephine twice. When I woke him— it was 5 A.M. in Paris—to ask him to pay for her costumes, he thought I was insane. Luckily, Ivan Harold Browning showed up to take Josephine off to dinner.

I advised Jack and Howard to forget the forty thousand dollars. "Find more money for the costumes, and take it out of her pay."

Howard left for New York on the next flight. "He has friends in the

Mafia," Josephine told me (though this had no basis in fact). "He'll get the money."

The following morning, Josephine and I came downstairs and found a limousine waiting to take us to her press conference. "They think I'm dead," she said, laughing. "This is not a car, it's a hearse."

She was equally critical of the journalists gathered to greet her. Wearing a Pauline Trigère dress and cape of brown and white homespun tweed, she sneered at questions about her youthful appearance— "That's the best you can do?"—and when a reporter inquired about her adopted children, she said, "Why don't you ask Jean-Claude, who is sitting among you?"

I obliged. I spoke of my brothers and sisters, said I was happy to be for the first time under the sky of America, but was soon interrupted by Josephine, who demanded of the reporters, "Are you interviewing him or me?"

Tickets were starting to sell, but the tension between her and the producers had not eased. While she and I were enjoying our luxurious suite, Jack and Howard were sharing one little room, and were so short of cash they would buy a single club sandwich to share at lunch. They also had a preacher staying with them, and every morning this man called on Josephine to see whether or not she had "the bad eye." If the answer was yes, the producers wouldn't talk to her, and I had to serve as go-between.

Josephine's contract stipulated that she was to be paid in cash—for each performance—five hours before curtain time. She had already sent to Nice for Joseph Bessone, her most recent business adviser. On paper, Monsieur Bessone represented "Lewston Incorporation Monravia," Josephine's dummy corporation based in Luxembourg. This company had been created in order "to cultivate the fame of Mrs. Josephine Baker, lyrical artist" and "to present her in the show business world." Since she was simply an employee of the company, and not its director, she couldn't be sued—successfully, anyway—no matter how much money she made.

When Monsieur Bessone arrived, not knowing a word of English, I got a new job as translator. (Josephine had decided she would no longer speak English to Jack or Howard.) A man who knew nothing about show business, Bessone adored his client, but wasn't flimflammed by her.

"Josephine loved schemes," he told me. "She knew how to spread discord and confusion. In France, it was impossible to find an interested publisher or producer anymore, so there was only America.

"The first time I saw her perform was at Carnegie Hall, and I realized what an American success could be. I was breathless, but so was the rest of the audience, watching a sixty-seven-year-old woman in a body stocking and a few feathers, slim as a sylph, looking half her age. She knew how to erase time, she knew it so well she died of it. Because she refused to recognize her own limits, she pulled once too often on the rope. She didn't care, it was enough for her to hear the bravos at the end.

"In Los Angeles, she was lost; that's why I came. You remember all the discussions with important people? Danny Kaye was interested in producing the movie about her life, we were very close on the numbers, but then he made the mistake of calling twice in the same day. She raised the price three times, and he dropped out. She was intoxicated with her own success, she thought she was Josephine with forty years less on her shoulders, Josephine who had not had cardiac crises, Josephine to whom the future belonged."

And to whom the past was a burden. From St. Louis, Richard, Jr., phoned, and she refused to talk to him, as she had refused to talk to his father when he'd come to the Villa Maryvonne. Richard, Jr., asked me to "tell Aunt Tumpy the people here want to give her a ticker-tape parade." It was the first time I ever heard her childhood nickname, but I was more moved than Josephine. "I will *never* go back to St. Louis," she announced.

Her costumes finally arrived, but she had greater things on her mind. She'd heard Ann-Margret was making ninety thousand dollars a week in Las Vegas. "So you see," she told me, "they're getting me for nothing."

Five hours before the curtain, as stipulated, she was paid. We left for the theater, me with half her money in my Jockey shorts, she with the rest of it in her bra.

When I got into my dressing room, I found I had forgotten to bring makeup. Josephine was not sympathetic. "Monsieur wants to go onstage, and Monsieur does not have makeup?" she screamed. "Too bad! Go find some!"

I was paralyzed, but I understood her fury. She was telling me, "You fool, don't you know you need makeup to get through life? If you don't have it, they will eat you alive." She had developed her own protection—makeup was only a metaphor for protection—against an ugly world.

Gene Bell, the black tap dancer, came to my rescue. "I showed you how to use a sponge, make your face smooth," he remembered. "Lupe, my wife, was there and she thought you looked very handsome, especially in your electric-blue velvet tuxedo."

After dressing, I walked to the wings. Josephine was standing alone near her quick-change booth (an improvised dressing room close to the stage) in her embroidered body stocking. She looked naked, very old and abandoned, like a character in a Fellini movie. She caught sight of me and said, "Let's go peek." Through a hole in the curtain, we peered at the audience. *"C'est du beurre,"* she whispered. "It's butter." A full house, but not a tough one. I laughed. The old pro had pronounced her verdict.

Everything about that night lives in my memory. Going onstage with her voice—*"Merde, mon chéri!"*—in my ear, and telling myself, she cares for me after all.

Even so, I was petrified. I have no ear for music, my German records had been made in a studio, so performing live seemed a suicidal act. Fortunately, I had a microphone to hold on to, a sort of electronic security blanket, otherwise I might have fled.

The lights dim, the orchestra plays a medley of songs Josephine has made famous, building up to "Ça, C'est Paris." As the music ends, the stage goes to black. A spotlight finds me. Josephine and I have been mother and son, but I'm getting my show business baptism from a general, not a mother. Her orders still ring in my ears.

"Mesdames et messieurs, bonsoir."

Look straight up at the balcony, Jean-Claude. Throw them your most beautiful smile, they're the ones who set the temperature of the room. (Fifty years before, she had discovered that the peanut gallery was generally crowded with people whose pockets may have been empty, but whose hearts were full. These were the ones with whom she felt most comfortable.)

"Buona sera, signore, signori.

"Buenas noches, damas y caballeros."

Slowly, I begin moving across the huge stage.

Down front are the Nazis who came to America to make their fortunes. Here is where you can make use of your years in Berlin.

"Guten Abend, meine Damen. Guten Abend, meine Herren."

Now you move to center stage. You've said hello to all the little satellite countries. Now you're addressing the citizens of this country. Now the smile has to explode, Jean-Claude, and the voice has to be very strong!

"And of course, good evening, ladies and gentlemen.

"I come to you this evening as a representative of my many brothers and sisters. We have been called the Rainbow Tribe."

("Sisters" is the cue—eleven violinists stand up and start to play, very softly, "J'ai Deux Amours." I choke up, my voice fills with tears.)

"We have been called the children of universal brotherhood. As you can see, time passes. *Le temps passe.*"

This is supposed to be a joke. When people think of Josephine and her tribe, they still conjure up pictures of a beaming woman surrounded by many babies. I am thirty years old and, dressed by Cardin, hardly the stock image of an orphan. The joke doesn't work, except to irritate Josephine because I tried it without asking permission. I walk back to the side of the stage. "My brothers and sisters have asked me to introduce to you the lady we all love so much."

Pause, Jean-Claude. Then shout the words out!

"Our MOTHER!"

The violins stop. The drum roll begins. I count nine beats. I bend over, gesturing toward the spot where she will appear, my hand reaching the floor as if I'm cleaning it. I look across the stage, smiling my most beautiful smile. The spotlight—the famous pink gel that keeps Josephine looking young jumps all over, as if searching for her, then stops abruptly.

By now, my nervousness is gone. Suddenly everything seems to be working. The audience is holding its collective breath, and all at once, she is there, just as lungs are ready to burst. People stand and scream, applauding, when I have barely finished shouting, "JOSEPHINE BAKER!"

"Is it for me?" she asks demurely, acknowledging the welcome. "Do you remember me?" Another ovation. It's a miracle. The tired old lady is gone, here's this vision of strength and youth, and I'm an idiot to have been worried for her. Then she touches the five-foot-high headdress she is wearing, and confides, "I can't move with this thing on." She sticks her head through the curtain so Yvonne can remove the burden, while keeping up a running commentary. "Ooh la la, I just got a pin in my scalp; in the old days, with the bananas, I did not have these problems."

I remember racing toward my dressing room to change, hearing on the speaker, "Jean-Claude, come help Mother," and reversing direction, somehow making it back in time to lead her down into the audience so she could hand out roses, read palms, flirt, seduce, enchant.

She told the crowd how when I was a young boy I had held on to her skirt because I was afraid to fall, "and today, it is I who need his strong arm. Because if I fall today, I won't be able to get up and come to you." Applause, during which she asks me, sotto voce, "How old are you?" "Twenty-six," I say. She turns with a mischievous look to the audience and says, "Jean-Claude, my oldest son, thirty-two years old, let's have big applause for Jean-Claude."

Sometimes she was so sharp, but other times she would sit on the apron, right next to the stairs that took her from center stage down into the house, and she would reminisce, and become confused. We had key words written in black ink all over the tops of the stairs to anchor her when she found herself drifting. Like a blind horse who still knows his way home, she was fine until she made a slip, and then the struggle to get back again, the flailings of the orchestra trying to follow her, were frightening. Still, she could put on a show so thrilling that you realized what she might have done if she'd taken the time to rehearse. But she was old, she was tired, she was spoiled.

There were also times when it was plain she was having fun. At the end of the first act, she'd be singing "Bill," when a black man, ostensibly a paying customer, would run up on the stage, and she, greeting him as her long-lost love, would knock his derby hat off, revealing a head covered with pink curlers and a hairnet. It was an old bit from the twenties, and it tickled Josephine as much as it did the audience.

During the intermission, she sent me out into the house to see what people were saying. In the lobby, two girls were selling record albums with Josephine's picture on the cover. I got on line, paid my ten dollars, and ran back to her. "Look what I just bought!"

She was furious. When she had played Carnegie Hall, the second-night performance had been recorded, and nobody had informed her. "I told you they're crooks," she said, and sent me to fetch Jack. He was apologetic, the album was to be a surprise for her, he had never intended to cheat her.

"I had no voice on the second night," she said, "because *you* forgot to have the air conditioning in the limousine turned off, so it must be a terrible record. Thank God Jean-Claude discovered your thievery!"

Suddenly, she has recovered her use of the English language, despite her vow to speak only French in front of poor hapless Jack.

It was touch-and-go whether she would return for the second act, but a truce was finally called. She did a number in jeans and metal-studded leather, like a Hell's Angel on a Harley-Davidson; she presided over a dance contest (her favorite part of the show), and there was a spectacular crossover in which she looked like a drawing of herself from the thirties, arrogant and triumphant in white satin, leading two rhinestone-collared white wolfhounds.

At one point I came on with a sealed letter and a red rose, supposedly from someone in the audience, and presented them to Josephine. She opened the envelope, and looking out into the house, said, "It's a love letter, nothing is more beautiful than love." The orchestra played the music from *Love Story,* Josephine pretended to finish reading, then kissed the rose and handed it to a woman in the front row. "Here, Madame, with my love. Hold it long enough to make a wish, then pass it to your neighbor. I call it my traveling rose."

The next-to-last number employed a choir of white-robed gospel singers holding lighted candles. Bessie Griffin, a huge-voiced gospel artist—"Jetting for Jesus" was the legend over her publicity pictures— came on with the choir, everybody sang "My Sweet Lord," and finally, Josephine did "My Way."

She was tired when it was over, and asked me not to let anyone in to her dressing room. I was standing watch at the door when Bob Brady, her "husband," who was not staying at the Beverly Hills but at another hotel, arrived with a tiny old lady in a pink satin suit. Her face dead white, she looked like a mummy. "Of course, Jean-Claude, you know Miss Swanson," Brady said. I went and told Josephine that Gloria Swanson was waiting with Bob, and she said to let them in. Then Jack Jordan arrived with a wildly excited Johnny Mathis, who threw himself at Josephine's feet, murmuring, "My queen, oh, my queen." Josephine enjoyed every minute of it.

So many people came back, Vincente Minnelli, Mayor Tom Bradley, Isaac Stern, the French consul. Flowers kept arriving, and there was a champagne supper party given by a fashion authority known as Mr. Blackwell.

Next morning, at a breakfast meeting, we got the word. And the axe. She was pruning away all competition. Gene Bell (whose dancing had been praised by a critic as "the evening's most successful segment") would no longer be appearing in both acts. "The public is bored by too much tap dancing," announced Josephine. Bessie Griffin, who had brought down the house, would also be cut back. "No encore, people don't like gospel except in church."

Me? She eliminated one of my two songs. I should have been prepared; last night, after my second number, she had made an entrance and cut off my applause. (I had been nervous when it was my turn to sing, but she had coached me. "Go to the fattest woman in the first row, charm her. 'Madame, I have brought you the most beautiful perfume in the world, the perfume of the Champs-Élyseés.' Then the music will start for the song 'Champs-Élysées.' " It had worked like magic—too well, maybe.)

The *Variety* review was hard on her. It described her "wobbling across the stage in one uncomfortable-looking, outlandish outfit after another," accused her of hitting "harsh, sour notes," and "forgetting words and beats."

But other critics—and the audiences—loved Josephine and the show. We heard that Marlene Dietrich had asked the theater manager about the lighting. "I'm not surprised," said Josephine. "That German cow has copied me all my life. The only thing left for her to copy will be my funeral."

On our second night, Gene Bell came in with a notice from *The Hollywood Reporter*. After much praise for Josephine ("unbelieveably beautiful," "expressive voice," "great talent"), the reviewer turned to me: "Jean-Claude Baker, one of Miss Baker's adopted children, handled the introductions with ease and also offered a couple of pleasant and bouncy songs." Elated, I ran to my mentor. "Maman, look what he said about me—"

I had thought she would be pleased because she had taught me how to behave onstage; instead, she was angry. "My name, Jean-Claude, do you know what it is to have my name? It took me fifty years to make it—and to keep it. And do you think it was fun? Don't you think I'm tired of singing 'J'ai Deux Amours' over and over like an idiot?"

I hadn't asked for her name. I wasn't listed in the program, even as Jean-Claude Rouzaud. But because she played the game of Universal Mother, because she'd worked out the introductions—"My mother!" "My oldest son!"—it was only natural that the press assumed I was Jean-Claude Baker. Nobody in America even knew that her children bore the name of Bouillon, not Baker. Leaving her dressing room, I was numb, destroyed. I had never tired of her singing "J'ai Deux Amours";

even when she improvised on the tune, it didn't occur to me that she was doing it out of boredom, that for her, the song was a martyrdom.

That night, introducing her, speaking of my "brothers and sisters," I felt like a fake. But the lights, the music, the applause, melted my rancor. And Josephine was superb. She asked Ella Fitzgerald to come up from the audience and join in singing "My Sweet Lord"—it was a way of keeping Bessie Griffin in her place—and when the last note ended, Josephine, in a simple black velvet dress that cost a simple five thousand dollars, knelt before Ella, putting her head on the great singer's knees. She was Mary Magdalene at the feet of Jesus. The audience screamed as the curtain fell and rose and fell again on the tableau.

When it came down for the third time and Josephine still hadn't moved, I knew something was wrong. Jack Jordan and I ran on, carried her off, and I got one of the little blue pills and put it under her tongue. Her jaw was frozen. We unbuttoned her dress, and she regained consciousness. She's dying, I told myself, and I was ashamed of the bad thoughts I'd had. This is Josephine, don't try to understand her, try to make her life easier. That's why you're here, and it's enough.

During the day there was constant madness and meanness; at night, when she and I were alone, she was different. We slept in the same bed, but there was nothing sexual about it. Once the lights were out, she talked—about Stellina, whom we both missed, about anything that came into her head. And I listened, spellbound. But I realized now that she was sick, and sometimes I would get into a cold sweat: What if she died in bed right next to me?

At intervals, I would rise on my right elbow and bend over her to hear if she was still breathing, and she would open her eyes, half amused, half upset. "You thought I was dead? Well, I'm not!" I would lie down again, and she would kiss my cheek. "I know you care for me, *mon chéri*." But with first light, she would rise, the madwoman again.

With seats selling out, she became impossible. Not only with her producers—she was still fighting about the Carnegie Hall record royalties—but with tycoons like Hugh Hefner and Bob Banner. Offered a TV movie of the week, she demanded three million dollars. "Plus hotel and airline tickets for my children." She saw it as a bargain, "because if I were to die, you would get a lot of free publicity."

She accepted an award from a black organization, but refused to lead off the dancing at their ball. "I'm too old," she said, "let my son Jean-Claude do it."

I asked a pretty black girl to dance, and got hell for it. "Why did you choose that girl? Leave my people alone!"

Again, I was lost. Didn't she preach that we must be color-blind?

One afternoon a friend of hers came by the hotel with a Yorkshire terrier puppy. "My patients took up a collection to buy him because they love you so much," he said. After he'd gone, she laughed. "He's the director of an insane asylum; I don't want to know how he got the money."

I named the puppy Moustique, and Josephine ordered him a hamburger. At the Beverly Hills Hotel, a room service hamburger cost seven dollars, and he ate only a little piece, so she put the rest in the refrigerator. Next day, when I was hungry, she told me to eat it. Again, I was resentful; she was feeding me leftovers from the dog.

After our last performance at the Ahmanson, she flew back to France so Princess Grace could name her Woman of the Year. (The award was being given by an American magazine.)

At some point during the few days she was at home, she was interviewed by the satiric weekly newspaper *Minute,* which printed a half-mocking, half-rueful piece reprising her life—the childhood, the military service, the career, the spending. "And the children, in spite of themselves, are dragged into this tragi-comedy. They are at Les Milandes when Josephine slaps the priest who reproaches her for having a virgin carved in her own image for the chapel. It is total dementia."

Now, the reporter said, Josephine's idée fixe was a college of universal brotherhood to be built on the island Tito put at her disposal. "I'm a woman who doesn't give up, and neither do my children. When we were expelled from Les Milandes, we were ready to go and live in a tent in Libya!"

Moïse was used by the paper to illustrate Josephine's "tragi-comedy." She had chosen him "to represent the Jews in her cosmopolitan community." As a child "he had to wear, all day long, a skull cap on his head." Now nineteen, he refused to be a symbol anymore, and declared himself a Catholic. To "Uncle" Marc Vromet-Buchet, he said, "I'm not Jewish, I'm from Brittany, and I have a brother!"

"It is true, it is difficult for a woman approaching 69 to bring about order in a home," wrote the interviewer. "Especially when the home does not really exist. The twelve children Josephine collected . . . never really were a family. . . . She wanted to make them into children of the world. But the world is not a home. The children of Josephine Baker have remained the children of their fathers."

In New York, I was staying with my old friend from Liverpool, Peter Brown. He was now president of the Robert Stigwood organization that had produced *Jesus Christ Superstar*. Josephine had asked me to find out if Stigwood would like to take over her tour.

Peter Brown said she was too demanding. "Like a lot of those old-time stars. She comes into a hotel and wants the curtains changed because they aren't blue. Producers don't mind that when a star sells tickets, but with Josephine, unfortunately, only a few old people remember her."

We were to resume the tour, opening at the Fisher in Detroit on October 21. Josephine didn't get back from France until October 20. On the way into the city from the Detroit airport, she asked the black taxi driver where he went to eat with his sweetheart, then told him to take us there. At the restaurant, she wolfed down chitlins and peach cobbler, and invited people at other tables to come see her show.

Some of them did. The show built. One night, Bobby Mitchell appeared backstage. "*Ma* Josephine." "*Mon* Bobby." They talked about the old days at the Casino and the Folies.

She and I could still get a good laugh. In Detroit, she sent me out for laxative chewing gum. I had never heard of that in Europe, and on the way back from the drug store, I tried a few sticks. Later in our suite, Josephine and I were running to the bathroom, laughing like little kids. I was discovering America.

On our last night in Detroit, so many people rushed the box office that the curtain was delayed for forty-five minutes. "You see, Jean-Claude," Jack Jordan said, "if she'd come to town a little earlier, we would have sold out every show."

Poor Jack, he was an amateur, a lover, a fan. I talked to him in 1979, and he told me about bringing Josephine back to America for the March on Washington and how he'd gone to Roquebrune ten years afterward to sell her on coming to Carnegie Hall. "She said, 'Nobody wants me, Jack, they've forgotten me. You just stay here with the boys and I'll fix you some food, I'm not going anyplace, forget about it.' And I convinced her, and that started the whole thing rolling again, and she said,

'I am going to take my boy Jean-Claude with me, because he has a lot of talent.' "

Jack had talent too, but he was no Shubert, no Nederlander, he couldn't be tough enough. Josephine needed a Pepito, someone to lock her in a room until she behaved.

The April in Paris Ball, held at New York's Waldorf-Astoria, is a fête beloved of the jet set; it raises money for French and American charities, and in 1973, Josephine was its star. She enjoyed the big suite with a sunken tub in the bathroom that the Waldorf's Claude Phillipe (god of the ball) had assigned to her. Bob Brady was in town, too, and they went everywhere together.

I remember lunching with them in Harlem, and Josephine's kissing every child in the place. Never had I seen her behave as she did in America. She seemed more natural.

The night of the ball, an interminable fashion show preceded Josephine's entrance. From where she and I stood waiting, we could see the audience, and suddenly, she erupted. "Look at those women shivering in those little fur stoles, so proud of themselves! God knows what they had to do to get them."

The outburst caught me off guard. She, who had gleefully used her body to get where she was going, had turned into a stony moralist. Her disapproval set the tone for that night's performance; she wasn't good, and cut the act short.

The next day, we heard from Paris that Marie-Hélène de Rothschild wanted Josephine to be part of the Bal à Versailles, another big charity party. "No!" Josephine said. "I will do nothing for the Rothschilds, they stole Les Milandes!" How? "They did not come to rescue me. You know, I met them when I arrived with *La Revue Nègre*." (This still did not explain to me why they should have saved Les Milandes forty-eight years later.)

That same day, it was reported in Suzy's column that Josephine was going to marry Bob Brady. "He put that in to get publicity for his paintings!" Josephine yelled. "I'm going to talk to him!"

But when Bob came by, she said nothing.

After the April in Paris Ball, Josephine and I went to the reopening of Chez Bricktop, and the next night, we saw a Broadway show called *Raisin*. (It was a musical version of *Raisin in the Sun*.) Debbie Allen was the ingenue. "That girl should play the young Josephine in the movie of my life," said Josephine.

Our next date took us back to the West Coast, and I thought we should go there as soon as possible. We had proved that only Josephine's presence on the scene could sell tickets. But she had decided on a detour to Istanbul, to celebrate the opening of a bridge across the Bosporus. "Jean-Claude, did you know it is a dream of mankind, to unite the Occident and the Orient?"

No, I didn't know, but I knew publicity in Istanbul would not help us sell the 3,734 seats in the Circle Star Theatre, twenty-five miles from San Francisco. Once again, it was I who was sent to California to smooth things over, while Moustique accompanied Madame to Turkey.

They may have made friends there, but Gasser Tabakoglu, Josephine's official translator, was not one of them. "She was nasty to me all during her stay," he says. "She had arrived claiming to be the official ambassador of UNICEF, but two days later, Danny Kaye came, and he was furious. He too claimed to be the official ambassador, not Josephine. They were supposed to open the bridge together, but now he refused. It was finally decided that Josephine would come from the European side and Danny Kaye from the Asian side and they would meet in the middle of the bridge. There were so many people following them—children carrying flowers and dressed in folk costumes, sword dancers, diplomatic leaders and army officers—that the bridge started shaking.

"Josephine and Danny Kaye cut the ribbon, and didn't speak to each other. And when she was asked about her children, she claimed she even had a Turkish child, which was not true. When I finally put her on the plane, with flowers and the little dog, I said to myself, 'Thank God she's gone!' "

Gasser's troubles were over when Josephine's TWA flight left the ground, but her producers' troubles were just starting up again. She was to fly to London, stay overnight, and catch an early-morning flight to San Francisco. When the customs agent in London told her Moustique would have to be quarantined—"Even the queen cannot come in with a foreign dog"—Josephine, who had been attempting to hide the fist-sized puppy under her blouse, flew to France. Next morning, she learned there was no flight from Orly that would get her back to the States in time.

Even if all had gone according to plan, the scheduling would have been tight. Josephine was to arrive in San Francisco only a few hours before her opening. A press conference had been scheduled at the airport. All day, we waited. No Josephine. It was hot, and I felt something bad was going to happen. I called London. She had come in on the flight from Istanbul, but after that, all traces of her had been lost.

Meanwhile, bulletins from the Circle Star were jubilant. Opening night was sold out. At 5 P.M., people were already arriving to have dinner in the restaurant connected to the theater. By 6 P.M., we decided to tell the press the truth. We didn't know where Josephine was.

Jack was a wreck. We'd messed up at the April in Paris Ball, lost money in Detroit; we were still coasting on six-month-old reviews from Carnegie Hall. If we flopped in San Francisco, it was over. Eight P.M. arrived, Josephine did not.

The next day, she got in, took one look at the theater-in-the-round, and exploded. "How can I change costumes in this livestock auction ring?"

"But Josephine," said Jack, "we're going to have an electric golf cart." "No," she said, "I'm not a cow." As though cows were customarily transported by golf cart.

We held a press conference, and she was cold but controlled—she'd been opening a bridge, mankind's dream, Danny Kaye was there, it's wonderful to be in San Francisco—until a pretty black girl asked, "Miss Baker, what do you think of black people in America today?"

She wheeled on the girl. "How can you use the words 'black people'? Don't you know black is the same as nigger? We are colored people!"

The girl remained composed. "Miss Baker, I am black, and black is beautiful. You have been away from home too long, I'm sorry for you."

A chill spread through the room, the press conference was over. That night, the show went well, though there were only three hundred people in the house; one of them was Alex Haley. Chauffeured by a theater employee, Josephine came on in the golf cart, like an Amazon on a horse, and caroled, "Hi, everybody, do you love me on my scooter?"

Afterward, they had kept the restaurant open for us, and we had dinner and champagne. We were faking it, trying to be cheerful, but it was like after a defeat in a war.

Back at the hotel, I was lying in bed, in the dark, filled with rage against Josephine. I had given up my club, my name, to go to America with her because she needed someone to protect her, and to put the blue pills under her tongue, but she was too crazy. To disappoint thousands of people, break her producers, wreck a show, it was too much. Idly, I considered strangling her. But she'd made enough front pages, and besides people would say I was her lover.

Josephine was psychic, she could always sense what I was thinking, and she came through the door from the bathroom and said, in her nice-little-girl voice, "Jean-Claude, don't look at Mother, I'm naked." I didn't believe it. The way she said naked, it was an invitation. I've seen her so many times naked, in the dressing room, in the hospital, but in the intimacy of the bedroom? Am I crazy? No, I'm not, she is the snake, she is temptation, when she says no it's yes, when she says yes it's no.

I look. She's standing in front of a mirror, her back to me, the only illumination coming from the bathroom. In that half-light, I can make out—dimly—the little neck, the little breasts. The face I can't see very well. Her head is bald, except for a few downy tufts of gray hair. She seems so defenseless, my anger disappears. I just feel sad.

We were booked for four nights. She had missed the first, only a few people showed up on the second, and the third day, Jack Jordan disappeared, taking with him the last five thousand dollars in the box office. I convinced Josephine to play the show anyway. "If Jack isn't here tomorrow, we can keep the costumes in lieu of salary." (Poor Jack had already paid for those costumes twice, but I was shameless.)

Only the tap dancer, dear Gene Bell, who was seventy-one years old in 1992, remembered San Francisco as a good time. "They gave us each a large dressing room stocked with liquor, and our names were written in gold on the doors.

"Josephine with the two dogs, and on the bicycle with rhinestones on her leather jacket—it was a killer show!"

It was a killer show, all right, it nearly killed Jack Jordan. He was still missing when we closed on Sunday. I had hired a security guard to watch Josephine's costumes. Even Yvonne Stoney was not allowed into the dressing room.

"San Francisco was a disaster," Yvonne says. "I felt so bad about it because Jack and Howard had struggled to bring her over. I mean, when she came to Carnegie Hall, she didn't have anything, they had to practically buy her underwear, and from the reception she got there, I thought she would kiss their feet, but she treated them like dirt."

It had been a long time since she'd kissed a man's feet. Yvonne remembers her saying, "Men fuck you and that's the end of it, they use you and abuse you and once they get what they want, they keep walking. I did all that when I was young, I don't need it anymore."

Josephine, says Yvonne, "was a shrewd businesswoman, she always came out on top. I remember after Carnegie Hall, she had me pack fifty-three thousand dollars in a paper bag, and then a shower cap, so she could hide it in her pocketbook, and not have to pay taxes on it. In San Francisco, she confiscated each costume as she took it off, before she walked out on us."

In time, Yvonne forgave me for double-crossing Jack. "You had to be on her side, you were her son."

A friend who was a director of Swissair loaned us a station wagon, and we sneaked the costumes to the airport. They were sent to Paris under the name of Jean-Claude Rouzaud. Josephine could show any nosy officials that she was traveling with nothing but her makeup and Moustique.

She and I were parting once again. "You were right," I told her. "I am going to stay in America."

"I knew it," she said. "But don't go to Hollywood, go to New York. If you make it there, you won't need me *or* old Europe. And try to find us a theater for around Christmas. I am the Universal Mother, we do a family show, and mothers will come and bring their children, it will sell out."

She could take your breath away. She stranded companies, audiences, managers, and drifted onto a plane that would take her someplace else without a care for the mess she left behind.

I went straight back to New York, and this time, Peter Brown had an idea for me. "I've booked the Palace for two weeks around New Year's Eve. Go to Nelle Nugent, she's Jimmy Nederlander's right hand, and tell her I'm willing to give you my option."

I put on my gray mink coat, very European, and go out into the snow. I take a taxi to the Palace, and beard Nelle Nugent in her office. I'm on a holy crusade to bring joy to New York, this dreadful city without human feeling. "Madame," I say, "my mother and I just finished a triumphal tour in America, we are free, and we would like the theater Peter Brown has been kind enough to offer us—"

"Triumphal tour?" says Nelle Nugent. "What the hell are you talking about? We lost seventy-five thousand dollars on your show in Detroit!"

I gape. I'm from France, I don't know the Nederlanders own the Fisher Theatre in Detroit.

She throws me out. I'm back in the snow again. I see the people in Times Square, the faces of all those monsters, I'm in a foreign land, trying to make myself understood in a language I don't speak well.

Suddenly I remember a restaurant called Le Mistral to which I've been with Josephine. I go there and request an audience with Jean Larriaga, the *grand seigneur* of the place. He appears, a short Frenchman, leads me to the bar, listens to my woes. "We went bankrupt, the producer abandoned us, Mother went back to France, she wants me to find a theater for Christmas because we need money . . ."

Next thing I know, he's put me at a table to have lunch with six other people, and a woman is asking me about my brothers and sisters, and how old the youngest is. I tell her Stellina is ten. "How nice," she says, and turns to the man next to her. "Jimmy, you must bring Josephine for Christmas, she has a little daughter the same age as our Christina."

I deduce that this man is in show business, and give him the same spiel I'd tried on Nelle Nugent, adding only that Nelle Nugent has thrown me out of her office. He is baffled. "Don't you know who I am?" he says. "I'm Jimmy Nederlander. I *own* the Palace."

Chapter 44

—

JOSEPHINE IS SICK BUT WON'T ADMIT IT

"It was her last chance to reconquer Paris"

orty-five minutes later, we were in his office, and it was Nelle Nugent's turn to gape. (Only recently, she told me that when I came back to the Palace with her boss, she thought, "How could this guy find Jimmy Nederlander so fast? I can't find him myself!")

Mr. Nederlander had me call Josephine. "I'm not talking to you," she said. "You're a traitor." I said Mr. Nederlander was booking her into the Palace, wasn't it wonderful? and he took the phone. "Miss Baker, your son is the fastest talker I ever met. I want you here tomorrow."

Impossible. She couldn't leave the children, she was booked for the ball at Versailles, but her Jean-Claude knew everything, he could get the press releases started. Mr. Nederlander agreed, yet I was worried. Why was I a traitor? Back at Peter Brown's, I called Marie Spiers and asked what was going on.

After San Francisco, Josephine had gone to spend a few days with Marie in Paris, and Marie had confronted her with a copy of *France-Dimanche*. "You're hiding something from me." The newspaper featured pictures of Josephine and Bob Brady ("twenty years younger, and an American millionaire"), along with a story about the "shadow" over their happiness. I was quoted as saying, "Maman is not divorced from Jo Bouillon," something I did not even know.

Josephine swore to Marie that there was nothing to the story. Again, it was "I don't know that man." She was going to appear at the Versailles ball after all (I had convinced Jean-Louis Barrault to approach her directly—he told her, "France needs you"), and since I had been invited too, I decided to fly to Paris for a couple of days. I could attend the party and, while in town, clear up the *France-Dimanche* mystery.

Upon my arrival, the first thing I did was get a copy of the "interview" I was supposed to have given. It was nothing but a blown-up version of the item from Suzy's column that had already appeared in London's *Daily Mail* and *France-Soir*. Although the editor of *France-Dimanche* was willing to clear me, Josephine refused to speak to him. She went to Versailles without me—she'd got my invitation canceled ("I don't know that person")—and stole the show from Liza Minnelli and Nureyev, and I went back to America.

By mid-November, the Palace contract was in Joseph Bessone's office. Josephine was to be paid thirty thousand dollars for her week's work, she was to open on New Year's Eve, and to be in New York five days earlier "for publicity purposes."

Now to my surprise, her nephew, Richard, Jr., took my place as whipping boy. "Aunt Tumpy used to tell me her children are bastards and giving her trouble, they don't have her blood, whereas I do, so she trusts me."

In December, Josephine wrote to Bob Brady about their "marriage," now three months old. "I too regret not having took [*sic*] the communion that beautiful and special day. . . ." She also told him that since I had talked to a "scandal newspaper," the family had written me off. "Not one of us wishes to see him again, he is a very bad boy. . . ."

I soon learned that was not the way the children felt at all. "I was surprised," Jean-Claude said. "She'd had you on a pedestal, and I said to myself, 'It cannot be, she used him and now she is discarding him.' Anyway, I felt a lot of affection for you, and you know, at the time, we were so fed up with her we had almost lost interest in her welfare."

Jari offered reassurance too. "For me," he said, "you were the brother who had logic, and who helped us a lot."

Josephine opened at the Palace on New Year's Eve. That morning, it rained. The journalist Dotson Rader, working for *Esquire,* covered the final rehearsal. Briefly, he spoke with Richard, who confided that "Madame Aunt" had never had a face-lift. When he saw her, Rader believed it. Her cheeks, he said, "like errant sand dunes invading an oasis, encroached sadly on her mouth when she was not smiling."

He sketched for his magazine a painful picture of a woman in the twilight of her days, wandering, distracted, working from some deep recess of will; when the body said no, the mind said no, and only the spirit insisted.

She ran out of breath. She forgot the name of her new dresser, and could not remember her lyrics, Rader reported. "Richard, sensing her confusion, brought her a cardboard schedule listing her songs and conversation. She had trouble reading it. She went on, leaning back, her sunglasses catching the stage lights . . . into another medley, and again she forgot the words . . . 'Smile when you're blah blah blah . . . and then I came back to New York and Billy Brice . . .'

"She had forgotten Fanny Brice."

Tommy Tune, the dancer/choreographer/actor, was at that opening. "I'd never seen Josephine, and it was not only New Year's Eve, but my night off from a show called *Seesaw,* so I went. There were many old European people in the audience, and this black guy dressed in a turban ran down the aisles passing out roses, and he said, 'Throw these to Josephine when she comes on, she will love it.'

"And Josephine started on and stopped and said, 'I can't step on all these beautiful roses,' and I thought, 'My God, how sensitive, how wonderful. And then somebody came out and sort of cleared her a path.

"My favorite moment in the show was when she sat down on the stage and started to recall this dance that George Balanchine had done for her. He'd said, 'Josephine, I see you with four men,' and she'd said, 'Well, I don't know, maybe that's too many men for me . . .' And she just drifted off into this reverie. The piano player was playing soft music, and she went away from us, into some memory we were not a part of. She was so at home on the stage she just went off. And then you could see her thinking, 'Oh, my God, I'm here at the Palace, what am I doing, talking about Balanchine and those four men, I must go on with the show.'

"You could see her return to reality, it was one of the great magic moments I ever experienced in a theater."

At the Palace, Dany Revel was her pianist, one of the fixed points in her changing world. He had known her since 1959, played for her in *Paris Mes Amours*. It was Dany who had come with her to the Regal in Chicago. "With her, many times I got tears in my eyes, and that's why I forgave her everything.

"In her own way, she was looking for perfection. She once stopped in the middle of the street and said, 'You understand, Dany, in life one can always do better.' To survive a long time, a hardness is needed. She dared to cut people out of her life, she tired everyone."

The New York Times's Howard Thompson raved about the show at the Palace, saying Josephine still had "luscious, honeyed tones in the middle register and hearty top ones belted out when she chooses. . . ."

Now Jack Jordan and Howard Sanders filed a $1.5-million damage suit against her, charging breach of contract in San Francisco. But in the teeth of lawsuits, she was unregenerate. After the last show at the Palace, she stole the costumes again. "I've never seen anything like that in my life," Richard, Jr., says. "She heard someone's coming with a warrant to take her costumes, and she calls up my brother Artie, and he brings his truck from Long Island. A sheriff came backstage later, but the costumes were gone. I said to Aunt Tumpy later, 'You are the biggest crook in the world!' "

As with Thelma Carpenter's "biggest gyp on the Nile," there is a certain amount of admiration in the description.

"From the Palace," Dany Revel says, "we went to the Raffles Club. I thought that was a step down, it was a private club, not ideal."

In the three weeks between her closing at the Palace and her opening at Raffles, she flew to Cuernavaca, and Bob Brady. But something went wrong between them. My own theory is that she discovered he was not so rich as she had believed. In any case, during the afternoon of January 15, she wrote a farewell note on paper with his letterhead, Casa de la Torre, and begged a favor. "One night, I was very ill, and you stayed near me, please do this again tonight. I only have pure thoughts, I probably will not come here again, so I would like to be near you one more night."

She calls him "my husband," tells him to throw himself into his painting and not drink too much, and announces her intention to sneak away "like a thief in the early morning . . . I won't be able to say goodbye."

Josephine is being so dishonest. She had started the game with him before our trip to Mexico—"He is gay," she had told me, "but a great host." Meaning, there would be free food, free beds, good company, nice parties. And when she's had enough, she's gone.

His letters to her were destroyed—after a fight with Richard, Jr., fearing blackmail, she burned them—and since he died before I could talk to him, we don't have his side of the story. But it seems to me he wasn't treated much better than I, though he did get a fond notice of dismissal.

People who didn't love her, who treated her as a business proposition, got a better deal. With Jimmy Nederlander, she showed up on time, she talked to the press, she signed autographs.

At Raffles, there was no Jimmy Nederlander to temper Josephine's whims, and little structure of any kind, so the show was pretty much a mess. The club, in the basement of the Sherry Netherland Hotel, was doing no business.

"And everybody was serving her with subpoenas," Richard, Jr., marvels. "I said, 'Aunt Tumpy, stop signing those autographs, you gonna sign one, we gonna go to jail.'

"We were living at the Hotel Navarro on Central Park South, and Aunt Tumpy was cooking rice all the time. And we had sweet rolls so stale we had to put water on them to soften them. She had been making thousands of dollars a night at the Palace—she would go to Armani and buy clothes, she bought that teacup puppy, Fifi, that cost five hundred dollars—and we were living in poverty."

Florence Dixon recalls those winter afternoons through a rosy haze. "We would sit on the floor of her apartment at the Navarro, and Josephine would put out pictures of the kids, and pictures of the Christmas dinner, with Sister there. I was spellbound.

"She didn't want anybody to know about her medical condition. We used to go to a lab and have her blood tested. She was supposed to send reports back to her doctor in France, but I don't think she ever did."

"Aunt Tumpy was very suspicious," Richard, Jr., says. "At the Navarro, she suddenly got the idea that terrorists were going to attack us, and suddenly I was moving trunks from one hotel room to another. She was suspicious of you, too, Jean-Claude. She said, 'He is scandalous, he is using my name, after all I have done for him, like he was a son of mine. Do you know, he tried to sing in my show?' "

I had finally made the acquaintance of Richard, Jr., outside of Raffles. Loving his father, I was happy to meet him, and we had a brief, friendly conversation. He told me of his troubles. "All the time at the Palace, and now at Raffles, she's complaining, 'Jean-Claude wouldn't do things that way,' and I've been saying, 'Why don't you get him back if he's so great?' "

He thought I should make peace with his aunt. I said no. "She'd have to ask my pardon on her knees."

I thought I was out of her life, but I wasn't. The manager at Raffles had made me welcome—I found out later that Josephine had told him to take care of me—and I went there almost every night, and stood at the bar. It was an exercise in masochism. She wasn't happy with the way the maître d' introduced her, and one night she reprimanded him in front of the audience. "That's it!" he said to me. "From now on, she can introduce herself!"

She never approached me and I didn't go to her, but a mutual friend, Jocelyne Jocya, was determined to effect a reconciliation, and prevailed on both of us to show up at the Village Gate where she—Jocelyne—was singing. "I have arranged everything for Sunday, Josephine's day off," she told me. "I have reserved a front table, you will arrive first, then she will come with Bessie Buchanan and Florence Dixon. The champagne is on ice."

Still, I fought with myself. If I gave in, Josephine would once again be getting away with murder. "She wanted to dominate, and make you afraid at the same time," Jacqueline Abtey had said. "When I discovered that, I knew it was time to leave her." Not being as smart as Jacqueline Abtey, I came to the Village Gate, sat at the table down in front, and waited. At midnight, I got up and went home.

Jocelyne says Josephine arrived a few minutes afterward, and was sad that I'd left. But she never called

In April, with Richard, Jr., she went west to appear at the Beverly Hilton Hotel for a weekend. "I thought, my aunt, the big star," Richard, Jr., says, "and then we went into that ballroom and it was empty. Only a few people came, Nina Simone, Lou Rawls's mother, Eartha Kitt, Diana Ross.

"Diana Ross is sitting there with her friends, and Aunt Tumpy goes up to her and cups Diana Ross's face in her hands, and kisses her on both cheeks."

Diana Ross has told me a less tender version of the face-cupping story. "Josephine came, stood in front of me, put her fingers into my hair, and pulled hard," she says. "I guess she wanted to see if I was wearing a wig."

"I was getting sick of the whole mess," Richard, Jr., says. "I finally just left California and never saw Aunt Tumpy again."

Back home on the Riviera, Josephine went to Joseph Bessone and said she wanted to buy a large property in Monaco. "I told her," he says, "the princess has been very generous with you, and I know she doesn't expect you to pay off the mortgage on the Villa Maryvonne, but if I were you, to show my gratitude, I would take care of that.

"Josephine paid off the mortgage. The princess was once again generous, she refused to take any interest."

In June, Sammy Davis, Jr., who was to headline the opening show at Monaco's new Sporting Club, withdrew in a fit of pique. He was replaced by Burt Bacharach, Desi Arnaz, Jr., Bill Cosby, and Josephine. The princess could always count on Josephine.

Her nephew, Richard, Jr., could not. At that time, she thought of him as an enemy who was planning to write a scurrilous book about her. "He told me he had frightful things to say about me and my sister," she confided to Florence Dixon. "He threatened to unveil the true Josephine Baker. The lack of family feeling among some of the young is deplorable . . . that boy is only thirsty for money and glory."

It was a thirst with which she was familiar. By mid-July, she and Dany Revel were back from a tour of Japan, and she was planning for the 1974 Red Cross gala. Again, in that act of cannibalism practiced by aging stars who feed on their own legends, the spectacular was to be a retelling of Josephine's life story.

Jean-Claude Brialy had agreed to act as master of ceremonies on opening night, and Josephine wove dreams. If the show were a hit, why not move it to Paris?

Marie Spiers came to spend her vacation in Roquebrune. "As soon as I arrived, Josephine said, 'Give me all your money, I need it,' and she took me and Christina Scotto (who was also staying with her) to Italy to buy beauty products. She claimed they were less expensive than in France.

"The Red Cross show was an absolute triumph. Afterward, again with my money, she went to Israel to cry at the Wailing Wall, and to comfort Golda Meir, who was no longer prime minister. She took Stellina."

Of all the children, Stellina, being the baby, was now closest to Josephine. "I was lucky," she says, "I think I had a wonderful mother, I never tried to judge her. I had ten years with her, and after she died, ten years with my father in Argentina, but for me he was a stranger.

"Once I said to him, 'You know something? You never wanted me, but be careful, because life is going to fool you. You love Marianne and all your other children, you think I'm the bad one, but the day you're alone, the one who will stay with you will be me.'

"When he was dying, he was hallucinating one time, he wanted to kill me, and afterward, he said, 'Stellina, it's not you, it's your mother.' And he cried. And he said all those things he never told my mother, things he thought and felt and never said. He had lived twenty years with all that inside. He died loving her."

Excited by the success of the latest Monte Carlo gala, Josephine got in touch with Gerard Oestreicher, an American producer. She said she would like to bring the production over "as soon as you arrange it with James Nederlander."

It didn't happen. Still, she didn't sit on her hands waiting. She was appearing at the Berns Theatre in Stockholm when she ran into Jack Jordan, who was convinced they were being led by forces they didn't understand. "I had to leave America because I lost everything, and I came to Stockholm to start again. We met. . . . There must be a reason."

"How strange life is," said Josephine. "Think! I was crossing the street . . . and you came down another road."

Then she accused him of lying, stealing, and leaving her stranded in San Francisco. As for the lawsuit, not only did she not owe him money, *he* owed *her* money!

She was on her way to South Africa, where she would tour for a month; after that, she would be appearing at the Palladium in London.

She had asked Dany Revel to accompany her on the South African tour, but Mrs. Revel said no. "My wife is a respected medium in France, and she said, 'I don't want you to go, *c'est tout noir.*' She didn't see death, just darkness. I felt like an idiot, but I didn't go."

Josephine shouldn't have gone either. The tour was a flop, houses a quarter full. The star criticized the apartheid laws but, said *Variety*, "she was willing to accept South African money."

She must have been glad to get back to London, where Dany was playing piano for her, the queen mother was in the audience—it was a command performance to help needy actors—and Josephine was a hit. She wore a new jumpsuit, and told old stories. "I started in 1924, and we were all beginners together—Pablo, Matisse, Hemingway. I used to look after them, picking up their clothes, getting them organized." As for the bananas, "I wasn't really naked, I simply didn't have any clothes on."

Two weeks before Christmas, Moïse got married. Josephine did not attend.

"He was the first of us to get married," Jean-Claude says, "and he wanted his mother at the wedding. It was touching. I remember she was in the kitchen doing the dishes, like a poor old woman with that plastic cap on her head, and Moïse said, 'Mother, why don't you want to come?' and she told him some kind of story—she had not been introduced to the girl, rules of etiquette had not been respected, whatever. She used any excuses she could think of.

"Moïse was very tense, hyper, and he said, 'For the last time, will you come to the wedding?' and she answered calmly, 'No, Moïse.' So he said, 'From this day forward, I will never set foot in your house.'

"It was so hard, but she preferred that, she preferred putting up a wall to talking, and there was no going over that wall."

"Moïse is marrying a chambermaid at the hotel where he's a waiter," Josephine complained to Jean-Claude Brialy. "It is a mistake to get married at nineteen with no experience in life." (The estrangement from Moïse had its bright side, she wouldn't have to part with any of the jewels she had been keeping "for my future daughters-in-law.")

"I wonder," Brahim says, "if she was not jealous of the women my brothers chose. Moïse's wife, Monique, was good-looking, a lovely girl, but Mother was furious."

Margaret had been planning to fix Christmas dinner, but Josephine protested. "No, Sister, you have worked enough, I'm going to take all of you to a restaurant." She also bought new clothes for all the children, spending one and a half million francs in a fancy store in Nice. "It was as though she had a presentiment that it would be her last Christmas," says Joseph Bessone. "Since she came back from America, she had gone nonstop. I told her she had to take more care of herself."

She didn't, she couldn't. Since America had not responded with a new offer, she turned her sights back home. No nibbles. Paris managers did not have faith in yet another Josephine Baker comeback.

And then, with her good fairy in attendance, her *baraka* working, whatever it was that always supplied her with a fresh chance, she met Jean Bodson, a patron of the arts. He took her to lunch and confessed that as a young man, he had been madly in love with her. "I own a little theater, not worthy of your talent, but it would be an honor to give it to you."

They went to check out his theater, Bobino, in Montparnasse, on rue de la Gaîté, and she was satisfied. "Oh! It will be perfect for my farewell. We could maybe move that column, build a staircase . . ."

Monsieur Bodson said he would redo the theater. By the time it was done, it had cost him a million dollars.

Now, every day, in Marie Spiers's apartment, Josephine rehearsed with Dany Revel at the grand piano. He had to go to play at the Hôtel Méridien at 6 P.M., but he gave Josephine his afternoons. He had written an opening number for her, a song with lyrics that began, "Here I am, back again, Paris, tell me, how do you find me?"

"For three months they were rehearsing," Marie says, "and while Josephine sang, she rearranged all my shelves. Pierre would come at night to see what she had learned." (Once again, Pierre was going to be her conductor.)

"She was beginning," Marie says, "to behave like someone reborn. She even found time to try writing her own life story [no Sauvage or Rivollet to help her this time], dictating a little bit every day to a secretary at Bobino. And she wanted to receive a lot of people again. She told me, 'It's too small here.' I found her an apartment two doors from mine, and she liked it, except for the bedroom. 'It smells of death,' she said. I signed the lease, and my son was upset. 'You are crazy,' he said."

Despite her bravado, Dany Revel knew that Josephine was worried. "It was her last chance to reconquer Paris. Then one day, we were rehearsing the opening, she was sitting on a chair, and she started to sing, and it was like a phonograph winding down, 'Heeere IIIII aaammm . . .' I looked over at her, and she had fallen asleep.

"I let her sleep, but wondered about her strength."

Still nervous that she wasn't quite ready to face the public, Josephine had asked to have the opening pushed back a week. Mr. Bodson was willing, but André Levasseur, who had designed the sets and costumes,

476 · *Josephine: The Hungry Heart*

said no, Dany Revel recalls. "She needed a few more days, even forty-eight hours would have given her some time to rest."

On March 24, the first preview took place. Her doctor had tried to prevent all extracurricular activities, but Josephine could never say no to the press. She permitted a TV news crew to come backstage. She was dressed for the finale of the first act in her army uniform with all her medals and ribbons. "The decorations you are wearing—" the interviewer began. Josephine never let him finish the question. "Won on the battlefields," she said.

She was asked about her family, and she laughed. "They are growing up. One of my sons, Luis, is getting married."

Had they been to the show?

No, they were studying. "At this moment, it is good they are not here, because when I'm with them, I forget everything, *tout, tout, tout.* Only my children count. And right now it is necessary that I have peace and tranquillity so I can give myself entirely to the public of Paris."

How did it feel to be back on a Paris stage?

"Good. Agreeable to find again my family. For me, family is everybody, but mostly the public who made me."

Heavily made up, without her big glasses, the bags under her eyes no longer hidden behind spangles, Josephine looked straight into the camera. "It is agreeable, because at least I can see what they think of me while I'm still alive."

Chapter 45

—

GOING OUT
IN A BLAZE OF
GLORY

"We always believed she was immortal"

The phone rang. Good news can generally wait till morning; at 2 A.M., it's always something else. "Jean-Claude, you must be strong," said the voice. "Josephine is dead."

It was April 12, 1975. I was thirty-one and I'd been living in New York, calling my Swiss bank when I needed money, taking voice lessons, tap lessons, and, like now, vacationing in Miami. I was giving myself the youth I'd never had.

In that room of the Pink Flamingo Hotel, I hung up and like a madman began to sing "J'ai Deux Amours" over and over in a loud, hoarse voice that sounded like somebody else's. Scenes from my life with her rushed through my head backwards, fuzzy and fast, as when you hit the rewind button on a VCR. It was 5 A.M., not yet light, by the time I had cried myself out and went downstairs to find someone to talk to. A night porter got me a cup of coffee.

I had seen the pictures of her in French newspapers, and reading about her projected comeback, I had stewed. Maybe she'll take Paris again, I had thought, but it's going to kill her. She had never apologized to me, but my fears for her had proved stronger than my pride. I had taken to phoning again. At first, she would pretend she didn't recognize my voice. "Who is this?" she would say. We would talk for twenty minutes, I would fill her in on Broadway and Hollywood gossip, the latest trend, the newest star, and then, suddenly, she would hand the phone to whichever child was passing by. "Here, it's your brother."

I wasn't the only one with a premonition of disaster. Marie went to all the previews at Bobino, and was alarmed. "She was very tired. Her doctor said, 'The heart is sick, but the children are the ones who are killing her.' That's why they weren't allowed to come to the show."

Josephine was missing her animals, but the management of Bobino was firm. "No dogs; who will take them out?" She asked Marianne to come and bring her a cat, but did not allow Marianne to stay. "She just did an *allez et retour,*" says Marie. Stellina was the only one of the children who spent a few days with Josephine before the opening. "I would go to eat with her in a little Italian restaurant across the street from Bobino," she remembers. "Maman was working very hard; she was tired, but very satisfied."

Josephine had convinced doctors, friends, even herself, that the children sapped her strength. "At the end, I think she wondered if she had done the right thing in adopting us," Jean-Claude says. "She had an illogical life, and she refused to admit it."

A year earlier, revelation—and with it, compassion—had come to Jean-Claude. "I went to see all her performances for the Red Cross gala. One night, after the show, we went to have dinner, and there were a dozen of us in the restaurant. That is when I finally realized what her life had been, through people like Maurice Bataille, whom she had wanted to marry. He would say, 'Josephine, do you remember?' and she would say, 'Oh, stop it, you silly!'

"She bloomed, she became a young girl again, and I was in tears. I thought, 'This is my mother, she made people happy before I knew her, in another life.'

"We did not go to see her perform at Bobino, because she did not want us there. In Paris, she did not belong to us, she belonged to her audience."

And to her company. Jean Pierre Reggiori, the youngest chorus boy—he wasn't yet eighteen—remembers her coming in every day with oranges. "She would say, 'My children, it's vitamins, eat them.' We adopted her, watched over her on the staircase. She would sometimes stumble, but we never let her fall."

Once again, the streets of Paris were covered with large colored posters of Josephine, the face retouched, smooth, ageless, the glittering body stocking, the plumes of feathers sprouting from a white turban. AVEC LE CONCOURS DE LA S.B.M. MONTE CARLO . . . JEAN-CLAUDE DAUZONNE PRÉSENTE JOSEPHINE, said the posters. Her first name was enough. For the French, there had been only two Josephines, the wife of Napoléon, and this one.

She had told reporters they would discover four Josephines at Bobino. "One of four years, one of twelve, one of twenty, and of course me. They don't look very much alike, but in the theater, illusion is what counts."

And she was still sweating to create that illusion. "She astonished me," says Alexandre, who was doing her hair and wigs. "She would come offstage dripping with sweat, and go to the stagehands. 'You must be tired, you have worked very hard, have a drink on me.' She was using a lot of perfume, telling me, 'You know, a woman must always smell good. I have had rains of perfume on my body.'

"She talked about the *Revue Nègre* and how Antoine had saved her opening night with his paper helmet. 'Now,' she said, 'I work only with wigs. You can put pins in my scalp, even if the blood is running, it doesn't hurt me.' "

But it did hurt her. She confessed as much to Liliane Montevecchi, then starring at the Folies-Bergère. "I went to see Josephine on a Sunday afternoon. Everybody in the house was crying, and we didn't know why, it was not a sad show.

"Afterward, in her dressing room, she took off her wig and said, 'I have such a headache. They pull my hair up under the wig to erase my wrinkles.' The few tufts of fuzz she had left had been pitilessly wound around pins, the skin pulled up tight with the hair, but she was willing to pay the price to present herself the way her public remembered her. She had a way to touch people's hearts, this woman. I don't know what it was, I never saw anything like it."

Olivier Echaudemaison, who was doing her makeup, says she was so tired she would fall asleep while he was working on her. "And when she woke up, she was totally surprised to see how beautiful she was. 'I don't recognize myself,' she told me."

"We had expanded the fifty-minute Monte Carlo show into a two-hour-long spectacle," says Jean-Claude Dauzonne, the director of Bobino. "We had enlarged the stage by covering the orchestra pit, and putting the musicians in the balcony. Mr. Bodson not only transformed the theater for Josephine, he paid her most pressing debts. (Even though no insurance company would touch her, he was willing to take the risk with her.) She was also receiving a substantial salary, plus a percentage of the take, and half the money was sent to her Swiss bank account."

Dauzonne had known Josephine since he was three years old. (His family had been friendly with Jo Bouillon's family.) "She liked me to come to her dressing room and talk while she got ready," he says. "Dany Revel had written her opening song, 'Me Revoila Paris,' and it gave me cold shivers. One of the lyrics was, 'And maybe, who knows, I will end my life on the stage.' I said, 'Josephine, I do not like that song.' I found it morbid, looking for sympathy. 'But no,' she insisted, 'it's wonderful!'"

"Altogether, she played fourteen performances, including previews. On the night of March 29, she stopped the show to announce with tears in her eyes that her son Luis had just got married, but because of her duty to her audience, she had not been able to be with him and his bride.

Luis had indeed made her a mother-in-law for the second time, but she was nicer to him than she had been to Moïse. "A few months before the wedding, I told her that she was going to be a grandmother," he says. "I think it gave her a certain joy, a certain sense of revenge against her own father; this time the roles would be reversed, this child would be born of a white mother and a black father."

"I believe she was happy about the baby," says Luis's wife, Michele. "But she and I didn't talk very much. At that time, I was shy, and she intimidated me. Then she went to Paris, and I never saw her again.

"We had invited her to our wedding, and though she couldn't come, she sent us a telegram saying her thoughts were with us, and she would pay for the wedding lunch. But since she died two weeks later, we ended up paying for it."

The press gala on April 2 was a triumph; in the wings, she whispered to Jean-Claude Dauzonne, "*J'ai gagné.* I have won."

Le Figaro agreed. "For the second time in fifty years, Josephine Baker has conquered Paris which one night in 1925 seduced her forever."

Six days later came the official premiere, attended by Princess Grace, assorted Rothschilds, *le tout Paris,* with a few exceptions. The faithful Joseph Bessone was missing. "She invited me to the premiere," he said. I said, 'I don't like to witness things that pain me, Josephine. You are going to leave your skin at Bobino, do not count on me to witness it.' In Paris, they killed her."

Backstage on opening night, she herself said the same thing to Jean Clement. "Those amplifiers are killing me, I'm going to die, because there is too much noise, my head hurts. Why do they do that? I have a good voice, I don't need all that noise."

The "noise" had been added not to augment Josephine's voice but to supplement the orchestra. A company called Festival had done a studio recording of the show—just audio, not video—and the tape was played every night in the theater. Besides fattening the band's sound, it provided a more reliable beat for the dancers. (With applause added, that sound track was released after Josephine's death. "We didn't want to film the show before the opening," says Jean-Claude Dauzonne. "So much was already on Josephine's shoulders."

In addition to her unhappiness with the clamor of the music, Josephine told Jean Clement, she was suffering because "my children are not nice with me."

Clement tried to tease her out of her mood. "Remember when Mistinguett said to you, 'Why do you want to adopt all those children?'

"And you said, 'I have to be an example,' and Miss said, 'You're crazy. Talk about examples, Christ came to save the world and they crucified him!'

"Josephine was not laughing."

Until the show began. Then everything changed. That opening night, I had sent her a telegram: PETITE MAMAN, I KNOW YOU WILL BE A BIG SUCCESS, AND YOU KNOW YOU ARE IN MY HEART. I PRAY FOR YOU. LOVE, JEAN-CLAUDE. She didn't need my prayers, she couldn't do anything wrong, she was continually stopped by waves of applause. "In her gypsy number, 'Donnez-Moi la Main,' Dauzonne says, "she went down into the audience, and there in the front row was Arletty, the actress who, after the war, had been censured for falling in love with a German. She was blind now, dressed all in white, and the famous pink follow-spot lighted both women as Josephine took Arletty's hand. 'How beautiful you are, Madame, *all* of France admires you.' "

Hippocrates wrote it: "Healing is a matter of time, but it is sometimes also a matter of opportunity."

"People were crying," says my friend Robert Boutin. "Next to me, Carlo Ponti turned to Sophia Loren and said, '*Regarde bien ça,* you won't see it twice in a lifetime.' "

There were thirty-four songs, and fifteen scenes from Josephine's life as she chose to remember it. It started like a fairy tale—"Once upon a time"—and proceeded to touch on Africa, Louisiana [*sic*], New York, France, the war, the Wailing Wall in Israel; there was even a skit in which she made fun of her bad time at Les Milandes. Dancers dressed as furniture movers came to haul away everything—including the pink sofa on which Josephine lay, showing off her beautiful legs—and soon nothing was left onstage but the star, singing "Au Revoir but Not Adieu."

At the end of the show, Jean-Claude Brialy came on to read a telegram from Giscard d'Estaing. The president sent Josephine fond wishes IN THE NAME OF A GRATEFUL FRANCE WHOSE HEART HAS SO OFTEN BEATEN WITH YOURS.

"She got a standing ovation of more than thirty minutes," says Robert Boutin. "People were screaming, 'You are the most beautiful, we love you, Josephine,' and finally, her voice strangled with emotion, she spoke. 'I had prepared something to say, but I can only tell you I love you and I know you love me.' "

Thierry Le Luron, then the most brilliant political satirist in France, told me he had gone to the theater that night out of respect for a national monument. "I went there thinking, well, I'm going to applaud the Eiffel Tower or the Arc de Triomphe, it will certainly be a little boring. In reality, it was sublime, people did not want to leave the theater, it was the crowning of Josephine's career."

At the Bristol Hotel, Mr. Bodson gave the opening-night party, and Princess Grace helped Josephine cut the many-tiered cake celebrating her fifty years as queen of the French music hall. She was wearing a cream-colored silk dress by Nina Ricci, a matching turban with a veil. During supper, the president of the city council presented her with the Grande Médaille de Vermeil de la Ville de Paris.

"She refused to go home early," Marie says. "She told me, 'I will stay until my last guest is gone.' "

It was 4 A.M. before she left the Bristol, and next morning, she was still euphoric. She phoned Marie and asked her to come to the theater that night. For the first time, Marie refused. "Tonight," she said, "I will sleep."

The second-night performance, which can be a letdown, was another triumph. After the show, the elated Josephine demanded that Dauzonne take her to Chez Michou.

"I want to see Bobby, that black American boy who imitates me," she said. Dauzonne refused—"Josephine, in two or three days, you can ask whatever you want of me"—and she was still sulking as he drove her home.

"When I put her in the elevator of her building," he told me, "I pushed the third-floor button and kissed her good-night. Her last words to me were, 'Oh, you young people act like old men, you are no fun.' "

Thursday, April 10, Marie Spiers: "Josephine always called me very early. That morning, I was happy not to receive her call. Thank God she is resting, I thought, and went to my boutique. Around 2:30 P.M., I phoned her apartment. Pepito's niece, Lélia, was working for her, and she answered. 'Madame is sleeping.' I said, 'What? She is still sleeping? Go wake her up.' Lélia left, came back, and said, 'I can't wake her, and she's snoring.' I called the doctor, and then hurried to Josephine's apartment."

Behind closed doors, the drama played out. "The doctor told me it was very bad," Marie says. In the bedroom, Josephine lay on her left side, one hand to her head, the plastic shower cap she had been wearing still in place. Her glasses had fallen to the floor. The bed was littered with newspapers, their front pages extolling her latest comeback. She had been reading these love letters when she collapsed.

"When I arrived at her place, I knew what had happened," says Jean-Claude Dauzonne. "It was the same way I had found my mother; she'd had a brain hemorrhage. Dr. Thiroloix chose the Salpêtrière hospital because it had the best emergency room in Paris, and we called an ambulance. Then I left to go to the theater; we told the radio and TV that Josephine had been hospitalized for exhaustion."

"The ambulance attendants asked me to remove Josephine's ring," Marie says. "It was the one with Pepito's crest, she had never taken it off since he gave it to her. The driver ran all the red lights, with the police helping us. Jean-Claude Brialy and André Levasseur were in the ambulance, but Brialy wouldn't sign Josephine into Salpêtrière, he said,

'Marie, you put this in your name.' So I signed, accepting responsibility for Josephine's bills."

Stellina Bouillon: "I was in my aunt Margaret's house, on Easter vacation from my school in England, and I had a dream that my mother was very bad, and I started crying and said, 'She is going to die, she needs you.' And Auntie said, 'Okay, if we don't have news by midday, I'll go to Paris.' "

Luis Bouillon: "With my Fiat coupe 124, I drove Aunt Margaret to the airport. On our way there, she asked me to stop by the Banco di Roma. I stayed in the car while she went inside."

Later, having arrived in Paris, Margaret realized she didn't even know where Josephine was. She went by taxi from hospital to hospital until she came to Salpêtrière. "I could see," she told me, "that Tumpy could not make it." The doctors conferred—if they operated, there was a 70 percent chance that Josephine would be permanently impaired—and Margaret made the decision. "Don't you touch my sister." (Later she told Florence Dixon, "If she had lived and been unable to talk or walk, she would have lost her mind.")

Marie Spiers and Margaret kept vigil through the night. Once, Margaret said, squeezing Josephine's hand, she thought she felt Josephine squeeze back.

At 5:30 A.M., on Saturday, April 12, Josephine died.

"She gave a few little sighs, then one long one, and it was over," Marie says. "I think deep in me, I was expecting it. What she had been doing was beyond her strength."

For two days, she had lain unconscious. Princess Grace knelt beside the bed, praying, as a priest gave Josephine the last rites. "She claimed many religions," says Jean-Claude Dauzonne, "but she had told us she was a Catholic. And that she did not want to be photographed dead."

The fiction she had created lived on. Her death certificate said she was the daughter of Arthur Baker.

Margaret and Marie had dressed her in the clothes she'd worn to the opening-night party at the Bristol. "We wanted her to go to Paradise the same vision we had seen after the premiere," says Alexandre. "In death, she had a great serenity, she seemed like she was sleeping."

"I chose the most gorgeous coffin in Paris," says Jean-Claude Dauzonne, "lined in pink, of course, since she always asked for a pink gel over her spotlight. Before we closed the lid, Margaret said, 'How beautiful you are, Sister,' and she began to sing a spiritual."

Margaret had not telephoned her brother Richard. "My father's French was still bad," says Guylaine, "and he and my mother were listening to the radio, and the announcer said, 'Josephine's light burned out this morning,' and my mother said, 'My God, Richard, your sister just died.' He was destroyed."

Jean-Claude Bouillon: "I had come home very late, it was 6 A.M., and Marianne was sitting on a low wall outside the villa, and I knew immediately that something weird was going on. The sun was rising, the light coming up, and she said, 'You know about Mother?'

"And she made a gesture with her arms meaning, it's all over. I went up to her, she was crying, and I was looking at the sky, and I did not understand.

"It was not until the next day that I realized my mother was dead. I had been drinking while she was dying at the Salpêtrière. For years afterward, I felt guilty. At the same time, we always believed she was immortal, Mother, she had survived so many things. But that moment I'll remember all my life, Marianne telling me of Mother's death, with a sign of her arms, in the dawn."

Brahim Bouillon: "She was always going away, and so she was just away again. I only realized later that this time she was dead. At the villa, our first reaction was, Are we going to be separated? Is Daddy coming back? Since the person who had brought us together had disappeared, we were wondering what would become of us. Rumors started that Princess Grace would take Stellina, that our father would come back and divide the family."

Me, as soon as I could get on a plane, I flew from America to Paris, and went to my apartment. Mara and Jari joined me there, and I tried to comfort them, but we were numb, we didn't understand she was gone. For us, she was still somewhere in the world, getting ready to go onstage, or making a speech about brotherhood.

I didn't want to go to the Salpêtrière and see her lying in a wooden box, and I was bitter toward those I thought had killed her, the frivolous jet-set delinquents who had dragged her around so they could be photographed with her. My brother Jean-Claude shared my feelings. "With age," he says, "people become infantile again, she wanted once more to be the twenty-year-old Josephine. That is why she let those people charm her."

But Jean-Claude and I both knew we could not entirely blame "those people." Josephine had been their avid accomplice. "For the past year,"

Margaret said, "her whole talk was of Paris, where she wanted to be."

Before leaving my apartment, Jari gave me a ticket for the funeral at the Madeleine. A ticket for a funeral? I was thunderstruck.

When I arrived at the magnificent many-pillared church on the morning of April 15, no one asked for my ticket. In fact, there were no crowds, the church was quite empty. The showman in me was disturbed by the poor turnout.

I sat in one of the front pews reserved for family, and a priest came up and said, "My son, she told me on her deathbed how good you were to her." Oh my God, I thought, on her deathbed, she talked about me?

The service began, with no more than twenty or so mourners in the vast domed space, but when the priest began to speak, everything became clear. He was eulogizing some other lady, one Madame Fougère. I was at the wrong funeral. I sat there fighting the urge to grin. "Maman," I thought, "even now you are teasing me."

Meanwhile, Josephine rode for the last time through the city. The procession started from the hospital, stopped in front of Bobino (its marquee lighted in her honor, her name blazing in the gray day), then wound its way to the church. The skies matched the somber mood of the people thronging the sidewalks and massed on the broad steps of the Madeleine; in pictures it looks as though flocks of birds had settled there.

Thousands of mourners turned out. Only three thousand could be seated in the church. Madame Fougère's actual son and friends having departed, another crowd filed in. There were Margaret with Jari and Mara (they were the only two of Josephine's children to come to Paris), and then suddenly, kissing each other, Alain Delon, Sophia Loren. It's not a funeral, it's an opening, with stars and photographers. I have a vision of Josephine, arms raised, palms up, calling out, "How do you like me?" and I say to myself, "Well, here she is!"

"If she had died before Bobino," said Jean-Claude Dauzonne, "it would have made three lines in the papers; as it was, her funeral was almost a national event."

Princess Grace arrived, and General de Boissieu representing the Legion of Honor. I saw Michel Guy, the minister of culture, and General Vallin. Madame Derval, the widow of Paul Derval, was there with Michel Gyarmathy.

Jo Bouillon, whom I had not yet met, appeared to be a man in pain. Arriving from Buenos Aires, he had spoken briefly to the press. "Too many memories come back," he said, "the past grips my heart."

All around us, there was an unchurchlike din. We could hear buzzing from the gallery, whispering on the main floor, and the sounds of flashbulbs popping as pallbearers carried the heavy ebony coffin up the aisle. The thing was like a Rolls-Royce, and again I had to fight the nervous impulse to break down and laugh hysterically. What a show, I thought; wherever she is, she must be laughing too.

As the press frenzy grew, Canon Thorel addressed the crowd. "Brothers and sisters, don't forget you are in the house of God." He gave the photographers five minutes more, then the church was still.

In front of the altar on a purple cushion were Josephine's military decorations, and everywhere flags of the army of France, and flowers. A heart of red roses said "From Daddy and the children," and there was a bouquet in the shape of a Star of David, but none of us knew who had sent it. Afterward, people who had not been able to get into the church came to pray for her, and each took a flower as a souvenir.

During the homily, the canon said Paris had suffered a blow to the heart with Josephine's passing. True, she had been a great sinner, "but aren't we all?"

At the end, we followed the coffin out of church, our steps echoing on the stone floor. Behind us, we heard sweet silvery notes rising from a harp. One last time, Pierre Spiers was playing for Josephine "J'ai Deux Amours." The sound mixed with sobbing, sublime and unreal.

We emerged into a sea, a crush, of people. It was the first time I had ever understood why Josephine enjoyed crowds. In spite of the fear that you're going to be crushed, you're drunk with excitement. "All her life, Josephine looked for love," said Lydia Jones, watching the scene on television. "Even on the steps of the Madeleine, she was still looking for love."

"After a blinding sun, it was a total darkness," says Jean-Claude Dauzonne. "We reimbursed Marie Spiers, we paid for the hospital, the funeral. I wanted Josephine one last time to come down the great steps of Paris, the steps of the Madeleine. It almost did not happen. We had to pull the priests' ears. At first they did not want to welcome her because of her 'past.' But Mr. Bodson was very generous to the church, and I told them, 'Think of the publicity it will give you.' Then they relented."

Unlike me, Princess Grace had found the events of the day unseemly. From the beginning, she had thought the funeral should be held in Monaco, so a compromise had been reached: there would be one funeral in Paris, another—more dignified—in Monaco. (To me, it's always seemed as though the princess kidnapped Josephine's body.)

Josephine's body was dispatched to Monte Carlo, to the Athanee, a funeral parlor. At home in Roquebrune, Marianne seemed to have aged overnight, changing from wild girl to composed young woman. She kissed me and said, "How strange life is, Maman is gone, but we get back two brothers and our father." (Moïse was once again welcome, as was I.)

Falling into my arms, Stellina cried. Jo Bouillon still wasn't sure who I was, but Stellina introduced us. "He is our brother from Berlin. He had a fight with mother a year ago, but she loved him."

"I left with ten children bearing my name in the family book," he said. "I come back, there are twelve, and they tell me you are the thirteenth, so please feel at home." (He had just been informed by Marie Spiers that Josephine had registered Noël and Stellina as Bouillons.)

The second funeral was set for Saturday, April 19, and on the eighteenth (a sad birthday for me), Mara and I stood guard beside her coffin at the Athanee. A steady stream of mourners came by, people from the region, chic Monte Carlo ladies, veterans dressed in their old regimental colors. Some could hardly stand, but they were there to give Josephine a last military salute. "She was one of us," they said. Old peasants with leathery faces and knotty hands, the kind of men I had grown up with, walked past, crying, and I knew they cried seldom. When their cows died, when hail ruined their harvests, not for women. But they cried for Josephine.

I remember a young blind girl brought by her mother. She had the child touch the coffin, as though she believed Josephine had special healing powers. I marveled at the way all these people had been changed by her, and I brooded, blaming myself for having killed her. If I'd begged forgiveness for the interview I never gave, if I hadn't been so stubborn, I would have been there to force the little blue pill between her teeth. ("My first reaction when I heard Josephine died was, somebody forgot to give her the pill," says Yvonne Stoney. "I knew it, I just knew it.")

We stood there, Mara and I, his heart filled with anger, mine with guilt.

Richard and his family came to Roquebrune. "We went to Josephine's house, but we weren't welcome," Guylaine says. "Jo said he and his children were having a family reunion."

"Not even my father was invited in," adds her brother Alain. "Jo Bouillon was very hard."

Once again, I saw Richard being turned away from that house, but I had to respect Jo's authority, his duties were not easy.

All the arrangements for the ceremonies were being handled by Princess Grace, and this funeral was more personal (no press allowed in the church) than the first. Jack Jordan came to say goodbye, and Jacques Abtey too.

Brialy, Levasseur, Dauzonne arrived from Paris; so did Maguy Chauvin and Marie Spiers. There was some whispering that a young woman hidden behind a heavy black veil was Stellina's birth mother. Princess Grace wore black, with dark glasses and a single strand of pearls, and the coffin lay inside the sanctuary, a prerogative generally reserved for royalty.

Just before the funeral, there had been a wedding in St. Charles, so we entered a church decorated for a celebration of life, not death, there was rice all over the floor. And in the silence—no jostling, no commotion here—the voices, pure and sweet, of a boys' choir rose in farewell to the woman who, the bishop reminded us, had wanted "the unity of God's children."

At the cemetery, to my surprise, the coffin, rather than being put in the earth, was hoisted onto an altar in the open air in the midst of a kind of Greek temple held up by four columns.

Then the family went back to the Villa Maryvonne, and I prepared lunch with a touch of feast about it because it was Mara's seventeenth birthday. We were worried for him, his grief and anger were remorseless. Marie Spiers, helped by Maryse Bouillon and her friend Jacky Ducos, set the table on the terrace, and after lunch and birthday cake, Jo Bouillon asked me to come with him to Josephine's room. It was still the only place in the house where one could talk privately.

I said I was sad that Josephine's blood relations had not been invited to lunch, and Jo said he hadn't known what to do. "When I left France, Josephine and I had friends in common. Each time I came back, more of them were enemies. I was afraid her family might want something, I felt I had to protect our children."

Jo told me he was worried about the depth of Mara's grief. "Please speak to him, I only want his good. They are all my children and I am going to try my best for them."

Eighteen months ago, in this same room, Josephine had asked me to help with Jean-Claude, and here again I was being asked to be the big brother, just like at home in St. Symphorien, I had been the big brother to my sisters. In a strange way, that's the only part of family life I do well.

I took Mara up to the hills above the villa, and heard him out. He was furious with Jo—"He abandoned my mother!" I told him Jo had come back to try and finish Josephine's job. "We're not here to judge."

We went home, had dinner, turned on the television, and there was Josephine. Prince Rainier had made a gift to France of the videotape of her last Red Cross gala, and tonight it was being shown nationwide. We had been feeling drained, the spirit of the house gone, and suddenly she was there with us, so alive the room was filled with her.

Jo recognized that the older children needed to talk about their mother as much as the younger ones did. They had all loved Josephine, and fought with her, and wanted to understand what had just happened to them. He suggested we all go upstairs and out onto the terrace. It was a soft night, the moon shone, and the bay of Monte Carlo shimmered at our feet the way Fredi Washington had described it on her first visit in 1926, "as if someone had thrown a handful of diamonds into the water." There was something jarring, out of kilter, about grief in the midst of so much beauty.

"Josephine touched us deeply," Jo said. "She hurt us, but we have to forget that, she wasn't aware of it, she was a very special human being, difficult to explain, and we are going to miss her a lot, but we have to be strong because she would have wanted it."

Then he told us a story. "We had just got married when your mother went on the road. It was after the war, and France had nothing. The Milandes château was in such bad shape we could not live in it, there was no money or material to repair it, so while she was away, I restored a little house on the grounds. I cut the wood, I painted it, hung curtains in the front windows, made a sign that said J'AI DEUX AMOURS, and put it over the front door.

"When Josephine came back, I picked her up at the train station, and driving home, I told her I had a surprise for her. I couldn't wait to see her reaction to the nest I had prepared for us. Well, she came in, dropped her coat, and started off to see her newborn piglets. I said, 'Josephine, have you seen what the sign says?' 'Yes,' she said, 'it's very nice.' She was already running toward the farm."

His voice was trembling. You loved her, and she hurt you, that was the price you paid for being with Josephine.

Jari, the most reasonable of all of us, doesn't quite agree. "She never hurt me. When we older ones were five, Daddy and Mother talked candidly to us. They said we were adopted, that our parents could not provide for us, and that Mother had taken us since she could not have children of her own. It helped us later on when we were growing up with a black brother, a yellow brother, a red brother. You were not shocked, you understood this other little child was from a family who could not feed him, and after a few months, he was your brother.

"I have always admired Mother as a great artist, but she was also the mother hen. Sometimes she wanted you to mature, become an important person; at the same time she tried to keep you a child.

"But once she passed away, life was different, we grew up. Like with green fruit, it was the time to ripen."

"She brought Paradise on earth," says Yvette Malaury. "If we are still here taking care of the castle, we don't do it for the owner, we do it for Josephine. Even when I am tired, and I have to climb the stairs to show the château to the tourists, she is the one giving me the will to go on. I hear her voice in my ear, '*Allez, allez,*' and I keep going."

Jacqueline Abtey thinks Josephine is taking bows in Heaven. "She probably sat down directly, without being invited, at St. Peter's right (unless she pushed her natural temerity and went directly to God himself). And she must be laughing, she must be thinking we are not so far from the truth about Josephine, she must be sending us some powerful and meaningful glances. A quick pirouette, and she will disappear behind the great curtain of Eternity, where all light is truth. The devil wouldn't have claimed her, he would have been too afraid she might convert him!"

As she had converted multitudes. Think of that young girl, newly arrived in Paris, Caroline Reagan's "bird of paradise." Jean Vergne, the great chef, remembered in his seventies his days as a fifteen-year-old apprentice in a restaurant kitchen, scrounging up pennies to go with his friends to see Josephine Baker, *la Perle Noire,* on the stage of the Folies-Bergère. "Ah, Josephine," he says, still smiling at the thought. "We were hungry kids, we wanted to bite her, we wanted to eat her raw."

Six months after we left her on the altar in the Monaco cemetery,

France-Dimanche ran an indignant headline: EVEN A DOG DESERVES A BURIAL, it proclaimed, over a piece that said Josephine's body was still awaiting inhumation.

For all this time, it had been stored in a stone shed where the gardeners kept their tools. It was left to Madame Armita to explain the delay. The princess, who had extended to Josephine the privilege of burial in Monte Carlo, was still considering various samples of black marble, but she had not yet decided on the right stone for the tomb.

On October 2, 1975, Josephine was finally laid to rest. I stayed away. I didn't want to see her put in the ground, I preferred to think of her lying under the sun of the Riviera in her little Greek temple.

Marie was there though, and Jo and the children, and faithful Jacques Abtey. "None of her 'good' friends from the old times," says Jacques. "But that's life, you understand. It was hard for me to grasp that she could just disappear like that, after having done all she had done. There was the hole in the earth, and the princess of Monaco standing motionless, facing me across the open grave for an hour. We were waiting for the priest to come, and he was late."

It was strange. She was buried exactly fifty years after she first danced onto a Paris stage. Fifty years to the day.

AN OPEN LETTER TO MY SECOND MOTHER

"You were a hustler; I'm a hustler too"

etite Maman,

It's over. Or is it? We still live together every night at Chez Josephine. For seven years, people have come trooping into my restaurant, and every so often, one of them asks, "Is Josephine cooking tonight?"

I laugh, thinking that you're probably cooking up something somewhere, but that would take too long to explain, so I just say, "Yes, in spirit."

You took your secrets with you when you left us. The sixty containers stored for you in Marie Spiers's name were sold by Jo through a Paris auction house, your treasure scattered to the four corners of the Earth. But the safe in your Paris apartment was already empty, your last will had disappeared, and most of the fabled jewels that had been stashed in a Monte Carlo bank vault were gone too. I hope Margaret got them, God knows she earned them.

Any other gems that surfaced were disposed of by Sotheby's in

Zurich. (Again, not under your name, because of all the financial claims still pending against you.) Even those few baubles amazed Jari. "The diamonds," he said. "I didn't think she had kept so much."

For me, *you* were the diamond. I loved you. When you were cruel, I blamed your actions on a racist society, and the injuries you had suffered. I wanted the verdict of history to read, "Guilty, but with an explanation."

We were both bastards, and in a way, I liked that; it made me a brother to little Tumpy.

"Maybe she did to us what had been done to her," says Jean-Claude number one, trying, like me, to figure out his life with you. "Maybe she broke down inside, asking herself, 'Who do they think they are? I did not live in a castle when I was a little girl, I lived in misery, and they should have a taste of it.' "

Jean-Claude remembers your devising an embarrassing punishment when one of the children stole a few pennies for candy. "Nobody confessed," he says, "and our mother had to break the pact that bound us. Like the master in slave times. So we were forced to march through the village with signs that said, I'M A THIEF hanging around our necks.

"Another time she locked me in the coal cellar of the château. It was dark, there were rats, and she would come and scream through the basement window, 'Confess!'

"Elvira and Caroline had survived so much hardship, and then had to adapt to a new life after slavery, and our mother must have lived with all that in her head, with a history of things not really buried, only covered by the ashes of time. Everybody was satisfied with the fairy tale of Josephine Baker coming out of poverty, sailing on a boat to stardom, but she had to live with her ghosts."

When I showed your birth certificate to Jean-Claude, it suddenly became clear to him why you always called Fifi, that little dog, "Freda." It is hard for us to understand how you could joke about your given name with a dog, but not share your past with us.

Trusting no one but yourself, you kept your own counsel, Mother. No wonder you fled St. Louis; Bob Russell's private railroad car was the golden coach that carried you to the ball. But why did you bury the springtime of your life? Why, over the next half century, did you pretend that the radiant girl I saw in pictures on the walls of the Hudgins' house, and in Fredi Washington's scrapbooks, never existed?

The world knelt at Josephine Baker's feet, but Tumpy was too busy to make peace with her past. A chameleon, you absorbed what you needed, in show business or in life, even if it meant stealing somebody's act, somebody's money, somebody's lover. Discovering you—not the fiction but the fact—I have been shaken as when I was a small boy, and the bigger kids told me there was no Santa Claus.

It was easy for me to love you because I was always so angry with my birth mother, with her passivity and the way she surrendered to other people's rules. One day when I was ten years old, I found her crying in her room. "Why don't you divorce Father?" I said.

"Don't ask me that," she said. "Without a father, your sisters would never find good husbands."

You were different, daring, you broke rules, you fought back. I admired that, while my affection for my real mother was tinged with scorn. (I didn't know then of her bravery during the war.) In the end, she died as she had lived, apologizing. She asked me to forgive her for not having been the mother I needed, then gathered a last breath to whisper, "Excuse me," as she died in the nurse's arms. *Excuse me.* I wanted to scream. I wanted *her* to scream. It was not in her nature.

Neither of you was very forthcoming about the past, but then, I didn't tell you everything, either. You never knew about my aunt Dinette, a beautiful Creole from Madagascar married to my mother's brother. When I was seven years old, she and Uncle Lucien and my cousins came to visit us in St. Symphorien, and those children, true high yellers, were the sensation of the neighborhood. They knew about crocodiles, and gave us presents of ivory and ebony. To me, maybe on some level you were the reincarnation of Tata Dinette, whom I adored and never saw again.

At that time I was called Yan-Yan (my little sister could not pronounce Jean Claude), but when I moved to Paris, I left Yan-Yan behind. Or so I thought. He stayed with me, despite myself, and in me, you knew him. As I knew Tumpy in you, before I ever heard her name.

For six months after you died, Jo Bouillon remained in Paris. I had offered him the use of an apartment that I owned there, and we went together to the fifth floor of number two villa Dancourt in Montmartre. He could not believe it. My apartment was right next door to the one he had lived in during the war, when he met you.

"Josephine would come there at any hour of the night and wake me up," he said. "After a while, I just left the door open. Often in the morning, I would find her fully dressed, sleeping beside me."

Eventually, Jo returned to Argentina, along with Jari, Akio, Stellina, Noël, and Koffi. I had told him I wanted nothing from the estate, but that I would keep the name of Baker. I said I approved of his decision to try and keep the family together, and I would help as much as I could.

Back in New York, I started a cable television show called *Telefrance-USA* (John J. O'Connor of *The New York Times* called it "The most ambitious, sophisticated weekly production on cable TV."), and even there, I felt your presence. Because of you, I won an Ace Award for a show called "Ladies and Gentlemen, the Legendary Josephine Baker."

"Josephine is still here trying to direct things," Jack Jordan said.

I kept in touch with Brahim and Jean-Claude when I visited Paris, and it was in Paris that I saw Jo for the last time. He was holding your grandchild, Marie-Audrey (Marianne's first baby) and he was happy. He died in Buenos Aires in 1984, with five of the children at his bedside.

As you had predicted I would, I liked New York, and in 1983 I became an American citizen. The three wishes of my childhood were coming true. I did not do my military service, I no longer bore my father's name, and even if there would never be a statue of me like Napoléon the Third on a horse, two out of three wasn't bad.

In 1986, I opened a Chez Josephine in New York, trying to re-create the ambiance of your first club at 40 rue Fontaine. I even have a pig, in memory of Albert, but mine is made of wood.

Fredi Washington, Maude Russell, Evelyn Anderson, Sweets Edison—they all drop in, they feel at home there.

In 1989, Brahim and I went to St. Louis for a "Bal la Baker," sponsored by Michel Roux, a successful businessman turned patron of the arts, and a one-time employee of yours. "When I was fourteen," he says, "I spent my summer vacation working at Les Milandes. Josephine got involved with everything; she would tell me how to dress a table even if she didn't know how to do it. She was like Leona Helmsley."

It was in St. Louis that Brahim and I met our cousins, Richard, Jr., and Clifford, and I begged them to share anything they could remember of your mother and grandmother. "Elvira would always be sitting in a rocking chair," Clifford told me. "I was only a little kid, I had nothing to say to her, and she had nothing to say to me. My grandmother Carrie's husband, Tony Hudson, was a nice guy, I enjoyed him, but it was a hundred years ago."

About you, his famous aunt, he was cool. "I would say she was an entertainer, that's all. She was a French citizen, what she did with her life over there was her business. So she adopted children? Fine. She was under no obligation to take care of or support her family here. I had no attachment to those children she adopted, they were her children.

"Entertainers find their lives where their audience is, so why shouldn't she have stayed in Europe?"

"Josephine is the great Cinderella story," says the actress Paula Laurence, who was a close friend of Bob Brady, and is currently a trustee of the Brady Museum in Cuernavaca. "We have to think of what an enormous inspiration she has been, not just for people of her race, but for oppressed and disadvantaged people all over.

"By her own ambition, by clawing her way through the world, she evolved into that incredible woman, but underneath, she was the same desperate, hungry, impossible to satisfy, rapacious creature she was in the beginning, or she could not have survived.

"She never changed, it was the fight, the challenge that captured her."

Are you smiling, Mother, or scowling at the way others remember you? Were you happy with my introduction to your movies *Zou Zou* and *Princess Tam Tam* at New York's Film Forum, in the winter of 1989? You broke the theater's box office record, but I can hear you now, demanding, "Why should that surprise you?" (The films, wrote historian Donald Bogle, "provide us with a rare glimpse . . . of the charisma that drove international audiences wild for almost six decades.")

Since I started this book, the children and I have become closer, and I have been urging them to write their own stories. People are curious, they ask me, "What ever happened to all those children?" I just say, "We're all alive, and no one is in jail."

In 1991, eleven of my brothers and sisters were reunited—for the first time since Josephine's death—on a French TV show. Noël, hospitalized for schizophrenia, was not there, but for him you are still "the lady with a lot of heart who thought about children."

Jari helps me in the restaurant, and recently, Koffi and his wife Diane came from Buenos Aires to visit. We went to Harlem to gape at William Spiller's house, and the building where Mama Dinks lived. We also had a reunion at Chez Josephine with your nephew Artie, who laughed when he met Koffi "The last time I saw you," Artie said, "was when Josephine brought you to Les Milandes in that shoe box."

For Koffi, you were a kind of Joan of Arc. "She fought for her ideas, even sometimes against herself. She was very ambivalent. 'I think white, but I'm black.' In her head, it was a difficult conjunction of ideas.

"She was very demanding of me because I was the darkest of the children. 'You are black, you have to be well dressed.' She wanted me to be proud of myself and fear no one. I like the color of my skin. It would be too sad, too monotonous to have only one color. The sky is blue, the sea green, the human race is the human race, not the white race or the black race.

"If Mother was still with us, she would be fighting against AIDS. I don't have her fame or strength, but in my own way, I can do a little to better the world, we all can."

Clearly, you did some things right, Mother. But you did some things wrong, too. You broke my heart. "Mother dropped you for Jean-Claude Brialy," Marianne told me, "because in France, you had no name, while Brialy was a star, he could help her."

It doesn't matter anymore. All your life, you were a hustler, and I'm a hustler too; secretly, I used to admire the way you delivered the blows; half the time your victims didn't know they were wounded until they saw the blood.

Following Balanchine's advice, I kept searching for you, and found behind your seven veils more than I've chosen to tell. As your friend Donald Wyatt says, "Even a legend deserves some privacy."

But some of the rumors about your adventures are too fascinating to ignore. Is it true that Charles de Gaulle, hero of the Resistance and legendary president of the French Republic, succumbed to your charms? Did you sleep with him? Marcel Sauvage told me he knew it for a fact.

I wouldn't bet against it. I don't forget that once you were a Goddess of the Macumba, and that you never liked to sleep alone. Even in death.

The baby of Luis and his wife Michele is buried with you. She was born after you died, and lived only a short time. "My mother had just left us," Luis says, "and it was like she was punishing us twice. I had the impression that she was stealing my child; she was alone in her grave, and she took her granddaughter so she would have company in eternity."

Seven years later, in 1982, when Richard was so ill he could no longer come to the telephone, I called Margaret. "You and he share Carrie's blood, I think you should make peace with your brother."

By the time I arrived in the town of Baillargues where Richard lived with his family in a kind of housing project, Margaret was already there. Richard was weak, he had not been out of bed for a long time, but he asked Margaret to shave him. I finished off the job with a touch of my electric razor, and a splash of my Vetiver cologne.

Then we went in to dinner. Margaret had prepared a feast like in the old days on Bernard Street, fried chicken, potato salad, ribs, lemon pie. I sat at the head of the table, and at the other end, in a high chair, was your eighteen-month-old great-niece (and my godchild), Nais. She was Richard's first French grandchild.

Richard was weak, but happy, and after the meal, he asked me and his son Alain to help him outside. Margaret said no. "You can't go out, it's going to kill you."

We went anyway.

When the neighbors saw him coming through the door, they surrounded him, kissing him, telling him how wonderful he looked. He led me to the front of the building and there, parked near the sidewalk, was an old gray Ford.

"Tumpy bought me that car, Jean-Claude," he said. "I have no money for insurance or repairs, but I keep it to remind me she could be generous. I know she hurt you, too, but you have to forgive her. The people that were good to her, she kicked them in the ass, and the ones that were bad to her, she fed them. That was Josephine."

That was Josephine. I must have heard it a thousand times from a thousand people. You were what you were, and Richard was right. I must forgive you for the bad times, say thanks for the good times, and move on. But you know what? I still miss you.

Richard and I bent over the rusty Ford, putting our hands on it, tears rolling down our cheeks. Back in the apartment again, I helped put Richard to bed, and then Margaret asked to be left alone with him. She was holding her Bible. You know your sister, Mother, she wanted Brothercat to be ready for the big trip.

I wandered into the living room. It was the end of the day. Nais was tired, but when Guylaine tried to take her to bed, she screamed. It was funny to see how this baby, who looked just like you, struggled. Pushing away her mother's hands, clenching her small fists, she pounded on the floor, banging her head, rage, will, life-force—whatever it was—giving her the strength to go on with the show long after her eyes drooped with sleep.

Then and there I knew Carrie was right.

Tumpy ain't dead.

APPENDIX 1

AKIO, single, works in a bank in Paris.

JANOT, single, works as a gardener for the Societé des Bains de Mer in Monte Carlo.

LUIS, married, two children, works for an insurance company in Monte Carlo and lives in Menton, France.

JARI, single, lives in New York. He now spells his name Jarry.

JEAN-CLAUDE, no. 1, single, currently writing a collection of short stories, lives in Paris.

MOÏSE, divorced, no children, currently lives in Israel.

BRAHIM, single, just finished his first novel. He lives in Paris and has changed his name to Brian.

MARIANNE, married, two children, lives in Paris.

KOFFI, married, two children, is a chef de cuisine. He lives in Buenos Aires with his family.

MARA, married, two children, works in a government tax office in Benson, France.

NOËL, single, lives in Paris.

STELLINA, single, lives and works in Paris for an airline.

MARIE-JOSEPH, widowed, one daughter, is an advertising executive in Dijon, France.

MARIE-ANNICK, divorced, two children, is a professor of French and English in Sens, France.

MARTINE, married, two children, lives in Istres, France.

APPENDIX 2

In the years between 1926 and 1975, Josephine recorded over 230 songs, singing in French, English, German, Italian, Spanish, and Portuguese, starting in September of 1926 for Odeon with a session that included "Dinah," "I Want to Yodel," and "I Wonder Where My Baby Is Tonight." My favorite, from *Princesse Tam-Tam*, is 'Le Chemin du Bonheur.' Her last album, *Josephine Baker at Bobino*, had Pierre Spiers conducting the orchestra. His son Gerard, who was playing drums with them, recalls that since Josephine first recorded "J'ai Deux Amours" in 1930, in C major, her voice had come down a full fifth, which is most unusual.

Telegram Josephine sent to German chancellor Willy Brandt from my home in Berlin on November 19, 1972, *prior* to her knowledge of the election results.

BIBLIOGRAPHY

PERIODICALS

Der Abend
African American
The Afro-American
Amsterdam News
L'Art Vivant
Beaux-Arts
Brooklyn Daily Eagle
Chicago Daily News
Chicago Defender
Chicago Star
Chronique du Pingouin
Constanze
Le Crapouillot
Daily Mail
Défense de la France
Esquire
Le Figaro
France-Dimanche
France-Soir
Gazetter and Guide
Herald Examiner (Chicago)
Hollywood Reporter
The Indianapolis Recorder
Journal du Jura
Le Merle Rose
Minute
The Nation

The National Observer
New Orleans Item
New York Daily News
New York Post
The New York Times
The New Yorker
Nippon Times
Paris Match
Paris-Soir
Paris-Magazine
Le Petit Journal
Philadelphia Independent
The Philadelphia Inquirer
Philadelphia Tribune
Pittsburgh Courier
Plaisirs
Philadelphia Afro-American
The St. Louis Argus
Le Soir
Sun Chronicle
Time
Tageblatt
Vanity Fair
Variety
Die Welt
Women's Wear Daily

WORKS ABOUT JOSEPHINE BAKER

Abatino, Pepito. *Josephine Baker Vue par la Presse Française*. Paris: Les Editions Isis, 1931.

Abtey, Jacques. *La Guerre Secrète de Josephine Baker*. Paris and Havana: Editions Siboney, 1948. Also unpublished notes and original manuscript generously supplied by Commandant Abtey.

Baker, Josephine, and Jo Bouillon. *Josephine*. Paris: Laffont, 1976.

Baker, Josephine, and Jo Bouillon. *Josephine,* Trans. by Mariana Fitzpatrick. New York: Harper & Row, 1977.

Bonnal, Jean-Claude. *Josephine Baker et le Village des Enfants du Monde en Perigord*. Le Bugue: PL Editeur, 1992.

Delteil, Caroline Dudley (Reagan). *La Revue Nègre*. Unpublished manuscript used with permission from Sophie Reagan Herr.

Guild, Leo. *Josephine Baker*. Los Angeles: Holloway House, 1976.

Hammond, Bryan, compiler. *Josephine Baker*. London: Jonathan Cape, 1988.

Haney, Lynn. *Naked at the Feast: A Biography of Josephine Baker*. New York: Dodd, Mead, 1981.

Hultin, Randi. *Jazzens Tegn*. Oslo: H. Aschehoug & Co., 1991.

Kuhn, Dieter. *Josephine*. Frankfurt: Suhrkamp Verlag, 1976.

La Camara and Pepito Abatino. *Mon Sang Dans tes Veines: Roman d'après une Idée de Josephine Baker*. Paris: Les Editions Isis, 1931.

Papich, Stephen. *Remembering Josephine: A Biography of Josephine Baker*. New York: Bobbs-Merrill, 1976.

Rivollet, André. *Les Fausses Canailles*. Unpublished manuscript used with permission of Rivollet estate, executor Bernard Houdeline.

Rivollet, André. *Une Vie de Toutes les Couleurs*. Grenoble: B. Arthaud Éditeur, 1935.

Rose, Phyllis. *Jazz Cleopatra: Josephine Baker in Her Times*. New York: Doubleday, 1989.

Sauvage, Marcel. *Les Mémoires de Josephine Baker*. Paris: Editions KRA, 1927. Illustrated with 30 drawings by Paul Colin.

Sauvage, Marcel. *Les Mémoires de Josephine Baker,* recueillis et adaptés par Marcel Sauvage. Paris: Correa, 1949.

Sauvage, Marcel. *Voyages et Aventures de Josephine Baker*. Paris: Editions Marcel Sheur, 1931. Preface by Fernand Divoire. Illustrated with photographs and drawings.

Worm, Piet. Text by Josephine Baker with the collaboration of Jo Bouillon. *La Tribu Arc-en-Ciel*. Amsterdam: Editions Mulder & Zoon N.V., 1957.

OTHER REFERENCES

Académie du Cirque et du Music-Hall. *Histoire du Music-Hall.* Paris: Editions de Paris, 1954.

Allen, Mearl L. *Welcome to the Stork Club.* New York: A. S. Barnes & Co., 1980.

Allen, Tony. *Americans in Paris.* Chicago: Contemporary Books, 1977.

Allen, Tony. *The Glamour Years: Paris, 1919–40* New York: Gallery Books, 1977.

Ambrière, Francis, et al. *Vie et Mort des Francais, 1939–1945.* Paris: Hachette, 1971.

Anderson, Jervis. *This Was Harlem, 1900–1950.* New York: Farrar Straus Giroux, 1981. Source of Lloyd Morris quotation, which originally appeared in his book, *Incredible New York.*

Arletty. *La Défense.* Paris: La Table Ronde, 1971.

Assouline, Pierre. *Simenon.* Paris: Juliard, 1992.

Barber, Noel. *The Week France Fell.* New York: Stein and Day, 1984.

Bechet, Sidney. *Treat It Gentle: An Autobiography.* New York: Da Capo Press, 1978.

Behr, Edward. *The Good Frenchman: The True Story of the Life and Times of Maurice Chevalier.* New York: Villard Books, 1993.

Berteaut, Simone. *Piaf recit.* Paris: Editions Robert Laffont-Trevise, 1969.

Bogle, Donald. *Blacks in American Films and Television.* New York: Garland Publishing Inc., 1988.

Boudard, Alphonse. *Le Banquet des Leopards.* Paris: La Table Ronde, 1980.

Bresler, Fenton. *The Mystery of Georges Simenon.* New York: Beaufort Books, 1983.

Bricktop with James Haskins. *Bricktop.* New York: Atheneum, 1983.

Brossat, Alain. *Les Tondues: un Carnaval Moche.* Levallois-Perret: Editions Manya, 1992.

Brown, Sterling. *The Negro in American Culture: The Carnegie Myrdal Study.* 1920.

Bushell, Garvin, as told to Mark Tucker. *Jazz from the Beginning.* Ann Arbor: University of Michigan Press, 1990.

Castle, Charles. *The Folies Bergère.* London: Methuen, 1982. Source of Camille Debans quotation.

Charles, Jacques. *Cent Ans de Music Hall.* Geneve and Paris: Editions Jeheber, 1956.

Charles, Jacques. *De Gaby Deslys à Mistinguett.* Paris: Edition Librairie Gallimard, n.d.

Chiaromonte, Nicola. *The Paradox of History*. Philadelphia: University of Pennsylvania Press, 1970; rev. ed. 1985.

Chisholm, Anne. *Nancy Cunard, a Biography*. New York: Alfred A. Knopf, 1979.

Coccinelle. *Coccinelle*. Paris: Editions Filipacchi, 1987.

Cody, Morrill, with Hugh Ford. *The Women of Montparnasse*. New York: Cornwall Books, 1984.

Coleridge-Taylor, Samuel, transcriber. *Twenty-Four Negro Melodies*. Boston: Oliver Ditson Co., 1905.

Coquatrix, Paulette. *Les Coulisses de ma Memoire*. Paris: Grasset & Fasquelle, 1984.

Covarrubias, Miguel. *Negro Drawings*. New York: Alfred A. Knopf, 1927.

Coward, Noel. *The Noel Coward Dairies*. Edited by Graham Payn and Sheridan Morley. London: George Weidenfeld and Nicholson, Ltd., n.d.

Cox, Beverly J., and Denna Jones Anderson. *Miguel Covarrubias Caricatures*. Washington, D.C.: Smithsonian Institution Press, 1985.

Cunard, Nancy. *Negro*. New York: Negro Universities Press, 1969. Reprint. Originally published in 1934 by Nancy Cunard, London.

Damase, Jacques. *Les Folies du Music-Hall: A history of the Music-Hall in Paris*. London: Spring Books, 1970.

Dance, Stanley. *The World of Swing*. New York: Charles Scribner's Sons, 1974.

de Gaulle, Charles. *The Complete War Memoirs*. New York: Da Capo Press, 1967.

de Gaulle, Charles. *Discours et Messages: June 1940–January 1946*. Paris: Plon, 1970.

Derval, Paul. *Folies Bergère*. Paris: Editions de Paris, 1954.

Deschamps, Fanny. *Monsieur Folies Bergère*. Paris: Editions Albin Michel, 1978.

Doman, James R., Jr., and Assoc. *The St. Nicholas Historic District*. Prepared for The New York City Housing & Development Administration. New York: 1973.

Driggs, Frank, and Harris Lewine. *Black Beauty, White Heat, 1920–1950: A Pictorial History of Classic Jazz*. New York: William Morrow and Company, Inc., 1982.

Duberman, Martin Bauml. *Paul Robeson*. New York: Alfred A. Knopf, 1989.

Dudley, Emelius Clark. *The Medicine Man*. New York: J. H. Sears & Company, Inc. 1927.

Ellington, Duke. *Music Is My Mistress*. New York: Da Capo Press, 1973.

Engel, Lehman. *The American Musical Theater*. New York: CBS legacy collection, 1967.

Fitch, Noel Riley. *Sylvia Beach and the Lost Generation: A History of Literary Paris in the Twenties and Thirties.* New York: W. W. Norton & Company, 1983.

Flanner, Janet. *Paris Journal, 1965–1971.* Edited by William Shawn. New York: Harcourt Brace Jovanovich, 1977.

Flanner, Janet. *Paris Was Yesterday: 1925–1939.* New York: Viking Press, 1972.

Fletcher, Tom. *100 Years of the Negro in Show Business.* New York: Burdge & Company, 1954.

Fox-Genovese, Elizabeth. *Within the Plantation Household: Black and White Women of the Old South.* Chapel Hill: University of North Carolina Press, 1988.

Georges-Michel, Michel. *Un Demi-Siecle de Gloires Théâtrales.* Paris: Editions André Bonne, 1950.

Georges-Michel, Michel. *Folles de Luxe et Dames de Qualité.* Paris: Editions Baudinicre, 1931.

Georges-Michel, Michel. *Nuits d'Actrices.* Paris: Editions de France, 1933.

Goddard, Chris. *Jazz Away from Home.* New York and London: Paddington Press Ltd, 1979.

Gordon, Taylor. *Born to Be.* New York: Covici-Friede Publishers, 1929.

Grun, Bernard. *The Timetables of History.* (based on Werner Stein's *Kulturfarplan.*) New York: Simon and Schuster, 1982.

Gun, Nerin E. *Petain-Laval–De Gaulle.* Paris: Albin Michel, 1979.

Gurock, Jeffrey S. *When Harlem Was Jewish: 1870–1930.* New York: Columbia University Press, 1979.

Handy, D. Antoinette. *Black Women in American Bands & Orchestras.* Metuchen, N.J.: The Scarecrow Press, 1981.

Harnan, Terry. *African Rhythm, American Dance: A Biography of Katherine Dunham.* New York: Alfred A. Knopf, 1974.

Hemphill, Elizabeth Anne. *The Least of These: Miki Sawada and Her Children.* New York and Tokyo: John Weatherhill, Inc., 1980.

Hughes, Langston, and Milton Meltzer. *Black Magic: A Pictorial History of Black Entertainers in America.* New York: Bonanza Books, 1967.

Hughes, Langston, and Milton Meltzer. *A Pictorial History of the Negro in America.* New York: Crown, 1967.

Jenkins, Alan. *The Twenties.* New York: Universe Books, 1974.

Johnson, James Weldon, ed. *The Book of American Negro Spirituals.* New York: Viking Press, 1925.

Kellner, Bruce, ed. *The Harlem Renaissance.* New York: Methuen, 1987.

Kessler, Harry Graf. *Tagebucher 1918–1937.* Frankfurt: Insel Verlag, 1979.

Kimball, Robert, and William Bolcom. *Reminiscing with Sissle and Blake*. New York: Viking Press, 1973.

Klurfeld, Herman. *Winchell: His Life and Times*. New York: Praeger Publishers, 1976.

Kluver, Billy, and Julie Martin. *Kiki's Paris: Artists and Lovers, 1900–1930*. New York: Abrams, 1989.

Leon-Martin, Louis. *Le Music Hall et Ses Figures*. Paris: Editions de France, 1928.

Longstreet, Stephen. *We All Went to Paris: Americans in the City of Light, 1776–1971*. New York: Macmillan, 1972.

Lottman, Herbert R. *The Purge: The Purification of French Collaborators After World War II*. New York: William Morrow, 1986.

Lotz, Rainer E. *German Ragtime & Prehistory of Jazz*. Chigwell, England: Storyville Publications, 1985.

Malraux, André. *Les Chênes Qu 'on Abât*. Paris: Gallimard, 1971.

Mauriac, François. *Paris Libéré*. Paris: Flammarion, 1944.

Maxwell, Elsa. *J'ai récù le monde entier*. Paris: Amiot-Dumont, 1955.

Maxwell, Gavin. *Lord of the Atlas: The Rise and Fall of the House of Glaoui, 1893–1956*. New York: E. P. Dutton & Co., Inc., 1966.

McAlmon, Robert. *Being Geniuses Together, 1920–1930*. Rev. ed. San Francisco: North Point Press, 1984.

Mellon, James, ed. *Bullwhip Days: The Slaves Remember*. New York: Weidenfeld & Nicolson, 1988.

Mezzrow, Milton "Mezz," and Bernard Wolfe. *Really the Blues*. New York: Random House, 1946.

Mistinguett. *Toute ma vie*. 2 vols. Paris: Rene Julliard, 1954.

Montgomery, Paul L. *Eva, Evita: The Life and Death of Eva Perón*. New York: Pocket Books, 1979.

Moulin, Laure. *Jean Moulin*. Paris: Presse de la Cité, 1969.

Murray, Albert. *Stomping the Blues*. New York: Random House, 1976.

O'Neal, Hank. *Berenice Abbott: American Photographer*. Commentary by Berenice Abbott. New York: McGraw-Hill, 1982.

Penissard, Monique. *La Japonaise*. Lausanne: Editions Favre S.A., 1988.

Peyrefitte, Roger. *Manouche: Her Life and Times*. New York: Grove Press, 1974.

Placksin, Sally. *American Women in Jazz: 1900 to the Present*. New York: Wideview Books, 1982.

Prasteau, Jean. *La Merveilleuse Aventure du Casino de Paris*. Paris: Denoel, 1975.

Pryce-Jones, David. *Paris in the Third Reich: A History of German Occupation, 1940–1944*. New York: Holt, Rinehart and Winston, 1981.

Redding, J. Saunders. *On Being Negro in America.* Indianapolis: Charter Books, 1951.

Riess, Curt. *Das War Ein Leben!* Frankfurt: Ullstein-Sachbuch, 1990.

Rim, Carlo. *Le Grenier d'Arlequin: Journal 1916–40.* Paris: Editions Denol, 1981.

Ringgold, Gene, and DeWitt Bodeen. *Chevalier: Films and Career of Maurice Chevalier.* Secaucus, N.J.: The Citadel Press, 1973.

Sablon, Jean. *De France ou Bien d'Ailleurs.* Paris: Robert Laffont, 1979.

Saint-Granier. *Ma Jeunesse Folle.* Paris: Editions de Paris, 1955.

Sampson, Henry T. *Blacks in Blackface: A Source Book on Early Black Musical Shows.* Metuchen, N.J.: The Scarecrow Press, 1980.

Sandahl, Pierre. *De Gaulle Sans Képi.* Paris: La Jeune Parque, 1947.

Shapiro, Nat, and Nat Hentoff. *Hear Me Talkin' to Ya.* New York: Rinehart & Co., 1955.

Simmel, Johannes Mario. *It Can't Always Be Caviar.* New York: Doubleday, 1965.

Singer, Barry. *Black and Blue: The Life and Lyrics of Andy Razaf.* New York: Shirmer Books, 1992.

Snyder, Louis L. *The War: A Concise History, 1939–1945.* New York: Julian Messner, Inc., 1960.

Stearns, Marshall and Jean. *Jazz Dance: The Story of American Vernacular Dance.* New York: Schirmer Books, 1964.

Steegmuller, Francis. *Cocteau.* Boston: Nonpareil Books, 1986.

Stuart, Lyle. *The Secret Life of Walter Winchell.* Boar's Head Books, 1953.

Taub, William L. *Forces of Power.* New York: Grosset & Dunlap, 1979.

Taylor, Frank, and Gerald Cook. *Alberta Hunter: A Celebration in Blues.* New York: McGraw-Hill, 1987.

Thurman, Wallace. *The Blacker the Berry . . .* New York: The Macaulay Company, 1929.

Thurman, Wallace. *Negro Life in New York's Harlem.* Girard, Ks.: Haldemann-Julius, 1928.

Valentin, Louis. *Piaf.* Paris: Librairie Plon, 1993.

Van Vechten, Carl. *Nigger Heaven.* New York: Alfred A. Knopf, 1926.

Von Eckardt, Wolf, and Sander L. Gilman. *Bertolt Brecht's Berlin: A Scrapbook of the Twenties.* Garden City, N.Y.: Doubleday, Anchor Press, 1974.

Waller, Maurice, and Anthony Calabresse. *Fats Waller.* New York: Schirmer Books, 1977.

Waters, Ethel, with Charles Samuels. *His Eye Is on the Sparrow.* Garden City, N.Y.: Doubleday & Company, Inc., 1951.

Weil, Alain, et Jack Rennert. *Paul Colin. Affichiste.* Paris: Editions Denol, 1989.

White, Palmer. *Poiret*. New York: Clarkson N. Potter Inc., 1973.

Willis-Thomas, Deborah. *Black Photographers, 1840–1940*. New York: Garland Publishing, 1985.

Woll, Allen. *Black Musical Theater: From Coontown to Dreamgirls*. Baton Rouge: Louisiana State University Press, 1989.

Wooding, Sam. *Like It Was*. Unpublished manuscript used with permission of Sam Wooding.

Young, Whitney M., Jr. *Beyond Racism*. New York: McGraw-Hill, 1969.

INDEX

ABOUT THE AUTHORS

JEAN-CLAUDE BAKER was born in Dijon, France. At fourteen, while working as a bellhop in Paris, he met Josephine Baker. Her bold inspiration led him to pursue a remarkably colorful career that has included success as a nightclub owner, television producer, and restaurateur. Mr. Baker first came to the United States on Josephine Baker's final American tour in 1973. He lives in New York City.

CHRIS CHASE lives in New York City.